The Middle East

SERIES IN CULTURE, COGNITION, AND BEHAVIOR

SERIES EDITOR
David Matsumoto, *San Francisco State University*

SERIES ADVISORY BOARD
Deborah Best, *Wake Forest University*
Michael Harris Bond, *Chinese University of Hong Kong*
Walter J. Lonner, *Western Washington University*

The Middle East: A Cultural Psychology
GARY S. GREGG

The Middle East

A CULTURAL PSYCHOLOGY

Gary S. Gregg

With a Foreword by

David Matsumoto

UNIVERSITY PRESS

2005

OXFORD

UNIVERSITY PRESS

Oxford University Press, Inc., publishes works that further
Oxford University's objective of excellence
in research, scholarship, and education.

Oxford   New York
Auckland   Cape Town   Dar es Salaam   Hong Kong   Karachi
Kuala Lumpur   Madrid   Melbourne   Mexico City   Nairobi
New Delhi   Shanghai   Taipei   Toronto

With offices in
Argentina   Austria   Brazil   Chile   Czech Republic   France   Greece
Guatemala   Hungary   Italy   Japan   Poland   Portugal   Singapore
South Korea   Switzerland   Thailand   Turkey   Ukraine   Vietnam

Copyright © 2005 by Oxford University Press, Inc.

Published by Oxford University Press, Inc.,
198 Madison Avenue, New York, New York 10016

www.oup.com

Library of Congress Cataloging-in-Publication Data
Gregg, Gary S.
The Middle East : a cultural psychology / by Gary S. Gregg.
p.   cm. (Series in culture, cognition, and behavior)
ISBN-13 978-0-19-517199-0

1. Ethnopsychology—Middle East.   2. Personality and culture—Middle East.
3. Islam—Psychology.   4. Religion and culture—Middle East.   I. Title.   II. Series.
GN502.G76 2005
155.8'2'0956—dc22   2004016417

Printed in the United States of America
on acid-free paper

FOREWORD

Recent years have witnessed an explosion in information technology. Scholars and scientists in all fields of study have at their fingertips more information than ever before and, in fact, more information than they can possibly manage. We are able to communicate and interact with others around the world effortlessly via the Web. Interest and research on people from different cultures and societies is at its highest in recent decades, and promises to become even more prominent in the future.

Despite the information explosion and increased ease of communication, there are still countries, regions, and cultures of the world about which we have little reliable information. Although studies of culture and psychology are prominent in the Far East (particularly Japan), North America, and Europe, they are still sorely lacking in Central and South America, Africa, Southeast Asia, and the Middle East. This gaping hole in the scientific literature is in fact largest in psychology, as psychological studies of the people of these cultural regions still lag far behind other types of scientific research.

The consequences of this lack of information are formidable. People's reactions to the events of September 11 demonstrated that ignorance about the lives of people from other cultures helps to promulgate stereotypes, misperceptions, and misunderstandings. Believing in uninformed stereotypes makes it easier to make negative attributions to groups of people when unfortunate events occur. Doing so also makes it easier to homogenize people, ignore their considerable individuality and diversity, and believe in the supremacy of one's ways of life, beliefs, and being.

It is in this light that I welcome Gary Gregg's *The Middle East: A Cultural Psychology* as the first book to be published in the Oxford University Press Series in Culture, Cognition, and Behavior. In this book, Gregg provides a broad overview of what underlies the psychological development throughout the lifespan of individuals living in Middle East and North African

(MENA) societies and cultures. Through his discussions of pediatric styles of childcare, the honor-modesty system, Islam, the tension between tradition and modernity, and the development of self and identity, Gregg does an outstanding job of highlighting aspects of development that appear to be similar panculturally—universal to all people of all cultures—as well as those that appear to be unique to the MENA region. Moreover, the work presented in this volume represents not only Gregg's own research, but also his understanding—remarkable in its breadth and depth—of all the relevant cross-cultural, cultural, and developmental literatures. He deftly crafts his message, juxtaposing the available scholarly literature from Europe and North America on questions and concerns about development with the concepts and material generated from his primary research on real-life MENA people.

There are several characteristics of this book that make it unique. For example, Gregg spends the first two chapters describing the social ecology of the region, which gives readers an excellent feel for that ecology and, moreover, for the general sociocultural milieu within which individuals in MENA live, work, and play. It is important background information that is not often available to cross-cultural, cultural, and mainstream psychologists today. Gregg's attention to concepts such as nomadism, peasant agriculture, urban commerce, and the widespread adoption of Arab culture and Islam provides a crucial context for understanding the material in the main sections of the book. This type of background material should be provided by *every* work on the psychology and development of *any* group of people in *any* area of the world and against which extracted psychological constructs should be interpreted and connected.

Gregg is not an armchair psychologist. In this day and age, psychologists interested in the cultural context of behavior can carry out their research at home in front of a computer, but Gregg chose to interact directly with the populations he is studying. Gregg's work is also unique because it brings the methodology of the *study of lives* tradition to the area of culture and psychology. He follows in the outstanding heritage of Erikson, Mead, Murray, Levine, and McAdams to go beyond simple verbal responses to questionnaires or behavioral responses to tasks by conducting comprehensive, in-depth, qualitative studies of the lives of numerous individuals living in MENA. Moreover, he brings the complexity, richness, and sometimes conflicting aspects of individual lives alive to the reader, all the while extracting psychological constructs and concepts that are vital to a complete understanding of their cultural psychological development.

Gregg's work is also notable in the theoretical frameworks of personality he uses. Although many views of personality in studies of culture today are dominated by the trait approach, Gregg revives the notion of different levels of personality organization. His three levels of psychological organization—corresponding to biological, social, and cultural influences—underscore the important fact that individual lives are complex, multilayered, and multifaceted.

The notions of *sentiments, motives,* and *social personae* are interesting, unique, and informative not only as theoretical contributions to the study of the psychology of MENA but also to all who are interested in the interaction between culture, personality, mental processes, and individual behavior.

Needless to say, Gregg's work makes numerous contributions—theoretically, empirically, and pragmatically. The two contributions that stand out in my mind are the messages he brings to the concepts of Individualism versus Collectivism (IC) and to contemporary studies of self and identity. He demonstrates amply that stereotypical descriptions of cultures (and, moreover, of individuals) as either individualistic or collectivistic are just too simplistic and most likely inappropriate. Gregg clearly shows that cultures have both individualistic and collectivistic tendencies, and that future theoretical and empirical research needs to work through this simple and perhaps misleading dichotomy. Gregg's research adds to a growing literature that suggests that selves and identities are comprised of a repertoire of schemata, including both independent and interdependent concepts, and that culture influences the content of these schemata via the contexts of the lives within which individuals develop. Despite the stereotypic and oversimplistic view of MENA cultures as being collectivistic, the individual lives of the people Gregg studied are incredibly rich, diverse, and full of fledgling individuality and autonomy. I agree with Gregg in his suggestion that oversimplified notions of independent/individual self-construals versus interdependent/sociocentric border on academic stereotyping, not unlike that done by political leaders throughout history to justify outright discrimination and aggression toward others. It is a path that concerned social scientists should not take, and one that Gregg's work argues against admirably.

Additionally Gregg's book is valuable because it makes available an interesting and important literature—two thirds of it by Arab-Muslim scholars—available to Western researchers and the informed public. And it helps us better understand Middle Easterners by seeing how they struggle to modernize their traditions without simply abandoning them for Western ones. The life span developmental framework that Gregg uses is perfect in highlighting these issues and concerns.

Gregg is a gifted writer; he brings the material to the reader as a novelist would bring life to characters, or as any artisans working their craft. The theoretical perspectives on culture, personality, self, identity, and development; empirical contributions of the study of lives approach; and the carefully crafted writing make this volume one that is sure to make a strong and lasting contribution to the scholarly literature on culture, psychology, and the Middle East/North Africa. This book is a befitting start to Oxford's Series in Culture, Cognition, and Behavior.

David Matsumoto
San Francisco

ACKNOWLEDGMENTS

This book had its inception in the seminar I taught on "Psychological Studies of Arab-Muslim Societies" at Harvard's Center for Middle Eastern Studies, and I thank Professors Susan Miller, Robert LeVine, Byron Good, and Mary-Jo Good there for their support.

Research for the book was supported by a sabbatical leave from Kalamazoo College in the 2002–2003 academic year. A Visiting Scholar appointment and a Mellon Grant made it possible to work at the University of Michigan's Center for Middle Eastern and North African Studies, and a Fulbright Fellowship supported crucial library research in Egypt and Morocco. Thanks to Professor Maissa el Mofti for welcoming me to 'Ain Shems University in Cairo and for many helpful conversations, and to Professor Farouk Sendiony and Elizabeth Coker at the American University in Cairo. Thanks also to Professor Mohammed Ezroura for welcoming me to Mohammed V University in Rabat, and to Dr. Mehdi Paes and Dr. Jamal Toufiq at the Ar-Razi Hospital in Sale (Rabat) for guidance early in my work there.

Great thanks to the Arabic tutors and research assistants who worked with me over the last three years: Laila al-Duwaisin (from Kuwait) and Faisal Shurdom (from Jordan) at Kalamazoo College, Yasmeen Hanoosh (from Iraq) and Marwan Gammash (from Saudi Arabia) at the University of Michigan, Ali Fadhel (from United Arab Emirates) at Western Michigan University, Hala Mahmoud in Cairo, and Laila Rabi'a in Rabat. Also to my Kalamazoo College students Shadi Houshyar, Natasha Ghazi, Maya Farhat, and Anna Maxbauer for bibliographic and library help, and for insightful comments on early drafts. Hala Mahmoud also deserves credit as coauthor of the section on indigenous psychology that appears in the Afterword.

Special thanks to Susan Schaefer Davis and Douglas Davis for their fine research, friendship, and patient encouragement of my work. And to Alison Geist for five years of collaborative work in Morocco, which she used to create more immediate and tangible results than I: the Near East Foundation-sponsored project now active in 40 villages, improving family nutrition, water sanitation, fuel-wood stove efficiency, and women's literacy.

Note on Photos ✤

All photos were taken by Gary Gregg and Alison Geist in southern Moroccan villages that continue to practice nonmechanized agriculture and herding of sheep, goats, and camels on the slopes of the High Atlas mountains. Few Middle Easterners today live in "traditional" settings like these.

CONTENTS

INTRODUCTION   *3*

PART I

Cultural Context of Development

1   Misunderstandings   *13*

2   The Social Ecology of Psychological Development   *44*

3   Honor and Islam: Shaping Emotions, Traits, and Selves   *90*

PART II

Periods of Psychological Development

INTRODUCTION TO PART II   *136*

4   Childbirth and Infant Care   *153*

5   Early Childhood   *179*

6   Late Childhood   *212*

7   Adolescence   *252*

8   Early Adulthood and Identity   *288*

9   Mature Adulthood   *325*

10   Patterns and Lives: Development Through the Life-Span   *359*

AFTERWORD: A Research Agenda   *369*

NOTES   *379*

REFERENCES   *421*

INDEX   *451*

The Middle East

INTRODUCTION

Since I began writing this book, the escalation of Israeli-Palestinian strife, the attack on the World Trade Center, and the wars in Afghanistan and Iraq have put the Middle East even more prominently onto the center stage of world history. Samuel Huntington has ominously predicted that the twenty-first century would see a "clash of civilizations" pitting Islam against the West, and Samuel Barber described globalization as culminating in a struggle of "Jihad versus McWorld." I hope this book might help put the daily headlines in a broader perspective, by describing psychological dimensions of traditional ways of life in Middle Eastern and North African societies, and of the impact of "modernization" and "underdevelopment." It will not offer psychological explanations for the region's economic and political problems, or for the Israeli-Palestinian conflict. But it will consider what Arab social scientists have been writing about the inner consequences of economic stagnation and political despotism, and about Middle Easterners' current attempts to "become modern" while conserving what they see as their authentic traditions.

The following chapters cover nearly all writings on the cultural psychology of Middle Eastern Muslim societies, and examine the patterns of psychological development, attachments, values, and identities that appear to be distinctive of the region. This work began when I first taught a seminar entitled "Psychological Studies of Middle Eastern Societies" and discovered that there was no summary of the region's cultural psychology I could assign my students, no review of the interesting studies I'd been reading, and not even a bibliography. As a result, the region is usually not covered in the cultural psychology courses now taught in most colleges and universities, and is rarely discussed at conferences of cross-cultural psychologists. Worse, Americans interested in learning about the area's cultural psychology find little other than ethnocentric writings on "the Arab mentality" that mistakenly attribute the Middle East's recent problems to the inertia of deep-seated psychological characteristics. I have therefore written this book with two purposes in mind: first, to provide cross-cultural researchers and students with a review of writings on psychological development in the Middle East; and second, to provide Westerners with psychological perspectives on the inner lives of Middle Easterners as they face a rapidly globalizing world, most of them living in conditions of economic and political "underdevelopment."

The book draws on my own background and experience. Trained as a personality psychologist in the "study of lives" tradition, I studied the development of identity among young adult Americans, and then spent five years in the 1980s in Morocco, conducting ethnographic research on the Berber-speaking Imeghrane confederation in the High Atlas and pre-Saharan area of Ouarzazate, and then life-history studies of identity among young adults living in villages and small towns. My synthesis of psychological writings is guided by my observations and interviews with over a hundred families in that region, and by my research on how individuals live their simultaneously modernizing and underdeveloping culture.

The Middle East as a "Culture Area" ✿

My review includes research on Muslim groups from Morocco to Pakistan and Turkey to Sudan—a huge and complex area whose cultures have been formed by millennia of mixing peoples, languages, ways of life, and religions. No homogenous shared culture—and certainly no shared "personality" or "mentality"—has resulted from this mixing. Nonetheless, I will discuss it as a *culture area*. This notion—and even the concept of "culture"—has come under increasing criticism as globalizing peoples, products, and ideas flow and mix with dizzying speed. I agree with these criticisms, and with the call to shift from studying the world's "cultures" to the process of "hybridization" that is taking place everywhere.[1]

But I believe that centuries of mixing three ways of life—nomadism, peasant agriculture, and urban commerce—in arid and semiarid lands, combined with the widespread adoption of Arab culture and Islam, have formed a "culture area" with distinctive patterns of development from infancy to old age. Abdelhamid Jabar's study of psychological needs in three Arab societies (chosen to reflect the historical importance of nomadic versus urban ways of life) led him to a similar conclusion.[2] The anthropologist Sherry Ortner and the Turkish historian Deniz Kandiyoti argue that the extended family systems found in the band of societies stretching from North Africa into China and India share "patriarchal" principles found in few other of the world's cultures.[3] These differ from each other in the way that "classic patriarchy"[4] has combined with agro-pastoralism and Islam in the Middle East, with the caste system and Hinduism in India, with rice agriculture and Confucianism in China, and with feudalism and Christianity in Europe—thereby forming four of the world's "Great Tradition" civilizations.

The Egyptian psychologists Khalifa and Radwan discuss the existence of common Arab psychological characteristics at length in their 1998 *Al-shakhsiyyia al-misriyya* (The Egyptian Personality) and conclude that the long interplay of culturally unifying forces has led to the sharing of some features throughout the region. Several survey studies support this view.[5] At the same time, differences appear in three subregions (the Persian Gulf, the Nile, and North Africa) and among individual nations. And throughout the Middle East, urban, rural, and Bedouin styles of life have created additional variation.[6] I have no doubt that the "culture area" concept brings a danger of oversimplification, and as Khalifa and Radwan point out, recent decades of population growth and economic change are probably reducing the extent to which Middle Eastern societies share a cultural psychology. I nonetheless believe we cannot dispense with the culture area notion, especially insofar as it helps understand the history by which family systems and life-patterns have evolved, and the hybridization that now affects every resident of the region.

The American anthropologists who developed the culture area notion in the 1920s and 1930s did so after analyzing the borrowing and refashioning of "culture traits" among native North American tribes. They never saw cultures as isolated and self-contained, and they did not think clear boundaries could be drawn between adjacent culture areas. They did believe that a predominant vision of life comes to guide a culture's borrowing (and rejection) of concepts, tools, and customs from their neighbors, and to guide how it revises these to fit its own conditions and worldview. But they also recognized that even small "simple" cultures encompass variations on their main themes and have individuals who at least try to live by divergent styles. Far from portraying a culture as homogeneous and cut off from its neighbors, the culture area concept can help (1) recognize patterns of psychological development that this region *shares* with neighboring culture areas (sub-Saharan Africa, Hindu India, and preindustrial southern Europe); (2) identify patterns that *differ* from those of neighboring areas; and (3) do justice to the great range of variation (male-female, urban-rural, country-to-country, and individual-to-individual) observed *within* the region. Viewing the region in comparison with its neighbors also helps take an important step away from ethnocentrically seeing it in the light of American middle class values.

Still, the "culture area" cannot be precisely defined. Studies from countries on the borders of the region—especially Turkey, Pakistan, Iran, and Sudan—suggest that in some respects they can be considered to be "in" the culture area but in other respects they fall "outside" it. Citizens of these border lands are correct to insist that they have distinct histories, customs, and outlooks that set them apart from other peoples in the region. Egyptians, Palestinians, Saudis, and others located in the region's core are equally correct to make the same claim. And during the last 50 years, dramatically differing forms of government have further increased cultural divergence. Still, the societies in this region share many characteristics with each other that they do not share with neighboring regions. I intend my definition of this "culture area" to be only a useful approximation that can serve as a bridge to closer study of the variations within it. In order to further simplify the book, I will not cover studies of Muslim Arabs living outside the region, or studies of Israel, or research on Jews, Christians, or Bahais living in majority-Muslim lands. The book also will not do justice to the important differences between Sunni and Shi'ite Muslims, or to the cultures of ethnic minorities, such as Berbers, Tuaregs, Druze, and Kurds.

I will, however, continually emphasize the diversity within the region. I adopt a notion of "culture" which views it not as a way of life *shared* by all those who live in it but as a constellation of values, meanings, and practices unevenly *distributed* to its members.[7] In addition, each chapter will discuss differences between men and women, and between more traditional and more modernized milieus. Personality may indeed appear as "culture writ small"— as an internalization of one's culture—but individuals have surprising latitude to select the elements of their heritage they regard as "their" culture, and to synthesize them in creative and idiosyncratic ways.

There remains the difficult problem of what to call this culture area. Only parts of it are "Arab"; it is only a part of the "Muslim" world; and "Middle East" usually refers to the countries of the eastern Mediterranean and Persian Gulf. In the book's first draft I used "Middle East" as the best of these inappropriate terms. But several Egyptian colleagues have convinced me to replace it with the awkward acronym MENA: Middle East and North Africa. While MENA is still not fully accurate, it has the advantage of not being a household word loaded with media stereotypes. It thus may help remind the reader that the culture area does *not* correspond to any of the primary identities—for example, "Arab," "Muslim," "Middle Eastern," "Saudi," "Algerian"—embraced by those who live within it.

Plan of the Book ❀

Chapter 1 discusses the stereotypes Westerners have developed about the Arab world, and examines five common misunderstandings of MENA societies that have been offered as explanations for the region's current problems. The next two chapters provide the background or "social ecology" of psychological development, summarizing studies of MENA social organization (chapter 2) and cultural values (chapter 3). The introduction to part II presents the model of cultural influences on personality development I use to synthesize the literature, and chapters 4 through 9 cover writings on psychological development by life-stage: infancy, early childhood, late childhood, adolescence, early adulthood, and mature adulthood. The final chapter provides a brief review of development across the life-span.

Given the size and importance of MENA, there is surprisingly little research on psychological development. Several widely read works, like *The Arab Mind,* by Raphael Patai, and *The Closed Circle,* by David Pryce-Jones, take highly ethnocentric "national character" approaches, treating Arabs as if they were a single person who could be put on an analyst's couch. (The 2002 edition of Patai's book features an introduction by Colonel Norvell De Atkine, director of Middle Eastern studies at the U.S. army's John F. Kennedy Special Warfare Center and School, who writes enthusiastically that "at the institution where I teach military officers, *The Arab Mind* forms the basis of my cultural instruction.")[8] Several of the most interesting, like Fuad Khuri's *Tents and Pyramids,* Abdelwaheb Bouhdiba's *Sexuality in Islam,*[9] Hamed Ammar's *Fi bina' al-bashar* (On the Building of Persons), Ali Zayour's *Al-tahlil al-nafsi li-al-dhat al-'arabiyyah* (Psychological Analysis of the Arab Self) and Mustafa Hijazi's *Al-takhaluf al-ijtima'i* (Societal Underdevelopment), are works of social criticism by MENA scholars which also examine the "Arab mentality." In addition, few MENA psychologists have participated in the last two decades' growth of "cultural" and "cross-cultural" psychology. This is due partly to their efforts to meet more urgent priorities, and partly to economic constraints.[10] The cost of the mostly Western journals and books in this area is prohibitive to many researchers and university libraries,[11] and as Omar Khaleefa points out, attending an international conference can cost several years' salary.[12]

In spite of serious economic and often political obstacles, researchers have carried out valuable field studies of child-rearing practices and of the forces shaping adolescent and adult development.[13] These studies lay out provocative debates about cultural influences on development and show important lines of convergence. Each of the life-stage chapters will end by highlighting a debate or disagreement which appears in the literature: the effects of strongly "interdependent" nurturing during infancy and its often abrupt withdrawal; the gender differentiation which intensifies near the end of early childhood, often coincident with circumcision;[14] the shift to possibly "authoritarian" styles of parenting in late childhood; the smoothness versus turmoil of adolescent maturation; the tension between Western and indigenous identities in early adulthood; and the relationship of societal and psychological development in mature adulthood.

Because I am writing partly for readers who may be learning about MENA societies for the first time, I make occasional use of autobiographies and novels to help bring patterns and numbers more vividly to life. This book does not, however, review the broad discipline of psychology in the region,[15] or cultural influences on mental illness and psychiatry. Two recent books provide excellent English-language introductions to these topics: Ramadan Ahmed and Uwe Geilen's *Psychology in the Arab World* (1998) and Ihsan Al-Issa's *Al-Junun: Mental Illness in the Islamic World* (2000).

Theoretical Framework ❀

To synthesize psychological studies of MENA I employ a framework based mainly on *dynamic* theories of personality development, especially those of Erik Erikson,[16] John and Beatrice Whiting,[17] Robert LeVine,[18] and Dan McAdams.[19] I also draw on Takeo Doi's writings on Japan,[20] Gannanath Obeysekere on Sri Lanka,[21] Sudhir Kakar and Ashis Nandy on India,[22] and Gilbert Herdt on New Guinea.[23] These differ from what Whiting terms "as-the-twig-is-bent" theories, which view development as a continuous process guided by reward, punishment, and the modeling of appropriate behavior ("social learning theory" is the leading example). While some aspects of development certainly are continuous, dynamic theories emphasize the importance of biologically and culturally patterned discontinuities: transitions in which established patterns of emotion, relationship, and self-conception must be transformed or suppressed in order to acquire new ones. The dynamic theories recognize that (1) developmental transitions often entail inner and interpersonal conflict, and that (2) earlier patterns may remain part of the new organization, and sources of tension within it. For Erikson, these discontinuities form the "developmental tasks" that define stages of human development.

I have divided the life-span into six *developmental periods*, condensing Erikson's eight-stage schema,[24] but I do *not* regard these periods as discrete "stages" with the timing and content he theorizes. I also distinguish three *levels of psychological organization* which emerge in succession, in adaptation to changing biological, cognitive, and cultural influences.[25] This model makes it possible to move beyond generalizations about "culture and self" to begin identifying cultural practices which have their main effects during specific developmental periods and influence specific levels of psychological organization. I sketch this model in chapter 3, where I discuss how we can best conceptualize the psychological consequences of "internalizing" the region's two primary value systems, and I then discuss it more fully in the introduction to part II.

My choice of this framework has two important consequences. First, while it is designed to account for cultural differences, it remains a Western theory of development whose applicability to MENA societies remains to be judged. Psychologists in many non-Western societies have criticized the importation of Western theories and sought to create "indigenous" psychologies which draw on their own traditions. Ahmed and Gielen call for this kind of "indigenization," for which the works of the Lebanese psychiatrist Mohammed Nablusi (*Nahu saykulujiya ʿarabiah* [Toward an Arab Psychology]) and the Egyptian psychologist Fuad Abu Hateb (*Mushkilat ʿilm al-nafs fi al-'alam al-thaleth hala al-watan al-'arabi* [Problems of Psychology in the Third World and the Arab Countries]) lay out blueprints.[26] By bringing together previous psychological studies (over two-thirds of them by MENA researchers) and putting them in a global context, I hope this Westerner's book may contribute to that project.

Second, I will pay relatively little attention to what many American textbooks now feature as the core of cultural psychology: studies of the effects of a culture's "cognitive schemas" on self-conceptions. This is because (1) little of that research has been done in MENA societies: (2) I believe it gives too much emphasis to cognition and too little to emotion and interpersonal relationships: and (3) it fails to take account of developmental discontinuities. Further, I believe much of this work—especially research based on scoring cultures on the dimension of "individualism" versus "collectivism"—to be especially inappropriate to the region, which, as Cigdem Kagitcibasi and Suad Joseph argue, has strong individualist *and* collectivist features.[27] I will, however, draw on other recent work in cultural psychology, especially that on culture-and-emotion, that shows that a set of universal emotions are shaped by each culture in accordance with its distinctive rules for displaying feelings.[28] I also will draw on recent studies of acculturation which show that the formation of multiple or "hybrid" identities is widespread and often adaptive. Both of these lines of research can account for discontinuity and tension in development.

Above all, I will not put MENA culture or character on the couch, for in no respect can the region be said to have a shared "basic personality." The life-history interviews I conducted in Morocco show not only a tremendous range of individual variation but also that the culture is not so much *shared* by those who live in the region as *distributed* among them. Different features are apportioned to men and to women; to the old and to the young; to city dwellers and to villagers or nomads; to the educated and to the illiterate; and to pious believers and to those who have strayed. Even within families, individuals internalize versions of their culture so divergent that they get in the way of understanding each other's lives. Culture is not to be found in a static system of shared values or meanings, but lives in patterned *dialogues* and *debates* about values and how they should be lived. The framework I adopt—based on six developmental periods and three levels of psychological organization—will help describe major cultural influences without minimizing the tremendous variety in individual adaptations to them. It also will help to examine how the two-sided process of societal "modernization" and "underdevelopment" is shaping the developmental tasks faced at critical periods in the life-course, and how the cultural dualities stemming from Western dominance of the globalizing world are affecting the course of individual lives.

At the beginning, however, it is important to consider the many ways Westerners have *mis*understood MENA cultures and psyches, which is the subject of the first chapter.

A Note to Readers ❀

I have written this book to be read cover to cover, with each chapter building on the previous ones. But for those who plan to read only parts of it, and for teachers who wish to assign selected chapters to their students, a brief overview of each chapter appears at its beginning. If you plan to read only some chapters, I recommend also reading the overviews of the others.

Cultural Context of Development

CHAPTER 1

Misunderstandings

This chapter briefly traces the history of Western images of the Arab-Muslim world, and reviews the most prominent "ministereotypes" created by Western writers, artists, and scholars. It then discusses the following five crucial misunderstandings of MENA societies, which lay blame for the region's current economic and political problems on its traditional culture or mentality.

1. *Despotism and strife stem from a tribal mentality equipped with modern weapons.*
2. *The "code of honor" monopolizes the Middle Eastern psyche, and subverts modernization.*
3. *Islamic "fatalism" breeds inaction and stalls development.*
4. *The momentum of tradition resists modernization.*
5. *Terrorism springs from a vein of fanaticism in Arab culture and the Arab psyche.*

Rejecting these misunderstandings opens the door to examining the region's problems in the context of its economic and political underdevelopment, which Hisham Sharabi argues has led to the formation of "neopatriarchal" forms of culture. Neither traditional nor modern, "neopatriarchical" cultures often refurbish oppressive traditions in efforts to adapt to conditions in which true traditions have been destroyed but economic and political modernization has faltered. In the postcolonial decades, the struggle for modernization in conditions of underdevelopment has influenced psychological development at all stages of life.

A Cast of Returning Characters ❀

Social psychologists have identified a simple, often automatic bias in our thinking—the "fundamental attribution error"—that easily leads to the creation of misleading stereotypes. In scores of experiments and field studies, researchers have found that we tend to explain our own actions as responses to situational pressures, but that we see the behavior of others as expressing their underlying personality traits. This process intensifies when we make inferences about groups rather than individuals, and especially when we characterize out-groups, such as other cultures or ethnic minorities.[1] This bias shapes how we think about all "foreign" cultures, but it especially plays itself out in the case of the Middle East. Scholars, journalists, and the public all appear eager to find psychological explanations for the region's purported economic and cultural backwardness, its despotic regimes and terrorist cells, and its religious "fanaticism."

Once one begins to seek psychological underpinnings for another culture's seemingly strange ways, another and more powerful process comes into play: projection. Freud and his early colleagues made much of our propensity to project our own "unconscious" interests, wishes, and fears into the ambiguous contours of the external world, and then believe we have found them there, in reality. This innocent process lets us perceive the stars to form constellations of creatures and heroes and the billowing clouds to unfold stories across the sky. But projection readily becomes pernicious when it uses a "foreign" culture or an ethnic group as its canvas. Jews then come to embody all the supposedly infectious forms of degeneracy "Aryan" Germans fear in themselves, and African Americans come to be stereotyped as shiftless addicts and welfare queens as they are made to represent the laziness and dependency white Americans fear might derail them from the hard work their success requires.[2] In a colonial context, projection does much of the dirty work of dehumanizing the colonized so the colonizers can go about their business with a sense of legitimacy. Thus the invention of the "savage" on the perimeters of "civilization," and of the "noble savage," equally a figment of projection.

Attribution errors and projection have powerfully shaped what Westerners believe they have learned about MENA peoples. Writings on the so-called Arab personality are especially rife with negative stereotypes, as Fouad Mogharbi,[3] Halim Barakat,[4] Sayyid Yassin,[5] 'Azet Hijazi,[6] and Mahmoud 'Awdah[7] have shown in detail. Yassin also documents how Arab intellectuals who launched the wave of "self-criticism" that followed the 1967 war with Israel laid some of the blame for Egypt's military defeat on weaknesses in their "national personality"—creating a cluster of "auto-stereotypes" that provided Western writers with quotations from Arab thinkers in support of their distorted views.[8] I therefore must begin by tracing how a set of conflicting stereotypes of the "Arab psyche" took shape in the writings of explorers, missionaries, and colonial officials, and then by examining five specific misunderstandings about purported psychological causes of the region's political problems. These misunderstandings are not merely historical curiosities but continue to be propagated by journalists, scholars, managers of international aid projects, and movie-makers. We need to see where they go awry—not so much to sweep them away and then get a clear view of MENA "as it really is" as to begin afresh to weigh what researchers have learned about patterns of psychological development.

Like His Picturesque Streets

Edward Said's *Orientalism* details the extent to which the West's "knowledge" of MENA societies was created in the service either of conquering and administering them as colonies or imagining them as exotic lands of freedoms and excesses prohibited in Europe. Few "Orientalists"—as those who studied the "Near East" and then the "Middle East" first called themselves—were content simply to pen accounts of the region's history and institutions; they sought also to penetrate the Arab mind and character. Not surprisingly, most discovered a negative mirror image of the rational, industrious, self-controlled European. Said quotes the assessment of the Egyptian mentality made by Lord Cromer, Britain's ruler of Egypt at the turn of the twentieth century: "The Oriental generally acts, speaks, and thinks in a manner exactly opposite to the European." While "the European is a close reasoner . . . a natural logician," Cromer wrote, "the mind of the Oriental . . . like his picturesque streets, is eminently wanting in symmetry . . . [and] singularly deficient in the logical faculty." Further, Arabs are "devoid of energy and initiative," are "lethargic and suspicious," and substitute "fulsome flattery" for serious discussion. "Want of accuracy," he concluded, "that easily degenerates into untruthfulness, is in fact the main characteristic of the Oriental mind."[9]

Or consider Andre Servier, who wrote his 1924 book *Islam and the Psychology of the Musulman* as "an intelligent study of Islam" intended to help France "found thereon a Musulman policy whose beneficent action may extend not only over our African colonies but over the whole Musulman world."[10] He gets right to the heart of the matter: "The Arab is devoid of all imagination. He is a realist, who notes what he sees, and records it in his memory, but is incapable of imagining or conceiving anything beyond what he can directly perceive."[11] At the end of the first chapter, Servier sums up his findings:

> The Arab has borrowed everything from other nations, literature, art, science, and even his religious ideas. He has passed it all through the sieve of his own narrow mind, and being incapable of rising to high philosophic conceptions, he has distorted, mutilated and desiccated everything. This destructive influence explains the decadence of Musulman nations and their powerlessness to break away from barbarism.[12]

Explaining that "Arab blood was impoverished" by marriages to Negro slaves, who "belonged to an inferior race, absolutely refractory to all civilization,"[13] Sevrier concludes that "in the history of the nations, Islam, a secretion of the

Arab brain, has never been an element of civilization, but on the contrary has acted as an extinguisher upon its flickering light."[14]

We might dismiss these portraits as relics of the bygone era of empire, except that milder forms reappear in the writings of social scientists throughout the century and to the present day. In his 1958 book *The Passing of Traditional Society,* Daniel Lerner cast modernization as challenging Arab society with "a rationalist and positivist spirit against which, scholars seem agreed, Islam is absolutely defenseless."[15] In a magazine article, he cutely characterized the conflict as "Mecca versus mechanization."[16] In the late 1960s and early 1970s the anthropologist Clifford Geertz described Moroccans as having "mosaic" selves[17] and wrote that in spite of Middle Easterners' frequent invocation of religion to justify modernization, Islam itself "can neither embrace nor understand" modernity.[18] Raphael Patai's recently reprinted book *The Arab Mind* argues that Arabs are so caught in a magical "spell of language" that they expect rhetoric to suffice where science and technology are needed, so they can neither see nor solve their pressing problems:

> In a pragmatically oriented community, the modal personality is strongly influenced by reality. . . . At the other end of the scale we find societies where reality does not exercise a high degree of influence on thinking and speech. Western peoples stand at one end of the scale, the Arabs near the other end.[19]

These ideas have continued to figure in the geopolitical thinking of statesmen, as Said illustrates with a 1974 essay in which Henry Kissinger divided the world into the developed societies and the developing:

> [The developed world] is deeply committed to the notion that the real world is external to the observer, that knowledge consists of recording and classifying data—the more accurately the better. . . . [The developing nations] have retained the essentially pre-Newtonian view that the real world is almost completely internal to the observer. . . . Empirical reality has a much different significance for many of the new countries than for the West because in a certain sense they never went through the process of discovering it.[20]

Servier thus condemns the primitives for being "realists" and lacking imagination, while Kissinger condemns them for overusing their imaginations and lacking an appreciation for reality. Some journalists have rejected this kind of "We're rational, they're not" view, but others have taken it as the key to making sense of the Middle East. In his widely read book *The Closed Circle,* David Pryce-Jones makes the pronouncement that "in the years of independence, the Arabs have so far made no inventions or discoveries in the sciences or the arts, no contribution to medicine or philosophy."[21] Turning to social scientists' writings for an explanation, he concludes that Arabs' preoccupation with honor and shame "is unsuited to a technical context because it prevents reason being an agreed value."[22]

A variant of this view holds that Arab civilization had a glorious past of literary and scientific creativity but then fell into a dark age of decline and decay. It now fails to measure up not only to the West but to its own classical ideals. As Western archaeologists rescued the treasures of the pyramids, deciphered hieroglyphic writings, and began to teach Egyptians their own ancient history, so Orientalists developed a sense of mission: to rescue the Arabs' classical age and catalyze a renaissance that would lead Muslims back into the light of progress. This view quickly found its political uses. Said documents how Napoleon took scores of scholars along on his military expedition to Egypt in 1798 and presented his forces as liberating the land from foreign rule. "We are the true Muslims," he proclaimed in Alexandria, come to regenerate Egypt's own traditions . "Napoleon tried everywhere to prove that he was fighting for Islam; everything he said was translated into Koranic Arabic, just as the French army was urged by its command always to remember the Islamic sensibility." When he departed he directed his deputy "always to administer Egypt through the Orientalists and the religious Islamic leaders whom they could win over."[23] A century later the American writer Edith Wharton toured Morocco and learned that "nothing endures in Islam, except what human inertia has left standing and its own solidity has preserved from the elements."[24] She praised the French general Hubert Lyautey and his administration for being "swift and decisive when military action is required"[25] and for dedicating themselves to the "preservation of the national monuments and the revival of the languishing native art-industries." An appreciative Lyautey told her: "It was easy to do because I loved the people."[26]

The Sheikh

The fantasy of restoring a degraded civilization to its former greatness animated the lives and writings of several British adventurers, peaking in the legend of "Lawrence of Arabia." Like Said's *Orientalism*, Kathryn Tidrick's *Heart Beguiling Araby* recounts how, in the imaginations of early nineteenth-century Romantic poets, "the East became a setting for the Romantic experience," beckoning to young Europeans questing to find themselves and thirsting for artistic inspiration. Throughout that century the image of the Arabian Bedouin as a noble savage was cultivated by writers who confidently believed that deep in the interior of Arabia's Nejd desert lived proud tribesmen with the purest Arab blood coursing through their veins, speaking the purest Arabic, and living in the purest liberty—their character combining virility, chivalry, tenderness, and a natural instinct for godliness.[27] Many great "Orientalist" writers and painters never left their imaginary dreamscapes to cross the Mediterranean; others took their dreamscapes with them. Richard Burton, a gifted speaker of 29 languages who made the pilgrimage to Mecca in 1853 disguised as a Pathan[28] doctor, wrote of the Bedouin as having a *societe leonine*, a "lionistic" society, in which "the fiercest, the strongest, and the craftiest obtains complete mastery over his fellows."[29] An accomplished swordsman who once challenged a fellow student to a duel at Oxford, "Burton was the first writer who explicitly admired the Bedouin's predatory character . . . [and in his hands] the detested bandit became a romantic rebel against society."[30] The Jesuit missionary Wilfred Palgrave crossed the Nejd in 1862 in disguise as a Syrian. He loathed the Bedouin, who he described as "at best an ill-educated child . . . [and] a degenerate branch of that great tree" of the Arab race, but he felt he found the pure-blooded, courageous, gentlemanly Arab thriving in the desert's oasis communities:

> patient, cool, slow in preparing his means of action, more tenacious than any bulldog when he has once laid hold, attached to his ancestral uses and native land by a patriotism rare in the East . . . sober almost to austerity in his mode of life. . . . [They are] the English of the Oriental world.[31]

In 1875 the nobleman adventurer Wilfrid Blunt and his wife traveled to Mesopotamia and met, in the person of a Bedouin tribe's sheikh, "that thing we have been looking for, but hardly hoped to get a sight of, a *gentleman* of the desert."[32] Three years later they set out on a "pilgrimage" to the Nejd in search of Palgrave's pure Bedouin and, hosted there by the region's emir, believed they had found a society of true aristocrats—practicing "shepherd rule"—that sadly had all but faded from British society. Blunt long had felt estranged from Victorian society, Tidrick writes, and "Nejd had seemed to him to be a unique repository of the traditional virtues, an example to the world of a society ruled with a light but confident hand by a rural aristocracy whose claim to legitimacy was based on birth and not on wealth."[33] Blunt bought an estate outside of Cairo where he presided as "sheikh" and dedicated himself to the cause of Arab regeneration. He schemed to lead a movement to end the rule of the Ottoman Turks over Arabia and reestablish the caliphate at Mecca, but the British government took no interest in his venture.

Then came World War I, and the strategic imperative to engage the Turks (fighting on the German side) on a second front suddenly provided Blunt's disciple—T. E. Lawrence—with an opportunity to carry out the plan. Lawrence had read and daydreamed about knights and chivalry throughout his youth, wrote a thesis at Oxford University on the Crusades, and hoped to become a knighted general by the age of 30. In 1916 he arrived in Arabia and, dressed in silken robes and carrying a golden dagger, he began coordinating the guerrilla war launched that year against the Turks. He later wrote in *Seven Pillars of Wisdom*: "I meant to make a new nation, to restore a lost influence, to give twenty millions of Semites the foundation on which to build an inspired dream-palace of their national thoughts."[34]

Tidrick points out that it was mainly officers and alienated aristocrats who felt lured by romantic fascination to the warrior Arab, and she insightfully suggests that two features of their childhoods probably gave Arabia the eerie sense of familiarity many of them described. First, as children in literate families, they grew up reading the Bible and the *Arabian Nights*, whose scenes came to life before their eyes in the Middle East. Second, most had boarding school experiences that stressed the virile values they believed they found among the Arabs: male solidarity, deference to authority, military toughness, and poetic romanticism. Reflected back through their writings—and through the Lawrence of Arabia myth created by the journalist Lowell Thomas and the poet Robert Graves—the Bedouin as gentlemanly ideal and the desert as setting for heroic and spiritual quests found a receptive public.

The romance of Arabia had little salience in late nineteenth- and early twentieth-century America, where a similar fascination with "becoming primitive" developed using America's own Wild West frontier as setting. At the very time that Native Americans were being destroyed in the West, the town and city-dwellers east of the Mississippi were romanticizing Native American culture and vicariously "going Indian." Studying the widespread phenomenon of spirit mediumship, the psychologist William James noted in 1890 with puzzlement that when mediums communicate with the spirit world they often turn into Indians as they enter their trances—seeming to draw unconsciously on shared cultural stereotypes. This also was the heyday of fraternal orders, with nearly a third of the adult male population belonging to groups like the Freemasons, the Order of the Red Man, the Odd Fellows, and the Knights of Pythias,[35] whose meetings were devoted mainly to initiating members through elaborate levels of hierarchy and to ornate titles. In some of these, men became figures in Old Testament landscapes, Greek or Roman warriors, medieval knights. In many they became Indians, using elaborate props to turn their lodge houses into warrior campsites where initiates would be put through ordeals to become "braves." When they awakened the next morning they went back to their mostly professional and white-collar office jobs. Lewis Henry Morgan, the first great American anthropologist, began studying the Iroquois in 1845 to devise rituals for his fraternal order, whose initiates were ritually reborn as adopted Red warriors while a chorus of white lodge members chanted for the destruction of White Men. As Morgan became a serious student of the Iroquois, he drifted away from his "boyish" fraternity brothers and was adopted into a real Iroquois clan. The historian Mark Carnes suggests that these rituals helped give American men a sense of rugged masculinity that their domestic lives and office, shop, and factory jobs increasingly failed to provide. Social scientists have now documented how around the globe colonizing peoples not only denigrate the colonized as savages but develop romantic images of them as living closer to the natural or spirit worlds, and as living happier, freer, more manly, or more virtuous lives than do the "civilized."

American interest in Arabia developed in the 1920s, when Lowell Thomas, who had covered World War I as a journalist and met the British general Edmund Allenby and T. E. Lawrence in Cairo, created a dramatic slide and film-illustrated travelogue lecture entitled "With Allenby in Palestine and Lawrence in Arabia," which he advertised in some venues as "The Last Crusade." The historian Joel Hodson has reconstructed much of the performance, which Thomas gave over 4,000 times, to an estimated four million people:

> The audience viewed the Pyramids from the air, saw massed bodies of cavalry. . . . and were introduced to *Allenby's crusaders* and *"The Army of Allah."* They were given aerial tours of contemporary and Biblical battlefields, *where the Scots defeated the Turks, and David slew Goliath,* and they saw *twentieth century crusaders* on the march, along the same roads *where the armies of Godfrey de Bouillion and Richard Coeur de Lion camped eight centuries ago.* . . . [In part 2] they were introduced to *Shereef Lawrence, the uncrowned King of Arabia, and his Arabian Knights,* and to *Auda Abu Tayi, a Bedouin Robin Hood.* . . . The performance ended with a description of the *capture of Aleppo and the downfall of the Ottoman Empire—Mesopotamia, Syria, Arabia and the Holy Land at last freed after four hundred years of oppression.*[36]

Thomas's magazine articles and 1924 book *With Lawrence in Arabia* fictionalized many aspects of his childhood and military adventures, but the book became a transatlantic bestseller and amplified his already grandiose legend. Beginning with *The Sheikh of Araby* in 1922 and followed by Rudolph Valentino's portrayals of Lawrence-like figures in *The Sheik* and *The Son of the Sheik,* Hollywood produced a series of "sun and sand" movies that established that "the stereotypical image of the sensuous Arab was from the beginning of commercial movie-making a proven box office draw."[37]

> The setting was the Saharan desert, but the story differed little in theme from earlier American Indian captivity novels: a white woman is captured and risks being ravished by a dark "primitive" abductor. . . . Sheik Ahmed (Valentino), himself first depicted as the seducer, rescues Diana from a villainous sheik. As with many adventure romances of the period, from Horatio Alger stories to Edger Rice Burroughs's *Tarzan of the Apes,* the hero turns out to have aristocratic origins. In *The Sheik,* Ahmed had been lost in the desert as a child twenty-five years before when his British father and Spanish mother (a device used to account for Ahmed's dark complexion) were killed.[38]

In 1962 the epic film *Lawrence of Arabia* set off a "Lawrence mania" of marketing:

> Lawrence "ghutra" scarves sold for as much as $75 and arabesque hats ranged from $30 to $60. . . . *Vogue* called the phenomenon

"Desert Dazzle." . . . One could also get the "Sheikh look" from Elizabeth Arden beauty products, including Lawrence of Arabia lipstick, nail polish, and "a Sheik-look Creme Rouge" that gave "sun-warmed complexion tones without dashing into the desert." . . . An issue of *McCall's* magazine devoted eight editorial pages to the "Lawrence look" at the beach in a photo spread entitled "How to be Sheik on the Sand."[39]

Movies and fashion had by then replaced the meeting halls and ritual initiation of "Indian braves" as the vehicles by which Americans could taste the mysterious effects of *mimesis*: that by imaginally becoming an alien Other, one can strengthen one's own sense of self.

The Harem

A third variant of the West's view of MENA comes mainly from writers and artists who found sometimes lifelong inspiration in the exotic colors, textures, scents, and rhythms of its daily life, and in the erotic delights they either tasted there or imagined flourishing behind harem walls. As Rana Kabbani (1986) shows, Western fascination with the eroticism of the Middle East goes back at least to Shakespeare's *Anthony and Cleopatra,* in which the "enchanting queen" of Egypt leads Anthony into an intoxicating passion that costs him his life. Anthony realizes the danger early on, breaks "these strong Egyptian fetters," and returns to Rome, where he takes up his duty and marries, but with regret: "though I make this marriage for my peace, in the East my pleasure lies." His Roman Octavia possesses "wisdom" and "modesty," but Cleopatra beckons with her beguiling "eros, eros"—"she makes hungry where most she satisfies."[40] "The dichotomy has now crystallized," Kabbani writes: "the West is social solidarity; the East pleasure, unrestrained by social dictates." Anthony dies kissing her:

> For Anthony, the East arrived in Cleopatra's barge. It was a mixture of new delights: the pomp of pageant, the smell of perfume and incense, the luxurious brocades that shimmered in the sun, and most notably, the woman herself—queen, love-object, mistress and despot—*was* the East, the Orient created for the Western gaze.[41]

For many Europeans, the East arrived in the *Arabian Nights,* a work first written by a French Arabic scholar named Antoine Gallard as a diversion, based loosely on oral tales that circulated throughout the Middle East and India. Published in the first decade of the eighteenth century, the *Arabian Nights* immediately became popular and spread the image of the *seraglio,* or royal harem, as a place of unleashed sensuality and violence. In the "frame story" that sets the tales in motion, the King Shahrayar finds his wife bedding one of his black slaves and kills her. Convinced of woman's essential lechery and deceit, he resolves to marry and deflower a virgin every night and then kill her in the morning. An intended victim, Sheherazade, tells the tales to captivate the king and avoid meeting her fate. In 1841 Edward Lane, who wrote an early ethnography of Egyptian life, published a family-friendly version of the tales, excising much of the sex and taming some of the violence. Later in the century, Richard Burton produced another version that he published privately for a circle of friends that included several reputed "libertines." Burton embellished the sex and the violence, appending his own thoughts about perverse Arab erotics. In all of these versions, Kabbani notes, the women characters are mostly "demonesses, procuresses, sorceresses, witches. They are fickle, faithless and lewd. They are irrepressibly malign and plot to achieve their base desires in the most merciless manner imaginable."[42] Thus were Arab women created for literate European tastes.

When Romantic poets and then painters looked outside repressive Europe for images of erotic liberation, they set off in search of the Arab women of their fantasies. In the mid–nineteenth century, the French writer Gerard de Nerval traveled in Egypt and Lebanon, "the land of dreams and illusions," in search of adventure, imagery, and the Eternal Feminine. "I must unite with a guileless young girl who is of this sacred soil that is our first homeland," he wrote, "I must bathe myself in the vivifying springs of humanity, from that poetry and the faith of our father flowed forth!"[43] He begins his account of buying a slave girl in his popular *Journey to the Orient* by observing: "There is something extremely captivating and irresistible in a woman from a faraway country." But soon after his purchase he realized: "I owned a magnificent bird in a cage,"[44] with whom he could not speak. He tried to teach her French, with little success but much fun: "I amused myself, too, very much, by having her pronounce complete sentences that she didn't understand, for example, this one: *Je suis un petite sauvage* [I am a little savage]."[45] When he left he turned her over to a Frenchwoman in Cairo, explaining: "She's lovely enough in Levantine costume, but she's hideous in the dresses and whatnot of Europe. Do you see me entering a salon with a beauty who could pass for a cannibal!"[46]

Flaubert traveled in Egypt in 1849, where he took up with a famous dancer/prostitute who later became the prototype for several of his female characters. Said writes:

> In all of his novels Flaubert associates the Orient with the escapism of sexual fantasy. Emma Bovary and Frederic Moreau pine for what in their drab (or harried) bourgeois lives they do not have, and what they realize they want comes easily to their daydreams packed inside Oriental clichés: harems, princesses, princes, slaves, veils, dancing girls and boys, sherbets, ointments, and so on.[47]

Dozens of other writers and painters, including Delacroix and Matisse, found inspiration in exotic, erotic, sometimes hashish-enhanced adventures in the

Middle East—a tradition carried on more recently by the American writers (Truman Capote, Tennessee Williams, William Burroughs, Allen Ginsberg, Jack Kerouac) who clustered around Paul Bowles in Tangier.

The Western public's fascination with what lay "beneath the veil" or "within harem walls" gave rise to a genre of pornography set in Arab lands,[48] and at the height of the colonial era—1900–1930—to the production of millions of postcards that purported to provide peeks into forbidden Arab interiors. In 1986 the Algerian writer Malek Alloula published a collection of these postcards created in his homeland during this era, entitled *The Colonial Harem*. After quickly exhausting the possibilities of naturalistic photos showing nondescript veiled figures from a distance, he explains, French photographers began hiring marginal women, often prostitutes, to pose as "authentic" Algerians in their studios. The first studio cards in this collection show girls and women looking out through barred windows, as if in prison; then they are captured at their window sills by photographers who have positioned themselves within. Next come numerous as-if harem scenes, with unveiled, often bare-breasted "Moorish" girls and women drinking tea, sitting near hookah pipes, and reclining in apparent anticipation of their lovers. Some of the photographers tried to convey authenticity by draping the women in layers of finery and jewels, though still often baring a breast, and some photos more than hint at lesbian love play. Alloula notes that "the colonial post card says this: these women, who were reputedly invisible or hidden, and, until now, beyond sight, are henceforth public; for a few pennies, and at any time, their intimacy can be broken into and violated."[49] Ultimately, he writes, they resemble trophies of war: "The raiding of women has always been the dream and the obsession of the total victor. These raided bodies are the spoils of victory."[50]

This fascination has hardly passed from the scene. The back cover of Cherry Mosteshar's 1995 book *Unveiled* proclaims in bold red print: "She was Trapped Behind the Veil of Hell," "A Nightmare World of Violence and Degradation" and "Now Her True Story Can Finally Be Told." Jean Sasson's 1994 book *Princess Sultana's Daughters* advertises itself as "intimate revelations" about "A Life of Unimaginable Wealth . . . Unthinkable Sexual Practices . . . and Terrifying Cruelty." And in 1997 Carla Coco published *Secrets of the Harem,* a large-format coffee-table book that purports to open the harems of nineteenth-century Ottoman Turkish rulers, "penetrating" the "complex organization" governing them in much the same imaginative way as did the Algerian postcards Alloula collected. Lavishly illustrated with paintings by European artists, the author sets out to describe "the welter of needs, desires, hopes and dreams of oriental women,"[51] as seen in "the most voluptuous place in the empire."[52] We learn about the Turks' origin on the steppes of Central Asia: "The pleasures of galloping on horses, raping girls, getting drunk, shedding blood and other acts of violence were mingled with feelings of tolerance and brotherhood." Somehow, though, "women enjoyed both consideration and freedom," which Islam greatly curtailed, giving them in its place the luxury and sensuality of harem life. The hookah-smoking concubine depicted in Frederick Bridgman's *Odalisque* thus shows how "the soft Levantine lovemaking replaced the rough love games of the steppes."[53] The topless African and European dancers in Vincenzo Marinelli's 1862 *Dance of the Bee in the Harem* illustrate a diplomat's report that they wore "garments so thin that they allowed 'all the secret parts' to be revealed,"[54] but only to a few eyes. Jean-Leon Gerome's 1859 *Guardian of the Harem* shows one of the "ugly, deformed and fierce-looking black eunuchs from Africa," among whom "homosexual love flourished."[55]

Inside the harem, "lesbianism was rampant,"[56] and women enjoyed "happy hours of oblivion"[57] brought on by coffee, tobacco, and opium, which Jean-Jules Antoine Lecomte de Nouy's 1888 painting *The White Slave* illustrates as the nude woman exhales wisps of smoke. Yet danger always lurked: a double-page spread of Fernand Cormon's 1874 *Jealousy in the Seraglio* shows a naked, dark-skinned woman peering with tensed joy at the bloody body of a white-skinned woman that an African eunuch has just knifed. The caption explains: "The harem, a wonderland of delights and pleasures, could become a treacherous place for the unfaithful concubine who displeased her master."[58] Two intoxicated women reclining together in Eugene Giraud's *Interior of a Harem* somehow illustrate that in the sixteenth century the reins of government "passed into the hands of the women and the palace slaves, who used their power recklessly and with great cruelty."[59] And somehow Delacroix's 1834 *Algerian Women*, which depicts three rather glassy-eyed hookah-smoking women attended by a black servant, illustrates how in the nineteenth century, "new sentiments were stirring, and the women, despite their poor education, were quite capable of thinking in addition to loving and procreating."[60] The book ends with "the elegant, ethereal princesses" wandering about the imperial palace "like ghosts, dressed in the best of French fashions," as an unnamed "new leader" transforms the empire into a republic and passes laws that "formally establish equality between men and women."[61]

Media Terrorists

In recent decades fiction has quickly followed the news in proliferating images of "Arab terrorists," as popular novels, TV shows, and movies have capitalized on the public's fascination and fear. Reeva Simon found few spy thrillers with Middle Eastern themes before the 1967 Arab-Israeli war, but these took off exponentially after it. By 1985 over 600 had been published in English: "Supermarkets, drugstores, bus stations, and airports were inundated with spy novels whose covers depicted petrosheiks and terrorists held at bay by macho "avengers," "destroyers," "killmasters," "executioners," "peacemakers," and assorted James Bond clones."[62] Historically MENA provided settings for "romantic" mysteries, but Simon found that most published after

1967 "fall into the 'paranoid' and 'vicious' varieties," featuring physically grotesque, vengeance-crazed, religiously fanatical villains.[63] Jack Shaheen has tracked Western media stereotypes of Arabs during this period, and his *Reel Bad Arabs* reviews nearly 900 films with Arab characters.[64] "Hollywood's sheikh of the 1920s became the oily sheikh of the 1970s and 1980s," he writes, "and now the fanatical 'fundamentalist' terrorist who prays before killing innocents."[65] Video stores and cable channels now offer hundreds of films with

> Western protagonists spewing out unrelenting barrages of uncontested slurs, calling Arabs: "assholes," "bastards," "camel-dicks," "pigs," "devil-worshippers," "jackals," "rats," "rag-heads," "towel-heads," "scum-buckets," "sons-of-dogs," "buzzards of the jungle," "sons-of-whores," "sons-of-unnamed goats," and "sons-of-she-camels."[66]

Romantic themes have all but disappeared.

Ministereotypes

The West has predominantly derogated Arabs as backward, irrational, fatalistic, and fanatical, but it also has reversed the stereotype and celebrated the Middle East as home to men more virile and women more sensual than overly civilized Europeans. The West thus has no single stereotype of the Arab but, as Tidrick puts it, many fluid "ministereotypes." Said emphasizes the political origins of these images and Tidrick the psychological, but together they show that every effort to know the Arabs[67] will be shaped by political and psychological forces that easily escape the notice of Westerners who believe their viewpoint to be "scientific," "objective," and "balanced." Just as the Orientalists' paintings and the postcards of Algerian women tell us more about the ways Europeans looked at them than the way they "really" looked, so Tidrick observes that the writings of the British adventurers tell us more about their romantic dreams and personal quests for identity than they do about the Bedouin. Discussions of the psychological characteristics of MENA peoples will prove to be especially "loaded" with political and personal motives: and this book can be no exception. The struggle to unearth and overcome attribution errors and projections can never fully succeed, but especially for an American writing or reading about the Middle East, it must be relentlessly carried on.

Misunderstandings ❀

Until the 1970s the Middle East did not occupy American imaginations the way it did European, but with dramatic front-page coverage of wars, dictators, and terror, it now looms large. After four decades of feminism, Bedouin manliness finds few admirers, and even if one wanted to, there are precious few Bedouin left to romanticize. The sexual revolution has eased the repressions that made "foreign" eroticism seem so lush and alluring, and AIDS has made quests for foreign liaisons more dangerous. Media portrayals of Arab men as terrorists, despots, and lechers and of Arab women as helplessly oppressed victims now stand unleavened even by stereotypes of the noble savage and erotic muse. Today both media and scholarly treatments continue to promote a range of serious misunderstandings about how psychological and cultural characteristics may doom the region to despotism and underdevelopment. I will discuss the five most widespread and entrenched of these misunderstandings.

Despotism and Strife Stem from a Tribal Mentality Equipped with Modern Weapons

In the introduction to her 1994 book *Passion and Politics,* the journalist Sandra Mackey writes: "Arab society is tribal. . . . The Arabs came to nationhood late, and they came with their tribalism intact. And it is as tribes that they largely manage their countries."[68] She believes tribalism animates an unstable tension of fission and unification that causes the Arab world so much strife: "The Arabs move rapidly back and forth between the realm of brotherhood and the recesses of betrayal, between unity and conflict. . . . It is this juxtaposing of conflict and unity that fuels the turmoil of the Arab world."[69] David Pryce-Jones's book *The Closed Circle* offers a similar tribalist framework for understanding MENA: "Far from creating approximations of Western social and political norms, the Arab order in its post-1945 independence has been reverting to basic tribal and kinship structures, with their supportive group values, as they were in precolonial days."[70] He elaborates: "Tribal society is a closed order. . . . Blood-relationship provides the closest social binding, greatly simplifying the common purpose. Aggrandizement and perpetuation of the tribe are ends requiring no justification." Competition within and among tribes creates "a zero sum affair. Pursuit of ambition by one family or tribe is necessarily loss and restriction to another." This leads to a "power-challenge dialectic" that, "surviving as a tribal legacy down the centuries . . . has everywhere perpetuated absolute and despotic rule." In his view, the problems of underdevelopment all stem from this: "The power-challenge dialectic continues to prevent the transformation of the collectivity of separate families into an electorate, of group values into rights and duties, of obedience into choice and tolerance, of arranged marriage into romantic love, and of power holder into a party system with a loyal opposition."[71]

Historical and anthropological studies show that while tribal peoples have long comprised a small percentage of MENA's population, they have exercised a disproportionate role in shaping its culture. Tribespeople have continually replenished and swelled the populations of towns and cities, and in many areas tribes from the hinterlands often swept away dynasties in decline and set up new ones. But as the great fourteenth-century historian Ibn Khaldun recognized, tribal and urban ways of life are antithetical in key respects, and tribespeople change when they come to town, losing over a couple of generations their "tribal" qualities of toughness and solidarity. Scores of community studies show that neither urban dwellers nor most village-dwelling agriculturalists can be termed "tribal" in any anthropologically meaningful sense of the term. In addition, studies of MENA tribes show just how difficult it is to define precisely what a "tribe" is. Many lack the genealogical organization boasted by some, and it was largely MENA tribes that convinced anthropologists that genealogies rarely described the actual organization of groups but provided an "idiom" by which groups try to make and reject claims on each other.[72] Furthermore, tribes rarely developed "despotic" rule, which mainly appeared with settled peasantries and urban-based states. Many studies of tribes show egalitarian, persuasion-based self-government at local, small- group levels where families are joined by kinship and day-to-day cooperation and many tribes devised schemes for rotating leadership among their component clans or fractions, so no one could dominate.[73] Authoritarian rule developed at the top of some tribes, especially when sheikhs and khans ruled peoples they had conquered or acted as agents of powerful sultans.

So it is not clear that tribes were ever "tribal" in the sense intended by Mackey and Pryce-Jones, or that tribes should be blamed for the despotism of states. It *is* clear that contemporary MENA societies should not be termed "tribal." Some of the rhetoric of tribal life continues to be used in political arenas, where it may sound archaic to outsiders, but this is a far cry from a still-tribal social system undermining modernization. In many MENA nations kinship and regional attachments guide the formation of important economic and political relationships, and the patron/client networks built from these may undermine attempts to create more democratic institutions. When I consider the character of patron-clientage in chapter 3, I will show that there are important tensions between unifying and fissioning forces at all levels of social organization, and that a kind of "power-challenge dialectic" does play itself out in interpersonal as well as political life. But these do not originate in an unperturbable momentum of tribal tradition, and the notion that MENA societies are still tribal—hence strife-torn and despotic—is simply the wrong starting point for understanding them.

The "Code of Honor" Monopolizes the Middle Eastern Psyche,
and Subverts Modernization

Mackey and Pryce-Jones both see the honor code, anchored in the region's tribalism, as providing MENA's predominant ethical system and psychological orientation. Mackey writes that Arabs "follow the general patterns found in the Bedouin's deep commitment to family and tribe, the dictate of vengeance, and the concept of honor."[74] She explains that "honor is the driving force of the Arab psyche. It is a demanding master that stalks its vassal with a broadsword called shame. . . . in Arab culture, pride constantly plays against defensiveness, creating within Arabs and among Arabs a level of ongoing tension."[75] The Bedouin so deeply internalized "the family's values and codes of behavior," she believes, that "he ceased to identify himself emotionally as an individual. Rather, his wishes reflected the wishes of his father, his interests matched those of the group."[76] Honor provided the glue:

> All different kinds of honor from bravery in battle to generosity extended to guests to the sexual chastity of his sisters and daughters interlocked to surround the Bedouin ego like a coat of armor. The smallest chink in that armor threatened to unhinge it, leaving the individual exposed to the greatest of all threats—shame. . . . In the end and at any cost honor had to be restored.

Honor thus wreaks havoc throughout the Middle East: "Honor builds from the individual to the nation to interstate relations and back down again in a constant battle of one Arab to get the better of another. This contest for honor fractures nations and divides countries."[77]

Pryce-Jones writes with equal certainty that "what otherwise seems capricious and self-destructive in Arab society is explained by the anxiety to be honored and respected at all costs, and by whatever means."[78] Reinforcing the power-challenge dialectic "from the top to the bottom of Arab society," the honor-shame system "effectively prevents the development of wider, more socialized types of human relationship . . . to Western concepts of contractual relationships."[79] He concludes: "The customary attachment of notions of honor to status and behavior, leading to pursuit of a military heroism that has long since been obsolete and make-believe in practice, continues to obstruct all reformist thought or experiment throughout the Arab world."[80] Mackey and Pryce-Jones are not just reading each others' works but the writings of scholars like Patai, who claims that the Arab psyche is governed by shame (fear of public censure) rather than guilt (fear of transgressing internal standards), which predominates in the West, and who attributes many social, political, and military problems to Arab leaders' preoccupations with "saving face" rather than adopting technological methods. A number of Western-trained MENA scholars also have written critically of their compatriots' preoccupation with honor and shame, so Patai, Mackey, and Pryce-Jones all have Arab intellectuals to cite. In chapter 3 I will argue that honor and shame indeed are crucially important features of MENA cultures, and that they shape the personality development of perhaps most individuals. But accounts like those given by Mackey, Patai, and Pryce-Jones grossly overstate individuals' immersion in their groups, and misconstrue the nature and role of the "honor code."

The notion that "primitive" peoples don't develop into individuals as Westerners do but remain enmeshed in the feelings and thoughts of their group has been around for a long time. Freud and other colonial-era psychologists believed that the development of civilizations proceeded along the same lines as that of individuals, so that the "thought" of primitive peoples resembled that of Western children and neurotics with childhood fixations. Others wrote that primitives had permeable rather than solid "ego-boundaries," their moral lives being governed by socially induced shame rather than the guilt that stems from violating principles of one's "own" conscience. In 1935 the anthropologist Alexander Goldenweiser wrote what should have been the last word on this outlook:

> Anthropologists are no longer surprised when new evidence is brought forth of the existence of full-fledged individuality among primitives. In the heyday of folk theory it was glibly assumed that the primitive individual was literally submerged, that no room was left for personality or self-expression in a society ridden by tradition, dominated by established habits and dogmas, shot through with inflexible patterns. No one any longer believes this. We know now that the very uniformity of primitive patterns should not be taken literally.[81]

But the simplistic West versus non-West dichotomy has come back in the view being advanced by social psychologists that Western societies have "individualistic" cultures that fashion "egocentric" selves, while most non-Western societies—including the Middle East—have "collectivistic" cultures that shape "sociocentric" selves (see chapter 9).[82]

Studies of MENA tribes show that however much they emphasize group loyalties, tribesmen have no difficulty identifying themselves emotionally as individuals, and in fact celebrate autonomy and independence as components of honor. "A real man stands alone and fears nothing," explained one Awlad Ali Bedouin to the anthropologist Lila Abu-Lughod, "He is like a falcon. A falcon flies alone."[83] Her *Veiled Sentiments* elegantly shows how a complex and subtle genre of poetry and song provide the Awlad Ali with vehicles for expressing and communicating the personal sentiments that the code of honor requires them to officially deny. And Mackey's suggestion that an individual's wishes automatically coincide with those of his or her father and group appears ludicrous in light of the literary and ethnographic accounts of prodigal sons, daughters who attempt suicide rather than accept arranged marriages, and nearly endemic intrafamilial strife. A recent American social psychology text cites the Moroccan proverb "If you cut off the ties of blood, you will have to worry on your own" as evidence that it is a "sociocentric" culture[84] but does not mention the commonly muttered proverb "Aqarib agarab," which means "Close relatives are scorpions." Evidence of "full-fledged individuality" among the most traditional MENA tribespeople and villagers could fill the rest of this book.

Scores of careful community studies show the honor-shame system to be far more complex than the accounts that blame it for MENA's strife and underdevelopment (see chapter 3). It varies dramatically from region to region and even from village to village; it takes on a different character for women and for men; its principles prove to be subject to continual dispute rather than consensus; it appears as one among several ethical systems guiding everyday life; and social action very often fails to follow its principles. The anthropologist Michael Herzfeld argues that it does not form a "code" that regulates behavior but a "poetics" by which people seek to stylize their public self-presentations in certain circumstances.[85] Pryce-Jones at least points out that the honor system is a circum-Mediterranean cultural pattern but fails to note that its great prominence among ancient Greeks hardly prevented them from inventing democracy, nor has it prevented Italians and Spaniards from becoming modern.

As for the argument that intense familial loyalties and the honor-shame system subvert reasoning, mastery of technology, and nation-building, one can look at the fate of Japan—long regarded as having one of the globe's most intensely interdependent family systems and most pronounced ethics of honor, shame, and "face"—which hardly remains mired in technological backwardness. What Japan, and indeed portions of the Middle East, shows is that familial attachments and sentiments of honor can fuel achievement, entrepreneurship, and modernization *under auspicious conditions*. MENA's honor-shame system certainly helps define its distinctive culture(s), and it often plays an important role in personality development. But it forms one thread of the culture(s), not its heart and soul, and cannot be blamed for the region's economic and political problems.

Islamic "Fatalism" Breeds Inaction and Stalls Development

Western diplomats and administrators of development projects often vent their frustrations with the pace of progress at religious "fatalism," which they view as a deep-seated cultural or psychological trait. At almost any capital city cocktail party or Peace Corps beer bash a voice or two will rise above the murmur of chat and pronounce: "These people are so used to sitting around waiting for God to do things that they won't get up and help themselves." Some Westerners know enough Arabic to dub this the "*insha' Allah* complex" or the "*maktoub* mentality." *Insha' Allah* means "God willing," and most Muslims utter this phrase after any reference to future events, such as, "I'll meet you tomorrow at 9 a.m., *insha' Allah*." *Maktoub* means "it is written" or "it is fated" by God and is often voiced to express feelings of resignation or helplessness before greater powers, such as while watching a flash flood sweep away a carefully cultivated field of barley. Many other common phrases (*fi yad Allah*, "it's in God's hands") convey similar sentiments, and everyday conversation is peppered with religious references that evoke God's presence and influence on the course of events: *bismillah*, "in the name of God," will be uttered at the beginning of any undertaking; *tebarakallah'alik*, "may the blessings of God be upon you," is used as a compliment; *allah ybarikfik*, "may God bless you" is used to mean "you're welcome." Westerners can read this saturation of daily life with God's power as a deep fatalism, or as a tragic sense of the precariousness of human undertakings, or as an infusion of every act with a spirit of worship. A few scholars, such as Patai, take it as fatalism and view Islam as providing a doctrine of predestination that gives comfort in times of hardship but has a "retarding effect" in times of opportunity, because "it makes people adverse to any effort directed toward seeking betterment."[86] Morroe Berger followed suit in his 1962 book *The Arab World Today:*

> Risk, uncertainty, free forms in art and literature, scientific exploration, philosophic speculation, the questioning of systems of government and of authority, all are leaps into the unknown and hence challenges to fate, to what has been laid down by religious and secular authority, to the perfection of Islam and to its completeness. This attitude shows itself in fatalism, authoritarianism, and the Arab view of the external world of nature.[87]

Some Arab writers also have made fatalism a target of criticism, as did Habib Ayrout in *The Egyptian Peasant,* long regarded in the West as the classic study of rural MENA society. The American-trained psychologist Sania Hamady also attacked fatalism in her 1960 book *Temperament and Character of the Arabs.* Writing this work as a "critical self-analysis" at a time of renaissance and emancipation, she argued that Arabs also need a "liberation from the self" and "a cleansing from within." In ten pages on predestination, fatalism, and resignation, she eloquently describes the demoralization wrought by poverty ("His fatalistic attitude is the result of a subsistence economy where people live in material want until death"[88]) and oppression ("The impact of fatalistic philosophy on the Arabs is therefore due not so much to the religious doctrine of determinism . . . as to the nefarious influence of political subjugation, economic poverty, and social tyranny"[89]), and she makes it clear that "landlordism and sheikhcraft are the main institutions that keep the people in the bondage of fatalism."[90] But she also makes blanket statements about fatalism in the Arab character: "He is little aware of the fact that he can, to a large extent, control his environment, contribute towards shaping his destiny, realize his wishes through conscious management and ameliorating his lot by his own actions."[91] Many Western authors have quoted and paraphrased statements like these, while ignoring her points about the heavy oppression of poverty, landlordism, and sheikhcraft (see chapter 9).

Yet religious fatalism provides an even less appropriate explanation for underdevelopment than does the honor code. As most scholars[92] recognize, Islam is remarkably flexible, and, like "honor," it takes diverse forms within a region, a village, or even a single family. Like other religions, Islam can be invoked to advocate or oppose modernization, to justify or condemn violence, to indict an oppressive government or cloak it in legitimacy. Whether it mobilizes initiative or counsels resignation appears to depend mainly on the presence or absence of real opportunity. Hani Fakhouri studied the Nile village of Kafr el-Elow in the mid-1960s (when Ayrout's book was reprinted to effusive reviews), just as an expansion of factories in the surrounding area was beginning to provide well-paying jobs and business opportunities. He conducted a survey among the supposedly fatalistic peasants and found that 90 percent believed a person's social position "is the result of his own efforts" and only 10 percent "the result of God's Will."[93] There were 18 small businesses in Kafr el-Elow at the end of World War II, 77 in the mid-1960s, and 283 when he returned in 1985. The latter two decades' growth in entrepreneurship, he notes, was accompanied by an intensification in religiosity.

John Waterbury's *North for the Trade* tells the social history of Morocco's Sous Valley region through the biography of a merchant named Hadj Brahim. The combination of gasoline pumps for wells drilled into an abundant water table and roads built by the French enabled the Berbers of this previously remote region to become the greengrocers of Morocco and by the 1960s to rival the wealth and influence of the traditional elite. In the process, they developed a religiosity resembling the Protestant ethic that the sociologist Max Weber believed helped give birth to capitalism in the West. The Soussis embrace orthodox Muslim beliefs and practices but use them to support a dedication to hard work, frugality, asceticism, and achievement that they regard as redemptive.

In the mid-1980s Alison Geist and I studied economic development among the Imeghrane, an agro-pastoral group on the southern slopes of Morocco's Atlas Mountains. The Imeghrane are part of the same Berber culture as the Soussis, but their terrain lacks most of the Sous Valley's resources, and we found it literally littered with failed entrepreneurial projects: farms and olive orchards hewn out of desert wastes that died when well-water turned brackish;[94] shops built for tourists who rarely stopped because the town down the road offered more spectacular vistas; fields of saffron abandoned after the owner's downstream neighbors stopped him from pumping water during a drought. We also discovered an important political difference. At Independence the Soussis swept out most of the local officials who ruled the countryside for the French and "milked" it for their own benefit, but in Imeghrane these men were restored to power by the new government, and their sons and grandsons continued to dispense access to government development projects as patronage, and to seize opportunities for themselves and their clients.

One of the more progressive men in Imeghrane's central cluster of villages owned a small cafe on a picturesque hill overlooking the weekly market, and began planning renovations when he heard that the road from the main highway was to be paved and would allow tourists to visit. But one day he returned from a trip to town to find that the governing official had bull-dozed his cafe to the ground and rewritten the deed for the coveted hilltop property to the head of a wealthy family in a neighboring village—an all-too-common typical example of what Hamady terms "sheikhcraft." Enraged, he attacked the official but was subdued by his paramilitary police, and after being told what could happen to him and his family he gradually resigned himself. When we saw him a few days later he bitterly muttered "Maktoub, maktoub" (It was written, it was written). We heard a great deal of this fatalism in Imeghrane—*after* human initiative and perseverance had been defeated by the superior powers of nature or corrupt rule.[95] Waterbury heard some of it in the Sous, and points out that no one attitude pervades all areas of a person's life: "Just when one becomes convinced that Brahim is a North African Ben Franklin, he abruptly becomes the Muslim fatalist or a grocery story J'ha [a trickster character], taking his customers or the government for a ride."[96]

The lessons seem clear: the opening of opportunity breeds a kind of achievement-oriented, "Muslim ethicist" religiosity; the closing of opportunity breeds resignation in the solace of religious fatalism. "Fatalism" plays no larger role in Islam than it does in Hinduism, Buddhism, Confucianism, or Christianity; nor is it any more a trait of Arabs than of any other peoples. And it no more retards development in the MENA than it has in Asia, where economic "miracles" have turned "backward" nations into "tigers" of the Pacific Rim. Contrary to the fatalist doctrine, a "Muslim ethicist" religiosity—in which worldly achievement is perceived as a kind of divine "calling"—animates much of the MENA's development (though this does not mean it is the primary *cause* of development). It also fuels discontent with the closing of opportunities by corrupt officials, wealthy elites, multinational corporations, and dictatorial regimes (see chapter 8).

The Momentum of Tradition Resists Modernization

Claims that the honor code or Islamic fatalism are to blame for the Middle East's economic and political underdevelopment often form part of a broader argument that "tradition" has a kind of inertia that the forces of modernization can only haltingly overcome. Patai says this quite explicitly: "In modern Western culture, the new is considered better than the old, and thus change in itself is considered a good; in tradition-bound Arab cultures, the old is regarded as better than the new, and thus the retention of the existing order is considered a good."[97] It may seem obvious that modern and traditional ways naturally oppose each other and that traditions have a weight of habit that acts as a naturally conservative force. But any intimation that Middle Easterners are "tradition-bound" misrepresents their reasoning, their motivations, and their current cultural struggles. A great many traditions are discarded the moment modern ways prove more convenient, effective, or enjoyable. Joseph Hobbs reports that the Ma'aza Bedouins of Egypt's eastern desert readily abandoned their traditional animal-skin water bags for plastic Jerry cans because they don't break when dropped, and in many areas, pastoralists now move their herds by truck.[98] Tourists often feel cheated when they sweat to get into remote areas and then see the extent to that "authentic" traditions have been discarded in favor of mass-produced and marketed ones. The Turkish novelist Orhan Pamuk has one of his characters write about a master mannequin maker who could not sell his exquisite works of art to the owners of fashionable stores because they were too authentic to tradition. "Turks nowadays didn't want to be 'Turks' anymore," explained a merchant who sold European-style clothes, "but something else." Another "pointed out that his customers did not buy an outfit but, in truth, bought a dream. What they really wanted to purchase was the dream of being like the 'others' who wore the same outfit." But the master and his son kept making mannequins, carefully observing the gestures of people in the streets, believing them to be the indelible repository of their cultural heritage. Then they saw the gestures give way:

> The gestures that he and his father called "mankind's greatest treasure," the small body movements people performed in their everyday lives, changed slowly and congruously, vanished as if under the orders of an invisible "chief," only to be replaced by a slew of movements modeled after some indiscernible original. Some time later, as the father and son worked on a line of mannequin children, it all became clear to them: "Those damn movies!" cries the son.[99]

One of the most stunning misrepresentations of tradition's resistance to modernity appears to have been the journalist Richard Critchfield's popular *Shahhat: An Egyptian*, which tells the intimate story of a "deeply traditional Egyptian . . . faced with sudden changes in his way of life."[100] Struggling to wrest a life from poverty in a Nile village near the temples of Luxor, Shahhat, as Critchfield portrays him, ineffectively alternates between fatalism, anger, and escape, a behavior Critchfield sees as widespread: "Shahhat is typical of the great mass of poor Egyptians, in his emotionalism and search for explanations to natural phenomena, not in modern logic, but in the sacred and profane supernatural." The peasants "developed a distinct mentality," he writes: "they preserved and repeated, but did not originate, create, or change."[101] In several passages, he suggests racialist explanations for Shahhat's reactions to the "cultural turbulence" around him: because he has some "Arab Bedouin blood" he "may be a little closer to the dark springs of life than the average fellah." In another passage Critchfield attributes Shahhat's temper to a "vengeful Bedouin streak in Shahhat's blood."

But as the political scientist Timothy Mitchell showed in a 1990 critique,[102] much of Critchfield's description of peasant life depends on paraphrase of Henri Ayrout's *The Egyptian Peasant*. In addition to describing the peasant as mired in fatalism, Ayrout wrote that the peasant "is like a primitive man or child," possessing "little individuality" and "atrophied intelligence." Oppressed by large landowners and despotic governments, he lives in misery but with such a "lack of education and culture" that "he does not feel the depth of his suffering."[103] Mitchell questions whether some of the incidents in *Shahhat* actually took place, but he objects most strongly to the way Critchfield saw village life through the lens of Ayrout's account of irrational, child-like, fatalistic peasants. Yet not only was *Shahhat* well received, Mitchell writes, but in 1981 Critchfield was awarded a MacArthur Foundation award for his "original" work.[104]

One reason for the continued misrepresentation of tradition is that a good many cultural battles in MENA societies are fought in the name of advancing modernization versus defending tradition, with rhetoric implying that the modern should be welcomed because it is modern and the traditional conserved because it has passed the tests of time. Nearly every aspect of life is now debated in terms of tradition and modernity, and it may be no exaggeration to say that MENA culture now consists of a "rhetoric of modernization," in which even mundane actions (for example, eating with one's fingers versus a fork) become statements of principle. But the fact that people may fight *for* a tradition does not mean that it has a momentum of its own or that those defending it are "tradition bound."

When we visited Imeghrane's sheikhs at the beginning of our fieldwork and asked how their lives had changed since they were boys in the 1930s, they voiced relief that tribal warfare had ended and delight that food had become more varied and plentiful—with no hint of nostalgia for violence or hunger. Imeghranis certainly "cling" to many of their traditions, but they successfully lobbied for a maternity clinic where their women could give birth in modern conditions. In their classic study *Becoming Modern*, Alex Inkeles and David Smith point out that life in premodern societies tends to be full of hardship and suffering, and that premodern peoples eagerly adopt modern tools and ways that ease their burdens. Around the globe, the frustrations of premodern peoples have intensified not when they have been presented with opportunities to replace the traditional with the modern but when their access to modernity has been blocked. This, rather than "Bedouin blood," may explain Shahhat's drinking and outbursts of violence.

Colonialism greatly complicated the process of "becoming modern," and the continuing domination by Western and Westernized elites continues to complicate it. Colonization typically took away the very resources and denied the very technologies traditional peoples needed to modernize, yet at the same time tried to get them to give up their core cultural and religious values for whatever Western mores each generation of soldiers, merchants, farmers, and missionaries took with them into the colonies. This has had two profound consequences. First, it has made the only "modern" life available to many traditional peoples a miserable marginal existence in a sprawling urban shantytown. Joseph Hobbs reports that the Ma'aza Bedouin have seen fellow tribesmen forced into slums, and their preference for the "freedom" of the nomadic life reflects not the momentum of tradition, but a carefully considered choice for better nutrition, sanitation, family solidarity, and even economic opportunity.[105] Second, colonized peoples often have embraced and defended some of their traditions as defining their identities, and used them to help rally resistance against the colonizers. This has been especially important throughout the Middle East, where Islam, the veiling of women, and (in some areas) Arab ethnicity helped mobilize anticolonial resistance.

Yet as cultural practices became "traditions to be conserved" against the assaults of the West, they were transformed in ways that made them no longer truly traditional. Believing that Muslim peoples had become weak because they had allowed their religion to degrade, reformers sought to "purify" Islam by ridding it of "superstitions." Nationalists embraced essentially *modern* forms of orthodoxy as the true tradition they fought for against their colonizers. Similarly, the veil became a modern symbol, as women began wearing them as statements of anticolonial protest—especially when other women, inspired by Western ideals, were unveiling and claiming equal rights as a strategy for strengthening the nation. And the pan-Arab nationalism that animated resistance in Lebanon, Jordan, Palestine, Egypt, Syria, and Iraq consisted of a fully modern philosophy for nation-building created by French- and American-educated intellectuals in the 1940s and 1950s. Far from being "bound" to tradition, MENA societies profoundly modernized their traditions in order to fight for them against their colonizers. The result may not much resemble the Western ideal of secular humanism,[106] but it is a modern, self-conscious reworking of tradition, and not tradition as spontaneously lived before colonization.

The process of revising and "inventing" tradition[107] has continued and perhaps intensified after independence, as it has around the globe. The Moroccan historian Abdullah Laroui has analyzed this process and argued that Arab "traditions" often turn out to be the creations of a traditionalist ideology issuing from a modernizing elite. "Tradition is a choice made in response to foreign intervention," he writes.[108] Not only are "traditions" attacked and defended as people jockey for power in families, communities, and nations but they are adapted for display to tourists and for performance on TV variety shows as "traditional"—paradoxically transforming them in the very act of preservation. In many areas of life, traditions come to be enacted modernly, and modern ways traditionally, and it becomes exceedingly difficult to disentangle what is truly traditional and what truly modern.

It is simply false to say that Westerners systematically welcome "the new" while Middle Easterners defend "the old." And even worse than being false, this way of thinking distorts the process of modernization and the nature of the struggles currently taking place in MENA societies. I will show that the cultural conflict between modernism and traditionalism—often taking shape as a conflict between Westernization and Islam—proves crucial to the organization of what Erik Erikson termed "psycho-social identity" for many Middle Easterners. But modernists often make themselves quite comfortable with the status quo, while many traditionalists seek reform and advocate radical change. Some of the most effective modernizers are illiterate villagers like our neighbor who turned his back on traditional agricultural ceremonies, saying, "Look, America's gone to the moon and we're sacrificing sheep to bring rain? We've got work to do!" And some of the most articulate traditionalists—including leaders of "fundamentalist" groups—are highly educated and worldly members of the urban elite. The cultural struggle of modernism and traditionalism must be seen as a debate over two philosophies about how to become modern: by following the West or by finding a Moroccan, or an Egyptian, or an Arab, or a Muslim path. From a psychological point of view, the most important feature of this struggle is that a great many individuals find themselves internally divided and uncertain, ambivalently drawn to modernism in some contexts and to traditionalism in others (see chapter 8).

Terrorism Springs from a Vein of Fanaticism
in Arab Culture and the Arab Psyche

When I first drafted this chapter, U.S. embassies in Kenya and Tanzania had just been bombed, and retaliatory raids had been carried out on targets in Sudan and Afghanistan. TV and newsmagazines were parading photos of the "master terrorist" Osama bin Laden, captioned with his ominous warnings that the holy war on Americans has just begun. As I revise it in the aftermath of the attack on the World Trade Center of September 11, 2001, American troops continue to search for bin Laden in Afghanistan, the United States has attacked and occupied Iraq, and the Israeli-Palestinian conflict has escalated to new levels of violence and despair. Western TV screens have been filled with a steady stream of horrific images: Taliban executions of veiled women in the Kabul soccer stadium, planes crashing into the World Trade Towers, carnage from Palestinian suicide bombings and Israeli reprisals.

There can be no doubt that guerrilla raids and attacks on civilians have profound cultural and psychological *consequences*, both in MENA and the West. But the *causes* of "Arab terrorism" are no more to be found in the culture(s) and psyches of ordinary Middle Easterners than are the causes of Irish Republican Army and Ulster Defense Force terrorism to be found in the Catholicism and Protestantism of ordinary Irish Christians, the causes of the Clear Path cult's sarin gas attacks in the culture and psyche of ordinary Japanese, the causes of 14,569 attacks carried out in Italy between 1969 and 1986 to be found in an Italian "mentality," or the causes of the militia movement and the Oklahoma City bombing to be found in the culture(s) and psyches of ordinary Americans.[109]

Walter Laquer traces the rationale and tactics of modern terrorism to mid-nineteenth-century Russian sources, elaborated late in that century by

Armenian and Hindu Indian nationalists.[110] In the second half of the twentieth century, terrorist groups have emerged in many societies around the globe, including those with reputations for nonbelligerence. From 1980 through 2001, the world's leading practitioner of suicide bombing were the Tamil Tigers of Sri Lanka,[111] who are culturally Hindu with a largely secularist ideology. Scholars studying terrorism, impressed by the range of societies in which it has emerged, have avoided psycho-cultural explanations in favor of an emphasis on (1) the psychological makeup of the individuals who become terrorists, (2) the group processes operating in organizations that carry out terrorist acts, and (3) official sponsorship of terrorism as a political strategy. Studies of individual terrorists find a tremendous range of life-paths that lead to violence, find psychological characteristics shared by a great many nonterrorists (i.e., threatened identity,[112] splitting and externalizing defenses[113]), and almost without exception conclude that "individuals who join terrorist groups show little evidence of psychopathology."[114] Jonathan Drummond argues that it is a critical conjunction of societal "tipping events" (signaling a group's victimization) with personal "triggering events" (individual victimization, loss, or humiliation) that leads a small percentage of political activists to become terrorists.[115]

Thanks to a half-century of research inspired by the Holocaust, wartime massacres of civilians, and genocides, we now know a good deal about the *group processes* by which "terrorist" killers are created; the main processes are as follows.[116]

1. Sanctioning of violence by authorities—often phrased in terms of a myth of historic mission and amplified by the motive of vengeance
2. Peer pressure to conform
3. Deindividuation of the actors
4. Denigration of the victims as subhuman
5. Training and baptism of a killing self
6. Routinization of the violent acts

When organizers can recruit individuals who live in despair, who have suffered personal loss or humiliation, and who have previous combat experience, these processes become all the more effective. They can be used in any culture to create cult-like groups that typically refurbish myths of warrior heroes to legitimate their attacks. But however well the myths play to their audiences, their claims to cultural authenticity mislead if taken for explanations for why such groups come into existence or carry out the actions they do. The available studies suggest that psychologically, terrorist groups resemble each other more than they do the cultures they claim to authentically represent, and that "fanaticism" is generated as cult-like groups get members to *sever* their ordinary social and family relationships.[117]

A good deal of evidence indicates that "Arab terrorism" has emerged mainly in milieus where the culture has been distorted or destroyed. Many terrorists, perhaps a majority, have come from Palestinian refugee camps, and more recently, from the war against the Soviets in Afghanistan. In 1986 the *Newsweek* reporters Ray Wilkinson and Rod Nordland investigated "the Middle East terror network" and concluded that "Terrorists are not born, they're made."[118] They found that Mohammed Abbas, who ran the Achille Lauro hijacking, had recruited his commandos from the Sabra and Chatilla camps; the surviving attacker of the Rome and Vienna airports had lost his father in an Israeli air raid there; another had lost his wife and daughter in an air raid on Chatilla; a teen-age guerrilla who called himself "Guevara" showed them shrapnel wounds from the battleship *New Jersey*'s shelling of Lebanese villages. It was the young men in the camps, writes the political scientist Barry Rubin, who responded to Yasir Arafat's plea: "Isn't it better to die bringing down your enemy than to await a slow, miserable death rotting in a tent in the desert?"[119] Many Taliban similarly had their origins in Pakistani refugee camps, some raised in religious orphanages that trained them for permanent armed struggle. The journalist David Lamb concludes: "If there is a common denominator in the character of the Arab terrorists, it is a sense of hopelessness."[120] And as the Palestinian psychiatrist Eyad El-Sarraj has observed, it is the emotionally scarred and despairing children of the first Intifaada who have grown up to become the suicide bombers of the second.[121] A recent study of young Palestine suicide bombers similarly pointed to the conjunction of symbolic political events (Ariel Sharon's visit to the Temple Mount) with personal injuries and humiliations suffered during the Intifaada.[122]

The traumas and addictive excitement of war often breed men who hunger for more. It was battle-scarred and betrayed World War I veterans who formed the Freikorps terrorists in Germany, whom many view as Nazi precursors. Vietnam veterans swelled the ranks of right-wing militias in the United States, and it was a veteran of the Gulf War who bombed the Federal Building in Oklahoma City. It now seems to be Afghan guerrilla fighters, encouraged by their defeat of a superpower, who provided the initial core of al Qaeda. From scores of studies we know that to grow up in a refugee camp or to come of age in a guerrilla war means to *not* live in one's culture, and as the readjustment difficulties of Vietnam combat veterans have shown, it often means to be profoundly alienated from ordinary family and social life. Recent studies have begun to focus on the disorienting experiences of "guest" workers and students in Europe, who often encounter racism and isolation alongside freedom and opportunity. While a great many work out cosmopolitan "hybrid" identities, the quest for authenticity leads a significant minority to Islamism, and some of those to hatred of the West. Given the roles of refugee camps, wars, and emigration in the backgrounds of many terrorists, and the ways violent groups require withdrawal from ordinary relationships, it appears clear that terrorists tend to be made in *estrangement* from their culture's mainstream rather than from thorough embedding in it.[123]

Yet if terrorism emerges from the confluence of individual suffering and state sponsorship, it readily takes on a life of its own. As Allen Feldman documents in his study of sectarian conflict in Northern Ireland,[124] terrorism creates a culture of violence that refashions the geographical spaces people inhabit, the types of characters the culture lauds and condemns, and the meanings people give to their bodies and feelings. Violence causes previously multisectarian or multiethnic communities to segregate and turns border zones into stages for the performance of violent rituals, as occurred with the creation of Israel and later in Lebanon's civil war. Bodies become tests of courage, weapons of violence, and scarred memorials to battle and torture. Political violence, Feldman argues, whether perpetrated by colonial powers on the colonized, by freedom fighters on their enemies, or by states on their citizens, profoundly changes culture.

The anthropologist Ghassan Hage writes that Palestinian youth participating in the *intifaada* have created a new "culture of martyrdom."[125] The groundwork was laid as the "highly masculine and competitive" youth culture came to celebrate daring confrontations with Israeli troops. Julie Peteet describes how by 1992 interrogations, beatings, wounds, and imprisonment had become rites of passage for Palestinian youth:

> Visits to families are punctuated by the display of bodies with the marks of bullets and beatings and are social settings for the telling of beatings, shootings, verbal exchanges with settlers and soldiers, and prison stories. . . . To the Palestinians, the battered body, with its bruises and broken limbs, is the symbolic embodiment of a twentieth-century history of subordination and powerlessness—of "what we have to endure" but also of their determination to resist and to struggle for national independence. A representation created with the intent of humiliating has been reversed into one of honour, manhood and moral superiority.[126]

Young men often describe these experiences as leaving them "nothing left to lose" and as inspiring them to join armed groups and to commit more daring acts. Hage detects "a suicidal tendency exhibited in those practices well before they materialize in the form of suicide bombing."[127] Then, "once the first act of suicide bombing occurred, it was immediately followed by a culture of glorification of self-sacrifice, that became further reproduced as more suicide bombings occurred, until this culture of glorification became an entrenched part of Palestinian colonized society."[128]

By 2001, 70 percent of 1,000 Palestinian nine- to sixteen-year-olds interviewed by the psychologist Fadal Abu-Hin said they wanted to be martyrs.[129] Hage joins a chorus of Palestinians in criticizing suicide bombing, but he suggests that two factors help explain the "paradox" of "a self aiming to abolish itself while also seeking self-esteem."[130] First is the "quasi-complete" lack of opportunities for Palestinian youth to build meaningful lives or even "to dream a meaningful life," which "produces a generalized form of premature social aging, even of social death." The second is "colonial humiliation"— being "psychologically demeaned" by both the general subordination of Palestinians and the personal humiliations of daily life: "being shouted at, abused, searched, stopped, ordered around, checked, asked to wait, 'allowed to pass,' and so forth." In response to unbearable social death, the culture of martyrdom provides youths with a meaningful death and with "an imagined enjoyable symbolic life following the cessation of their physical life." The anticipated attack thus helps annul the sense of humiliation. Echoing Peteet's observations about scars transforming humiliation into honor, Hage suggests that terrorist organizations' ability to transform social death into meaningful after-life and humiliation into potency may be "their primary function and the secret of their success."[131]

Wherever violence becomes organized and chronic enough to remake culture, the psychological consequences can be widespread and deep. In Latin America, army attacks, police torture, death squads, and guerrilla movements became so pervasive that by the 1980s anthropologists began terming some of them "cultures of terror."[132] In addition to the armed strife in Palestine, Algeria, and Lebanon, many MENA citizens are affected on a nearly daily basis by the terror that some governments use to rule them, as its objective is not just to eliminate dissidents but to create pervasive fear and mistrust. Samir al-Khalil's *Republic of Fear* gives a powerful account of Saddam Hussein's Iraq as a society virtually created by the state and as a culture built on fear of the *mukhabarat*, the secret police. The use of state employment and state terror as the carrot and stick of autocratic rule has shaped the modern cultures of many MENA nations, creating generalized dependency and insecurity. The mixing of autocratic rule and secret police with traditional beliefs in supernatural beings and Western media imagery readily creates the sort of "magical realist" atmosphere evoked in the novels of Gabriel Garcia Marquez, Salman Rushdie, Tahar ben Jelloun, and others, in which reality and fantasy braid dismayingly together into a cultural landscape that is neither traditional nor modern.

The challenge to cultural psychology, then, is not to "explain" terror by finding its cultural roots[133]—especially since people become terrorists primarily in milieus where traditional culture has been undermined. Rather, cultural psychology's so-far-unmet challenge is to investigate how political violence, by both militia-like groups and governments, affects the psyches of those who grow up and live in its shadows (see chapter 9).

Underdevelopment ❀

Many of these misunderstandings have been created by distorting important forces at work in MENA societies. Tribally based values *have* shaped the region's cultural heritage(s); social life often *is* animated by something like a "power-challenge dynamic"; honor and shame *do* anchor a central ethical/etiquette system; Islam *does* pervade life in a way that makes God continuously present; contemporary culture *does* take shape as a debate about tradition and modernity; the heritage *does* celebrate the daring and glorious deeds. All of these features influence psychological development and personal identities, which this book will explore. Specifically, it will examine how Middle Easterners are seeking to adopt modern ideas, technologies, and styles of life, and to preserve their cultural heritages, in conditions of *underdevelopment* or *dependent development*.

Underdevelopment in MENA has to do with the fact that most of the nations that have oil are sparsely populated, and that most of the nations with large populations lack not only oil but also the other resources (water, coal, minerals, wood) needed to fuel industrialization. It has to do with the region's high rate of population growth, that contributed to the 2.3 percent *decline* in per capita GNP between 1980 and 1993, the worst performance of any region in the world. "Real wages and labor productivity today are about the same as in 1970," write the economist Alan Richards and the political scientist John Waterbury: "rising poverty, joblessness, and social unrest are direct results of this growth failure."[134] Underdevelopment has to do with the fact that many governments have grown as what political scientists call "rentier states": financing themselves by directly controlling oil revenues (or in some cases foreign aid), they provide modern sector jobs through development projects and public services, thus bypassing the need to tax their citizens and be held accountable to them. Al-Khalil estimates that 60 percent of the urban labor force in Iraq depended on the state, meaning Hussein's Ba'th Party, for their jobs.[135] Underdevelopment also has to do with the support Western powers and the former Soviet Union have provided to antidemocratic regimes, and with the saturation of the region with marketing images of Western life-styles that the majority of people cannot afford.

Above all, underdevelopment does *not* perpetuate tradition: it is an active process of change that renders people unable to live either traditional or modern lives. Underdevelopment challenges those living it to create new forms of culture by selectively blending elements of the old and the new, and the result challenges observers to understand it with concepts other than "traditional" and "modern." Ahmad Zaid describes how the importation of a kind of pseudo-modernity has provoked a great variety of reactions, producing a "third" culture that is neither traditional nor modern.[136] The historian Hisham Sharabi uses the term *neopatriarchy* to describe this "absence equally of genuine traditionalism and of genuine modernity."[137] "Over the last one hundred years," he writes, "the patriarchal structures of Arab society, far from being displaced or truly modernized, have only been strengthened and deformed, in 'modernized' forms."[138] From families to regimes and all along the networks of fluid protofamilial patron-clientage that link them, neopatriarchal forms of relationship adapt to conditions of underdevelopment, yielding a society of "forced consensus based on ritual and coercion" from top to bottom, one that is "incapable of performing as an integrated social or political system, as an economy, or as a military structure."[139] Sharabi cites the Nobel Prize–winning Egyptian novelist Naguib Mahfouz on the central psychological consequence for the average man: "In this new society he has been afflicted with a split personality: half of him believes, prays, fasts and makes the pilgrimage. The other half renders his values void in banks and courts and in the streets, even in the cinemas and theaters, perhaps even at home among his family before the television set."[140]

The Lebanese social psychologist and novelist Halim Barakat offers a similar analysis, emphasizing the damaging role played by most MENA regimes: "In a society that is neither modern nor traditional, the state—by restricting public involvement and appropriating the vital functions of society—has become a force against, rather than for, the people and society."[141] A 2002 United Nations Development Program (UNDP) assessment by a commission of Arab scholars reaches similar conclusions. In spite of impressive economic, health, and education gains, citizens of MENA countries have the least freedom and "voice and accountability" of any region in the world: "The wave of democracy that transformed governance in most of Latin America and East Asia in the 1980s and Eastern Europe and much of Central Asia in the late 1980s and early 1990s has barely reached the Arab States."[142] The "freedom deficit" has stifled private sector initiative and civic participation, and caused the region to be "richer than it is developed."[143] The estimated one million scientists and professionals who have emigrated from the Arab world have impressive accomplishments, but MENA lags behind other developing regions in research and development. And a survey of youth conducted by commission staff found 51 percent wishing to emigrate—nearly all to Europe, the United States, and Canada.

Barakat writes that with governments deliberately undermining modern institutions they can't control and imposing oppressive policies in the name of modernization, many populaces find themselves left "with very limited options except to seek refuge in their traditional institutions (that is, religion, sect, tribe, family, ethnicity) to express their discontent." This has "solidified rather than diminished the conditions of dependency, patriarchal and authoritarian relationships, socioeconomic disparities, and alienation that have endured throughout the post-independence period."[144] Far from being static, Arab culture always has been shaped by dynamic struggles between "the old and the new," and this has intensified in recent decades. Today, Barakat concludes, "conflict between sets of value orientations is the greatest indicator of the complexity and contradictory nature of Arab culture at present. The task of understanding such a culture is rendered even more difficult by its transitional state; an intense internal struggle of becoming is underway."[145] The psychological dimensions of this "struggle of becoming" are the central topic of this book.

CHAPTER *2*

The Social Ecology of Psychological Development

Part 1 of this chapter reviews traditional forms of social organization in MENA societies, which historically provided the environments in which development took place, and set the overall designs of infant care, child and adolescent socialization, and adult roles and life-paths. Patterns of family, gender, and kinship relations developed from centuries of interaction among pastoral, agricultural, and urban ways of life, and broadly resembled those found throughout the Mediterranean, including those in the southern European societies Westerners view as providing their own classical heritage. Ethnographies from nearly all MENA societies suggest that three characteristics are especially important:

1. *The organization of marriage, family, and kinship systems is "endogamous": marriages with "close" relatives are preferred, especially with a man's father's brother's daughter.*
2. *The nature of social groupings is "segmentary": family, kin, village, tribal, and neighborhood groups tend to split into smaller competing groups in some circumstances, and unify into larger cooperating groups in others.*
3. *The basic building-block units of society are not families or lineages but "patronymic associations"—fluid, flexible family-like groupings extended by patron-client relations with nonkin, which sometimes come to resemble what anthropologists term "lineages."*

Ethnographers repeatedly emphasize the flexibility of social groupings in MENA, and that relationships both within and beyond the family cannot simply be taken for granted but must be negotiated dyad by dyad. These dyads are generally hierarchical—of senior-junior, master-apprentice, teacher-student, patron-client types—and take family-like forms, in that they tend to be enacted with etiquettes of authority-deference and of protection-dependence that are extended from family contexts.

This broad pattern of family and kin relations sets the social ecology of psychological development in traditional milieus. Children learn the rudiments of these interaction styles with their immediate family members, and then progressively extend them to more distant kin and then nonkin. As the etiquettes are mastered and internalized, they shape many of the region's culturally distinctive psychological characteristics. Yet in spite of the culture's official values subordinating the individual to the group, the fact that group relationships are so open to negotiation creates a surprisingly wide field of play for individual initiative and character. Part 2 of this chapter describes the profound changes that colonization, independence, urbanization, education, and underdevelopment have brought to traditional patterns of life. As the UN's recent Arab Human Development Report documents, in spite of dramatic economic growth and improved health and literacy, the majority of MENA citizens currently live in conditions of underdevelopment characterized by: (1) economic stagnation aggravated by high rates of population growth; (2) continued rule of undemocratic regimes and absence of basic civil rights; and (3) sharp cultural duality of Western versus indigenous styles of life. The processes of "development" and "underdevelopment" are simultaneously changing the social environments in which psychological development takes place at all stages of the life-cycle.

Introduction ❀

In every society, psychological development is embedded in the organization of families and styles of familial interaction, in the relationships among the kin-groups, villagers, and townspeople who make up its primary communities, in conditions of cooperation or strife with neighboring groups, and in the nature of the political process by which groups govern themselves or are ruled by others. In turn, these features of *social structure* usually take shape as adaptations to the society's ecological setting and to the technologies at its disposal. Some psychological characteristics, then, may be traced ultimately to the society's systems for organizing people to produce and distribute food, material goods, and services and to reproduce itself biologically and culturally—all together making up the *social ecology* of development.

The anthropologist Francis Hsu, for example, sees the Chinese family system as adapted to its agricultural technologies, its land-tenure systems, and its dynastic rule, and he views personality as built around familial roles and the values and feelings associated with them. Backed by the Confucian emphasis on filial piety, sons came into adulthood by embracing their duty to conserve the property and the "Big Family" that ancestors had built. They thus typically developed in submission to and then identification with their fathers, who embodied the authority of the ancestors worshiped at household shrines. This system "deprives the younger generation of any feeling of independence," Hsu writes, "while at the same time it enables them to *share* whatever wealth and glory is due to their immediate or remote ancestors."[1]

This contrasts markedly with the Native Americans of the central plains—to take a second example—who lived as mobile hunters and gatherers, had no family lands to conserve through inheritance, and continually changed the composition of their camping groups. Matrilineal kinship systems developed in this context, giving women a good deal of familial authority and social status, and adolescents were allowed greater latitude for romantic liaisons and for choosing their own spouses. Young men came into adulthood by going off on solitary vision quests in which they acquired personal guardian spirits, and by establishing highly individualized reputations as hunters and warriors. The full range of human affection flowed in both the Chinese and American plains worlds, but through very different patterns of attachment, authority, and initiative. Personality developed through different systems of family and community roles, and self-conceptions were defined within different worlds of meaning: ancestors and land versus guardian spirits and brave deeds.

This chapter will describe the broad outlines of MENA's social structure and political economy, focusing on aspects which most directly shape psychological development. The remainder of this introduction lays out what may be *the* crucial difference between traditional and modern societies: that in most traditional societies, authority and domination tend to be exercised directly, in face-to-face personal relationships, while in modern societies authority and domination tend to be vested in impersonal institutions, such as schools, corporations, and bureaucracies. Part 1 reviews MENA's *traditional* social ecology, focusing on a mixture of pastoral nomadism, peasant agriculture, and urban commerce found throughout the ancient Mediterranean and stretching into Central Asia. Part 2 considers how the traditional pattern is changing as MENA societies are both becoming *modern* and becoming *underdeveloped*.

It will be important to keep in mind that I will use all of these notions—*culture area, pattern, tradition, modernization,* and *underdevelopment*—as useful simplifications. The area cannot be precisely defined, the pattern shows endless variation, there never was a period of "true tradition," and modernization and underdevelopment are controversial processes, better assessed in the cool light of history than in the heat of the present. But some important influences on psychological development do appear to be characteristic of the region, and distinguish it from the neighboring areas of sub-Saharan Africa, Hindu India, or preindustrial Europe, and these terms help describe them.

"Traditional" MENA Societies ❀

Industrialized societies are dominated by corporations, schools, government agencies, and other large organizations. Many sociologists regard the "rationality," "impersonality," and "regimentation" of these bureaucracies as the defining features of modernity. The general separation of family and firm means that individuals form relationships by different principles at their place of work (and school) than they do in their homes and personal lives. Work relationships tend to be more formal, contractual, and based on calculations of self-interest. Managers learn to view their employees as "resources" and to pay, promote, and fire them not on the basis of kinship ties or personal feelings but as they contribute to the organization's productivity. As the sociologist Anthony Giddons points out, this separation leaves individuals free to cultivate friendships and families as "pure relationships," based solely on shared interests, feelings of affection, and other emotional ties.[2] Nearly all Western psychological theories of development assume that the ability to sustain satisfying *pure relationships* is the healthy outcome of childhood and adolescent socialization—and many scholars take this as the psychological hallmark of modernity. Giddons suggests, however, that we might reasonably expect "pure relationships" to be quite unstable, and to make for especially fragile friendships and families.

This differs dramatically from most preindustrial societies, where family based groups typically perform the functions of the firm, and often those of the school, the political party, the welfare agency, the police, and the army. Where families are managed as production systems—and often as political parties, police forces, and so on—emotional ties take on a different character from those built as pure relationships: personal feelings of affection and animosity merge with calculations of resource deployment and strategic alliance. Many important life choices—including one's vocation and spouse—may be made by family elders, a situation that requires everyone to adopt broadly "collectivistic" values rather than "individualistic" ones.

In MENA societies, family and kin-based groups continue to play this kind of encompassing role in many, perhaps most, lives. From this arises some of the most dramatic differences between MENA and "modernized" societies. Relationships between husbands and wives tend to take on a different emotional character where marriages are arranged, romantic love is disparaged as a danger to the social order, and passion is distinguished from a type of love which grows from a lifetime of collaborative work. Parent-child relationships take on a different character as well: even where they attend school, many children begin contributing to their family's subsistence at an early age, and are educated as "apprentices" to their parents and elders. Rather than teaching their children to find their own ways in the world, parents more often nurture the formation of lifelong bonds of loyalty and interdependence. Patterns of authority and domination also differ in ways that have important psychological consequences. Many preindustrial societies are "gerontocracies," in which seniors (typically in their forties and fifties) are supported by the labor of juniors, whose lives they control. Most are "patriarchies," in which men exercise authority over women and assign them much more of the labor of subsistence. In addition, an unequal distribution of land and herd wealth sets up a range of relationships by which senior men dominate and sometimes exploit poorer kinsmen and neighbors.

Pierre Bourdieu argues that the face-to-face character of these forms of domination brings about the most important difference between premodern and modern cultures.[3] The social ecology of the industrialized West operates by what he terms "mediated forms of domination," in which the control of labor and extraction of profit are carried out by seemingly impersonal institutions. By contrast, most preindustrial economies rely on "elementary forms of domination," in which this authority must be exercised in a face-to-face manner. Managers of modern corporations and bureaucracies "are able to dispense with strategies aimed *expressly*. . . and *directly*. . . at the domination of individuals."[4] They carry out policies formulated by experts and exercise institutional rather than personal authority over those they supervise, so that seemingly objective assessments, market forces, and other impersonal priorities control employees' lives. In elementary systems of domination, however, "relations of domination are made, unmade and remade in and by the interaction between persons."[5] That is, seniors must personally dominate juniors, men personally dominate women, and the wealthy personally dominate the poor—often within networks of family and kin ties in which feelings of affection and friendship also flow. If one seeks to understand traditional MENA societies in comparison to the modern West, this must be the starting point, because "elementary forms of domination" remain predominant in many areas of the former, while "mediated forms of domination" prevail in much (though certainly not all) of the West.

This creates important psychological differences, as the patriarch who directly dominates, exploits, protects, and nurtures his sons, brothers, women, nephews, neighbors, sharecroppers, and servants must be both hardened and softened in profoundly different ways from the corporate executive who finishes his spreadsheet projections, hires or lays off hundreds of workers, and then goes home to a separate family life and circle of friends who share his recreational and aesthetic interests—pursuing the pleasures of "pure relationships," to use Giddons's term. And so must the members of the patriarch's household and network of clients differ in similarly dramatic ways from the executive's labor force. Westerners may enjoy the freedom to direct their lives in accordance with their inclinations, so that identifying one's interests and talents becomes a major task of psychological development and often a source of strength for those who can cultivate them. But Westerners also find themselves exposed to forms of insecurity and anomie that exact great psychological costs, especially for the poor and poorly educated. In MENA societies, individuals more frequently face the developmental task of accommodating to relationships and life decisions they have not chosen. But as they are embedded in familial and community networks, they may be better protected from many "modern" sources of distress.

Psychologically, the interpersonal styles and etiquettes by which face-to-face relationships of domination are worked out become especially important, because as children and adolescents master them they internalize core cultural attitudes, values, and emotions (see chapter 6). In enacting styles of greeting and conversing, deference and authority, apprenticeship and comradeship, bargaining and intimidation, young people come to feel as others do in similar situations. Or at least they learn what their culture *expects* them to feel, for it must be kept in mind that many, perhaps most, members of a society do not internalize these feelings in just the way prescribed by their culture's ideals. People inevitably develop strong personal reactions to the relationships of authority in which they find themselves embedded. Their reactions *against* what they are expected to think and feel can play as large a role in their psychological makeup as the attitudes and emotions they are supposed to internalize.

The anthropologist Eric Wolf has insightfully noted that early culture-and-personality researchers often took the etiquettes and styles by which face-to-face relations of domination are negotiated as expressions of "national character" and treated them as the primary data from which a psychological portrait of a culture could be sketched.[6] He quite correctly criticized the notion that a society *has* a "national character" but suggested that "patterns of interpersonal etiquettes" have important psychological consequences as they "indicate the way in which the parallelogram of social forces in one society differs from that of another."[7] That will be the objective of this chapter: to describe the "parallelogram of social forces" in MENA societies, within which psychological development takes place.

This approach has important limits, however, and comes with the danger of "reductionism." Not all psychological characteristics can be traced to a region's social ecology. Religion can influence social organization of its own accord, as can be seen in Northern India, where Muslims prefer to marry within their kin-group, and Hindus marry outside of it. And since a region as large and complex as MENA does not have a single social ecology, it is important not to overstate its uniformity. Perhaps most important, individuals within any society show a great variety of psychological characteristics, and the patterns they share by virtue of its social ecology do not standardize their feelings and actions into anything like a "national character." In fact, social ecology is perhaps best seen as setting the forces which *produce variation* among individuals.

This chapter does not offer a general introduction to MENA societies and cultures; such introductions can be found in three excellent books I urge the reader to consult: Daniel Bates's and Amal Rassam's 1983 *Peoples and Cultures of the Middle East*, Dale Eickelman's 1989 *The Middle East: An Anthropological Perspective*, and Halim Barakat's 1993 *The Arab World*. This chapter sketches a framework for the discussion of influences on psychological development in subsequent chapters. Here I will focus selectively on six themes:

- The symbiotic relation of agricultural and pastoral ways of life
- The tensions between honor-based and religion-based ethical systems which provide the primary etiquettes of interpersonal relationships
- The "dialectic" of rural and urban ways of life
- The "endogamous" organization of marriage, family, and kinship systems
- The "segmentary" nature of social groupings
- The centrality of "patronymic associations"—family-like group-ings extended by patron-client relationships—to both social life and individual life-cycles

The picture to emerge will be one of great flexibility and fluidity, in which it is not so much social groupings which endure through time but strategies for forming them.[8] This applies even to families, where kinship does not automatically lead to cooperation and loyalty. Historically, this fluidity has been rooted in the region's scarce and continually shifting resources, and in the imbalance between humans and resources that nearly all groups chroni-cally face.

Part 1: Traditional Social Ecology ❈

Agro-Pastoral Symbiosis

MENA culture(s) formed from the long interaction of three ways of life: nomadic pastoralism, settled agriculture, and urban trades and commerce. This combination emerged with the Neolithic invention of grain cultivation and domestication of animals in roughly 9,000 to 5,000 B.C. Irrigated agri-culture needs intensive labor but also yields surpluses that can be stored, traded, and taxed, so it can support complex forms of social organization. It requires cooperation at village or regional levels but frees enough people from agricultural labor to build irrigation systems, towns, temples, and empires. Sheep, goats, camels, and cattle raised mainly on surrounding range lands added dairy products and a little meat to diets and provided wool, skins, and other raw materials for clothing and tools. Agricultural surpluses also allowed some people to specialize as craftsmen, merchants, and governors. From these elements the basic pattern of Near Eastern civilizations took shape.[9]

Perhaps the most important ecological feature of the Mediterranean basin and its arid hinterlands is the tremendous year-to-year variability of rainfall. Annual averages are meaningless in many areas, and some regions that aver-age over 200 millimeters—which should support rain-fed cultivation—only get that much every third or fourth year. Villages in the Imeghrane "tribe" we studied in the pre-Saharan foothills of Morocco's High Atlas mountains depended on irrigation from springs fed by the Atlas snow pack. But the farmers never knew how much water to expect, how much would still flow in late spring and summer, or even which of their four springs might dry up. When rain did come, it often fell in cloudbursts that turned the normally dry river-bed into a raging torrent for a few hours and washed away laboriously tilled fields. This variability similarly affects pastures and herding patterns, as rain may turn one valley into a verdant meadow of grasses and wild flowers and leave a neighboring one parched. Historically, aridity and variability together introduced great flux and fluidity—and often strife—to all social arrange-ments. Families, extended kin-groups, villages, and tribes tended to divide and combine in response to shifting resources, and men had to be ready to defend their resources against attack and fight their way into those controlled by others.

Towns and cities developed in ancient times with the building of irriga-tion systems, and then around regional market centers, trade routes, and stra-tegic positions. Yet town life could be equally unpredictable, as townspeople depended for food on their control of surrounding agricultural communities and their control of caravan and shipping routes, both of which tended to be precarious. Tribes and armies often severed these links, and towns swelled as villagers fled into them or emptied as their residents sought refuge in villages. In premodern times only about 10 percent of the populace lived in cities, but city-dwellers played a crucial role in fashioning and standardizing features of the culture and disseminating them to the villages and hinterlands.

Fluctuating ties of mutual dependence linked these three ways of life. The cities lived on food produced in the countryside, agriculturists also herded livestock, and most pastoralists relied on agriculture and urban crafts. Agri-culture-less "simple"[10] or "proper"[11] nomadism can be found only among the reindeer herders of the tundra, some horse and small ruminant herders of Central Asia, cattle herders (such as the Maassai) in East Africa, and camel herders in the Arabian and Saharan deserts. MENA nomadism is "invariably symbiotic," dependent on some kind of interdependence with agricultural production, and so Khazanov terms it "seminomadism."[12] The foundation of life was therefore *agro-pastoralism*, with agricultural and pastoral produc-tion combined in myriad ways. One common form was "transhumance," in which families live in settled villages where they cultivate fields but a portion of the household herds livestock on the surrounding rangelands.

In many areas, nomadic tribes ensured access to agricultural products by running a kind of protection racket in which they forced villages to be-come their clients. The villages gave foods to the tribe, who then refrained from raiding them and protected them from raids by other tribes. Pastor-alists also came to own fields in villages, which villagers cultivated as sharecroppers. Some incorporated members of ethnic minorities—Jews, "gypsies," and "blacks"—as clients and slaves who worked as blacksmiths, leather-workers, barbers, house-builders, well-diggers, and personal ser-vants. The Tuareg of the Sahara developed a feudal or caste-like society, with a "nobility" of camel-mounted warriors dominating "vassal" groups of sheep and goat herders and "slaves" they kept as craftsmen, servants, and cultivators of oasis fields.

For towns to thrive, pastoralists' domination of villages had to be reversed. This meant the rulers of settled peoples typically had to extract enough surplus from agriculture and trade to support an army to dominate and perhaps even tax the pastoralists. In addition, many towns developed at tribal boundaries as sacred sites, becoming religious and trade centers for the surrounding pastoralists, who agreed to leave them in peace—such was the situation of Mecca at the time of the Prophet.[13] In some of the more fertile areas (especially in what are now Lebanon, Egypt, Turkey, Pakistan, and Iran) feudal-like systems developed, especially in the eighteenth and nineteenth centuries, in which "lords" and their armed agents terrorized and exploited impoverished peasants. Large parts of the Euphrates valley in Syria were depopulated in the late eighteenth century by Bedouin raids and attacks by soldiers-turned-bandits. When Turkish armies regained control, urban merchants bankrolled poor peasants and city-dwellers to rebuild and cultivate fields as sharecroppers. The financiers got title to the lands and became urban "lords" who owned villages and, in some cases, whole groups of villages and virtually owned the landless peasants who lived in them.[14]

In other areas, villagers lived as members of formidable "free" tribes. After the settled tribes of the Moroccan Rif mountains declared themselves a republic in the 1920s, it took a combined Spanish-French force of over a half-million troops to "pacify" 20,000 tribesmen on horseback.[15] One of the key features that shaped MENA societies is that until this century (and in some cases during it), large portions of the population lived beyond the day-to-day control of urban governments, usually in a form of organization anthropologists term "tribal," in which every adult male, with the important exception of protected clients, was potentially a fighter.

Agro-pastoral symbioses played different roles in the formation of traditional MENA cultures from those they played in Europe, India, or sub-Saharan Africa. Transhumant pastoralism certainly influenced the rural cultures of southern Europe, but generally in areas dominated by cities, states, and empires. Self-governing "tribes" of nomads did not provide European cultures with values, literary ideals, or models of social organization as they did in MENA. The development of feudal systems in Europe marked a further departure from the agro-pastoral-urban mix that continued to prevail in much of MENA until this century. To the east, India developed as a society of settled agriculture, with "Aryan" invaders establishing themselves above the indigenous inhabitants in the fifteenth to tenth centuries B.C. and fashioning the caste system, which stands in sharp contrast to the social fluidity and ideological egalitarianism of MENA. Sub-Saharan Africa, with its ecological diversity ranging from desert to rain forest, became home to a great variety of cultures based on different ways of life: hunter-gatherer bands roamed in both deserts and rain forests, cattle-herding nomads dominated the Sahel, the wetter western and central regions were home to shifting "swidden" agriculturists, and settled fishers and farmers lived in many areas. The nomadic pastoralist/warrior groups tended to be localized in particular areas rather than spread throughout the region, and they did not shape a pan-African culture to the extent that the agro-pastoral symbiosis and Islam combined to do in MENA.

Honor and Islam

The symbiosis of agriculture and pastoralism often was forged by military might. Raiding was endemic among many nomadic tribes, but if this was motivated by economic and political objectives,[16] the nomads celebrated the daring, the fight, the victory, and the honorable rules of engagement in a wealth of poetry and song that came to anchor an ethos of honor, modesty, and shame that pervaded all ways of life. Michael Meeker has explored the warrior ethos of Bedouin culture by analyzing the raiding poems recorded by the Czech ethnographer Alois Musil, who lived among the Rwala Bedouin of Northern Arabia immediately after World War I and rode with some of their raiding parties.[17] Sometime during the first millennium B.C., the Bedouin developed saddles for their camels and "gradually converted their beasts into formidable mounts of war. . . . Such an advance enabled the North Arabian Bedouins to enter our own era with a popular military capacity that was truly awesome in its setting in the desert and steppe."[18] In the seventh and eighth centuries they conquered and carried the new religion of Islam to what is now Morocco and Spain in the West and to Central Asia and Iran in the East. This gradually forged a "cultural uniformity," Meeker writes, whose main characteristic was neither Bedouin nor Islamic values but the tension between them:

> The cultural uniformity which we now find in the arid zone, however, does not reflect the traditions of a people bent upon violence. On the contrary, it does reflect by and large a *moral reaction* to the threat of popular political turmoil. The process of Islamization itself can be viewed in part as a moral response to the problem which arose from the circumstances of Near Eastern pastoral nomadism.[19]

The historian Maxime Rodinson[20] and the anthropologist Eric Wolf[21] have studied the social conditions in which the Prophet lived in seventh-century Arabia and have called attention to the Islam's antitribal themes. Mecca was a town of merchants built around a tribal pilgrimage center, and both authors emphasize the extent to which the religion Mohammed recited and taught there opposed its vision of a peaceful brotherhood of believers (*dar al-islam* means "house of submission/peace") to the violent tribal solidarity of actual brothers and cousins (*dar al-harb* means "house of warfare").

As "traditional" MENA Muslim cultures took shape over the following centuries, they tended to incorporate both the honor-based ethic of the nomad warrior who lives free "like a falcon" and the ethic of the pious believer who lives in a peaceful community under the rule of law. In the following chapter, I will show that the "honor code," born of warriorhood, and Islam, born of peacemaking, remain the two predominant ethical and interpersonal etiquette systems in MENA societies, and shape the course of psychological development from early childhood.

The Dialectic of Tribes and Cities

In the fourteenth century, the North African philosopher-historian Ibn Khaldun wrote what has become the classic interpretation of MENA society as a product of pastoralism, Islam, and urbanity. He developed a cyclical theory to account for the rise and fall of dynasties, several of which he had observed firsthand. His theory posits that the dynastic pattern displays a broader cultural dynamic, rooted in an underlying dialectic between opposed social-psychological principles: *hadara*, which can be translated as *civilization, urbanity,* or *high culture,* and *'asabiya,* a term built from the root word for "nerve" or "sinew" and meaning *group solidarity, strength,* and *toughness.* These principles animate settled urban and Bedouin ways of life, respectively.

In Ibn Khaldun's view, *'asabiya* arises from two features of Bedouin life. On the one hand, hardship toughens the men who live it, accentuating their natural aggressiveness. "They are the most savage human beings that exist," he writes: "compared to sedentary people, they are on a level with wild, untamable animals and dumb beasts of prey."[22] On the other hand, the formation of primary social groups (family, lineage, tribe) on the basis of male kinship extends and develops natural familial feelings of affection into a wider sense of group "nobility." As a conjunction of virile strength, familial compassion, protectiveness, ascetic endurance, and self-control, *'asabiya* anchors the traditional archetype of honor. Among the Bedouin, *'asabiya* easily becomes a fearsome archetype, but Ibn Khaldun believed that self-imposed Islam restrains their ferocity without undermining their fortitude. This religious tempering yields people who are closer to virtue than are city dwellers.

Bedouin hardly feel content with their difficult lives, however, and so they seek the comforts of civilization—which their military prowess enables them to conquer and then assimilate. But once they are established as an urban-based dynasty, the group solidarity (*'asabiya*) begins to dissipate, and moral corruption and physical weakness ensue. As urbanites, they become "accustomed to luxury and success in worldly occupations and to indulgence in worldly desires."[23] In the third or fourth generation the dynasty weakens and collapses from within. Ibn Khaldun likens this rise and decline to the human life-cycle, and suggests that families—or at least prominent "houses"—also traverse this cycle, typically in four generations: the builder embodies the qualities that created his glory, his son tries to preserve them but lacks his father's direct experience, the third generation must rely on imitation, and the fourth lacks the qualities and effort demanded by glory. A rising branch of the family or "house" then seizes control, and the original collapses.[24]

This theory stresses three key points about the nature of family and larger political groups. First, even though prominent "houses" may claim that their prowess derives from "pure" or "noble" genealogies, it actually stems from the feeling of group solidarity ('asabiya), manufactured by hard work, "individual qualities," and "group effort." Society has a kin-group structure, but kin solidarity must be *achieved*, and once achieved proves difficult to sustain. Second, a social grouping often referred to as a "house," consisting of a familial core but extended to include distant kin and nonkin "clients," forms the primary building block of society. And third, every community consists of families that are rising as houses and houses that are declining into mere families. However much a herding camp or village or an urban neighborhood may look "timeless" to an outsider, most churn with competition and change.

Since most MENA residents traditionally grew up and lived out their lives in the interdependent relationships of families and houses, these fluid groupings established the parameters of psychological development. And even though styles of parent-child, sibling-sibling, and patron-client interaction may be shared from household to household, it is important to keep Ibn Khaldun's *dynamic* theory in mind: rising households play these rules differently from those seeking to maintain their predominance, and differently from declining or fallen ones—creating important variation within the culture.

Marriage, Family, and Kinship

The industrialized West prides itself in allowing young people to choose their marriage partners based on attraction and affection. Historically, Europeans have seen "Oriental" marriage—practiced in MENA, India, and China—as more primitive because parents arrange them, and because grooms customarily pay a "brideprice" to the bride's family, suggesting that he purchases her. This view is incorrect. The anthropologist Jack Goody[25] has assembled impressive evidence that historically there was a broad resemblance of marriage systems throughout the "post Bronze Age, pre-industrial, literate societies" of Eurasia (Europe, China, India, and MENA), based largely on their systems of agriculture.[26] In addition, he shows the term "brideprice" to be inappropriate, because the groom's payment is usually used to provision the bride with a dowry of household goods, jewelry, and other property. A portion of this sometimes went unpaid at marriage but was payable in the event of divorce, to act as a deterrent to separation. Goody urges Europeans to see their heritage as shared with all of Eurasia, and as differing from many African marriage systems on the one hand and the practices of modern Europe on the other.

Goody's argument extends a thesis about fundamental differences between sub-Saharan African and Eurasian marriage systems that was first advanced by the economist Esther Boserup,[27] who saw the widespread sub-Saharan practice of polygyny (men taking multiple wives) as related to the importance of women's labor in agriculture. She distinguished between two broad patterns of agriculture: "female" systems, based mainly on hoe cultivation of shifting fields in conditions of low population density (common in sub-Saharan Africa) and the "male" systems based on irrigation and animal traction (common in the high-density areas of Eurasia). The high value of women's labor in "female" systems leads to polygyny as a strategy to harness women's labor and production, and to the payment of bridewealth at marriage, which compensates women's fathers for the loss of their daughters' labor and reproductive power.[28] In "male" systems, by contrast, marriage tends to be monogamous and to be accompanied by some form of dowry, either direct, in which the woman's family provides her with goods to take into the marriage, or indirect, in which a substantial portion of the groom's payment is used to endow her. Goody provides much evidence for Boserup's thesis, but he believes that it is the inheritance of property, rather than the value of women's agricultural labor, that shapes marriage practices.[29] In sub-Saharan shifting agriculture, property tends not to be privately owned, and so it is not inherited, while most Eurasian agriculture entails private ownership, hence inheritance of family lands. Women inherit in most Eurasian societies, either at their parents' death or at marriage via dowry—leading ultimately, Goody argues, to a preponderance of monogamous marriage, to preferences for marriages with close relatives, and to greater male control over the arranging of marriages and over women's sexual contacts and reproduction.

The anthropologist Sherry Ortner describes the same pattern of family and gender relations but suggests that it is not rooted so much in types of agriculture or inheritance as in the influence of states. Noting that the Eurasian association of family honor with men's control of women's sexuality is not found in pre-state societies, she argues that it is the agents of states making senior men responsible for their families that endows them with the authority from which arises "the absolute authority of the father or other senior male over everyone in the household—all junior males and all females."[30] Deniz Kandiyoti also contrasts sub-Saharan and Eurasian forms of "male dominance," arguing that the "classic patriarchy" of the latter evolved from the labor demands of peasant agriculture combined with state control and taxation of family heads. She suggests that these "Great Tradition" societies have developed distinctive forms of family and gender relations as women and men have negotiated what she terms a "patriarchal bargain" tailored to the specifics of their mode of subsistence and religious values.[31] MENA marriage and family systems generally follow Eurasian rather than sub-Saharan practices, with some important exceptions. As is well known, Islam permits a man to take up to four wives, but polygyny is in fact rarely practiced, so the vast majority of marriages are monogamous. Marriages with "close" relatives are often preferred (in ancient Egypt, even between brother and sister), but especially within the male kin-group, which sets MENA apart from India and China, where marriages were made outside the immediate male kin-group.

Before getting into more detail, it may be helpful to introduce some basic kinship terminology. A *nuclear family*, of course, consists of parents and their children, and in the West each nuclear family ideally constitutes its own self-sufficient household. An *extended family* adds other relatives, in the West typically a grandparent or two. In much of MENA, the traditional ideal household consists of a large extended family, headed by a patriarch and including his grown sons and their wives and children. Typically each nuclear unit has its own rooms, possessions, and some separate finances, but they cooperate on many household tasks. A *joint household* consists of adult siblings, with their spouses and children, who continue to live together as an extended family after the death of the patriarch. Quite rare in the West, they are not uncommon in MENA, where they may appear at a crucial point in a family's "life-cycle." Ideally, a nuclear family grows into a large extended one as the children marry and sons bring in their wives and then their children. When the patriarch dies, the brothers may choose to remain together as a joint household, perhaps until their mother dies or longer. Joint families have many efficiencies of scale that help keep them united but also easily develop imbalances among the nuclear families that cause strife. At some point, the brothers decide to divide their inheritance, and a careful costing out and division of property ensues—not infrequently with acrimony and intrigue—and the cycle begins again with new nuclear units. While few families actually follow this ideal cycle, many at least approximate it—with two important consequences for psychological development. First, many children grew up in large households with grandparents, aunts, uncles, siblings and cousins, which means they had many caretakers and family relationships. Second, while divorce after children may have been rare, births, deaths, and household divisions brought continual flux to family relationships, and often stressful disruptions.

Most traditional MENA societies can be described as having kinship systems that are *patrilineal*, meaning that descent and rights are reckoned in the male line,[32] *patrilocal*, meaning that a newly married couple lives with the husband's father's family, and *patriarchal*, meaning that men have authority over women and senior males over juniors. These three characteristics need not go together, but they do coincide and reinforce each other in most of the region.[33] Traditionally, marriages were arranged, with mothers doing a good deal of scouting and consulting and fathers making the final decision and carrying out the formal negotiations, which resulted in a contract specifying their terms and the amounts to be paid in gifts.

In contemporary Western societies, one's kin-group is termed a *kindred*. It consists of one's immediate nuclear family and whatever grandparents, aunts, uncles, and cousins a person keeps contact with, and it has two important features. First, it is not a "corporate" group: it is not named, it does not have rights to properties or resources, and its members do not have specific loyalties or duties to each other. Second, it is *bilateral,* in that it is reckoned on both the father's and mother's side, and our terms "aunt," "uncle," and "cousin" do not differentiate between relatives on the father's or mother's side. Further, parents can pass their property to their children however they wish. In most traditional MENA societies, relationships reckoned along male lines had social and political importance that relationships along female lines did not—and therefore are *patrilineal* rather than bilateral.[34] In the industrialized West, most newly married couples set up their own households, but most of traditional MENA was *patrilocal,* meaning that the wife moves into her husband's father's household. This sets up an important gender difference in the socialization of children: much is done to build a son's loyalty to his father's household, while many girls grow up expecting to leave it. The difference in spouses' ages becomes important as well. Traditionally, women married around the time of menarche (often at age 15 to 17 in conditions of malnutrition), but men after they had established reputations as competent adults, and perhaps contributed to the marriage payment. Women then tended to be five to fifteen years younger than their husbands, likely to outlive them, and therefore ultimately dependent for their well-being on their sons rather than their husbands. Many researchers have pointed out that this contributes to the cultivation of an especially strong emotional interdependence between mothers and sons, which is sustained throughout adulthood.[35] That is, mothers tended to raise sons not to go out on their own but to stay at home, supporting their mothers, being nurtured by their mothers, and accepting the wife their parents choose for them.

Unlike the Western-style kindred, joint and extended families live together in households and function as corporate groups: often named, they hold rights to resources and property and share social and political obligations in their village, tribal section, or neighborhood. In many areas, households descended from a common male ancestor are united in named *patrilineages.* A *lineage* consists of all of the descendants in one line (a patrilineage if in the male line, a matrilineage if in the female line) from an ancestor who lived perhaps three or six generations ago. The existence and role of patrilineages in MENA has been a topic of dispute among researchers, set off by repeated observations that many groups that describe their own social organization as lineage based often don't behave in the ways they say they do.

As the dust of this debate settles, it appears clear that MENA groups vary in the prominence of lineages: some do not "have" them, and in others they may be more or less prominent depending on their functions. Patrilineages tend to be strongest when they hold rights to pastures, farmland, springs, wells, or other resources; when they form neighborhoods or herding camps; when they are named; when their leaders represent them at village or tribal councils; and when they have collective responsibility for defense of their members and for exacting vengeance should a member be robbed, attacked, or killed. Like households, lineages also may develop a store of honor and prestige—which many scholars, following Pierre Bourdieu, term "symbolic capital"—that its members share but also must uphold by "stricter observation of tradition" and "going one better in purism" than others.[36] Individuals in all MENA groups thus tend to be enmeshed in networks of kin that extend beyond their nuclear families, and the boundaries between kin and outsider tend to be blurred, fluid, and flexible.

Endogamy

Most of the world's preindustrial cultures are kinship based, and most have rules encouraging or requiring *exogamy:* that people marry someone from outside of their kin-group, which often means outside of their lineage. Many encourage marriages between *cross-cousins,* (in a patrilineal society, a man's *mother's* brother's daughter, who belongs to a different lineage) and regard marriage with a *parallel cousin* (a man's *father's* brother's daughter, who belongs to one's own lineage) as incest. Many seemingly simple societies have worked out complicated rules of exogamy that marry men to women of other lineages, and the anthropologist Claude Levi-Strauss earned his renown by explaining these as systems that link men *across* lineages via exchanges of women.[37]

As different as they are in so many respects, societies of China, India, and sub-Saharan Africa tended to be patrilineal and, when they had lineages, to practice lineage exogamy. Following Levi-Strauss's lead, many anthropologists have seen this as promoting a wider social integration of groups that might otherwise fission in strife, on the assumption that having sisters and daughters living among other lineages will restrain one's treatment of them. They therefore have puzzled over MENA societies, most of which encourage marriage *within* the patrilineage. In fact, the ideal often is said to be for a man to marry his patrilateral parallel cousin, his father's brother's daughter (in anthropologese, his FBD). Other "close" marriages also tend to be approved, including of cross-cousins (such as a man's MBD) and second cousins, especially on the father's side. In fact most men marry someone other than their FBD, as the quirks of demography often don't provide men with eligible FBDs and because many other considerations come into play, such as the potential spouses' characters, health, and personal wishes. In general, wealthy and prestigious households are more likely to arrange FBD marriages than are the poor.

One of the most important consequences is that by keeping rather than exchanging women, FBD and other "close" marriages build groups of individuals linked by relationships through their female kin as well as their male kin. Fredrick Barth found that Basseri pastoralists of southern Iran describe their herding camps in patrilineal terms, but they actually are "united by patrilineal, matrilineal, and affinal [marriage] ties, which often reinforce each other." Further, he notes, his patrilineal diagram of a camp's kin structure "could with equal success be re-drawn to give an impression of a group built around matrilineages."[38] Abner Cohen observed that the lineage-like *hamula* groups making up the Arab villages he studied on Israel's borders are demarcated in "the idiom of patriliny" as having a unity based on being "from one sinew" but typically are glued together by other sorts of relationships, and the *hamula* can look like "a group of men who are mainly linked through their marriages to one another's daughters."[39]

The patrilineal reckoning of relationships easily obscures the fact that networks of female kin often form the core of extended households and of larger groups that cooperate on a daily basis. MENA families thus tend to be highly *patriarchal*, in that senior males clearly exercise authority over women and juniors, but at the same time families tend to be highly *matrifocal*, in that women and especially mothers play crucial roles in organizing the work of daily life and in providing the emotional nexus of interpersonal relationships. This is crucial for understanding how families shape the psychological development of their members. As Sharabi emphasizes, "the female in Arab society may play only a limited role in public life, but her influence 'backstage' . . . is profound."[40] Traditional MENA cultures recognize this duality in viewing the father's semen as responsible for a child's bones and the mother's womb for its blood, a complementarity expressed by regarding patri-groups as body-like, with male bones (in some areas lineages are called *'adem*, "bones"—*ikhs* in Berber North Africa—or *fukhdh*, "thigh bones") and female blood.

A number of theorists, including Levi-Strauss,[41] Robert Murphy and Leonard Kasdan,[42] and Barth,[43] believe endogamous and "close" marriage practices tend to build intense family and patri-kin loyalties at the expense of overall societal integration. A key feature of MENA's ecology is that resources are scarce, continually shifting, and unpredictable—easily setting families and lineages into competition. The relatively low density of family ties *between* kin-based groups may allow strife to escalate more readily than in societies that "exchange" women by exogamy. Ecology and kinship strategies thus may cause some of the fission and feuding that commentators have misattributed to "tribalism" or a preoccupation with "honor." In both tribal and nontribal settings, the "code" of honor often provides an ideology for conflict over resources. Feuds in the cluster of villages we studied in Imeghrane were said to have begun as disputes over women and personal insults. But after I charted the lineage and irrigation systems of adjoining villages, it became clear that these points of honor were being used as pretexts to escalate longstanding struggles for the control of water.

MENA residents and anthropologists give various reasons for favoring FBD marriages, including two quite practical ones. First, since daughters inherit half a share of their father's property, FBD marriages can help keep a household's property intact. Second, FBD and other "close" marriages are said to have a better chance of succeeding: the bride and groom already know each other, she knows her mother-in-law and gets to stay close to her own mother, and a host of relatives can moderate his treatment of her and intervene to patch things up should they quarrel. Since young people often know their cousins and second cousins well, they can lobby through their mothers to marry someone they like and trust.

Ladislav Holy emphasizes that MENA cultures also attach important moral and symbolic meanings to FBD marriages. Noting that a man often is said to have not just a right to marry his FBD but a *duty* to do so, Holy points out that an FBD marriage announces the fathers' and son's affirmation of the patrilineal principle. By turning ideology into fact, it publicly commits them to upholding society's core ethical values: it reproduces the solidarity of brothers, and by keeping the women in the household or lineage, it "covers" them and underscores the family's honor. Viewing honor as a form of "symbolic capital," Holy urges that FBD marriage be seen "as preventing the alienation, not of the group's material property, but of its whole symbolic capital of which the material property is just one specific manifestation."[44] That is, the building and conservation of honor "provides the key to understanding the meaning of the preference for in-marriage."[45]

Brothers, Cousins, and Virgins

Holy also emphasizes that two key moral principles converge in endogamous marriages: that of loyalty among male relatives, and that of men's duty to control "unharnessed" female power.[46] The sociologist Germaine Tillion developed this point of view in the early 1960s, arguing that this pattern is neither Arab nor Muslim but arose as a distinctive characteristic of Mediterranean societies.[47] For many decades, ethnographers who studied rural communities in southern Europe had little contact with those who studied MENA, but in the 1960s and 1970s they began documenting a wide range of commonalities. The notion took shape that until the Renaissance or industrial revolution, the northern and southern shores of the Mediterranean formed a culture area, with the sea linking rather than dividing them. Important features of family organization, the honor "code," religious belief and practice, and men's control of their daughters' and sisters' virginity appeared to be circum-Mediterranean, as much a part of the West's classical heritage as of MENA.

Tillion proposed that three broad types of society can be found on the globe.[48] Modern society at least aspires to be a "republic of citizens." Most preindustrial societies, organized by matrilineal or patrilineal kinship but practicing exogamy, she terms "republics of brothers-in-law," because marriages tend to establish cooperative relationships between a man and his wife's brothers. In the Mediterranean, the Neolithic revolution brought a new cultural adaptation in which marriages with close patri-kin became acceptable and then preferred, creating what she terms a "republic of cousins." In the competition between groups of warring, raiding, and feuding male kin for resources and prestige, a distinctively circum-Mediterranean machismo then developed:

> From Gibraltar to Constantinople, on the sea's northern and southern shores alike, among Christians and Muslims, among town-dwellers and country people, among settled and nomadic populations, there is to this day an enhanced sensitivity, both collective and individual, to a particular ideal of virile brutality and a complementary dramatization of feminine virtue. The two are welded into a notion of family pride that thirsts for blood and extends beyond itself into two myths: ancestry and posterity. The entire paraphernalia is regularly accompanied by what, in sociological jargon, is termed endogamy, which may go as far as incest.[49]

Tillion argues that the industrial revolution transformed southern Europe's republic of cousins into republics of citizens, a development that was centered in the cities and disseminated to the countryside, but gradually and incompletely, so that ethnographers can still study rural communities where feuding, close marriage, and the virtual seclusion of women continue. On the Mediterranean's southern, Muslim shore, however, no such transformation took place, and continual rural to urban migration tended to reinforce the republic of cousins in cities rather than to disseminate the republic of citizens to the countryside. And as others have pointed out, colonization produced a defensive intensification of many traditions as distinctive of national, Arab, or Muslim identities, adding another reason to seclude and veil.

In a classic 1971 article, "Of Vigilance and Virgins," the anthropologist Jane Schneider developed a similar argument about the cultural unity of the premodern Mediterranean, a unity that "centers around the interdependent concepts, honor and shame, and around related practices governing family integrity and the virginity of young girls" and that she believes "derives from a particular set of ecological forces."[50] Tracing the interaction of agriculture, pastoralism, and state institutions throughout the region, Schneider shows that Mediterranean societies historically have been characterized by intense struggles for scarce resources (land, water, and women) among distinctively small, "fragmented," patri-kin-based groups, often linked in fragile and shifting alliances. Again, the scarcity of resources combined with their continual variability makes it chronically difficult to maintain control over them and for dominant groups to maintain a balance of persons to land, water, and pasturage. Often aggravated by endogamous marriage preferences that tend to encapsulate rather than link patri-kin and by inheritance rules that divide rather than conserve parental property, the forces of fission repeatedly tear at even the smallest units: the lineage, the joint or extended family, and the nuclear family itself. In some of the more pastoral areas this fostered heroic raiding cultures, and in some of the agricultural regions it spurred endemic family- and clan-based feuding—both of which have been seen to anchor the honor code and to provide it with poetic material and inspiration. Schneider argues that the Mediterranean's deeply cherished values of family and kin loyalty in fact represent attempts to mask and contain a resilient underlying "individualism." These ecological and political conditions thus pattern relationships within families:

> It is typical of the Mediterranean that the father-son relationship is somewhat strained and potentially competitive; that brothers are not emotionally close after they marry; that the most enduring and solitary bonds are those uniting a mother and her children and, in lesser degree, those between cross-cousins and between a mother's brother and his sister's children. . . . In other words, the conditions which have fragmented the economic and political structure into its minimal, nuclear family components, have also fragmented the family.[51]

And here she sees the honor code's primary ideological function:

> Against great odds, and in spite of the centrifugal forces described above, the Mediterranean societies do generate nuclear family solidarity and, in some places, lineage solidarity. . . . Central to this social order are codes of honor and shame. Honor as ideology helps shore up the identity of a group (a family or a lineage) and commit to it the loyalties of otherwise doubtful members.[52]

Control of women's fertility emerges as a natural, central, and practical strategy for building the patrilineage, so women emerge as key symbols in the ideological system:

> Men not only want to control the sexuality of women; women are for them a convenient focus, the most likely symbol around which to organize solidary groups, in spite of powerful tendencies towards fragmentation. . . . I suggest that the sanctity of virgins plays a critical role in holding together the few corporate groups of males which occur in many traditional Mediterranean societies.[53]

Thus in a historically deep and geographically broad context characterized by endemic competition among small, family- and patri-kin-based groups, the honor "code" evolved to construct manhood in accordance with two core dimensions: an aggressive, agonistic stance toward outsider men, and a protective stance with regard to insider women whom the men regarded as sacred and vulnerable. In the face of strong fissioning forces that drive men apart, making women sacred helps cement men's group loyalty.

I will examine the nature of the honor "code" in the next chapter, and I put "code" in quotation marks here because it should be understood neither as a uniform code of values nor as about only honor. As Bourdieu[54] and

Michael Herzfield[55] argue, it is better viewed as an interpersonal etiquette, a system of sentiments, and a poetics that guides men's public self-presentations (and the responses of women and juniors to them). In light of research showing significant variation in its style and in the moral sentiments it associates with men's actions, and especially in light of research on women's place in this world of honor, I will show that it is better termed an "honor-modesty system." The crucial point here is to see the role this system plays in forging loyalties among men whose interests often diverge, binding them together in protection of vulnerable land and women, in opposition to other threatening alliances of cousins.

Lineages and Patronymic Associations

Throughout MENA, men use patrilineal relationships to build not only households but larger forms of association, including clans, tribes, and urban neighborhoods. Many tribes use genealogies to organize their component groups, so that (using anthropological terms) a *tribe* might represent itself as descended from a founding ancestor, its component *clans* as descended from each of the ancestor's sons, and each clan as consisting of several *lineages* descended from the clan founder's sons. No tribal organization turns out to be this simple, however, as they typically have more levels and asymmetrical segments.

Emile Durkheim described "segmentary" societies in the 1890s, citing the Algerian Kabyle as an example,[56] but it was E. E. Evans-Pritchard's analysis of the "segmentary lineage system" he observed among the cattle-herding Nuer in central Africa that made this notion so influential in anthropology.[57] He argued that the lineage system brings stability to "acephalous," government-less societies by setting up balanced or "complementary" oppositions of sometimes-feuding but sometimes-cooperating segments at each level.[58] Feuds were breaking out and being resolved all the time as Nuer groups raided each other, and Evans-Pritchard believed that each feud strengthened another group unity: that leaves on a twig (families within a lineage) would join after one had been raided to fight the leaves on the raider's twig; subsequently all the twigs on a branch (lineages in a clan) might join to fight a clan (joined twigs) on an opposing branch; after a short peace, the unity of a branch might be broken by one of its twig's raids on another. Shifting raids and feuds kept the component units roughly equal in power, he believed, and thereby safeguarded the autonomy of all from the domination of any.

The accounts of informants from many MENA tribes suggest that they traditionally had segmentary lineage structures—with the "leaves" consisting of camping groups among nomads and hamlets or neighborhoods in settled communities—and that raiding and feuding sustained the kind of shifting fissioning-and-fusing process Evans-Pritchard described. But more detailed fieldwork showed that things rarely work that way. Emerys Peters's study of camel herders in Cyrenaica (now mostly in Libya) was the first of many to document that acts of violence do not always lead to fission, that lineage loyalties may not be automatically activated, that alliances based on principles other than patri-kinship are forged to cross-cut segments, and that some powerful groups dominate others in spite of supposed genealogical equality.[59] On the basis of his studies of Bedouin tribes in the Sinai, Emmanual Marx argued that alliances created to pursue and defend resources form the basis of tribal organization, with tribesmen codifying alliances by representing them in terms of close patrilineal kinship.[60] Further, many ethnographers have found that living tribesmen cannot fill in the genealogical chain that links their group to tribal, clan, or lineage ancestors, and these units sometimes are named for territories or nicknames, suggesting that all upper level groups may be agglomerations united under a fictive ancestor or common place of origin.

Studies of lower level groups (herding camps, hamlets, and village neighborhoods) typically have found that half to 80 percent of the families have patrilineal links with each other but that the others have been incorporated without patri-kin ties. Ibn Khaldun had recognized that while prominent "Houses" tend to claim pure genealogies, they actually incorporate nonkin clients who come to share the feeling of group solidarity and pride in the group's noble descent. Genealogies only build solidarity when they preserve interaction, he argued, for considered by itself, "a pedigree is something imaginary and devoid of reality. Its usefulness consists only in the resulting connection and close contact."[61] In light of all this evidence, most MENA ethnographers have come to view a segmentary lineage system as an *ideology* or *cultural idiom* that groups have worked out to map their own organization, and perhaps to describe how their political affiliations should work, even if they rarely do.

Debate continues about the existence and importance of patrilineages. Marshall Sahlins provides an important perspective on this debate by suggesting that a segmentary lineage system tends to develop as "an organization of predatory expansion," "a social means of intrusion and competition in an already occupied ecological niche."[62] He focuses on Evans-Pritchard's work, which he criticizes for presenting the Nuer as "having" an overall social structure derived from segmentary lineage principles rather than as using those principles to create higher level alliances in a particular historical circumstance, one in which they were expanding and fighting their way into other tribes' territories. The principle by which patrilineally related leaves on a twig or twigs on a branch come to each other's aid works mainly on the tribe's borders, he argues, where a massing of reinforcements from otherwise dispersed segments can carry the day militarily. With a decrease in intertribal competition, segmentary lineage systems fade in salience, as segments return to their more dispersed lives and other cross-segment bonds anchor whatever degree of pan-tribal integration may exist. Sahlins points out that segmentation and complementary opposition characterize many social systems, and argues that segmentary lineage systems tend to develop in tribal groups in conditions of intertribal competition.

Much of Sahlins's analysis may apply to MENA tribal societies. Our studies of the agro-pastoral Imeghrane showed that new settlements—both agricultural "homesteads" and herding camps—tended to be made by extension of patrilineage relationships, but that over a couple of generations these settlements coalesced as territorial groups with interlineage cooperation. While the first generation needed support from lineage-mates in the "home" village, the third generation was more likely to resist the claims of now more distant "home" relatives and draw on those sharing the new territory (even though of other lineages or clans) for assistance. This dialectic of lineage-based expansion and territory-based consolidation probably played itself out in many MENA regions, bringing segmentary lineage relations and other forms of integration to the fore in different historical periods and circumstances. I once observed to one of the senior men in the village where we lived that lineages were no longer very import there after decades of peace and government control, and he commented, "Yes, but if trouble comes, you'll see the lineages *ghadi inod*" (will stand up/appear). The psychologist Mustafa Hijazi conducted field observations and interviews during Lebanon's civil war in the 1980s and found militia groups reinventing lineage-like relationships among fighters and their families, even as they fought for a society that would be liberated from those very traditions.[63] Luis Martinez and Ali Kouaouci describe a similar formation of lineage-like militant groups in Algeria's civil war in the 1990s.[64] Lineage-like organizations may be less the *cause* of contemporary strife than *responses* to it that reinvigorate traditional social principles.

The work of Peters, Marx, Sahlins, and many others indicates that MENA societies should not be seen simply as composed of lineages nested within clans. But their cultural ideology stresses the value of patrilineal ties—providing a *strategy* for forming and legitimizing social groups in some circumstances. Ethnographies consistently show that endogamous and FBD marriages represent one strategy for building a cooperating network of kin, but alongside other strategies, including "alliance" marriages with unrelated households.[65] Many studies, including ours of Imeghrane villages, suggest that poorer families try to marry "up" within the village but often can't, and that large and powerful families try to marry "in the house" or to close patri-kin much of the time but also make occasional alliance marriages with powerful households in other villages or clans. Powerful households may also take poor but promising young men from opposing lineages under their wing, as "clients." One such young man, an ambitious and capable brother in a prominent Imeghrane joint family, quarreled with his brothers and struck out on his own, taking his share of his inheritance with him. When the leading household of an opposing lineage saw him struggling to make a go of it, they loaned him enough cash to finish his new house, and gave him a part-time job as a truck driver. If the relationship thrives, intermarriages probably will follow in a decade or so.

The crucial point is that patrilineal relationships and loyalties tend to be made real and have important consequences, but (1) they often have to be built and sustained with effort in the face of many fissioning forces; and (2) they reflect not *the* structure of MENA families or societies but the use of one important strategy among many. As Holy points out, the fact that acts that affirm patrilineal loyalties have an honor-building cultural cachet means that people often prefer to speak in this idiom rather than in others, even about relationships that are more strongly anchored in friendship, strategic alliance, or patron-clientship.

Segmentation

Many MENA communities do, however, have a "segmentary" organization—regardless of the extent to which this involves ties of kinship—and segmentation itself helps account for some of the apparent "instability" of social groupings. The Imeghrane provide an example of how smaller groupings are nested within larger ones. They are composed of eight "tribes" or "tribal factions," themselves composed of smaller segments. Imeghrane-s say they are an agglomeration of families from all over the region. They rarely claim descent from the founder their segment was named for, or even know anything about when he lived or who he might have been. Many segments were named for territories they occupied. What mattered to them, at least before "pacification" in the 1930s and in some areas still today, was to organize the segment into five units, or five "fifths," and to allocate responsibilities equally to the fifths or rotate leadership among them, thus preserving a rough equality.[66] Imeghrani-s readily explained the gerrymandering of kinship and residential groups required to fashion five roughly equal fifths, and they rarely represented these as descendants of brothers or cousins. Still, the system had an overall segmentary character, because of the association of each level with a set of resources and activities.

At the lowest level (see table 2.1), the household owned land and livestock, functioned as a production unit, and ate together from supplies kept in a single storeroom whose key the senior male typically carried. Households belonging to a "lineage" generally abutted each other and formed a neighborhood in the village, and many daily activities were carried out with neighborly cooperation that amounted to de facto "lineage" cooperation. In the past, a man's lineage provided the vengeance group responsible for defending him, though here too the Imeghrane tried to equalize things by customarily defining this as a man's 10 or 40 nearest male relatives. In some villages, each "lineage" got an equal share of the irrigation water, which then had to be divided among its households. In some areas "clans" had rights to specific pastures or herding camps. Villages typically consisted of three or four "lineages," which cooperated on a range of activities, from defending the

Table 2.1 Segmentary Organization of the Imeghrane

Segment Level	Resources and Common Interests
Imeghrane confederation	Territory (pastures, water sources, fields, villages), political unit with elders' council and rotating leader (*amghrar* or *sheikh*)
"Tribe" or "fraction"	Water sources, pastures, political unit with elders' council and leader
Village	Fields, water sources, pasture rights, political unit with elders' council and head-man, mosque, school, and cemetery
Lineage	Water rights, pasture rights, neighborhood within village
Household	Fields, livestock, water rights, dwelling, common food store, and "hearth"
Nuclear family	Room(s) in household

village's water sources and maintaining its irrigation canals to building a mosque and paying an imam to teach its children and conduct religious services. Villages also shared the surrounding pasturelands, which were used for daily herding of animals corralled at home, and often had rights to distant pastures used by transhumant shepherds.

Each of the tribe's eight subtribes or "fractions" had a mostly contiguous territory, enclosing its water sources and pastures, to defend. Most of the more important summer pastures belonged to a "fraction," sometimes subdivided by villages or lineages. The "fraction" was also a primary political unit, having an *amghrar* (Berber) or a *sheikh* (Arabic) who acted as an intermediary with government officials and who traditionally had been responsible for raising contingents of men for rare tribal-level conflicts, and sometimes for collecting his fraction's share of the tribe's tax. Each individual thus belonged to nested segments: a nuclear family, in many cases an extended household, a patri-"lineage," in some cases a "clan" with branches in several villages, a "fraction," and the Imeghrane "tribe."

One can see how scarce and shifting resources and continual imbalances of family composition gave rise to conflicts at each level—over inheritances, water rights, farm plots, pasture rights, and so on. Historical circumstances occasionally united the entire tribe. It is not important whether the Imeghrane's units are "real" lineages and clans, but it does matter that the overall structure—anchored in its adaptation to its resources—is "segmentary." A segmentary structure, whether represented with a mythic genealogy, in an idiom of territories, or as a set of alliances, differs markedly from a stratified society such as existed in India (based on caste), in medieval Europe (based on feudal estates), or in the modern West (based on social class). All of the nested groups to which one belongs are both unified by shared interests in defending and using resources, and fractured by lines of potential strife over diverging interests in other resources. While the individual may appear to be firmly enmeshed in widening circles of loyalties, all is in fact shifting, fragile, and precarious—leaving great room for individual maneuver and initiative.

Patronymic Associations

As the American anthropologists Clifford Geertz, Hildred Geertz, Lawrence Rosen, and Dale Eickelman all have emphasized, each relationship within a segment must be negotiated on a person-to-person basis, even when it involves family ties. The basic social groupings are neither just families nor true lineages but show features of both. Hildred Geertz refers to them as "patronymic associations."[67] She studied a prominent familial network in the Moroccan town of Sefrou that other Sefrouis characterized with the French term *grand famille*. At first glance, it looked to be a classic endogamous patrilineage, with 9 percent of marriages FBD and 69 percent within the group. Traditionally, the families making up the *nas Adlun*—the "people of" or "descendants of" a man named Adlun—occupied a neighborhood within the town walls centered on *derb Adlun*, or "Adlun street," with their own mosque, public bath, and Quranic school for their children. That is, *some* of the *nas Adlun* lived there, along with a number of their sharecroppers, servants, and other dependents who were not actually kinspeople.

When Geertz studied them in 1968, 36 of the 145 *nas Adlun* adults lived in the quarter; the others had moved into houses in Sefrou's new suburbs, and some to other Moroccan cities. She found great disparities in wealth: of the 61 living men, "one was wealthy, nine were well-off, twenty-eight were of average income, and twenty-three were poor or even with no means of support."[68] In the center of the quarter sits the dar Hamid, the "house of Hamid," home to 12 of the 36 descendants of Hamid, grandfather to the elder men. Nested within the *nas Adlun*, the members of this house often are referred to as *nas Hamid*. A prestigious and conservative lineage-like group, the *dar Hamid*'s high rate of endogamous marriages had produced "a ramifying thicket of ties in which no one person is linked to anyone else in a simple, one-dimensional way."[69] Its eldest male had the highest prestige and income (from fields worked mainly by sharecroppers), but the most influential man was a younger cousin of his named Moulay Ali, a well-connected mover and shaker who did not live in the quarter but kept a house there:

> Despite the fact that he rarely enters Dar Hamid, its inhabitants are dominated by his invisible presence. . . . Nearly every member of Nas Adlun is a client of Mulay Ali in one way or another. Within Dar Hamid there is no one who has not at one time or another been obliged to beg a favor of him, no one who is not in some way beholden to him. In countless small and large ways his net of transactions, debts, and obligations covers the entire house.

In consequence he is the de facto head of the house of Hamid. His authority binds together the people in it, even though he is not a resident. Seen from the vantage point of Mulay Ali, the house itself is not a unit but merely a shelter for part of his network of client-kinsmen that extends throughout the town.[70]

The people of *dar Hamid* were coming to be called *nas Mulay Ali,* "the people of Mulay Ali."

Geertz initially tried to diagram the *nas Adlun* as a patrilineage but found that she—and her Adluni informants—could not: "The genealogical tree was a failure."[71] They described the *nas Adlun* as a group of overlapping and more inclusive "name clusters"—*nas Hamid, nas Mulay Ali, nas Adlun.* Abner Cohen had made similar observations about the patrilineage-like *hamula* groupings that organized family and village life in the Palestinian "border villages" he studied, and he chose to describe them as *patronymic groups,* groups named for a founding or influential male, rather than as lineages.[72] He subsequently wrote of them as *patronymic associations* in recognition of their fluid and shifting boundaries. Hildred Geertz follows Cohen and argues that networks like the *nas Adlun,* which typically do not include all the kinspeople that a lineage should but do include people who are not kin, ought to be viewed as patronymic associations rather than as lineages.

In patronymic associations, ties of kinship, friendship, and patron-clientage thoroughly intermingle and merge. Americans, she points out, tend to view family relations, friendships, and patron-client relationships as fundamentally different, as operating in separate spheres of life. For many Moroccans, however, "the social ties of friendship and patronage intergrade with family, and many of the same norms apply to any of them."[73] Her points apply generally to family and social life in MENA societies: in spite of both modernization and underdevelopment, most people grow up, come of age, and live out their lives enmeshed in the interdependent relationships of patronymic associations. And the fluidity of these relationships opens the door to talent, initiative, and ambition—traditionally for men, and increasingly for women—creating a social milieu that, beneath its collectivistic rhetoric, proves surprisingly individualistic.

Patrons and Clients

Of the three types of relationship—family, friendship, and patronage-clientage—the latter is probably the least familiar to Westerners, but it is a crucial ingredient of social relations throughout MENA and in many other developing societies. A woman in a poor Imeghrane household learns that the regional governor will be visiting the sheikh, and since she knows that the women of the sheikh's household will be overwhelmed with preparations, she shows up and offers to help. At the end of the day, the sheikh's wife or

---

mother gives her some grain and vegetables to take home, not as payment but as a counter-gift that both women recognize to be not quite equivalent to the value of the woman's help. This initiates a "patron-client" relationship: if the counter-gift underreciprocates the woman's help it effectively says, "you can call on me if you need other things"; if it overreciprocates her help it says, "I'll expect your assistance again." When the young Imeghrani man who broke away from his brothers accepted a loan and a job from the *grand famille* of an opposing patronymic association, he became their client. The patron expected that the generosity of the interest-free loan would be repaid in other ways, probably in the form of political support in disputes that pitted the two patronymic associations against each other. All parties recognize that this could require the young man to betray his patronymic ties and would therefore constitute an act of loyalty to the patron that merited further counter-gifts. The young man expected the job to open doors of opportunity that his elder brothers seemed determined to keep closed to him. Real friendship might develop in either of these cases, so that genuine affection might accompany a rather careful monitoring of gift and counter-gift. And these types of relationships might be established between powerful and poor members of the same patronymic association, so that a family tie might merge with the reciprocal exchange, and perhaps also with feelings of friendship. Many people view it as a duty of well-off families to take on their poor relatives as clients before they take on outsiders. Traditionally, patron-client relations of this sort play a key role in managing the chronic imbalances of household resources and available labor.

As one might imagine, patron-client relationships can be quite unstable, since both patron and client have incentives to get more than they give, and actual values cannot be calculated. Since clients typically enter the relationship in a weaker position, they easily feel resentment as well as gratitude, and patrons may resent having to take care of "good-for-nothing" relatives who would "eat" them into poverty. In addition, patrons may use intimidation and coercion to force poorer or weaker individuals into clientage and to make the exchange exploitative. The de facto head of a patronymic association like the *nas Adlun* has wealth, prestige, and connections with government officials and can work behind the scenes to make life miserable for a poor relative—or rebellious son—who wants to make it on his own. Patronage easily becomes domination, and clientage subordination, and the cultural etiquettes guiding patron-client interaction draw on the many signs of authority and deference that characterize the familial hierarchy.

To Be "First Among Equals"

A group of prominent American anthropologists have argued that Morocco and MENA generally should be seen neither as class societies nor as a kinship societies, and they emphasize the ways fluid social networks are negotiated dyad by dyad. In the first edition of his text on the region, Dale Eickelman summarized their work as follows.

> I worked with the initial assumption, shared for the most part with ... Clifford Geertz, Hildred Geertz, Lawrence Rosen and Paul Rabinow—that Morocco's social structure was best conceived with persons as its fundamental units ... [and that] persons are not arranged in layerlike strata or classes but are linked in *dyadic bonds of subordination and domination* which are characteristically dissolved and reformed. The relatively stable element in this type of social structure is not the patterns that actual social relations form, but the *culturally accepted means* by which persons contract and maintain dyadic bonds and obligations with one another.[74]

This is crucial. In spite of a widespread belief in the equality of men, large disparities in wealth exist in all communities. In most areas (and there are important exceptions)[75] disparities traditionally did not make for a class-based culture, since poor households tended to be linked not to other poor households but to better off households within patronymic associations. Patron-client relationships tend to be formed between richer and poorer or stronger and weaker, and so, as Eickelman describes, they typically entail "subordination and domination." The "culturally accepted means" by which these relationships are built and maintained tend to be extended from authority/deference relationships within the immediate family, with kinship terms often used to describe them. And as Hildred Geertz notes, the means used to manage patron-client relationships are drawn into the exercise of authority *within* the family sphere, making for an important degree of continuity as one moves from the familial core of the patronymic association out to its peripheries of patronage-clientage.

The organization of society as nested chains of hierarchical dyads is characteristic of many—though not all—preindustrial societies. Extensive research has been done in Japan on the character of senior/junior *oyabun-kobun* relationships, which link parent and child, teacher and student, master and apprentice, manager and employee, emperor and citizen in similar styles of hierarchy.[76] The work of the psychiatrist Takeo Doi[77] and others shows that the "culturally approved means" by which these are maintained have profound psychological importance, as children are socialized to the kind of hierarchical interdependence they entail from birth. Many Arab scholars have studied this continuum of familial-protofamilial-patron/client relationships of authority and deference, and argue that it plays a similar role in shaping psychological development in MENA societies.

Modernizing forces certainly are affecting these networks of hierarchical dyads, but in complex ways whose effects are not clear. The anticipated destruction of *oyabun-kobun* relationships by modernization in Japan has not occurred, and modernization theorists have had to recognize that supposedly "premodern" cultural systems may actually promote industrialization. This could occur in MENA societies as well. At the present time, the modernization of some sectors, which appears to be creating an educated and Westernized elite, is underdeveloping other sectors and, in the view of a number of MENA scholars (especially Hisham Sharabi[78] and Abdullah Hammoudi),[79] reinforcing rather than undermining familial-patron/client networks. Specifically, many governments use patronage networks to govern, funneling money, jobs, educational and entrepreneurial opportunities through networks of the regimes' clients. This strengthens the clients' positions as powerful patrons to their clients, and so on down the line to the poor farmer who trades his vote in the next election for some UN food relief during a drought, because the village headman administers the distribution.

But what looks to an anthropologist like a traditional reciprocity system looks to those committed to modern notions of justice—as are many in MENA—like corruption. More important, Sharabi, Hammoudi, and others argue that the reinforcement of patronage networks undermines the creation of a "civil society" that could promote democratization, and that it sustains dangerously patriarchal models of political association.[80] The Lebanese sociologist Fuad Khuri's *Tents and Pyramids* provides a detailed analysis of the familial-patron/client system and comes to similar conclusions. Many societies have pyramid-like structures, he writes, consisting of a relatively stable hierarchy of offices with authority inhering in the offices rather than in the personal strength and charisma of the office-holders. He believes that MENA societies largely lack these and more closely resemble "a Bedouin encampment composed of tents scattered haphazardly on a flat desert surface with no visible hierarchy."[81] This equality paradoxically gives rise to a struggle for preeminence, to be "first among equals," which takes shape as a general imperative he sees at play in all spheres of society, from family (to be the "Mulay Ali" of the *nas Mulay Ali*) to religion (to be the *imam* of a community of believers) to politics (to be the sheikh of a tribe or emir of a state) to games of leisure (to be the third "imam" stone of a *khnat* group in backgammon). In every context, a man must *achieve* his status as first among equals, Khuri emphasizes, "through the strategic manipulation of custom" backed by "sheer physical power": "The tone of voice, the hands and the legs, the eyes, the seating order are all manipulated to assert your position as dominant or dominated."[82]

An aspiring "first among equals" uses intimidation, affection, generosity, and ingratiation to forge bonds among the group he dominates, and then by forming clientage relations with more powerful players.[83] The primary tactic consists of building relations of domination and subordination on models of familial interdependence, protection, authority, and deference—"a complex process of generalizing kinship terms to the whole universe around the actor. It is a process in which people become brothers and sisters, aunts and uncles, nieces and nephews, first and second cousins."[84] This works informally, by both parties spontaneously using kinship terms to cover a range of feelings and motivations: "kinship terms are used to convey friendliness, animosity, anger, formality, seriousness, sarcasm, intimacy, politeness, disrespect, status, hierarchy, equality, closeness, or distance. It is a world in itself."[85] An ambitious man begins by unifying his family and kin under his authority, and Khuri views endogamous, FBD, and close marriages—all more common in wealthy and prominent families—as strategies for building internal solidarity. Noting that the term for "elite" (*khassa*) means "private," while that for "common" (*amma*) means "public," he explains that: "As people move up the social ladder, they turn inwardly rather than outwardly, thus becoming *khassa* (the private ones) rather than *amma* (commoners) . . . endogamous behavior is an instrument to attain 'enclosure' and therefore internal solidarity."[86]

Khuri writes as a social critic, and in a mood of pessimism. He believes the continual creation of these inwardly turned networks to be "a recipe for autocratic rule," the phrase he uses as the title of his concluding chapter:

> There are no pyramids and therefore no standardized rules of succession to high office. Government belongs to the powerful, the conqueror. And power rests in the control of solidarities, endogamous groups, which militates against the rise of a "public" that holds the ruler accountable for his actions. . . .
>
> The political agony of Arab countries can be summarized in one sentence: no ruler, whether king, president, prince or sultan, is held accountable for his policies. Only a strong public could make the ruler accountable. Hence, the word "republic." "The public" has not yet emerged in Arab countries; "the private" prevails.[87]

Khuri's analysis of the logic of familial-patron/client networks takes us from political economy into the terrain of psychology. He in fact refers to this logic as a "mental design," and he not only describes the strategy and tactics of becoming first among equals but also, like Hammoudi, explores the emotional complexities that go with oscillating between acting as a dominant "first" in some contexts and as a deferential "equal" in others. He recognizes that a potentially transformative "public" is emerging in some cultural spheres, but he often writes as if the mental design of Bedouin tents awaiting a "first" dooms MENA societies to autocratic rule. At the end, however, he gets to the crux of underdevelopment in the region: governments that deliberately suppress civic life and rule through patronage. Here the actions of regimes, their elite clients, and their secret police have profound effects on psyches. He repeatedly emphasizes that the society of "tents" leaves the isolated one vulnerable, and if the "mental design" itself does not inspire fear, the presence of secret police and absence of civil rights certainly does.

The economist Alan Richards and the political scientist John Waterbury also underscore the predominance of "clientalist politics" in most MENA societies. And they point out that many groupings that initially appear to be traditional turn out to have been assembled in response to modern states and economic markets: "One trap we must avoid is seeing [apparently] older forms of political organization and action as direct reenactments of their forebears. Tribe and tribal loyalty in the twentieth-century Middle East are qualitatively different from their seventeenth- or eighteenth-century anteced-ents. So too are sects, ethnic groups, families, and coteries."[88] Political parties, unions, interest groups, and other forms of civic association "have not yet pro-vided effective means to protect members from the new order," so "people retreat into or invent 'security groups' as much to protect themselves as to promote their interests."[89] Some groups take shape as "clusters of cronies"— Richards and Waterbury cite the cases of Iraq and Syria, where Saddam Hussein and Hafiz al-Assad built regimes based on "clan" ties.[90] Modern patrons tend to be "brokers" between bureaucracies and individuals:

> He may help procure a birth certificate, a work permit, a commer-cial license, a passport, or any of the other vital pieces of paper that the modern state routinely requires but does not routinely deliver. He may help place a son in secondary school or the university, find a migrant a job in a public agency or factory, get the courts to drop charges for a misdemeanor, or swing a loan through the agricultural credit bank.[91]

Modern states and economies thus have paradoxically preserved traditional-appearing patronymic associations and patron-clientage networks, and so the "first among equals" strategy often thrives alongside the "fair competitive achievement" strategies that schools and modern organizations are supposed to put into play.

The Social Ecology of Psychological Development in Traditional Milieus

To the extent that we can speak of "traditional" MENA societies, these char-acteristics—a symbiosis of settled agriculture and nomadic pastoralism, a dialectic of rural and urban ways of life, patriarchal (but "matrifocal") fam-ily systems built by preferences for "close" and often endogamous marriages, and segmentary social groupings ("patronymic associations") built of both kin and patron-client relations—have shaped the ecological parameters of psychological development. Chapter 3 examines how these parameters have anchored the region's preeminent ethical systems—those of honor and Islam—which have pervasively organized social interaction, personal moti-vation, and identities. And chapters 4 through 9 consider how, in traditional settings, these parameters influenced psychological development at each life-stage. They especially appear to influence:

- Infant-care and child-rearing practices that set up important developmental discontinuities and sharply differentiate trajectories for boys and girls
- The pattern of authority, subordination, and emotional interdependence within families, which powerfully shapes development in middle and late childhood and early adolescence
- The formation of late adolescent and early adult identities in terms of the sometimes contrasting poetics of honor and modesty on the one hand and religious piety on the other
- The character of protofamilial relationships with patrons and clients, which influences the trajectory of adulthood
- The psycho-social stresses adults typically face, their common expressions of distress, and the anxiety management techniques they employ to manage them
- Patterns of development and individuation in mature and later adulthood

In the following chapters, it will be crucial to keep four points in mind. First, these ecological parameters do not shape all of a person's character: individual temperament and idiosyncratic events play large roles in everyone's development. Second, they do not influence all individuals in the same way, and do not yield anything like a shared "basic personality" or "national character." In fact, apparently shared ecological factors often generate important variation in developmental trajectories, leading even siblings within the same family to *not* share psychological characteristics. Third, cultural values, child-rearing practices, personal motives, and adult identities cannot simply be interpreted as reflections of the social ecology. Some beliefs and practices may best be seen as efforts to resist ecological imperatives—several scholars have suggested, for example, that Islam's creation of a brotherhood of believers seeks to transcend the fractious world of segments based on the brotherhood of kin.

Finally, these ecological parameters appear to set into play a complex dynamic of collectivism *and* individualism, of "sociocentrism" *and* "egocentrism." It would be misleading to place MENA cultures at any point on an individualism-collectivism continuum, as the shifting character of segmentary allegiances fosters both a strong sociocentrism and an equally strong individualism. The anthropologist Charles Lindholm argues that observers have generally failed to recognize how individualistic these societies are:

> The cultural heritage of the Middle East . . . is structured by an ancient antagonism between unstable urban civilization and armed peripheries. This fluid and unreliable setting has favored an entrepreneurial ethic of risk-taking, individual initiative, adaptiveness and mobility among opportunistic co-equals who struggle over ephemeral positions of power and respect, constrained only by participation in a framework of elastic patrilineages.[92]

In addition to influencing family relationships and child-rearing practices, then, the ethnographic literature suggests that ecological factors foster continually waxing and waning tensions between sociocentrism and egocentrism, and between the ideals of honor and religious piety. This constellation of ecological parameters and cultural tensions differs from those characteristic of Northern Europe, of Hindu India, and of sub-Saharan Africa and gives the MENA "culture area" its distinctive psychological textures.

While there have been no direct studies of psychological characteristics associated with these features of social ecology, Abdelhamid Jabar's 1978 *Derasat moqarana fi al-shakhsiyia* (Comparative Study of Personality in Qatar, Iraq, Egypt, and America) represents an intriguing attempt to assess some of them. Starting from Ibn Khaldun's contrast of Bedouin and "civilized" ways of life, Jabar reasoned that Egyptian culture has historically been dominated by "civilization," Iraqi by a mixture of the two, and Qatar by the "Bedouin." He gave the Edwards Personal Preference Inventory, which measures 15 psychological needs identified by Henry Murray as basic components of personality, to samples of high school and university students in those three societies,[93] and to students at an American university. He found that the Arab samples differed from each other on only a few of the psychological needs, and while these fell short of confirming his hypothesis, some of the differences fit his predictions about the greater influence of the Bedouin way of life on Qataris (who scored higher than Iraqis on needs for independence, authority, and aggression).

However, the American and Arab need profiles differed on nine of the fifteen needs, with Qataris higher on needs for order, dominance, nurturance, endurance, and aggression and Americans on needs for affiliation, intraception, exhibitionism, and heterosexuality.[94] Jabar concludes that the data show a common Arab culture with relatively small variations resulting from ecological factors. And the overall pattern—with Americans showing higher need for affiliation and the Arabs and Americans *not* differing in needs for achievement, autonomy, or change—clearly contradicts the stereotypes discussed in chapter 1, and also the notion that MENA cultures might be characterized as "collectivist" in contrast to an "individualist" West.

Part 2: Modernization and Underdevelopment ❀

MENA societies have never been static, but they have undergone profound transformations over the last two centuries that are changing important aspects of the picture I have just sketched. In the nineteenth and early twentieth centuries, European colonization destroyed their political and economic systems, in many cases seizing their most valuable resources. Many colonial administrations ruled the vast, less productive areas indirectly, through rural and tribal "notables," giving them the power to turn leadership into domination, to intensify their exploitation of farmers and tribesmen, and to make their positions less subject to the cycle of ascent and decline described by Ibn Khaldun. The aftermath of World War I saw national boundaries imposed on core regions, carving them into states that often did not correspond either to a resource base or to the social groups constituting them. Cities began to swell with migrants from the countryside, and the military power of nomadic tribes effectively came to an end.

Led by a largely Western-educated generation, the nationalist movements that spread in the 1920s and 1930s sought to modernize their countries as well as to fight their colonizers. Arguments by the philosopher Mohammed Abduh that Islam could incorporate modern science without losing its authenticity gained wide popularity, and Qasim Amin's case for women's equality also spread. In 1923 the Egyptian feminist Huda Sha'rawi returned from an international women's conference in Rome and publicly removed her veil at the Cairo railway station. Other educated women followed suit as they became active in public life, and an Arab women's conference was held in Palestine in 1929. In Turkey, a republic was declared in 1923 with Mustapha Kemal (Ataturk, "father of the Turks") as president. To build a Western-style secular state, he moved the capital from Istanbul to Ankara, replaced Islamic laws and courts with a European legal system, secularized the education system, replaced the Arabic script with the Latin alphabet, discouraged veiling, and passed a law requiring men to wear European-style hats rather than traditional fezes. In Iran, Reza Shah set out to build a Western-style nation from a land with far less infrastructure than Turkey. He built a professional army and used it to forcibly settle nomadic tribes, curb the influence of religious leaders, and enforce a law against veiling. His son Mohammed Shah tried to use oil revenues to catch up to the West in a decade but also to make himself king in the manner of ancient Persian rulers.

Many MENA nations achieved independence in the 1950s and undertook large-scale development programs to modernize agriculture, manufacturing, transportation, communications, education, and health care. Under various ideological banners, new regimes sought to forge national and pan-Arab unity by settling tribes, reforming "feudal" landlord-tenant systems, extending and Arabizing education, and mobilizing the masses in political parties. This wave of modernization tended to be anti-Western but largely secular, emphasizing "Arab nationalism" and "Arab socialism" rather than Islam. By the mid-1960s many of these efforts were faltering, and regimes began turning to rule by patronage rather than popular participation, sometimes rehabilitating "notable" Big Men to prop them up. Some destroyed political parties and civic organizations that had begun to press for democratic reforms and more equal sharing of opportunities and wealth.

Israel's quick and decisive victory in the 1967 war brought about a crisis among Arab leaders and intellectuals, who engaged in an intensive reevaluation of their postindependence ideologies and culture. Some wrote analyses of "the Arab personality" that now appear Eurocentric in the ways they scrutinize their own cultures through Western-trained eyes. Oil wealth brought dramatic increases in prosperity to some nations but also financed oppressive regimes, especially in Iran and Iraq. By the 1980s a different kind of crisis was increasingly felt by populaces in countries that lacked petroleum, one brought on by a poverty of natural resources and rapid population growth. With both Western-style capitalism and Soviet-style socialism discredited and Arab unity in shambles, political Islam—or "Islamism"— gradually emerged to provide a new model of modernization and a new critique of corrupt regimes.

A Statistical Profile

The population of the region has tripled since the late 1950s, continues to grow at about 2.8 percent—higher than any region but sub-Saharan Africa (at 3.0 percent)—and will double again by about 2020. Richards and Waterbury point out that "within just three generations (of twenty years each) the region's population will have increased *twelvefold*."[95] As a result, MENA is overwhelmingly young: half the population is under 20, and in some countries, under 15. Population growth has greatly diluted the benefits of substantial economic growth. MENA has about two-thirds of the world's petroleum, so per capita gross domestic product (GDP) is moderate to high in the Gulf oil states (Bahrain, Oman, Qatar, Saudi Arabia, and the United Arab Emirates). It is quite low elsewhere: in 1992, around $2,000 in Algeria, Iran, Tunisia and Turkey; about $1,000 in Jordan and Morocco; only $660 in Egypt.[96] Most important, between 1980 and 1993 per capita GDP *declined* 2.3 percent for the region as a whole, the worst performance in the world (sub-Saharan Africa declined 0.8 percent). The 1990s saw some recovery, so that per capita GDP for the region was about $1,650 in 1997.[97] Assessed in terms of purchasing power, GDP per capita was about 20 percent of that of the industrialized nations in the OECD (Organization for Economic Cooperation and Development) in 1975, but fell to just 14 percent by 1998.[98]

Roughly a third of MENA people lived in "absolute poverty" in 1990, compared to about 25 percent in Latin America, 11 percent in East Asia, and about 50 percent in sub-Saharan Africa and South Asia.[99] But only 2.5 percent live in "extreme poverty" (under $1 per day), the lowest percentage of any developing region, and in spite of its concentrations of oil wealth, MENA has one of the most equal income distributions in the developing world.[100] Given the great significance of "informal," unmeasured sectors of the economy, unemployment is even more difficult to assess, but official estimates generally range between a little under 10 percent (Egypt, Syria, Turkey, Iran) to 15 percent (Morocco, Tunisia, Jordan), with a few higher (Algeria at 26 percent).[101] More important, rates are very high among the young—64 percent of Algerian 15- to 19-year-olds, and 46 percent of 20- to 24-year-olds—most of whom reside in urban areas: and in many countries unemployment *increases* with education.[102]

At the same time that economic progress has been stagnant or slow, MENA populaces have become more urban and better educated, and have higher aspirations. With a little over half of its population living in cities, the region is currently more urbanized than sub-Saharan Africa, South Asia, and East Asia. Nomads have declined from an estimated 10 percent of the population in 1960 to less than 1 percent today, and the percentage of farmers has decreased significantly during this period: from 67 percent to 31 percent in Algeria, from 58 percent to 46 percent in Egypt, from 54 percent to 36 percent in Iran, and from 54 percent to 32 percent in Syria.[103] By 1960 the 35 million city-dwellers constituted a third of the population: by 1990 this had grown to 135 million, or 55 percent: and the urban population is projected to reach 350 million in 2020.[104] As of 2000, Cairo was a city of 14 to 16 million people. This urbanization has mixed effects: in the 1970s Saad Ibrahim noted that immigrants to the cities often retain their rural life-styles, so that "rather than modernizing its traditional and rural inhabitants, the Arab city is itself being traditionalized and ruralized."[105]

Health has improved dramatically, with life expectancy increasing nearly 20 years since the 1960s, to 68 years for the region (ranging from 45 years in Somalia to 75 in the United Arab Emirates).[106] And while infant mortality rates remain "high" at 58 per 1,000 births in 1992 and higher than Latin America (44 per 1,000) and East Asia (39 per 1,000), infant mortality has dropped dramatically, with most countries at one-third to one-fourth their 1960 rate (many of these countries then exceeded 150 per 1,000). Current rates range from around 10 (Qatar) to 75 (Yemen),[107] though variation by income and region within countries remains great, so some impoverished areas still have rates in excess of 100 per 1,000. In calories available per person, the region ranks second, at 3,000, behind the developed OECD countries (at about 3,400) but well ahead of South Asia (at 2,200) and sub-Saharan Africa (at 2,100). Yet, as of 2002, developmental stunting continued to affect 15 percent to 25 percent of children, and many more in strife-torn areas: over 30 percent in Sudan and over 50 percent in Yemen.[108]

Public education has expanded dramatically, mainly in the last two to three decades. MENA got a later start than some other regions, and in 1990 had an adult literacy of about 55 percent of men and a little over 40 percent of women.[109] This put it behind East Asia (75 and 65 percent), Latin America (85 and 70 percent), and Europe (95 percent for both men and women) but slightly ahead of sub-Saharan Africa (50 and 40 percent), and South Asia (45 and 30 percent). Most MENA countries have eschewed adult literacy campaigns to devote their resources to educating children, with impressive progress. In 1990, for example, only 14 percent of Moroccan men and 1 percent of women over 60 could read and write, but 78 percent of 10- to 14-year-old boys were literate and 56 percent of girls. For the region as a whole, secondary school enrollment more than doubled for men between 1970 and 1991 (from 24 to 56 percent) and more than tripled for women (from 15 to 56 percent)—which compares favorably with Latin America and East Asia. By 2000, the MENA continued to lag behind other developing regions in primary school enrollment but was a bit ahead in secondary school and university enrollment.[110]

The expansion of education has many important effects. For one thing, it raises aspirations, and the great majority of youth now hope to work with their minds rather than their hands. In many areas, children of rural families have done exceptionally well in schools, which, alongside the army, now provide them with an important route of upward mobility. For another, it means that most children are growing up and coming of age in schools, which brings a constellation of opportunities and challenges that are largely absent from traditional patterns of socialization. It also means that most MENA countries have growing numbers of educated but unemployed and underemployed young people, most trying to get lives in urban areas, which makes them a volatile political force.

In addition to providing health care and education, governments have to respond to popular demands for jobs, and many regimes have done this by expanding public sector employment, in some cases providing jobs for most secondary school graduates (Egypt in the 1970s and Algeria in the 1980s).[111] Jobs as teachers, health care workers, agricultural extensionists, postal clerks, technicians, and bureaucrats of all sorts tend to be prized, because even when they pay little they offer steady, secure work and high status. By the 1990s public sector jobs accounted for about 30 percent of employment in Egypt, over 40 percent in Jordan and Bahrain, and over 50 percent in Saudi Arabia and Algeria,[112] and al-Khalil estimates they accounted for about 60 percent of urban employment in Iraq.[113] In many countries these jobs provide the foundation for a new middle-class culture, not of entrepreneurs and businessmen but of technicians and bureaucrats who hold their jobs, in varying degrees, as clients of governing regimes.

A recent Moroccan high school graduate once explained to me his family's strategy of getting its sons employed in different ministries, so the family could get help from them when they needed it. Patronage networks build both from the bottom, where poorly paid or avaricious clerks may want a gift in exchange for providing a driver's license or an inoculation that should be free, and from the top, where control of large projects, budgets, equipment, and promotion decisions enables managers to build extensive clientage relationships with their subordinates. In these settings, traditional patron-client reciprocity becomes "corruption," and populaces come to perceive the agencies that are supposed to modernize their societies as predatory.

A second crucially important and volatile source of income has come from largely temporary migration to the Gulf oil states and Europe. In the mid-1980s, 3.5 million Middle Easterners worked as laborers in Saudi Arabia and the Gulf oil states, two million of them from Egypt, 750,000 of them from Yemen, and nearly 400,000 of them Palestinians and Jordanians.[114] Another 750,000 worked in Iraq. Turks and North Africans mainly went to western Europe as "guest workers": 1.5 million held jobs there in the mid-1980s, totaling 3.5 million persons, counting the families that accompanied some of them.[115] They make three to ten times what they could working at lower level jobs at home, and the wages they remit to their families make an enormous contribution to some countries' economies: $6 billion to Egypt in 1992, $3 billion to Turkey, $2 billion to Morocco, $750 million to Jordan, and $500 million to Tunisia. Migrants are almost entirely young and male and come predominantly from rural areas, so they significantly reduce both the unemployment rate and rural poverty. As the UNDP assessment notes, emigration has helped keep income inequality lower than in other developing regions. No good estimates are available, but it is clear that remitted wages have accounted for a substantial proportion of private sector investment in many MENA countries.

The cultural effects of migration are matters of much debate, and ultimately not yet clear. Certainly those who go to conservative Gulf states have different experiences from those who work in Germany, France, or Holland. The latter typically encounter an appealingly liberated style of life, of which they can taste little if they are to save their earnings for back home. At the same time they run into a good deal of class condescension and racism. Some migrants return believing in the superiority of European ways, others in their decadence, and others feeling an ambivalent attraction and repulsion—and no one knows in what proportion. There can be no doubt that the merchandise that migrants buy with their remittances fuels the taste for modern consumer goods, even in remote villages. Since the "Big Men" of prominent houses more easily get their sons and nephews passports and jobs, migrant labor generally increases their power as patrons and intensifies the dependence of nonmigrant families on them. In one remote High Atlas village of the Imeghrane, the migrants all came from the houses of the three powerful families leading each of its patronymic associations, and several had used their remittances to start well-digging businesses in the rich agricultural plains around Meknes, where they hired mostly sons of poor families from their home village as laborers on slightly modified versions of traditional sharecropping contracts. These arrangements appear to further entrench "traditional"-appearing familial-patron/client networks at the same time that they disseminate "modern" technologies, goods, tastes, and styles.

As many scholars have pointed out, this modernization is not primarily driven by structural changes in MENA economies. Improved productivity in agricultural and other sectors has largely been offset by population growth, so that most countries have become less able to feed themselves, and manufacturing and high-tech sectors remain especially weak. Research and development for the entire region totals about that of the Ford Motor Company, and has declined slightly since 1980. The UNDP report cites this as one of the region's key weaknesses.[116] Outside of the Gulf oil states, most countries are resource poor and import a large portion of their energy, raw materials, and consumer goods, paying with remitted wages and foreign aid–supported public sector jobs. The region as a whole also spends a great deal on weapons—9 percent of its GDP in 1990, compared to less than 4 percent in Africa, South Asia, East Asia, and Latin America. Between 1978 and 1988, MENA governments spent $180 billion on imported weapons, three to five times the amounts spent by other regions, most with much larger populations.[117] Most indigenous economies cannot begin to support the improved standard of living that many in the world now enjoy—and with per capita incomes of $700 to $2,000, they lag far behind the United States (at over $20,000) and are only somewhat better off than the world's poorest regions. Rural poverty remains high, and large, densely packed shantytowns have grown on the edges of most cities.

The agro-pastoral symbiosis that historically provided the foundation of MENA cultures is declining in importance. But with a third to half of their populations still rural, with the cities growing with rural migrants, and with high rates of cyclical country-city migration, rural and even "tribal" ways of life continue to influence the creative mixing of cultural styles now taking place. Media and multinational marketing now play important roles in this mix. Egypt has emerged as the center of the Arabic-speaking world's movie, music, and television industry, and throughout the region families now gather around their TVs after dinner to watch Egyptian entertainers and soap operas. Most also get American, European, and Indian movies. Satellite TV has brought a flood of new European and Arab channels, including the widely watched al-Jazira news.

All of these modernizing forces have psychological consequences. Perhaps the most important arise from transformations in family life. As Mohammed Guessous points out, the traditional family performed nearly all social functions for its members, especially the socialization of children, occupational training, and the formation of core values. Larger institutions, from tribes to religious orders to craft guilds, modeled themselves after families. Modern institutions remove many of the family's core functions—especially socialization and occupational training—and operate by principles that often conflict with those rooted in families. This both "disarticulates" the family from other institutions and transforms the relationships among family members.[118] El Mustafa Haddiya's studies of rural and urban Moroccan students lead him to conclude that the conflicts between family and school become serious for most rural students, who pursue education with a determination to improve their family's standard of living and find the modern world they're introduced to estranges them from the environment they increasingly see as "backward."[119] But while rural students tend to remain committed to their families, the media-driven youth culture in the cities further undermines the family as a source of life-style values, and estranges many students from their parents as well as their underdeveloped conditions.[120] Many studies find that educated and salaried middle-class families are having far fewer children, and raising them not only in more nuclear-like households but by different principles. More and more marriages are chosen rather than arranged, and even when husband and wife are deeply devout they probably have a more companionate relationship than was the norm in the past. It is not yet clear, however, to what extent the "trend" toward Western-style families and child-rearing will diffuse throughout society, or form a distinctive style of the privileged that the "popular" classes reject.

Cultural Dualities

Developing societies often are said to have a dual economy: a modern sector of firms, financial institutions, and bureaucracies, and a subsistence sector in which most production goes for household consumption, labor is organized by age and gender, and exchanges of products and labor are often carried out by barter or by cycles of gift and counter-gift. These sectors may exist geographically side by side, with a timelessly traditional-looking village of subsistence farmers located within a kilometer or two of a modern factory. The modern sector may form a small island in a great sea of subsistence agriculture, or the subsistence sectors may appear as islands in modernized societies—as parts of Appalachia do in America. "World systems" theorists have pointed out that the dual economy notion is deceiving, because a great many individuals and perhaps most households in developing countries participate in both, linking modern "core" sectors with traditional "peripheral areas," often to the disadvantage of the latter. Most MENA societies have dual economies that support contrasting ways of life, and, more important for my purposes here, these support a series of cultural dualities that go along with them: traditional versus modern, backward versus advanced, native versus Western.

As a result, people have two (or more) ways of doing just about everything: bathing, dressing, speaking, eating, marrying, building a house, circumcising a son, treating an ailment. Every act invariably makes a statement about who one is and who one aspires to become. Everyday social life therefore proceeds as a more or less muted or heated debate about ways of life, and I believe it no exaggeration to say that MENA does not have a traditional culture that is modernizing but a new culture, neither traditional nor modern, that consists of the debate. As Aziz Krichen writes of Tunisia:

> With the establishment of the protectorate begins what one may call the era of dualism. Dualism in the economy with the traditional sectors and modern sectors; dualism in the demographic distribu-

tion split between French colonists and indigenous populations; dualism of the State with the two-headed structure of the Palace of the Bey and the Residence Generale; dualism of urban spaces with the contrast between the medina and the European-style city; dualism of the military; dualism of the administration, justice, education, religion, press, artistic and sports activities, etc.... Even foolishness was affected by this phenomenon with psychiatrists on one side and sorcerers and witch doctors on the other.[121]

The point Krichen makes at the end appears to be critically important for the younger, educated generation, for there is a deep dualism about how to conceptualize the human mind, and about how to explain and even experience one's thoughts and feelings. On the traditional side, religion offers a theory of the psyche as a battleground of divine and demonic forces, and provides a series of self-care techniques based on purification and Quranic recitation that promise a measure of control over disturbing dreams, daydreams, immoral wishes, depressive moods, dissociative states, and the like. On the modern side, public education is disseminating the rudiments of a supposedly scientific theory of mind that attributes disturbing experiences not to the mischief of Satan or *jinn*-spirits but to an "unconscious" and that attributes the paralyses and losses of speech or sensation that frequently occur among adolescents not to being "hit by a *jinn*" but to "imagination" or "hysteria." This generation's struggle for a theory of mind and emotion, and for techniques of self-control receives little attention, but it may be one of the most important features of the current cultural debate.

Underdevelopment and the Psychology of Modernity

Economically, most MENA countries can be said to be "middle-income developing nations," undergoing dependent development or *underdevelopment*: they have been incorporated into the world system as "semiperipheral" regions, supplying resources (mainly petroleum and labor) to core areas (mainly the industrialized West) and consuming Western and Asian products ranging from wheat to Disney TV shows to Walkmans to tactical fighters. Cities have grown as satellite centers, peripheral to the core economies of the West, but serving as core areas in relation to their peripheral hinterlands, which supply them with foodstuffs and labor, and purchase products manufactured in or imported through them. This clearly has improved overall standards of living, health, and education, in spite of prodigious population growth. It has transformed family and social relationships, and widely disseminated modern tastes and aspirations. But it has not created Western-like social orders, reducing families to nuclear or subnuclear units or substituting "mediated" forms of domination for face-to-face varieties and "pure relationships" for kin and client ties.

"Tradition" and "modernity" mix and often clash, here beside the main square of Marrakech. Next to the square sit two landmarks: the twelfth-century Koutoubia mosque and a Club Med Hotel.

Growth also has not led to the creation of Western-like liberal democracies, supported by civil rights and free presses. In many nations, indigenous elites acquired colonial properties and enterprises at independence and maintained them in a similarly exploitative manner. The Algerian psychiatrist Franz Fanon presciently decried the failures of decolonization in his 1963 *Wretched of the Earth:*

> The national middle class which takes over power at the end of the colonial regime is an underdeveloped middle class. . . . The national bourgeoisie of underdeveloped countries is not engaged in production, nor in invention, nor in building, nor in labor; it is completely canalized into activities of the intermediary type. . . . To them, nationalization quite simply means the transfer into native hands of those unfair advantages which are a legacy of the colonial period.[122]

Preoccupied with defending these advantages and "filling its pockets as rapidly as possible," Fanon writes, the postindependence elite also fails politically, often turning to single-party rule. "It does not create a state that reassures the ordinary citizen, but rather one that rouses his anxiety," he writes: "it makes a display, it jostles people and bullies them, thus intimating to the citizen that he is in continual danger." Independence soon turns into authoritarian rule, Fanon writes, and the populaces become disenchanted: "The peasant who goes on scratching out a living from the soil, and the unemployed man who never finds employment do not manage, in spite of public holidays and flags, new and brightly colored though they may be, to convince themselves that anything has really changed in their lives."[123]

According to the five-level rating system devised by the van Asbeck Centre for Human Rights at the University of Leiden, most MENA states are classified as level 3, meaning that "political imprisonment, torture, political murder occur," or level 4, meaning that "murders, disappearances, and torture are a common part of life." Jordan and Saudi Arabia are scored as level 2, meaning that there are "limitations of a secure rule of law," and Baathi Iraq, Sudan, and Taliban-ruled Afghanistan fell into level 5, in which there is "state terror directed toward the whole population."[124] The 2002 *Arab Human Development Report* directly blamed undemocratic governments for a good share of the region's underdevelopment.[125] It is difficult to describe to those who have not experienced it how palpable and pervasive the fear of government authorities can be. The Lebanese psychologist Mustafa Hijazi's *Al-takhaluf al-ijtima'i* (Underdeveloped Society), offers a frequently cited analysis of the pervasive psychological consequences of centuries of subjugation, first by despotic sultans, beys, pashas, and local Big Men with armed entourages and then by colonial regimes and, after independence, by new generations and styles of tyranny. In chapter 9 I review his analysis, along with writings by other Arab social scientists during the era of "self-criticism."

Life in MENA societies is changing, but we have no yardstick of tradition and modernity by which to measure it. This psychological inquiry must therefore begin with the recognition that the great majority of its citizens are neither traditional nor modern nor en route from tradition to modernity—even though many now describe themselves in precisely these terms. Youth are fully committed to "modernity," but a great many now believe that their societies should not become modern on the Western model but, as the sociologist Ali Lila put it after studying Egyptian youth, should "modernize from within tradition."[126] At the present time we have a very poor understanding of the psychological dimensions of life lived in patronymic clientage networks, with annual per capita incomes of $1,000 to $2,000, under undemocratic regimes, buffeted by seductively marketed Western life-styles on the one hand and appeals to the authenticity of one's own cultural heritage on the other. It is here especially that Western psychology may be most lacking in appropriate concepts.

It was the late eighteenth-century poet Goethe who captured the psychological nature of modernity, perhaps in part because he witnessed its birth in other parts of Europe from his home in "backward" Germany. In *Wilhelm Meister* and *Faust* we find the vision of inner-driven growth of personality that later animates the theories of Freud, Jung, Erikson, and most contemporary models of "life-span" development (which also expand it to cover women's as well as men's lives). Youths create dreams for their lives from deep inner sources that Freud a century later termed "unconscious," and development is set in motion by pursuing them. Goethe's Wilhelm declares: "Deep within us lies this creative force which can create what it is meant to be, and does not rest until out of us, or in us, in one way or another, that thing has been represented. . . . Man is not ever happy until his vaguer striving determines his limit."[127] A man's dream and the passion to live it typically crystallize in his love for a woman, but initially at least, for a woman who proves to be less a real person than what Jung later called an "archetype," representing the feminine side of his own character, shaped to complement his dream (women, Jung theorized, developed similar archetypes of men). The dream fails, or he fails the dream, but from its tragic collapse a new dream and a new passion arise, and with the talents developed and self-knowledge gained from the initial dream's pursuit, this one forms truer to the youth's emerging talents and to the real woman who revives his love. Wilhelm thus defies his parents' decision that he go into business and sets off to become an actor (his childhood passion), perhaps ultimately to play Hamlet. Renewed after failures by loves for an archetypal "Amazon" figure, Wilhelm perseveres and eventually plays Hamlet to cheers. But he soon discovers his success stemmed from the match of his own and the Prince's character, and that he cannot play parts that don't so directly express his own personality—and therefore cannot become a true actor. He returns home to make a new life, but the contrast with his friend Werner, who became a banker at his parents' bidding, is stark: Werner recognizes that Wilhelm has become "a personality," while "if I had not during this time gained a good deal of money, there would be nothing about me at all."[128]

This romantic vision of life holds that (1) personality should grow toward self-expression in a life's work and toward a capacity to love, and that (2) this growth is set in motion and sustained by the discovery and pursuit of one's personal dream. Herein lies the psychological essence of modernity. Not that premodern peoples never nurture dreams and pursue them, but modernity makes this the very point of life, with the corollary that a free society should allow "equal opportunity" for all "pursuits of happiness." Goethe's vision was hardly the sort of touchy-feely, self-actualization philosophy of contemporary pop-psych books, but was deeply tragic. Nor was it simply individualistic or egocentric, for while an individual may need to break away from family and tradition to pursue a dream, Goethe showed the path of tragedies and revised dreams leading toward deepening social commitments. But worse than the tragedies wrought in pursuit of dreams are lives lived with dreams not pursued.

Modernity nourishes personal dreams. This is the aspiration that modernity is spreading around the globe, and has spread among the young people of MENA societies. It is an aspiration more fundamental than wishes for cars and clothes and stereos. And it is this aspiration to pursue sharply or nebulously defined dreams that clashes so devastatingly for many with the hard realities of underdevelopment: with the power of Big Men, with the needs of dependents, with the imperatives of honor, and with the confines of poverty. I do not know how to describe in psychological terms the consequences of a dream dashed not by the logic that unfolds during a person's pursuit of it but by the undermining of one's ability to pursue it. This occurs in Western societies as well as in underdeveloped ones but appears to be especially widespread where population growth has undermined economic growth and many young people find themselves with neither work nor civil rights. The spiritual consequences are great, and it may be in the spiritual realm that compensatory dreams get formed.

I perhaps should apologize for speaking here in imprecise terms, and for discussing such a crucial issue in literary rather than psychological language. But the life-history interviews I have conducted with young Americans and Moroccans convince me that this business of dreams lies at the heart of modernity, modernization, and underdevelopment, and I do not find myself in possession of psychological terminology that does it justice. I sometimes suspect, however, that "dependent development"—a phrase coined to characterize the economies of peripheral regions dominated by industrialized cores—may also describe trajectories of psychological development pursued after the defeat of dreams either by traditional Big Men or by bureacracies.

CHAPTER *3*

Honor and Islam
Shaping Emotions, Traits, and Selves

This chapter describes the primary value systems of MENA societies. Ethnographies from nearly all MENA cultures suggest that the region is characterized by two predominant value systems and their associated interpersonal etiquettes and self-care practices: that of "honor-and-modesty" and that of Islam. Neither are distinctive to MENA, but their conjunction in that region gives it much of its cultural—and psychological—character. These values intertwine and merge at many points, but they also remain surprisingly autonomous and self-contained and often come into conflict, as Islam articulates higher principles that indict exploitative pursuits of honor and tyrannical rule. From toddlerhood on, these systems are learned in different settings and in different languages and they cultivate different kinds of sentiments and motives. The designating of sacred places (mosques and tombs), objects (the Quran), and activities (prayer, recitation) that can only be entered in conditions of purity, together with the organization of daily, weekly, and yearly time as oscillations of pollution and purity, work to elaborate honor and Islam as contrapuntal, if not contradictory, systems.

Psychologically, the internalization of these value systems—most important during middle childhood—appears to shape universal emotions, traits, and self-conceptions into culturally specific sentiments, motives, and social selves. The notion of sentiment refers to emotions as modified by culturally specific display rules and by cultural values that infuse them with moral meanings. The term "motive" refers to culturally distinctive needs, life-goals, and themes that organize and modify the expression of temperamentally based personality traits. And the concept of social persona or social self derives from G. H. Mead's analysis of the way people come to fashion images of themselves by taking the perspective of the larger society—what Mead terms the "Generalized Other"—on the repertoire of roles they play within it.

Because the cultural values of honor-modesty and Islam can coincide or conflict, the social selves often formed from these value-etiquette systems may merge or clash depending on person and circumstance. Importantly, these social selves do not complete personality but interrogate one as to who he or she will be and issue a challenge to prove one's self in their terms—which sets the developmental task of identity formation. They also set the developmental task that may recur throughout the life-span: to integrate pursuits of honor and piety into a whole, or at least into a balanced, life.

Introduction ❈

Just as psychological development is rooted in family and social relations, so it is rooted in a culture's primary value systems. In all MENA societies, ethnographers describe the "code" of honor and the Muslim religion as providing the primary value systems. Many characterize the culture as animated by a tension between these two sets of principles, and some speak of them as organizing personality, self, or identity. Raphael Patai, for example, suggests that individual personality typically has a "Bedouin substratum," by which he essentially means the honor code, and an "Islamic substratum."[1] Life-histories and autobiographies also suggest that Islam and the honor code play central roles in the organization of personality for a many. As value systems, as strategies for negotiating personal relationships, and as rhetorics for making and performing selves, honor and Islam shape emotions, thoughts, and the decisions that guide life-courses. While the two converge at many points, they tend to be learned and enacted in different contexts, with contrasting vocabularies. They thus easily take shape as separate systems that sometimes merge and cohere and at other times diverge and conflict.

Neither are distinctive to MENA societies. Historically, the honor-modesty system was circum-Mediterranean, with important features of it extending well beyond the Mediterranean's shores. Ethnographers often describe it as having two complementary axes: one emphasizing hostility and performative bravado toward outsider men and the other emphasizing protection and seclusion of insider women. During the colonial era, the first axis appears to have been "exported" to some of the frontier areas of Latin America, though without the more pronounced forms of female seclusion as practiced in the Mediterranean. The second axis prevails throughout the so-called purdah zone that stretches through northern Hindu India and into Bangladesh, though without the more pronounced forms of *machismo* or *egoismos* cultivated in the Mediterranean. Matters of honor, shame, and modesty certainly figure large in the cultures of Southern India and Southeast Asia, but as Louis Dumont has shown, the challenge-and-riposte individualism that underlies the honor-modesty system gives way in India to notions of hierarchy associated with the caste system, with its elaborate etiquette of avoidance and deference.[2] Sub-Saharan African cultures again show great variability, but ethnographers generally have not described them as organized around an honor-modesty system articulated along these two axes.

The geographic distribution of Islam does not coincide with that of the honor-modesty system, which antedated it throughout MENA. As the fastest-growing world religion, it has spread into large areas of sub-Saharan Africa and Southeast Asia, though in India it gives way to Hinduism and Buddhism, which not only map out very different spiritual quests but provide different systems of caring for the mind and body. Thus the honor-modesty system clearly can thrive without Islam, and Islam can thrive in societies that do not so strongly embrace the honor-modesty system. It is their conjunction in MENA that gives the region much of its cultural—and psychological—character. This chapter examines the values and interpersonal etiquettes associated with these two *cultural discourses* and describes the psychologically integrative role they appear to play in individuals' personalities.

Honor in the Mediterranean ❀

Anthropologists have studied the "honor code" for nearly a century, and most have come to view it as a defining feature of a circum-Mediterranean culture area, rooted, as Jane Schneider argues, in the region's ecology and political economy.[3] Many fieldworkers have noted that the honor code comes to be deeply internalized, so that people automatically respond to events and build reputations, personalities, or selves in its terms. Peristiany introduces his *Honor and Shame: The Values of Mediterranean Society* by writing that the study of honor and shame "is also a study of the basic mold of social personality," of the "ideals of a society and of their embodiment in the ideal type of man."

Peristiany repeatedly describes honor not just as a code of behavior but as something that inheres in a "type of personality" or a "social persona."[4] Its core quality is, to use the Spanish term, *machismo*, defined by the *American Heritage Dictionary* (1992) as "a strong, sometimes exaggerated sense of masculinity stressing attributes such as physical courage, virility, domination of women, and aggressiveness." Among the Greek Cypriots he studied, Peristiany found men to be generally "agonistic" in struggle with other men for prestige, and since "prestige that is hard to gain can be easily lost. . . . a true man is always on the alert, constantly prepared to prove himself."[5] Like Schneider, he sees the honor code as anchored in the political economy of fluid, family-based, face-to-face competition for resources that characterizes the region, and he finds it in Homer's epics much as he witnessed it in the isolated village he studied.

Indeed, the psychological importance of honor was perhaps first explored in *The Republic*, where Plato theorized that the human psyche is composed of three often-warring parts: an appetitive part that blindly seeks to sate hunger, thirst, sexual, and other bodily desires; a rational part that always seeks to do the Good but often lacks the willpower to hold sway; and a spirited part, "the part that loves honour and winning,"[6] that in response to unjust treatment becomes "boiling and angry,"[7] and that reacts to immoral appetites with feelings of shame.[8] Plato believed he saw this "lion"-like quality in well-born dogs—such a dog has "keen senses, speed to catch what it sees, and strength in case it has to fight it out with what it captures"[9]—and in well-born horses and young men. If tamed as reason's ally, honor "makes the whole soul fearless and unconquerable,"[10] but if not it can bring a man to ruin: "Doesn't his love of honor make him envious and its love of victory make him violent, so that he pursues the satisfaction of his anger and of his desires for honors and victories without calculation or understanding?"[11]

This part of the psyche may seem difficult to grasp in Western middle-class cultures that discourage *machismo* mentalities. But as Peristiany points out, honor-based subcultures flourish in them, for example street gangs, whose family-like bonds of loyalty, defense of women and turf, and daring raids and whose ethic of vengeance parallel the Mediterranean honor code. According to James Gibson's *Warrior Dreams*, post-Vietnam novels and films increasingly build stories around Rambo-like characters who set out for vengeance after their women or children have been attacked. Coaches of contact sports cultivate sentiments of honor and shame to motivate endurance and aggression. And the rhetoric of political and corporate leadership often draws heavily on the vocabulary of honor. The honor code thus forms part of the West's classical heritage, and even though psychologists pay it little attention, variants of it remain woven through Western cultures.[12]

Researchers studying Mediterranean societies disagree sharply about what kind of a social or psychological "thing" honor is, however, and they use a variety of terms to characterize it. Here too, autobiographies and life-histories suggest that Peristiany is correct to emphasize that it forms not just a "code" of values but an "ideal type of man," a "social personality," and a "persona." Honor, he writes, is fundamentally performative in nature:

> In this insecure, individualist, world where nothing is accepted on credit, the individual is constantly forced to prove and assert himself. Whether as the protagonist of his group or as a self-seeking individualist, he is constantly "on show," he is forever courting the public opinion of his "equals" so that they may pronounce him worthy. . . . The entire society watches for the young shepherd's first quarrel, that is, for his first chance to prove himself.[13]

I believe this simple example—"The entire society watches for the young shepherd's . . . first chance to prove himself"—provides the key to conceptualizing honor in psychological terms.

Honor as a "Code" of Values

A classic account of honor as a "code" comes from J. K. Campbell, based on his fieldwork among Greek pastoralists:

> The intrinsic principles of honour refer to two sex-linked qualities that distinguish the ideal moral characters of men and women: these are the manliness of men, and the sexual shame of women. . . . In general, the qualities of manliness are obvious and familiar. "To be a man" the individual must show himself to be courageous and fearless. He must be strong in body and spirit. . . . The manliness of the men in any family protects the sexual honour of its women from external insult or outrage. The women must have shame if the manliness of the men is not to be dishonoured.[14]

Ahmed Abou Zeid's study of Egyptian Bedouins[15] presents a classic account of the MENA honor "code." A group's honor—in which its individual members share—rests upon the "nobility" of its genealogy and the purity of its blood line, its dominance over peasants and clients, the heroic acts of its ancestors and senior men, the generosity of its stronger members toward weaker ones, hospitality to strangers, the protection of its women from outsider men, and the compliance of its women with the rules of self-concealment and chastity. The code thus encourages sporadic attacks on other groups, with "raids on large hostile camps . . . still regarded as the most daring action of chivalry and heroism that enhances the prestige of the young man and his group."[16] At the same time, it enjoins a making-sacred of the group's women:

> In Bedouin usage, the word *beit* covers both the tent and its occupants who always form one family. . . . It is often referred to as the *haram* (sanctuary) and is regarded in this sense as a sacred thing. It is also *haram* (taboo) and thus strangers are forbidden to come near it without the permission of its members. For the *beit* is, in the first place, the abode of the *h'aram* (womenfolk) . . . [who are] always regarded as something sacred and to be protected from desecration. In fact, much of the honour of the *beit* and the lineage depends on observing this sanctity.[17]

These two relational stances—aggressive toward outsider men and protective of "sacred" women—define the honor code's core dimensions.

Problems with Abou Zeid's and other classic formulations arise at three critical points. First, he characterizes the honor code as "a solid body of values that control the patterns of behavior in Bedouin society and act as an effective check on social relations."[18] While most ethnographers report that tribesmen express the attitudes he describes, they find the universe of Bedouin values to be much more complex and flexible. The concept of "honor code" resembles that of "segmentary lineage system," in which it is repeatedly offered as a map of social relations in MENA tribal groups but rarely as the only map, and it often proves to be a poor guide to social action as it unfolds on the ground. Second, Abou Zeid chooses to set aside individual honor and shame in order to analyze their "communal connotations."[19] Yet it is precisely in the great range of differences between individuals that the picture becomes more complex. Third, while many writers regard the honor code as *the* overarching value system of MENA societies, ethnographies show tremendous variation in customary law, in the vocabularies of honor, and in the personal qualities and acts held to be honorable.

Game, Sentiment, Syntax

Pierre Bourdieu's analysis of "the game of challenge and riposte" among men in Algeria's Kabyle region[20] provides one of the most subtle treatments of honor as a rule-governed system. In a kind of smoldering war of each against all, men continually tease and test each other, and these provocations sometimes turn serious and demand a response. As a challenge implies equality, it acknowledges the challenged man's standing, and this animates social life:

> This stake [*nif*, which means "point of honor"][21] for the Kabyle is worth more than life itself. *Nif* is also the desire to overcome one's rival in man-to-man struggle; it is that "jealous emulation," that struggle for glory of which Hume spoke with reference to Greek cities. . . . *Nif* is above all in the action of defending, cost what it may, a certain public image of oneself.[22]

Bourdieu also separates the two core dimensions of honor, which the Kabyle term *nif*, assertion and defense of one's public image, and *hurma,* protection of one's home and women. Threats to *nif* set in motion the "dialectic of challenge and riposte," while threats to *hurma* invoke a more deadly "logic of outrage and vengeance."[23] These complementary dimensions are symbolized in gendered terms: *nif* refers to the "sacred of the 'right hand,'" symbolized by "rifles" and a man's male kinsmen; *hurma* refers to the "sacred of the 'left hand,'" symbolized by the house[24] and consisting of a man's women, land, and home and everything feminine—including his personal vulnerabilities and private feelings.[25]

Bourdieu sometimes describes this as a "system of values."[26] But he anchors it in the priority "to conceal the whole domain of intimacy," including "the body and all its organic functions, the self and its passions, sentiments and affections."[27] And in addition to "values," he uses a wide range of terms to refer to honor, including "game," "logic," "rhetoric," "ethos," and "sentiment." Each of these implies a rather different theory of culture—or of the honor code's position in Kabyle culture. He concludes, however, by emphasizing the terms "ethos" and "sentiment," sketching a psychological view by suggesting that the "values of honor" may serve as "unconscious models of behavior":

> In practice, the system of the values of honour is lived rather than clearly conceived. Thus, when they spontaneously believe that such and such a mode of conduct is dishonouring or ridiculous, the Kabyles are like someone who picks out an error of language without being in command of the syntactical order that it infringes.[28]

On the one hand, this still mixes a great many concepts: sentiment, code, value, unconscious model, behavior, syntactical order. On the other hand, he has grasped a crucial point: these components (sentiment, value, unconscious model, cognitive syntax) are widely, deeply, and nonconsciously internalized and, above all, *felt* to cohere, even if attempts to make them explicitly cohere often generate dispute. In his later writings, Bourdieu begins describing this sort of system as a *habitus*, a term he applies to the important terrain between social rules and individual spontaneity where he believes culture is mostly lived. With Algerian honor and gender relations in mind, Bourdieu sees habitus as the embodiment of interpersonal politics, as "a permanent disposition, a durable manner of standing, speaking, and thereby of feeling and thinking."[29] It is culture become "second nature," become a grammar by which people read their experiences and negotiate their relationships.

The honor code thus has the feel of a coherent system of values but in fact occasions endless debates about what its terms mean and how they should be applied. At what point does honorable strength become shameful bullying? At what point does honorable protection of clients, juniors, and women become shameful tyranny? At what point does honorable generosity become shameful vulnerability to exploitation? As Peristiany points out, a man of honor "may, without falling from grace, break a number of rules considered minor in relation to those of honour,"[30] but debate often rages as to whether the rules broken are major ones. And as Abou Zeid notes at the end of his discussion, "it is difficult to say where exactly lies the line at which honourable deeds may find their sense reversed and become a source of disgrace."[31]

Honor and Inequality

Julian Pitt-Rivers's classic article on honor in Andalusian Spain describes more of the code's social complexity. In that hierarchical social setting, he finds the honor code composed of the same core elements I have discussed: "The ideal of the honourable man is expressed by the word *hombria*, 'manliness.' . . . The contrary notion is conveyed by the adjective *manso* which means both tame and also castrated." There too, honor "is bound up with the fear of ungoverned female sexuality, which has been an integral element of European folklore ever since prudent Odysseus lashed himself to the mast to escape the sirens." Thus: "The honor of a man is involved therefore in the sexual purity of his mother, wife and daughters, and sisters, not in his own"[32] and this entails seclusion: "The honorable woman: locked in the house with a broken leg—the ancient and still popular saying goes."[33]

But the system has different meanings depending on one's status: among lower status men, honor accrues to individual qualities and achievements, while among the elites it accrues more to inherited wealth and power and depends less on women's sexual modesty. The linkage of honor and shame also differs—he could have said "reverses"—depending on whether the relationship in question involves equals or unequals: "The concepts of honor and shame are therefore either, according to context, synonymous as virtue or contraries as precedence or humiliation."[34] That is, among equals men can gain honor insofar as they safeguard their women's virtue, but in hierarchical context to be a patron to clients is honorable and to be a client of patrons is shameful.

By thus seeing the honor code within the framework of patron-client relations, Pitt-Rivers calls attention to a key contradiction: "In the struggle for life success depends in reality upon the ability, much less to defend one's rights against equals, than to attract the favour of the powerful."[35] This analysis extends to the entire Mediterranean and MENA: the majority of men must find honorable ways to enact and justify dishonourable client roles. As Abu-Lughod, Khuri, and others have emphasized, the representation of patron-client relations via etiquettes of familial deference, alongside demonstrations of *machismo* in the game of challenge-and-riposte and in control of one's women, combine to compensate for the humiliations of clientship. In the final analysis, Pitt-Rivers views the honor code as a kind of false consciousness that legitimates the power of the elite by conceding them a degree of honor they have not actually won by daring deeds.[36] Pit-Rivers thus takes an important step in seeing that wealth can create honor, especially in feudal-like milieus. But he does not call sufficient attention to the ways the poor also can use honor to resist the wealthy. Peristiany observes that among Cypriot villagers "hierarchical relations are resented and resisted as, whenever the superior stresses his rank, the inferior stresses his manliness. *Ki' esy moustaki ki' ego moustaki*: we both have a mustache, we are equals in our manliness."[37]

Honor and Religion

None of these ethnographers consider religion as providing an alternative system of values—which suggests the extent to which honor can appear to be an autonomous system. But ignoring religion downplays the pervasive disagreement about *where* honor reverses into disgrace, and *which* system of values should take precedence. As Eric Wolf,[38] Maxime Rodinson,[39] and others have shown, the core Muslim ethical vision—from its inception—emphasizes the universalist values of allegiance to the brotherhood of believers explicitly against tribal values of allegiance to the brotherhood of blood, to the patrilineal kin-group. Throughout the Mediterranean, religion readily enters into disputes of honor.

In his essay "Honour and the Devil," discussing rural Greece, Campbell focuses on two important aspects of the honor code's complexity that I have so far not mentioned. First, he observes that the villagers embrace and live by two conflicting value systems: the honor code and Orthodox Christianity. "The difficulty for the Sarakatsani is that they affirm so unambiguously that existence has only two aspects of transcendent value, honour and dependence on God. . . . How is this opposition of values resolved or accommodated?"[40] He then proposes a provocative answer to this question: "By associating The Father, The Son, and The Mother of God in a holy archetype family, the institutions and relationships of the Sarakatsan family, even the concept of honour and the duty to defend it, are given a categorical quality and a divine sanction."[41] Campbell sees this assimilation of the earthly family to the divine archetype as tempering the "amoral ruthlessness that unrelated men may show towards one another"[42] when animated by the honor code. He also points to a second mechanism of resolution, the Devil: "The Devil is the symbol and the efficient cause of all those many tensions and hostilities that prevent the Sarakatsani from living in the values of Christian fellowship. . . . It is the Devil who schemes to separate family from family."[43] He stops just short of fitting together the pieces of this cultural puzzle but comes close to saying that it is the Devil, "with the assistance of women," who introduces factious envy and strife and ultimately legitimates the struggle for honor.

From Code to Rhetoric

In 1980 the anthropologist Michael Herzfeld criticized what he saw as a growing tendency to overstate the extent to that Mediterranean societies share an honor code.[44] The convergence of findings that showed cultures throughout the region to make ethical and character judgments in terms that translate as "honor" and "shame," he argued, led to the unwarranted assumption that these terms have the same meanings in all languages and societies. Ethnographers had failed to look into the details of honor- and shame-related concepts in their local contexts. His own analysis of honor in three Greek communities adds another dimension to our understanding of it. First, he notes that "honor" was defined in contrast to two archetypes of dis-honor, both of which carry the connotation of being polluting entities: threatening outsiders (especially the "wolf"-like Turks) and insiders who fail to meet their social obligations and often are suspected of possessing the Evil Eye. As Campbell describes the Devil as a figure of antihonor, so Bourdieu points out that among the Kabyle the *amahbul*, or lunatic, plays this role.[45]

Second, Herzfeld shows how a group of four terms commonly used to define honor are associated differently in three Greek communities: *sinithisi*, social custom: *filotimo*, social worth/honor: *egoismos*, masculine assertiveness;[46] and *khoui*, exaggerated self-aggrandizement. All of these communities associate honor with conformity to "custom" but differ on the others. He lists their linkages as follows.[47]

Village	*Concept of Honor*
Glendi	Custom and egoismos and aggrandizement
Sarakatsani	Custom and egoismos and *not* aggrandizement
Pefko	Custom and *not* egoismos and *not* aggrandizement

These communities thus do *not* share an "honor code." But Herzfeld notes that they form a continuum: Pefko, which values conformity to custom, is a lowland agricultural community that emphasizes the importance of kindred relations; Glendi, which values even flamboyant self-assertion, is a mountain pastoral community that emphasizes large patrilineages; in between lies Sarakatsani, a mixed agro-pastural community. He suggests that J. Schneider may be correct to see similar gradations through the Mediterranean, based on agricultural versus pastoral ways of life.

Herzfeld's critique should end attempts to describe the honor system as a shared "code" of values, in favor of views that treat it more like a language or an artistic genre, consisting of themes or elements that can be combined into a variety of configurations. His *Poetics of Manhood* takes an important step in this direction by emphasizing its performative character:

> There is less focus on "being a good man" than on "being *good at being a man*"—a stance that stresses *performative excellence*, the ability to foreground manhood by means of deeds that strikingly "speak for themselves." . . . There must be an *acceleration* or *stylistic transfiguration* of action: the work must be done with flair; the dance executed with new embellishments . . . and the theft must be performed in such a manner that it serves immediate notice on the victim of the perpetrator's skill: as he is good at stealing, so, too, he will be good at being your enemy or your ally—so choose![48]

He also sees the tension between honor and religion that intrigues Campbell and links these to a pair of kinship ideologies, which yield "two contrasted definitions of the social self." The family as kindred (reckoned along both male and female lines) "foregrounds principles of 'European' and 'Christian' identity," while a man's male ancestors define a patrilineage identity.[49] He observes that these two kinship idioms and social identities come to the fore in different circumstances: kindred relations and person-categories in the course of everyday life, and patri-lines and group categories in times of crisis. (This analysis fits social psychologist Henri Tajfel's theory of "social identity,"[50] according to which group conflict shifts participants' identities from personal to group characteristics, and sets stereotyping in motion.) He thus sees the honor system as comprising a rhetorical system for performing a certain kind of masculinity, but as one persona in a repertoire of at least two—patri-kin-based honor and kindred-based religion—between which most men shift.

Honor and Modesty

In *Veiled Sentiments*, Lila Abu-Lughod broadens our understanding of honor in another dimension. She also views it as an ideology, but she then investigates how it works for the weak in an Egyptian Bedouin group: for women, juniors, clients, and dependents. She first describes the Awlad 'Ali's "network of honor-linked values":

> First, there are the values of generosity, honesty, sincerity, loyalty to friends, and keeping one's word, all implied in the term usually translated as honor (*sharaf*). Even more important, however, is the complex of values associated with independence. Being free (*hurr*) implies several qualities, including the strength to stand alone and freedom from domination. This freedom with regard to other people is won through tough assertiveness, fearlessness, and pride, whereas with regard to needs and passions, it is won through self-control. . . . One man explained, "A real man stands alone and fears nothing. He is like a falcon (*shahin*). A falcon flies alone. If there are two in the same territory, one must kill the other."[51]

Then she shows how the Awlad 'Ali's ideology of equality covers a reality of inequality, of the dependence of the many on the few. Here the "natural" hierarchy of family life provides a rubric for escaping dishonor:

> The fundamental contradiction between the ideals of independence and autonomy and the realities of unequal status is mediated by a conceptual device: all relations of inequality are conceived in the idiom of relations of inequality within the family. . . . The familial idiom downplays the potential conflict in relations of inequality by suggesting something other than simple domination versus subordination. . . . Even more important, the familial idiom suggests that the powerful have obligations and responsibilities to protect and care for the weak.[52]

The kinship terms and the gestures and tones of voice that show the "natural" deference of women to men and juniors to seniors within the family are extended to construct extrafamilial relationships of "domination and subordination,"[53] much as Khuri details in *Tents and Pyramids*.

Abu-Lughod then reinterprets the meaning of *hasham*, which is usually translated as "shame." *Hasham* does means shame, but it also can mean to show respectful deference to one's elders and modesty vis-à-vis one's body and desires. Honor comes from strength and autonomy, but women and juniors do not shame themselves when they voluntarily defer to familial seniors; they *accrue* honor: they *tahashsham*, which in these contexts does not mean "to be shamed" but to show "modesty" or "deference." By extending these familial terms and etiquettes beyond the family, the weak and dependent show honorable modesty and deference to their social superiors:

> The categories of person from whom a young man might *tahashsham* are his father and male agnates of his father's generation, together with men of the same generations from lineages of equal status to his own, and his older brothers. . . . Clients *tahashsham* from their patrons and from anyone of the same status as their patrons. Women *tahashsham* from some older women. . . . and from most older men. . . . They do not, however, *tahashsham* from men who are clients, no matter how old, especially if they have known them for a long time. The general rule is that persons *tahashsham* from those who deserve respect.[54]

The honor code thus generates not only "shame" as its dishonorable antithesis but a "modesty code" as its honorable complement:

> One way those at the bottom resolve the contradiction between their positions and the system's ideals is by appearing to defer to those in authority voluntarily. . . . The weak and dependent, who cannot realize many of the ideals of the honor code, can still achieve respect and honor through an alternative code, the modesty code.[55]

This formulation fundamentally changes our understanding of honor, away from the oversimplified honor-versus-shame dichotomy and beyond the male game of "challenge and riposte," to incorporate the range of stylized male-female, senior-junior, and patron-client interactions. That is: the *poetics* of masculine honor generate the complementary *etiquettes* of the modesty code. The total pattern is more appropriately termed the *honor-modesty system*.

Abu-Lughod subtitled her book "Honor and Poetry in a Bedouin Society," and her point is to show that alongside the culture's dominant *discourse* of honor-modesty exists a second discourse, a genre of oral poetry woven improvisationally into daily life that articulates sentiments of fondness, loss, and vulnerability that—as Bourdieu also emphasized—the imperatives of honor and modesty require be concealed. Driven by the self-presentational rhetoric of the honor-modesty system, the discourse of ordinary life for those confronted with loss, poor treatment, or neglect . . . is one of hostility, bitterness, and anger; in matters of lost love . . . the discourse is one of militant indifference and denial of concern. Poetry, on the contrary, is a discourse of vulnerability, expressing sentiments of devastating sadness, self-pity, and a sense of betrayal, or, in cases of love, a discourse of attachment and deep feeling.[56]

People usually keep the contexts for showing these emotions separate, using poetry—"the discourse of intimacy"—to express and share feelings with others from whom "one does not *tahashsham*."[57]

Abu-Lughod puzzles over the reasons a culture might so cherish a genre that expresses sentiments that its own values hold to be deviant, and she suggests that poetry also has practical uses in negotiating personal relationships. On the one hand, its singing can plead for succor or protection from the strong, to whom direct appeals cannot easily be made. On the other hand, the strong person who also speaks poetry may demonstrate both complexity of character and exceptional self-mastery, and thereby enhance his or her honor. But the poems still voice "oppositional," "antistructural" messages, often about illicit love, not easily reconciled with values of honor-modesty. "Thwarted love, especially between a man and woman from different tribes, is the theme of the most poignant Bedouin love stories," which, she reports, "are recounted as true tales of the distant past."[58] In one a boy and girl from different tribes fell in love, and her enraged father's brother's son claimed her as rightfully his. The boy was sent off on a caravan but died on the return journey, and when his body was brought home the girl joined his kinsmen's wailing. Her cousin discovered she had gone to his enemy's camp, followed her there, and beat her to death on his grave, and then insisted she be buried a kilometer away from him. "After a while, a palm tree sprang from the head of the boy's grave, and a tree sprang from the head of the girl's. The trees grew and grew until their fronds crossed high in the sky." Her cousin hired a woodcutter to chop down the trees, but his ax broke on the trunk. Later in his sleep the boy appeared to him in a vision, and parted with the poem: "Love must bring forth fruits that join each other in their sky."[59] Abu-Lughod points out that the story brands the girl a "slut," and so affirms the power of the patriarchal order, but at the same time portrays her as a heroine: "Their defiance ends in a victory of sorts. People who listen to such tales admire the behavior of lovers and do not condemn it as immoral, and they appreciate the poetry that expresses the lovers' feelings."[60] The Awlad 'Ali regard poetry as "risqué, against religion, and slightly improper" but still feel "thrilled" by it: "For Awlad 'Ali, poetry represents what is best in their culture, what they consider distinctively Bedouin."[61]

Abu-Lughod rejects the view that the honor-modesty system forms a kind of social mask, while the discourse of poetry enables people to reveal their "true" feelings. She also rejects the "hydraulic" view that emotions excluded from the discourse of honor and modesty "erupt" in poetry.[62] Noting that many cultures develop antistructural discourses that seem to subvert their dominant values, she suggests that "Awlad 'Ali's poetry of self and sentiment be viewed as their corrective to an obsession with morality and an overzealous adherence to the ideology of honor."[63] She concludes:

> Poetry reminds people of another way of being and encourages, as it reflects, another side of experience. . . . The vision is kept alive by those who benefit least from the system that the honor ideology maintains. And maybe the vision is cherished because people sense that the costs of this system, in the limits it places on human experience, are just too high.[64]

Honor and Modesty as a Cultural Pattern

This takes us far beyond Abou-Zeid's early analysis of honor as a "code" of values. The general evolution of anthropology from models of culture that hold it to consist of roles, norms, and values toward models that view it as constituted of discourses or performative rhetorics has enabled ethnographers to better describe the honor-modesty system, which decades of careful fieldwork has explored. As we assemble this literature, we see the system as anchored in the construction of a *machismo* style of masculinity in a context defined by a core contradiction between an ideology of equality and autonomy, and a reality of inequality and dependence. Honorable manhood is built on two primary interpersonal dimensions: antagonistic, "challenge-and-riposte" relations with men of roughly equal status, and control, concealment, and protection of women and dependents. By his own actions, a man can win or lose a significant measure of honor, and ascend or fall in his community's hierarchy of status. But preserving honor also requires the wealth to serve as a patron to many clients, and so honor appears to accrue naturally to wealthy households and to flow from them.

Community studies show that the personal qualities viewed as honorable vary from locale to locale, depending largely on ways of life. They also show more dispute than consensus about the points at which honorable actions turn into dishonorable ones. Further, the honor system exists alongside at least two other ethical/discourse systems—Islam and romantic literature—both of which may voice critical responses to it. The honor system is not all-encompassing, but it appears that its predominance or "hegemony" requires some important emotional, moral, and spiritual yearnings to be expressed through other discourses.

Of particular psychological importance, the "code" of honor generates not only dishonor as its opposite but a code of modesty and deference as its complement. As Khuri and Abu-Lughod emphasize, the extension of the family's "natural" relations of honor-deference appears to help "resolve" the contradiction between the region's egalitarian ideology and its reality of dependence and subordination. Psychologically, this extends emotional interdependencies established in childhood (see chapters 4 and 5) through the range of hierarchical dyadic relationships that knit society together. Further, the honor-modesty system's images of manhood emphasize implicit and explicit symbols of "phallic" strength—physical prowess and potency versus weakness—on the patrilineal axis, and deep reverence for the nurturant maternal bond on what several ethnographers describe as the family's "matrifocal" axis. As most individuals move from being juniors in all of their relationships to being seniors in at least some of them, the honor-modesty system structures the development of self-presentational styles throughout the life-course. And since many persons act in some relationships as juniors and in others as seniors, it defines the pattern by which they shift continually among self-presentational styles.

Honor, Modesty, and Personality

Even though the ethnographers who have studied honor in the circum-Mediterranean are not psychologists, nearly all of them speak of it as deeply embedded in personality or self. But they use a bewildering variety of terms to describe its internalization: *code, value, game, syntax, persona, rhetoric, discourse,* and so on—indicating the difficulty of figuring out what it amounts to psychologically. Psychology, for its part, offers no simple answer. For one thing, there continues to be fundamental disagreement about the basic constituents of personality. More important, psychologists generally have tried to define the constituents of personality as universal human characteristics—emotions, traits, drives, and so on—that lie behind or below culture. Most theories allow for cultures to influence overall levels of "anxiety" or "depression," to enhance or dampen "extroversion," or to increase or decrease the prevalence of "obsessive-compulsive" styles—but do not account for culturally distinctive personality characteristics. Yet this is precisely what the ethnographic reports suggest: that the honor-modesty system fashions personality in a distinctively circum-Mediterranean/MENA manner.

Psychologists continue to take sharply opposed views of the universality-versus-cultural distinctiveness of emotion. "Naturalists" emphasize that all humans share the physiological processes involved in emotion[65] and that all humans possess a set of biologically based emotional responses.[66] Cultures may influence how people express these, but the naturalists believe that for basic emotions, indigenous emotion terms can be translated into a single scientific vocabulary. "Constructivists," by contrast, argue that even the most basic emotions are socially fashioned, and that they must be studied as "statements about, and motivations for the enactment of cultural values."[67] Richard Shweder makes this case by showing the general nonequivalence of an

Indian scheme for classifying emotions with physiological theories of them. As an example, he argues that *lajya* cannot be translated as "shame," as it often is, or as any other English emotion term.[68] Rather like the Arabic *hasham*, *lajya* entails "modesty," "respect," "loyalty," and other virtues associated with maintaining social harmony—even and especially when this requires women (with whom it is especially associated) to "bite their tongues" and "swallow their rage." As part of this complex net of meanings, *lajya* cannot be translated.

I will take a "both-and" position on this debate between naturalist and constructivist theories of emotion. I believe people in MENA societies develop personalities around the same universal emotions and traits as do Americans, Japanese, Indians, and others. But they also come to experience and express these with textures of feeling and to configure them in culturally distinctive ways—and this confers meanings that cannot be translated. Following Ekman,[69] many psychologists now view universal human emotions as having culturally specific "display rules," and this provides one way of conceptualizing how psychological states might have both universal and local features.[70] The crucial question is whether the local features merely add culturally specific shadings and ornamentation, or more fundamentally transform an underlying universal emotion into something that seems not so universal.

The answer depends almost entirely on context: in some instances it is important to look through the culturally specific features to see a universally shared emotion, while in others the universal emotion should be viewed as a vehicle for the expression of culturally specific feelings. The same holds for more enduring dispositions or drives: in some circumstances psychologists may investigate the universality of personality traits; in others they may study culturally specific patterns of needs or motivations. And when they study the self or identity, they similarly may focus either on universal or culturally specific features. When a young Moroccan I interviewed says his failure to find employment makes him feel "pessimistic," "weak," and "tired" of life, it makes sense to view him as experiencing the universal syndrome of *depression*. But when we look at the textures of his feelings, the meanings they have for him, and the role they play in his personality organization, they appear to script a culturally distinctive and meaningful sense of *tragedy*, which is firmly anchored in the honor-modesty-shame system.[71] Personality theories generally have not taken account of this dual character of emotional experience, and need terminology to describe the development of both universal and culturally specific features. The question here, then, is how to conceptualize the culturally specific characteristics formed by internalizing the values/rhetorics of honor-modesty as a kind of "second nature."

The honor-modesty system could be viewed as an elaborate set of display rules that ornament universal emotions with Mediterranean-MENA stylings. But ethnographers consistently report that it runs much deeper: that individuals come to literally em-body it in their most spontaneous thoughts, feelings, facial expressions, gestures, tones of voice, and so on. They see it adding such important culturally specific meanings that the universal emotions essentially serve as the raw materials for the cultural pattern. Bourdieu intends the term *habitus* to capture precisely this internalization of a culture's performative style as automatic bodily habits, as schemas for conceptually ordering the world, as etiquettes of social interaction, and as a syntax of self-presentation. But his habitus concept doesn't yet give us psychological terminology. Drawing on the convergence of studies of individual lives and ethnographic research, I will suggest that the region's honor-modesty system creates three sorts of culturally specific psychological entities: *sentiments*, *motives*, and *social personas*. I will use these terms in contrast to "emotions," "traits," and "selves," terms that psychologists typically employ to describe universal characteristics.

Specifically, I will adopt a three-level model of personality organization based on the theories of Robert LeVine, and I will view the honor-modesty system—alongside Islamic piety—as integrating an important middle level of personality, "above" a level consisting mainly of *core* affective tensions and temperamental traits and "below" a level consisting of the self-representational system that Erik Erikson terms *identity*.[72] (See the introduction to part II for a fuller explanation of this three-level model of personality organization.) This view parallels that of the personality theorist Dan McAdams, who argues that the great array of personal characteristics psychologists study can be grouped into three levels. Level 1 consists of the "decontextualized, and relatively nonconditional constructs called 'traits,' which provide a dispositional signature for personality." Level 2 consists of motives, values, attachment styles, personal strivings, and so on, "that are contextualized in time, place, or role," and level 3 encompasses personal identity, as embedded in a life-narrative.[73] According to this view, people in MENA societies can be expected to share temperamentally based emotions and dispositions with members of all cultures but also to develop characteristics distinctive to MENA that then serve as dimensions of individual difference *within* MENA cultures. The three-level model of personality organization makes it possible to identify cultural influences at each level. I believe that the honor-modesty system (and also Islamic values and practices) especially shapes level 2. And to describe the level 2 structures shaped by the region's two predominant value systems, I will use the term *sentiment* rather than "emotion," *motive* rather than "trait," and *social persona* (or *social self*) rather than "self."

SENTIMENTS

The honor-modesty system cultivates a cluster of feelings centered on honor, shame, and modesty, which are much more than basic emotions: they are saturated with conceptual and moral meanings, and they always are situated in configurations of interpersonal relationships. To underscore this, I will follow the leads of Bourdieu and Abu-Lughod and use the somewhat archaic term *sentiment* to describe honor-related feelings, rather than familiar terms like "affect," "emotion," or "value." In the 1920s the American psychologist William McDougall outlined a theory of personality as an organization of sentiments, which he defined as "acquired conative trends."[74] He did not explicitly view sentiments as culturally distinctive, but he chose the term to describe linkages of affect, moral principle, and action that are more complex and enduring than comparatively simple emotions or traits. And he emphasized that a distinction must be made between a momentary emotional experience and a longer-lasting sentiment—a "wave of patriotic emotion" versus an enduring "love of country"; an "emotion of outraged honor or justice" versus an enduring pursuit of honor or justice.[75] Even though a single word may name both the emotional state and the sentiment, the sentiment entails an active, continuous pursuit or avoidance of the state, and this infuses the state with moral value. The sentiment of honor (or modesty or shame) thus includes not just the feeling of honor but also a feeling *for* honor, in the sense that one admires, respects, or cherishes it, as well as a feeling *for* honor in the sense of having good taste about it—as an architect may have a feel for interior light, an athlete may have a "feel for the game," or a poet a "feel for language."

The honor-modesty system thus can be said to shape universal human emotions into culturally distinctive *sentiments*, which should properly be described in native-language terms. I will use the English translations "honor," "modesty," and "shame," both for ease of discussion, and because no single Arabic term captures the meaning of any of them. But it is important to keep in mind that as lived in MENA contexts, these sentiments have subjective textures and meanings that members of other cultures do not and perhaps cannot fully share. On a daily basis, a Westerner may experience moments of "self-esteem," "propriety," and "embarrassment" in a manner that roughly parallels a Middle Easterner's experiences of honor, modesty, and shame, but the resemblance does not run very deep.[76]

MOTIVES

The sentiments constituting the honor-modesty system also appear to develop into culturally distinctive *motives* or *needs* that define important dimensions of individual difference. That is, some individuals become more highly motivated to accrue and display "honor" than are others, and the same holds for "modesty" and for susceptibility to "shame."

Psychologists typically refer to dispositions of this sort as "traits," but they have not been very precise in defining the term, since some use it to refer to regularities of behavior and others to motives or needs that underlie behavior. They also have not been precise in distinguishing "trait" from other constructs, such as motive, need, drive, or value. For more than 50 years, researchers who adopt the trait-as-behavioral-regularity view have used factor analytic techniques to identify the dimensions underlying people's ratings of themselves and others on exhaustive lists of trait adjectives,[77] and they have come to a broad consensus that human personality is composed of five basic, universal traits: (1) surgency (or extroversion), (2) agreeableness, (3) conscientiousness, (4) emotional stability (or neuroticism), and (5) culture (or intellect or openness to experience).[78] Increasing evidence that at least some of these have substantial heritability suggests that they may arise from individual variation in human temperament. Researchers have tried to name these factors with universal, nonculturally specific terms, and a growing body of studies from non-Western societies—including Turkey and Pakistan (see chapter 9)—supports this "Big Five" structure of traits.

The contrasting trait-as-underlying-motive approach was pioneered by Henry Murray,[79] who created the Thematic Apperception Test (TAT) to identify basic *needs* or *motives* and measure their strength. Unlike the trait-adjective ratings used by the "Big Five" researchers, the TAT relies on the process of "projection." It consists of a series of ambiguous black-and-white drawings and pictures, for which subjects are asked to make up stories. Murray theorized that the content of the stories will be influenced by the strength of an individual's underlying needs, and scoring systems have been devised to measure the strength of various needs as the amount of imagery related to them that appears in a person's stories. He proposed a set of 16 basic needs, and while these have come to be spoken of as *traits,* he conceptualized them as *motives* that influence the long-term course of lives, that can be expressed through a variety of specific behaviors, and that may well not yield short-term consistency of behavior. A few personality psychologists have distinguished *traits* (like the Big Five) from *motives* (like needs for power, affiliation, and achievement) as different kinds of psychological structures, exerting different effects on behavior and life trajectories.[80] David Winter and his colleagues recently published findings from longitudinal studies of personality that underscore the importance of distinguishing motives from traits. Defending the "underlying motive" position, they in fact argue that traits should be seen as behavioral styles through which higher order motives are expressed.[81]

While traits as conceptualized by Big Five researchers are probably not culturally distinctive, motives probably are, and I believe the honor-modesty system fashions a set of *needs* or *motives* that define important dimensions of individual personality in the MENA culture area. Ethnographers speak of the honor-modesty system in terms similar to those used by psychologists for "level 2" personality processes (values, attachment styles, personal strivings, interpersonal strategies, etc.), and they similarly emphasize the honor-modesty system's sensitivity to context—especially in viewing it as a grammar or syntax of social performance. I believe that the concepts of *need* or *motive* best describe how honor, shame, and modesty become psychological dispositions. Probably MENA researchers could operationalize these dimensions and measure a "need for honor," a "need for modesty," and a "sensitivity to shame" from TAT stories and then investigate the relationship of these needs to a range of formative influences and life outcomes, as has been done with power, affiliation, and achievement motives in the West.

Like most American psychologists, Murray and his successors sought to define needs in universal, culturally nonspecific terms, but his original list appears to combine some that one would expect to be universal and some that may be culturally distinctive. McAdams's level 2 processes similarly appear to include some that probably are defined universally, and some that are culturally specific. Needs for power, affiliation, and achievement have been intensively studied as the core of Murray's set, and affiliation and power are often discussed as manifestations of fundamental, universal human drives toward agency and communion. The "achievement motive" has been studied in many cultures, but it remains unclear whether it should be viewed as a universal motive, stronger in some cultures and weaker in others, or as a distinctively Western or modern one, which some non-Western or traditional cultures simply may not create. I suspect it is best seen as the latter: as forming an important component of an achievement-popularity-self-esteem configuration that plays a prominent role in modern societies analogous to that played by the honor-modesty system in the traditional MENA.

Had the pioneering work of Murray and his colleagues been done in MENA, I believe it likely that honor, modesty, and shame would have emerged among the most prominent needs or motives (along with an equally prominent set of spiritual/religious needs). Motives related to honor, modesty, and shame would appear to give personality a distinctive organization there—not by creating a shared "national character," an "Arab mind," or a "basic personality" but by defining the key dimensions on which people differ.

SOCIAL PERSONA

Most ethnographers cast the honor-modesty system as shaping not just sentiments and motives but also selves. They often speak of it, as does Peristiany, as creating a social self or a persona or, as do Herzfeld and Abu-Lughod, as providing a discourse for composing and performing a self. It operates automatically and nonconsciously, they say, like the syntax that enables one to hear the grammaticality of a sentence or like an aesthetic that yields a visual experience of proportion or disarray. At the same time, most ethnographers choose language that indicates that the honor-modesty system does not create *the* self, and they either imply or say that important aspects of experience or personality fall outside of those patterned by the honor-modesty system. What kind of integrative pattern is this, and what role does it play in the organization of personality?

Here study-of-lives interviews provide some clues, as they enable one to trace how individuals draw on features of the honor-modesty system to interpret and manage their emotional lives, and to fashion and present selves. In telling their life-stories, most of those I interviewed repeatedly configured themselves within interpersonal relationships and fields of sentiments clearly internalized from the honor-modesty system. Yet individuals varied in quite idiosyncratic ways as to what features of the honor-modesty system they selected and embellished. For my interviewee Mohammed, it was a recklessness at fighting that he admired in his great-grandfather, a legendary "Big Man" in his oasis village. It had gotten his great grandfather killed, and it almost destroyed him when his toughness got out of control and he became *jahal*, "wild," "rabid," "ignorant." A religious reconversion finally enabled him to tame his misanthropic rage with prayer. For Hussein, it was his timidity and his great desire to "stand up" (*waaqif*) to authorities who often made him stop in his tracks (*tawaquff*), paralyzed by fear, and his feeling that he needed someone to "stand up with/for him" (*waaqif ma'aaya*) in his dealings with threatening authorities. He repeatedly placed himself in relational triangles consisting of a powerful tyrant figure, a vulnerable victim figure, and a defender/challenger figure, who, though initially weak, finds strength and courage to confront the tyrant on the victim's behalf. His memories and accounts of his life sometimes cast him in the victim role and sometimes in the defender/challenger role; they cast his father in all three roles; and the books, films, folk tales, and Quranic suras he liked nearly all organized their action around similar triangular dramas. These two men internalized "the" honor-modesty system in very different forms, each tailored to his personality and life-history—as did all of those I interviewed.

In all of the life-narratives I elicited, the idiosyncratically internalized honor-modesty system showed two important features. First, it constructed a whole configuration of self-in-the-world, governed by a set of game-like rules, much as Bourdieu describes. Second, it crystallized as if in the view of others, as if witnessed by "society" in general. Theoretically, G. H. Mead's notion of *social self* consists precisely of such a matrix of social positions and game-like interactions, and his theory provides the best account we have of the psychologically integrative nature of the honor-modesty system. Mead believed that as children play at social roles, they learn not only how to enact the requisite behaviors but increasingly to take the perspective of other players in the "game" on their own performances—thus constructing representations of "Me." Individuals take on progressively more complex roles as they grow into adulthood, broadening the context in which they see themselves acting until they consolidate an encompassing social self by viewing themselves from the overarching perspective of the "generalized other"—essentially a map of the social structure and its interactional rules and etiquettes. The honor-modesty system does precisely this: it integrates more elementary emotions and attachments into a culturally specific system of sentiments and motives, *seen as if in the gaze of a Generalized Other*. It coalesces within individual personalities neither as merely the mask of a false self—though it may feel this way at times—nor as one's "authentic" self, though it also may feel this way at times.

But while the honor-modesty system may integrate personality in the form of a social self/persona, this does not *complete* personality, because rather than assigning an identity, it challenges the person to formulate one and stake his or her claim to it. Here is where the example cited by Peristiany provides the key: "The entire society watches for the young shepherd's first quarrel, that is, for his first chance to prove himself." The Generalized Other—the eyes of all as the young man perceives them turned on him—casts a challenge and awaits his response.

Mead recognized that the social self, the "Me," does not incorporate all of one's personality, and that some other part of the self may see and feel displeased with the role(s) that the Generalized Other assigns or the judgment(s) it renders. He therefore postulated the existence of an "I" pole of the self that is not frozen by social categories and can respond either by accepting the "Me" and playing it to the hilt or by struggling to revise the "Me." As Mitchell Aboulafia[82] has pointed out, this resembles Sartre's view, according to which one finds oneself as if "thrown" into a world and a body and a society, as fixed by the "gaze" of an amorphous societal "they" into a particular position or persona, and consequently is forced to choose what one will stand for. Mead's notion that an individual, as "I" must react to the "Me" he or she comes to perceive from the perspective of the Generalized Other also leads into the heart of Erik Erikson's theory of identity. As Peristiany's example (and my life-history interviews) shows so clearly, the Generalized Other challenges and interrogates—it takes shape aggressively in the psyche as a kind of internalized grand inquisitor. It does not just inquire "What will you become?" but demands "Prove that you are this or that !"—a man of honor or a woman of honorable modesty. It integrates personality as being about honor, modesty, and shame, as the local culture configures these, but it does not assign an honorable identity: that must be defined, claimed, won, tested, and proven.

The consolidation of an honor-based social persona thus signals an essential milestone in the acquisition of one's culture, and the arrival of the developmental task of adolescence and early adulthood: to formulate and publicly establish an honorable identity.[83] The honor-modesty system thus creates *a* social persona but not *the* social persona. Islam, romantic poetry, and perhaps other "discourses" may fashion others. As individuals differ in the family and community environments that socialize them, so they differ in which of these social selves becomes predominant in their character. A few appear to achieve remarkable syntheses of alternate discourses, while others—like Si Ahmad of Mahfouz's Cairo Trilogy—keep them compartmentalized and continually shift among them. For many people in MENA societies, I believe Islam fashions a second social persona that sometimes converges with that built of the honor-modesty system but sometimes diverges from and may even indict it, as was the case with my interviewee Mohammed, who reformed his honor-driven delinquency by a religious reconversion.

Islam ✸

The great majority of MENA citizens are Muslims. This does not just mean that they believe in and practice Islam but that they live in a Muslim culture that weaves religion into the textures of daily life in ways that make the divine continuously present. Most idioms of speech—greetings, farewells, congratulations, exclamations, expressions of sympathy, shock, well-wishing, and celebration, and all references to the future—use religious phrases, so daily conversation rarely carries on long without invocations of God. Devout Muslims pray five times a day, and in rural and many urban areas, the rhythm of daily activities is keyed to the calls to prayer. Islam provides a theory of mind and emotion, and throughout the day and week Muslims monitor states of personal pollution and purity, not only as a religious obligation but also as a kind of mental hygiene that enables them to interpret and manage psychological distress.

Islam is learned and practiced in many sacred contexts set apart from the mundane—in Quranic schools, mosques, saints' tombs; in the month-long Ramadan fast in which everyday rhythms reverse; in celebrations, pilgrimages, and sacrifices associated with the Great Feast (commemorating Abraham's sacrifice), the Prophet's birthday, and the Hajj (pilgrimage to Mecca); in rituals associated with circumcision, marriage, childbirth, and death; and in solitary prayer and recitation. So as much as it threads through daily life, Islam is most directly practiced in withdrawal from this-worldly affairs and in a psychological reorientation to God, the Prophet, the Quran (written and recited in classical rather than vernacular Arabic), the earth's axis (Mecca), the Night of Destiny (in which the Quran was first revealed), and the judgment day. Worship in sacred sites, in a sacred frame of time, and in states of purification sets religion in counterpoint to the rather dirty business of ordinary life. God, the Prophet, the saints, and religious teachers form what might be termed a "Sacred Other," parallel to society's Generalized Other, from whose perspective a believer sees himself or herself fixed in a gaze that casts a different challenge from that of the honor-modesty system, which offers a different kind of "home" from the patronymic Big House, and that provides a different discourse for creating and performing one's self.

In this section I will examine features of religious practice that most deeply affect the development and organization of personality and that provide techniques for "the care of the self." Throughout MENA, there is continual debate among religious scholars and ordinary believers about what beliefs and practices are "true Islam." Reform movements have sought to rid "folk Islam" of its many unorthodox elements, including devotion to "saints," the entering of trance states, exorcism, and the use of esoteric knowledge and powers that may amount to "sorcery." I will focus on practices believed to be Islamic by their practitioners, and leave questions of orthodoxy aside. After briefly describing Islam's "Five Pillars," the Quran, and the significance of

Quranic recitation, I will examine the Prophet's role as the ideal man, as a healer, and as a source of compassion. I will follow this with a discussion of "saints" and the paths by which *baraka*—divine blessedness—flows into and through the world, of the purification and pollution system and its use to manage emotional distress, of dreams and anxieties about Satan's mischief, of attacks by *jinn* spirits and the Evil Eye. Finally, I will sketch how Islam may pattern sentiments, motives, and social selves.

The Five Pillars

Muslims often begin explaining their religion to non-Muslims by listing its five pillars, as follows.

SHAHADA, THE TESTIMONY OF FAITH

By pronouncing "La ilaha illa allah wa mohammed rasul allah" (There is no god but God, and Mohammed is His Prophet), a person becomes a Muslim and reaffirms his or her faith.

SALAT, PRAYER

A Muslim should pray five times a day, at daybreak, midday, afternoon, evening, and night, and whenever possible he or she should join the community at Friday prayers. One performs a brief purification ritual, mentally formulates one's *niyya* (the "intention" to pray with all one's being), kneels facing Mecca, and performs a prayer that has two phases. First one performs the mandatory two to four *rak'as*, or bowings, each consisting of a prescribed litany and movements: a recitation of *Allahu akbar*, "God is most Great," with open hands held at the side of the face; a recitation of the Fatiha (the Quran's brief opening sura) and other Quranic passages while standing upright; a bowing from the hips; a return to standing; a kneeling prostration; a return to kneeling; and a second prostration. Then one may address personal pleas, praises, or vows to God. The prayer ends with a recitation of the *shahada*, the testimony of faith. The twelfth-century religious scholar Ghazzali explained the meaning of the prostrations:

> The dearest of your members, which is your face, gets hold of the humblest thing, which is dust. . . . Whenever you place your self in the place of lowliness, know that you have placed it in its proper place and have returned the branch to the trunk, for of the dust were you formed and to it you return.[84]

The Pakistani scholar Allahbakhsh Brohi emphasizes that prayer provides "protection against the defilement and contamination that affect man's life":

> If five times a day he were to remove himself from the corrupting taint of worldly transactions in which he is apt to lose himself, and

were to make an effort consciously to identify himself with the pursuit of the supreme goal for that he has been created . . . then there can be no doubt that he would succeed in adhering to the path of righteousness.[85]

SAUM, FASTING

During the lunar month of Ramadan a Muslim should not consume anything (including water and tobacco smoke) from daybreak to dusk. Since the lunar calendar is about two weeks shorter than the Gregorian, Ramadan moves through the seasons so that the time of fasting shortens with the days in winter and lengthens in summer. At dusk, families usually gather around a special protein-rich break-fast meal (if possible, with dates, buttermilk, hard-boiled eggs, a hearty soup or stew and a sugary pastry desert) and wait to eat until they hear the call from a minaret or, in some cities, a siren or cannon shot. After breaking the fast, people in many cities go out for a stroll and, in some areas, to take in popular entertainment that lends an almost carnival atmosphere to the evening. They return a couple of hours later for the dinner meal. Most people awaken an hour before daybreak for a third light meal, and in some towns and cities criers or horn-blowers walk the residential quarters to awaken people for this meal.

Ramadan is regarded as the holiest month, and it is said that during it the gates of heaven open wide and those of hell shut. The twenty-seventh day is the "Night of Destiny," when God first commanded Mohammed to "Recite!" what became the Quran, "the recitation." The entire Quran is recited in mosques, and many men (and a few women) stay up through the night to listen and recite. Ramadan ends when religious scholars see the first sliver of a new moon, and there is a joyous celebration of the 'ayd al-fitr, known as the "little festival," which involves a communal morning prayer, a family feast, gifts of new clothes for everyone, visits to relatives and friends and, in many areas, visits to the graves of the dead.

Fasting on winter's short days may not be very taxing, but for farmers, herders and others who do hard physical labor in desert climates, summertime fasts can be agonizing. Children often want to fast along with the adults, and parents commonly insist they eat but also praise half-day, then full-day, then longer successes. A male should fast the whole month after his first nocturnal emission, and a female after her first menstruation, so fasting marks the attainment of biological maturity. A great many teen-agers have mastered the whole fast by this point without parental pressure, and feel a sense of pride. As with prayer, the prescribed behaviors provide merely a foundation for deeper meanings. Most Muslims view the fast as a demonstration of self-mastery and as a purification that promotes mental and physical as well as spiritual health. Ghazzali described three degrees of observance of the fast: the least spiritual entails simply following its rules, and yields little more than month-long discomfort; the second requires abstaining from improper thoughts, and from the five actions said by the Prophet to annul the day's fasting: lying, backbiting, slandering, uttering a false oath, and casting a glance of passion.[86] The highest requires abstaining from all worldly aspirations and hopes, and thinking of nothing but God and the judgment day.

ZAKAT, TITHING

Muslims should give between a fortieth and a twentieth of their year's yield to the poor of their community, and those with means are expected to be the most generous. In some communities, religious organizations collect and distribute the tithes, but much of the giving is done privately. Better off families often give to poorer relatives and members of their own patronymic associations—reinforcing patri-kin and patron-client loyalties.

HAJJ, PILGRIMAGE

Muslims are enjoined to undertake a pilgrimage to Mecca sometime during their life, if they are able. All dream of it, but few from distant lands can afford the expense. The pilgrimage is undertaken in the last month of the Muslim year, Dhu l-Hijja, and, as with prayer, the pilgrims must enter a state of consecration, wearing only two unsewn white sheets and refraining from washing, shaving, cutting their hair, and acts of bloodshed. Also as in prayer, they formulate and declare their *niyy'a* or "intention," to perform the pilgrimage wholeheartedly. The pilgrim first enters the Great Mosque and its *haram*, or "sacred space," and performs seven circumabulations around the Kaba, a cubic structure of quarried granite believed to have been built by Ibrahim (the biblical Abraham) at God's direction, and to be the center or navel of the world, the point at which the seven heavens come closest to earth. At the time of the Prophet, the Kaba was the center of a Bedouin pilgrimage site at Mecca, surrounded by "pagan" idols, which he destroyed after conquering the city. At some point, the pilgrims kiss the Black Stone, a dark red-brown stone mounted in one corner of the Kaba and believed to have been brought to Ibrahim by the angel Gabriel, originally white but turned black by contact with pagan sin and impurity. After the last circumambulation, they press their chests and arms against a sanctuary point near the Black Stone, absorbing (many believe) the *baraka*, or divine blessedness, that permeates the Kaba and the *haram*. They pray two *rak'as* and drink water from the nearby Zamzam well, originally the valley's only source of water. This reenacts the incident in which God tested Ibrahim by ordering him to abandon his wife Hagar and son Ismail, whom Gabriel saved from thirst by creating the well. The water also is believed to be full of *baraka*, and many pilgrims bottle some to take home, to use as medicine and ablution after their deaths. After leaving the mosque, they engage in a "running" between two hills where many believe Adam and Eve once rested.

On the next two days they travel through a series of "stops" or "standings" that take them to the plain of Arafa below Jabal al-Rahma, the Mount of Mercy, where they pray and hear a sermon, and then back, in great celebration, to the village of Mina, where they throw pebbles collected along the way at three pillars marking the spots at that the Devil tempted Isaac to disobey Ibrahim. This "Stoning of the Devils" is the first of several rituals by which the pilgrim exits the state of consecration. Each pilgrim sacrifices a ram at the site believed to be where God commanded Ibrahim to sacrifice his son Ishmael and then allowed a ram to be killed in his stead. They eat some of the meat, also believed to be rich in *baraka*, and leave the rest for the poor.[87] On this tenth day of the month, Muslims the world over celebrate the *'ayd al-adha*, or sacrificial feast (often called the "Great Festival"), in which the head of each household sacrifices a ram in reenactment of the Ibrahimic sacrifice, and three days of feasting follow. Men's heads are shaved and women's hair cut, ending the state of consecration or purity. Upon returning, the pilgrim is addressed with the title *hajj*. As with the other four pillars, the behaviors prescribed in the pilgrimage are believed to hold deep spiritual meanings for those devout enough to experience them. Ghazzali taught that

> the pilgrim who sets out for the Kaba should bear in mind that he goes to see the Lord and that, by the Lord's own promise, the sight of the House will be accepted as a claim to being vouchsafed the sight of the Lord's face in the world to come.... So the pilgrim must impress upon himself the magnitude of his undertaking and make sure of his single-mindedness in his task and the purity of his motivation. He is to cut his ties with his own small world and, in doing so, he must make good the wrongs he has done with sincere repentance.[88]

Or, as the ninth-century scholar Bistami wrote, "on my first pilgrimage I saw only the temple; the second time, I saw both the temple and the Lord of the temple; and the third time I saw the Lord alone."[89]

Recitation

Quran means "recitation." It was begun on the Night of Destiny when the angel Gabriel brought God's command to Mohammed, asleep at his retreat on Mount Hira: "Recite!" Terrified, he replied, "What shall I recite?" Twice more Gabriel commanded and Mohammed asked "What shall I recite?" Finally Gabriel replied:

> Recite in the name of thy Lord who created,
> Who created man of blood coagulated.
> Read! Thy Lord is most beneficent,
> Who taught by the pen,
> Taught that which they knew not to men.[90]

The revelations soon stopped, plunging the Prophet into a period of doubt and confusion. But his wife Khadija believed he had been chosen as God's prophet and sustained him. Finally Gabriel brought another revelation, "The Daybreak," in which God reassured Mohammed and all Muslims: "Did He not find you an orphan and give you refuge, going astray and guided you, found you poor and made you rich? . . . Do not oppress the orphan and do not repel the beggar."[91] More revelations followed, and 20 years after the Prophet's death in 632 these were compiled as the Quran in order of decreasing length, after the brief *Fatiha*, "The Opening":

> Praise belongs to God, the Lord of all Being,
> The All-merciful, the All-compassionate,
> The Master of the Day of Doom,
> Thee only we serve; to Thee alone we pray for succour,
> Guide us in the straight path,
> The path of those whom Thou hast blessed,
> Not of those against whom Thou are wrathful,
> Nor of those who are astray.[92]

Recitation of the Quran remains the high art of Islamic civilization, appreciated by the educated and the illiterate alike. Every village and urban neighborhood has reciters who can be heard in mosques, at public celebrations, and on quiet afternoons. The most talented appear on radio and television, and cassette tapes of their recitations play in homes and merchants' stalls across the region. Even those lax in prayer and fasting may be moved to tears by a powerful recitation. The art has developed over centuries into well-defined styles of pronunciation, cadence, and voice tone that impart emotional force to the images, warnings, and promises of the text. The Quran has a much more poetic character than the Bible, which is built around histories and narratives. Quranic suras often juxtapose fragments of well-known stories (of Adam and Eve, Abraham, Moses, Jesus, etc.) with images of heaven and hell, exhortations, and announcements of social laws, and they use rhythm, assonance, and rhyme to unify the text. Since the latter qualities cannot be translated, readers of English versions usually have great difficulty following its meanings. Muslims often insist that the Quran cannot be translated, since its meanings reside in the language. As Kristina Nelson observes, the Quran does not so much state a set of meanings that then can be enlivened by recitation but uses "the very sound of the language to convey specific meaning." She explains: "This amounts to an almost onomatopoeic use of language, so that not only the image of the metaphor but also the sound of the words that express that image are perceived to converge with the meaning."[93] It is not meant to be read, she points out, but to be recited and heard.

Revealed, written, and recited in classical Arabic, whose standard it sets, the Quran differs from all spoken dialects, some as much as modern English differs from Shakespearean or French from Latin. Recitation also draws on scales, melodies, intonations, and phrasings of Arabic music, but modulates these in ways that set it apart from song. To emphasize this distance from everyday speech and music, the rules of recitation specify detailed features of pronunciation (mouth, tongue, and lip positions, voicing, duration, etc.) coordinated with types of consonants, a more nasal style than ordinary speech, prescribed tempos, the insertion of sounds following some final syllables to give them emphasis, the phrasing of meaning units in single breaths—all of which seek to simultaneously "beautify" the voice in recitation and achieve a tone of *huzn*—"sorrow," "sadness," or "grief."[94] Many religious scholars argue that recitation should bring the reciter and the audience to a weeping state that mixes awe, humility, and ecstasy. A complex and subtle state, "*huzn* is the awareness of the human state vis-à-vis the creator," Nelson writes: "with *huzn* one knows true humility, awe of the divine, human frailty and mortality."[95]

The rules leave latitude for individual reciters to use the unique qualities of their voices, to improvise rhythmic and melodic features, and to add repetition and omit phrases. To an outsider, recitation takes life in the boundary area of song and chant, edging toward one or the other, depending on the reciter, without quite becoming either. In recitation, the human voice can become hauntingly beautiful. Nelson writes: "Recitation of the Quran should be an engrossing religious experience. . . . The role of the reciter is not only to transmit the meanings of the text, but to stir the hearts of listeners with those meanings."[96] The emotional and spiritual qualities brought about by recitation are difficult for an outsider to comprehend or describe, but it is clear that they form a set of sentiments as culturally distinct as those of the honor-modesty system. Certainly Muslims differ markedly from one another in both the extent to which they have "religious experiences" and in the nature of the experiences they have, but spiritually momentous events are not limited to a privileged or devout few. Recitation brings God's voice into this world, and literate believers follow styles of recitation when they read the Quran in solitude, their inner voices echoing exalted forms. And since all of those who pray follow recitation styles when they repeat the *Fatiha* and other Quranic verses, nearly everyone participates in coming near to God's voice.

Further, most Muslims find particular passages to be especially beautiful and moving, and the life-history interviews I conducted suggest that these often provide important linkages between idiosyncratic psychological themes and the shared religious heritage. My interviewee Mohammed, for example, had lost his mother at the age of seven, and he attributed his nearly ruinous adolescent descent into delinquency to the lack of someone who would nurture him with "compassion." He described his reconversion experience as follows.

One night I was sitting like this and thinking about how I came into the world: a human being came out of my own mother's belly/womb, and he was clean . . . he didn't know anything about smoking or drinking or lying or stealing. Why now had I sullied myself and filled my head with all these things: I smoke, I drink, I live without purpose, I lie. Why didn't I stay like I was born, clean? Why! From that time I decided, that's it, I must stop all this and become clean again. . . . I asked myself what to do and I decided to become clean like the first time I came out of my mother's womb. I must start praying and devote myself to religion.

He turned to reading the Quran in the solitude of his room, and passages about "betrayal, orphanhood, and poverty," especially those in The Daybreak, moved him to tears. He explained:

Here Allah, the Great, the Merciful, calls out to the Prophet and instructs him, because the Prophet had been through that state—orphanhood and poverty. He calls upon the daybreak: by the light of day and by the dark of night, your Lord has not forsaken you, nor does he abhor you. The life to come is better than this ephemeral one, which will end. But up there, in Allah's home, the orphan who has lost his parents receives compassion, commiseration, clemency, and kindness.

When I interviewed him, he had become an admired reciter in his village, and dreamed of reciting on radio or TV.

Each person I interviewed felt moved by different passages and images, each speaking to his or her personality and life-history. The Quran and its recitation thus provides richly varied themes, out of which individuals selectively invest some with deeply personal meaning. Even as it shapes shared feelings of *huzn* ("sorrow," "sadness," and "grief" but also awe and ecstasy), recitation provides the materials for a flourishing of individual differences in religious experience and meaning.

The Prophet

Muslims regard the Prophet as human rather than divine, and unlike Jesus he lived a full life span. These factors perhaps enhance the spiritual and psychological role he plays as the ideal man, and it is widely taught that Muslims should take him as their model. In him the power of *baraka*, divine blessedness, and the power of physical prowess—proven in battle and with many wives—converge. "Servant" of God, he founded a community on new principles, and Islam can be said to flow from or through him: the Quran, which he received from God and recited, the *sunnah*, or proper behavior he exhibited in his life, and the *hadith*, his advice and teachings that provide guidance in living by the Quran. "His life, as understood traditionally, is read by the devout throughout their earthly journey in a thousand literary forms," writes philosopher Seyyed Hosein Nasr:

the Prophet is the infallible guide and the source of all spiritual guidance in Islam; and his *Sirah* [biography], *Sunnah,* and *Hadith* constitute the ship that carries those who aspire to the spiritual life across the waters of earthly existence to the shore of that land which bathes in the Divine Presence.[97]

As Annemarie Schimmel puts it:

> Muhammed indeed constitutes the exemplar and model for every Muslim believer, who is called to imitate him in all, even seemingly insignificant, actions and habits. . . . It is this ideal of the *imitatio Muhammadi* that has provided Muslims from Morocco to Indonesia with such uniformity of action: wherever one may be, one knows how to behave when entering a house, which formulas of greeting to employ, what to avoid in good company, how to eat, and how to travel.[98]

Identification with the Prophet and attachment to Islam's early history are promoted by the practice of giving religious names. Most first-born sons are named Mohammed, and others Ahmad (Mohammed's eternal name), Hamed, or Hamid, all derived from the root $h*m d$, which means "to praise." Some are named after the Prophet's relatives: men Ali (his cousin and son-in-law), Hassan or Hussein (Ali's sons); women Khadija or Aisha (two of his wives) or Fatima (a daughter and Ali's wife). God has 99 names, formed of superlative adjectives (i.e., *akbar*, "The Greatest"), and many of these are given as names with the prefix *abd*, which means "servant of": Abdullah, "servant of God," Abderahaman, "servant of the compassionate" (or Rahama for a girl), Abdelatif, "servant of mercy" (or Latifa for a girl), and so on. Not all names have a religious origin (Sa'id, or Sa'ida for a girl, means "happy"), but most do, and they establish a personal link with the Prophet, his family, and his milieu, or with God.

The power of the Prophet to act as a compass point for lives also is anchored in children's memorization of the Quran at special schools attached to community mosques, usually when they are age six to eight. Attendance at these schools may be declining, but a great many children still go before or during their first years in public school, and the majority of the current generation of adults studied at them. The term for "memorize," *hafid*, means "conserve" (so that *muhafada* means "conservative"), and the objective of Quranic school education is to inscribe proper recitation. For this purpose, the Quran has been divided into 60 roughly equal parts, and children memorize and recite one at a time. Children learn the Arabic script, which they write on slates, but generally do not discuss or study any matters beyond memorization—which has been a topic of controversy among modern educators. Perhaps more important, the imams and *talebs* who teach in Quranic schools have a reputation for treating the children harshly, beating them not only for misbehavior and inattention but for poor memorization. It is difficult to know what effect memorization under these conditions may have, though it is clear that the medium of fear is often intended to be part of the Quran's message. In fact, the traditional model of childhood held that the first, indulgent phase of childhood must come to an end around the age of six or seven, and that enrollment in Quranic school marks a shift in how a child, especially a son, should be treated: boys and girls should increasingly be separated; the father should become more distant, formal, and punitive; and a fear of God should be inculcated (see chapter 6).

Compassion

Every sura in the Quran begins "Bismillah al rahman al rahim" (In the name of God, the Compassionate, the Merciful), and a pious Muslim will utter or write this phrase before any undertaking. While God certainly can appear strong, wrathful, and awesome, I was continually struck by the way young Moroccans spoke of God and the Prophet as sources of compassion in an often harsh and heartless world. The villagers with whom we lived also experienced God as a source of mercy, sustenance, and shelter. This appears poignantly in one of the sermons recorded by Richard Antoun in a Jordanian village. This particular sermon was occasioned by a visit to the imam by a village woman who complained that some of her relatives were not fulfilling their obligations to her, apparently because they were giving patrilineal relations precedence. That Friday, the imam used terms built of the r^* h^*m root to metaphorically set out the Muslim life-course as one in which the individual is sundered from the womb (*rahim*) by the cutting of the umbilical cord, sustained through earthly life by compassion (*al rahma*) that flows through bonds with uterine or blood kin (*rahem*), and finally returns to the source of Being (*al rahman*, "The Merciful," *al rahim*, "The Compassionate") at death. Antoun points out that the imam chose *rham* as the sermon's root metaphor precisely in contrast to the predominant patrilineal idioms of kinship:

> Rahm is a maternal symbol par excellence, and in its social relational denotation it is bilateral . . . stressing the maternal line and at the same time the balanced lines of kinship—both female and male, mother and father. . . . In a village with three clans and numerous (twenty-eight) patrilineages the preacher chose the womb, the most intimate maternal symbol, to stress the kinship of all.[99]

Like the family, the village (or tribe or neighborhood) has complementary patrilineal and matrifocal characters, the latter reinforced by religion, often against the exclusivity of the former. The imam emphasized that "general kinship" consists of "the kinship (blood kindred, mercy) of religion founded upon genuine brotherhood among true believers."[100] Such "maternal" symbols and meanings run prominently through Islam, often unrecognized by outsiders, who mainly see its patrifocal imagery. But the fact that God is, above all, *al rahman al rahim*, "the Merciful and the Compassionate," gives God a kind of androgynous character—not that Islam explicitly genders God but that God appears to emanate both traditionally paternal authority and traditionally maternal compassion.

Baraka *and Saints*

"Divine blessedness," *baraka*, flows into and through this world as a kind of empowering and healing substance, and when we examine common beliefs about this process we move into a border region between what observers often term orthodox and folk Islam. *Baraka* is widely perceived as flowing into local communities and daily life through a variety of channels. Fresh water, especially from springs and wells, contains *baraka*; grain and bread contain it, and may be referred to as *baraka*; some meat has *baraka*, especially that of a ram and especially from its shoulder; dates, honey, and milk are especially rich in *baraka*; *baraka* is stored in silver and money, so beggars often beg for "a little *baraka*." While an absence of *baraka* does not necessarily cause illness, *baraka*-rich foods can strengthen anyone weakened by illness or injury.

Persons also may possess *baraka*, which appears as what Westerners would term "charisma." The Prophet had the greatest *baraka*, which appeared in his beautiful physique and countenance, in his magnetic character, and in a radiant luminosity many believe emanated from him. It is also believed that his descendants have inherited *baraka*, though it manifests itself more strongly in some than in others. Some say that Morocco's King Hassan, a descendant of the Prophet like Jordan's King Abdullah, had *baraka* that made bullets bend around him in a coup attempt. Individuals not descended from the Prophet may also come to possess *baraka*, and any who manifest it may come to be popularly recognized as "saints."[101] Saints can pass their *baraka* to adepts—often accompanying a moment of spiritual enlightenment—so that spiritual power and wisdom are sometimes passed along centuries-deep chains of "Sufi" teachers and students. In addition, possessors of *baraka* also may be granted dispensations from social norms. Most regions have legends of saints who acted as divine fools, publicly flouting conventions of sexual and personal decency, whose acts and utterances are said to embody principles higher than social norms.

In fact, the "worship" of saints, though questionably orthodox, forms a central feature of Islam throughout MENA. Some anthropologists see this as a Mediterranean custom, incorporated into Catholicism in southern Europe. In many areas, the landscape is dotted with the domed tombs of saints, nearly all of them possessing *baraka* that can empower and heal. Some are believed to heal specific diseases or troubles a psychologist probably would term "mental illness." Pilgrims come seeking cures, and may pray for the saint's help and vow to return and make a sacrifice if the help is given; they may sleep in the tomb, hoping to be visited by the saint and healed; or they may take some dirt or other substance associated with the site and ingest it to absorb its *baraka*. Infertile women may sleep in the tombs of local saints, hoping that the saint will visit and impregnate them or open them to their husband's semen. Some people become "tied" to a particular saint, usually after he (or occasionally she) has appeared to them in their sleep, and thereafter regard him as a patron who can intercede on their behalf with the Prophets and God. They may visit the tomb on a yearly basis or when they feel a need. Many religious brotherhoods or "Sufi" groups follow the "path" and teachings of a particular figure they regard as a saint, and adepts may make annual group pilgrimages to the tomb—often on the Prophet's birthday—that are modeled more or less closely on the pilgrimage to Mecca.

Women appear much more likely to be spiritually "tied" to saints and to turn to them for help. Since they may feel unwelcome at mosques, many observers have suggested that women have developed "saint worship" as an alternative focus for their religiosity. Some women say that while men can stand in the mosque and petition the Prophet and God directly, women need intercessors to do this for them. Similar arguments are made about some of the less orthodox "Sufi" brotherhoods. Composed largely of undercaste blacks and poor people, these engage in music-aided trance dancing (for example, the "whirling dervishes"), during which some perform spectacular feats of

Mosque and tomb of a "saint" reputed to cure madness,
paralysis, and other symptoms by driving out the jinn spirits
that cause them.

self-mutilation (slashing their heads with knives, walking on broken glass or hot coals, etc.) and pacify demons that possess them. The torch-lit nighttime dancing and trancing at their pilgrimages sometimes become shockingly licentious. Members of the North African Aissaoua brotherhood, for example, become possessed by animal spirits when they enter trances, and act like wild beasts, even biting into the uncooked meat of the sacrificial animal, which Islam firmly prohibits. But their special relationship with the animal *jinn* spirits enables them to charm snakes and to cure scorpion and snake bites. Members of these groups also perform as musicians at weddings, circumcisions, and other ceremonies.

Saints also historically served important political roles. Many saints' tombs and their living descendants were located on boundaries between hostile tribes and villages. The descendants were not members of the tribes and did not take up arms to fight, except sometimes to rally jihads against invaders. The living heads of the descendants often served as a mediators in local disputes, and their compounds provided "sacred" spaces where weekly markets could be held in peace. The saints also often symbolized the illegitimacy of despotic rule. Countless legends tell how saints proved their *baraka* in struggles with despots, the power of divine blessedness showing itself miraculously superior to brute force. Michael Gilsenan has described a similar opposition of *baraka* and brutality in northern Lebanon. In a nearly feudal arrangement, a group installed as beys by the Ottoman Turks two centuries earlier had evolved into landowners whose toughs kept the peasants taxed in poverty with beatings and murders. Lineages of saints lived in villages throughout the region, and legends tell of how they periodically humbled the landowners. "'The sheikh [holy man/religious leader] was the only man whose hand the *bey* kissed,' as it is put locally."[102] The miracles of humbling—a bey once bent to tie his shoe and could not stand until the saint arrived and gave his permission—show that "divine authority is utterly opposed to worldly power and oppression,"[103] since "the sheikh can vividly demonstrate the other, 'underlying' reality by being even more forceful than the lord."[104]

The two groups vividly displayed the opposition in their ways of life. In contrast to the landlord's imposing palaces and lavish hospitality (all creating debts his clients would be expected to repay with loyalty and service), the religious sheikh lived an ascetic existence in "an austere and unadorned" peasant dwelling, with "only the courtyard, the whitewashed walls, a few naked light bulbs, and a Quranic text." He took in anyone who came to him, and shared whatever he had: "Men might eat and drink, learn and listen, pray and meditate, sleep and talk all within his house thanks to his *baraka* . . . made possible by his sacred qualities and his favor with God."[105] But Gilsenan shows that the reality behind the appearances was more complex:

How was the miracle of the endless river of religious bounty maintained? It was in large part funded by the very lord who represents all the principles of what the saint's life is the antithesis. For it was the lord who sent the sheikh sacks of wheat and grain and seed, even money when necessary, and who leased out land to other members of the family.[106]

Saintly life-styles and legends continue to provide folk prototypes for religious critiques of tyranny, from which Islamism may now benefit.

In many MENA regions *baraka* remains a powerful force—spiritual, medical, and political—even in seemingly "modernizing" milieus. It is a force the young Moroccans I interviewed seek to tap, usually right alongside their vigorous efforts to acquire scientific knowledge and master technology. By culturally prescribed dietary practices, regimes of self-care, religious observances, and identifications with the Prophet (and sometimes other charismatic models), they seek to empower themselves against all manner of threats to their physical, emotional, and spiritual well-being. This system perhaps differs most from those commonly practiced by Westerners in the way it merges or at least interlinks health promotion, mental hygiene, spirituality, and political critique—with the notion and experience of *baraka* at its core.

Satan, Jinns, *and the Evil Eye*

Then there are the forces of anti-*baraka*: Satan, the devil; *jinn* spirits (from which we get "genie"); and the Evil Eye. Concentrations of *baraka* tend to draw these forces to them, rendering many of the things that possess *baraka* precarious, vulnerable, and in need of protection, and making some of them dangerous to approach. Where Christianity tends to see all evil as issuing from the Devil (with demons sometimes acting as his agents), evil appears to have more distributed origins in MENA, stemming from an array of agents who act largely on their own. Islam provides techniques for protecting things and humans from these invisible threats. Some methods are taught in the Quran or recommended by the Prophet, while others are based on unorthodox "superstitions."

Satan causes a good deal of mischief by whispering temptations that can lead one off the path of virtue: thoughts of lying, stealing, cheating, and so on. He especially whispers illicit sexual thoughts and tries to distract people from praying or keeping their "intention" (*niyya*) focused during prayer. The devil becomes especially bold when people sleep and can cause a person to dream of committing forbidden sexual or violent acts. As my interviewee Hussein explained to me, a nocturnal ejaculation is frequently referred to as being "hit by Satan." But since some of the most destructive acts are believed to be committed by *jinn* spirits and glances of the Evil Eye, Satan can appear as a more mischievous and less heinous figure than the Christian devil.

Jinn spirits (called *zar* in some areas), are said in the Quran to have been created alongside humans. They live in a kind of parallel universe, sleeping underground by day and emerging at night, where they sometimes appear in the guise of animals or leave tracks in the sparks of fires. This makes wells, caves, drains, and latrines dangerous, as *jinns* usually live in or pass through them, and it also makes dusk and night dangerous times. Some take up residence in empty or ruined buildings, but a few usually live in each household, sharing space with the humans there and often settling in under the threshold. Most *jinns* just go about their own business, but they can be mischievous if they come across a human alone, and they anger quickly if disturbed. A mischievous *jinn* might, rather like a "poltergeist," cause little troubles that make a person nervous or frightened. An angered *jinn* might cause a person to have an accident, or it might "hit" someone, causing him or her to "fall" and lose consciousness for a moment. A very angry or malicious *jinn* can possess a person and make him or her fall into a fit that resembles an epileptic seizure. They also are believed to cause some illnesses, and especially may be blamed for women's infertility or reproductive difficulties.

To take a psychological view, the actions of *jinn* spirits are invoked to explain a variety of unusual feelings and behaviors. A person who becomes nervous may experience himself or herself as in the presence of a *jinn*. The momentary losses of attention or control that cause accidents may be attributed to a *jinn*. And it is only in recent decades that medical explanations for fainting and epilepsy have been popularized, and both traditionally were understood as caused by *jinns*. Yet some "falls" and seizure-like fits do not have medical causes and appear to be nonconscious dramatic imitations of those that do. Among other things, then, *jinn* spirits provide a system of "folk" explanations for events that may have medical and psychological causes.

A variety of precautions can be taken to live peacefully with the *jinns*, and many are woven into daily customs and etiquettes. By saying *bismillah*, "In the name of God," before stepping over the threshold to enter a house, or before hauling water from a well or throwing hot water down the drain, one alerts the *jinns* and announces oneself as a believer. Many people refrain from sweeping after dusk, in order to not derange and anger them. If one feels a *jinn* hovering about, one can recite verses from the brief sura "The Dawn": "I seek refuge in the Lord of the dawn; From the evil of that He has created; And from the evil of intense darkness when it comes" or from the Quran's last sura: "I seek refuge in the Lord of men; The King of men; The God of men; From the evil of the whisperings of the slinking devil."[107] Families try not to leave members alone for long periods, and a host never leaves a guest alone. *Jinns* are attracted to many *baraka*-rich substances, and iron and salt repel them, so an iron tool may be placed beneath the grain in a family's storehouse, and bystanders often try to force an iron key into the clenched fist of seizure victims. *Jinns* flock to blood, so salt is sprinkled on the bloody ground around sacrificed animals.

Jinns also can be pacified. When people move into a new house they perform a ceremony that includes a small sacrifice (usually a chicken), whose blood is a gift to the *jinns* living there. Incenses not only provide nice aromas, but please the *jinns* and keep them content. It is believed that there are three types of *jinns*: Muslim *jinns*, which are most common and generally benign unless mischievous or angered; Christian and Jewish *jinns*, which can cause serious accidents and illnesses and may "hit" and possess people; and pagan *jinns*, which can be especially malign. Some *jinns* have names and distinct personalities, and when a person discovers one of these has taken up residence, the person may keep its favorite incense burning or dress in its favorite color.

One of the most infamous is a *jinniya* (female *jinn*), known throughout North Africa as Aisha Qandisha. Reputedly Sudanese in origin, Aisha Qandisha typically appears to men as an irresistibly ravishing beauty, into whose arms they fall, failing to notice her camel's or goat's feet. By then it's too late, and she turns into a hideous *'ajouz*, or "crone," to whom the man is then "married," meaning that he finds himself impotent with other women (including his wife) without Aisha's consent. Vincent Crapanzano has studied the Hamadsha brotherhood, a low-status and unorthodox "Sufi" order in North Africa, most of whose members are married to or possessed by Aisha Qandisha. They follow the eighteenth-century saint Sidi Ali ben Hamdush, who was said to dance himself into ecstatic trances, reciting "Allah! Allah! Allah the eternal! Allah the adorable!" and to perform miracles.[108] Hamadsha placate the *jinniya* and cure others possessed by her by dancing themselves into trances and then slashing their heads or performing other self-mutilating (but miraculously unscarring) acts as she instructs them.

The *jinns* appear to have three important psychological effects. First, they form a central part of a folk theory of mental illness. The patterns of experience and behavior that a psychiatrist would diagnose as schizophrenia, depression, multiple personality, hysteria, and epilepsy are commonly attributed to *jinns* and then treated with religious practices. Only a few people try these treatments, but cures at saints' tombs, exorcisms, and publicly performed trance-dancing ceremonies make the whole process widely known. Second, less serious ailments, emotional conflicts, immoral and unnatural thoughts, and nightmares are often attributed to Satan and *jinns*, to sorcery that uses them as intermediaries, or to a glance of the Evil Eye. Since the primary precaution one can take consists in scrupulously performing one's religious obligations, troubling experiences like these motivate people to greater piety and devotion. Nearly all of the young educated Moroccans I interviewed described some illness, injury, dream, symptom, or uncanny experience that they suspected may have been caused by an invisible being or force. They preferred scientific explanations for their difficulties and many had sought modern medical treatments. But they often lacked "modern" interpretations, and several had turned to more regular purification and prayer in efforts to calm their minds.

Third, children are taught from toddlerhood that these beings—and also *ghoul-s* (ogres) and *afrits* (giants) of various sorts—are real. In contrast to the hard work many Western middle-class parents do to convince their children that there aren't monsters in the closets or under their beds, traditional MENA parents evoke fears of them to control their children: "Don't reach up there, there might be a *jinn.*" This appears to shape a general *externalization* of anxiety: a tendency to respond to anxiety by sensing it as arising in response to an external, perhaps invisible threat—and then to respond with protective measures.[109]

Pollution and Purification

Religious practices provide a comprehensive system of "self-care" that centers on monitoring states of pollution and restoring conditions of purity. Pollution and purity are largely not brought about by sin and virtue, so they are not *moral* states. Pollution results inevitably from the physiological processes of life: sweating, urinating, defecating, spitting, blowing one's nose all increase one's degree of minor pollution, and sexual ejaculation puts one in a state of "major" pollution. Adulterous sex without ejaculation does not bring major pollution, while intercourse with one's spouse does, so the system clearly separates the morality of sexual acts from their polluting consequences. The brief washing ritual performed before the five daily prayers restores a state of purity, though major pollution requires more complex bathing, traditionally performed at public baths on the night before Friday prayers.

Purification creates something like a protective field that safeguards one against the whisperings of Satan, the mischief and anger of *jinns*, and glances of the Evil Eye. It also makes it easier for *baraka* to flow into and empower one. Only prayers performed in a state of purity may be accepted and answered, and the Quran should be handled and recited only in a state of purity. Careful purification before sleep will help ward off nightmares and immoral dreams, and may enable one to receive "true" dreams predicting future events or even to receive a vision of a saint or the Prophet. As the dirty business of daily life corrodes this field, a person becomes increasingly vulnerable to invisible forces. While it is essential to keep in mind that individuals differ greatly in the extent to which they make use of this system, for a great many it sets up a nearly continuous self-surveillance[110] in which anxiety and emotional distress are interpreted as pollution and vulnerability to external forces, and managed by purification and other ritualized protective and calming strategies. Many traditional hygiene practices are modeled on the purification ritual (for example, washing hands before meals and the mouth afterward; washing upon arising and before retiring), and this more deeply embeds it in the rhythm of daily life.

Care of the Self

With the Prophet as a model for identification, religious phrasings woven into daily interaction, *baraka* as an empowering substance that flows through earthly conduits, a theory of mind based on external invisible forces, and the division of the day and week into cycles of pollution and purification, Islam provides a comprehensive self-monitoring, self-care, and emotional management system. *By no means* does this imply that most anxieties are attributed to invisible forces, that most emotions are managed by religious practices, or that Muslims are any less aware of their "true" feelings and the "real" reasons they have them than any other people. But every culture provides techniques for interpreting and managing ambiguous, unpleasant, uncanny, and immoral feelings, and these may facilitate misperceiving their "real" causes. The mixture of orthodox and folk techniques practiced by many in MENA provides this sort of system, and appear especially to manage difficult feelings evoked or suppressed by the play of honor and modesty.

For example, in response to a TAT card, my interviewee Hussein began composing a rather stereotypic "honor violation" story in which a man becomes enraged upon hearing that his wife has been accosted in their home, and he said the picture showed her holding him back from attacking the assailant because of her fear that he will be arrested and jailed. Apparently disturbed by the character's near loss of control, Hussein then said he had to "leave the picture aside a little to talk about the religion of Islam." He explained:

> The Prophet said that when one of you becomes angry, go wash/ purify as if you're going to pray. He said: when one of you becomes angry, when his blood rises, he should go perform the ablution, because when one purifies one cools. He said to you: the thing that angers you comes from Satan, it is of Satan. Satan was created from fire, and what puts out fire? It's water. . . . So you should go wash/ purify with cold water, so that the fire inside you will be extinguished by the water.

Note that he did not just say the man should splash some cold water on his face to come to his senses. Rather, in a few brief sentences he marked out the coordinates of the religious worldview, imaginatively tracing the steps of a technique prescribed by the Prophet that gives anger a concrete representation as fire and then "extinguishes" it with another concrete representation, of cool water. Evoking Satan associated Hussein's anger with "evil" and "pollution," which the water cools, "purifies," and turns to goodness. Hussein's aside thus shifted his distress out of the secular realm, where the "honor code" celebrates the anger that fuels vengeance, and into a sacred realm where the Quran and the Prophet's teachings provide him a pacific system of images and concepts in which he can represent and then "extinguish" it. With his identity reanchored in Islam's core concepts and symbols, Hussein felt calmed, returned to the picture, and completed his story.

Nearly all of those I interviewed struggled to interpret and manage inner turmoil and uncanny experiences in modern versus religious frameworks.

"Pop psych" versions of Freudian, humanistic, and behaviorist theories have not been disseminated as they have in the West, and even with high school educations, few of my respondents had much exposure to supposedly scientific models of mind, emotion, and behavior. While those I interviewed do not constitute a representative sample, I believe the kind of struggles they described are widespread among adolescents and young adults—both male and female—and maybe they always have been. Gilsenan makes the following intriguing observation:

> In this village, and I suspect in many other villages and towns of the Muslim world, the sheikhs [religious teachers] are associated informally with what might be viewed as an extended rite of passage for those in transition to full adult male status. That is to say, those who tend to make up the bulk of their followers or attendants, who go to the rituals, and sit in their reception rooms are very often the unmarried (or only recently married) young men. My suggestion is, and it is only speculative, that the sheikhs were, and in our case still are, often most important for providing a moral and ritual framework and sanction for a group that for many different reasons is central to the problems and ambiguities of sexuality and honor.[111]

I believe that the need for a system to monitor, interpret, and manage emotional distress draws many youth to their religious heritage and may contribute to the current "return to Islam." An underappreciated but crucial feature of Islamism is the *jihad al-nafs*, or the inner "war against desire," that many young people have enjoined to resist the largely Western media-marketed temptations that beckon them away from the straight path they need to stay on in order to succeed in schools, marriages, and careers. I will return to this "war against desire" in later chapters.

Religion and Personality

I have selectively highlighted features of Islamic belief and practice that appear to have pronounced psychological importance. Like the honor-modesty system, these pervade the rhythms and etiquettes of daily life and form a loosely integrated system of propositions, a logic, a syntax, a habitus, a rhetoric, and a discourse in which selves can be constructed and performed. The psychological importance of this system clearly varies from person to person: from the Muslim brothers and sisters who devote every thought and action to living their religion and bringing the kingdom of God to earth to Mahfouz's Hajj Ahmad, who believes and prays as earnestly as he drinks and commits adultery, to Khadija, the young Moroccan I interviewed who felt split between a God-fearing "Muslim" self and an unbelieving "French" self. The significance of religion not only differs between individuals but within them over time as religious practice waxes and wanes throughout the life-span, as Michael Gilsenan and many others have noted.

I believe that, like the honor-modesty system, Islam cultivates a set of culturally distinctive *sentiments, motives,* and *social selves.* But perhaps because ethnographers have written less on the psychological aspects of Islamic spirituality than they have on honor and modesty, it is more difficult to delineate these. By combining ethnographic and theological accounts with my own fieldwork and life-history interviews, I believe some hypotheses can be tentatively advanced, as follows.

SENTIMENTS

Islam encompasses a rich variety of traditions, but a set of sentiments appears at the center of perhaps all of them. These include, at least, sentiments of purity and pollution, a sense of *baraka* (blessedness) and its depletion, a sense of receiving divine mercy and compassion, an "awe" or "fear" of divine power and judgment, and, closely allied with this awe, sentiments of righteousness and propriety associated with taking the Prophet as one's model and staying on "the straight path" of virtue. These may converge into a sense of oneness or union with God, which overcomes a sense of estrangement from the divine. And as Mernissi[112] and others have suggested, the primary negative sentiment threatening all of the positive ones may be *fitna,* which means "chaos," "disorder," "loss of control," and "insurrection."

For most Muslims, the sentiment of purity entails more universal emotions of security, tranquility, and perhaps what Western psychologists call healthy narcissism. Pollution, by contrast, entails more universal feelings of anxiety, vulnerability, threatened abandonment, and perhaps guilt. The sentiment of *baraka,* blessedness, entails feelings of strength, vigor, vitality, fecundity (especially for women), and security, while its absence or depletion is associated with weakness, exhaustion, depression, and bodily vulnerability. Purification and *baraka* may flow together in prayer, fasting, Quranic recitation, and other religious practices, and pollution and depletion of *baraka* may especially be associated with anxiety over attacks by invisible beings and forces (Satan, *jinns,* the Evil Eye, sorcery). Awe at or fear of God's overwhelming power is an important theological notion that appears central to most Muslims' spirituality, as is the allied sense of *huzn*—tragic sadness evoked by Quranic recitation. But closely related to these is the sentiment of receiving God's mercy and compassion, evoked at the beginning of every Quranic sura—"In the name of God, the Merciful, the Compassionate"—and at the start of every undertaking.

By no means do these exhaust the range of religious sentiments Muslims may experience, but they may be those that Muslims share with other Muslims, regardless of the particular region or tradition in which they are raised. And while they may have parallels in other religions, I doubt the parallels are very close.

Islam thus appears to shape at least four psychological needs or motives as important dimensions of individual variation in MENA societies. Using rough translations of indigenous terms, these might be named needs for purification (*tahaara*), blessedness (*baraka*), propriety (*akhlaaq*), and mercy (*rahma*).

Many individuals appear to be careless about pollution and purification, or perform the rituals in a perfunctory manner. But others have a strong "need for purify": they feel perhaps more disturbed by the sometimes grimy feel of pollution, or more strongly yearn for the sense of security that comes from divine protection against the whisperings of Satan and mischief of *jinn* spirits. Individuals similarly differ in the extent to that they experience religious practices as infusing them with *baraka*, divine blessedness, or explicitly undertake them in the hope of being strengthened or healed by *baraka*. Physical illnesses, infertility, exhaustion, interpersonal defeats, depression, and existential malaise may all lead one to seek *baraka*—from foods, medicines, saints, prayer, or others sources. A wide range of (universal) emotions or traits thus may lead an individual to develop a stronger need for *baraka*. A similar range of emotions may lead an individual to perceive and seek the divine as a font of *rahama*, mercy, and *hanan*, compassion, and as a refuge and haven from social strife, life disappointments, sinful acts, or the terror of mortality. The sentiments of sadness (*huzn*) evoked by Quranic recitation and of supplication to the Prophet or saints probably intensifies the "need for mercy." And while some individuals, like Mahfouz's Si Ahmad, compartmentalize their sin and devotion, others appear to be especially motivated to follow the prescribed rules of morality (*akhlaq*) and to stay on the *tariq mustaqim*, the straight path of righteousness. The sentiment of awe and fear of God also evoked in Quranic imagery and recitation probably fuels this "need for propriety." All four of these needs may be counterpoised to the negative, unpleasant, threatening experience of *fitna*— disorder, chaos, loss of control, insurrection—which also may shape a basic need or motive. Liability to *fitna*, and the need to avoid it, may well be an important dimension of individual difference in its own right, intensifying any or all of the other motives.

Purity, blessedness, mercy, propriety, and perhaps *fitna* thus describe five relatively independent emotional-theological themes within Islam that I suggest probably shape culturally distinctive "motives," the strength of which differs from person to person. Clearly I write speculatively here, as the research that might identify these as motives has not been done. But I believe that the available ethnographic and life-narrative evidence points to these characteristics as dimensions of individual variation.

SOCIAL PERSONAS

I believe religious belief and practice also creates a social persona that, for most individuals, coexists alongside the social persona formed by internalization of the honor-modesty system. Islam defines a different cosmology, a sacred system of time, space, and causality that contrasts with the profane parameters of daily life. Spiritual existence is oriented toward Mecca; time is anchored in the Prophet's life and recitation of the Quran (and in the lives of earlier prophets); and human and historical events are caused by uneven flows of *baraka* (divine blessedness) through this world, all of which reflects the mixture of divine, prophetic, saintly, Satanic, and invisible forces in the affairs of this world. MENA cultures certainly weave the profane and the sacred tightly together in time and space, but often as contrasting places and moments; and when one contacts or participates in the sacred, one locates oneself within a different cast of characters, operating by different rules, on a stage laid out to an eternal scale of space and time. To draw again on G. H. Mead, a Muslim comes to perceive himself or herself from the perspective of a sacred Generalized Other: God casts a judging but also compassionate and forgiving gaze; Satan whispers temptations to stray; *jinns* threaten mischief or even to take over one's body; the Prophet provides a model of personality and life; and saints may act as healers, teachers, and intercessors. As a young person gains mastery of this religious world and its self-care practices (largely in late childhood, I will suggest in chapter 6), he or she internalizes and enacts a sacred persona that may shift or even reverse some of the key features of the honor-modesty system.

Periods of Psychological Development

Introduction ❁

The previous two chapters described the social ecology in which life-span development takes place: forms of family and social organization and two preeminent value systems. While these characterize MENA as a "culture area," none are simply contained within it, as the culture area took shape from the historical overlap of a semiarid ecological zone stretching from Morocco into Central Asia, the circum-Mediterranean culture from which the West traces its own roots, and Islamic culture that has spread through much of Africa and South Asia. In chapter 3 I briefly sketched a three-level model of personality organization to suggest that the value systems of honor-modesty and Islam especially influence middle-level characteristics—*sentiments, motives,* and *social personas.* I ended by emphasizing two crucial points: that these form not shared traits but culturally distinctive dimensions of individual difference; and that they do not complete psychological development but set the task of fashioning adult relationships and identities.

Part II examines writings that more specifically address psychological processes. This introduction presents the model of development I will use to organize, interpret, and synthesize the writings. It combines a *life-stage theory of development,* based mainly on the work of Erik Erikson, with a theory of *three levels of personality organization* based on the writings of G. H. Mead, Robert LeVine, and Dan McAdams. This introduction also considers a set of ecological characteristics that probably have shaped prevailing cultural models of child care in MENA societies, and that influence psychological processes throughout the life-span. The following six chapters then examine influences on psychological development in successive periods of life: infancy, early childhood, late childhood, adolescence, early adulthood, and mature adulthood.

Surprisingly few observational studies have been conducted of child-rearing practices in MENA societies, and even fewer on child development. Elizabeth Fernea's 1995 compilation *Children in the Muslim Middle East* contains useful articles on children's legal and health status, adoption and orphanages, themes in children's literature and textbooks, and children's games and music, but only 3 of the 39 focus on psychological aspects of child care and development. Earlier collections of psychological writings (Brown and Itzkowitz's 1977 *Psychological Dimensions of Near Eastern*

Studies, a 1985 special issue of *Anthropological Quarterly* on constructions of self in MENA, and Fernea's 1985 *Women and Family in the Middle East*) contain only three articles on psychological development, all on older children. Most of the information we have comes from anthropological field studies that include observations of child-rearing. Fortunately, nearly all accounts converge in their descriptions of the main influences on childhood, adolescent, and adult development in MENA. Unfortunately, the available literature tells us very little about the range of individual and local variation, and we must be cautious about inferring that patterns of *influence* yield corresponding patterns of *development*. This is especially important because researchers who largely agree about the cultural patterning of each stage frequently disagree about the psychological effects of its key features.

Periods of Life ❀

The six periods roughly correspond to Erik Erikson's developmental stages. I have condensed his scheme to six periods partly because the literature on MENA is not specific enough to distinguish all eight. Thus the chapter on "early childhood" covers his stages 2 and 3, and that on "mature adulthood" encompasses middle and late adulthood. More important, I am not convinced that his model fully fits MENA societies, either in the timing or the content of stages. I do concur with Erikson's notion that the conjunction of biology and culture set typical "developmental tasks" in each period, and I will emphasize both the distinctive ways in which MENA societies pattern universal "tasks" (such as maternal attachment in infancy) and the "tasks" that appear distinctive of the region (such as broadening maternal attachment to an extended-family "house"). I also will follow Erikson in highlighting culturally patterned discontinuities that appear to define developmental tasks.

While it is important not to link developmental periods to specific age ranges, some approximate correlation is needed simply to organize the material. Infancy, therefore, will cover roughly the first two years of life, early childhood the age three to seven range, late childhood from about seven to puberty, adolescence from puberty to the late teens, young adulthood from the late teens to midtwenties, and adulthood from the midtwenties on. It is important to keep in mind, however, that these are very rough correlations.

Levels of Personality Organization ❀

My synthesis of the psychological literature also draws heavily on the work of Robert LeVine, who for 50 years has studied culture, child care, and child development in sub-Saharan Africa and South Asia. In particular, I will adopt the distinction he makes between two *levels* of personality organization, which he terms "genotypic" and "phenotypic." LeVine follows the psychologists Gordon Allport and Kurt Lewin in using the biological relationship between genotype and phenotype as an analogy to distinguish core personality characteristics shaped in infancy and early childhood from the more manifest or surface characteristics developed later. The analogy holds that just as the physical environment influences which features of an animal's genetic endowment (genotype) come to be expressed in its actual body form and behavior (phenotype), so the cultural environment influences both whether and in what form core psychological characteristics formed in early childhood may be developed and expressed in a human's adult personality.

LeVine uses these terms *only* as an analogy: he does not intend "genotype" to refer simply to inherited traits. He explains that personality genotype

> refers to a set of enduring individual behavioral dispositions that may or may not find socially acceptable expression in the customary (or institutionalized) behavior of a population. Its major characteristics are early acquisition (through the interaction of constitution and early experience); resistance to elimination in subsequent experience; and capacity for inhibition, generalization, and other transformations under the impact of experiential pressures. . . .
>
> Three broad classes of dispositions comprise the personality genotype:
>
>   (1) Basic, probably genetically determined, parameters of individual functioning. . . .

(2) The motivational residues of early experience. The child's representations of his wishes and fears concerning other persons in his early life provide unconscious prototypes for his emotional response to others in subsequent environments. . . .

(3) Adaptive organizations that monitor and regulate responses to stimuli coming from the external environment and from internal needs[1]

Personality genotype thus encompasses the "emergent self," "core self," "subjective self," and "verbal self" that Daniel Stern believes emerge in succession in infancy and early childhood[2] and the "personal dispositions" Dan McAdams theorizes form "Level I" personality characteristics.[3] By contrast, *personality phenotype*

> refers to the observable regularities of behavior characterizing an adult functioning in the variety of settings comprising his environment. . . . One of the most important integrating characteristics of the personality phenotype is a self-concept, an internal mental representation of the self that includes boundaries between, and identities with, the self and other individuals, groups, and ideologies. In his functioning as a member of society, the individual uses this enduring self-concept to monitor his own behavior and to determine the extent to which each of his behavior patterns is ego-syntonic, that is, consistent with his image of himself.[4]

The phenotypic level thus depends for its coherence on what Erikson terms "psycho-social identity," consisting of a system of values, a social ideology, and commitment to a set of social roles or life-style that embody them.[5] As for the relationship of phenotype to genotype, LeVine explains that

> the phenotype is not independent of the genotype; in a sense, it *is* the personality genotype modified by prolonged normative experience, through the deliberate socialization by parents and through direct participation in the wider social system. . . . In their phenotypic expression, genotypic dispositions may be suppressed and disguised for purposes of social adaptation and conformity, but are not thereby eliminated.[6]

LeVine thus intends this distinction to enable cultural psychologists to describe developmental conflicts and discontinuities, and the inner and interpersonal tensions they may create. It also provides a conceptual framework for describing the processes by which genotypic-level characteristics are transformed into phenotypic-level ones—what Gannanath Obeysekere terms "the work of culture."[7] Because of the danger of mistaking "genotypic" to literally mean "genetic," I will use the term *core personality* to refer to this level, and use Erikson's term *identity* to refer to the "phenotypic" level.

As suggested in the chapter 3, however, writings on the region's honor-modesty system and on Muslim religiosity suggest that a third level of psychological organization must be added to this model, between core personality and identity: that of G. H. Mead's *social self.* My study of life-history interviews with young adult Moroccans also shows the need for adding this level of organization, which makes one deeply a member of one's culture and challenges the individual to formulate an adult identity within it. I will refer to it as *social persona* (or *social self*). The resulting three-level model converges with that recently proposed by Dan McAdams to encompass the range of characteristics described by personality theorists: level 1 (dispositional traits), level 2 (needs and motives), and level 3 (an identity anchored in a life-story).[8]

A Conceptual Framework ❀

Linking the six-period model of development with the three-level theory of psychological organization provides the theoretical framework I will use for synthesizing psychological writings on MENA societies. The observation that core-level tensions appear integrated into more complex units at the level of social persona and that social personas are integrated into the more complex life-stories and ideologies that constitute identity accords well with a developmental view that focuses on two probably biologically based transitions (one around age five to seven, the other around puberty) that cultures almost universally read as signals of readiness for crucial social role transitions.

This model also nicely incorporates Erikson's view that identity develops via three processes: *introjection* in early childhood, *identifications* in middle to late childhood, and *ideological belief systems* in late adolescence or early adulthood. It also gives increased importance to the period of late childhood, which has largely been neglected in favor of early childhood and adolescence since Freud unfortunately called it the "latency" stage nearly a century ago. Many lines of research now indicate that this is a crucially important period, especially for the development of social competence and a sense of self-worth. The following chapters, then, describe social and cultural forces in MENA as acting in specific developmental periods, on specific levels of psychological organization.

Like all general and simplifying frameworks, however, this one also *over*generalizes and *over*simplifies. It is crucial not to draw sharp boundaries between levels or periods, and not to link levels of organization too tightly with developmental periods. Individual variation is too great to postulate a rigid developmental timetable. One way of loosening the linkage of levels and periods is to conceptualize them in terms of the apprenticeship-competence-expertise sequence now used to characterize some developmental processes. A loose schedule of cultural influences on personality then might be postulated along the lines shown in table 1.

The use of "apprenticeship-competence-expertise" terminology has some obvious drawbacks. It suggests that affective tensions, moral sentiments, and self-representations can be regarded as *skills*, and that a set of culturally useful skills can be identified at each period. Yet it also calls attention to the ways these personality characteristics do have strategic uses and develop as interpersonal and intrapsychic tools.[9]

Table 1 Developmental Periods and Levels of Personality Organization

	Infancy	Early Childhood	Late Childhood	Adolescence	Early Adulthood
Core (level 1)	Apprenticeship	Competence	Expertise		
Social persona (level 2)		Apprenticeship	Competence	Expertise	
Identity (level 3)			Apprenticeship	Competence	Expertise

Early culture-and-personality theorists like Ruth Benedict and Margaret Mead argued that all societies contain roughly the same range of human temperaments but that each culture favors a subset of temperamental qualities and cultivates them toward its ideals, in ways that often make the ideals difficult to achieve for those born with different traits. Their cultural relativism did not consist of the belief that human nature is so plastic that culture can mold it in any direction, but that individuals who flourish in a culture that prizes their temperamental qualities might founder in one that favors those they lack—and conversely, those who become deviants in one culture might well have developed into ideal men and women had they been born into another. As simple as it is, the model diagrammed in table 1 provides a framework for considering how traits created at earlier periods of development may be selected for and against at later periods—presenting individuals with easier or more difficult adjustments.

The "configurationist" school also viewed culture as resembling a collective work of art, and Edward Sapir likened an individual's acquisition of culture to the mastery of a musical instrument and repertoire. There can be no expression of individuality, he argued, without achieving proficiency at the skills and formal principles of a cultural heritage. Conversely, once one acquires proficiency, one can begin to innovate and cultivate a distinctive style. "Expertise" should be viewed in this light: not just as a higher level of skill but as the ability to adapt, vary, create, and individuate. This is precisely the challenge that the acquisition of culturally distinctive characteristics at the *core* and *social persona* levels of personality presents to an individual as he or she fashions an adult *identity*: to adapt, vary, create, and individuate.

Ecological Influences on Child-Rearing ❀

Ethnographic data from around the globe have identified several factors that influence child care and child development. The most important appear to be climate, subsistence base, kinship structure, and household organization—and consideration of these can help place MENA child-care models in comparative context.

Climate

John Whiting has documented a broad and potentially important difference between "sling" cultures, located primarily in the tropics, and
"cradle" cultures, located in colder climates to the north and south.[10] Since
the risk of protein-calorie malnutrition tends to be higher in tropical
regions, he believes that sling carrying represents one element of an
intensive and extended maternal caretaking that is adapted to minimizing
infant exertion, distress, and caloric expenditure and to maximizing the
coordination of hunger and nursing. In sling cultures, mothers (and other
caretakers) typically carry their infants on their backs or hips in slings, and
often take them into their beds to sleep. Cradle cultures lay, carry, and put
their infants to sleep in cradle-like structures (such as those used by Native
Americans). Slings maximize body-to-body contact and nonverbal,
kinesthetic communication; cradles create physical separation but facilitate face-to-face interaction.

   John Whiting and Beatrice Whiting believe these two pragmatic
designs for infant care have different psychological consequences.[11] Cradle
cultures make infants both helpless and in control of their caretakers and
generally tend to foster a relation of "ambivalent dependency" of infants
on their mothers.[12] In cradle cultures—and Whiting has the West, eastern
Europe, and Native Americans specifically in mind—"independence and
self-reliance are highly valued and at the same time dominant-dependent
behavior is subtly rewarded."[13] Sling cultures tend to create a different sort
of core emotional conflict. Especially when they minimize fathers' involvement in child care, sling cultures foster a "symbiotic identification" of
mother and infant that for men tends to create a "cross-sex identity
conflict." Here the Whitings join with Nancy Chodorow,[14] Gilbert Herdt,[15]
and others in viewing this sort of child care as facilitating the development
of an early feminine/maternal identification, which then must be suppressed or renounced and replaced by a culturally constructed masculine
identification—often by the sort of "protest" hypermasculinity that David
Gilmore terms a "man the impregnator-protector-provider" model.[16]
MENA (and circum-Mediterranean) societies sit on the northern edge of
the sling culture zone, with cradles coming into use in some of the moun-
tainous areas.[17] Its folk models of childhood follow those of sling cultures

in their general outlines, but in a less pronounced manner than societies between the latitudes of 30 degrees north and 30 degrees south.

Subsistence Base

Two bodies of research suggest that peasant agriculture and nomadic pastoralism are associated with two clusters of psychological characteristics, which are shaped throughout the life-span. The great majority of MENA populations have pursued these ways of life until the middle of the twentieth century, and they appear to have influenced these peoples' models of infant and child care.

The first cluster concerns differences between agricultural and pastoralist societies in fostering independence and emotional expressiveness. In a classic study, Robert Edgerton and his colleagues found large and important psychological differences between farmers and herders in four East African tribal societies. Within each culture they interviewed and tested individuals from both a farming and a pastoralist community, and found that these groups differed on two primary dimensions: "open versus closed emotionality" and "direct versus indirect action."[18] The more open and direct pastoralists scored high on scales of affection, sexuality, direct aggression, fear, bravery, brutality, and depression, while the closed and indirect farmers scored high on scales of anxiety, conflict avoidance, emotional constraint, hatred, impulsive aggression, and indirect action.[19]

With regard to emotionality, Edgerton writes that "the emotions of farmers may well be strongly felt . . . but they are not openly expressed. . . . For the most part, farmers seem to succeed in closing off their emotions to others, for it is only now and then that suppressed feelings break through in impulsive, uncontrolled fashion." By contrast, "pastoralists display their feelings easily, openly, and seemingly 'naturally.' . . . The good and the bad, the joyous and the sad, the soft and the harsh—are all expressed with far greater freedom."[20] With regard to action, "the farmers are characteristically indirect. Not only do they avoid direct expression of their feelings, when they do speak and act, it is with a careful eye to obscuring their motives, to veiling their meanings, and to avoiding confrontation over any potentially contestable issue." Again by contrast, "pastoralists strongly value independent and direct action. They make decisions as individuals, openly pursue goals, and typically say and do what they wish—directly."[21]

The largest and most telling difference concerned the pastoralists' valuing of independence. "It would appear that independence of action is a pastoral trait, par excellence,"[22] Edgerton concludes. By contrast, ethnographers long have regarded parental emphasis on obedience to be especially marked in agricultural societies.[23] Interestingly, Edgerton also found high respect for authority among the pastoralists, and resentment of authority to be typical of farmers: "Pastoralists expressed a sincere and deferential respect for the authority of various persons; in contrast, farmers expressed contempt, ridicule, or disrespect for the same categories of persons."[24] While this might seem to contradict the pastoral emphasis on independence, Edgerton points out that herders continually have to adjust to changing conditions, and probably need both guidance from elders and the ability to act decisively on their own. The overall pattern of findings suggests that different forms of authority and obedience are exercised in farming versus pastoralist groups, with independence perhaps complementing authority among the herders.

These farming–pastoralist contrasts have two implications for understanding traditional MENA cultures. First, they suggest that there may be important differences within the region between nomads and settled agriculturalists, and probably between both of those ways of life and urban dwellers. And second, to the extent that MENA culture was forged from the symbiosis of agriculture and pastoralism—and especially from the many "transhumant"[25] populations that traditionally combined agriculture and pastoralism—one might expect to find a mixture of these contrasting values and emotional styles. Perhaps the strong tendencies toward individualism within a framework of "collectivist" familial values noted by Schneider, Clifford Geertz, Kagitcibasi, Joseph, and others derives from the combining of these two ways of life. I believe that practices often viewed as inconsistencies in the region's child-rearing practices—encouraging both independence and obedience—are better viewed as evidence of contrasting ecologically based imperatives.

The second cluster of psychological characteristics concerns what many ethnographers term the "envy–Evil Eye complex," which appears to have emerged in the Mediterranean with the Neolithic revolution—the so-called birth of "civilization" that came with the cultivation of wheat, domestication of animals, invention of metallurgy, creation of towns, and rise of states. While this complex appears most prominently in European

Mediterranean and MENA societies,[26] it spread to much of central Europe and India, and to Mexico and Central America after the Spanish brought it there.[27] It did not take hold in most of sub-Saharan Africa (where a "witchcraft complex" appears to be widespread), in China, or in Southeast Asia. The complex centers on the belief that people are prone to cast glances of envy upon the good things possessed by others (newborn babies, healthy children, abundant fields, robust flocks of sheep, fine animals, nice houses, etc.) and that a glance of envy can damage, destroy, or kill whatever it falls upon. In response, the complex entails an array of practices aimed at preventing oneself from casting a glance of envy (avoiding direct praise, and using invocations of God's blessing as congratulations and compliments, which protect the admired object) and, more often, aimed at protecting one's valued possessions from the envious glances of others (using amulets, charms, and disguises of various forms). Some observers have noted that this looks like *paranoia*: people "project" their own envy and hostility, perceive it to be directed at them by others, and resort to "obsessive" defenses to protect themselves. And in keeping with psychoanalytic hypotheses that paranoia originates in disturbances in early attachment relations or harsh toilet-training, some have expected Evil Eye cultures to impose stresses in these early periods.[28]

In a series of classic articles, George Foster developed the thesis that conditions of settled peasant agriculture tend to intensify the human inclination to envy to the point that beliefs about it and protective practices become prominent features of the culture.[29] Foster believed this arises from two characteristics of most peasant societies: their productivity tends to be limited by land or water,[30] and they tend toward pronounced social inequality, whether hidden behind outward uniformity or blatantly displayed. Such societies thus tend to be "deprivation societies": not cultures of shared poverty but cultures "in which some people are poor while others are not, in which the well-being and power of those with plenty is visible to, and resented by, those with little."[31] This gives rise to worldviews entailing an "Image of the Limited Good," according to which

> life is played as a zero-sum game, in which one player's advantage is at the expense of the other. . . . The person who is seen or known to acquire more becomes much more vulnerable to the envy of his neighbors. He knows that his neighbors may convert

their envy into direct or indirect aggression, because they see his success as being at their expense. He therefore is likely to fear the consequences of their envy.[32]

Cross-cultural studies provide qualified support for Foster's thesis. John Roberts examined the association of Evil Eye beliefs with other cultural characteristics in 186 societies[33] and found no evidence of its association with infant child-care practices (such as early weaning or toilet-training) that might support the "paranoia" explanation. He did find associations with intensive settled agriculture, patrilineal descent, cultural complexity, social stratification, and concentrated political authority. "These associations provide a pattern of social inequality, strong and focused authority, and indications of the importance of property," he writes, adding that this combination probably underlies both envy and the Evil Eye.[34] While the Evil Eye was not associated with early socialization, Roberts did find it correlated with the use of physical punishment in later childhood, and he concludes by suggesting that in addition to settled agriculture and inequality, "strong" and "capricious" authority appears to be associated with it.[35] After reviewing the large literature on the topic, Vivian Garrison and Conrad Arensberg also reject the paranoia explanation and build on Roberts's findings to argue that it is a generalized "patronal dependency" and associated "risk of seizure" that gives rise to fear of envy and protective rituals.[36] These take archetypal form in the circum-Mediterranean but also characterize other regions where the Evil Eye appears. They conclude that the Evil Eye arises mainly from "personal patronage, the *personalismo* of the sheikhs, land-lords, and other protectors, mediators, and sanctioners of opposing peasant and peasant-and-nomad clienteles, at work in the stratified but unstable 'state societies' with tribal tributaries in the region."[37]

The Evil Eye complex remains strong in traditional milieus in MENA (and has not disappeared from many European Mediterranean societies). While it is not caused by early child-care practices, it clearly influences them: many infant illnesses and deaths are attributed to it, and fear of the Eye motivates a range of protective measures.[38] As mentioned in chapter 3, toddlers are taught to fear the Eye, along with *jinn* spirits and ogres and the whisperings of Satan, which together anchor a system of self-care based on interpreting some anxieties as vulnerability to invisible threats. Further, if herding ways of life tend to foster independent action and open emotionality (as Edgerton found), the "image of limited good" and fear of envy in village life may foster group compliance and more circumspect styles of emotional expression.

These broad nomad-versus-peasant contrasts may capture important differences between traditional groups within MENA. At the same time, MENA cultures have formed from centuries of interaction between these ways of life, and movement of peoples from both into towns and cities—a process that has greatly accelerated in recent decades. The resulting culture appears to contain psychological features associated with both. And if Garrison and Arensberg are correct, wherever "patronal dependency" and "risk of seizure" remain in force, as appears to be the case in many *populaire* (working class) and *bidonville* (slum) urban milieus, then some complex of envy and rites of protection also should appear.

Kinship

Francis Hsu has argued that cultural psychologists have overestimated the effects of early infant and child care and given too little attention to how kinship and family organization deeply shape the development of early attachments into the relationships that anchor adult personality.[39] Compared to discrete child-care practices that may have only limited and transient effects, Hsu believes the overall patterning of father-child, mother-child, spousal, and sibling dyads within a specific kinship system exerts pervasive, long-term influence on emotional and social development. Patrilineal, matrilineal, and kindred systems differ in how they allocate nurturing and disciplinary roles, and patrilineal cultures may differ significantly in which dyadic relations they emphasize as anchoring group loyalties and personal identities. He suggests that Westerners emphasize the husband-wife pair, the Chinese the father-son pair (and line of paternal ancestors), Hindu Indians the mother-son pair, and Africans the solidarity of brothers, siblings, and/or age-mates.

This can lead to oversimplification, but Hsu's approach gives appropriate weight to culturally stressed patterns of emotion and authority within families. MENA cultures traditionally stressed the patriarchal character of authority and the matrifocal nature of nurturance and compassion, and it appears that three important influences on development can be traced to the specifics of mother-child, father-child, and brother-sister relationships. All form features of the predominant cultural model of socialization, which individual families may follow more or less closely. First, many researchers have noted that women's positions in their husbands' families—with their status, emotional intimacy, and future security often depending more on their children (and especially sons) than on their husbands—encourage them to cultivate intensely interdependent bonds with their children.[40] When added to the concern with infant survival, these considerations lead to a style of infant care that has been described as "symbiotic" (see chapter 4) and seen as laying the foundation for emotional interdependencies sustained throughout life.[41] Second, there are many descriptions—and criticisms—of the distant and harsh "patriarchal" authority exercised by fathers and other senior men over women, boys, and junior men.[42] Ethnographic reports indicate that fathers tend to be warm and playful with infants and toddlers but then adopt a reserved, commanding, and often fearsome persona when their children reach roughly the age of five to seven (see chapter 6). Third, Suad Joseph emphasizes the importance of (older) brother–(younger) sister relationships, especially during adolescence, when brothers become responsible for supervising and protecting their sisters (see chapter 7).[43] She believes these are the main roles in which boys develop adult masculinity and girls adult femininity, and because they entail both intimacy and authority, brother-sister relationships give both siblings practice in the fusion of love-and-control that probably will characterize their marriages.

Household Organization

Household residential patterns also play a key role in development, as they set the range of those who may play caretaking roles, the size and character of child cohorts, and the general level of social interaction. LeVine notes that residential patterns can determine how similar early interaction patterns are elaborated into very different adult interactional styles. Among the Kenyan Gusii, he reports, each of a man's several wives occupied a hut with her children at some distance from other wives and neighboring families, and visiting was infrequent. This appeared to develop the low-verbal-engagement mothering into a rather cool style of social interaction: "The Gusii . . . were reticent about interpersonal encounters outside the domestic group, believing excessive sociability to be dangerous for a person of any age, and their conversational interaction was governed largely by a code of restraint." The West African Yoruba followed a similar infant-care model in polygynous households but resided "in a bustling compound sharing hearth, yard, and veranda with other mothers and children and having frequent encounters with visitors." As adults, they "adhered to a cultural ideal of sociability and gregariousness in which extended greeting, cheerful interaction, lengthy and hilarious conversations, and expressions of concern for the welfare of others were mandatory as well as commonplace."[44]

Though polygamy was practiced infrequently, MENA patterns traditionally paralleled the Yoruba style: the ideal household consisted of large extended or joint families, each nuclear family possessing some private spaces but all sharing a kitchen, courtyard, and other communal spaces. Village and urban neighborhoods tended to be built as clusters of kinsmen (and clients) in adjoining dwellings, so that a great deal of visiting went on between neighbors and socializing in semiprivate alleys or square-like areas between dwellings. The belief that a person left alone was vulnerable to *jinn* attacks intensified socializing, as good manners and care demanded that people always provide company to each other. So in spite of the fact that a great deal of the region is sparsely populated, both urban dwellers and villagers live in some of the most dense and crowded habitations to be found anywhere, and grow up in milieus of animated sociability.

Summary ❀

At the outset, then, we can provide a rough sketch of the broad MENA model of child-care, which operates especially in infancy and early childhood to shape *core-level* psychological characteristics. This model clearly appears to be a variant of what Robert LeVine and his colleagues term a "pediatric" model observed throughout sub-Saharan Africa and in many premodern societies, which evolves into what can be termed an "apprenticeship and obedience" model in early childhood (see chapter 4). The MENA variant of this model includes the following elements.

1. The use of slings to provide nearly continual contact facilitates close and perhaps "symbiotic" maternal attachment based on tactile and kinesthetic (rather than face-to-face) communication.
2. The historical combination of agrarian and pastoralist subsistence bases probably leads to mixed encouragement and discouragement of direct emotional expression, and mixed encouragement and discouragement of independent action.
3. The pattern of kinship relations promotes a high degree of differentiation and perhaps complementarity in typical child-mother (intimacy-based), child-father (authority-based), and sister-brother (intimacy- and authority-based) interaction styles.
4. The setting of large household compounds facilitates gregarious social interaction, based on a sharp separation of public and private spheres, and on generation- and gender-linked principles of avoidance and etiquette-governed interaction.

As is the case in every society, a child's (and an adolescent's and adult's) socialization into this world is neither automatic nor always easy, and the difficulties a person typically faces become the "developmental tasks" that characterize a period.

Because there are relatively few direct studies of psychological development in MENA societies, the following chapters will review the many rich accounts of *cultural models* of child-care and life-span development. Thanks to work underway by psychologists at expanding university systems throughout the region, the picture of development that can be drawn in a decade or two will be much more detailed than it is today. And the issues engendering debate undoubtedly will change.

CHAPTER *4*

Childbirth and Infant Care

Studies in many MENA societies show that mothers throughout the region traditionally followed "pediatric" models of infant care broadly similar to those of many preindustrial societies. Adapted to improving the chances of survival in conditions of high fertility and infant mortality, this type of infant care entails nearly constant maternal caretaking, nursing on demand and to sooth distress, and dampening rather than eliciting excitement. This differs from "pedagogic" models typical of industrialized societies, which encourage face-to-face interaction, protoconversations, exploration, and excitement—all of which appear to be adapted to preparing infants for schooling.

MENA's pediatric style of infant care maximizes tactile and kinesthetic communication while minimizing face-to-face interaction. It also minimizes separation and facilitates the development of a secure attachment, "basic trust," and the formation of an interdependent bond that some observers describe as "symbiotic." It appears to provide the psychological foundation for a strong bond of maternal interdependence that is cultivated to last through-out life—similar in some respects to that described by Sudhir Kakar for Hindu India and Takeo Doi for Japan. Weaning tends to be abrupt, however, often coinciding with the birth of a new baby and a dramatic decrease in maternal caretaking. The chapter concludes by focusing on the disagreement between researchers who view this pattern as setting up an often traumatic "dethronement" that undermines the separation-individuation process and those who view it as fostering secure attachments that are broadened at weaning to the extended household, setting up a kind of group self that anchors subsequent familial interdependence and loyalty.

All studies find that modernization is changing this "pediatric" pattern, generally toward a "pedagogic" one. But it remains unclear how infant care practices may be changing among the large numbers of urban poor, who may be unable either to follow traditional styles or adopt pedagogic styles.

Introduction ❁

Studies in traditional MENA milieus provide near-consensus that parents follow variants of a "pediatric" model of infant care observed throughout sub-Saharan Africa, South Asia, and in many preindustrial societies, which appears to be designed to nourish and protect babies in conditions of high infant mortality (see the discussion of sources at the end of this chapter). This contrasts with American and European "pedagogic" models that assume survival and prompt active interaction and exploration. Researchers disagree, however, on the psychological consequences of MENA's pediatric pattern. Some argue that the common practice of long "indulgent" nursing and "sudden" weaning undermine the separation-individuation process and the subsequent development of psychological autonomy. Others believe it promotes the formation of secure mother-infant bonds and then a healthy widening of a toddler's circle of attachments to the extended household. This chapter will briefly describe *pediatric* and *pedagogic* styles of infant care and then examine field studies that report on conception and birth, swaddling and carrying, and nursing and weaning. It then will consider how modernization (especially education, improved health, and smaller family size) and underdevelopment (especially slum living conditions) are changing traditional patterns and conclude by focusing on the disagreement among researchers about the traditional pattern's effects on attachment and long-term psychological development.

Cultural Models of Child Care ❁

LeVine and his colleagues emphasize the importance of the *cultural models* of child care and development that guide the socialization of children. These consist of three features: a "*moral direction,* a *pragmatic design,* and a set of *conventional scripts for action.*"[1] The *moral direction* refers to the overall goals caretakers seek for their children, which may change in adjustment with children's ages and may differ for subgroups (boys versus girls, wealthy versus poor) within a society. In MENA, for example, maternal care practices come to symbolize the family's obligation to nurture and protect its members, fostering a sense of moral indebtedness that perhaps resembles that described in Japan. The *pragmatic design* refers to the general techniques and strategies parents use to care for and socialize their children, and to the schedule by which these change as they grow. MENA parents traditionally took precautions to shield their infants from the ever-present dangers of *jinn* spirits, glances of the Evil Eye, and other supernatural beings, which are held responsible for illnesses, accidents, and deaths. They then taught their toddlers to fear *jinns,* ogres, and *afrit* (monsters), both to control them ("get away from there, or the *jinn* will get you!") and to instruct them in the rudiments of the Islamic system of self-care that anchors adult piety. The *conventional scripts* consist of sequences of behaviors parents employ in specific situations. Distinctive greetings, gestures of deference, and eating arrangements, for example, display the age and gender hierarchy of MENA family relations.

Many researchers now follow the distinction LeVine and his colleagues make between the two broad cultural models of caretaking in infancy and early childhood: a pediatric model aimed mainly at ensuring infant survival (found mainly in traditional or pretechnological milieus), and a pedagogic model aimed at fostering exploration and learning (favored in the West and in modernizing sectors of "developing" societies).[2] In industrialized societies, infant mortality rates tend to be low, children are expensive to care for and contribute little labor or income to their families, and aging parents usually do not depend economically on their children. These conditions favor a preference for relatively few children, and since their survival is rarely in

Middle Easterners traditionally followed a "pediatric" model of infant care that emphasizes protection and dampening excitement rather than early stimulation. Their "sling-carrying" style—common to hotter regions around the globe—facilitates nearly continuous physical contact and kinesthetic (body-to-body) rather than face-to-face communication.

doubt, parents begin training them from infancy in the attitudes and skills they will need to compete in school and the occupational marketplace. In most preindustrial societies, by contrast, parents need many children to contribute labor to the household and to care for them as they age. High infant morality rates intensify the pressure for high fertility and encourage caretakers to adopt nurturing, protective infant-care practices that enhance the chances of survival. This typically involves maximizing the nearly exclusive attention mothers give their babies, with training for social roles put off until later:

> The goal of agrarian mothers, then, is to maximize the number of surviving children by spacing births to prolong the period of exclusive maternal attention, including breast-feeding and cosleeping. . . . The mother gives most attention to each child in turn before it is weaned, particularly in the early months before its survival is regarded as assured.[3]

In pedagogic models

> infant care is construed less as nurturance for a child at risk than as mental and social stimulation for a child with a future. Maternal attention is devoted to talking and playing with the baby, creating extended "protoconversations" before the baby is capable of speech and responding to the baby's initiatives for social interaction.[4]

On the basis of work in sub-Saharan Africa, LeVine and his colleagues contrasts the pediatric and the pedagogic as shown in table 4.1.[5]

In Western families following pedagogic models, days are organized to provide alternating periods of exciting interaction and solitary sleep:

> The well-rested baby is seen as ready to be stimulated by toys and social interaction, specifically by the proto-conversations in which the mother talks to the infant, eliciting a (vocal and motor) re-

Table 4.1 *Models of Infant Care*

Feature	Pediatric Model	Pedagogical Model
Goal	Protection	Active engagement, social exchange
Means	Soothing	Stimulation, protoconversation
Temporal distribution over first 30 months	Decreasing	Increasing
Cultural script	Modulate excitement Commands	Elicit excitement Questions, praise

sponse that she interprets as a conversational turn in a continuing "play dialogue." . . . These are deliberately educational interventions. As Heath concluded from a study of middle-class urban parents and children in the southeastern United States, "Before the age of 2, the child is socialized into the initiation-reply evaluation sequences repeatedly described as the central structural feature of classroom lessons."[6]

By contrast, in cultures that follow pediatric models, nearly continual contact with the mother, cosleeping, immediate soothing of crying or distress, nursing on demand, and the avoidance and dampening of excitation all serve to minimize the infant's caloric expenditure and thus appear to be well adapted to conditions of poor nutrition and vulnerability to infectious diseases. Comparison of mother-infant interaction in a rural East African culture (Gusii) and suburban Boston found that 93 percent of interactions with 9– to 10–month-olds in Gusii involved holding, versus 25 percent in Boston, and that talking and looking constituted 11 percent and 1 percent of interactions in Gusii, versus 29 percent and 43 percent in Boston. Videotaped interactions during the first six months revealed the contrast in styles shown in figure 4.1.[7]

American mothers thus engage in a great deal more face-to-face contact with verbal questioning and praise, but their highly interactive style also generates much more emotional distress, which LeVine and his colleagues defined as "fussy vocalization, crying and/or moving away from the setting,"[8] than does the Gusii mothers' style. While pedagogic strategies prepare children for typical classroom interactions, pediatric strategies entail much more kinesthetic communication and physical coparticipation in activities, and

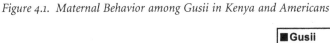

Figure 4.1. Maternal Behavior among Gusii in Kenya and Americans

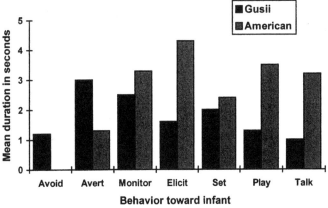

prepare children for "apprenticeship" forms of education, in which they learn by imitation or even by having their limbs moved through the motions being taught. Analysis of videotaped mother-child teaching interactions showed that "the Gusii child's orientation to the task was often maintained by the mother's use of physical control measures such as tugging and restraining— rarely used by American mothers. The Gusii children did not resist being pulled and pushed, but the American infants did in almost every instance."[9]

A good deal of ethnographic evidence now shows the contrast between a pediatric emphasis on tactile/physical communication associated with nurturance, protection, and soothing and a pedagogic emphasis on face-to-face verbal communication, stimulating play, and preparation for school captures many of the most important differences in infant care between "modern" versus "traditional" cultures. Virtually all accounts indicate that MENA parents traditionally followed variants of the pediatric model. But ethnographers also have documented important differences *within* modern and *within* preindustrial cultures. In America, for example, verbal mother-infant communication occurs less frequently in working-class families than in middle-class families. In southern Africa, Kalahari foragers engage in more verbal interaction than do mothers in other African societies—as much as do working-class Americans.[10] It therefore is crucial to describe both (1) variations of the pediatric model observed within MENA societies, and (2) the frequent divergence of child-care practices from the cultural model's ideals.

In many preindustrial societies, a pediatric model of infant care leads into what might be termed an *apprenticeship and obedience* model of child-rearing.[11] In contrast to "modern" classroom-based formal education, which emphasizes independent work and competitive achievement, learning in preindustrial societies tends to occur alongside parents or older kin, and to emphasize imitation, cooperation, and compliance with directions. Ethnographic accounts indicate that traditional MENA societies followed variants of an apprenticeship-and-obedience model—that reformers have sought to change and traditionalists to conserve.

In the large "traditional," "underdeveloped," or "peripheral" sectors of MENA societies, parents continue to follow pediatric models that resemble those described for parts of sub-Saharan Africa and for most of India. Descriptions of infant and child care in medieval Europe show broad similarities, but potentially important differences appear in the European use of cradles and cribs rather than slings, in the practice of infanticide by "exposure," and in the extensive use urban and aristocratic families made of wet-nurses. In contemporary MENA, modernized, urban-industrialized sectors certainly are expanding, and educated parents living in nuclear units are choosing to have smaller families and adopting pedagogic models like those of Europe and America. There are few data by which to gauge the rate of this change, and, perhaps more important, ethnographic accounts make it clear that change is not simply unidimensional.

Most MENA societies are becoming increasingly stratified by class, and observers report that in the slums ringing most cities, some traditional pediatric practices appear to remain entrenched while others are being abandoned—but without the adoption of modern pedagogic practices. In poorer urban areas, households tend to be continually in flux, rarely matching either traditional extended or modern nuclear forms. Caretaking arrangements often have to be improvised, and child-care practices may not closely follow any single model. In rural areas, many households and villages have been nearly emptied of able-bodied young adult males, who have emigrated to the Gulf States, Europe, and major cities for work. At the same time, the extension of schooling to rural areas takes older children away from the farming, herding, cooking, and child-care tasks they traditionally performed. In many respects, the countryside remains a repository of traditions, but emigration and schooling together shift household work loads, caretaking responsibilities, gender roles, and exercises of authority in important but often unpredictable ways. It is therefore impossible to estimate the percentage of families following pediatric or pedagogic strategies, mixing the two, or diverging from both. My account will focus on the more traditional pediatric patterns by which the majority of the current generation of adults were raised. I will draw often on Hamid Ammar's 1954 *Growing Up in an Egyptian Village*, which continues to be the most comprehensive account of child-rearing and was enriched by his daughter Nawal Ammar's restudy of the village in the mid-1980s.[12]

Conception and Birth ❀

Throughout MENA, insemination is likened to cultivation, a view affirmed by a verse of the second Quranic sura: "Women are your fields: go, then, into your fields as you wish."[13] It is widely said that the man provides the seed that the woman nourishes in her womb, and that physically the child gets its bones from its father and its blood (or sometimes flesh) from its mother. In many rural areas, this view is metaphorically extended to term the patrilineage one's "bone." Friedl summarizes the theory of conception prevalent in southwestern Iran, which closely matches that described by Hilma Granqvist for Palestine,[14] Carol Delaney for rural Turkey,[15] and Janice Boddy for northern Sudan:[16]

> God willed that men have seeds and that women have a womb, the child-bag. Upon ejaculation of seed-fluid, a man's seed falls into the woman's womb, which contains blood. . . . Although children might not know what their father's seeds look like or consist of, the concept of growth-out-of-a-seed is familiar even to the very young. Seeds provide the link between father and children, just as they do between last year's wheat and this year's."[17]

The Quran teaches that God created life by breathing spirit into a lump of clay, and Granqvist reports that Palestinians believe this occurs at each conception. As one of her informants described it: "When God wishes to feed a woman with a child, the angel Gabriel goes, brings his hand full of dust from where the child will die. He kneads the dust and [as the man ejaculates] puts it before the door of the woman's womb, and God draws and paints."[18] The man's seed carries some of his qualities to the child, but the woman's temperament (hot versus cold, wet versus dry, and clean versus dirty) and the purity of her womb also shape many of its characteristics. In the village Friedl studied,

> if the mother's humoral disposition is warm, the child, referred to as such from the moment of conception, will be a "child" in the narrow sense, that is, a boy. If the mother's humoral nature is cold, it will be a girl. If the womb is clean, the child will be beautiful, with light, clear skin, but if it is not clean, the seed might not mix properly with the blood, or else the womb might not be able to take care of the child. If a child nevertheless grows in a "dirty" womb, it will be dark-skinned and ugly.[19]

In traditional contexts, motherhood fulfills a woman's destiny, confirms her adult status, and solidifies her marriage—all of which are put in jeopardy by failure to conceive. If a woman passes a year of marriage without becoming pregnant, anxiety intensifies, and she may begin seeking diagnoses and remedies for her problem. "A woman who does not bear children," reports Hamid Ammar, "is called 'akir'—one who literally 'kills' her offspring; and the woman who has stopped bearing is referred to as 'mushahira'—being 'bound' or literally affected (in some way) by the moon."[20] With the birth of a first child, many women come to be addressed as "mother of so-and-so,"—um Hamed if her son is named Hamed—which clearly conveys new status and respect. Whatever fear and ambivalence a woman may feel privately, pregnancy usually brings approval, an easing of work burdens, and indulgence of moods and cravings.[21] "Pregnant women are said to be unreasonable, quarrelsome, and teary," Friedl reports, and these emotions are attributed "to a female weakness in reason that is heightened during pregnancy because the womb is taking care of an increasingly big and heavy load."[22] She also becomes vulnerable to jinn spirits and the Evil Eye, and may conceal her pregnancy as long as possible. Before the birth she may move back into her parental home so her female relatives can help with the delivery; or her relatives may come help her in her husband's home, or she may deliver with her mother-in-law's help. In cases of close marriage, these relationships may overlap in a single dwelling or adjoining households. In many communities, a midwife will be summoned to deliver the baby, while the woman's female relatives also attend.

Increasing numbers of women give birth in rural clinics and urban hospitals, but perhaps the majority still deliver at home, in less-than-sanitary conditions, without anesthetics, and without emergency care should it be needed. Sanitary conditions at some maternity clinics may not be much better, anesthetics in as little use, and the emotional environment much worse.[23] Several ethnographers have reported that childbirth is said to be "women's jihad," citing the Prophet as saying that a woman who dies in childbirth, like a man who dies in war against foreign invaders, will go directly to Heaven.[24] The root *j*h*d* actually means to exert effort, and *jihad* conveys this, so it means something more like "to exert great effort in a sacred cause."

Announcements and celebrations of the birth typically depend on the baby's gender and health (as they do in much of India and did in the European Mediterranean): "Very good news, such as the birth of a healthy boy, is announced loudly to the outside and spread further to all the interested. Less good news, such as the birth of a healthy girl, is spread more slowly and quietly. Problems such as obvious birth defects leak out of the delivery room slowly."[25] In many areas, a naming ceremony is held on the seventh day and a ram (or other animal) sacrificed.[26] In the Egyptian village studied by Hamid Ammar, the baby is passed over the animal's blood seven times:

> "Blood flowing" is supposed to ward off the effects of the "evil eye." It is also considered as a sacrifice for the child's life, saving the child's life by giving the life of an animal. The traditional support for this is the story of the Prophet Abraham whose son Ismael was saved by a heaven-sent ram.[27]

Nawal Ammar found that by the mid-1980s villagers had abandoned this ceremony, most citing its increased cost.[28]

Most names have religious, family, or historical importance, and so signify character and destiny within the culture.[29] Names are usually taken from the Prophet (Mohammed), his family (Ali, Aisha), or prophets (Brahim, Youssef) or constructed as "servant of" attributes of God (i.e., Abdelkrim, "servant of the Generous"). Children also may be named after grandparents or after family members or previous children who have died. In some areas, children may be named after mythic, historical, and literary figures, and more recently after popular entertainers. Ethnographers working in rural or poor urban areas report that a few children are given humorous or "ugly" names to protect them from the Evil Eye.[30] Al-Sa'ti found that religious and folklore-based names decreased in Egypt between 1950 and 1975, while "modern" names increased from 20 to 40 percent for men and from 44 to 62 percent for women.[31] Nawal Ammar found that villagers had diversified children's names, naming more of them after national leaders and cultural figures.[32]

After the birth, the mother and baby usually observe a 40-day period of seclusion, during which her relatives care for her as she cares for her baby.[33] This is treated as a kind of liminal, betwixt-and-between period, both sacred and polluted. Angels hover around and protect the baby, but the loss of blood—said to be "black" or "dirty" like no-longer-productive menstrual blood[34]—and the opening of the body puts the mother in a state of pollution.[35] Granqvist reports that Palestinian women say that "for forty days her grave is open," a saying that Delaney also reports among rural Turkish women.[36] Both are in a heightened state of vulnerability, the baby especially to the Evil Eye and the mother to *jinn* or *zar* spirits. Nawal Ammar reports village women continuing the period of seclusion in the 1980s and continuing to fear spirits and the Eye.[37] Thus the woman is protectively enclosed or "covered" during the period in which her body is "open," impure, and vulnerable. Bathing on the fortieth day purifies her, and she begins resuming her normal routine, including intercourse with her husband. This contrasts with most of sub-Saharan Africa, where postpartum sexual taboos of up to two or three years are observed—a practice that Whiting[38] and LeVine[39] believe represents an adaptation to especially high infant mortality rates, and a probable cause of polygynous marriage. In these societies, several ethnographers report that many new mothers try to avoid frequent intercourse until their child has been weaned, to delay another pregnancy.

Swaddling ❀

Infants are generally swaddled[40] and alternately laid on blankets and held in their mothers' arms. Friedl reports that cradles are used to hold and sometimes transport children in the mountains of southwestern Iran, but in most of MENA, infants are carried in slings, and gradually moved from the chest to the hip and to the back. In the areas using slings, infants spend most of their days in physical contact with their mothers, or sometimes with other family caretakers. Prothro reports that 95 percent of the almost 500 Lebanese mothers interviewed swaddled their newborns, usually for the first five months: "Strips of cloth, new or used, are wrapped around the child until he is snug and relatively immobile. In some instances the child's arms may be left free, but in most cases—at least in the early months—his arms are wrapped at his side."[41] This was practiced equally in urban Beirut and rural Beqaa, and by Arab Muslim, Arab Christian, and Armenian Christian mothers, who said it kept the child warm or its body and legs straight. Palestinian mothers told Granqvist they usually swaddle their infants for about four months in the summer, and about five in the winter.[42] 'Alia Shakri reports similar practices in Egypt,[43] and Susan Davis in Morocco.[44] Judith Williams reports that in the Lebanese village she studied swaddling began during the first week and continued intermittently for a year, though "even quite a young baby will spend many of his daytime waking hours unbound and out of the cradle, carried about loosely wrapped in a blanket."[45] Mothers again give "a preponderance of health explanations for the practice: swaddling keeps the baby warm, makes his limbs straight and strong; it is also easier to keep a child clean."[46]

In the two decades before this research, a fierce debate had raged about the psychological effects of swaddling, catalyzed by Geoffrey Gorer's argument that prolonged constriction of infants shapes the depressive, guilt-burdened, rage-prone, tragic contours of the so-called Russian character:

> It was through the study of swaddling practices that I discovered what appear to me to be some of the most important clues to the interpretation of Russian behavior; and the derivatives of the swaddling situation became for me as it were the thread that led through the labyrinth of the apparent contradictions of adult Russian behavior.[47]

Most researchers eventually concluded that swaddling in Russia and eastern Europe usually was not practiced in as constrictive a manner as Gorer believed and that it does not have the profound effects he inferred. Others argued that swaddling forms only one part of a larger pattern of infant caretaking and that the comparatively low levels of physical contact and social interaction experienced by many Russian infants resulted from a confluence of swaddling, the use of cradles, and cultural beliefs about infancy. Still Prothro explored the possibility that swaddling might affect personality development by dividing his sample of children into those swaddled less than and more than five months and comparing ratings of their dependence, aggression, conscience, and achievement motivation—and found no differences. Our informal observations in Imeghrane suggest that while swaddling certainly does not promote motor activity and exploration, it usually does not cause any more discomfort than the bundling of American babies in cold weather or the carrying of them in "snuggly" packs or carseat carriers. As Williams reports, infants rarely are swaddled all the time, and caretakers usually respond to signs of distress.

Nursing ❀

Throughout the region, mothers are reported to nurse frequently and on demand. Extended breast-feeding is believed to strengthen the infant and to transfer good qualities from the mother's line[48] and is widely—and correctly—believed to provide some contraceptive protection. Granqvist reports:

> as soon as a little child cries or shows the slightest sign of restlessness, it is at once laid to the mother's breast. Very often a woman who is nursing a child has an opening in her dress over each breast and thus she can feed it at once. And she does it unhesitatingly in any place, at any time, and very often.[49]

Cederbland writes: "Free suckling habits are the rule before weaning. A child is given the breast as soon as it cries. Breast children are often seen playing with, biting and nipping their mother's breasts as if they were playthings."[50]

Williams reports that while many mothers said they nursed five or six times a day, she observed them nursing much more frequently, often to soothe their infants:

> Perhaps what matters more than the frequency of feedings, be it five to six times a day, or fifteen to twenty—and the latter figure is much closer to reality—is that the breast is given not only at every cry but at every sign of restlessness. The child is instantly quieted. . . . The quiet child in Haouch is, as elsewhere in the Arab world, the ideal child. . . . In Haouch, during the first few months of childhood especially, the breast is endlessly available and the chief principle is the maintenance of quiet. The breast or bottle is often pressed upon a quite uninterested but fidgety baby.[51]

Davis similarly reports that Moroccan infants "are nursed on demand (even three or four times an hour), and are never allowed to cry more than a few seconds without being pacified, usually with the breast."[52] In Iran, Friedl notes, "older babies still are nursed on demand, even if they are fed other food, too. The frequent nursing has taught the infant to demand the breast not only when hungry or thirsty but also when sleepy, cranky, stressed, or in pain. A mother's breast is a hiding place, warm, dark, and safe."[53] The length of nursing varies greatly from child to child, but most women try to continue well into the second and often into the third year. Al Nawayseh reports two years or more to be part of the traditional model of infant care throughout Jordan,[54] as Davis, Abdeslam Dachmi, and Mohammed Qabaj report for North Africa.[55] The Lebanese mothers interviewed by Prothro said they had nursed their five-year-olds for about a year, and his data showed that boys were nursed longer than girls. (His researchers' ratings of maternal "warmth" also showed higher scores for mothers of boys than of girls). Williams reports that few infants are nursed for less than a year, and boys often for two: "Most women say they nurse until they are pregnant again. . . . The generally longer nursing period of the boy in Haouch is quite frankly explained in terms of the grater value placed upon him and the greater concern for him."[56] Najoui Sa'idallah reports that Egyptian peasant and Bedouin families relied on natural breast-feeding, for 12 to 18 months for girls and 18 to 24 months (but sometimes up to three years) for boys.[57] Other Egyptian studies, however, found no difference in the nursing of boys and girls.[58] Nawal Ammar reports that village women tried to nurse for two years, but many did not succeed because they became pregnant again, their milk dried up, or their infants weaned themselves. Over three-quarters of women in both the 25-to-34 and 35-to-45 age cohorts reported nursing for at least a year.[59] The rural and poor urban Sudanese mothers interviewed by Badri said they had nursed for an average of 15 months, and middle-class urban mothers 9 months, with "a new pregnancy" being the most frequently cited reason for weaning.[60]

Between 1976 and 1980, the World Fertility Survey conducted surveys of nursing practices with probability samples of over 15,000 mothers in Jordan, Egypt, Tunisia, and Yemen.[61] They reported that 87 (in urban Tunisia) to 98 percent (in rural Egypt) of babies were nursed in their first months of life. In urban areas, between a quarter (in Yemen) and a half (in Egypt) were still nursing at one year, and in rural areas between a half (in Yemen and Jordan) and 72 percent (in Egypt) continued to nurse. Only 4 to 17 percent still breast-fed at two years, and 1 to 8 percent (in rural Egypt) did so at three years. Nursing was generally longer in rural than urban areas, and especially so in agricultural families (an average of 20 months in rural Egypt, compared to 10 months in urban Egyptian families in which the husband had a modern occupation). Mothers reported nursing boys only slightly longer than girls. Mother's education has a powerful relationship to the duration of nursing, as in many other developing countries (see table 4.2). Studies by Egyptian researchers generally confirm Hamid Ammar's account of rural practices: nearly all mothers maintain close physical contact with their infants (including carrying and cosleeping) and breast-feed on demand for 18 to 24 months, stopping when they perceive they have again become pregnant. Lower class urban mothers tend to follow this traditional pattern, though they more often supplement breast-feeding with formula. Work outside the home, however, causes mothers to shift away from traditional practices. Urban middle-class mothers more often use bottle-feeding or supplement breast-feeding with formula, more often schedule the times for feeding, and wean an average of six months earlier.[62]

These data generally support ethnographers' reports that the traditional cultural model prescribes nursing for two years but also indicates that even in traditional milieus many children are not nursed that long, mainly because some wean themselves and others are weaned when mothers become pregnant. In addition, modernizing influences—especially mothers' education and urban residence, but also mothers' employment and use of contraceptives—dramatically shorten the duration of nursing. Educated mothers more often schedule feedings rather than nurse on demand, even in rural areas.[63] Nawal Ammar reports village women's continuation of nursing-on-demand but noted earlier supplementing of breast milk with prepared foods, and less

Table 4.2 Average Duration of Breast-Feeding in 1970s (months) by Mother's Education

	Urban Egypt	Rural Egypt	Jordan	Tunisia	Yemen
None	16	20	12	17	13
10+ years	10	14	9	8	6

maternal responsiveness than Hamid Ammar described. At least some mothers let their children cry when they knew hunger wasn't the cause, some expressing an attitude quite at odds with the pediatric model: "'Crying,' told me one informant, 'teaches the child that it cannot get everything it wants in life.'"[64] At least some educated urban mothers say they struggle against their inclinations to comfort and nurse crying infants.[65]

Nursing also is regarded as the maternal act par excellence: "a woman in the eyes of the people is specially compassionate, quite otherwise than a man," Granqvist reports: "the mother's breast is a symbol of compassion. It is said: 'A man's breast has no milk.' This means that compassion is not to be expected from a man."[66] Hamid Ammar concurs, noting that "the mother's breast is the symbol of compassion. . . . It is because women can provide their babies with milk that they are considered to be endowed with compassion."[67] He also reports that mothers offer their breast not only when their infants are hungry or fidgety but whenever it becomes "compassionate," or full. The association of breast-feeding and compassion ramifies throughout the culture, especially in rural areas. In Imeghrane and many other regions, each adult woman in a household should own a cow that she feeds and cares for and whose prized, baraka-rich dairy products she processes and provides to the men and children. Boddy notes this symbolic elaboration in northern Sudan and reports that women often said of themselves, as do women in Imeghrane, nihna behaim, "we are (like) cattle"—which she correctly sees as expressing a powerful ambivalence about their status: on the one hand, women are treated like baby- and food-producing beasts; on the other they perform the sacred function of nourishing life, which men shelter and protect at society's inner core.[68] As Ammar points out, these symbolic elaborations of nursing help forge a lifelong bond:

> Nothing is more binding in the mother-child relationship than the memories of "stomach enveloping" and "breast feeding" which are symbols invoked by mothers to remind their sons or daughters to be obedient, or to come to their help in old age. "I enveloped you for nine months and have fed you with my breast" is supposed to be one of the most effective and compelling entreaties.[69]

Other MENA researchers confirm the importance of these meanings.[70]

A MENA "Pediatric" Model ❋

Quantitative data comparable to those LeVine collected from Yoruba and Gusii or Mary Ainsworth from Ghanda are not available for MENA children, but the *traditional* model(s) of infant care and mother-child interaction clearly follow a similar pediatric model. Cederblad writes that "the child's first year may be characterized by a very intensive, almost symbiotic contact with the mother, who carries the child with her everywhere she goes, and sleeps with it beside her. The child's oral needs are probably satisfied optimally as far as sucking and physical contacts are concerned."[71] Davis notes that a great deal of mother-infant communication takes place through their physical contact, and that while mothers talk to their babies, they rarely have the kind of stimulating, face-to-face "conversations" typical of American mothers. Swaddling, nursing on demand and to quiet crying, carrying, and cosleeping coalesce to establish a protective, soothing, excitation-dampening maternal bond during the first year or so.[72] Friedl concludes that in Iran, "because the environment is considered potentially dangerous for an infant, the mother's prime responsibility is to protect and defend the baby, rather than to educate or entertain him or her."[73]

Educated, middle-class urban families are clearly shifting away from this pediatric model toward a pedagogic one. Not only do they rely less on breast-feeding and wean their infants earlier (though usually more gradually) but they also place greater emphasis on independence by having their infants sleep separately, teaching them to wash and dress themselves, and toilet-training them a good deal earlier.[74] These changes appear to be related both to the changed values that come with education, daily schedule changes associated with women's work outside their homes, and the generally smaller family size and greater housing space available with middle class or professional incomes. Nawal Ammar found village mothers following the basic pediatric pattern Hamid Ammar described 35 years earlier, but in attenuated forms—especially earlier and more gradual weaning, an earlier end to cosleeping, less immediate responsiveness to crying—all signaling further change toward a pedagogic model. The situation in poor urban milieus is complex and unclear. The quantitative data suggest a pattern "between" rural and middle-class urban practices, but ethnographic descriptions suggest that many poor families cannot practice features of the traditional model they continue to believe in and often improvise in ways that deviate from the pediatric but not in the direction of the pedagogic model.

The traditional pediatric model does not produce "passive" babies, and certainly not deprived ones.[75] Most are born into densely peopled communities of extended family and adjoining households, where visiting among neighbors and kinswomen (with their children) is common. After the 40-day seclusion period, most infants are progressively introduced to wider kin and neighborhood circles, so protective pediatric strategies typically develop into more gregarious styles. As the anthropologist Judy Brink notes of an Egyptian village:

> In large extended families adults and children, who are consistently loving and nurturing, surround infants and engage them in almost constant social interaction. These infants do not have toys to play with and do not form attachments to blankets or dolls as do American infants. They learn to play with people, not inanimate objects.[76]

Few MENA families are polygamous, and while there may be little intercourse for considerably longer than the required 40 days, postpartum abstinence does not typically last nearly as long as in many sub-Saharan societies. Mother-infant interaction appears to be somewhat less exclusive than in sub-Saharan Africa, and because birth spacing appears to be shorter, the nearly exclusive mother-infant bond (including cosleeping) tends to be of shorter duration. In addition, while most fathers do little infant care, ethnographers report that many have some affectionate, playful interaction with them on a daily basis, and in this regard MENA more closely resembles Hindu India's variant of the pediatric model than that observed in polygamous African societies.

Accounts of infant care among both Muslims and Hindus in the Indian subcontinent suggest a similar pediatric pattern. Except for colder northern regions, Indians generally use slings rather than cradles, they have similarly high levels of physical contact, sleep with their infants, and breast-feed on demand and to soothe distress. Mothers may continue nursing through the first trimester of a new pregnancy. There too, the birth of a boy gives cause for greater celebration than of a girl, and boys receive more warmth and indulgent care. The disparity in male-female mortality rates is even higher in

While mothers in traditional milieus do most of the caretaking of infants and toddlers, fathers typically spend some affectionate and playful time with them each day.

northern and central India than in the MENA,[77] indicating better care and feeding of boys, infanticide of girls, or both. Unlike babies in the arid MENA region, most Indian infants are ritually bathed every day. Observers report that infants do not always find this a pleasant experience, but it may provide an experiential foundation for the bathing purification rituals important in many sects of Hinduism.[78]

Historical sources suggest that infant care in the preindustrial Mediterranean followed a similar pediatric model, with bourgeois and noble families differing from the general populace in important respects. The Western view that infants need unindulgent, highly scheduled and structured care—much criticized by psychologists and educators in this century—did not gain ascendancy until the seventeenth and eighteenth centuries. Medieval parents generally sought to keep their infants in as womb-like conditions as possible—keeping them lightly swaddled and warm, nursing them on demand and to soothe distress into and beyond the second year, bathing them in warm water (when possible), and often sleeping with them. They differed from MENA mothers in using cradles rather than slings, especially in colder areas, which generally promotes less body-to-body contact and more face-to-face interaction, but we have no medieval-era norms for this.

In noble and urban families, however, babies often were given to wet-nurses, usually peasant women, sometimes for extended periods. The fact that many cities regulated the wages of wet-nurses testifies to their prominence, and Charles de La Ronciere reports that in the bourgeois homes of early Renaissance Tuscany,

> infants were rarely nursed by their mothers. Most were turned over to wet-nurses, only 23 percent of whom lived in their employer's home. Three out of four young children spent their first months away from home; indeed, 53 percent were not reclaimed by their families until they were at least eighteen months old.[79]

According to Shahar, records show that eighteenth-century Hamburg had 4,000 to 5,000 wet nurses in a population of 90,000, and that in eighteenth-century Paris a majority of infants may have been cared for in the homes of wet-nurses.[80] Records and written accounts indicate that peasant women nursed their own babies, and wet-nurses assisted only when mothers had insufficient milk or died. Though the evidence is fragmentary, it suggests that in the advantaged classes, nursing, close physical contact, and cosleeping did not form part of a pattern of cultivating a lifelong mother-child interdependence.[81]

Ethnographers report that boys in MENA generally receive more devoted treatment than do girls (though the quality of care also depends on birth order, the baby's temperament, and the family's welfare at the time),[82] and infant and child mortality rates indicate that girls are more likely to die than boys. Amartya Sen reports the overall female-to-male ratio to be about 0.95 in Egypt, 0.97 in North Africa, and 0.90 in Pakistan (compared to 0.94 in

China and 0.93 in India, two countries with pronounced gender bias).[83] Sub-Saharan Africa, which does not appear to have gender bias in infant care, has a female-to-male ratio of 1.02. Dachmi believes that traditional North African mothers tend to create overly symbiotic bonds with their male infants and insufficiently symbiotic bonds with their girls, but his case studies testify to the great individual variation in mothering styles and to the importance of birth order and other factors. His young patient "Fatoum" developed a range of psychosomatic symptoms in response to her mother's neglect, and Dachmi found her mother despondent that Fatoum was her third daughter without having given birth to a boy and that her husband and his family had threatened to reject her. When she did have a boy, she further withdrew to devote herself to him. Fatoum's older sister had apparently not been neglected in this manner, and eventually provided Fatoum with caretaking her mother did not.[84]

The immediate effects of MENA's pediatric model appear to be to facilitate the development of "secure attachment" and of what Erikson terms "basic trust," to soothe distress and modulate emotional excitation, and to build a strong bond of compassion and interdependence between mother and infant. When done as the model prescribes, pediatric strategies probably do enhance survival and provide psychological buffering against the sufferings of often-chronic skin, respiratory, and intestinal diseases. The longer term psychological effects of pediatric infant care have mainly to do with the meanings of maternal caretaking as these are elaborated during later childhood, adolescence, and adulthood. To the extent that the pediatric model's idealized bond of compassion is realized, this probably lays the emotional, tactile, and kinesthetic foundation for the rich metaphors of maternal compassion that weave throughout the culture. It establishes a core of "indulged dependence" that appears as a feature of most hierarchical dyadic relationships. This broadly resembles the sort of interdependence described by G. Morris Carstairs, Sudhir Kakar, Alan Roland, Stanley Kurtz, and others for Hindu India,[85] and by Takeo Doi, Richard Beardsley and colleagues, George DeVos, Takie Lebra, and others for Japan.[86] As the maternal bond is subsequently elaborated, it also probably anchors the protective secluding and covering of virgins and mothers that characterizes circum-Mediterranean cultures. And it probably inspires the vision of life as begun with a sundering from the *rahim*, womb/maternal compassion, as sustained by the compassion of *rahem*, kindred/uterine kin, and as culminating in a reuniting with God, *al rahaman*, the Merciful, *al rahim*, the Compassionate,[87] that distinctively characterizes Arab-Muslim cultures.

Debate: Weaning and Its Discontents ✻

Weaning marks the key transition from a period of intensely protective maternal caretaking to wider social interaction within the household. Especially when a mother has another child, weaning effectively ends the pediatric period. This happens frequently, as throughout the region women often try to continue nursing until they become pregnant again and then wean abruptly because they believe that pregnancy poisons the mother's milk for the nursing child.[88] While the shift from nearly exclusive maternal care to a wider circle of caretakers tends to take place gradually, most ethnographers describe the act of weaning as typically abrupt and often traumatic. Hamid Ammar reports that "mothers in Silwa recognize weaning as a 'traumatic experience' for the child and do their best to absorb the child's attention in other directions."[89] Marriane Cederblad writes that "weaning, although begun late, is a traumatic period in the baby's life. The child is moved away from the mother's bed in conjunction with weaning so that it will 'forget' the breast."[90] Davis writes that in the Moroccan town she studied,

> the process of weaning is very abrupt; the mother chooses a day, paints her breasts with liver bile or hot pepper to discourage the child, and from that point does not nurse it again. . . . It is recognized that weaning is difficult for the child . . . [and] women say of a newly weaned child "now he knows that *ghder* (treachery, betrayal) exists in the world."[91]

Egyptian researchers have identified "sudden," "arbitrary/inconsistent," and "gradual" styles of weaning in all milieus, but sudden weaning with the use of bitter herbs on the nipples (by about one-third of mothers) is commonly reported in rural and more traditional urban families, and gradual weaning is more common among urban working and educated mothers.[92] Sa'idallah reported that Egyptian peasant and Bedouin mothers did not differ in weaning styles, with about half taking a "gradual" approach and half weaning "suddenly" with bitter herbs.[93] Al Nawayseh reports the widespread use of bitter herbs to wean infants quickly in traditional Jordan.[94] Lebanese mothers told Prothro that they weaned their infants in "one or two days." Many said they used bitter substances on their breasts or sent their infant to stay with a relative for a few days, both of which are regarded as "severe" weaning practices in cross-cultural comparisons.[95] "Lebanese are abrupt weaners by world norms," he reports, and "Lebanese infants often respond unfavorably to this abrupt treatment."[96] The mothers' reports showed the same pattern observed in studies of Americans—the longer children are nursed, the more likely they are to experience distress at weaning: "Of 131 children weaned at eleven months or later, 70 had *much* emotional upset over weaning. Of 231 weaned before eleven months, only 30 had *much* emotional upset over weaning."[97] Friedl's observations are worth quoting at some length:

> Weaning is a traumatic affair for most children and their families. The intention of mother's weaning strategies are to make her breasts so distasteful that the child gives up nursing on its own, without

fuss—a strategy that never seems to work smoothly. Behrokh colored her breasts bright red with ink to frighten little Leila: Leila would lift her mother's skirt, look in horror at the red blotches, start to scream, drop the shirt, lift it again, throw a tantrum, and start all over again. Amene said, "Pheew, yecch, ugly, dirty, hit it!" whenever her two-year-old son was nursing, to make an "enemy" of her breast. He played along by hitting the breast and saying "pheew," but then laughed and continued to nurse, occasionally, for another six months. Shahrbanu put pepper on her nipples to hurt her weanling's mouth; he screamed and pummeled her for almost a week. Zari daubed her breasts with bitter juice of an herb to make her weanling spit, as did Afi with lime juice: the children licked, spat, howled, then nursed anyway. Banu hid her breasts under buttoned garments to make them "unaccessible like a buried treasure." Her son poked a hole in the cardigan, ripped her shirt, and found the pot of gold, she said.[98]

In Imeghrane, weaning typically was done in a day or two, usually with the mother putting foul-tasting herbs on her nipples. Tantrums and regression (from walking to crawling, for example) were common, and many children who had eaten little solid food before being weaned lost weight and weakened before they developed appetites for it. Our analysis of census and household survey data in selected villages suggested there may even be an increase in mortality in the second year, possibly following weaning. As in Lebanon, some infants are sent to stay with relatives in other households or even in other villages until they "forget their mother's milk."

Ethnographers consistently report that Indian mothers similarly continue nursing as long as possible, but observers differ in their perceptions of whether weaning tends to be gradual or abrupt. Prolonged breast-feeding and abrupt weaning is practiced in most of sub-Saharan Africa, and this combination has given rise to much debate about its effects on personality development. A couple of now classic studies[99] found that while weaning often occasions short-term distress (especially if it occurs in the second year, when attachment is most intense), most children have attachments to other caretakers and it causes no long-term difficulties. Attachment, these studies concluded, is based in the overall pattern of communication, not just nursing.[100] LeVine and colleagues nonetheless conclude from a variety of developmental indices that the second year of life "can be a difficult emotional transition period." The Gusii child

> is no longer cared for as a baby, is sometimes yearning for the mother . . . , and is often not ready to become part of the children's group. Furthermore, weaning in the middle of this year poses a nutritional problem, because the replacement of breast milk with protein-rich foods (cow's milk, meat, eggs) is by no means universal.[101]

Ethnographers continue to make observations like Friedl's:

> The baby likely will sate itself on tea and sugar, it likely will have cried itself to sleep more or less hungry long before dinner is ready; tough food such as meat, rare as it is for everybody, or bread, cannot be chewed easily by the weanling—by the time the baby has swallowed a few half-chewed bites dinner will be over. Not only is the inadequate food supply traumatic for the child but so is the sudden withdrawal of the maternal pacifier, which had helped the younger baby to cope with frustrations. So many weanlings are "weak, thin, cranky," that this conditions just about describes a weaned child in Deh Koh; a postulated norm ascribed to a developmental stage perpetuates parental behavior that brings about this norm.[102]

North African psychologists have engaged in an instructive debate about this pattern of prolonged breast-feeding and abrupt weaning.[103] In *Sevrages et Interdependence* (Weaning and Interdependence), the psychiatrist Assia Msefer works with a theory drawn from Klein and Winnicott that holds that healthy development requires mothers to cultivate an illusion that their infants possess them and can depend on their protection, and then to gradually undertake a process of disillusionment that allows a toddler to separate, discover reality, and form relationships with others. She argues that what I have termed the pediatric pattern, terminated by abrupt weaning, tends to intensify fear of abandonment and to promote an illusory idealization of the mother and defensive dependence on this idealized image in all of its rich cultural elaborations. Because women ultimately depend on their sons, they tend to cultivate interdependence with them more intensely and for a longer duration than they do with daughters. She believes that because women's power, enjoyment, and self-regard are traditionally so constrained to reproducing, nurturing, and feeding, nursing tends to become the primary anchor of mother-son interdependence, highly sensual and deeply enjoyed by both. This leaves boys especially unprepared for weaning, she believes, and for the displacement by a new baby that often occasions it.[104]

Msefer thus believes boys maintain their attachment in the face of loss by developing an idealized image of the mother, who becomes "the priceless object" and "mysteriously symbolizes the community of the family."[105] This marks the first and crucial step in the reproduction of the patriarchal order. "A woman is idealized to the extent that she is a mother, and devalued to the extent to that she is a woman,"[106] she writes, so that the idealized mother "has no need of individuality."[107] This anchors the matrifocal character of the patriarchal order, as the son "internalizes an idealized image of his mother, which justifies the fact that he solicits her to choose his wife, and to make general decisions about his family life."[108] Defensive as it is, she believes this "dependent attitude" consists of ambivalent, oscillating inclinations to submit and revolt. Msefer also suggests that prolonged and abruptly terminated indulgence roots the pervasive fear of the Eye, the *jinn* spirits, and other malevolent beings, which represent both the sense of vulnerability that the mother once soothed and rage at her loss that has been projected.

Rouchdi Chamcham also draws on Winnicott to make a similar argument, suggesting that an extended period of indulgence terminated by "the brutality of weaning" often creates a developmental crisis that is not easily resolved: "Most infants pass on to the following stage without having integrated their impulses, or resolved problems related to their dependence, their sense of success, their self-esteem, their self-affirmation, their individuality, or their control and sublimation of aggression."[109] Dachmi makes this case in even stronger terms, drawing on the psychoanalytic writings of Klein, Lacan, and Mahler, as well as Winnicott, to argue that the overly symbiotic nurturing of boys undermines the separation-individuation process, and that the trauma of abrupt weaning prompts a splitting of maternal representations, producing via projection both celebrated images of the Good Mother and the culture's terrifying ogresses and female *jinns*.[110] In traditional North Africa, he concludes,

> when the individual has to dissolve and disappear into the group, individual narcissism into familial and group narcissism, and the individual ego-ideal into the group ego-ideal, the individual ego— when it is totally based on external reality and crushed by the super-ego—cannot in any case aspire to autonomy and independence.[111]

Camille Lacoste-Dujardin believes "symbiotic" and highly sensual mothering undermines individuation,[112] and Ghita El Khayat-Bennai similarly views the "symbiotic" attachment of the first year, broken by "brutal" weaning, as creating "a grave syndrome of abandonment" that, because of the difficult transition to adult foods, appears to increase mortality in the second year (as LeVine noted among Gusii).[113] But both also note that in traditional large families the loss may be eased by mothering from the many other women in the family's interior: Lacoste-Dujardin suggests that this fosters immersion in the familial group rather than individuation.[114] The psychologist Abedelatif Chaouite develops this latter point to take issue with the trauma and undermined-individuation view. He concurs that weaning does tend to be sudden and requires an infant to make a difficult transition, but he rejects the interpretation that it amounts to "a weaning trauma that leaves in the Moroccan an indelible mark of an intense frustration" and critically "affects the personality of the adult Moroccan."[115] Rather, he believes that families typically recognize the significance and difficulty of the transition, and rally around to take the mother's place as primary caretaker.

The expansion of the toddler's attachments entails "a veritable restructuring of its entire relational universe," but "to the infant's benefit. It brings about its social integration." In place of the mother-infant dyad, "weaning introduces the infant to the enlarged, culture-bearing group."[116] While ethnographers report that fathers rarely perform tasks like diapering, they concur that fathers often spend a good deal of time holding and playing with young children, especially in the six-month to two-year range, and we certainly saw Imeghrane fathers (and uncles and grandfathers) make extra efforts to entertain those being weaned. Chaouite also draws on Winnicott to make the intriguing suggestion that, especially in the absence of attachments to toys and things, the familial group serves as a "transitional object" that facilitates a gradual, developmentally appropriate process of dis-illusionment, still anchored in a continuing relationship with the mother, who hardly withdraws completely at weaning. Since weaning typically takes place during the second year when the toddler is learning to speak, the intensely physical relationship with the mother progressively gives way to primarily verbal relationships with family group members and an identification with the household.

Chaouite believes the extended family continues to play an important psychological role for adults: "It continues to offer a substitute for the warmth and security of the first object relation. It could be said that 'the group bosom' replaces the maternal bosom, and serves in the traditional social structure to regulate individual and group tensions, and to protect one against the threats of depression."[117] He suggests that the identification with the household forms a "group self" that serves as a psychological "bridge" from the interdependent maternal dyad to the larger society beyond the family. Yet this strength also brings a danger: that one may lose the support of one's family group, a "narcissistic wound" that always hovers in possibility.

Western developmental psychologists concur that the establishment of a style of attachment is one of the most important features of infancy and early childhood. A variety of procedures have been developed for assessing attachment style: the most prominent is based on the work of Ainsworth (who studied Ugandan as well as American children),[118] which distinguishes "secure" attachment (roughly 60 to 65 percent of middle-class American one-year-olds) from three forms of "insecure" attachment: "avoidant" (associated with unavailable and rejecting styles of parenting), "resistant" (associated with inconsistently available parenting), and "disorganized" (often associated with parental neglect and abuse).[119] It is clear that cultures differ in the percentages of these attachment styles that their parenting yields, and in the *kinds* of attachment they promote.[120] I have been unable to locate research on these specific attachment styles in MENA societies, and because infants acclimate to particular kinds of parental interaction and separation, procedures that have become standard for assessing attachment in the West—such as the "Strange Situation"[121]—would probably need to be revised for use in MENA contexts.

Still, a close examination of the sharp difference of opinion over the traumatic versus developmental effects of "symbiotic mothering" terminated by abrupt weaning suggests a synthesis of researchers' seemingly opposed views. First, all observers seem to concur that this sequence creates a developmental discontinuity, and as Erikson and others have emphasized, it is the synchrony of culturally patterned discontinuities with biological and cognitive changes (walking and talking, in this case) that fashions a milestone developmental "task." But individuals—rather than "the culture"—go through the weaning transition. They bring their individual temperaments and idiosyncratic experiences to it, and they pass through it via diverse routes. The task probably generates individual variation, producing both the culturally specific norm of health (secure attachment to extended family members and to the family as a group) and pathological distress (basic mistrust, anxious attachment, and a "splitting" of maternal images). As psychotherapists, Msefer and Dachmi see a good deal of pathology, while Chaouite observes mostly nonclinical families, and these different sources of data probably shape their contrasting views.

It may be relevant in this regard that Cederblad found a lower prevalence of behavior disorders among Sudanese (and Nigerian) children than among Swedish (including psychosomatic symptoms, anxiety, depression, aggression, lying, stealing, hyperactivity, and tics), in spite of their objectively more stressful environments, with poor nutrition and health, a lack of toys and recreational facilities, inadequate schools, and frequent physical punishment. She believes that a range of supportive factors increase the resilience of Sudanese children, especially strong attachment fostered by "the early mother-child relation" that can have "far-reaching preventive effects," the extended family system that provides support when parents cannot, the low rate of divorce, and the strong religious beliefs that "give a sense of coherence to adults and children" and "increase stress resilience."[122]

Second, Msefer, Dachmi, and Chaouite all believe that the extended family typically becomes an important "object" to the weaned child. And here Mediterranean ethnographies suggest that over and above people's attachments to individual members of their households, they become attached to the "house" as an idealized, honor-bearing entity that persists through generations as individuals come and go. Many of the Moroccans I interviewed showed strong attachments to their "houses," which also served as what some theorists refer to as a "self object": an Other in which one participates and derives a sense of self (Dachmi's "narcissisme familial"; Chaouite's "group self"). This certainly does not coalesce in early childhood, but configurations of attachments, anxieties, and idealizations developed then may provide the experiential foundation of later identities and loyalties.

Third, ethnographers working throughout MENA and the circum-Mediterranean describe the house as built symbolically of a patriarchal skeleton protecting a near-sacred matrifocal heart and bosom, and the experiential foundation of these gender-based metaphoric elaborations also may be laid in the first three years. The culture's extensive repertoire of body idioms used to characterize family, house, patronymic association, and larger groupings (up to and including the state) may be rooted in the physical, tactile, and kinesthetic experiences of early childhood. Intensely physical pediatric infant care and the weaning transition do not *cause* these idioms to develop, but they probably do shape emotional and relational contours of core personality, which adults then can draw upon as they imagine and represent their social groupings and communities and their identities within them.

Sources ❀

The most extensive English-language accounts of traditional child care continue to be Hilma Granqvist's *Birth and Childhood Among the Arabs*,[123] based on fieldwork in a Palestinian village in the 1920s, Hamed Ammar's *Growing Up in an Egyptian Village*,[124] based on fieldwork in a Nile village in the 1950s, and Edwin Prothro's *Child Rearing in Lebanon*,[125] based on interviews with mothers and testing of their five-year-olds in Beirut and three Beqaa Valley towns in the 1950s. Egyptian researchers followed Ammar's work with a series of large questionnaire studies in the 1960s and 1970s, including several directed by Mahmoud Abdelqader,[126] Naguib Askandar,[127] and teams from Egypt's National Research Center.[128] 'Alia Shakri summarized these (and other studies) in 1992, emphasizing that they generally confirm Ammar's fieldwork but also find important urban-rural and social class variations.[129] Sa'idallah's comparative study in the early 1980s of nomadic Bedouin, settled Bedouin, and village families in rural Egypt found both similarities and differences among these groups, as well as important differences between social classes.[130] In the mid-1980s, Nawal Ammar restudied the Egyptian village her father studied 35 years earlier, and her dissertation, *An Egyptian Village Growing Up*, documents important changes and continuities that probably have occurred throughout the region.

Mohammed Johari's 1992 *Al-tifl fi al-turath al-sha'bi* (The Child in Popular Tradition) and Naif Al Nawayseh's 1997 *Al-tofal fi al-hiyat al-sh'abia al-ardania* (The Child in Popular Life in Jordan) provide important background on traditional views of children in Egypt and Jordan respectively, as does Mohamed Sijilmassi's 1984 *Enfants du Maghreb* for North Africa. Samia Sati's 1979 study of naming in Egypt documents parents' shifting hopes for children in response to historical events and modern opportunities.[131] Erika Friedl's *Children of Deh Koh* and "Child Rearing in Modern Persia" provide recent observations from a rural Iranian village, and Judy Brink's "Changing Child-Rearing Patterns in an Egyptian Village" gives an account of current attitudes and practices in rural Egypt. Homa Hoodfar's "Child Care and Child Health in Low-Income Neighborhoods of Cairo" presents observations of a poor urban milieu, and Susan Davis's *Patience and Power* provides a description of the life-cycle in a Moroccan small town. John Akin and colleagues' "Breastfeeding Patterns and Determinants in the Near East" reports findings from surveys of mothers in Jordan, Tunisia, Yemen, and Egypt in the late 1970s. Marianne Cederblad's 1968 *Child Psychiatric Study on Sudanese Arab Children* assessed psychiatric symptoms in all of the 1,700 children in three villages near Khartoum, and contains a brief but useful description of early child care. Her followup 15 years later enabled her to track changes with urbanization (see chapter 6) and compare Sudanese children with Nigerian and Swedish counterparts.[132] Gasim Badri interviewed 150 Sudanese mothers of five-year-olds in the mid-1970s, documenting urban-rural differences and social status.[133] Several North African psychologists have discussed the possibly traumatic consequences of the predominant pattern of infant care, which entails "symbiotic" maternal caretaking ended by abrupt weaning, especially Assia Msefer's *Sevrages et Interdependences*, Abdeslam Dachmi's *De La Seduction Maternelle Negative*, Ghita El Khayat-Bennai's *Le Monde Arabe au Feminin*, Rouchidi Chamcham's "L'enfant marocain," and Abdellatif Chaouite's "L'enfant Marocain: Horizon d'une pensee psychologique."

CHAPTER *5*

Early Childhood

When "pediatric" infant-care practices successfully protect against the many threats to survival, they cultivate basic trust and a "symbiotic" interdependence similar to that Sudhir Kakar describes for Hindu India and Takeo Doi for Japan. In traditional MENA milieus, weaned toddlers then move into much less predictable worlds: of hunger that is less reliably satisfied, of nearly continuous ailments and discomforts, and of fears of dangerous creatures and invisible beings—conditions found many preindustrial societies. Toddlers often find themselves competing for attention, affection, and prized foods, and for boys, at least, this competition may be intensified by shaming comparisons with siblings, relatives, and peers. Girls take on housework and caretaking responsibilities that both curtail their freedom and enable them to make valuable contributions to the household; boys are mostly left to play.

Observers report that many toddlers develop an interactional style of "assertive dependency" in response to the diminution of secure care, which cross-cultural research suggests is common to large families in complex agricultural societies. This style appears similar to the "amae"-ing that Doi describes in Japan, where he believes that assertively evoking caretaking and indulgence not only sustains an important measure of interdependence but represents a step toward learning to manage the "master-apprentice"-type relationships that are characteristic of Japanese society. Boys and girls in MENA also are taught to "hashim": to show modesty and politeness calibrated to situations and kin relations. Learning "hashim" and assertive dependence appear to lay a foundation for interaction styles later used to negotiate kinship and patron-client relationships, and for gender-appropriate styles of honor and modesty.

As extended family members rally around to provide nourishing care in conditions of scarcity, security in an increasingly frightening environment, and compassion in response to physical discomfort and emotional distress, toddlers readily develop attachments to relatives and to the familial "house," which can serve as personality-anchoring "transitional" and "self" objects. As children are enclosed—protectively and controllingly—by a circle of men with whom they have relatively little but typically affectionate contact, a broadened and increasingly idealized matrifocal interdependence easily deepens during this period. Traditional MENA milieus appear to facilitate "core" personality orientations anchored in this matrifocal interdependence and in its extension throughout the extended family hierarchy—via "apprenticeship-and-obedience" styles of caretaking (often by siblings, grandparents, and others) and via "assertively dependent" styles of eliciting nurturance. Deliberately evoked fears of visible and invisible dangers reinforce the protective dimension of matrifocal interdependence and may facilitate "externalized" styles of managing anxiety.

As with infant care, it is not clear how "modernizing" influences are affecting this traditional pattern. All studies show important social class differences in socialization, and suggest that middle-class urban families are moving toward Western-style pedagogic models. The situation in poor urban families appears complex, as many cannot follow either traditional or modern models.

The chapter ends with a discussion of circumcision, which is typically performed toward the end of this period for boys, and in some areas for girls (mainly Egypt, Sudan, and Somalia). Accounts indicate that many children experience circumcision as a potentially traumatic injury, but neither its immediate nor long-term psychological effects have been well studied. By design it inscribes a purifying mark that charts a boy's destiny as a masculine man and, for the girls who undergo it, as a fertile, feminine woman. The theories of Nancy Chodorow, John Whiting, and Gilbert Herdt may help explain the meanings of circumcision and its influence on the subsequent course of gender development, especially for men: that boys must renounce and "repress" feminine senses of self that have been developed during intense maternal infant care, and that girls must renounce strivings held to be masculine in order to sustain their early feminine identifications.

Introduction ❀

The loose coordination of weaning, walking, and talking mark the transition from infancy to toddlerhood, or from what Margaret Mead termed the "lap child" to the "yard child." I will treat this as the beginning of early childhood, a period that typically lasts until the ages of five to seven, when important, biologically driven cognitive and emotional transitions take place. My definition of these periods also corresponds to those that Qabaj reports are recognized in North African folk beliefs about childhood.[1] Most cultures time major shifts in child-rearing with these transitions—including in modern societies, entrance into formal schooling at the age of five or six.

Hamid Ammar identifies several characteristics of the postweaning period in traditional milieus that other MENA ethnographers have observed as well: a decline in maternal attention as older siblings take over caretaking responsibilities, a "preoccupation" with food, sibling rivalry and competition, entrance into older children's play groups, fears of spirit beings (ogres, *jinn* spirits, Satan, the Evil Eye) and visible dangers (like jackals and scorpions), and circumcision (for boys throughout MENA and for girls in some areas). In addition, important gender differences are established during this period, and by its end male and female development diverges in important respects. In more traditional milieus, boys and girls are treated in increasingly different ways, assigned different tasks, and guided into different social environments. Gender identities are underscored, usually toward the end of this period, by the circumcision of boys and, in some areas, of girls—rites that "purify" them. These influences appear to be especially important for further shaping features of *core* or *level 1* personality, some of which establish attachment and interaction styles that subsequently will be elaborated into social personae, and some of which may require suppression or transformation in order to acquire the sentiments, motives, and social personae associated with the honor-modesty and Islamic ethical systems (see chapter 3).

Many of these influences on development differ from those typically studied as shaping American middle-class children during this period: parental and preschool promotion of cognitive development, play with same-age peers, nuclear versus single-parent rearing, television viewing, and play with toys. The Western children studied by developmental psychologists generally are not chronically hungry or cared for by older siblings, and their parents generally try to discourage sibling rivalry and to reassure them that monsters and bogeymen do not exist. Western children experience nothing comparable to circumcision in early childhood (though one could speculate about the whether injuries and medical procedures might have similar effects). These features make early childhood in MENA much different—at least in more traditional milieus—from that depicted in Western developmental psychology texts. We can again use LeVine's terminology to capture these differences in broad terms: while Western middle-class parents continue to follow a *pedagogic model* that appears to be designed to prepare their children for school, MENA parents traditionally shift gradually from a *pediatric model* of infant care to an *apprenticeship-and-obedience* model of child-rearing.[2]

Toddlers in traditional milieus receive much of their care from older siblings and amble about in mixed-age groups of children—which Barbara Rogoff believes provides important opportunities for "apprenticeship" learning that is nearly absent in Western middle-class contexts.[3] Further, in such traditional milieus, caretakers typically manage children by giving directions and expecting obedience rather than offering choices and encouraging exploration. Apprenticeship-and-obedience models appear to be common to many preindustrial societies—including Hindu India, most of Africa, and premodern Europe—but, as the Whitings' research shows, there are important variations in how apprenticeship learning and obedience are practiced.[4] As Davis describes, MENA parents begin teaching the concept of *hashim* during this period, and the rudiments of modesty and politeness toward seniors that *hashim* entails[5]—beginning the child's development of level 2 characteristics that become a central focus of socialization in late childhood.

It also is clear that the traditional pattern is changing. Many studies show that higher status, more "modernized" families are moving toward variants of the pedagogic model.[6] Part 1 of this chapter will examine patterns of attachment and social behavior, and part 2 will focus on gender development and the diverging developmental paths of boys and girls. The chapter concludes with the debate over the processes by which gender identities develop, and over the role that circumcision rites may play in "inscribing" them.

Part 1: Attachments and Social Behavior ✿

Maternal Caretaking

After weaning, toddlers remain mainly in the company of women, girls, and other small children. The division of labor by gender tends to be nearly total, with men working outside and women inside,[7] and houses are designed to separate men's spaces (usually an outer room or verandah) from women's (courtyards, kitchens, and rooftops in the cities, though wealthier families have additional rooms). Toddlers spend nearly all of their time in the women's areas, especially houses' central courtyards or the alleyways outside the house, under the loose supervision of slightly older siblings, cousins, or neighbors. Ethnographers report that fathers spend little time with their infants and toddlers and do little caretaking, but many point out that their attachment and influence may be significant. Davis writes: "Moroccan men are more open about displaying affection toward small children than are their American counterparts."[8] Badri notes that MENA fathers' reputation for being "severe and aloof" does not characterize their relations with infants and toddlers.[9] Fathers often lavish affection on toddlers at the beginning and end of the day, and yard children often wander freely into the men's areas. Badri reports that nearly all of the Sudanese mothers of five-year-olds he interviewed

> described the relationship between the father and his children as a relationship of love and affection, irrespective of the sex of the child. ... Moreover, the majority of the mothers said that their husbands carried their children, played with them and kissed them. ... Furthermore, the mothers reported that the child usually got excited when the father came back home.[10]

Older sisters or female cousins from age 5 to 15 often become a toddler's primary caretakers, carrying them on their backs, cleaning and feeding them, and taking them along on errands. Toddlers may sleep with these caretakers, or with grandmothers or aunts, who also may help out during the day. Mothers certainly continue to provide some care and affection, and Prothro found that the majority of Lebanese five-year-olds had never been apart from their mothers for as long as 24 hours.[11] But the amount of labor required to run a household remains very large, and mothers may have little time and energy available for personal attention to any weaned child. Williams notes that

> in the customarily very large Haouch families, as the younger child is displaced by the arrival of the next one, he becomes a part of what struck me as a rather undifferentiated, anonymous group of inter- mediate children. . . . By the age of one and a half or two, when a new baby is born, the child's arena shifts from the mother's side to the neighborhood world of children. A five- or six-year-old sis- ter, or if such is unavailable, a cousin or reluctant older brother, is charged with the small child's care. Lugged on the older one's back or hip or safely settled on the periphery of the play group, he thus spends the better part of his waking hours.[12]

Friedl notes that in the Iranian village she studied, "toddlers are in a sort of limbo: they are considered 'sweetest' in this phase, and their parents become very attached to them, but at the same time their physical care is most ne- glected, especially if they must compete with older siblings and new babies."[13] Prothro also found that Lebanese mothers spend much less time with weaned children, and the decrease in quantity appears to reflect a change in feeling as well. He asked whether the mothers found infants or older children a greater source of pleasure, and almost three-quarters said they preferred infants. Badri got the same response to this question from Sudanese mothers, and reports that a large majority disapprove of their toddlers "following them and stick- ing close."[14] Prothro believes that infants experience a "cultural discontinu- ity" in the transition to the postweaning world:

> The early period of attention and general indulgence is followed by one of comparative indifference and reserve. The security and ha- ven of the mother's arms are followed by a state of much less emo- tional warmth. . . . [In the second or third year] the "dethronement" of the infant not only follows weaning, but is also quite commonly coincidental with the birth of the next child. Thus the child learns at an early age to associate indulgence with oral gratification, and deprivation with the presence of a sibling.[15]

In the mid-1980s Sigman and Wachs assessed the nutritional status and coded samples of caretaking of 153 Egyptian and 110 Kenyan toddlers for a year beginning at 18 months of age.[16] Both samples were from farming communities, but parents in about half of the Egyptian families had nonfarm occupations and a quarter were "high SES" (socioeconomic status). They found generally similar patterns of caretaking in Egypt and Kenya, with two noteworthy exceptions that, they suggest, may be related to nutritional differences: with an average daily intake of 1,119 calories, the Egyptian toddlers fell below recommended minimums, but were not malnourished, as were the Kenyan infants, with an average intake of 848 calories. First, maternal caretaking declined over the year in both cultures, but there was a corresponding increase in sibling caretaking in Kenya that did not occur in Egypt. Second, Kenyan mothers gave more intensive caretaking to their most poorly nourished toddlers, while the poorly nourished Egyptian toddlers received *less* caretaking.[17] It was not clear whether this reflected a rejection of toddlers in poorer health or the negative health consequences of decreased caretaking.

On the basis of her 1983–84 study of child-rearing in an Egyptian village, the anthropologist Judy Brink believes the general pattern of toddler care resembles that described by Whiting and Edwards as "inconsistent

Many ethnographers report that early childhood can be a difficult period of emotional distress and poor health, especially for toddlers who have been displaced by a new infant (such as the girl in the rear) and weaned to unclean water and food.

nurturance" in North India (other ethnographies of India lend support to this view).[18] Weaning brings the "wonderful world of indulgence" to an end: she writes:

> A new infant typically occupies the mother and weaned children are turned over to child caretakers. As soon as children can walk they join groups of children who play in the street and children no longer spend all their time with the mother. . . . As in India the uneducated mothers respond intermittently to their children's demands for comfort, care and attention and often only after delays and persistent crying. . . . Most mothers are inconsistent, sometimes hitting the child and sometimes giving in.[19]

She believes this encourages an aggressive style of dependency, as toddlers often must evoke maternal caretaking.[20] Survey studies of Egyptian[21] and Syrian[22] parents indeed find that a majority of mothers in traditional milieus at least sometimes resort to hitting their toddlers. Friedl gives a similar account of Iranian toddlers:

> A weaned child is supposed to participate in adult routines for eating and sleeping. As adult routines (late bedtime, late dinners) and diet (tough, chewy foods, much consumption of tea and sugar) are unsuitable for young children, toddlers often deteriorate physically, becoming weak, cranky, and demanding. Their only strategy for gaining attention is whining; yet, because whining is considered "normal" for this age, it is largely ignored or punished.[23]

It is important to emphasize that the development of an "assertively dependent" interaction style varies by household composition, the mother's education, the child's birth order, and other factors. But when mothers have many children and much work, toddlers easily may find maternal affection to be a "limited good" for which they compete with other siblings. At the same time, they may find the diffuse affection of multiple caretakers to be bountiful.[24] Nawal Ammar makes the interesting observation that by the 1980s, at least some toddlers compensated for their "deprivation from mother" not only by "forming other primary family bonds" but by eating candy bars, watching TV, and playing with toys.[25]

Poor Health and Fears of Invisible Beings

Hamid Ammar and Friedl note the general sickliness of two- to four-year-old children in the villages they studied, and report that parents view this period as one of nearly continuous illness and discomfort. Ammar believes that decreased postweaning care contributes to the high mortality rate among one- to four-year-olds,[26] and LeVine and colleagues found that rural Kenyan children show declines on some developmental measures in the year or so after weaning.[27] Nutrition, sanitation, and health care in many rural villages and urban neighborhoods remain poor, and the fact that weaned children drink more water, crawl and play in areas with manure and garbage, eat with dirty hands, and share food with other children exposes them to illnesses from which nursing provided a measure of protection. Cederblad's team's medical examination of Sudanese children found over one-third of three- to six-year-olds to be "weak and ill" with serious health problems. A quarter had recurrent diarrhea or blood in their feces, reflecting the high prevalence of parasites. Nearly a quarter had vomiting and lack of appetite.[28] Friedl describes conditions in Deh Koh that resemble those we observed in many Imeghrane villages:

> Toddlers have "colds, fever, diarrhea all the time," says Hurijan. . . . According to various physicians who have practiced in Deh Koh over the years, children suffer from avitaminosis, protein deficiencies, subnutrition, chronic internal parasitic infections including giardiasis and amoebiasis (in 1994 100 percent of Deh Koh's children were infected, many with multiple intestinal infections), respiratory infections, eczema, cuts and bruises, bone fractures, eye diseases, toothaches. . . . All drinking water in Deh Koh is polluted with parasites, according to administrative officials. Eating dirt [a sign of malnutrition] is as much a part of children's expected behavior as whining.[29]

Infectious diseases such as polio, mumps, whooping cough, measles, and chicken pox traditionally struck in these years and killed many children already weakened by poor nutrition. Only in the last decade or two have vaccination programs begun to reach most poor and rural children. In the large Imeghrane village we studied, women who had completed their childbearing had birthed an average 8.4 children, nearly three of whom died before age five. Most women had experiences like that of Asiye, in the village Friedl studied:

> My son had just learned to walk and talk when he got measles. He was burning with fever, lying on my skirt folds while I was baking bread. I had no choice: seven, eight people to feed every day. I cried, looking at him burning up next to me. Once in a while I put my ear to his chest to see if his heart was beating still. When it stopped, I let him lie there, next to me, until I was finished with the bread. Then I washed him and we buried him.[30]

In traditional milieus, many childhood ailments are believed to be caused by *jinns* and the Evil Eye, and anxious parents take a great many precautions—including, unfortunately, leaving them dirty and unkempt so that the Eye won't be drawn to them. Toddlers' environments are full of dangers: glowing embers and precariously balanced pots of boiling water, scorpions and snakes, open wells and irrigation canals, butane stoves and lights, and, in the new cities, cars, electric appliances, and construction sites. They also find themselves in a world alive with invisible dangers. As they learn to walk and talk, parents frequently invoke the dangers of *jinn* spirits, *ghouls* (ogres), *afrits* (giants), strangers, and lunatics to control them. Before television, nights often ended with elders telling fairy tales that featured these beings, and by the age of five or six, most children have known or seen the frightening spectacle of people said to be possessed (who have epileptic seizures or display seizure-like fits of psychological origin). "The instilling of fear is one of the expedients that parents constantly use to repress their children and make them docile," Hamid Ammar writes. "Parents also scare their children by threatening them with dangerous creatures like scorpions and snakes. They scold them by saying, 'May you be bitten by a scorpion or a snake.'"[31] He also reports: "Fear responses were quite striking during the Rorschach testing of the children, as revealed by the frequent occurrence of responses such as 'silowa' [ogre], 'ghoul,' 'scorpion,' 'snake,' 'wolf,' 'fire,' and 'blood,' many of which do not actually match the blots chosen."[32] Williams makes similar observations about the use of fear in Haouch, noting that "the ferocious beast is also a common threat but so is the doctor and his needle!"[33]

Toddlers' newfound legs and speech thus carry them into an enchanted but dangerous wider world. They hear some charming fairy tales of poor peasant girls who miraculously marry princes, but truly malevolent forces tend to prevail in the tales they're told, which often resemble those collected by the Grimm brothers and often don't end sweetly. They also prevail in their parents' threats, in the illnesses, deformities, seizures, and deaths they learn are caused by spirit beings, and probably in fears for their own health. Western psychologists know relatively little about the effects of poor health, untreated chronic ailments, and nearly continual exposure to heat, cold, and insects when *not* associated with a syndrome of abuse or neglect. But illnesses, injuries, discomforts, and deaths of other household members, together with the protective measures and disciplinary use of invisible beings, probably increase a sense of bodily vulnerability and form the foundation for the *externalized* interpretation and management of anxiety that religious and folk practices later elaborate into systems of self-care.

Hunger, Food, and Blessedness

In a pair of paragraphs that easily go unnoticed, Hamid Ammar remarks on "the striking interest and respect" toddlers develop for food:

> This shows itself in the children's ordinary conversation, in the amount of details they give in relating folk story with food themes occurring in it, in their excessive delight in telling about a good meal that they had or that they are going to have. . . . Feasts and ceremonies are first recalled as occasions for excessive good food. Even in

both adults' and children's dreams, food is an important element in their manifest content.[34]

Prothro also was struck by this preoccupation. He gave the five-year-olds a "Uses Test," designed to assess children's "cultural orientation" by asking what a series of common objects are used for:

> The most striking feature of the responses of Lebanese children was the frequency with which they referred to food or to eating. For them hands and mouth are to eat with, birds and trees provide food, and even mountains are places to grow food. There were more food responses than all other pleasure, comfort, play or enjoyment responses combined.[35]

American children, by contrast, gave more "play" responses than any other kind. Prothro believes this partly reflects the farming life of the Beqaa Valley families, who gave a higher percentage of food responses than the Beirut children. It also may reflect the real scarcity of food, though he points out that "middle-class" children did not give fewer food responses than the "lower class" children. Food also has rich cultural meanings, as Ammar points out, and is considered "almost sacred."

> Bread is not only filling, but also possesses an aura of sacredness, being believed to be the essence of life. The name given to bread is "*aish*" which literally means life. . . . Bread, like written words on paper, which might contain something from the Koran, must be respected. . . . Children are also enjoined to kiss bread if it falls from their hands on the ground. . . . They are punished if they throw bread from their hands when angry or annoyed, as this might make the "*baraka*" fly from the house.[36]

Prothro rejects the notion that most children experience weaning-related fixations on food, but he does believe the "noticeable decrease in [the] general warmth of his [the young child's] treatment at or shortly after his weaning" may create anxiety about food, especially since the older children who care for the younger children may not be responsive to their hunger. Perhaps most important, "the mothers report that food was an important part of their disciplinary technique. Reward frequently consisted of praise and affection combined with food, and punishment was often followed by the withholding of food. From the time of weaning, then, food was a symbol of warmth, affection, and social approval."[37] This continues throughout early childhood, Prothro notes in his conclusion, as "mothers who wish to reward their children often give them something to eat, and food occupies an important place in the thoughts of the children."[38] In Imeghrane families, we observed both chronic hunger and the widespread giving and withholding of food as a disciplinary technique, forming an often silent but nearly continuous form of communication between parents and children. At family lunches and dinners, the senior male (or female) removes the meat—if any—from the collective bowl and sets it aside to cool, and then distributes bites to each person at the end of the meal. They apportion the quantity and quality of bites in accordance with gender and age, and also as reward or punishment for comportment. Mothers supply many of the most valued and nutritional foods, especially dairy products and sweets, and give and withhold them both to nurture and comfort and to reward and punish. Similar practices—and meanings associated with food—have been reported in many preindustrial societies and have been noted as an important feature of socialization in India.[39]

During early childhood, then, food continues to come primarily from the mother and other household women, both because women and children often eat apart from the men and because women work with food nearly all day long and intermittently give morsels the children. Prothro assumes that mothers are consistent enough to effectively reward the well-behaved children, but Friedl, Brink, and other observers believe that assertive enactments of dependence (that may be seen negatively as "whining") work better than good conduct, especially when mothers have heavy work loads and many children. Lebanese mothers told Prothro their toddlers often do not sit down for regular meals but eat their way through the day as food is being prepared, which essentially continues the practice of feeding on demand, but with the provision of food less certain and more contingent. Again, Western psychologists do not know much about the effects of chronic hunger or the use of food as a disciplinary technique. At a minimum, however, these combine to intensify anxiety about getting enough to eat, and to infuse the giving and receiving of foods with a rich complex of emotional, moral, and religious sentiments that surround the sharing of meals and giving of hospitality. Even though mothers provide less continuous caretaking in early childhood, the matrifocal core of the household is built around their power as providers of *baraka*-rich foods.

Sibling Rivalry

Ethnographers report that parents recognize and expect sibling rivalry,[40] that many regard it as a developmentally constructive force, and that some actively evoke it to control or motivate their children. Hamid Ammar reports:

> It is assumed in Silwa that the knee-baby is always jealous of the lap-baby, and the yard-baby is jealous of the knee-baby, and that this jealousy is irrespective of sex. . . . It is acknowledged that the youngest child becomes jealous immediately [when] his mother's abdomen becomes enlarged on pregnancy and he is usually told of the forthcoming event. The mother hums phrases expressing her sympathy

with the child's jealousy and anxiety in store for him. The custom, though not so common now as it was twenty years ago, is for the older child after the birth of a new baby to wear round its neck one, two, or three cubes of sulphur called cubes of jealousy, wrapped in a piece of leather. This is supposed to minimize the dangers of excessive jealousy, as although jealousy is a healthy drive for growth, its excess might have ill effects on the child. It could induce diarrhea, swellings, lack of appetite, temper tantrums, and sleeplessness.[41]

He notes that younger children are often given deprecating nicknames to help appease the jealousy of the older, but this may be reversed to motivate the older, as was the case in which a four-year-old was called "the stupid one" and his two-year-old brother "the clever one."[42] Villagers said rivalry helps makes a man desirably "hot" rather than "blunt," or not easily provoked, and visitors often greet children by asking "Who is better, you or your brother?"

Prothro also reports that rivalry "is openly encouraged by the shaming of one child by comparing him with another."[43] Hamid Ammar views this as "a cultural means of motivating the child to abandon his babyish attitudes and behave according to his age," and he notes: "The sense of importance and worthiness is continually hammered into children's minds through comparing them either with their sibling or with other children."[44] He also reports that the villagers expect boys to become competitive as they near the end of this period and that parents resort to provocations when competitiveness seems lacking. Parents do not provoke competition from girls, whom they rarely tease with sibling comparisons. Nawal Ammar reports that rural parents in the 1980s continued to use the kind of shaming sibling comparisons Hamid Ammar reported, but with somewhat older children (again, mainly boys), and mainly to stimulate achievement in school.[45]

Few ethnographers have written extensively on these practices, but sibling comparisons and provocation of competitiveness may help sow the seeds of the social imperative Khuri characterizes as being "first among equals." Prothro notes that Lebanese parents use sibling comparisons to shame boys into more compliant or competitive behavior, and he points out that the Arab proverb "I against my brother, my brother and I against my cousin, my cousin and I against the stranger" not only expresses the defensive nature of family solidarity against outsiders but assumes a hostility that erupts when external threats are absent.[46] While it would be reductionistic to take sibling and peer rivalry as the *cause* of adult interpersonal strategies, I believe many parents see it as providing natural training in skills they think their children—especially boys—will need later in life. That is, the folk model of early childhood includes scripts for provoking sibling/peer competitiveness (at least for boys), which helps lay a foundation for one of the culture's major moral directions: striving for honor.

I also believe that the "aggressive dependency" that strikes some observers as resulting from "inconsistent nurturance" may not derive simply from caretakers lacking the time, energy, or concern to intervene more consistently but from an important recognition: that in worlds of "limited good," children—especially boys—need to become assertive, competitive, clever, and persistent. I prefer the term "assertive dependency" for this style of evoking caretaking, and I believe it lays an interpersonal foundation for building the clientship relations with both kin and nonkin patrons (see chapter 2).

Children's Social Groups

The literature on MENA cultures contains few studies of the social behavior of young children. But the Whitings' classic "Six Cultures" study made systematic observations of 3- to 6- year-olds and of 7- to 11-year-olds, and some of their findings *perhaps* can be extrapolated to MENA. A sample of children in each culture was observed for at least 14 five-minute periods over several months, and instances of the following peer-interaction behaviors were coded.

Acts sociably	Suggests responsibility
Insults	Offers support
Offers help	Seeks attention
Reprimands	Assaults sociably
Seeks dominance	Touches
Suggests help	Assaults

A multidimensional scaling analysis showed that these behaviors form two dimensions. One contrasted cultures that scored high on "offers help," "offers support," "suggests responsibility," and "touches" with those that scored high on "seeks help" "seeks dominance," and "seeks attention." The Whitings termed this dimension *nurturant-responsible versus dependent-dominant* and found it to be associated with cultural complexity: in the three simple cultures (Kenyan, Mexican, Philippine) children tended to be at the nurturant-responsible end, and in the three complex cultures (Okinawan, Indian, American) they tended to be at the dependent-dominant end.[47]

The Whitings suspect that this difference may partly have to do with the differences they documented between simple and complex cultures in women's participation in agricultural work and their children's contribution to subsistence production and household chores. Women play a greater role in food production in the simple cultures, and their children begin carrying wood and water, taking care of animals, preparing food, and cleaning at the ages of three to five. In complex societies, women are assigned primarily to household tasks, and children typically begin these chores a little to much later. Three- to four-year-olds typically performed only one of these chores in the complex cultures, and two to five of them in the simple ones. Children in simple societies therefore take on greater responsibility, in cooperative contexts, at earlier ages.

By the Whitings' criteria, MENA societies are all complex cultures, and one would expect their children's social behavior to be more "dependent-dominant" than "nurturant-responsible." Ammar reports that boys in Silwa are given "no serious tasks" until the age of five, when they may be asked to carry messages and run errands, and that they do not begin helping with farm work until the age of seven. Girls typically assume major infant-care responsibilities and household work at their mothers' sides by the age of five.[48] Williams gives a nearly identical account of girls' tasks and boys' freedoms in Lebanon.[49] Observational accounts like Brink's that describe MENA children as displaying "aggressive dependence" would appear to fit the Whitings' characterization. Of the six cultures studied, MENA societies most closely resemble that of Khalapur in Muslim North India, which had the highest "dependent-dominant" score. The close association of dependence and dominance might seem paradoxical, but it is important to keep in mind that the MENA's Big Family clientage systems repeatedly have been characterized as built from negotiated dyadic bonds of dominance and dependence.

Gender differences certainly appear here: ethnographers consistently report that girls in MENA societies tend to be given many more household and child-care chores than are boys, and at much younger ages, and to have much more daily contact with the mothers, which may provide more opportunities for both maternal affection and control. The young girls we observed in Imeghrane villages appeared much more "nurturant-responsible" than boys, and boys much more "dependent-dominant," but we collected no data on this. Davis's description of gender differences among toddlers also roughly fits these terms.[50]

The other dimension identified in the Whitings' analysis contrasted cultures in which children scored high on "acts sociably," "assaults sociably," and "touches" with those in which they were high on "reprimands" and "assaults." The Whitings termed this *sociable-intimate versus authoritarian-aggressive* and found it to be associated with household organization: children in cultures with mostly nuclear families (Mexican, Philippine, American) scored at the "sociable-intimate" end of the continuum, while those with mostly extended or polygynous families (Kenyan, Indian, Okinawan) scored at the "authoritarian-aggressive" end.[51] They believe this has much to do with the quantity and character of fathers' involvement with their wives and children. In the extended/polygynous family cultures, fathers have much less contact, and it tends to be in formal settings and when the father exercises his authority. In many cases, these cultures set up "dual households," in which the men spend most of their time in one area, perhaps also taking their meals and sleeping there, while the women and children occupy separate areas, which further discourages informal, intimate relationships between them. Reports from the Six Cultures ethnographers indicated that "overt aggression between husband and wife was most common in the cultures with extended families."[52] In the three nuclear family cultures, "a man slept in the same bedroom and usually in the same bed as his wife. It was also customary for the whole family to eat at the same time and place. . . . Children who grew up in the three nuclear family cultures interacted with their fathers more frequently than children in the three extended family cultures."[53] The Whitings believe that greater interaction with fathers, especially in informal contexts in which they need not represent the authority of their parents and their extended patri-kin group, facilitate more "sociable-intimate" behavior.

As MENA societies traditionally follow the patrilineal-extended pattern, they should be expected to facilitate more "authoritarian-aggressive" social behavior than "sociable-intimate." Both polygyny and corporate lineage groups are much rarer in MENA than in sub-Saharan Africa (and Kenya), but the segregation of men and women, both inside and outside the household, is often more pronounced. Again, MENA households most resemble those of Khalapur in North India, which is also part of the "purdah zone"[54] stretching across northern India and into Bangladesh, in which women are often veiled and secluded. The Whitings note: "The social distance between husband and wife in Khalapur was perhaps the most extreme."[55] Indeed, MENA ethnographers note relatively high levels of competitive aggression among children, and that older siblings and cousins are expected to act as parental authorities with younger ones, often carrying out this role with zest as they get older and begin to be given responsibility for maintaining the family's honor in the community.

Data from the Six Cultures study thus converges with ethnographic observations to suggest that MENA children—at least boys—tend to be more "dependent-dominant" than "nurturant-responsible" and more "authoritarian-aggressive" than "sociable-intimate" in their social behavior, similar to those in the northwest Indian village of Khalapur. Sub-Saharan Africa contains a sufficient mixture of simple and complex societies, and of cultures with nuclear and extended families, that no generalizations can be made. Preindustrial European societies certainly were complex rather than simple, and families more likely to be extended than nuclear, so children there also would be expected to have been "dependent-dominant" and "authoritarian-aggressive."

There clearly are important differences, however, between rural and urban families and between social classes. Askandar and colleagues note that socialization during this period tends to be generally "permissive" in rural milieus but is characterized by greater "firmness and harshness" in cities, though with different goals and means for middle-class and poor families.[56] Sa'idallah found that compared to rural families, "popular" urban Egyptian parents separate boys and girls earlier and more consistently, conceal sexuality (which rural children witness early), and enforce sexual modesty earlier.[57] Haddiya observes that socialization in rural villages appears quite similar across families during the first four years of life but then diverges in accordance with a family's wealth, education, and occupation.[58]

Many studies have found that better off urban families, especially those with more highly educated mothers, are shifting from pediatric and apprenticeship-and-obedience models toward pedagogic ones: they are having fewer children, decreasing physical contact (especially cosleeping), weaning earlier and more gradually, toilet-training and teaching cleanliness and self-care earlier, relying on modern rather than traditional medical care, providing more and more equally distributed food, more often using "encouragement" and deprivation of privileges rather than corporal punishment, emphasizing educational achievement, and so on.[59] In spite of a broad trend toward practices associated with pedagogic models, the available data suggest that compared to Western middle-class norms, the traditional pediatric model continues to guide a great many MENA parents—probably most. And if the Turkish psychologist Cigdem Kagicitcibasi is correct, MENA cultures (like many developing "majority" societies") may be creating forms of family structure that allow individuality in the public world but sustain "connectivity" in the private, avoiding the familial and community fragmentation common in the West.[60]

Juad BenJalloun's study of children's places in traditional and modern Moroccan architecture suggests other unintended but important consequences of modernization.[61] Traditional urban houses were built around a central courtyard and typically opened onto small alleyways where other kin lived. Toddlers were forbidden access to many rooms during the day and usually played with siblings and sometimes neighbors in the courtyard, where some adult could always keep an eye on them or listen for trouble. At around age six or seven, they'd be allowed into the alleyway on their own, where parents could count on neighbors to keep loose surveillance over them. Rural houses similarly had enclosed courtyard-like spaces and opened onto village common areas—often with the mosque, well, and threshing-grounds, and usually older teens or adults in the vicinity. Toddlers were relatively safe in these spaces (though scorpions and *jinns* frequented them too), unlikely to break things, and always within a glance of adult supervision. The densely packed apartments in modern cities, by contrast, have no courtyards and open down flights of stairs onto often busy streets. Toddlers easily create messes and break things in the house, and often no one will check on them in the street. Ben Jalloun believes this leads to more constrictive parental control inside the house, with less autonomy for the children and more frequent parent–toddler conflicts. For those who are sent into the street to roam with older children, however, it probably increases what I have termed assertive dependency and competitiveness, and may amount to neglect.

Aside from the elite's move toward pedagogic models, the nature of the changes underway is not well studied or understood. Immigrants to cities and city-dwellers assigned to jobs in other areas lack the extended family networks that often provide a great deal of child care and socialization. Mothers who work outside the home must devise different patterns of child care from those who stay home. And poor families filling the sprawling slums outside many cities often can neither follow the traditional pediatric model nor adopt a pedagogic one, and must resort to many improvised approaches.[62] Their socialization practices should *not* be seen as falling midway between traditional "pediatric" and emerging "pedagogic" models, and their frequent reliance on provisional arrangements may mean they cannot follow any specific model.

Part 2: Gender Development

The differential treatment of boys and girls begins with greater celebration of a boy's birth and more intensive and prolonged maternal nurturing. It continues in early childhood with the earlier assigning of girls to work tasks and caretaking of younger children,[63] and with the provocation of boys to competitive assertion and greater indulgence of boys' "assertive dependence." It appears to increase markedly around the ages of five to seven: the Sudanese mothers Badri interviewed believed boys and girls must be raised differently but said they did not see temperamental differences between their five-year-old boys and girls, and "a number of mothers volunteered the information that differences between the sexes appear after the age of seven."[64] Grotberg and Badri report: "Both boys and girls are raised with similar practices, with no gender differences. Gender differences seem to come after ages six or seven."[65] The end of early childhood often loosely corresponds to circumcision for boys and, in some areas, for girls—rites that confirm gender identities by removing tissues that are considered gender-inappropriate from their bodies. Boys are circumcised throughout MENA, usually between the ages of three and seven[66] (though in some areas it is customary done at birth). In some areas girls undergo circumcision or, "female genital cutting" (FGC) usually between the ages of five and ten. Ethnographers have collected good information on the meanings that "being circumcised" come to have for adults, but the psychological effects on both boys and girls remain unclear and subject to debate.

Female Circumcision/Genital Cutting

Female genital cutting appears to have originated in the ancient civilizations of the Nile, long before the spread of Islam. Its more extreme forms—which include infibulation (nearly complete suturing of the vaginal opening)—are known as "Pharaonic circumcision" and may have originated among the pastoralists of the horn of Africa (in areas now mostly in Somalia).[67] Some form of female circumcision continues to be practiced mainly in Nilotic and Somali societies, especially in Egypt and northern Sudan, and in some cultures of West, Central, and East Africa, often in a checkerboard pattern in which some groups do and others do not perform it. It was practiced by some Bedouin groups on the Arabian Peninsula near the horn of Africa, but not by the large Rwala and al Murrah tribes. It also is not practiced by the Tuareg of the Sahara, the pastoralist Fulani or Hausa south of the Sahara, the agriculturalists of highlands Ethiopia, or the cattle-herding Nuer and Dinka of southern Sudan and Ethiopia. This means that in spite of the fact that the Muslims who practice FGC generally believe it to be part of their religion, it is *not* practiced in most Muslim societies (including the Palestinian village studied by Granqvist)[68] and *is* practiced in many that are not Muslim. It appears not to be practiced in any society that does not also circumcise men.[69] In most MENA societies, no "initiation" ceremony is held for girls until their weddings.

Janice Boddy's ethnography of a northern Sudanese village—"Hofriyat"—provides the most detailed account of Pharaonic circumcision as it was traditionally performed:

> A circular palm-fiber mat with its center removed was fitted over a freshly dug hole in the ground. The girl was seated on the mat at the edge of the hole. As kinswomen held her arms and legs, the midwife, with no apparent concern for sterile procedure, scraped away all of her external genitalia, including the labia majora, using a straight razor. Then she pulled together the skin that remained on either side of the wound and fastened it with thorns inserted at right angles. (Fresh acacia thorns produce a numbness when they pierce the skin and may have helped relieve the pain.) These last were held in place by thread or scraps of cloth wound around their ends. A straw or hollow reed was inserted posteriorly so that when the wound healed there would be an opening in the scar for elimination of urine and menstrual blood. The girl's legs were then tied together and she was made to lie on an *angarib* [rope bed] for forty days to promote healing. When the wound was thought to have healed sufficiently the thorns were removed and the girl unbound.[70]

When she conducted fieldwork in the 1970s and 1980s, midwives had begun to use sterile equipment, to inject a local anesthetic before performing the surgery, and to apply an antiseptic before bandaging the girls. The circumcision of two sisters she observed in 1976 ended as follows.

> Women gently lift the sisters as their *angarib*-s are spread with multicolored *birish*-s, "red" bridal mats. . . . Amid trills of joyous ululations we adjourn to the courtyard for tea; the girls are also brought outside. There they are invested with the *jirtig*: ritual jewelry, perfumes, and cosmetic pastes worn to protect those whose reproductive ability is vulnerable to attack from malign spirits and the evil eye. The sisters wear bright new dresses, bridal shawls, and their family's gold. Relatives sprinkle guests with cologne, much as they would do at a wedding; redolent incense rises on the morning air.

Newly circumcised girls are referred to as little brides (*'arus*); much that is done for a bride is done for them, but in a minor key. Importantly, they have now been rendered marriageable.[71]

Infibulation almost certainly guarantees a girl's virginity at marriage, and a midwife must cut through the scar tissue to enable her to give birth. The midwife also reinfibulates the woman after the birth, and when the confinement period ends, the mother is re-presented to her husband as if a new bride.

Boddy reports that a much more minor procedure that "consists in removing only the prepuce or hood of the clitoris"—known as "Egyptian" or "*sunnah*" (orthodox) circumcision—was becoming popular in Sudan's larger cities, but not in the rural villages. Local men who worked in the Gulf states came back advocating the *sunnah* procedure, but senior Hofriyati women vehemently opposed it: "each depicted sunna circumcision by opening her mouth, and Pharaonic, by clamping her lips together. 'Which is better,' they asked, 'an ugly opening or a dignified closure?'"[72] Boddy discovered that women's adherence to female circumcision had less to do with maintaining women's honor by reducing their sexual desire (an objective many men cite) than with protecting their fertility—on which both their social positions and senses of identity rest: "Informants assert that it is performed on young girls so as to make their bodies clean (*nazif*), smooth (*na'im*), and pure (*tahir*), this last term furnishing the Sudanese colloquial for circumcision in general: *tahir* ("cleaning" or "purification"). . . . Circumcision prepares her body for womanhood."[73] Boddy found that associations of "women," "fertility," and "enclosure" run throughout the culture: women should be enclosed within their patrilineages by endogamy, they should be enclosed within the household's walls, their bodies enclosed within clothing and veils, and their wombs enclosed within their bodies. Openings at any boundary invite defilement, pollution, and *jinn* attacks that can damage a woman's honor, health, and reproductive capacity. From the women's point of view, circumcision and infibulation are practiced to maintain the enclosure of the womb, and so protect women's reproductive powers:

> Thus Pharaonic circumcision is for women in Hofriyat an assertive, symbolic act. Through it they emphasize and embody in their daughters what they hold to be the essence of femininity: uncontaminated, morally appropriate fertility, the right and the physical potential to reproduce the lineage or found a lineage section. In that infibulation purifies, smoothes, and makes clean the outer surface of the womb, the enclosure or *hosh* [household compound] of the house of childbirth, it socializes or, in fact, culturalizes a woman's fertility.[74]

Female circumcision may not take on precisely these meanings in all of the cultures that practice it. The less extreme *sunnah* procedure is referred to as a "purification" and may more often be advocated for reducing a woman's sexual drive. Hamid Ammar reports that Silwa's midwife said it is done "to prevent any suspicion on the bridegroom's part that the bride is not a virgin."[75] Boddy notes that men may stress the control of female sexuality as its rationale, while women may emphasize protection of fertility. Regardless of its meanings, the procedure certainly can be a terrifying and traumatic one. The Egyptian physician and feminist Nawal El Saadawi begins her autobiography with the following recollection.

> I was six years old that night when I lay in my bed, warm and peaceful in that pleasurable state that lies half way between wakefulness and sleep, with the rosy dreams of childhood flitting by, like gentle fairies in quick succession. I felt something move under the blankets, something like a huge hand, cold and rough, fumbling over my body, as though looking for something. Almost simultaneously another hand, as cold and as rough and as big as the first one, was clapped over my mouth, to prevent me from screaming.
>
> They carried me to the bathroom. All I remember is that I was frightened and that there were many of them, and that something like an iron grasp caught hold of my hand and my arms and my thighs, so that I became unable to resist or even to move. I also remember the icy touch of the bathroom tiles under my naked body, and unknown voices and humming sounds interrupted now and again by a rasping metallic sound that reminded me of the butcher when he used to sharpen his knife before slaughtering a sheep for the *Eid*.
>
> I strained my ears trying to catch the rasp of the metallic sound. The moment it ceased, it was as though my heart stopped beating with it. . . . I realized that my thighs had been pulled wide apart, and that each of my lower limbs was being held as far away from the other as possible, gripped by steel fingers that never relinquished their pressure. I felt that the rasping knife or blade was heading straight down towards my throat. Then suddenly the sharp metallic edge seemed to drop between my thighs and there cut off a piece of flesh from my body.
>
> I screamed with pain despite the tight hand held over my mouth, for the pain was not just a pain, it was like a searing flame that went through my whole body. After a few moments, I saw a red pool of blood around my hips.
>
> I did not know what they had cut off my body, and I did not try to find out. I just wept, and called out to my mother for help. But the worst shock of all was when I looked around and found her standing by my side. Yes, it was her, I could not be mistaken, in flesh and blood, right in the midst of these strangers, talking to them and smiling at them, as though they had not participated in slaughtering her daughter just a few moments ago.

They carried me to my bed. I saw them catch hold of my sister, who was two years younger, in exactly the same way they had caught hold of me a few minutes earlier. I cried out with all my might. No! No! I could see my sister's face held between the big rough hands. It had a deathly pallor and her wide black eyes met mine for a split second, a glance of dark terror that I can never forget. A moment later and she was gone, behind the door of the bathroom where I had just been.[76]

Serious medical complications have been well documented, especially from Pharaonic circumcision, including infection, chronic irritation, infertility, and sometimes death. Many writers like El Saadawi have protested against the trauma of its infliction and the loss of sexual responsiveness it brings. But no studies of its effects on personality development are currently available.

Male Circumcision

The circumcision of boys is practiced by all MENA Muslim cultures. A few have been reported to circumcise boys a week after birth, approximating Jewish and Christian practices, and a few to perform the rite as an adolescent test of endurance, as is done in many sub-Saharan societies. But the great majority perform it between the ages of three and seven, with ages varying in part because the feasting and entertainment costs favor collective ceremonies during which all boys in an acceptable age range in a family, a neighborhood, or a village are circumcised together. Around the globe, most societies that circumcise boys do so either earlier or later than this, and the timing in MENA—when boys are old enough to be terrified but not old enough to show their bravery—suggests that it must have distinctive meanings and effects there. Ammar reports that fathers in Silwa encouraged their sons not to cry, but many ethnographers indicate that it is not at all done as a test of "manliness." Cansever and Ozturk separately report that in Turkey,[77] and the Davises and Crapanzano that in Morocco,[78] boys often are told lies to conceal their impending circumcision from them, and then caught by surprise and taken off to it, as was Saadawi. One of the men Crapanzano interviewed recalled:

I did not think it was going to happen. I thought I was the favorite son and was going to a feast. . . . I was given a good *jallaba* and a *burnous*, and was put on a horse and led around the village. I was taken to the mosque, and then home. The barber was hidden in the room so that I wouldn't see him. When I was brought in, two men held me tightly. The barber came and sharpened his scissors. [Demonstrates.] He took the foreskin and put a little bit of sheep manure under and twisted the foreskin around it. This was to protect the head (*ras*). He cut it with a single stroke. And the skin jumped off, and I jumped. I cried terribly. A woman put me on her back and danced in front of the oboes. . . . They sacrificed a bull for me. They made a lot of bread and invited a lot of people and had a feast. I sat in a corner. The guests gave me money. . . . The scissors were really hard. When he cut, I jumped in the air. I thought I would kill him. I thought that had I been big, I would have killed him. Who can look at a person who has caused you blood and pain. No one can take that. . . . I thought at the beginning that he had cut it off.[79]

The collective village circumcision we observed in Imeghrane certainly was a terrifying affair for the boys. Most were carried screaming by a male relative (fathers are said to be emotionally unable) into an incense-filled, tent-like enclosure, flanked on one side by a chorus of men loudly chanting Quranic suras ("to drown out the boys' cries," several explained) and on the other by ululating women. The sponsor sat with the boy on his lap and held his legs apart while the barber—a "black" from a village of African-origin craftsmen and sharecroppers—made the cut. The howling boy was then wrapped onto the back of his waiting mother, who (wearing spangles on her dress and a mirror on her forehead to deflect *jinns*) carried him quickly back to their house. Several of the boys we saw lost consciousness. Some of the men I talked with that day said they did not remember their circumcisions, and a few recalled it as something "ordinary," after which they delighted in the attention and gifts. Many recalled intense fear and pain, and a good number still felt angry that they had been told lies—especially, they said, when slightly older children had been teasing them that they were going to have their penises cut off.

The circumcision of boys is also said to be a purification that marks them as members of the Muslim community and readies them for marriage, and in most communities the ceremony resembles that of a wedding.[80] In Silwa and some other communities (including Imeghrane), the boys are draped with a girl's scarf or shawl, ostensibly to help ward off *jinn* spirits, but as these are removed just before or after the procedure and the boy addressed as "bridegroom," it also clearly symbolizes a passage from girlishness to masculinity. And like many other societies that circumcise boys, the foreskin is regarded as a bit of feminine tissue that must be removed to masculinize the penis. Nothing is done to teach the boys these meanings at the time, though as observers of younger boys' circumcisions a few years later they will begin to pick them up. And as Crapanzano insightfully points out, the boys' status in the family and community does not change: "Symbolically—and in fact—the boy is led from the woman's world back to the woman's world,"[81] where within a few days he is treated much as before. This makes for a seemingly strange rite of transition, since there is no transition.

The psychological effects of circumcision for boys are also difficult to ascertain, especially since it takes place in a single incident rather than in the all-day-every-day interaction patterns that shape social behaviors like sibling rivalry or assertive dependency. The fear and pain certainly make it traumatic for some, but perhaps no more significantly so than that associated with burns, cuts, scorpion bites, and other childhood injuries. But like other injuries and assaults, it can be expected to intensify anxiety and a sense of vulnerability. In the early 1960s the Turkish psychologist Gocke Cansever conducted a small study of circumcision, administering a battery of psychological tests to six poor and six middle-class children about a month before they were circumcised, and again three to seven days afterward. She observed a decrease in IQ scores, as estimated from the Goodenough Draw a Person test, and noted that the boys drew smaller figures after their circumcision, indicating (she believes) increased "insecurity," and "inadequacy." She also believes their postcircumcision sketches and the explanations they gave of their figures' "three wishes" showed signs of confused sexual identification and regression to more "oral" affects and needs. The children's version of the Thematic Apperception Test showed increased aggressive imagery (incidents of explosion, bleeding, cutting, death, being devoured) and an increase of aggression toward self and mother figures (but not toward father figures, society, siblings, animals, or objects). "According to these results," she writes, "the females were held responsible for the damage; they were perceived as the castrators, and aggressive wishes were aimed at them."[82] Rorschach protocols showed increased "constriction," suggesting a diminution of affective response and withdrawal from human figures and increased perception of "broken, damaged, disfigured objects and figures," which she interprets as evidence that "the children perceive the operation as castration."[83] Cansever also notes important child-to-child variation: "When one child reacted to the operation with an aggressive rebellion from within, the other regressed to a state of passive submission. When one became interested in sexual organs, the other seemed concerned over oral deprivation."[84]

This is a very small study, using projective techniques not recognized as valid by all psychologists, and Cansever offers her conclusions tentatively. But they are intriguing, especially vis-à-vis the role the rite may play in reproducing patriarchal orientations. She believes the findings support the psychoanalytic view that circumcision tends to be experienced as a castration, but, contrary to the Freudian formulation, that boys appear to perceive females as the mutilators rather than fathers and to direct their hostility toward them. Tentatively, she suggests that "the child held the investigator and the co-operating mother responsible for the mutilation and thus displaced all his fury to the female figures."[85] Ultimately, however, she believes the as-if castration experience may stimulate a boy's "masculine strivings."

A decade later the Turkish psychologist Orhan Ozturk conducted interviews with about 150 university students, health aids, and psychiatric patients and with the parents of 30 children whose circumcisions he observed. While 20 percent of the adults did not recall the procedure, 40 percent said they had been "greatly afraid," and 22 percent said they had been "specifically afraid that their penis might or would be cut off entirely." Nearly 90 percent recalled that adults had commonly threatened children with castration as a punishment. Together, Ozturk believes, circumcision and castration threats "provide a widespread exposure of the child to an intense focus on the penis and to the possibility of injury to it."[86] He reports that all of the children he observed were "terribly frightened of the experience; however, this fear subsided when the children were taken to bed, where their parents were waiting, many gifts were given, and entertainment was provided."[87] Interviews with parents showed that 19 of the 30 children developed behavioral problems in the following four to six weeks, usually "increased aggressive behavior" but including "tics, exhibitionism, obsessive-compulsive reactions, and stuttering"—which apparently did not cause serious pathologies.[88] He did not assess aggression toward male and female figures, but parents reported heightened fear of the father in twelve children (and decreased in one) and decreased fear of the mother in eight children (and increased fear of her in five). Yet when he asked the adults in his sample how they would feel had they not been circumcised, they gave answers like

> "One would be crippled, and defective." "No girl would marry him." "I would be afraid of women." "I would be afraid of impotence." "I would be very inhibited in sexual relationships." "It would be dirtiness." "You couldn't even go to bed with your wife." . . . They called the uncircumcised person "an alien," "a man with a foreskin," "a coward," "a woman," "a weakling."[89]

He reports that 55 percent of the men he interviewed "believed circumcision increased their sexual potency."[90]

In view of the age at which it tends to be performed, Ozturk believes circumcision primarily helps consolidate a boy's masculine gender identity. He notes the contrast between the "castration-danger effect" that tends to occur during and immediately after circumcision and the social meaning of masculinization that develops subsequently: "The sense of 'I am castrated' immediately after or at the time of the circumcision is later altered to, 'I'm not castrated and I never shall be.'"[91] A frightening and painful mock castration thus serves as a kind of innoculation that ultimately helps build a sense of masculine prowess. Crapanzano also calls attention to the disjunctive character of the ceremony: that the boy returns to the status of boy, typically with heightened anxiety:

> It declares passage where there is in both ritual and everyday life no passage whatsoever—only the *mark* of passage, the mutilation that is itself an absence, a negation. It is a precocious rite. The boy is declared a man before he is . . . physically a man, or treated as a man. . . . It gives him, if I may speak figuratively, a preview of man-

hood—a preview that is, however, dramatically arrested. He is in his "manhood" deprived of his manhood.[92]

This is a crucial point: the rite declares the boy a marriageable man but typically leaves him with heightened anxiety about his bodily vulnerability. Cansever, Ozturk, and Crapanzano together suggest that circumcision at this age does not so much confer a sense of manhood as set in motion a striving for a distinctly "phallic" manhood that will not be confirmed until much later, perhaps with proof in fighting, with marriage, or with the birth of a son.

In terms of its immediate effects, then, both male and female circumcision generate and amplify individual differences, as Cansever's and Ozturk's studies amply demonstrate, even though they are small. Some children, especially among those whose parents prepared them for the procedure (55 percent of Ozturk's sample) rather than deceiving them, may experience it as a triumph.[93] For some proportion of others, the fear and pain mount to unbearable, traumatic intensities. Boddy reports that over half of the adult women in Hofriyat regard themselves as possessed by *zar* spirits and participate in trance-dancing/possession ceremonies in which the spirits take over their bodies. Whether or not spirit possession should be viewed as a form of multiple personality disorder (MPD), the finding that over 90 percent of American MPD cases originated in extreme and often bizarre forms of sexual abuse[94] at least strongly suggests that Pharaonic circumcision may increase the propensity to dissociative experiences. The symptoms attributed to spirits (paralyses and the loses of sensation and speech that Freud and others termed "hysterical") and spirit possession itself are abundant in MENA societies that do not practice female circumcision, but they appear to be especially prevalent in the milieu Boddy observed. As to the long-term meanings of circumcision, however, there is great cultural consensus that it "purifies" the body, transforming women's bodies into vesicles of fertility rather than sexuality, and enhancing and guaranteeing male potency. In terms of its meanings, then, the bodily mark(s) of circumcision signify both religious purification and sexual/reproductive potency, effectively fusing Islamic spirituality and the honor-modesty system.

Debate: Routes to Masculinity and Femininity ❀

Theories of Gender Development

Here we encounter a debate between two types of psychological theory, which view gender development—and circumcision—in entirely different ways. On the one hand, social learning theories draw on the work of B. F. Skinner and Albert Bandura and emphasize that children learn sex-appropriate behaviors and attitudes by watching others model them, by being rewarded for performing them, and by being punished (or ignored) for failing to act in sex-appropriate manners. These yield a picture of developmental continuity and generally disregard circumcision as a significant event. On the other hand, psychodynamic theories draw on the work of Freud and post-Freudians and focus on the role of the child's sexual desires, its fears of punishment, abandonment, and castration and its attachments to parents and identifications with parental figures. These theories emphasize developmental discontinuity and often view circumcision—when it occurs after infancy as a rite—as a pivotal event. In fact, these two theories explain different features that constitute "gender."

Most psychologists now regard a person's gender as constituted of three surprisingly independent components, which tend to be formed by different processes and on different time schedules: *gender role behaviors, gender identity,* and *sexual orientation.* Social learning theories provide good accounts of how boys and girls learn what their society considers to be gender-appropriate roles and behaviors but do not offer very good explanations of how gender identity or sexual orientation develop. Psychodynamic theories, by contrast, have mainly sought to account for gender identity and sexual orientation and have little to say about the learning of specific roles and behaviors. Psychodynamic explanations of sexual orientation currently look inadequate or wrong, as sexual orientation appears both more biologically based and culturally determined than it does the outcome of parent-child interactions.[95] Psychodynamic accounts of gender identity, however, continue to have many adherents.

The MENA child-care and socialization practices described earlier entail the modeling/reinforcement/punishment-driven learning of *gender role behaviors:* how to act as a boy or a girl. Nearly all observers report that boys and girls still play together and may share beds during early childhood, are cared for by women and girls, live primarily in women's spaces, and go to the women's public bath with their mothers. But toward the age of five to seven, parents increasingly instruct their children about the behaviors appropriate for boys and girls and begin rewarding compliance and punishing deviance more seriously. Equally important in terms of social learning are the tasks assigned to boys and girls and the environments in which they carry them out. Girls get more responsibilities at younger ages than boys, and by age five or six they may spend a good many hours each day helping their mothers and watching younger children, which appears to promote more "nurturant-responsible" orientations. By contrast, boys at the same age are less likely to have responsibilities that require cooperation or caretaking, less likely to be closely supervised, and more likely to be prodded or teased into competition—a situation that appears to facilitate "assertively dependent" or "dependent-dominant" orientations. Both the direct process of parental modeling, reward, and punishment and the indirect process of separating boys' and girls' social environments intensify in later childhood—though attendance at coeducational schools clearly subverts traditional forms of gender differentiation.

The construction of masculine and feminine *gender identities* (beyond the basic sense of biological maleness and femaleness that usually solidifies before the age of three) appears to be a more complex process. And many anthropologists continue to turn to psychodynamic theories—especially those based on the work of Nancy Chodorow[96]—to account for it. According to orthodox Freudian theory, both boys and girls start out "as if" boys, attached to their mothers. Around the ages of four to six, boys' attachments become sexualized, and they enter the Oedipal phase. Their fear of paternal punishment or castration mounts until they surrender and repress their desires for their mothers and identify with their fathers—and this identification then motivates further strivings to become masculine. In the 1930s, the psychoanalyst Abram Kardiner was one of the first to revise this theory in light of cross-cultural evidence, arguing that the Oedipal triangle is primarily about attachment and dependence rather than sexual drives. As a boy seeks to maintain an interdependent attachment with his mother, he and his father (and perhaps other siblings) become rivals for her care, and the boy feels increasingly threatened with separation. He resolves this by identifying with his father and maintaining a more vicarious attachment to his mother. The much and justly criticized Freudian account of female development begins with a girl's discovery that she has been castrated, which leads her to wish for a penis and turn away from her mother toward her father. Freud believed women never fully resolve their version of the Oedipal complex but that a feminine identity consolidates when she sublimates her wish for a penis into a wish for a baby and identifies with her mother.

The orthodox Freudian theory does not provide an adequate account of either male or female development in the West, let alone in other cultures. But as a number of feminist psychologists have pointed out, it sought to make sense of some important and puzzling clinical observations. In perhaps all societies, sons may feel rivalry with their fathers for their mothers' affection, and in highly patriarchal societies, the father's authority may crystallize not just in fantasies of bodily injury or castration but in actual beatings, injuries, and real threats of castration. In this context, boys may readily come to identify with the "aggressor" father figure, especially when he also acts as a protector. And given that many patriarchal societies invest the phallus as a symbol of power, some little girls may indeed feel something like "penis envy" that expresses their desire for the freedoms and prestige their brothers enjoy.

Current anthropological theories, following Chodorow, trace the development of gender identities to earlier patterns of attachment and separation. Boys and girls start out "as if" girls, almost symbiotically attached to their mothers. They experience themselves as nearly a part of their mothers and experience the world through her postures, scents, tones of voice, and gaze, developing a core sense of self that is fundamentally feminine. This does not mean feminine as opposed to masculine, because there is yet no duality, but simply feminine by virtue of participating in and with the mother's femaleness.

Then the developmental tasks of boys and girls diverge. Girls must eventually shift their erotic and love attachment from their mothers to men, while retaining their core feminine sense of self and identification with their mothers. By contrast, boys must shift their identification and sense of self from its early femininity to an achieved masculinity, while retaining their sensual attachment to women. Chodorow believes that by sustaining their empathic identification with their mothers, girls separate in a less definitive way than do boys, and mature with a greater capacity for empathic involvement with others:

> From the retention of pre-Oedipal attachments to their mothers, growing girls come to define and experience themselves as continuous with others; their experience of self contains more flexible or permeable ego boundaries. Boys come to define themselves as more separate and distinct, with a greater sense of rigid ego boundaries and differentiations. The basic feminine sense of self is connected to the world, the basic masculine sense of self is separate.[97]

This is the origin of Carol Gilligan's widely known theory that women develop in interdependent connection with others, while men develop via separation and pursuit of autonomy.[98] But Chodorow also seeks to account for the genesis of misogyny, which she traces to the difficult psychological work boys must do—with their cultures' help—to suppress their earliest "feminine" sense of self. Many cultures help boys achieve a kind of compensatory masculinity by scripting a path by which they can turn against, deprecate, and control supposedly weak, dependent, and irrational "women" as a vehicle for turning against the "feminine" in themselves. The anthropologist Gilbert Herdt draws on this theory to describe the development of hypermasculine warrior identities in some Melanesian cultures, which put boys through brutal initiations that entail symbolically removing bad female fluids they received from their mothers and introducing good male fluids that will stimulate the growth of manly qualities.[99]

The Mediterranean anthropologist David Gilmore also draws on Chodorow's theory, suggesting that

> the main threat to the boy's growth is not only, or even primarily, castration anxiety. The principal danger to the boy is not a unidimensional fear of the punishing father, but a more ambivalent fantasy-fear about the mother. The ineradicable fantasy is to return to the primal maternal symbiosis. . . . From this perspective, then, the manhood equation is a "revolt against boyishness."[100]

His comparative survey of cultures finds a "quasi global," machismo-esque image of manhood that he terms the "Man-the-Impregnator-Protector-Provider" model. But this exists in more and less pronounced forms, with greater and lesser misogyny, and it appears to be little developed in a few cultures that seem to facilitate men's incorporation rather than repression of their early "femininity." Gilmore believes that environments that require men to become warriors intensify the Impregnator-Protector-Provider line of development: "The data show . . . [that] manhood ideologies are adaptations to social environments, not simply autonomous mental projections or psychic fantasies writ large. The harsher the environment and the scarcer the resources, the more manhood is stressed as inspiration and goal."[101]

John Whiting also has developed a variant of this theory. It emphasizes a boy's need to shift identifications from the mother to the father, not so much to resolve psycho-sexual conflicts as to take advantage of father's greater status, power, and control of resources. He hypothesizes that in cultures that emphasize exclusive, prolonged mother-infant bonds, boys often develop a "cross-sex identity conflict"—an ambivalence of feminine and masculine senses of self. Viewing male puberty rituals that involve genital mutilation as attempts to clarify and solidify masculine identity, he found a worldwide association of genital mutilation rites at puberty with long mother-infant cosleeping, which he used as a proxy for the general intensity and exclusivity of the relationship.[102] Cultures that practice circumcision often regard the foreskin as a bit of "female" tissue that must be removed to complete a male, suggesting that circumcision symbolically removes "feminine" characteristics.

As much as they provide complementary theories of different components of gender, social learning and psychodynamic theories stand opposed on one critical issue. Social learning approaches yield what Whiting terms an "as the twig is bent" account of development, in that they show how boys and girls are little by little nudged toward contrasting masculine and feminine ideals. Psychodynamic approaches postulate important discontinuities in development, especially in the case of boys, for whom patterns of emotion and attachment nurtured in infancy (a core "feminine" sense of self, according to Chodorow) must be reversed in later ones. Most important, the psychodynamic theories hold that the earlier patterns do not just vanish but continue to be important components of personality and must thereafter be actively resisted, pushed to the margins of awareness, and defended against. Some set of defensive strategies, usually deployed so automatically and unconsciously that they are termed "mechanisms," then become woven into personality.

Chodorow, Gilmore, and Whiting all view more machismo forms of masculinity as having a defensive and compensatory character, and misogyny as arising from the projection onto women of the supposedly passive and weak "feminine" senses of self nurtured in them by intense maternal infant care. They note that in many cultures these forms of masculinity are defined in contrast to a pair of "split" stereotypes of women: an idealized, vulnerable but often sacred virgin or mother (and in some cases, a virgin mother) that they protect; and a despised, dangerous, usually sexually wanton woman that they guard against or persecute. These images enable a manly man to preserve a set of worshipful feelings toward a maternal figure and a set of rejecting and derisive feelings toward an abject figure of woman-gone-astray.

Gender Development in MENA Societies

This theory plausibly describes the general lines of development that lead toward the version of the Impregnator-Protector-Provider model of manhood that MENA shared with the preindustrial Mediterranean. The pediatric style of infant care and cultivation of matrifocal interdependence within the wider world of women plausibly facilitates the development of an early "feminine" sense of self—though probably not in as intense a form as may occur in polygynous, long postpartum sex taboo societies in sub-Saharan Africa. Available descriptions of male circumcision rites indicate that they often include symbolic defeminizations (draping the boy in a girl's scarf before the procedure; regarding the foreskin as "feminine" tissue) and masculinization (explicitly treating the boy as a "bridegroom")—even though the boy is not removed from the world of women, as is done in many cultures, and even though the ceremony is not staged as a test and proof of manliness. In addition, adults' threats to castrate or circumcise boys as punishment, older boys' teasing that younger ones will be castrated—amplified by the shock and betrayal experienced during circumcision—may infuse the rite with meanings about "castration anxiety." Reports by Ammar, Dachmi, and a few other observers that women sometimes play with infants' and toddlers' penises to soothe or entertain them and that the women may kiss the boys' penises before the ceremony, taken together with recollections by some of Crapanzano's informants that immediately afterward they were placed naked on their mothers' naked backs,[103] suggests that circumcision may have more classically "Oedipal" meanings for some individuals. That is, these observations may support Ozturk's thesis that, at least in some cases, the rite works to masculinize by a kind of innoculation effect, heightening "castration anxiety" in the short run but in the long run conferring the message "I am *not* castrated" and "I am a fully masculine male." While they do not focus specifically on circumcision, Hijazi, Bouhdiba, and Hammoudi all propose that the prevailing cultural model for rearing boys into men entails "feminizing" or "emasculating" them by forcing their subjection to harsh authority (usually in the 7-to-12 age period—see chapter 6), which then motivates them to achieve and prove their manhood via competition with peers, domination of women and juniors, and identification with figures of authority[104]—a sequence that at least parallels these interpretations of the circumcision rite. (It is important to keep in mind that variants of this sequence are widely practiced in modern Western societies by armies, sports coaches, fraternities, and other groups that "make men."[105])

Again, it is not the culture that undergoes circumcision but individual boys, and, like weaning, the rite clearly creates and amplifies individual variation. It is likely that for some boys its primary psychological meanings concern emerging sexual feelings and castration fears; that for others it primarily concerns a reversal of a "feminine" core self; and that for still others it partakes of neither of these developmental trajectories. Further, the meanings of circumcision probably are not internalized at the time it is performed but crystallize gradually—especially as older boys witness younger boys' circumcisions—as a kind of cultural road map to masculinity. Masculine roles still remain to be learned, mainly through social modeling and reinforcement, and manhood must be achieved and proven via the performative rhetorics of the honor-modesty system. But as Whiting theorizes, the achievement and proving of masculinity probably always occurs more or less against a diffuse, underlying sense of "femininity," or perhaps against a sense of bodily vulnerability readily experienced as "effeminacy." This forms the core of Bouhdiba's theory of masculine development in MENA societies, which Afsaneh Najmabadi endorses on the basis of her study of the genre of tales she calls "wiles of women" stories:

> The boy, initially part of the women's world, is marked to exit that world to the world of men. To become a man, he has to prove that he has outgrown his originary contamination with womanliness, has ended his in-between-ness, through denouncing the women's world, at times through becoming contemptuous of it or even hostile towards it. A boy becomes a man by repudiation, by disavowal of femininity. . . .
>
> The world of the father turns out to be an ambivalent, if not dangerous, zone. This fearful ambivalence contributes to engendering a desire to return to the world of the women, to the presumed safety of the domain of the mother (imagined as a lost paradise). To become a man, the boy needs to fight off this desire for return and to enact repeatedly his disassociation from the feminine.[106]

As Crapanzano emphasizes, this repudiation of the feminine certainly is not accomplished by undergoing circumcision, but circumcision probably takes on this meaning as boys grow into more mature understandings of its significance.

It is not clear, however, that social learning and psychodynamic theories can be stitched together to provide a useful account of the role of female genital cutting rites (FGC) in women's gender development, especially since (1) the practice of Pharaonic circumcision is limited to a few areas, (2) the less extreme "Egyptian" practice appears mainly to symbolize the danger of female sexuality, and (3) the great majority of MENA women are *not* circumcised. Chodorow's theory that girls develop into women in continuous connection with their mothers, sisters, and babies clearly applies to the segregated and enclosed realms in which they live out most of their lives. At the same time, it is plausible that an "envy of maleness" as an experience of vulnerability to male power, and the persistence of socially condemned "masculine" strivings, creates an important discontinuity in girls' development, and that FGC contributes to feminine identity by helping suppress these.

The fact that the *jinn* or *zar* spirits that possess women usually turn out to be male, so that in possession women experience and perform themselves as men, suggests that "masculine" strivings remain powerfully active beneath their fertility-centered identities as mothers. Boddy observed trancing Hofriyati women become a British military officer waving a cane and smoking cigarettes, a pair of Arab warriors mock fighting with swords, a Turkish pasha, a European doctor, a Catholic priest, an archaeologist in khaki pants and pith helmet, an airplane pilot, a railway engineer wearing a man's suit and blowing a whistle, a whisky-drinking English gentleman, and even Basha Birdan, who Boddy suspects may be Sir Richard Burton, the translator of the *Thousand and One Nights* who traveled in the area in the nineteenth century.[107] These *zar* "antiselves," nearly all intrusions from surrounding out-groups, certainly open wide the enclosures that symbolically create Hofriyati women as sacred mothers, and turn them, briefly but dramatically, into foreign men.[108]

The lack of research on circumcision makes it impossible to even speculate about its short-term psychological effects, though descriptions of the rite make it clear that children's reactions vary tremendously. The long-term effects appear to center on the "manifest" value of the bodily mark as an increasingly meaningful symbol of masculinity or femininity, on the "latent" meaning that boys have been defeminized and (where practiced) girls demasculinized, and, for boys, possibly on a "latent" threat of castration (or "inoculation" against it) that motivates subsequent pursuit of masculinity.

Sources ❁

The primary sources of information on early childhood in MENA societies are the same as those on infancy: Hamid Ammar's *Growing Up in an Egyptian Village* and Nawal Ammar's followup, *An Egyptian Village Growing Up*, Shakri's "Al-tanshi'a al-ijtima'iyya" (Socialization), Abdelqader and 'Afifi's *Al-dirasa al-midaniyya 'an al-asalib al-sha'ia al-ijtima'iyya fi al-rif al-misri* (Field Study of Socialization in Rural Egypt), Askandar, Ismail, and Rachid's *Kayfa nurabi atfalana* (How We Raise Our Children), Prothro's *Child Rearing in Lebanon,* Davis's *Patience and Power,* Friedl's *Children of Deh Koh,* and Brink's "Changing Child-Rearing Patterns in an Egyptian Village." Badri's interview study of Sudanese mothers in the 1970s and Grotberg and Badri's followup eight years later provide important data on urban-rural and social class differences.[109] Al-Aharas's 1979 survey study of 400 rural and urban Syrian parents covers both early and late childhood.[110] Williams's study of Lebanese adolescents (*The Youth of El Hacimi Haouch*) also contains some observations on this period. Beatrice and John Whiting's *Children of Six Cultures* provides data on core dimensions of children's social behavior during this age range, which perhaps can be extrapolated to MENA societies.

The once popular hypothesis that culturally patterned toilet-training practices play a key role in shaping development has largely been abandoned.[111] Davis reports that, unlike weaning, "toilet training is very relaxed,"[112] and studies by the Egyptian researchers Hamid Ammar, Nawal Ammar, Badri,[113] Abdelqader and 'Afifi,[114] Sa'idallah,[115] and Askandar, Ismail, and Rachid[116] and the Moroccan Abdsalam Dachmi[117] indicate that toilet-training is not rushed and is done gently, except perhaps in lower class urban families (one study found that 40 percent of poor Egyptian parents used threats or punishments[118]). I therefore do not discuss toilet-training as an important influence on development in MENA societies.

There are surprisingly few studies of psychological consequences of circumcision. Esther Hicks's *Infibulation*, Boddy's *Wombs and Alien Spirits*, and Nawal El Saadawi's *Hidden Face of Eve* provide ethnographic and first-person accounts of female circumcision (which activists now insist be termed "female genital cutting" [FGC]). Descriptions and interpretations of male circumcision come mainly from Vincent Crapanzano's essay "Rite of Return" and from studies by two Turkish psychiatrists, Gocke Canserver's "Psychological Effects of Circumcision" and Orhan Ozturk's "Ritual Circumcision and Castration Anxiety."

CHAPTER 6

Late Childhood

Late childhood appears to be crucial for shaping the sentiments, motives, and social personae related to the honor-modesty system and to Islam—the second level of personality organization in the model I have adopted. During this period most children come to see and sense themselves as embedded in worlds animated by honor and Islam. They master a set of cultural etiquettes and moral imperatives associated with them, which come to be automatically experienced as a kind of second nature. Ethnographic studies suggest that the honor-related etiquettes shape sentiments and motives of deference, hospitality, assertive dependence, "'ar" (a gesture imploring aid), intimidation, and mediation, and that religion-related practices develop sentiments and motives of purity-pollution, "baraka" (divine blessedness), awe/fear of God, divine mercy/compassion, and "fitna" (chaos, disorder). Mastering these etiquettes so that they become second nature signals that a child has developed "'aql," which means both "reason" and "social maturity."

For most boys, this period traditionally entails an important developmental discontinuity: a shift from the world of women to that of men, and from a more "feminine" sense of self to a "manly" one. The path to masculine prowess typically begins with circumcision and winds through a period of forced submission, deference, and sometimes harsh discipline. Abdelwaheb Bouhdiba believes that masculinization follows a distinctive trajectory in MENA societies, in which boys adopt the cultural idealization of the Mother as a font of nurturance and protection, preserving their early interdependent bond in mythic form as they move into the intimidating world of men. Less has been written about the psychological dynamics of girls' development. They appear to experience a potentially profound disempowerment as their lives are increasingly circumscribed by men because they supposedly embody the forces of chaos and disorder ("fitna") and lack the reason ("'aqel") that would enable them to achieve self-control. Yet girls also appear to experience greater continuity in sustaining their female-centered relationships and sense of self—

which may provide them with important sources of self-confidence and esteem.

Urbanization, education, and media are changing this traditional pattern, but in unclear and inconsistent ways, especially because of diverging ways of life among educated elites, "popular" classes, and the urban poor. In addition, MENA nations now diverge tremendously in economic development and in the kinds of educational and media environments they provide. Several studies suggest, however, that schooling is broadly transforming the traditional "honor-modesty" system into a family-based achievement orientation—in which educational and career achievement brings family honor—similar to that described in several Asian cultures.

The chapter ends with a discussion of the possibly authoritarian character of parenting. Many Arab social critics see traditional "patriarchal" authority as "authoritarian" and as dangerously anchoring authoritarian politics in the psyche. But MENA's patriarchal model may differ in important ways from the "authoritarianism" that has been studied in Western societies: several studies have found higher parental control and emphasis on respect for authority in MENA cultures than American, but not the full authoritarian syndrome. Control appears to be counterbalanced by high levels of warmth, which Cigdem Kagitcibasi suggests may signal "authoritative" rather than "authoritarian" styles. Still, the process theorized by the authors of The Authoritarian Personality may also be occurring in some MENA families: as "modernization" undermines traditional family control, patriarchal authority may readily become authoritarian.

Introduction ❀

Freud characterized the 7-to-12 age range as a "latency" period in which children acquire new intellectual and social skills but retain the personality organization that he believed crystallized in the 5-to-7 period. Psychologists have long recognized the incorrectness of this view, but "late childhood" continues to be greatly under-studied in comparison to infancy, toddlerhood, and adolescence, and its importance for the cultural shaping of emotions and self remains poorly appreciated. I believe writings on childhood in MENA societies (see the section on sources at the end of this chapter) converge to indicate that a pair of potentially complementary *social personae* (or *social selves*) coalesce during this period, organized around the culture's predominant value orientations: the honor-modesty system and Islam. As discussed in chapter 3, the internalization of these orientations shapes culturally distinctive sentiments, motives, and social selves that arise from seeing one's self from the perspective of society's primary roles and values. These form a second *level* of psychological organization, which may entail transformation, suppression, or further elaboration of *core* characteristics. There is little research on how these important developments take place, however, and Western theories—which emphasize the effects of classroom performance, nonkin peer groups, media, and nuclear or single-parent home environments—have little relevance, at least to traditional MENA milieus.

LeVine notes that most preindustrial societies emphasize compliance and obedience during this period, and that learning occurs largely in "apprenticeship" contexts in which children work alongside their parents and older siblings. This appears as a natural extension of the pediatric model: though the goal shifts from survival to contributing to the household's subsistence, it continues to contrast with the encouragement of exploration and preparation for formal schooling typical of pedagogic models. In apprenticeship contexts, parents and elders often teach young children by guiding their limbs and hands through the appropriate motions (which LeVine and colleagues found American toddlers will not tolerate), building on the kinesthetic interdependence fostered in infant care.[1] MENA families in traditional milieus appear to follow variants of this *apprenticeship and obedience* model[2]—which was broadly shared throughout the preindustrial Mediterranean and formed part of the West's classical heritage. According to Johari, MENA popular tradition holds "respect for parents" to be the primary value instilled in children and encourages instilling fear—initially of animals and spirit beings, and then of authority figures—as a necessary means.[3] According to Grotberg and Badri, the basic principles of parenting in Khartoum include:

1. Parents in general do not encourage curiosity, exploratory and manipulative behavior of their young children; however, high-income parents answer more questions from their children than do low-income parents.
2. Parents discipline their children strictly and with physical punishment, but low-income parents discipline their children more strictly than high-income parents.
3. Parents insist on prompt obedience; children are taught to be polite and submissive to adults.[4]

Shakri reports several Egyptian studies in which parents endorse this model,[5] and many researchers report and criticize parents' widespread reliance on physical punishment during this period.[6]

An often quoted MENA proverb holds that parents are slaves to their child during its first seven years, the child slave to the parents during the next seven, and during the third seven he—and the proverb is usually cited for boys—must find his own way into adulthood. People chuckle at this exaggeration, and some object to its moral, but it captures an important feature of the culture's predominant model of childhood: that children younger than six or seven lack the *'aqel* (meaning both "reason" and "social maturity") to learn much, and that the foundation of character needs to be laid before puberty arrives. MENA parents tend not to romanticize this period as a time of freedom, and Hamid Ammar goes so far as to write: "In adult eyes, the period of childhood is a nuisance, and childhood activities, especially play, are a waste of time"[7]—though Nawal Ammar notes that with less need for children's labor in the 1980s this attitude had begun to change.[8]

Because they differ so greatly, I will treat traditional milieus in part 1 of this chapter and modernizing ones in part 2. In traditional milieus, this is a period in which children must master the moral imperatives, lines of authority, and etiquettes of the kinship system, which means they accommodate to and internalize what Hisham Sharabi terms its prevailing forms of "authority, domination, and dependency."[9] Children also learn the principles and practices of Islam and begin using these as interpersonal etiquettes and as techniques of physical and emotional self-care. Gender differentiation increases steadily, so that boys' and girls' developmental paths further diverge. In modernizing milieus, schooling replaces key features of family socialization, replacing most apprenticeship learning with classroom instruction, and replacing some traditional values and identities with modern ones.[10] Still, some traditional socialization continues in modernizing milieus, and may even be intensified.

Many Arab scholars see this period as a critical one in which "authoritarianism" is internalized as a psychological structure, with dire consequences for adult political participation. But others—especially the Turkish psychologist Cigdem Kagitcibasi—believe that traditional family authority is not inherently "authoritarian" as this has been conceptualized by Western psychologists. This chapter will therefore culminate in a discussion of the debate over the nature of familial authority and "authoritarianism" in MENA societies.

Part 1: Traditional Milieus ❀

From the perspective of their modern and often Western educations, many Arab writers criticize traditional socialization practices, especially the emphasis on obedience, rote memorization, and physical punishment. But it is important to keep in mind that in many traditional MENA milieus boys were raised to fight. Unlike China, India, and several other traditional civilizations, a large percentage of MENA populations lived beyond the daily reach of state authorities, and each adult male shared responsibility to fight for his family, village, or kin-group. Some often-criticized MENA socialization practices appear common to cultures that raise boys to fight, including the sectors of modern societies that celebrate the ethos of combat, such as contact sports, the military, and youth gangs. The model of "character building" by which adults treat children harshly in order to toughen them, and instill fears that they then demand their children conquer, is found in many cultures. If this is to be criticized as brutal or as antithetical to "modern" ideals, it nonetheless should be understood in relation to the imperative of raising boys to fight.[11] And, as mentioned in chapter 2, some of the "inconsistencies" criticized by observers may be rooted in the conflicting imperatives of agriculture (conformity and indirect emotionality) and pastoralism (independence and direct emotionality)[12] that MENA societies historically combined.

Kinship Relations and the Politics of Honor

By the age of six or seven, many children will have been cared for, comforted, ordered about, reprimanded, entertained, and taught by a variety of older siblings, grandparents, and aunts and uncles. Williams observes that in a Lebanese village

> the lesson of kinship is the clearest and most elaborate he must learn. When he is very small, he is addressed by members of his family not by his own name but by the one that describes his relationship to the speaker: the grandfather calls his small grandchild *jiddi* (my grandfather) and the aunt addresses him as *ammti* (my father's sister) or *khalti* (my mother's sister). His own name is withheld as the relationship to the speaker is emphasized and only when he has learned his kinship lesson is he called by his given name.[13]

He or she will have learned terms of address and gestures of respect due to elders, and at least observed the hospitality ceremonies performed for guests. Households and neighborhoods tend to be dense with social interaction, and the child who earlier played with family members rather than toys increasingly learns more adult styles of interaction. Sharabi and Ani write:

> The child is trained in sociability by being made to participate in conversation and to take part in social ceremony. . . . He comes to accept as natural the need to assert himself in social gatherings, and to imitate the grownups in their gestures and manner of speaking. A boy who is silent is ridiculed for not taking part in conversation: "Poor boy, he has a mouth to eat but not a mouth to speak." . . . To say that "Samir is a clever boy" (*Samir walad shatir*) means that he knows how to get along with others, i.e., how to manipulate his environment, which consists of parents, siblings, relatives, neighbors."[14]

Throughout late childhood, the web of kinship expands to encompass more of the patronymic association (see chapter 3). Williams writes:

> His world quickly becomes peopled with kin of specific designation, each with a specific set of mutual rights and obligations. Thus, the father's brother carries almost as much authority as the father and, in the latter's absence, as much . . . so the mother's sister and female maternal relatives in general, are mother substitutes; cousins are

members of the child's first peer group and . . . often remain the closest friends of adolescence.[15]

Expectations for *mu'addab* (propriety) increase steadily with age. According to Ammar:

> Whilst in the first five or six years the child's respect for its parents and elders is inculcated mainly through physical gestures and intimacy, the respect later on is expected in terms of a decrease in word intimacy and physical proximity. Moreover, certain manners must be observed, such as walking behind the father or an elder and not abreast of him, standing up or at least sitting properly on the ground on his approach. . . . Whether in attending to the hand-washing of guests, the distribution of tea amongst them, or in shaking hands with them, a fairly definite order of precedence is observed by the child.[16]

From the repeated exchanges of everyday life, intrigues played out behind the scenes, and ceremonies that punctuate routines, children learn to maneuver within this web of patronymic relations. As Hsu emphasizes, this shapes a child's personality and sense of himself or herself. Indeed, nurturance, punishments, and rewards become increasingly contingent on a child's social abilities. The literature contains many anecdotes and few studies of this process, but evidence converges to suggest that two aspects have particular psychological importance. First, children learn to judge degrees of "closeness" and to adjust their actions accordingly. Second, they learn not simply their position within the web but a repertoire of interpersonal etiquettes with which they can negotiate and continually adjust their relationships.

Hamid Ammar emphasizes the importance seniors increasingly place on distinguishing between private and public norms, allowing informalities in private they would punish in public. Above all, children learn that they represent their household in public and to more distant kin. "For the Haouch youngster the world of people is quickly sorted out into relatives, 'those from our house,' and strangers," writes Williams, "all the child's actions bring pride or shame not to himself but to the family."[17] Ammar notes that the child's growing responsibility for its family's reputation is stressed by the frequent use of "we" by family members when "I" might suffice, and by the way praises and curses intended for a child may be addressed to its family. Boys often quarrel, he reports, by hurling insults at each other's fathers, ancestors, hospitality, and livestock.[18] In addition, children are often asked not their names but "Whose son are you?" and they spontaneously introduce themselves as "the son of so-and-so."[19]

All of these practices help further develop a familial "sense of self," elaborating an identification with the household as an honor-bearing but vulnerable self object. And this may be based less on the child's actual (but private) relationships with family members than on the style of his or her public self-presentations. To the extent that the family may have rallied around and become a kind of transitional object at weaning, this learning to act within the web of kinship and to carry an awareness of one's self as a representative of a familial "we" appears to be an important developmental continuity—leading toward the organization of the sort of *social self,* described by G. H. Mead, based in MENA on the principles of honor and modesty.

This familial/kin-based social self consists not just of an identification with one's "house" but of the repertoire of values, etiquettes, and strategies needed to maneuver within the patronymic association and larger community. This repertoire certainly varies for pastoralists, villagers, and city-dwellers, for wealthy patrons and poor clients, and for men and women, but ethnographic accounts suggest that most children learn a core set common to these milieus. These include the following.

DEFERENCE

The principles of *adab* (politeness/respect) require that relations with seniors be marked by formal gestures of deference, graded according to the degree of distance and the formality of the occasion (juniors kiss seniors' hands, rise to greet them, use formal terms of address, serve them, carry out their instructions, defer to their opinions and wishes, etc.).

HOSPITALITY

Children learn to perform the rituals of hospitality as both hosts and guests. Elaborate forms of hospitality may be given only to distant kin or outsiders, but simple gestures form part of everyday social intercourse within the household and neighborhood. Serving a grandparent, for example, may simultaneously entail deference and hospitality. Hospitality also implies reciprocity, and becomes an important strategy for building and managing patron-client dyads.

ASSERTIVE DEPENDENCE

In the last chapter I cited ethnographers who have noted that crowded and busy household milieus often encourage weaned children to develop styles of aggressively eliciting caretakers to attend to them and indulge their dependence. At least some observers report that children in this period refine these styles and enact them to attract attention, caretaking, protection, and favors from a widening array of family members and kin. Styles of evoking seniors' responsibilities to juniors may subsequently figure in the negotiation of patron-client relationships.

'AR

Assertive dependence may develop into various forms of an interpersonal strategy known in North Africa as *'ar,* which entails making a personal sacrifice of some sort that morally compels another to protect, help, or grant one's request. In precolonial eras, it sometimes was employed as a ritualized political act: an exile from one tribe might sacrifice a ram at the doorstep of a neighboring tribe's sheikh and request his official protection. Some tribes even sacrificed to Foreign Legion commanders, a kind of "crying uncle" they hoped would compel them to make peace on terms short of total surrender. Interpersonally, 'ar typically takes the form of ritualized pleading—often "Allah yarham al-walidayn" (May God bless your parents)—accompanied by verbal tones and postures conveying mild supplication, which amounts to an exceedingly emphatic "please." In dire circumstances this may be combined with dramatic gestures of deference, such as kissing the addressee's hand, kneeling, or urgent invocations of God's protection. It entails some sacrifice of honor, however slight and brief, which morally presses the petitioned person to comply.

Teen-agers sometimes 'ar in slightly jesting tones to cajole a cigarette from a friend, or a harried office worker might 'ar to convince a taxi driver on his break to take him on an errand. But whether subtly intimated or dramatically performed, 'ar plays a role in the negotiation of most hierarchical relationships. A would-be client might employ it to solicit a more powerful person as a patron; a client might resort to it in order to resist exploitation or intimidation by a patron; or a patron might turn to it to convince a client to comply with an onerous request. I have observed children in this age range use 'ar-like gestures with adult family members and older siblings to elicit favors or try to get out of trouble, and also to mollify younger siblings whom they have bullied or teased to tears.

PROTECTION

If deference, hospitality, assertive dependence, and 'ar mainly provide children with strategies to enact with seniors, children also begin learning styles by which they may act as seniors toward juniors. This typically begins when they are assigned to watch over younger children, a role that may include nurturing, comforting, and disciplining. Nurturing is generally assumed to be an older girl's responsibility and disciplining to be an older boy's. Girls do more child care, but in many households older boys do a great deal of it throughout late childhood and into adolescence. This caretaking extends into the community, where they not only protect younger children from physical dangers but ensure that they do not cause trouble that embarrasses the family. By the end of late childhood, most boys will be expected to defend younger ones from neighborhood bullies and to both protect and "police" their sisters from older boys.[20] And as protection also entails comfort and emotional support, it probably develops both boys' and girls' capacity to nurture.

INTIMIDATION

In many traditional milieus, children may need to learn to intimidate other children, and this may especially occur in large households where sibling comparisons intensify rivalries and older children get rights over younger ones. Children caring for younger siblings may be punished for bullying them, but also for failing to keep the younger ones in line. "A brother in particular is an effective authority," Williams writes of rural Lebanese families, "especially in the absence of the father. By the time he reaches adolescence his word carries considerable weight not only with younger children but with his sisters as well."[21] Boys especially learn intimidation in physical contests and sometimes fights with peers. Much of the play during this period entails testing strength, agility, endurance, and courage, and children learn how far to push and allow themselves to be pushed.

Seniors often encourage intimidation that remains within bounds. No family can afford a hothead who starts trouble with kinsmen and neighbors, and so aggression may be quite strongly discouraged and punished (as Prothro reports of Lebanon and Badri of Sudan). But boys also may be shamed and punished if they back down from a challenge, or if they continually run to their parents to intervene in peer conflicts. Pastoralist, agricultural, and urban communities differ in their approval and encouragement of intimidation, but in most milieus it is one of the interpersonal styles learned during late childhood—framed always by a sense of responsibility to the household.

MEDIATION

The interpersonal politics of patronymic associations include a range of mediation tactics that avoid, diffuse, and resolve conflicts, and children begin to learn them during this period. Many observers note that as relationships between boys and their fathers grow more distant and as girls come into conflict with their mothers, children may ask their opposite-sex parent to intervene on their behalf. Quarreling parents may similarly use children to take messages between them or enlist older children to plead their cases. Throughout late childhood, children may call upon kin, peers, and even nonkin to mediate difficulties, and they increasingly play mediation and go-between roles themselves. This too appears to provide an important strategy for the negotiation of adult relationships.

G. H. Mead likens socialization to the learning of an organized game (like soccer), in which by gaining an understanding of game from its multiple positions, the player (i.e., the child growing into adulthood) comes to perceive himself or herself within the larger configuration of positions, strategies, and styles. Mead refers to the overall configuration as the Generalized Other and the self-conceptions that arise from taking its perspective on one's self as the *social self*.[22] I believe that this familial/kin-centered "we" consolidates in late childhood with mastery of this repertoire of etiquettes, forming an honor-oriented *social self* or *social persona*.[23] By the end of late childhood, then, most children automatically construe persons, events, and relationships in its terms, and automatically respond with the requisite etiquettes and styles.

A great deal of expertise, however, remains to be acquired in adolescence and adulthood.

Fathers

As described by many MENA scholars and writers, the cultural model of fatherhood prescribes a shift from warmth, affection, and playfulness in early childhood to distance, formality, and discipline during this period. Brink notes that "Egyptian fathers are effective as disciplinarians because, while they are loving and affectionate with infants and very young children, they assume a more stern and authoritative relationship with older children. A man's power and authority in the home are unquestioned by both his wife and children."[24] Ahmad Ouzi writes that the traditional Moroccan model holds that continuing the gentleness and succor accorded infants and toddlers into this period will yield weak manliness and that distance and physical punishment are essential to forming the "toughness" adult responsibilities require.[25] In *Palace Walk*, the Egyptian novelist Naguib Mahfouz describes the onset of Ahmad Abd al-Jawad's fearsome paternal authority through the eyes of his youngest son, Kamal:

> He was often amazed to remember that this same father had been sweet and kind to him not so long ago, when he was a small child. Al-Siyyid Ahmad had enjoyed playing with him and from time to time had treated him to various kinds of sweets. He had done his best to lighten Kamal's circumcision day, hideous though it was, by filling his lap with chocolates and candy and smothering him with care and affection. Then how quickly everything had changed. Affection had turned into severity, tender conversation into shouts, and fondling to blows. He had even made circumcision itself a means for terrifying the boy. For a long time Kamal had been confused and had thought they might inflict the same fate on what he had left.
>
> It was not just fear that he felt toward his father. His respect for him was as great as his fear. He admired his strong, imposing appearance, his dignity that swept everyone along with it, the elegance of his clothing, and the ability he believed him to have to do anything. Perhaps it was the way his mother spoke about her husband that put him in such awe of him. He could not imagine that any other man in the world could equal al-Siyyid Ahmad's power, dignity, or wealth.[26]

Eickelman's life history of a Moroccan *qadi* (religious judge) portrays this sort of "stern" father:

> What I remember most of my childhood is the cane. When we were young, my brother and I were beaten three times daily by my father:

morning, noon, and night. Each night he required us to stand before him and recite five *hizbs* [verses] of the Quran. Other children were expected to recite one. If we made a mistake, then we would be beaten again.[27]

Williams reports that the Lebanese children she studied are "chiefly controlled by verbal threats and physical punishments" and notes that they "quickly learn that of the two parents the father is the more fearsome and formidable figure. For the mother, eventual punishment by the father is a favorite and most effective threat."[28] Friedl makes similar observations about the Iranian village she studied:

"Threat in the eye, warmth in the heart," our grandmother-neighbor summed up the right parental attitude toward children in Deh Koh. Without *tars*, threats, fear, proper respect due to elders, to anybody in a higher position of authority than oneself, the society would crumble, people say. It is a quality ordained by God to make ordered life possible, and ought to be instilled in children early. This is a father's duty. "Respect makes children mind their manners," said a father whom I had asked to explain *tars*. "When my father called me or gave me an order when I was a boy, the only possible answer was, 'Yes!' Anything else would have brought a blow. This is *tars*."[29]

Ammar describes the Egyptian village he studied as an "authoritarian patriarchal society" that raises its children by "harsh discipline."[30] He too notes that fathers' affectionate treatment of their young children typically gives way to distance, formality, and harshness during this period, which parents perceive to be "the most appropriate for punishing and disciplining the child. . . . The concentration of punishment at this period is justified on the grounds that the boy or the girl at this stage is neither too young nor too old to learn."[31] He writes at length about the use of fear to control children, not only in early childhood by evoking the specter of ghouls, ogres, *jinns*, and scorpions but in later childhood by curses and beatings. "The instilling of fear is one of the expedients that parents constantly use to repress their children and make them docile," he writes, and parents often cite the saying "'Fear is a blissful thing' (*al khof baraka*)."[32] He continues:

Punishment may be in the form of fulminations or curses, or it may be corporal. . . . Punishment can also take the form of denouncing the boy as a girl, or condemning him as a homosexual, and also through depriving him of his food or his share of meat. . . . Corporal punishment is not uncommon either by beating, striking, whipping or slapping. . . . The father's authority cannot be flouted; and a change in the tone of his voice must be seriously considered.[33]

Indictments of parental authoritarianism appear prominently in many published North African autobiographies and literary works. In *Mountains Forgotten by God*, Brick Oussaid recounts his boyhood as a shepherd in Morocco's Middle Atlas mountains, where the hardships of poverty, illness, and weather were only intensified by being sent to school, where a "tyrannical" teacher regularly humiliated his students—"He soon had a nickname for each of us: 'Come here, you crud.' 'Get up, nigger.' 'Repeat, the ape in the back.' 'Your turn, cripple!'"—and beat them: "According to his mood he hit us on the hand, and then, when they were swollen, came the agony of being beaten over the fingernails."[34] Eickelman tells us that as a household head and enforcer of the law, the religious judge came to view his childhood beatings "as a sign of his father's concern for him." Not so Oussaid, who eventually became an engineer and emigrated permanently to France: "We just barely survived. We were grave and fearful because, hurt and mistreated, our hearts and spirits were broken."[35] And not so Abdelkrim Ghallab, a renowned nationalist leader, who in *Le Passe Enterre* recalled beatings from his father and Quranic school teacher. A public square in Fes, he writes, gave him and his friends a few moments of freedom between home and mosque:

> At home . . . family life was lived in submission to severe rules that the children could neither disobey nor challenge; the authority of the father who imposed these laws never would have tolerated resistance or disobedience.
> At the mosque, the *fqih* reigned in terror over the children; as soon as one aspired to get a little freedom, the *fqih* would order he put his feet in the air, and beat them twice as hard with his stick, and thus return the child to the level of his terrorized classmates.[36]

Mahfouz similarly describes Ahmad's everyday intimidation of his family: "The brothers took their places politely and deferentially [at the breakfast table], with their heads bowed as though at Friday prayers. . . . No one dared look directly at their father's face . . . their fear itself made them more nervous and prone to the very errors they were trying so hard to avoid."[37] In his autobiographical novel *The Simple Past,* the émigré Moroccan writer Driss Chraibi rails at the brutality of his father, whom he derisively calls "Lord," and of his religious teachers: "Four years at Koranic schools taught me law, dogma, the limits of dogma, and *hadiths*, with cudgel blows to the head and on the soles of my feet—administered with such mastery that even till the Judgment Day I never will forget them."[38]

These accounts do justice to the way many fathers cultivate fearsome personas, instill fear, and enforce their authority. And they convey the predominant model of paternal authority during late childhood. Still, Mahfouz's patriarch Ahmad, and the father of the religious judge Eickelman interviewed, carry this model to what many MENA fathers would regard as an unnecessary extreme, and nearly all would condemn Chraibi's "Lord" as abusive. As Friedl and most other observers emphasize, the cultural model emphasizes balancing "threat in the eye" with "warmth in the heart." As much as they believe in inculcating fear, they also believe that "too much fear and punishment will make young children unbecomingly quiet, shy, fearful, weak, small, tearful, and dumb, and at a later age sneaky, uncooperative, and generally unsuccessful in life."[39] Ammar notes that alongside proverbs like "If you don't beat the child, nothing good would come of him" are an equal number such as "The stick makes the boy dumb."

In evaluating these accounts, we must neither underestimate the psychological effects of fearsome authority nor infer that fear reigns in all, even in most, families. Many fathers simply do not seek to enact this sort of persona, and there appear to be subcultural differences throughout the region. Maissa Al-Mofti found that while Egyptian Nubian fathers do punish their children, they also tend to be much more involved with their upbringing and more often express affection, provide guidance, and encourage independence than do fathers in other Egyptian families.[40] Based on my own fieldwork and interviews, I believe that most children encounter a fearsome authority figure like Mahfouz's Ahmad, if not in their own father then in an uncle or a teacher. But most also have relationships with men who treat them much more compassionately—sometimes their fathers (who may ardently protect them from the kind of harsh treatment described earlier) and sometimes grandfathers, uncles, teachers, or imams. The young Moroccans I interviewed experienced and articulated multiple prototypes of senior-junior relationships: the Ahmad-like authoritarian-protector model certainly appeared at the center of these, but it was accompanied by much more egalitarian, nurturing, and mentor-like models, which most of my interviewees extolled.

Sub-Saharan African cultures again show too much variation in both what behaviors parents seek to control and how they control them to generalize about paternal authority. Some even devised "age-set" organizations that appear to have minimized intergenerational tensions.[41] Ethnographies of Hindu Indian areas suggest that paternal control, while no less demanding of conformity to kinship and caste etiquettes, was exercised more by threats of rejection and induction of guilt than by fear and physical punishments (though these were not unknown). They also suggest less sharp differentiation of paternal and maternal roles in exercising authority.[42] For higher caste Hindus, entrance into late childhood was marked by "second birth" ceremonies, after which boys began formal religious instruction. This often was demanding and tended to be carried on in atmosphere of gravity, but not of fear and beatings as reigned in many Quranic schools. The traditional MENA model of distant and fearsome fathering is probably best seen as a circum-Mediterranean one, closely related to the region's honor-modesty system. Historical studies of childhood in northern and central Europe do not yield a clear picture of fathering in preindustrial eras, but it was early twentieth-century studies in Germany that led to the theory of authoritarian parenting and the "authoritarian personality"—which I will discuss at the end of this chapter.

Mothers

The predominant cultural model prescribes no fundamental change in mothering during late childhood, as it does in fathering. It encourages a mother's continued indulgent nurturing as a natural and needed counterweight to the father's new responsibility to impose authority, especially for boys. As Mernissi, Bouhdiba, Msefer, El Khayat-Bennai, Lacoste-Dujardin, Sharabi, Dachmi, and others have pointed out, women have two important structural reasons for sustaining relationships of interdependence with their children—especially sons. First, when lacking intimacy and companionship with husbands,[43] women naturally turn to their children for emotional ties. Second, a woman's future security depends in many respects more on her sons than on her husband. Her husband probably will die well before she does: her son(s) will then inherit his property, and she will depend on them. In addition, her power and status in the household ultimately depend on her control of the daughters-in-law her sons bring into it. And until they marry, a woman's daughters provide her primary workforce and social companions throughout the day, and the arrangement of "close" marriages may enable them to sustain those roles. Mothers thus have strong practical reasons for building a sense of indebtedness and loyalty in their children. Mothers do not act in calculated, Machiavellian ways but simply respond to the conditions governing women's life-spans, which make it "natural" to use nurturing, indulgence, and protection to build interdependent loyalties.

Fathers may create an atmosphere of anxious formality, but during the father's absence—which may be most of the day and evening—a relaxed air of informality and intimacy readily forms around the mother as she goes about her domestic tasks. Her physical nurturing of 7- to 12-year-olds may remain intense, as she grooms them, feeds them, and cares for them when they fall ill. Children typically learn folk health care practices from her (and other women) during this period, and she typically becomes the interpreter of their dreams—introducing them to more complete and subtler knowledge of "psycho-spiritual" forces: to *baraka* (divine blessedness) and its deprivation, to the effects of heat and cold and purity and pollution, and to the workings of saints, *jinns*, sorcery, and the Evil Eye.

As Bouhdiba and Ouzi note, a mother and her children of this age may share their status as juniors and victims of patriarchal control and conspire to circumvent the father's authority.[44] She may protect her children from excesses in his severity, and her children may begin using her to help bring him to see things their way. They also may begin helping her exert influence in the household, by providing information from areas she can't easily enter, or by appealing on her behalf to more powerful adults. The emotional interdependence forged in infancy thus ideally develops into an alliance built both on personal intimacy and exchanges of influence.[45] Lacoste-Dujardin notes that boys may spend less time with their mothers during this period, but their emotional bond typically deepens, and she suggests that "mother and son constitute the only heterosexual couple that remains a stable unit in this patrilineal and patriarchal society."[46]

Mahfouz brings this prototypic mother to life in the person of Amina, Ahmad's wife. Married before she turned 14, she endured years of solitude and loneliness as the secluded mistress of an empty house until she began to bear children. Ahmad went out with friends every night, and she learned to awaken herself at midnight to care for him as he returned:

> It had occurred to her once, during the first year she lived with him, to venture a polite objection to his repeated nights out. His response had been to seize her by the ears and tell her peremptorily in a loud voice, "I'm a man. I'm the one who commands and forbids. I will not accept any criticism of my behavior. All I ask of you is to obey me. Don't force me to discipline you."[47]

When she began to bear children, she turned all her attention to them:

> In their early days in the world, though, they were tender sprouts unable to dispel her fears or reassure her. On the contrary, her fears were multiplied by her troubled soul's concern for them and her anxiety that they might be harmed. She would hold them tight, lavish affection on them, and surround them, whether awake or asleep, with a protective shield of Qur'an suras, amulets, charms, and incantations.[48]

And as they grew, the oven-room became center of the warmth and care she radiated:

> The oven room, although isolated, had a special claim on Amina's affections. If the hours she had passed inside it were added up, they would be a lifetime. Moreover, the room came alive with the delights of each holiday in its season. The blaze of the fire gleamed from the depths of the oven through the arched opening, like a flaming firebrand of joy in the secret recesses of the heart. . . .
>
> If Amina, in the upper stories, felt she was a deputy or representative of the ruler, lacking any authority of her own, here she was the queen, with no rival to her sovereignty. The oven lived and died at her command. The fate of the coal and wood, piled in the right-hand corner, rested on a word from her. The stove that occupied the opposite corner, beneath shelves with pots, plates, and the copper serving tray, slept or hissed with flame at a gesture from her. Here she was the mother, wife, teacher, and artist everyone respected.[49]

And when Ahmad left for work in his shop, the mood lightened, and Amina became the center of family life:

> the family gathered shortly before sunset for what they called the coffee hour. . . . This hour was well loved by them. It was a time to enjoy being together as a family and to have a pleasant chat. They would cluster under their mother's wing with love and all-embracing affection. The very way they sat leaning back with their legs folded under them showed how free and relaxed they felt.[50]

Few accounts better convey the contrasting styles of relationship and emotional tone associated with the division of men's and women's spaces within a household, or the deep association of woman-as-mother with warmth, food, nurturance, and festivity, and with the inner core of the household—the *silat ar-rahim*—the uterine/compassionate tie that bonds them from within. Bouhdiba believes that as a "haven" in a world of "emasculation," mothers and children often develop a sense of complicity:

> By a subtle but very natural strategy, mothers and children have decided since time immemorial to combine their efforts to hold in check if possible, in any case to circumvent and to compensate for, whatever is abusive in patriarchal power. . . . He is not unwilling to do this, for he knows that his work will be rewarded with gratitude. But above all what pleasure there is in outwitting the father, or taking revenge, with such delicious and relatively safe complicity![51]

In this prototypic world, children in the 7-to-12 age range develop with a complementarity of threatening paternal authority and protective maternal nurturance. But how do real families match up to the prototype? From my own fieldwork it is clear that some match almost perfectly. One young man who described his family in precisely these terms even offered a sociological view: In most families, he said, the child stays distant from same-sexed parent, who acts as disciplinarian, and seeks out closeness with the other one, who more freely expresses "fondness." "His father grabs him and beats him but his mother gives him compassion/kindness—that's the reason." But many families do not match the prototype. Just as not all fathers play the fearsome authority, so not all mothers are able or willing to play the nurturing protector. In the agricultural villages we studied, many mothers were simply too exhausted from house and farm work to devote much time to their 7- to 12-year-olds. We also observed a handful of seriously disturbed mothers who neglected and abused their children, and the perhaps psychotic mother of a women I interviewed abused all of her children, while their unusually compassionate father tried to protect and comfort them. One young man's mother died when he was seven, and he grew up with no one to soften his father's ferocity—which he blames for turning him from an "A" student into a bitter-at-humanity delinquent and destroying his once bright future. Another's father was 50 when he was born, and he recalls him fading into ill health and resignation during his late childhood. His much younger mother ran the household and acted as the disciplinarian he feared.

Exceptions abound, and while ethnographic accounts do not contradict the cultural model, they generally do not show mothers treating their 7- to 12-year-olds with the continuous nurturance and compassion it prescribes. Prothro found that while Lebanese mothers allowed and encouraged dependency to a greater extent than American mothers, they also allowed greater "'laissez-faire' kind of independence," that they scored a little lower on overall warmth than a sample of American mothers, and that they reported more frequent use of physical punishment—especially with boys—than did the Americans.[52] It may be that the cultural prototype is realized more often in well-off urban families of the sort Mahfouz creates in his Cairo Trilogy and in which many writers and scholars grew up. More probably the prototypic nurturant-protective bond may be built not so much of the routines of daily life as of occasional and dramatic incidents. That is, it may be the well-remembered times when mothers cared for sick or injured children, when they saved them from blows or comforted them afterward, when they allowed them liberties their fathers have forbidden, and when they sacrificed to fulfill their wishes that forge the idealized tie of compassion.

This divergence of ethnographic accounts from the cultural prototype only underscores the importance many scholars accord to the prototype's *idealization* of the mother. Bouhdiba especially emphasizes this point, writing: "In an Arabo-Muslim setting the mother appears even more as a font of affection, all the more precious in that it is a restful oasis in the arid social desert."[53] In his view, the world of patriarchal authority has a profoundly matrifocal emotional core, which many observers have failed to appreciate. Repeatedly threatened with "emasculation" by intimidating patriarchs and challenging peers, Bouhdiba believes boys especially develop an idealized, "mystified" image of their mothers, and more generally, of "the Mother" as a near-sacred source of nurturance and compassion—recall the "sermon on *raham*" recorded by Antoun—that coalesces as a psychological "kingdom of Mothers" at the heart of the patriarchal order. Bouhdiba in fact views this idealization as a linchpin of the patriarchal system, constraining women to the role of nurturing mother and men to the role of her guardian. Even in families where fathering and mothering diverge from the prototypes, then, cultural values associated with the honor-modesty system and Islam may encourage children to represent and experience their fathers and mothers as approximating its contours.

Gender Differentiation

Throughout late childhood gender differentiation further increases, mainly in terms of the spaces in which boys and girls move and the activities in which

---

they take part. But while much has been written on the plight of girls, few scholars address their psychological development. In general, girls' development appears to be more continuous: most begin taking on household responsibilities and "apprenticeship" learning of skills within the world of women during early childhood, and in traditional milieus all three of these—responsibilities, relationships, and skills—intensify during late childhood and culminate in marriage soon after puberty. Circumcision marks an important transition in the areas that practice it, but the symbolic meanings that continue to build a girl's sense of womanhood derive from the interior spaces she increasingly occupies and from the food preparation, serving, and child-care tasks she increasingly masters in preparation for marriage.[54] Parents more rigorously enforce the rules of deference and propriety, but fathers may not feel the need to assume the fearsome persona with their daughters and may remain informal and emotionally spontaneous with them.

Girls probably experience a growing discontinuity between their skills and importance to the household on the one hand and their inferior status in it on the other. During late childhood, girls gradually find themselves more segregated from boys, restricted to the household and its immediate vicinity, burdened with longer hours of work, and increasingly subservient to the men of their households. Under the direction of senior women, most are subjected to less harsh discipline and to little of the testing of courage and insults to their developing "femininity" that boys typically face. They also learn more skills at younger ages than boys, and find a good deal of cooperation and support within expanding networks of women. Many become their elders' companions and then participants in what men see as "women's" religious practices: placating household *jinn* spirits, venerating and visiting the tombs of saints, and making use of religiously based healing.

Boys appear to be liable to considerable discontinuity as they enter this period. The transition may be marked by circumcision, but then also by their fathers' increasing formality and harshness, by being enrolled in Quranic school, and by being given male work responsibilities—for many, for the first time. They thus shift from helping their mothers and accompanying them to the public bath and saint's tombs to participating in a range of men's activities: work, the public bath, and the mosque, often in their fathers' company. They remain free to hang out with the women and younger children in the interior rooms but may be teased and chased away if they don't begin spending more time with the men and with peers in the neighborhood. With both male authorities and peers they face tests of strength, courage, endurance, and self-control and may be teasingly or humiliatingly insulted as "donkeys," "women," or "homosexuals" or even, as Mahfouz and Bouhdiba note, threatened with castration. The household's women increasingly serve them, and they often get increasing responsibility for policing and disciplining their sisters. As discussed in chapter 5, Whiting and Gilmore believe that it is mainly during this period that boys in many cultures shift their primary identifications from mothering

In traditional milieus, boys often begin "apprenticeship learning" in late childhood, like these young shepherds.

to fathering figures, adopting "hypermasculine" orientations in proportion to the exclusiveness of their earlier maternal ties and to the culture's efforts to socialize them into a warrior ethos.[55]

By the end of this period, the segregation of boys and girls is especially pronounced in more traditional urban milieus, though less extreme among some farmers and nomads and among "Westernized" elites. Public schooling, of course, introduces dramatic changes as it becomes universal.

Peers and Play

Few accounts are available of children's peer groups and play, but several scholars have sought to make much of the lessons they believe children learn from the games they play—at least in traditional milieus. Traditional parents refrain from playing with children of this age (though they do with younger ones) and neither provide them with toys nor organize their play. In both villages and cities, children associate mainly with relatives and neighbors, so most relationships continue to be governed by principles of familial hierarchy. Out of parents' sight, however, the tone of interaction changes. Ammar emphasizes that with parents, "subservience, respect and fear are expected," while in the company of other children, "rivalry and reciprocity

Girls typically begin "apprenticeship learning" earlier than boys, and by late childhood provide a good deal of care to infants and toddlers.

on equal terms are the norms." Parents punish disobedience, while peers mock and ridicule those who lag in "social maturity."[56] He writes:

> If restraint and docility are the keynotes of child behavior toward adults, a free and impulsive life reigns amongst children themselves. . . . If two boys or more start quarreling with each other, they should fight the issue out for themselves. . . . On being punished or rebuked by his elders, the child is expected to obey, while if he shows any submissiveness, if wronged by his "pals," he would be punished by his parents and would be asked to retaliate for himself.[57]

Ammar believes children's groups to be as important to their socialization as family interaction at this stage, a view in keeping with the recent arguments of Harris[58] and others. His and other ethnographic accounts suggest that children gain vital experience with peers in the interpersonal strategies—assertive dependence, 'ar, protection, intimidation, mediation, and so on—they later will use to build networks of personal relations. In practicing these strategies, they probably internalize feelings, values, and concepts central to the honor-modesty system, in ways that complement what they learn in family interaction.

Ammar and Friedl studied children's games in rural villages, and note that boys and girls play separately and differently. Not only do girls have less time for play but also "much of little girls' traditional play is imitation of their mothers' work: making mud-bread, collecting grass, making fire, washing, spinning on a stick spindle, baby-sitting."[59] Older girls engage in loosely structured cooperative or turn-taking play, in generally more sedentary activities than boys. But they are hardly all sugar and spice: Friedl reports that many girls' rhyming games focus on personal possessions, sexual organs, and excrements: "A rich body of immodest, bawdy, *zesht* [improper, obscene, ugly] language is placed in the context of play, beyond reprimand."[60]

Both also found that boys' play often consists of vigorous games in large groups, usually organized by the oldest. "Most of the boys' games are aggressive, requiring exertion and brute strength,"[61] Ammar writes, and he describes many that involve contests of strength, wrestling, and speed. Many pair an older and younger boy, who compete with other older-younger pairs—a little like the "chicken-fighting" American children do in swimming pools, in which smaller ones sit on the shoulders of older ones and try to knock each other off their "horses." Other games pit two groups against each other, each consisting of a leader and his followers, and Friedl points out that in most of these the boys don't function as teams but as agglomerations of leader-follower dyads. Ammar and Friedl both note that many boys' games set up contests—such as breaking apart a chain of boys who have linked arms—in which the loser is punished, usually by being beaten or ridden like a donkey.

Ammar, Friedl, and the Iranian political scientist Cosroe Chaqueri make much of the ways these features of children's games link the interpersonal politics of families, communities, and nation-states. Ammar emphasizes two points. First, the formation of leader-follower groups that compete with other carefully equalized leader-follower groups[62] mirrors—and provides training in—the village's politics, based on competition among groups forged by family and lineage solidarity.[63] Second, the games provide an important training and proving ground for maleness: "Through the tough and rugged manner of play," he writes, "boys gain their manly skill and endurance."[64] They are egged on to assert themselves courageously and often are belittled as "donkeys" or "women" when they lose. This further appears to follow the Whiting-Chodorow-Herdt-Gilmore theory that many cultures script the building of masculinity via an expunging of "feminine" weaknesses. In several games boys who fail at feats of strength or agility are punished until they either break free or "confess 'He is a woman' or say 'He is in God's protection' (a woman's phrase)."[65]

In penalty punishment "'donkey-riding," "scoring a donkey" or confession of "womanhood" is found in boys' games and does not occur in girls' games. Confession of "womanhood" . . . should be the last resort for a boy when pain from punishment is no longer bearable, and is almost a means of vindicating manhood. One also notices that, if two teams are playing and one team withdraws from playing when it is the other team's chance to be "in, " the latter jeers at the withdrawing team by shouting: "You are women, you just want some 'henna' in your hands. "[66]

Ammar reports that boys' play entails a good deal of obscene, sexual, and explicitly phallic imagery,[67] but he does not mention the rhyming duels that Alan Dundes studied in Turkey.[68] This genre of sexual insult game resembles the African game of "Dozens" played by African-Americans, and is found in Greece and North Africa and probably throughout MENA. In the game as it is played by 8- to 12-year-old boys, success "depends upon an individual's skill in formulating appropriate retorts to provocative insults," which consist of sexual threats to himself or to the women of his household:

> One of the most important goals is to force one's opponent into a female, passive role. This may be done by defining the opponent or his mother or sister as a wanton sexual receptacle. . . . A more indirect technique is to disparage or threaten the opponent's mother or sister, which is a serious attack upon his male honor. . . . Of course, the victim normally does not simply remain passive. Rather he tries in turn to place his attacker in a passive, female role.[69]

Dundes offers a psychoanalytic interpretation of this dueling play as dramatizing a conflict he believes to be generated by boys' striving for masculinity and dominance over women in a context in which they are dominated by adult men and elder boys as if they themselves were women: "Turkish male verbal dueling serves in part as a kind of extended rite of passage. Like most if not all puberty initiation rites, the duel allows the young boy to repudiate the female world with its passive sexual role and to affirm the male world with its active sexual role."[70] At points, Hamid Ammar suggests that it is in this sort of peer play that boys learn to confront and begin to conquer the fears—of beatings, animals, and chthonic beings—instilled in early childhood, and throughout this period by parents and elders. "During childhood the instilling of fear is one of the expedients that parents constantly use to repress their children and make them docile," he writes, "Yet I noticed that older boys, as well as adults, were highly ashamed of admitting fear of anything; to be courageous like a lion is the sign of a daring male."[71]

Friedl and Chaqueri call attention to the games that mimic the "authoritarian" relations on local and national rule and seem to make punishment the "high point."[72] Hamid Ammar describes a game of this sort, called "The Rule of the Whip," in which boys draw lots with a palm frond to score points:

These things are necessary for the game: a palm-tree branch (used as a cane), a ring of rope and a very small stick. The player cannot participate in the benefits of the game until he scores a one and the person is thus "sweetened. " Further scores are: six for a "Sultan" who holds the ring of rope, four for a "Minister" (vizier) who holds the cane, and three ones for the small stick. Directly a Sultan and a Minister are scored, the former can command the latter to beat any "unsweetened" boy with the cane (usually from one to ten strikes on the soles of the feet). The small stick, when it is scored, is the "stick of mercy" and the holder can lessen any of the Sultan's penalties. As the game continues, the different symbols of command, execution and mercy change hands . . . and thus give ample chance for retaliation, conspiracy and altercation.[73]

Friedl notes that the leaders in boys' games are usually named after adult rulers—"head," khan, or shah:

In one game, the leader chooses an aggressor to hit the players who in turn defend themselves as best they can within the boundaries of a defined space, until the leader, who stayed out of the fights, orders the aggressor to stop. The sixteen-year-old who explained the game to me jokingly remarked that it resembled the traditional chief and his rifleman, a hand-picked, loyal executor of the chief's orders, and the villagers who were subject to the chiefs' arbitrary demands and violence. This and similar games were interpreted as a playful dramatization of the traditional chief-peasant relationship that structured social life in Deh Koh until about 1965. . . .

Two games label the leader a shepherd, the players sheep, and the enemy a wolf, thus furnishing a metaphor for the hierarchical and authoritarian relationships among men. The same authoritarian, hierarchical theme is expressed in the setting of a "shah" who orders his vizier to investigate the complaints of a leader of a tribal camp about a theft. The thief is identified, and the vizier administers a punishment.[74]

David Hart reports similar games played by Berber children in the Rif mountains of Morocco: "the competition is cutthroat, and the winner emerges by hook or crook, any way he can, while the losers are ridiculed as 'donkeys' or 'dogs.'"[75] The games he observed include *awzir*, or "minister":

Each boy throws a pair of sandals or babouches into the air. If they both fall face down, the boy who threw them is the "king" (*malik* or *ajiddjidh*). If they both fall face up, the boy who threw them is the "minister" (*awzir*). If one sandal falls face down and the other face up, however, the boy who threw them is a "dog" (*aqzin*), and the "minister" then asks the "king" how many times the "dog" should be beaten across the soles of his feet. The "king" may state any number, and his will is carried out by the "minister."[76]

Chaqueri describes other games in this genre, including several "riding" games, such as "Gav, Gusaleh, Panier," or (Cow, Calf and Cheese), in which a "least intelligent" child

> is chosen through a guessing game. He is kept under a blindfold by a master until the others hide out of his view. Then the master calls the players in hiding by their names one after the other. Each respondent must whistle or clap his hands. The "least intelligent" player must tell where each of the players is hiding. Those whose hide-outs are correctly identified are named the "females," the rest are called the "males," whatever their real sex may be. Then, the "males" are rewarded by riding on the back of the "females."[77]

He also observed describes the ancient game "Shah-Vizier Bazi," first described by Herodotus. In this game, which is

> played, in the twentieth century, by a group of children no fewer than three, a match box is thrown in the air in turn by all the male participants. He who has the match box standing up is the "King," he who has it on the side is the "Vizier," and the rest who have it sitting flat are the "commoners." Chosen in a game of chance, the "King" has the right to have his "Vizier," or henchman, inflict *whatever punishment* he desires on his subjects, the "commoners of the game."[78]

Viewed psychologically, these games certainly show boys' efforts to master the fear and threats of humiliation to which they are subjected. Not only can they learn to endure insults, punishments, and humiliations as temporary, playful events but they begin rehearsing the dominant roles in which they inflict them. The use of "sultans," "ministers," and other political figures provides a degree of play-enabling displacement from the family elders and teachers who discipline them, but, as these observers note, it also may create a dangerous first phase of political socialization, modeling political relations on familial authority.

Ammar, Friedl, and Chaqueri thus regard boys' peer play and organized games as providing an important arena for establishing a sense of masculinity defined by three complementary axes: (1) the negotiation of hierarchical senior-junior, leader-follower, ruler-commoner dyads; (2) courageous physical competition against equals; and (3) domination of girls and "womanly" boys. These of course form the core features of the honor-modesty system, and elder children use its principles—especially intimidation, protection, and mediation—to control and protect younger ones, and boys to police and control girls. Juniors use complementary principles—especially deference, aggressive dependence, and 'ar—to evoke indulgence and protection from elder children and to moderate their bullying.

In a manner very much like that described by G. H. Mead, then, these accounts suggest that peer groups and games probably become instrumental in late childhood for the formation of a social self based on internalization of the honor-modesty system. The games appear to provide precisely the kind of rotation of roles and variation of scenarios that Mead believed facilitates learning to see one's self from the perspective of a Generalized Other. Ammar, Friedl, and Chaqueri are probably right to emphasize the way many games reach beyond the family and local community to imagine the society at large, which children at this age are beginning to see impinge on their families, and into which they will soon venture. And they may be right to worry that these childhood imaginings of the political order are so hierarchical and tyranni-cal. Writing in reflection on the Iranian revolution, Chaqueri takes this point the farthest, arguing that the games "propagate the imperial complex," that they "introduce into the child's mind the Manichaen notion of rulership/ repression as an 'inevitable' phenomenon."[79]

The contrast between girls' and boys' play also deserves to be empha-sized. Both Ammar and Friedl write that girls' play tends to be much less aggressive and competitive than boys' and that while it is not free of teasing, obscenity, and insult, it rarely entails leaders, followers, and punishments. Girls' worlds are being increasingly circumscribed during late childhood: they are falling increasingly under the authority of their brothers and cousins (who are proving their manliness in explicit contrast to women's weakness)—and this cannot fail to affect how they are construe themselves as girls-becoming-women. But, as Susan Davis notes in her ethnography of Moroccan women, the more cooperative solidarity and competence at adult skills emphasized in their play may provide foundations for constructing surprisingly positive social selves, even within the confines of patriarchy.[80]

It is important to point out again that similar strategies of peer masculin-ization remain common in modern Western societies, and that traditional MENA boys' play with peers resembles the pledging-initiation cycles of Ameri-can student fraternities and the socialization of children into sports teams[81] (which authorities often endorse as training in "leadership"): juniors must prove themselves by withstanding the humiliations and hazings of their senior peers, and then get their turn at humiliating and hazing new juniors. Still, if MENA's social order is, as Eickelman writes, woven of "dyadic relations of domination and subordination," then much of the learning of attitudes, styles, and strate-gies appropriate to both stances appears to be rehearsed in late childhood play.

Religion

Religious knowledge and practice grows steadily during late childhood,[82] and with the onset of puberty a young person should adopt all the prescriptions for adults. Traditionally, most boys and a few girls began to attend Quranic school around the ages of six to eight, where they learned to write the Arabic script and memorize the Quran under the notoriously harsh rule of a religious teacher—often the imam of the local mosque. Many wealthier families hired a religious tutor to teach in their homes, and sometimes including daughters. Poor families' need for a son's labor in the fields or a shop kept many boys from Quranic school.

Quranic education was perceived to buttress the formal and fear-inspiring persona many fathers adopted. The Iranian reformer Ahmad Kasravi recalled his first Quranic teacher as possessing only "a certain skill in beating his pupils on their hands and feet, to the satisfaction of most of the pupils' fathers, who considered beating an even more important part of education than learning to read."[83] The Moroccan psychologist Abdelwahad Radi writes: "The Quranic school, above all, is an institution whose mission is 'social conservation.' It is this function that is the most appreciated by the families . . . rather than the learning of the Quran itself."[84] Entering Quranic school thus has a ritual quality to it, and Ammar quotes other well-known fatherly statements of "advice" to their sons' teachers:

> I have given you the child of my blood, the fruit of my loins, and given you power over him, and made him obedient to you. . . . Teach him the Koran, History, Poetry, Traditions, and appreciation of eloquence. Prevent him from laughing except on proper occasions. . . . Do not be too kind to him, or he will take to idleness. Improve him kindly, but if that will not suffice, you can treat him harshly.[85]

Others report fathers traditionally turned their sons over to the religious teacher with a more draconian instruction: "You kill/sacrifice him, I'll skin him."[86] Ammar notes that parents may notify the teacher of their son's misbehaviors,

> whereupon the Shiekh would give the boys concerned a lesson on the importance of obedience to parents, or threaten them, or even thrash them in front of their parents. . . . In cases of serious offenses such as offending one's father or swearing at religion, or mentioning the mother in swearing, two strong boys would hold the offender's feet in a turban . . . and lift them in front of the Shiekh, who would administer the striking as he deems fit.[87]

Fathers or other senior males also traditionally begin taking their sons to the public bath for the major purification on Thursday nights, and to the mosque on Friday for the weekly sermon—which some of those I interviewed recalled as an important step in joining the world of adult men. So it was for Ali Hashemi, the moderate Iranian mullah whose life-history Roy Mottahedeh uses to tell the story of the Iranian revolution:

Around his sixth birthday Ali stopped going to the bathhouse with his mother and started to go with his father. It wasn't the only important change at that time in his life; learning to pray, learning to write, and learning to sit quietly with his father's friends were just as new and took more hours each week than a visit to the bath. But somehow he remembers the change at the bathhouse best: one week he was sitting with a lot of talkative, sweating half-naked women, the next week he was sitting with a lot of solemn, half-naked men while his father explained to him that in this bathhouse, as in so many others in Iran, a painter had put a picture of the devil on the ceiling. He had done so because the devil was supposed to torture men in a place of fire and steam like the bathhouse.[88]

In this manner, formal religious learning is elaborated in other settings, and a range of hygiene and "folk" health-care practices loosely coalesce as parts of religious life.

While Quranic schooling taught key religious principles—especially about pollution and purification rituals, prayer, and the *hadiths* (traditions or sayings of the Prophet, to be taken as models of comportment)—it consists mainly of memorization. The Quran is divided into 60 *hizbs*, or parts for memorization, and students would work on one at a time, copying the teacher's writing onto slates and reciting them over and over. Many writers have described the terror in which they sat through Quranic school, but some children who were blessed with good memories and voices found themselves praised and encouraged and thrived there. A woman I interviewed had been sent to Quranic school by her devout grandfather and became its star student. She was never beaten, often praised, and her ability led to her being enrolled in public school. She became the first woman teacher from her community.

Whether they flourished or suffered, memorization "inscribed" key images and poetic verses from the Quran in the minds of most, as well as an appreciation for the beauty of Quranic recitation. Many reformers criticize Quranic schools for emphasizing rote memorization at the expense of critical thinking, but knowledge of religious figures and texts and verbal fluency with them are skills crucial to adult social life. Rhetorical eloquence is not only greatly admired but also an important tool in the negotiation of relationships and a key ingredient of a man's reputation—and is also appreciated in women. As Ammar writes, "a learned man is to this day judged by the amount of the Koran and the number of prophetic traditions that he can quote, and the number of proverbs and maxims he can bring into the argument."[89] A child who succeeds in memorizing the Quran is greatly admired, and traditionally, Fernea notes, this "was an occasion for family gathering and celebration, which might also include the city neighborhood or, in rural areas, the entire village."[90]

If children often memorized the Quran in conditions of fear, they typically mastered fasting for the month of Ramadan by their own volition, with encouragement and praise rather than threats. The onset of puberty (a boy's first nocturnal ejaculation and a girl's first menstruation) signals the time at which a young person should keep the entire fast, but most do so before that time, motivated by the desire to be grown up and participate with the family and community. Parents often gently discourage younger children from fasting for long periods, but many begin practicing for part of a day, then a day or two, and gradually increase the duration until they fast the entire month. They recite portions of the Quran throughout Ramadan, and some boys may attend the all-night recitation on the Night of Destiny, where they may begin to appreciate what they first learned under duress.

By memorizing the Quran, using the pollution-purification system to manage their bodily and emotional health, enacting daily religious etiquettes, practicing the self-mastery required to fast the month of Ramadan, and participating in the religious celebrations that mark the passage of the year and major life-transitions, children come to deeply internalize religion during late childhood. In addition to sentiments and motives related to states of purity-pollution, the literature suggests that children develop a sense of acquiring *baraka* (divine blessedness), an awe and often fear of God, a sense of receiving divine mercy and compassion, and an anxiety about *fitna* (chaos, disorder). As I suggested in chapter 3, this probably consolidates what G. H. Mead termed a "social self"—a self seen from the perspective of a Generalized Other constituted of God, the prophets, divine and demonic beings, and the community of believers into which the child is maturing.

Part 2: Modernizing Milieus ❀

The patterns I have been describing characterize more traditional milieus, studied mainly in the 1950s through the 1980s. There can be no doubt that "forces of modernity" are transforming these patterns, but it is difficult to gauge just how, especially in light of the growing differences between social classes. Al-Aharas's survey of 400 Lebanese families found that educated parents have fewer children and follow child-rearing styles that are based more on "encouragement" than "severity."[91] The available data consistently show middle-class families moving generally away from the "apprenticeship and obedience" model, with fewer parents viewing obedience as their primary goal, and more saying they encourage independence and use praise and reasoning to shape their children's behavior.[92] Poor urban families, however, appear to continue their reliance on physical punishment, and this appears to be less leavened by "reasoning" and by the often positive contact of apprenticeship learning than in rural families.[93] Fewer children attend Quranic schools, and formal classroom instruction by strangers has largely replaced apprenticeship learning from parents and kin. One of the most significant changes is that nearly all children now spend this period in public schools, and in the peer cultures fostered by them. But if higher status families are abandoning practices conserved by the poor, they also may be conserving traditions the poor lack the resources to sustain. In addition, there are contrasts at all social levels between those who choose Western versus devout life-styles. It simply cannot be said that higher status families "modernize" more rapidly.

Cederblad and Rahim studied the effects of urbanization by following up her 1960 study of psychiatric symptoms in rural villages outside of Khartoum that had by 1980 become suburbs of the city.[94] Medical exams of 245 children and interviews with their mothers found that many features of traditional family life had been preserved, including polygyny, large family size, little divorce, few women working outside the home, and 100 percent circumcision of both boys and girls, but that incomes, housing, sanitation, nutrition, and overall health had improved considerably. In 1965, 30 percent of boys and 10 percent of girls were in school, but in 1980 that had increased to 90 percent of the boys and 60 percent of the girls. Behavioral disturbances, however, increased—most markedly among children in poor families and among school-aged boys. The researchers point out that while the poor families were objectively much better off than they had been in 1965, they felt poorer. While all families shared a rural life-style in 1965, urbanization had brought social stratification, and the style of housing, clothing, and job status required to feel a respectable member of the community had escalated beyond the means of poorer families. They suggest that school-aged boys bear the brunt of this stratification, as they move out into the unfamiliar outside world with expectations that they will succeed in school and become providers to their families. The higher prevalence of behavior disturbances in urban than in rural communities, they note, has been found in many societies.

Schooling

Public schooling has introduced dramatic changes in all of the late childhood socialization processes described earlier. Throughout the region, educational success has become the primary route of upward mobility, which for many means moving from subsistence into modern economic sectors. Yet schooling has only recently become available in some areas, and it brings failure and disappointment to many of those whose aspirations it initially raises. It also may conserve some traditional socialization processes—such as "rote" learning—by embedding them in modern-looking institutions. Schools replace the apprenticeship style of learning, in which children participate in adult tasks, with classroom instruction and testing by a professional, often an outsider to the community. It replaces mixed-age, kinship-based play with age-based peer groups. It virtually creates adolescence as a developmental period, and makes possible the creation of youth cultures. The activities it introduces—especially sports, and especially soccer—displace the traditional games and semiorganized play described earlier. Schooling also decreases gender differentiation, dramatically in the countries with coeducational schools.

All of these features give formal education the potential to be deeply subversive of the traditional culture, undercutting the control that patronymic associations exert over children. As children's futures come to depend on their school achievement rather than on the subsistence resources their familial network controls, families come to depend on children's earning potential in the modern sector. Parents become unable to teach their children the skills they need or provide sufficient material resources for them to make decent modern lives. Many cannot knowledgeably guide their children into a world that is both modernizing and underdeveloping. Further, new forms of peer relationships provide less training in negotiating the senior-junior dyads that traditionally served as prototypes for adult relationships. Mustafa Haddiya used surveys and interviews to study 500 Moroccan students in a poor rural area[95] and found that parents overwhelmingly embraced education as the route to better lives, but most were unable to support their children in their studies. He reports sharp contradictions between the traditional values practiced at home and the modern values taught at school. But the schools didn't practice those modern values: teachers unhappily posted far from their urban homes resented their deprivation, saw their pupils as culturally handicapped, and mistreated them with insults (that 96 percent reported) and beatings (that 76 percent reported).[96] In addition, 93 percent of the children said they felt frightened at school most of the time, and 96 percent said their teachers' treatment of them most resembled that of their fathers.[97] (It should be noted that the Moroccan parliament recently passed a law prohibiting both parents and teachers from striking children, which the United States and several European countries still have not done.) Haddiya reports that students found the transitions between family and school confusing and that schooling gave them an urban outlook that alienated them from the world of their farming community. But as the urban outlook became their primary frame of self-reference, it induced feelings of inferiority and humiliation.[98]

At the same time, many children continue to participate in apprenticeship-style learning outside of school, and many are taken out of school after the equivalent to our sixth or eighth or tenth grade to pursue traditional vocations. Patron-client-style relationships also may thrive within the schools. One young man I interviewed explained how, as a poor but straight-A student who moved in with relatives in Casablanca to attend high school, he struck up a friendship with a wealthy, less intelligent classmate: the classmate took him to cafes and bought him presents, and he let the classmate copy his schoolwork. And as Haddiya suggests, the *style* of education in many primary schools may not differ dramatically from that of traditional Quranic schools. Gerald Miller studied Moroccan primary classrooms in the early 1970s and found a preponderance of rote, prescribed, nonquestioning behavior and minimal innovation beyond the facts. He concluded: "Although there has been a recent modernization of the primary school curriculum, a closer analysis suggests that the lasting lessons learned have changed little from those taught for centuries in the traditional Quranic schools."[99] Many classrooms still are not dramatically different. A second-grade teacher I interviewed stressed that her main task is to instill *adaab islamiyya*, or religious propriety, which, she explained, consists of proper forms of address, cleanliness, respect, orderly sitting, and "love for the teacher." In their classic study of "modernization," Inkeles and Smith argue that schools modernize less because of the knowledge they teach than because of the principles of bureaucratic organization learned in them.[100] It remains difficult to assess the extent to that the traditional principles of authority, dyadic interdependence, and gender differentiation may be preserved within MENA schools.

Perhaps most important, education appears to be transforming the honor-modesty code into an achievement ethic, in which school achievement has become a major source of familial and personal honor. In a manner perhaps resembling that reported for Japan and other Asian countries, this may recruit family and group-based motives to fuel individual achievement.[101] These processes probably begin to coalesce in the higher primary school grades, toward the end of late childhood. In addition, public education is not undermining religion as many predicted but appears to be encouraging a "Muslim ethicist" religiosity that, like the "Protestant ethic" described by Max Weber, regards achievement and earthly success as a kind of religious calling.[102] I believe this little-appreciated development to be crucial for understanding the broad "return to Islam" among young people in MENA societies.

Debate: The Question of Authoritarianism ❧

Many ethnographers, and especially Arab reformers, have viewed the patriarchal family as "authoritarian." They believe that the authoritarianism learned mainly in this period of childhood carries into the political sphere, providing psychological support to Strong Men and dictators. The notion that political authoritarianism might be rooted in familial authoritarianism was first developed by the Frankfurt School's analysis of Nazism—especially in Erich Fromm's *Escape from Freedom*[103] and T. W. Adorno and colleagues' book *The Authoritarian Personality*.[104] The latter collected empirical data to support the theory that a set of psychological traits cohere in an authoritarian personality syndrome, and that those who develop this syndrome tend to support totalitarian leaders and ideologies from a deep emotional affinity. The syndrome entails a psychological need for subordination to a powerful leader figure, rigid moral values, an inability to tolerate emotional ambivalence, derogation of the weak, and an eagerness to persecute deviants and ethnic out-groups. The study did not, however, spell out the nature of authoritarian parenting in any detail, beyond describing it as distant, demanding, punitive, and intolerant of ambiguity and ambivalence. More recently, Robert Altemeyer has collected an impressive body of data showing that the syndrome of "right-wing authoritarianism" continues to exist in Canada and America and is correlated with growing up in families that practice fundamentalist religions, shelter their children from people who are "different," and make greater use of physical punishment.[105] A good deal of evidence also shows that people tend to become more authoritarian in times of economic and political crisis.[106] Debate continues about the extent to which psychological authoritarianism may influence the course of political events, but the theory remains in good currency as a partial explanation for the wide appeal of Nazism and of other totalitarian movements.

A second body of research on parenting styles has conceptualized authoritarian child-rearing in a different way. Diana Baumrind and others have conceived parenting in terms of two largely independent dimensions: high versus low warmth (or "warm and responsive" versus "rejecting and unresponsive") and high versus low control (or "restrictive and demanding" versus "permissive and understanding").[107] These two dimensions yield four parenting styles:

	High Warmth	Low Warmth
High Control	*Authoritative*	*Authoritarian*
Low Control	*Permissive*	*Uninvolved*

The authoritative style is essentially defined as the ideal, and observations of American nursery school children found it associated with "energetic-friendly" patterns of interaction, high self-esteem, and little antisocial behavior. Children of authoritarian children were found to exhibit more "conflicted-irritable" behavior, which means being moody, unhappy, aimless, fearful, and alternately aggressive and withdrawn. Permissive parents had children more likely to be "impulsive-aggressive," and the children of uninvolved parents showed evidence of neglect, including insecure attachment, low self-esteem, aggression, and poor social and academic skills. Baumrind followed up on her original subjects in adolescence and found continued relationships between parenting style and personality, especially for boys: sons of authoritarian parents had worse academic records, weaker social skills, and lower self-esteem than boys with authoritative parents.[108]

Can MENA child-rearing be said to be "authoritarian" in either of these senses? A number of scholars appear to believe it can, though they do not refer directly to either body of research. Halim Barakat, who has sharply criticized psychological generalizations about Arabs, sees the region's political authoritarianism as having roots in its patriarchal family organization:

Political socialization takes place in the home, resulting in the congruency of political orientations among members of the family. Also, rulers and political leaders are cast in the image of the father, while citizens are cast in the image of children. God, the father, and the ruler thus have many characteristics in common. They are the shepherds, and the people are the sheep: citizens of Arab countries are often referred to as *raiyyah* (the shepherded).[109]

Sharabi makes a similar argument:

> The values and attitudes of patriarchal relations internalized in early childhood underlay the "modernized" surface and determined the deep structure of personality and orientation. . . . A central psychosocial feature of this type of society, whether it is conservative or progressive, is the dominance of the Father (patriarch), the center around that the national as well as the natural family are organized. Thus between ruler and ruled, between father and child, there exist only vertical relations: in both settings the paternal will is the absolute will, mediated in both the society and the family by a forced consensus based on ritual and coercion.[110]

Bouhdiba sharply indicts "paternal authoritarianism":

> There is the terrible image of the father: *Ab*. This all-powerful, all-serious colossus cannot but represent an impenetrable wall between the child and his father. . . . A Muslim upbringing was, of course, authoritarian. As such it was no different from many other things. The authority relationship has deep roots in our traditional society. It binds not only man to woman and parents to children but also teacher to pupil, master to disciple, employer to employee, ruler to ruled, the dead to the living, and God to man.[111]

Hijazi, Hammoudi, Zayour and many others make this argument.

These formulations do not mean, however, that the relationships observed in Western studies hold in MENA societies. The parenting styles theory has been criticized as applying only to Western middle-class milieus, and some studies have found "authoritarian" parenting to produce more well-adjusted children in poor and dangerous communities.[112] Ruth Chao argues that the notions of "authoritarian," "controlling," and "restrictive" are ethnocentric and misleading when applied to Chinese parenting.[113] She cites studies in which Asian parents score mainly as "authoritarians" but their children perform better in school than those of "authoritative" whites, and she suggests that the "strictness" that signals parental hostility and mistrust in white middle-class families signals parental concern and caring in Asian families.

Some research has been conducted in MENA using translated versions of the "F scale" devised to measure authoritarianism for *The Authoritarian Personality*. In the 1950s Edwin Prothro and Louis Melikian administered this and other scales to university students in Lebanon and Egypt,[114] and in both studies the Arab students gave more authoritarian responses than had Americans. Three aspects of these findings, however, raise doubts about whether this indicated the full syndrome of authoritarianism. First, Prothro noted that scores were higher on the items asking directly about authority and obedience than on the indirect questions designed to tap underlying psychological orientations.[115] Second, F-scale scores did not correlate highly with the Political and Economic Conservatism scale, as they did in American samples, suggesting that endorsement of obedience to authority may not shape political ideologies in the same way. Third, Melikian also administered a scale measuring "nonauthoritarian" attitudes that had shown strong negative correlations with the F-scale in American samples, and found much lower correlations in the Egyptian sample—which suggests that "the Moslem authoritarian . . . has more nonauthoritarian traits than the United States authoritarian."[116]

In the 1960s Cigdem Kagitcibasi carried out a more comprehensive study of authoritarianism in Turkey.[117] She sought to separate features of authoritarianism likely to reflect social norms (i.e., loyalty to parents and state, rejection of out-groups) from a "core" personality trait of dogmatism and intolerance she believed would be universal. A sample of Turkish students scored higher on measures of respect for state authority, general respect for authority, and rejection of foreigners than did a sample of American students, reflecting Turkish social norms. They also scored higher on core authoritarianism, which she believes is probably due to "stricter discipline within the Turkish family." But the Turkish students actually scored slightly lower than Americans on a measure of authoritarian family structure: they were higher on the "control" items in this scale but reported as much or more "affection" in their families as did the Americans—in accordance with ethnographic accounts that describe Turkish families as both warm and restrictive. Most important, generally lower intercorrelations among the scales in the Turkish sample indicate that these features do not form a personality syndrome there as they do in America, echoing Melikian's earlier findings among Egyptian students. Though these were neither large nor flawless studies, they suggest (1) that Middle Easterners *value* authority more highly than do Westerners, but (2) that the authoritarian personality *syndrome* may not be widespread—or at least was not in the generation that came of age in the 1950s and 1960s.

I have located few MENA studies using Baumrind's typology. El-Feky surveyed 400 Kuwaiti couples with children, all university or graduate students, and as he predicted, this affluent and highly educated sample strongly preferred the "authoritative" style.[118] But he suggests that traditional views influenced their next-strongest support for "authoritarian" styles. Karakitapoglu-Aygun's survey of Turkish and American students found the Turks to perceive greater "authoritative" family control than the

Americans but equal "authoritarian" control.[119] El-Feky believes Baumrind's typology applies to high-status MENA parents, but there are many reasons to suspect that it might not fit less-elite groups. For one thing, the presence of a distant, fear-inspiring father does not mean that a household, especially an extended one, lacks warmth. For another, ethnographic reports indicate that parents typically exert great control in some contexts but leave children quite free in others, so they may be "restrictive" and "permissive" at the same time. And perhaps most important, as Chao suggests of China, some aspects of "strictness" that look authoritarian to Western eyes may convey involvement and concern in MENA families. Karakitapoglu-Aygun concurs with Chao and suggests that styles of control Americans would perceive as authoritarian Turks would perceive as authoritative.[120] In light of these considerations, we simply do not know the extent to that the predominant models of parenting are "authoritarian" or "authoritative."[121]

Here the Frankfurt School's theory proves especially useful. Fromm and Adorno and colleagues tended to see traditional, preindustrial family relations as patriarchal and often harsh, but not as authoritarian in the sense they studied in conjunction with Naziism. They saw authoritarianism as emerging from a transformation of traditional authority in modernizing conditions. As industrialization and urbanization undermined the traditional bases of patriarchal authority (for example, control of the skills, resources, and social statuses children must acquire to become adults), many parents resorted to harsher means to enforce obedience for weaker reasons ("Because I'm your father and I say so!"). And as children moved into an adult world in which the security afforded by traditional attachments had broken down, and Depression conditions turned the modern world's freedoms into empty promises, many "escaped" into the authoritarian world of the Nazis. Similar dislocations may have contributed to the rise of Shinto Nationalism in Japan at roughly the same time, and may be affecting MENA societies in recent decades. Sharabi in fact argues that it is conditions of "neopatriarchy"—in which true tradition has been destroyed but modernity not achieved—that transform *patriarchal* forms of authority into *authoritarian* ones.[122]

All this underscores the importance of distinguishing between traditional models of patriarchal authority and the modern syndrome of authoritarianism. Patriarchal authority certainly was prominent in MENA societies, but, as Kagitcibasi points out, families also tended to provide warmth and nurturance. Participatory and protodemocratic relations also were common: the give-and-take discussions Mahfouz portrays Ahmad's family as enjoying in his absence may be a prototype, and the lively political discussion on "the Arab street" may be another. In addition, many traditional relationships were based on egalitarian principles, and ethnographers almost universally testify to the importance of "egalitarianism" as a cardinal value throughout the region. Islam's core vision of a "brotherhood" of believers seeks to forge a wider egalitarian community—which the mosque symbolizes in traditional communities. Khuri actually argues that it is the *absence* of a hierarchical vision of the social order that leads to despotic rule, as individuals struggle to become "first among equals." If the young Moroccans I interviewed all had encountered at least one fearsome authority in their childhoods, they also all had developed some important nonpatriarchal relationships. Throughout the course of our conversations, they sketched out a variety of prototypes for human association, some more "democratic" and some more "authoritarian"—any of which they could draw upon to imagine political communities.[123] Perhaps most important, nearly all of them voiced criticisms of their parents and of other authority figures, in contrast to the idealization and refusal to admit ambivalence about authorities found to be a component of the authoritarian syndrome.

The egalitarian values of MENA are embedded in many types of social association, especially at "grassroots" levels, where—at least outside the reach of sultans and feudal-like lords—leadership tended to be temporary and loyalty based on consent. Most local groups relied on a *jemʿ*, or council of elders, consisting of the senior male from each household, to discuss and make consensus decisions on collective matters. In addition to patriarchal authority, traditional MENA societies also relied on "protodemocratic" or "protorepublican" forms of political organization. It is at *higher* levels of political organization, not at the "grass roots," that despotic methods have so often been used to impose a Strong Man's rule.

Hamid Dabashi argues that three "cultural paradigms" of political-religious authority crystallized in MENA in the first centuries after the Prophet's life, each anchored in a "remembered persona of Mohammed." These initially took shape as sects: the Sunni sought to routinize the Prophet's charismatic authority, the Shi'i to reinvigorate it in a succession of charismatic individuals, and the perpetually revolutionary Khariji to reject both of these in favor of the anarchic free choice of individuals. These ideologies have not remained confined to sects, however, but have become woven as internal debate into the "the character and culture traits present in every Muslim individual and community."[124] Sects and regimes came and went, but

> what remained constant was the simultaneous and unrelenting presence of all these three complementary/contradictory fixations on the institutional, individual, and negational conceptions of authority. As institutional (Sunni) forces of authority sought to stabilize, routinize, and systematize the social and moral life, the individual (Shi'i) forces would shift the balance of obedience away from centralized piety and invest it in one charismatic figure or another. Borrowing from both, just to deny them both legitimacy, the negational (Khariji) forces of obedience sought (temporary) relief from any sustained organization of obedience, whether administered by the state apparatus or claimed by the individual charismatic.[125]

An individual Muslim's outlook on authority, he concludes, depends on whether circumstances put him in a Sunnite, Shi'ite, or Kharijite "state of mind."[126] Anchored as is each in a "remembered persona of Mohammed," none are democratic. But at the same time none are inherently "authoritarian." Most important, Dabashi shows that there is not simply *a* traditional model of authority but that tradition encompasses multiple and conflicting models—which might be modernized in a variety of ways, including more truly authoritarian and more truly democratic ones.

Populist movements throughout MENA have sought to expand the public sphere and organize it according to more democratic and republican principles, while dictatorships have repeatedly tried to destroy the public sphere and control the political process by neopatriarchal use of intimidation and patronage. Khuri points to the warring militias in Beirut, the House of Saud's rule in Saudia Arabia, the Ba'th regimes in Syria and Iraq as examples of groups that have successfully dominated the modern political landscape by organizing themselves in accordance with traditional principles of enclosure and endogamy.[127] Sharabi emphasizes the role of the *mukhabarat* (secret police) in sustaining MENA "neopatriarchies," and Kanan Makiya (writing as "Samir al-Khalil") has described how the Iraqi regime has used *mukhabarat* to sow a Hobbesian fear in each person of all others, in the midst of which the leader figure, magnified by propaganda into the Leader, appears to provide a measure of security. Makiya emphasizes that the Iraqi Ba'th Party did not just build on tradition: its "Leader syndrome . . . was a *new* conception of authority for modern Iraq uniquely associated with Ba'thi experience."[128] To create this authority, the regime combined terror with a vast system of patronage financed with oil revenues to eliminate the institutions of civil society, both traditional and modern:

> Their project was to destruct the social reality they inherited into a new set of equally weighted constituent elements—frightened, rootless individuals, alienated from their traditional groups (kin, tribe, sect, class)—and then to reassemble these fragments within a new state-centralized network of relationships. The undifferentiated Leviathan-like mass that emerged was in principle either hostile to or sealed off from any other "partial," non-Ba'thist sense of belonging.

Dislocated from traditional groupings, he continues, "the ideally formed Ba'thist individual lacks the civilizing attributes of bourgeois society and consequently is left suspended in a no-man's-land, one that is both characteristically modern and terrifyingly primitive."[129] After a time, he writes, people began "'choosing' to surround themselves with pictures of Saddam Hussein, hoping in this way to 'ward off evil.'" As they silenced themselves in front of their children and required others to mouth the regime's propaganda, its "raw power" was "turned into a new kind of authority, one that rules inside each soul."[130] The new authoritarianism thus appears not as a resurgence of tradition against modernity but works from the outside in, from *modern* forms of propaganda, terror, and dependence.

These considerations suggest that the region's postindependence totalitarian regimes have not come to power by the momentum of a traditional authoritarianism. Many of them have consolidated their rule by wiping away more egalitarian traditional forms of association. This does not mean that psychological orientations toward traditional patriarchal authority are irrelevant, however. Like Hijazi, Barakat, and Sharabi, Makiya sees the respect traditionally given to threatening-but-protective authorities as helping to confer legitimacy on regimes that have forced themselves on populaces. In addition, political actors deliberately use patriarchal rhetoric and style themselves as embodying traditional strengths and virtues. Abdellah Hammoudi sees the roots of the much less draconian "Moroccan authoritarianism" in traditional relationships, but he too does not regard these as having their own modernity-retarding momentum. Rather, he traces their deliberate top-down rehabilitation in the 1960s and 1970s: after a florescence of democratic aspirations and reforms initiated during the independence movement, he writes, monarchical patronage and coercion "forced people back into the 'politics of the notables,'"[131] disseminating the nonideological *style* of the rural Big Man throughout new political institutions. Conspicuously displaying piety, self-mastery, charity, distance from women, respect for elders, and protection of dependents, "the notable constitutes a cultural reincarnation, which has penetrated almost all spheres of life."[132] The political sphere thus has been created as a competition among patron-client networks, managed by patronage and occasional violence from the top, operating on an authoritarian model of dominant-subordinate dyads rather than on the principles of equality, representation, and consensus that also form part of the fabric of tradition.

The question about whether late childhood socialization is "authoritarian" thus has a three-part answer. The first concerns individual differences. Not every family follows the patriarchal model, and more than a small minority of children develop during late childhood in milieus that diverge from it. Individual children respond differently to it, as Mahfouz shows so well in the characters of Ahmad's children—especially Yasin, who so fails to develop his father's self-control that his sexual escapades cause scandal after scandal, and Kamal, who becomes an intellectual and criticizes the whole social order. The Moroccan religious judge whom Eickelman interviewed appears to have responded to his father's harsh treatment in a classically authoritarian manner, refusing to criticize him and viewing his thrice-daily beatings as having been for his own good. But Nawal El Saadawi rebelled against patriarchal authority and became one of Egypt's leading feminists and dissidents.

Second, the authoritarianism evident in the politics of many MENA nations should not be seen as tradition perpetuating itself by its own psychocultural momentum. In the absence of free speech, we have no idea how much popular support the autocrats have, or the extent to which Islamist opposition may be authoritarian. Only the Iranian regime came to power as the result of a popular movement, and as I write this it is under attack by large numbers discontented with its totalitarianism. As Sharabi, Makiya, and Hammoudi emphasize, a good deal of current authoritarianism appears to stem from the confluence of individuals defensively fashioning "neopatriarchal" outlooks in conditions of underdevelopment, and ruling elites "rehabilitating" patriarchal models in authoritarian manners. These are *modern* processes, even when rhetoric appeals to the strength of tradition.

Third, the emergence of social classes is bringing about well-documented differences in family size, birth spacing, and child-rearing philosophies. More educated, better off parents are generally moving away from the patriarchal model and adopting more Euro-American middle-class styles of parenting. At the same time, less educated, poorer parents in underdeveloped sectors now find the traditional bases of their authority eroded, as they cannot teach their children the skills or provide them with the resources they need to make decent lives in the modernizing world. As they lose these potent means of controlling and guiding their children, they may turn to harsher and more truly authoritarian means—much as the Frankfurt School theorists believed occurred among the working and "petit bourgeoisie" classes in Germany.

In the United States, countless surveys have found education and socio-economic status to be the strongest predictors of authoritarian values and ethnic prejudice, and working-class families' greater emphasis on conformity and use of physical punishment is well documented.[133] While the authoritarian syndrome certainly can be found among the educated and well off (who provide some of its most charismatic leaders), it is mainly produced in poorer, lower status milieus. While patriarchy appears to be softening among MENA's educated elites, it may be hardening into authoritarianism in families mired in underdevelopment. To the extent that this stratum becomes politically active—with aspirations raised by education and media but frustrated by lack of success—it may readily give support to authoritarian ideologies and figures.

In the final analysis, reform-minded scholars are probably correct to see patriarchal child-rearing as *potentially* dangerous, as it creates a model of fearsome and harsh but ultimately protective and empowering strength that can be fashioned into an authoritarian political style. But they are probably not correct to see traditional patriarchal authority as leading directly to modern authoritarianism. So the debate remains, and we do not presently know *how* dangerous traditional patriarchy may be, or to what extent underdevelopment may be *creating* modern authoritarianism.

Sources ❀

The primary English-language sources on late childhood continue to be Hamid Ammar's *Growing Up in an Egyptian Village* and Nawal Ammar's *An*

Egyptian Village Growing Up, Prothro's *Child Rearing in Lebanon*, Badri's *Child-Rearing Practices in the Sudan*, and Grotberg and Badri's followup study (using a similar methodology), Williams's *Youth of El Hacimi Haouch*, Brink's "Changing Child-Rearing Patterns in an Egyptian Village," and Friedl's *Children of Deh Koh*. Cederblad and Rahim's 1980 followup to her 1965 psychiatric study of Sudanese children provides especially valuable data on the effects of urbanization.[134]

Arabic sources include Al-Aharas's interview study of 400 Syrian parents of 7- to 12-year-olds,[135] Askandar's interview study of 100 lower class and 100 middle-class Egyptian parents,[136] and S'adallah's ethnographic study of 30 rural Egyptian families (comparing nomadic Bedouin, settled Bedouin, and farmers),[137] which provide empirical portraits of general patterns and important urban-rural and social status differences. Several studies directed by Mahmoud Abdelqader[138] and teams from Egypt's National Research Center[139] provide additional data on parental attitudes and socialization practices, and Abdelhamid Jabar's *Al-itijahat al-walidia fi tenshia al-atfal* ("Parental Socialization Attitudes") document differences related to parents' educational levels. Shakri's *Al-tanshi'a al-ijtima'iyya* (Socialization) summarizes many of the Egyptian studies carried out in the 1950s through 1970s, including some master's and doctoral dissertations, many of which provide data on urban-rural and social class differences. Maissa Al-Mofti conducted questionnaire studies of sixth-graders in the mid-1980s to complement earlier parent surveys and to assess rural-urban contrasts[140] and the distinctive socialization practices of Nubians in Upper Egypt,[141] and Mustafa Haddiya used questionnaires, interviews, and a TAT-like procedure to study schoolchildren in rural and urban regions of Morocco.[142]

These studies are supplemented by a relatively rich literature on children's games, including, in addition to chapters in Hamid Ammar's and Friedl's books, Nawal Ammar's dissertation, Cosroe Chaqueri's *Beginning Politics in the Reproductive Cycle of Children's Tales and Games in Iran*, Alan Dundes's article "The Structure of Turkish Boys' Verbal Dueling Games," and a chapter in David Hart's *Aith Waryaghar of the Moroccan Rif*. Life-histories (such as Dale Eickelman's *Knowledge and Power in Morocco* and Roy Mottahedeh's *Mantle of the Prophet*) and autobiographical writings (such as Driss Chraibi's *Simple Past*, and Abdelkrim Ghallab's *Le Passe Enterre*) also provide important accounts. One of the best portraits of traditional family relations comes from the Egyptian Nobel Prize–winning writer Naguib Mahfouz's Cairo Trilogy, especially its first volume, *Palace Walk*. In addition, a number of social theorists have written descriptions of development that cover this period, including Halim Barakat's book *The Arab World*, Abdelwaheb Bouhdiba's *Sexuality in Islam*, and Hisham Sharabi's *Neopatriarchy*, and discuss the "authoritarian" character of fathering and nurturant style of mothering that together form the nexus of the traditional cultural model.

CHAPTER 7

Adolescence

Ethnographic studies show that in traditional milieus, adolescence was brief for most boys and nonexistent for most girls. Yet for both boys and girls, the years after puberty entailed important transitions and psychological development, especially in acquiring expertise at the honor- and religion-based practices they typically mastered in late childhood and in honing the "social selves" they fashioned in terms of these two ethical systems. Because they married in their early teens, girls probably experienced greater discontinuity, as menstruation, deflowering at one's wedding, moving out of one's parents' home, and childbirth often came within a couple of years. Boys probably experienced greater continuity in their familial relationships but disjunction between deferential subordination to elders, dominance over juniors, and aggressive competition for status and honor with peers. Like other Eurasian civilizations, MENA prohibited premarital sex and prescribed arranged marriages and, like other preindustrial Mediterranean cultures, made the seclusion and virginity of daughters/sisters into a point of family honor— turning the suppression of sexual and romantic feelings into a major developmental task during this period. Yet in spite of MENA's strong "collectivist" values rooted in emotional interdependencies nurtured from infancy, the literature suggests that many girls and boys experienced sharp conflicts between their own "individualistic" desires and the control their elders exerted in the name of group interests.

The formation of a household-based "group self" probably helped cement adolescents' allegiances, especially during this period in which both boys and girls came to shoulder so much responsibility for their group's work and honorable reputation. Religious devotion provided young people with schemas for accommodating to the fates imposed by nature, by the logic of honor, and by the authority of patriarchs. And the richly elaborated symbolism of gender—opposing outside and inside, seed and soil, bone and flesh, right and left, white and red, and so on—provided identity-anchoring links between bodily processes, spiritual qualities, and the rhythms of the cosmos.

Modernization and underdevelopment have created "adolescence" as a developmental period, with family-based, apprenticeship-style socialization increasingly being replaced by formal schooling. As described in the previous chapter, this appears to be catalyzing a transformation of the honor-modesty system into a family-fueled achievement motivation that resembles that described for some Asian cultures. Most traditional symbols of identity are being replaced by media-influenced youth cultures, introducing a new source of strife with parents. Marc Schade-Paulsen's study of Algerian "rai" music shows how these subcultures can be "transgressive" yet conservative at the same time. Mixed-sex education in most countries has increased opportunities for romantic and sexual contacts, but these remain saturated with anxiety and mistrust. And in many countries, the traditionally direct transition from child to adult has given way to widespread and realistic fear of being unable to acquire any adult role.

Researchers offer contrasting accounts of whether adolescents are being thrown into "crisis" by social dislocations and cultural contradictions or make generally smooth transitions to adulthood sustained by family ties and religious values that have remained more resilient in MENA societies than in many others. These views cannot easily be resolved, though there certainly are individual differences: some youths make smooth transitions to adulthood while others struggle mightily. As Mounia Benani-Chraibi suggests, a good deal of strife may be kept latent during ordinary or "cool" times by family and community control, and emerge into the open in "hot" times of political upheaval.

Introduction ✤

Many observers of MENA societies see adolescents coming of age in a crossfire of cultural conflict, their aspirations raised by education and global media but dashed by economic underdevelopment and political despotism, their imaginations fired alternately by the calling to usher in the modern and by the calling to conserve the authenticity of their traditions. Youths put themselves on the front lines of nationalist movements in the 1920s through the 1950s, of leftist and prodemocracy protests in the 1960s and 1970s, and of Islamist movements in the 1980s and 1990s. They have done much of the fighting in the civil wars in Lebanon and Algeria, the Iranian revolution, and the Palestinian Intifaada. High schools and universities have convulsed with political ferment for decades and are closely watched by authorities. All of this suggests that MENA adolescents experience high levels of inner turmoil and constitute an especially volatile political force. Unfortunately, there are relatively few psychological studies to confirm this assessment (see the sources discussed at the end of this chapter).

American ethnographers seem somewhat surprised to have observed less psychological disturbance and generational conflict than they anticipated. Davis and Davis write:

> [Erik] Erikson's account of an adolescent identity beleaguered by contradictory role expectations sounds like it should work well in the rapidly changing Moroccan setting, but in fact we have not seen much of the "role confusion" of which Erikson writes. Zawiya youth seem to us surprisingly good at negotiating the twists and turns of daily life.[1]

While some Arab researchers report continuity and relatively little distress, autobiographies and literary works portray more inner turmoil. Mahfouz's depictions of Si Ahmad's children in his Cairo Trilogy illustrates the variety of youthful struggles with paternal authority and cultural tradition. Yacine wants to emulate his father but lacks Ahmad's self control and discretion and careens from scandal to scandal. Fahmy sneaks out to join an anti-British demonstration and is killed by soldiers' fire. Mahfouz's own voice perhaps speaks through Kamal, whose study of philosophy leads him to subvert the foundations of patriarchy. A number of Arab researchers also perceive turmoil and describe a widespread "crisis of youth."

A pair of contrasting portraits thus emerges. One portrait shows a family-centered, collectivistic culture in which adolescents mature into adulthood enmeshed in thick networks of social support and control, and consequently with relatively little inner turmoil or rebellious testing of convention. The other portrays a patriarchal society dis-integrated by economic underdevelopment and deformed Western ideals of freedom and consumer culture, which provokes adolescent individualism, rebellion, and inner struggle. Part 1 of this chapter considers adolescence in traditional milieus, with separate sections on girls' and boys' development, and part2 discusses modernizing milieus. The chapter concludes with an examination of the conflict between "smooth transition" and "discontinuity and crisis" views of MENA youth.

Theories of Adolescent Development

Western theories generally view adolescence as a period in which teen-agers separate from their families and move into their own peer, romantic, and work relationships. They thus emphasize the attainment of personal autonomy and self-regulation as the primary psychological task of adolescence. According to the Freudian view, puberty reawakens "latent" Oedipal attachments, which must be "worked through" in order to separate from one's parents and develop an autonomous, well-integrated ego. This view has few adherents today, but many psychodynamic psychologists emphasize the destabilizing effects of adolescent sexuality and ambivalent feelings about familial dependence and parental authority. Many also see an intensified narcissism among adolescents, evident in egocentric outlooks and heightened concern with self-esteem. The Piagetian view emphasizes the cognitive leap adolescents make into "formal operational thought" that enables them to reflect on their beliefs, actions, pasts, and futures in adult terms, and to reevaluate the norms and etiquettes they have learned. Piaget also believed this leads to an "egocentrism" of outlooks and concerns, which gradually becomes "decentered." Both theories thus view adolescence as beginning with a destabilization of a youth's orientation to the world and with an intensified preoccupation with the self.

Over the last two decades, many psychologists have adopted reinforcement and social modeling theories to account for development during the teen years. They tend not to view adolescence as entailing the kind of developmental discontinuities that the Freudians and Piagetians believe define it as a developmental stage. They do see potential conflict between the incentives that shape behavior in different settings, especially home versus school versus peers. In general, these researchers have focused on factors of particular importance in American society: (1) parenting styles, (2) achievement motivation, (3) peer popularity versus rejection, and (4) popular media. Clearly, most of these influences on adolescent development were irrelevant in traditional MENA milieus, where parents had different aims and where schools, same-age peer groups, and modern media did not exist.[2] These influences are becoming important on an almost a daily basis, however, as smaller families, education, and mass media become universal.

All of these theories have been criticized as products of Western societies that value individual autonomy and as not applicable to "collectivistic" cultures that emphasize lifelong familial loyalty and interdependence. Indeed, the ideal of personal autonomy as the "healthy" outcome of adolescence appears to be woven into most Western theories, and *is* inappropriate to much of MENA. But the processes by which biological, emotional, and cognitive changes destabilize earlier forms of psychological organization, and by which group loyalties create conflicts between social milieus, probably determine the course of adolescence in MENA as well as in the West.

In MENA societies, two major developmental tasks of this period appear to be (1) the extension of interpersonal styles associated with honor-modesty and Islam beyond the patronymic association and to nonkin patrons and clients, and (2) incorporation of the young person's adult strength and sexuality within these etiquettes and systems of self-care. Together these entail an elaboration and honing of the *social personae* shaped by honor-modesty and Islam— when things go according to cultural plan—developing "expertise" at this middle level of psychological organization. Many Western psychologists also emphasize the formation of what Erik Erikson termed a "psycho-social identity" as the central developmental task of late adolescence and early adulthood. My life-history studies of identity suggest that the consolidation of social personae indeed defines the nature of the identity-development task and sets it in motion during this period. But largely because the consolidation of an identity is seen to complete the transition into adulthood, and most writings on identity deal with people in their late teens and twenties, I will devote the following chapter to writings on this topic. It is important to keep in mind, however, that identity formation gets well underway during adolescence.

Adolescence in Traditional Milieus ❀

Researchers typically define the beginning of adolescence as the onset of sexual maturation ("puberty"), though cultures may or may not recognize this as beginning a transition, and they may or may not synchronize changes in social roles with it. Ahmad Ouzi's linguistic analysis of terms used for youths of this age led him to conclude that traditional Moroccan (and probably MENA) society did not recognize "adolescence" as a developmental period. He believes the rapid transition of children into adult roles did not allow for the kinds of psychological development held to characterize adolescence in industrialized societies, and he suggests that a major psychological task consisted of subordinating individualistic strivings to family and community authority.[3]

Schlegel and Barry report that about two-thirds of the societies they surveyed hold public initiations into adulthood, about equally for boys and girls.[4] In many societies this begins a period of youth—much more often for boys than for girls—that may last two to four years, until marriage. Several African cultures held initiation rites for boys every five to seven years, and those initiated together formed an "age-set" with various social and ritual responsibilities. Like most complex agricultural societies (China, India, medieval Europe), MENA societies do not hold initiation rites for adolescents. However, the onset of sexual maturity signals to both boys and girls that they should begin fully observing purification practices and keep the entire fast of Ramadan—which served as an informal and perhaps semipublic rite of passage. Unlike many initiation rites, these are not forced: most adolescents perform them as personal accomplishments that demonstrate their acquisition of social maturity, 'aqel. In some areas, puberty also brought changes of dress—such as wearing the burqa mask in parts of Arabia[5] and adult makeup styles in parts of North Africa[6]—and greater seclusion for women.

Adolescence in the MENA societies ended with marriage, as Schlegel and Barry say it does in nearly all traditional societies. But since most girls were married soon after puberty (and many before), the wedding itself can be seen as an initiation ritual that marks a direct transition from childhood to adulthood. Early marriage of girls is not unusual: Schlegel and Barry report they are married within two years of puberty in 60 percent of the societies they examined.[7] While nearly two-thirds of societies allow premarital sexual intercourse,[8] traditional MENA cultures—like most complex agricultural so-

---

cieties—did not.[9] And while nearly 60 percent of societies allow boys to take initiative in selecting their spouses, and nearly 50 percent allow girls to do so, marriages in MENA traditionally were arranged—also as in most complex agricultural societies. Schlegel and Barry found "subordination" of both boys and girls to their fathers to be much more pronounced in pastoral and agricultural societies—and MENA historically combined these means of subsistence—than in foraging and horticultural ones.[10] In general, then, adolescence in MENA societies followed the broad outlines of a Eurasian pattern (Europe, India, and China), rooted in family control of land, livestock, and reproduction, which emphasized patriarchal authority, sexual restraint, and arranged marriage.

In traditional settings, the psychological themes central to late childhood continue to be important: adolescents become fuller participants in the adult relationships of their patronymic associations, honing the etiquettes they mastered in late childhood and performing them to display their 'aqel, or "social maturity." They also more skillfully use the interpersonal strategies they have learned to pursue their own interests, negotiating dyadic interdependencies—entailing authority and deference, assertive dependence and nurturance, vulnerability and protection—both within and increasingly beyond the household. Their responsibility for conserving their family's honor increases markedly, as the virginity of postpubertal girls becomes a symbol of family honor, and the vigilance and courage of its teenaged boys a source of its strength. Land and livestock also are sources of power and honor, and in many traditional milieus adolescent boys were called to fight to defend or extend the household's holdings. Identification with the "house" ideally intensifies and provides the "we-self" or "self object" that holds their loyalty in the face of diverging interests, and sustains them through renunciations imposed for its sake. Adolescents remain enmeshed in the same patterns of patriarchal authority imposed in late childhood, though they increasingly are expected to comply less from fear than from internalized loyalties.

New developmental themes also come to the fore, especially as a consequence of physical and sexual maturity. In traditional milieus, at least, boys' rough games evolve into the more serious business of performing manhood, which may embroil them in deadly games of challenge and riposte, dramatic displays of filial loyalty, or ascetic feats of religious devotion. Ethnographers consistently report that sexual matters are neither concealed from children nor branded as sinful, and that by late childhood most are familiar with bawdy talk and romantic poetry and song. Both boys and girls are generally expected to develop romantic interests and "crushes" but to refrain from pursuing them. Girls are seen to have weak control over their sexual desires, so their fathers and brothers intensify their efforts to seclude them. Boys may be encouraged to "hunt" girls and get sexual experience with outsiders, but they also are warned about the explosive scandals that could result.

Wikan's description of the contrast between girls' and boys' adolescence in Oman holds for many traditional milieus, though it perhaps overstates boys' freedom:

> At the age of twelve to thirteen, both boys and girls are thought mature and ready to assume full adult responsibilities. Whereas girls are then married off, boys wait an average of ten more years before they arrange for their own marriage. . . . Whereas boys in their teens become masters of their own lives, girls become the subjects of a new and unknown master, their husband—and often of his mother too. Boys enter a stage of increasing freedom and experience; girls enter one of increasing work and confinement, but also of gratifying responsibilities and chances of self-actualization.[11]

Girls in Traditional Settings

For girls, the stricter control imposed at puberty often brings an abrupt end to mixed-sex play, and in some areas fuller veiling and seclusion. In the Omani village studied by Wikan, for example, girls begin wearing the burqa mask at puberty and marry soon after.[12] Several ethnographers (Wikan, Boddy, Delaney) have emphasized the way these practices and the symbols associated with them link female fertility with the powers of nature—conferring value on adolescent girls and disempowering them at the same time. It is impossible to estimate how many girls experience puberty as an enriching fruition of their reproductive powers, but many do not. Soumaya Naamane-Guesseus writes that even in Casablanca in the 1980s, many girls experienced their first menstruation in ignorance and distress, and their sexual maturity as a source of anxiety.[13] In 1965 Nawal El Saadawi described her reactions to her first menstruation:

> I stayed in my room for four days in a row, not having the courage to face my brother, or my father, or even the servant boy. . . . My mother has undoubtedly betrayed my new secret . . . I closed the door on myself to explain this strange phenomenon to myself. . . . Was there no other way for girls to mature, other than this unclean way? . . . God undoubtedly hates girls, so he tarnished them all with this shame. . . . I withdraw within myself, hiding my dejected existence.[14]

Certainly not all girls had such negative reactions, but even though menstruation signals fecundity its cultural meanings tend to be negative. Menstrual blood is regarded as polluted and polluting, and while menstruating women do not have to remove themselves from social interaction (as they do in some cultures), it is nonetheless a period of uncleanliness, as it was traditionally throughout the Mediterranean. Restrictions vary from place to place: Delaney reports that the Turkish women she studied do not make bread

In traditional settings, adolescent girls provide much of the work required to run their households, like these girls grinding grain for couscous.

when they are menstruating because they view it as a procreative activity subject to contamination. They also avoid pregnant women, as menstrual blood's "noxious odor" could "penetrate bodily boundaries and bring about a miscarriage or deform the fetus."[15] Abu-Lughod reports that "Bedouin women exaggerate the uncleanliness of menstruation by abstaining from bathing or even hair combing while menstruating."[16] And, she notes, its significance is elaborated among the Bedouin (as in some other MENA groups) by the contrasting colors worn by men and women:

> The uncleanliness associated with menstruation is not restricted to the days when a women is actually menstruating; rather it taints all females from the onset of menarche until menopause, and even after. Men are symbolically associated with purity, the right (the sacred), and the color white. . . . The quintessential item of Awlad 'Ali

Adolescent boys (like this teenaged shepherd) do much of the farm work and herding for their households, and begin to share responsibility for defending their family's resources and honor.

men's clothing is the *jard*, a white woolen blanket worn over the robes and knotted at one shoulder like a toga. Women are associated with uncleanliness, the left, and the colors red and black. . . . They never wear white.[17]

Puberty signals the time for arranging a marriage. The cultural model holds, Wikan writes, "that love is created through consummation of marriage."[18] The preference for "close" marriages combined with mothers' frequent behind-the-scenes efforts enables many girls to influence their parents' choices, and often to stay close to their families. "If they are close by," a Bedouin woman explained, "daughters can eat with you and come visit you often. If they give birth, their mothers are near them. If they get sick, they're near their mothers."[19] Girls also may welcome arranged marriages with outsiders, as did the young Iraqi girl described by Elizabeth Fernea, who was married outside her family, to a teacher, at the age of 15.[20] And many restrictive families still allow their teen-aged children opportunities to meet and work out romance-based marriages. Elaine Hazelton summarizes the Jordanian Bedouin Jawazi al Malakim's account of her traditional marriage in these terms: "Even though they were of different tribes, they had occasionally seen each other and talked at a well while performing their duties. They had even arranged to meet at various times before Hassan finally asked his uncle, who knew Jawazi's father, to propose the marriage."[21]

Other girls were married to men they knew and despised, however, or to men they first saw on their wedding night. Some accepted their fates, but others resisted, a few to the point of running away or committing suicide. Davis reports the following from the life-history of a rural Moroccan woman:

> My father died, God bless his soul, and my mother gave me [to a man] while I was still small. . . . When he had the wedding, I ran away. . . . They came and caught me; they brought me back. I ran away again, and they slapped me into irons, on my legs they put a chain—on my legs they put iron rings like those for animals. A girl friend helped me and we took them off one leg and I hung it around my neck and I had the iron ring in my hand and I ran away from the village [and eventually got her mother to break off the engagement].[22]

A few girls took "dishonorable" routes of flight. The following song was recorded from a young Moroccan prostitute in the High Atlas mountains in the 1930s:

> Poor naive young man, stop hassling me! . . .
> You say you want me to be your wife
> After just one night of my love-making.
> Well, I know how long your desire would last!
> And what can you offer that's sweeter than freedom? . . .
> What can you give me, tell me that, naive young man?
> Days without meat, without sugar, and without songs,
> The sweat and dirt of hard work,
> The dung of the stable, stinking clothes,
> And that awful smoke in the dark kitchen,
> While you're off on the mountain, dancing the dance of the rifles?
> And you'll keep after me, all the time
> To bear boys, boys, and more boys!
> Can't you see I'm not made for all that? . . .
> I'm like a flower with a seductive scent
> That only blossoms for a pleasant reason,
> To receive, when it chooses, each night and each day,
> The freshness of the dawn, the caress of the sun.[23]

These certainly are exceptions to the rule of parental authority, but stories of teen-age daughters' rebellion circulate in every community and testify to the "individualistic" strivings that readily surface against the grain of family loyalty.

Weddings as Girls' Rites of Passage

In traditional milieus, the marriage ceremony serves as a rite of passage into adulthood, publicly celebrating a girl's value, as she is made beautiful with gowns, jewels, and intricate henna designs. El Khayat-Bennai emphasizes that a girl's socialization from the age of four or five aims—from the skills she is taught to the collecting of her trousseau—at building anticipation of her fairy-tale-like wedding day. (She also reports the saying that "a woman only goes out into the world three times: from her mother's stomach, to her husband, and to the cemetery.")[24] Girls at an Egyptian Bedouin wedding attended by Abu-Lughod sang to the bride:

> Fair and her bangs hanging down
> A girl you'd say was a lowland gazelle
> Fair, unblemished with not a mark on her
> Like the moon when it first appears
> She takes after her maternal and paternal aunts
> Gold threaded with pearls
> If you want love from a girl of our tribe
> Put down nineteen hundred pounds
> Her father doesn't care about money
> What he wants [in a man] is importance and honour.[25]

Even more important, her deflowering proves her virginity and publicly certifies her honor. Abu-Lughod describes waiting with the guests as this ritual was carried out:

> I jumped as the guns went off and the men rushed away. The women streamed in to surround Selima, dazed and limp in the arms of a relative, singing and dancing with relief. The cloth with its red spot of blood, a faint mark, was waved above our heads. Selima's maternal aunt exclaimed, "Praise God! Blessings on the Prophet! How beautiful![26]

The next day, another girl explained: "For us Bedouins . . . this is the most important moment in a girl's life. No matter what anyone says afterward, no one will pay attention as long as there was blood on the cloth."[27] As a middle-aged Egyptian explained to Nayra Atiya as she recalled her wedding night: "Blood has to come out. It stands for honor. . . . A girl's honor is worth the world. Her happiness is built on it. It's destroyed without it and can never be repaired."[28]

Marriage ceremonies make use of many of the same symbols as other rites of transition (birth, circumcision, burial), especially colors associating biological processes with social values and spiritual qualities. Abu-Lughod reports that the bride is covered with a man's white *jard* (signifying purity) to be brought to the groom's house for the ceremony ending in her deflowering, but thereafter she dresses as a woman:

From then on she begins to wear married women's clothing, which consists of two critical pieces: the black headcloth that doubles as a veil and the red woolen belt. These represent Bedouin woman-hood. . . . The red belt that every married woman wears symbolizes her fertility and association with the creation of life. . . . The red belt cannot be worn if the black veil is not also worn. . . . Black is a color with numerous connotations, most of which are negative. . . . Veils literally blacken the face; thus, they symbolize shame, particularly sexual shame.[29]

We observed similar practices and meanings in Imeghrane. Delaney describes the rich color symbolism in traditional Turkish society:

The colors of red and white . . . are very important in Turkish cul-ture and appear to symbolize aspects of procreative sexuality. They are prominent at *sunnet* (circumcision) and at marriage, two cer-emonies whose expressed aim is procreation. A red and white flag is planted at weddings and at the completion of a new house: both occasions have to do with the creation of a new procreative unit. Red stands for *kizlik* (virginity) as well as menstruation, childbirth, and the procreative potential that is represented by henna (sacred soil) in the wedding ceremony. It also symbolizes the blood that nurtures the child in the womb. . . .

White, the color of milk, is another symbol of nurture and sus-tenance. . . . White is also the color of semen and thus can represent the male's generative or creative power, which is allied with the di-vine. Finally, white is the color of purity and honor. It is the color of the cloth people don on the hajj at Mecca and of the shroud in which the corpse is buried.[30]

Boddy describes a similar system of color symbolism in the Sudanese village she studied, with white representing semen, milk, and purity; black repre-senting decay and disease; and red representing a mixture of meanings that give it both positive (fecundity) and negative (pollution) associations with "feminine blood."[31] Women are positively associated with the whiteness of milk, and as they nurse infants so they care for dairy animals and process dairy products, providing their families with these strengthening foods, rich in *baraka,* divine blessedness. Every adult woman should "own" her own cow (that also was the ideal among the Imeghrane we studied)—providing a complementary power to that of men, who slaughter animals and provide their *baraka*-rich red meats.

Puberty and early marriage thus typically brought a set of new circum-stances, largely beyond the girl-woman's control, and potentially disequili-brating of her previous personality organization. Within the space of a couple of years, a girl could find herself with a woman's body, married and sexually active, and living in a new household under her husband's and mother-in-law's authority. And a new source of anxiety comes with these changes, for the fate of her marriage, her status in the community, and her completion as a woman depend on conceiving a child within the first couple of years. These transitions clearly create and amplify individual differences: ethnographies and autobiographies make it clear they were liberating and fulfilling to some, imprisoning and traumatic for others—and, as Boddy makes clear, most women experienced an ambiguous mixture of stress and fulfillment. If all goes according to the cultural model and the girl passes the tests of virginity and fertility, the symbols and meanings that organize her wedding and child-bearing can confirm her identity as an honorable adult woman, tempering other representations of her as a dangerous source of pollution and *fitna* ("chaos/disorder"). If the transitions do not go according to plan, the potential for social conflict and psychological distress appears to be great. The strong association Boddy found between marital/reproductive failures and spirit possession suggests that possession often represents an attempt to repair damaged selves and fashion alternative identities.

Boys in Traditional Settings

Boys in traditional milieus may have some years of "youth" between sexual maturity and marriage. The cultural model assigns teen-aged boys a heavy burden of work and keeps them dependent and deferential to elders' authority. But it also expects them increasingly to take on "policing" responsibilities for the in-group's boys and women, and in many areas it encourages raiding or feuding with out-group competitors. These provide arenas in which they can hone, test, and perform the components of honorable manhood described in chapter 3, and assimilate the symbolic associations of masculinity: outside rather than inside, right rather than left, seed rather than soil, bone rather than flesh, pure rather than polluted, white rather than red.[32]

In pastoralist societies young men herded, raided, clandestinely courted, and celebrated all of these in poetry and song—cultivating the *'asabiyya* (toughness/fortitude) Ibn Khaldun portrays as the heart of Bedouin character. Meeker has shown how the poetry of the Rwala Bedouin associated manhood with weapons and acts of war, and with the "beastly energies" of their mounts.[33] In agricultural villages, boys worked hard under the close supervision of elder men, and their scope for acts of daring and the "challenge-and-riposte" contests for honor varied greatly from community to community. Where sultans and feudal-like lords dominated peasant cultivators, honor appears to have centered on self-control and filial piety rather than individual initiative and bravado. In the Nile village Hamid Ammar studied, paternal and state authority were strong, fighting was rare, and the adolescent boys struck him as "timid, apprehensive, and withdrawn."[34] By contrast, in the agricultural Algerian Kayble region studied by Bourdieu and the Moroccan

Rif studied by Hart, feuding was endemic, and most men had killed by the time of their marriages.[35]

Ibn Khaldun regarded urban life as the soft antithesis of tough Bedouin life, but, especially since city populations were continually replenished by migrants from the countryside, the ethos of marital masculinity thrived in them as well. In many cities, the youths of each "quarter" (usually centered around a prominent patronymic association) formed groups that combined features of benevolent associations, defenders of the neighborhood's women, and street gangs. They sometimes fought with youths from other quarters and enforced conventional morality in their own quarter with rough justice, providing adolescent boys with an arena in which to test and demonstrate their manliness. Sawsan El Messiri describes the *futuwat*—which "literally means youth, but implies gallantry and chivalry"[36]—of Cairo's popular quarters as an ideal type or identity combining "cleanliness, intelligence and alertness" but above all "physical strength . . . accompanied by bravery."[37] Each group was led by a sometimes-married man in his twenties, and many *futuwat* were teen-aged apprentices in traditional crafts and businesses. "Supporters come from various categories," El Messiri writes, and "are referred to as 'followers' (*atba'*), 'boys' or 'lads' (*subyan*), a clique (*shilla*), and 'those who stand for you' (*mahasib* and *mashadid*)."[38] He describes their fighting spirit:

> The *futuwat* within and among different localities are in constant competition to assert their supremacy, their quarrels taking on the proportions of feuds. To end a feud between two equally renowned *futuwat* is difficult because any appeal for reconciliation would be answered by the saying, "We are *gad'an* (tough and brave) and men do not give up their revenge." In a quarrel it is expected that a *futuwa* will beat and be beaten by others. But to be attacked and run away, or not hit back, would identify a *futuwa* as a "woman" (*mara'*), which is the most humiliating insult he could receive.[39]

The *futuwat* served as protectors of circumcision and wedding processions, and took these celebrations of male prowess to provoke fights with youths from other quarters.

In many areas, then, adolescent boys were expected to prove their worth by doing much of the hard work of herding, farming, and craft production but also to prove their manliness in combat and to take the lead in protecting and policing the women, juniors, and vulnerable members of their families and communities. They continued to be excluded from the inner circles and prerogatives of adult men, and were kept in dependent, deferential, junior relationships to their fathers, their patrons, the council of elders, and religious authorities. Many accounts suggest that they readily chafed at this state of affairs, and local communities are rife with tales of prodigal sons. The cultural model's emphasis on filial piety presumes rebellious inclinations that must be tamed.

Traditional communities often gave youths roles in rituals and festivals that recognize their prowess. In the main Imeghrane village we studied, the annual festival celebrating the Prophet's birthday featured teen-aged boys at three crucial points. Those who had been studying the Quran joined the chorus of reciters who initiated the festival. Then after the imam cut the sacrificial ram's throat at the mosque, four strong youths picked it up and ran it to the irrigation canal before it died, mingling its baraka-rich blood with the water to help ensure a plentiful supply of water the following year. Later in the afternoon, villagers gathered at the threshing grounds, large bowls of cous-cous containing the ram's meat were laid out in the center, and the senior men danced and sang around them. An old man with a stick was posted to guard the cous-cous from older children and younger teens, who darted out to steal handfuls. The villagers laughed and cheered as the youths nimbly avoided the old man's wild swipes and devoured the cous-cous—clearly dramatizing the village's dependence on the vitality and daring of the maturing generation.

Abdallah Hammoudi has studied an even more dramatic festival celebrated in some of Morocco's High Atlas villages, in which the senior men leave the village and the unmarried youth take over. In a "time of freedom" lasting three days, they perform an obscene masquerade that includes a mock wedding and a procession in which masked characters break into the houses occupied now only by women.[40] Hammoudi interprets this "rite of transgression" as dramatizing the generational conflict smoldering beneath the surface of deference, a "revenge of the sons" enacted as a kind of caricature of the patriarchal order—all of which is said to bring good fortune to the village. Festivals like this may not be found in much of MENA, but other more orthodox rites also feature youth as bearers of the community's future. Young men swell the ranks of the Ashura procession in Iran that commemorates the martyrdom of two of the Prophet's grandsons.

Masters and Disciples

As Ammar and Gilsenan note, many teen-agers and young men become devoted to religion. They join religious brotherhoods or pass their free time with the local sheikh or imam in prayer, chanting, and discussions of the Quran and *hadith*. This often serves "as an extended rite of passage for those in transition to full adult male status," Gilsenen believes, as they learn more deeply the Islamic cosmology, gain expertise at the etiquettes of piety, and begin participating visibly in the community's religious life.[41] Hammoudi makes even more of the relationship of master to disciple, seeing it as providing an ideal prototype for the array of dyadic relations in which a young man finds himself uncomfortably the "junior" partner. He points out that the etiquettes of deference and submission required of the junior—from hand-kissing to serving—amount to ritual emasculation and feminization. The religious master-disciple prototype both takes this to an extreme and idealizes submission as the path to empowerment:

> Signs of femininity—in the form of submission and service—are displayed in the relation of domination between father and son or superior and subordinate. But in no other sphere of life does this negation of virility become more extreme than in the process of mystical initiation, where the obligatory passage through a feminine role on the long path to masterhood, under a guide's authority, reaches an unequaled level of expression and stylization.[42]

In the period of submission, the disciple acquires power from the master, and in many folk histories of the miraculous enlightenment of saints and holy men, this entails a transfer of bodily substances from the master to the disciple. Analyzing the reproductive metaphors used to describe this process, Hammoudi writes:

> The disciple is so to speak impregnated through a teaching process that resembles procreation. The master transforms into a saint the young man who rushes to him in a sense-awakening encounter; he basically feminizes his disciple in order to produce charisma: it is a metaphor of insemination, gestation, and birth.[43]

Hammoudi points out that "while the master dominates with all of his authority and appears ruthless, he also often displays tenderness and motherly attention toward a disciple who is being tested."[44] The disciple's empowerment eventually enables him to rebel against the master and surpass him: "Submission is replaced by authority and passivity by overflowing virility—which according to some is a sign of divine force. This again clearly resembles the reversal required of a son when he separates from his father or when the father dies."[45] Hammoudi sees this prototype woven throughout the culture, idealizing submission as the route to empowerment and dominance. "The schemata of submission, ambivalence, rebellion, and access to masterhood," he writes, "are enacted on a daily basis, in the present and historically all at once."[46] He suggests this forced deference serves as a cultural means of motivating dominance (again, a strategy not uncommon in Western societies): juniors become "agreeable and modest in the father's (or master's) presence; virile and domineering in relation to others, in particular women and boys of the same generation."[47] And he offers the crucial insight that the master-disciple prototype makes "emasculating" subordination honorable, by endowing it with the promise of empowerment.

This process of playing the deferential junior in some circumstances and the dominant senior in others appears to be continuous with the games of dominance-subordination that younger boys play in many traditional milieus (see chapter 6). In adolescence the play becomes real, as does the empowerment, at least in youths' growing authority over juniors and women, and sometimes in raids and feuds. Hammoudi believes that alternating between deference and dominance creates a "fundamental bipolarity," leading "every individual to endorse within himself two selves in permanent tension."[48] He underscores the pervasiveness with which "the ambivalence of the chief-subordinate, master-disciple, and father-son relationship operates at the very heart of social life," and that therefore "dualism is omnipresent: everyone is alternately a chief and a subordinate."[49]

Individualism and Familial Loyalty

If the traditional cultural pattern prescribed greater continuity for boys than girls, it appears that boys more readily experienced conflicts between loyalty to their families and the imperative to establish themselves in their wider communities. Meeker argues that Arab Bedouin societies were among those in which segmentation, pastoralism, and raiding amplified "individualistic" ambitions in its young men, and consequently intensified conflict between adolescent sons and fathers.[50] Charles Lindholm also underscores how surprisingly "individualistic" MENA cultures are in the latitude they allow individuals to achieve their social statuses.[51] Even a youth's disobedient or rebellious acts are sometimes admired as signs of strength, courage, and promise.

Misfits, rebels, and prodigal sons often could choose to leave. My interviewee Mohammed's father had fled his family's poverty to a *zawiya* (religious lodge/school), where he became an imam and then made his own life. When Mohammed's own delinquency brought him to the brink of failure, he impulsively enlisted in the army without consulting anyone in his family. Luqman, the imam of the Lebanese village Antoun studied also made a dramatic rebellion as a youth, secretly enrolling in school after his father had told him to quit and work with his brothers on the farm. Their conflict came to a head during a harvest season that coincided with Ramadan, when Luqman's insistence on fasting and praying cut into his ability to work, and his father ordered him out of the house. His mother and a brother moved out with him, and they scraped by for a couple of years. Then the village imam left, and a devout village elder named Mustafa Basboos filled in:

> One Friday morning, against the advice of many of his friends and to the amazement of the assembled worshipers, he [Luqman] strode up to the minbar from one side and Mustafa Basboos strode up from the other and both proceeded to deliver the sermon at the same time. With his evangelical delivery and surer sense of learning Luqman apparently drowned out his rival and proceeded to give a sermon on hypocrisy. After the sermon those who had opposed him recognized his talent and congratulated him. . . . In August 1952 at the age of twenty-four Luqman was hired as imam of the village. . . . A year later Luqman married a woman from his own clan.[52]

These examples show that in spite of their usually deep and sincere familial loyalties, it is not uncommon for boys—like girls—to resist parental plans for their lives. Many ethnographic accounts suggest that individualistic strivings often come to the fore during adolescence, even in traditional milieus. The master-disciple schema appears to define a path to virile manhood that moderates this tension, by representing subordination as a step toward the acquisition of prowess and toward eventual dominance.

Adolescence in Modernizing Milieus ❀

The whole range of "modernizing" forces—education, urbanization, industrialization, reduction in family size, and global media saturation—are greatly extending the years between childhood and adulthood, creating a period of adolescence that increasingly resembles that studied in Western societies. Most important, young people whose futures no longer depend on learning their parents' skills, on inheriting their parents' fields and herds, and on accessing their parents' patron-clientage networks gain a great deal of power to define and act in their own interests—especially when they can read and their parents cannot. In addition, many of the traditional means of accruing and displaying honor, and many of the rituals and symbols that traditionally anchored identities, have faded or shifted their meanings.

Traditional patterns continue to be lived by a smaller and smaller fraction of MENA youths, but a good many traditional characteristics can be discerned beneath the surfaces of modern clothes, music, and street slang. In the 1970s, Amad and colleagues' survey of Egyptian students found them to "vacillate" in acceptance and rejection of their parents' authority, but large majorities valued respect for elders, concurred with parental control over their movements, and endorsed traditional Egyptian values, especially religious ones.[53] More recently, Barbara Mensch and colleagues examined the gender-role attitudes of 660 unmarried 16- to 19-year-old Egyptians who participated in a representative national survey, and found that "by and large, young people appear to conform to traditional notions of what it means to be male and female."[54] Ninety-two percent of boys and 88 percent of girls agreed with the statement "A wife needs her husband's permission for everything," and 87 percent of boys and 84 percent of girls agreed that the husband alone should be the family breadwinner. Both boys and girls mentioned being *mu'addab* (polite and well-bred) as the most important characteristic they wanted in a spouse, followed by piety, with "love" ranked fifth. Girls wanted more shared decision-making than did boys, but at rates that made them just "less conservative" than the boys. Further, the expected associations between indicators of "modernity" and "modern" attitudes did not appear: adolescents with more education, urban residence, and higher socioeconomic status did not generally have more "modern" attitudes, and on some points they voiced marginally more traditional views.[55] The researchers express surprise at the consistency of adolescents' attitudes.

The survey did not gauge the extent to which adolescents' traditional attitudes represent cultural continuity, or the deliberate return to tradition that many young people are choosing. Yet, as many scholars have pointed out, the so-called return to tradition is not truly traditional but a modern fashioning of "traditional" life-styles in a context of proliferating cultural identities. Observers can find it dizzying to sort out what remains truly traditional, what has been recently invented as "tradition," and what is truly modern. It is clear that MENA youth are not simply "becoming modern" at different rates but are embroiled in pervasive debates about what modern ways they should adopt and what traditional ways they should conserve. I discuss how this debate shapes the formation of identity in the next chapter, but, as Haddiya's studies show, even rural adolescents get fully caught up in it.[56]

It is crucial, however, not to see MENA adolescents simply as en route to "becoming modern." For many, the promise of modernity is being overwhelmed by economic underdevelopment. Especially in nations like Egypt, Algeria, and Morocco—which have large populations and limited resources— a large proportion of educated urban youth are not facing the many choices opened before them by "modernity" but are filled with anxiety about getting *any* meaningful place in society. Ouzi's survey found this over 20 years ago, and the situation has worsened in a number of countries. In the early 1990s Mustafa Haddiya found 88 percent of a sample of 800 Moroccan high school students voicing generalized fears for their futures, 80 percent specifically citing the prospect of not finding a job.[57] Lack of work often means continued dependence on parents, an inability to marry, and only partial integration into the community of adults. This point deserves restating: the shift for many MENA youth has not been from a traditional world in which they moved directly from childhood to adult roles to a modern world in which childhood and adulthood are separated by years of "adolescence." Rather, many face the ominous threat of having *no adult status*—of becoming *hiyateen,* "those who lean on walls," as they are called in Cairo.

Education

Education brings profound change, at least for the increasing numbers of adolescents who stay in school. As Davis and Davis note, "the perception of today's parents that children need a rather long period of schooling and the parents' willingness to support their children's continued study have helped create the potential for an 'adolescent' period in Zawiya."[58] Schooling raises aspirations, and nearly all of those who make it past primary school set their sights on white-collar or professional jobs. Academic success thus becomes the primary vehicle for achieving honor within and for one's family. The interdependent ties most adolescents have with their "house" appears to fuel an achievement motive in ways similar to those described for Asian cultures,[59] facilitating the transformation of the honor-modesty code into a group-based achievement ethic. This represents an important psychological change, as an achievement ethic requires a different configuration of sentiments, motives, and social personalities from that required by the traditional honor-modesty system.

Schooling, especially in rural areas, introduces new sorts of conflicts. In the rural Lebanese village Williams studied in the 1960s,

> schooling for the boy is often a disruptive event. He is sent to school burdened with his family's and sometimes his own unrealistic expectations. Many an illiterate fellah father envisions unlimited possibilities for his "educated" son. The vision is often shared initially by the boy himself. It is vague in all respects but one: whatever the occupational aspiration, be it modest such as "clerk" or "employee" or more ambitious such as "teacher" or "doctor," it must not involve manual labor. A few years later he leaves school, ill-prepared for anything but manual labor.[60]

Haddiya came to nearly identical conclusions after studying rural Moroccan students in the 1980s: they and their parents saw education as the ladder out of poverty and backwardness, and the students embraced urban aspirations and values. But as this became the framework for their self-evaluations, it estranged them from their rural environment, leaving the majority who drop out or fail especially dissatisfied.[61]

Davis and Davis estimated that by the mid-1970s parents in the town of "Zawiya" were sending all of their children to school, but they found that youths' "raised aspirations are likely to be met only by a few, however, and many will be disappointed by their inability to complete school or to obtain a higher level job than their parents have."[62] They estimate that only 3 percent of the children entering elementary school in the 1980s passed the baccalaureate exam that entitles them to study at a university. "Such low success rates, combined with very poor job prospects even for the lucky few who continue on to college, have produced increasing frustration and cynicism," they report.[63]

In the mid-1970s Ouzi used sentence completion tests to indirectly assess the "psychological orientations" of 200 high school juniors and seniors in a variety of Casablanca neighborhoods. His sample thus represents the 5 percent of Moroccan youth who got this far in school and were anticipating university study—that is, those who were most successfully "becoming modern." He found generally positive senses of self-efficacy, positive views of teachers, strong and supportive peer relations, and broad optimism about the future. At the same time, however, he found widespread fear, focusing primarily on the baccalaureate exam—on which their and their families' futures depended—and on family economic crises that could force some of them out of school. A majority also said they feared their fathers, who continued to exercise often harsh authority over them, as well as the police and security forces who kept them under surveillance.

Most MENA cities are now crowded with young men who have left school and not found steady jobs. They know they have failed to honor their families as they once hoped, and their families often feel resentful of the sacrifices they made for grown children who now "just sit and eat," as my unemployed interviewee Hussain said his father puts it to him. Youths often direct their anger at poor teachers and facilities, at corruption and favoritism in the schools, and at a lack of parental support.[64] While these complaints may rationalize failure, they also contain a good deal of truth. Ouzi rails at the primary education system as he saw it in the 1970s, describing students as being "locked in a prison," forced into rote memorization of useless information, and "subjected [an] to unbearable hell-fire" of insults and beatings that demoralize many and cause high dropout rates,[65] which Haddiya reported in the 1980s.[66] And like their counterparts in poor American communities, many MENA youth come from families that cannot afford supplies or help them with their studies and that need them to work when they should be studying. Few have rooms of their own or quiet places to study, and rural youth often have to crowd in with relatives or share cramped rented rooms to attend high schools in towns and cities.[67]

Girls face three additional difficulties. They usually have more housework than their brothers, and so have less time to study. Men may harass them as they walk to and from school, putting their reputations at risk. Their parents may decide to arrange a marriage and take them out of school at any time, especially if they fear for their reputations. A now-married woman told Davis and Davis how these problems can come to a head: she complained to her older brother about a student who kept harassing her on the street. Her brother fought him and drove him off, but when she finished the school year her parents forbade her to continue.[68] Several studies have found girl students to score higher on measures of anxiety than boys, which Abdelkhalek and Nil attribute to parental confinement and surveillance that "shackles" adolescent girls.[69] Education also brings girls new opportunities, and many have fought to seize them. El Saadawi describes the victory she won over her mother when she went out without permission and had her hair cut short. Her mother beat her, but she held her ground defiantly: "I pitied her when I saw her face sink in defeat and weakness. I felt a strong desire to hug her, kiss her, and cry between her arms . . . to say to her: 'Reason does not lie in my always obeying you.' . . . I looked in the mirror and smiled over my short hair and the flash of victory in my eyes.'"[70] These battles have been common (some of my interviewees told similar stories), and adolescents' victories not unusual.

Most of the Moroccans I interviewed gave angry accounts of the hardships and injustices they experienced as they struggled to succeed in school and keep their dreams alive, and these usually overshadowed all other aspects of their adolescence. None said they had been troubled by matters of popularity, athletic ability, or personal appearance, as Americans so often do when they recall their teen-age years. The Moroccans feared being forced into early marriages, being cheated by students with better connections, being trapped in unemployment or "useless" farm labor, and failing to make good on their parents' sacrifices. As Hussein saw it, "they send you to school and put a satchel of worries on your back." At the same time, for many of those who succeed, education provides upward mobility and a "modern," if not quite "Western-style," adolescence.

Sexuality

MENA societies continue to be among the world's most restrictive in opposing premarital sex. Yet, as Bouhdiba emphasizes, Islam embraces, celebrates, and sanctifies erotic pleasure, with the Quran, *hadith,* and theological literature all showing a "fundamental hedonism."[71] Islam envisions a "profound complementarity of the masculine and the feminine," he explains, which are united in procreative sexuality legitimated by marriage—sexuality then becoming "an act of piety" and "a prefiguration of heavenly delights."[72] Islam does regard sexuality as a dangerous force that needs careful regulation, for when it flows outside the bounds of marriage and reproduction, it "violates the order of the world [and] is a grave 'disorder,' a source of evil and anarchy."[73] Islam therefore

> remains violently hostile to all other ways of realizing sexual desire. As a result, the divine curse embraces both the boyish woman and the effeminate man, male and female homophilia, auto-eroticism, zoophilia, and so on. Indeed all these "deviations" involve the same refusal to accept the sexed body and to assume the female and male condition. Sexual deviation is a revolt against God.[74]

At the same time, MENA urban cultures have long embraced a hedonism that overflowed these boundaries, and developed a literary form that celebrated forbidden pleasures: *mujun,* "the art of referring to the most indecent things, speaking about them in such a lighthearted way that one approaches them with a sort of loose humor."[75] *Mujun* was practiced by men at both taverns and private parties, sometimes culminating in sex with dancing girls and serving boys. Forms of *mujun* could be found throughout MENA, Bouhdiba writes, and in all levels of society: "A desperate love of pleasure that spread beyond the courts and wealthier classes of the city, *mujun* was an *ars vitae,* a permanent *carpe diem.*"[76] Indulgence in illicit pleasures by those who enforced the laws was duly noted, and Bouhdiba quotes the classical writer Yaqut's description of the weekly orgies hosted by a government minister, and his comment that "next day . . . they returned to their usual puritanism."[77] Mahfouz makes this duality a central theme of his Cairo

Trilogy, as the patriarch Ahmad enforces puritanical discipline in his home, indulges his large appetites for wine, women, and song on his houseboat, and prays at the mosque, all with equal intensity. And in many areas, explicitly erotic singing and dancing—often by entertainers who also work as prostitutes—remain integral to circumcisions, weddings, and some pilgrimages.

Thus if Islam forbids many forms of sexuality, the forbidden is never far away, and adolescents in many areas traditionally had exposure to literary *mujun* and illicit sex. Bouhdiba's point is that MENA cultures do not just restrict sexuality but provoke and restrict it at the same time, creating a situation for young people that confers an aura of great promise and equally great anxiety. Restrictions are brought most strictly to bear on girls, who may still have their "blood of honor" displayed on their wedding nights. Boys, on the other hand, may be expected to "hunt" girls, and to get some sexual experience before they marry. The promise of the Quranic vision of sexual complementarity is thus undermined by the patriarchal social order, Bouhdiba writes, which suppresses women's sexuality and develops men's in misogynistic forms:

> Puberty is the moment when sexuality comes to the forefront, when one takes one's leave of the female world, where having become a man, one is expected to behave as a man. . . . The gap between the sexes in Arabo-Muslim society is now consummated. . . . Woman herself, like her world, is derealized. At puberty the child becomes aware of this too. From that moment on, he is trained to direct all his energies towards the cult of a life shared with other males and towards the systematic depreciation of femininity.[78]

Returning to a Moroccan community in which they had worked for many years, Davis and Davis were able to investigate teen-age sexuality in some depth. They report that masturbation is disapproved of because "there is a general sense among Muslims that sexual experience without a partner is shameful."[79] There appears to be no widespread belief that "semen loss" is debilitating and leads to illnesses, as is found throughout India and Southeast Asia, but Ben Jelloun reports that many men associate masturbation with impotence.[80] Like menstruation, ejaculation causes major pollution that must be purified with a more extensive washing ritual than that performed prior to daily prayer, and, as Wikan suggests, men may prefer to avoid this (especially when they must take the time and expense to go to a public bath). Nocturnal emissions are widely attributed to the mischief of the devil, and many men may perceive masturbation as succumbing to Satan's temptations. Davis and Davis found that adolescents discussed it "only very covertly and with great shame," and they believe it is not widely practiced.[81] Fewer than 5 percent of the adolescent boys interviewed by Pascon and Bentahar in the 1960s volunteered that they masturbate.[82]

Homosexual play appears to be somewhat more common, at least among boys, and tends not to be strongly condemned as long as it does not continue into adulthood. Davis and Davis write:

> Homoeroticism is tolerated and fairly common in late childhood and early adolescence. . . . The homoerotic contact that seems to occur fairly commonly among teenage males is usually casual, sporadic, and of short duration. Local adults tend to regard such activity as childish play, and the boys involved do not consider themselves homosexual.[83]

Pascon and Bentahar report that about 20 percent of the Moroccan boys they interviewed in the 1970s volunteered they had had sex with other boys,[84] and Davis and Davis estimate that "more than half of local boys have had at least some experience of group masturbation or exhibition.[85] Not even rough estimates are available for girls, and no girls told Davis and Davis they had had sex with other girls, even though many spoke candidly about heterosexual play.

Attitudes toward homosexuality are complex and varied. Like much of the European Mediterranean, MENA cultures traditionally strongly condemned men who did not marry and beget children but also contained traditions that celebrated romantic and sexual love of boys by men. They also tended to sharply distinguish between the "passive" role in male-male sex, which is abominable because "feminine" and subordinate, and the "active" role, which was more acceptable because dominant and "masculine."[86] In Oman (and perhaps other areas), there is a recognized semipublic role, called *xanith*, for transsexual or transvestite men who dress in women's clothing and effect feminine postures and gaits, socialize with women, and serve as "passive" partners or prostitutes for other men. Wikan describes the *xanith* as a "third gender" and reports that there were about 60 men in the small town she studied (2 percent or more of adult men) who had been *xaniths* at some point during their lives. Some enacted it until they married, and if they successfully had intercourse on their wedding night, became full-fledged men, avoiding the women whose companions they been as *xaniths*. Some moved in and out of the role, and some began to play it after they married and fathered children—including a son of a prominent political leader. Villagers gave a "deceptively simple" explanation for how some boys come to be *zaniths*:

> Men say that when young boys at puberty start being curious and exploring sexual matters, they may "come to do that thing" together, and then the boy "who lies underneath" may discover that he likes it. If so, he "comes to want it," and as the Soharis say, "An egg that is once broken can never be put back together."[87]

Many observers report that boys are more or less expected to get some sexual experience, and many do with prostitutes. "Though anti-Islamic *par excellence,*" Bouhdiba writes, "prostitution was nevertheless profoundly rooted in Arabo-Muslim mores."[88] In MENA towns, "the red-light district is part of the familiar landscape." Often situated between old and new neighborhoods, such districts become shortcuts for shoppers and school children, so "one sees there every day children between twelve and eighteen, often clutching their school satchels."[89] Viewed as an "outlaw" and often deprecated by the men who visit her, the prostitute nonetheless is "more or less institutionalized, very often legitimated, sometimes legalized," serving as a "safety valve" for desire that flows outside the bounds of marriage. Most important, "Prostitution is a *de facto* institution by which boys are initiated into sexual life. Indeed, the clientele is largely made up of adolescents. . . . The sexual life of the young Arabo-Muslim is very often, if not almost entirely, taken over by organized prostitution, whether public or not."[90]

More than a third of the village youth interviewed by Pascon and Bentahar said they had visited prostitutes.[91] Only about 5 percent had had sex with women other than prostitutes. As Davis and Davis report, a boy's first encounter might come at a family or community celebration (a naming ceremony, circumcision, wedding, etc.) for which musicians and dancers—sometimes also prostitutes—are hired to entertain and typically dance with explicitly sexual movements and lyrics. They describe a naming ceremony they attended:

> The most obviously enthusiastic spectators throughout the evening were late adolescent males, who often clapped in time to the drum and chanted familiar refrains. . . . Three times the dancers worked the crowd for money, with the older dancer approaching one person after another and dancing directly in front of him. This places her midriff directly in front of the seated male's face, and given the nature of her movements has the unmistakable implication that she's taunting him with her sex. . . . We learned the next morning that most of our neighbors had stayed until dawn and that the party warmed up in the wee hours, with one of the male musicians donning a female dancer's robe. . . . At celebrations where dancers are present, it is common for arrangements to be made for all interested males to pay for brief access to them in a nearby room at the conclusion of the party.[92]

Even small towns and rural villages often have women, usually poor and divorced or widowed, who have sex for money. Wikan describes a married woman in Oman who worked as a prostitute, keeping her husband in the dark about it. Her neighbors condemned her behavior but accepted her: "She is always friendly and hospitable, does not gossip, is kind and helpful," explained one woman: "only in this one respect is she not good."[93] My interviewee Hussein described his awkward first visit to a prostitute. He was 16, and a cousin near his age convinced him to go:

He and I agreed to have the experience from her. I led the way, and I was frightened. I talked to her, I told her there were two of us, and she said, come in, come in. I was frightened someone might see me, someone who knew me . . . and that some trouble would start and people would gather and see me, or the police would come knock and take me away.

He felt guilty afterward, and recalls apologizing to her: "I felt like she didn't want me, and I said, 'You did that just to satisfy me . . . I'm sorry, I've wronged you. I'm sorry, I'm very sorry.'" Now in his twenties, still single and living at home, he visits a prostitute every three or four months—with less fear and guilt but also with little joy.[94]

Romance

Most observers report that both boys and girls are expected to have crushes. Williams writes that the Lebanese villagers she studied recognize a period of *za'lan*, being "love-sick" or "love-crazed":

The symptoms are clear and unmistakable: elaborate attention to appearance and clothes, disinterest in work and school; giggly, whispered conversations among small clusters of girls; speculative, laughing gossip in large gatherings of teen-agers; among the boys, less talk perhaps, but much hanging about the water tower and the village common where, late in the afternoon, the girls come and go. Any oddity of behavior at that age is, indulgently and not without humor, ascribed to being *za'lan* or *za'lani*.[95]

Outside of the more conservative MENA countries, teen-agers attending school explore the uncertain terrain of romantic relationships with their classmates—more actively in cities than in towns, and in towns than in villages. The small-town teen-agers Davis and Davis studied could avoid watchful eyes much more easily than could their parents, and engaged in more clandestine flirting, if not public dating. In many areas, high school students develop romances by exchanging love letters and sometimes meeting briefly on the way home from school or in shopping districts. Some of these romances lead to marriages, as more and more parents allow their children initiative in finding spouses. A few lead to ruined reputations, pregnancies, and violence. As Davis and Davis note, most are carried on in an atmosphere of anxiety and suspicion:

Girls fear that boys are apt to entice them into sexual activity and then leave them. . . . Most girls over sixteen can give specific examples of this occurring locally. Girls also fear physical punishment or possibly rape as a consequence of their heterosexual activity, if discovered. Several older adolescents said that a couple found in an isolated setting by a group of young men might be physically or sexually abused.[96]

Ouzi reports that over 70 percent of the high school students he studied showed "orientations to the other sex" that were negative and troubled.[97] While they overwhelmingly endorsed "the family" as the basic unit of society, a majority also viewed married life as limiting and full of discord. Images of women were highly stereotypic, centering on a lack of self-control and untrustworthiness, and a good number of the sentence completion and TAT responses he elicited echoed the traditional view that "any meeting of a man and a woman is accompanied by a third, the Devil." Economic development and the "opening to the West" do not seem to have changed traditional views, Ouzi writes, so that romance remains a matter of anxiety and confusion, and boys and girls "view each other with feelings of fear, ignorance, and embarrassment."[98]

According to Davis and Davis, boys are expected to aggressively "hunt" girls but at the same time to regard those who respond to them as dishonorable and not worthy of marriage. This situation resembles the American "double standard," they note, "in which the girl suspected of sexual activity was stigmatized while the boy was excused or envied."[99] As in much of MENA (as traditionally in the European Mediterranean), girls who leave their houses are subject to frequent flirtation or harassment:

> The physically mature and attractive girls of Zawiya are approached regularly in a sexually suggestive manner by males of adolescent age and beyond. To be known to have walked in the fields beyond view of houses, or to have been seen in conversation with a boy in Kabar, or to have visited his house when his parents were not there is taken as evidence of loss of sexual purity.[100]

A 16-year-old Iranian girl told Friedl: "We girls have to be very careful on the way to school. . . . The school principal tells us to keep the veil and the headscarf tightly wrapped. . . . for our own protection. And who wants to cope with a dirty-eyed suitor when you are in tenth grade?"[101] My interviewee Khadija, who dresses in Western styles, grew outraged as she described the daily harassment she experiences:

> It's the most repugnant thing I have to deal with. . . . When I go by a cafe and it's full of the servants of God, I need cotton balls for my ears! Everyone has something to say, and they'll even trip my feet. You have to change your route, because you're going to hear some ugly words: *bint zenqa* [streetwalker], or something like that cuts/wounds you, which touches your feelings. So, do you go fight with him? Do you go insult him? What are you going to do with him? You have nothing you can do with him.

My interviews generally support Ouzi's and the Davises' observations that many adolescents explore romantic relationships, but these tend to be fraught with suspicion and anxiety.

The lengthening of adolescence and the mixing of boy and girl students, combined with the dissemination of Western models of romance in movies, TV, popular music, and magazines, has significantly changed the context within which adolescents must deal with sexuality and romance. The traditional means of controlling these—segregation of the sexes, nearly constant surveillance by seniors, and early marriage—have greatly weakened in most milieus. Media images appear to be especially powerful because many of them resonate with the poetic celebrations of romantic love and hedonism that have been woven into the heritage for centuries. Adolescents thus face the challenge of managing sexuality and romantic attachments in the face of greatly intensified temptation, at a time when ethnographies and opinion surveys show that the overwhelming majority want to become modern *and* stay loyal to familial and religious principles. Many researchers conclude this produces widespread distress—evident not so much in open conflicts with parents as in the fear and anxiety surrounding relationships between boys and girls.[102]

Rai *Music and North African Youth Culture*

Marc Schade-Poulsen's study of *rai* music in Algeria provides a psychologically insightful account of the youth culture that flourished there alongside the rise of Islamism in the 1980s and 1990s. *Rai* developed in the late 1970s in the "cabarets" of Oran, where young musicians used accordions, electrified instruments, and eventually drum machines and synthesizers to modernize traditional musical styles.[103] On top of dance rhythms, a *rai* singer voices a simple but moving "key phrase," referred to as the song's *nakwa*, or "identity card," by the musicians. Other lines—known as *zirri'as*, or "grains to be dispersed"—fill in a story-like context or evoke vaguely related memories or sentiments.[104] The lyrics express emotions ranging from love and lost love to lust, anger, and even piety:

> "I didn't think we'd break apart."
> "In spite of all, I still want you."
> "I love kisses in the neck that go down to the breasts."
> "The hand drum, and hashish, and we'll have a good time."
> "There is no God but God, and there is destiny."[105]

In the 1980s *rai* became the most popular music in Algeria, and spread throughout North Africa and the Arab-speaking world. A variant of *rai* designed by Western producers to suit European dance styles became a popular genre of "world music." Schade-Poulsen reports that *rai* had a distinctly generational character from the start and was created largely by and for the first postindependence generation: the singers used the titles *chab* or *chaba*—"youth" (male or female)—in contrast to the titles of *sheikh* or *sheikha* used for popular singers, which conveys a sense of being an older master. In the "cabarets," men and women in stylish European clothes drank and danced together. A witty master of ceremonies presided over the performance, and patrons gave him money to dedicate requests to friends. Requests sometimes came so quickly that most *rai* songs were never finished but were broken off so a new one could begin.

Some of the women were prostitutes (*qahbas*) but many were "free women" (*maryulas*) who might be a man's mistress or lover. A man who frequented *le milieu* ("the scene") explained: "When you see a beautiful woman and you know she can be laid, she is *maryula*. But a *qahba* is one who walks, who makes her living like that." An M.C. added that the free woman "smokes, drinks, dances, gads about but for pleasure not money. She is *zahwaniya*"(an expression having the sense of being merry, joyous, fond of good living, a lighthearted person).[106] Two popular *rai* singers formed their stage names from this term: Cheb Zahouani (a man) and Chaba Zahouania (a woman). The cabaret scene resembled the kind of entertainment that long had been available to men at brothels, and the M.C.-dedication format had long been practiced at traditional weddings. But the clubs provided an atmosphere more like that of Western discos: "Here, men took 'free women' out, talked with them, had fun with them. Here, couples publicly fondled each other, kissing and displaying public behavior that was very rarely witnessed outside such places."[107] And the musicians sang mainly of love and lust: "For those who knew *rai* well, images of the beach, the forest, the loose belt, and the railway were concrete images of immodest relations with women or of immodest behavior associated with consuming alcohol."[108] As the genre grew, performers and fans began to distinguish between "dirty" and "clean" *rai*: the latter speaking to the unfulfilled, unrequited, and blocked loves that teens and young adults repeatedly suffered.[109] And *rai* quickly moved beyond the cabarets. The spread of cassette recorders in the 1980s took *rai* into young people's homes, where teens could listen when out of earshot of their parents. Some hosted dancing parties in the late afternoon, at which girls would arrive in conservative dress, change and put on makeup for the party, and then change back before going home for dinner. Cassettes also filled the streets with *rai* as the soundtrack of urban life.

Western media portrayed *rai* fans as rebels and revolutionaries. A French magazine article was titled "Rai—Algeria Wants to Make Love, the Arab Blues Against Fundamentalism."[110] But Schade-Poulson found musicians and fans had surprisingly conventional values:

> A man should be strong, in good shape physically, and open and generous toward others rather than keeping to himself or excluding others from his life. Mention of the expression *mrubla* [disorderlies]

made people laugh with pleasure, for it implied gangs of youths, staying awake at night, chasing women, fighting other groups, and drinking out of the same small glass in good company. . . . [And] having a relationship with a "free girl" required a man to be able to defend his position with money and his prowess in the physical fights that broke out in the cabarets.[111]

They contrasted themselves to sons of the elites, whom they termed *tshi-tshi*:

This expression was synonymous with rich, spoiled youngsters who were snobbish, drove their fathers' cars, went abroad on holidays, and imitated Western lifestyles. According to the stereotype, they avoided military service, were physically weak, and obtained women only because of the money and cars they possessed. Once they got hold of a woman, they let her go around as she pleased. All in all, they had become effeminate through their imitation of the West and their possession of Western consumer goods.[112]

These values fall quite in line with the honor-modesty ethic and resemble the *futuwwa* figure that El Messiri says manifests the values of the Cairo "son of the homeland." The fans opposed neither traditional family values nor religion, Schade-Poulson reports, but followed the cultural model in separating their pursuits of pleasure in spaces away from their families and during the period of youth.

He also notes that while the Western media portrayed *rai* as articulating demands for freedom, the songs about love mainly voice regret over the damage that illicit liaisons wreak on "the peacefulness of the home" and especially on a man's relationship with his mother.[113] Many portray women as treacherous in quite traditional terms—as unloyal, caring only for money and material goods, and prone to use sorcery to manipulate men. In *rai* lyrics and his interviews, Schade-Poulsen found these stereotypes combined with both a "nostalgia" for virtuous women of the past and an idealization of European women and their freedoms. Some songs directly praise European women, even using "brunette" and "blond" to make the contrast.[114] The *rai* musicians and their fans thus operated with three images of women:

The first image was the *maryula*—the "masculine" woman, close to men, a woman of pleasure and lust who might lead a man into contact with unregulated and impure parts of himself and of society. The second was the woman with *hijab* [veil], who would not be interested in the world outside the home, who would obey her family and husband, and who would not seek the freedom of the world of consumption. The third was the European or Western woman, the only one capable of loving, that is, a woman being "like a man" ought to be: intelligent, trustworthy, and not interested in material affairs.[115]

This mixture testifies to two important aspects of adolescence. First, as the Davises and Schade-Poulsen emphasize, most young men and women now want to develop romantic relationships and choose their own spouses but face daunting difficulties, especially in the atmosphere of fear and mistrust. Second, the racial legacy of colonial domination—the allure of blond, white European women—has been reinforced by media and marketing images, and continues to affect at least some men's romantic dreams (several of the men I interviewed frankly said they yearned for European women). *Rai* music speaks to these matters, voicing the ambivalent reactions of young men (and occasionally women) to the neither-traditional-nor-modern world in which they come of age. While the music urges "Dance! Drink! Love!" the lyrics often lament the costs of delinquent pleasures. "*Rai* revealed how major contradictions existed between young people's aspirations to enjoy leisure and to establish themselves as individuals within a couple," Schade-Poulsen writes, "while at the same time having to manage codes of respect."[116]

Rai *and Islamism*

Islamists murdered several popular *chebs* in the 1990s, and forced most of the "cabarets" to close. But Schade-Poulsen sees less distance between them than did European journalists. "During my fieldwork," he writes, "no one contested the basic values structuring the moral organization of Algerian society." *Rai* gave voice to "transgressive" sentiments but phrased these in an indirect style that "implied that even here a certain moral code was being upheld." Born of the postindependence generation's new freedoms, *rai* sang simultaneously of their appeal and dangers. In this it converged with the Islamists' critique of social decay and "deregulated" gender relations. As antithetical as are *rai* and Islamist ways of life, a short step of repentance brings a hedonist back onto the straight path. This pattern characterized the life-histories of some of Schade-Poulsen's informants—and several of the young men I interviewed. And as he notes, this follows a quite traditional model of male development:

> the consumption of alcohol was an initiation rite for youngsters, together with smoking and going to the brothel. To drink was a sign of virility and a proof of reaching adulthood. Drinking, however, was not done in the family, for this would be to mix the profane (the street) with the sacred (the home). Only after this youthful stage would drinkers become practicing believers, most often after marrying. . . . Youth was made for the pleasurable, old age for serious things.[117]

Other teens choose to stay firmly "on the straight path," and for them *rai* music confirmed the dangers of illicit sexuality and Western morals. Ali Lila describes how Egyptian youth have come to feel that the West-centered promises of both socialism (Nasser) and capitalism (Sadat) have failed, and turned to religion in order to "modernize within tradition."[118] While only a minority of adolescents became Islamist activists, the 1980s and 1990s saw a great increase in the number who followed Islamist teachings and sought to reregulate contact between men and women. They oppose popular music and dancing, adopt religious rather than Western clothing, and avoid physical and eye contact between men and women. In many high schools and universities from Morocco to Turkey, a majority of girls now cover themselves in headscarves and sometimes full veils, and a large but difficult-to-estimate percentage of boys are choosing to live by religious precepts.

Islamist teachings provide many adolescents with a powerful analysis of their economic and sexual anxieties and bring an inner awakening and a sense of self-control and virtue. As Richard Mitchell emphasizes in his history of Egypt's Muslim Brotherhood, Islamism not only opposes despots and defends traditions but preaches a deeply personal form of renewal:

> The essential step in the renaissance, and more important than "practical reform," is a vast "spiritual awakening" among individuals. . . . The reason for "the weakness of nations and humiliations of peoples" is that hearts and souls become weak and emptied of "noble virtues and the qualities of true manhood." The nation that is overwhelmed by "material things" and "earthliness," and that has forgotten "hardship and struggle on behalf of truth," has lost its self-respect and hope.[119]

For many young men and women, "regaining spiritual balance" means gaining mastery ('aqel) over desires (nafs) in the face of temptations perceived to issue from the West. According to many Islamists, the struggle against inner desire constitutes the "greater jihad" (the j*h*d root meaning "great effort"), and the "lesser jihad" consists of struggle against tyrants and foreign attacks. This inner dimension, so often not seen by Western observers, is a psychologically crucial feature of Islamism, as it provides a coherent system of beliefs and practices for managing the emotions that beckon youths to betray their heritage, their families, and their goals.

Debate: Storm and Stress versus Smooth Transition to Adulthood ❀

As in most complex societies based on peasant agriculture, MENA adolescents traditionally were given little latitude for romantic or sexual liaisons, or for pursuing personal ambitions rather than the roles assigned by family patriarchs. But observers repeatedly report that adolescents did not adapt readily to paternal authority, and several ethnographers suggest that MENA and Mediterranean social structures may provoke greater adolescent strife than in Hindu Indian or in some African cultures. Studies of MENA adolescents yield two contrasting portraits: one depicting them as making relatively smooth transitions into adulthood, guided through conflicting values and anxieties by their strong familial attachments; the other depicting them as in grave crisis, with clashing values and uncertain futures causing serious personal disturbances. We can render this conflict of interpretations a little less extreme by noting that ethnographies of villages and small towns appear to be more likely to report smooth transitions, while studies of urban-based youth cultures appear to be more likely to show strife and turmoil. In addition, Western researchers, perhaps mindful of the high levels of delinquency and distress in their own countries, appear to see more continuity, while Arab researchers, who have lived amid the dramatic changes underway in their societies, more readily perceive crisis. There probably is truth to both portraits. Ouzi, for example, concludes that the urban high school students he studied were troubled in several spheres of their lives but generally showed strong self-esteem and social integration—though he suggests that their peers who had left school would show more troubled profiles.[120] Still, the divergence of views remains.

Ahirshaw criticizes psychological studies for attributing the "crisis of youth" to individual problems (divorce, harsh parenting styles, sexual conflicts, school failure, etc.) and argues that these should be seen in the context of the larger social and cultural conditions that intensify them. In particular, he points to the role of population growth and economic underdevelopment in darkening youths' futures and intensifying their fears; to the gap between generations in control of economic and political institutions; and to the still-traditional nature of most families, which provide positive networks of support but also inculcate "mythical" orientations to self and others, and lose the ability to teach the skills and attitudes required by larger society. Conflicts are further intensified, he believes, by the pervasive cultural dualities within which Arab youth are forming personal values and identities, specifically the contrast of tradition and modernity, associated, respectively, with Arab and colonial societies and embodied in the dual use of Arabic and English or French in schools, in workplaces, and on the streets.[121] Nearly all of the Arab researchers who write of crisis (and this includes Lila on Egyptian youth,[122] Shebshun on Tunisian youth,[123] and Ahirshaw,[124] Ouzi,[125] and Rabia'[126] on Moroccan youth) focus on this conflict of traditional and Western values, on the conflict of familial values with those learned in school and peer groups, on the anxiety surrounding romantic relationships, and on despair at getting jobs and places in the world as adults.

Ammar, Williams, the Davises, Joseph, and Kagitcibasi are probably correct to emphasize the resilience of MENA family networks and their ability to protect youths from "modernizing" changes that have wrought disorganization in other culture areas. I believe many youths successfully transform the values of honor-modesty into a family-driven, "Muslim ethic" achievement orientation that effectively surmounts many of the conflicts they face and enables them to "modernize within tradition."[127] But an achievement ethic requires opportunity in order to be sustained, and economic underdevelopment combined with politicized cultural dualities may amplify tensions to individual and collective flash points—and religion then readily provides a critique of corrupt secular powers (see chapter 3). Bennani-Chraibi's observation—that in politically "cool" times adolescents appear beset by relatively minor conflicts but that during politically "hot" times they appear torn by inner and interpersonal strife—helps reconcile the "smooth transition" and "crisis" views.[128] The demographer Ali Kouaouci suggests that the chaos that followed the outbreak of the Algerian civil war of the 1990s—which claimed an estimated 100,000 lives—was fueled in large measure by the rage of a swelling population of educated youth, stuck at home with little hope of jobs or marriages.[129] Erik Erikson, having witnessed Europe's counter-cultural youth movement in the 1920s, the rise of Nazism in the 1930s, the complacency of the 1950s, and the student movements of the 1960s, continually reminded psychologists that history can turn apparent stability into strife and creative conflicts into destructive ones with astonishing speed.

Sources ❖

Many studies describe the social conditions of youth, and the dilemmas faced by the first postindependence generations, but there are relatively few psychological studies.[130] Neither Sharabi[131] nor Barakat[132] nor Bouhdiba[133] write explicitly about "youth," nor do Mernissi[134] or Ahmed[135] in their books on women. Elizabeth Fernea's recent collection *Children in the Muslim Middle East* contains three brief chapters on adolescents, but none deal with psychological development.[136] Hamid Ammar's *Growing Up in an Egyptian Village* includes a brief but useful chapter on "Adolescence, Sex, and Marriage," and Friedl's *Children of Deh Koh* ends with a series of informative anecdotes about teen-aged boys and girls. Meeker's *Pastoral Son and the Spirit of Patriarchy* suggests a series of broad links between pastoralism, father-son conflict, and religious belief among the cultures of East Africa and MENA. A handful of field studies give more extended treatment of teen-age boys and their attainment of manhood. Gilsenan's *Lords of the Lebanese Marches* contains observations about young unmarried men in a near-feudal village setting. Sawsan El Messiri's *Ibn Al-Balad* includes an important analysis of the youth of traditional Cairo neighborhoods—especially of the *futuwa*, or "tough guys," who help protect and maintain order in them. Abdullah Hammoudi's book *The Victim and Its Masks* shows the father-son tensions played out in a "transgressive" festival in rural Morocco, and his *Master and Disciple* develops a provocative analysis of the master-disciple relationship as a script for constructing adult masculinity.

Several ethnographies of women include descriptions of girls' teen-age years. Unni Wikan's *Behind the Veil in Arabia* provides a psychologically insightful account of girls' transitions into adulthood in a traditional Omani village, and Carol Delaney's *The Seed and the Soil* describes puberty, seclusion, and marriage practices in a rural Turkish village. Janice Boddy's *Wombs and Alien Spirits* gives a detailed account of girls' circumcision, marriage, and childbirth in a Sudanese village, and of the fertility-related symbols and meanings that appear to define their identities. Lila Abu-Lughod's *Veiled Sentiments* deals mainly with the adult women of an Egyptian Bedouin group, but her analyses of honor-modesty and gender symbolism pertain equally to adolescents. The sociologist Soumaya Naamane-Guessous's study of female sexuality in Casablanca included interviews with 65 adolescent girls, and forms the basis of her 1988 *Au-dela de Toute Pudeur,* which describes the cultural practices and meanings associated with puberty, seclusion, and marriage. The psychiatrist Ghita El Khayat-Bennai's book *Le Monde Arabe au Feminin* and the anthropologist Camille Lacoste-Dujardin's book *Des Meres Contre Les Femmes* provides psychodynamic analyses of women's development within patriarchal families. There are two American ethnographies: Judith Williams's 1968 *Youth of Haouch el Harimi, A Lebanese Village* and Susan Davis's and Douglas Davis's 1989 *Adolescence in a Moroccan Town.* The Davises, who carried out observations and interviews in the medium-size town they call "Zawiya," provide the most extensive account of adolescence currently available. In addition, Alice Schlegel and Herbert Barry's *Adolescence: An Anthropological Inquiry* surveys data from 175 societies and helps put traditional MENA patterns in a global context.

Some Arab researchers find youth managing the transition to adulthood with relatively little distress. Hamid Ammar saw adolescents in the Nile village he studied in the 1950s as making relatively smooth transitions into marriage and adulthood. "Unlike many Western societies," he writes, "youth in Silwa do not express in their attitudes that sense of being torn between youthful autonomy and parental insistence on dependence."[137] Mensch and colleagues' recent survey of gender attitudes among Egyptian adolescents similarly found more evidence of consistency than change.[138] Other studies, however, by both Western and Arab researchers, portray youth as caught up in conflict and crisis. Paul Pascon and Mekki Bentahar conducted an attitude survey of rural Moroccan youth in the 1960s and saw them caught in a "crisis" brought on by social change: education had modernized their aspirations, but economic underdevelopment greatly limited their opportunities and left them subject to traditional patriarchal authority.[139] A decade later, Ahmad Ouzi used sentence completion and TAT tests to study Moroccan high school students, and his *Saykulujiyyat al-murahiq* (Psychology of Adolescence) describes them as possessing positive senses of self and peer relations but as experiencing high levels of distress in other areas. El Mostafa Haddiya's interview studies of Moroccan adolescents focused on conflicts between school and family values and on youths' struggle for positive identities in the face of uncertain futures.[140] Marc Schade-Poulsen's study of Algeria's *rai* music subculture portrays its youths as ambivalently struggling with modernity and tradition.[141] Ali Lila's *Al-shabab al-'arabi* (Arab Youth: Reflections on the Phenomenon of Religious Renewal and Violence) describes Egyptian youths' rejection of the West, "return to religion" and pursuit of "modernization within tradition."[142] Mounia Bennani-Chraibi's study of urban Moroccan youth, *Soumis et Rebelles* also depicts turmoil, especially evident in ambivalent identities that alternately idolize and demonize the West.[143] Ahirshaw's 1994 *Al-montor sikologiyya li-azmat al-shabab fi al-watan al-'arabi* (Psychological Theories of the Crisis of Arab Youth) reviews three decades of Arab studies and finds most researchers concluding there is a widespread "crisis of youth."

CHAPTER *8*

Early Adulthood and Identity

Ethnographies of traditional MENA milieus suggest that a relatively clear-cut framework for identity was provided by two key contrasts—of gender (male versus female) and religion (Muslim versus non-Muslim)—that were woven through language, the etiquettes of daily life, ritual celebrations, and the cosmology of invisible beings. Age also appears to have provided salient contrasts, and in many areas, so did the contrasts between nomadic, village, and urban styles of life described by Ibn Khaldun. But if these core contrasts assigned what G. H. Mead termed a "Me" self in late childhood and early adolescence, identities based on them remained to be achieved. By late adolescence and early adulthood, the "I" increasingly responded, both by investing selected features of these contrasts with individuating personal meanings, and by improvising upon them in innovative ways. Distinctive acts of honor, modesty, and fertility (or of dishonor, immodesty, and troubled fertility), as well as poetic self-presentations and personalized forms of piety, confirm and individualize identities in early adulthood—and continue to do so throughout adulthood. Even in the most traditional communities, multiple cultural discourses (of honor-and-modesty, of piety, of sentimental poetry) appear to have facilitated the fashioning of multiple identities.

In modernizing and underdeveloping milieus, many of the traditional symbols organizing space, dress, and interaction have been lost, replaced by markers of achievement and social class. Colonization and postindependence Westernization have introduced a new duality that appears to have become the central axis of identity: tradition, which can appear either "backward" or "authentic," versus Western-style modernity, which can appear either as "progress" or "degeneration." Many studies show that people tend to develop dual identities, based on discourses of authentic tradition and of progressive modernity, and that the contradictions between these are readily experienced as troubling and sometimes "schizophrenic." Several researchers argue that the chaotic clash of competing values undermines identity formation and causes chronic psychological distress for many. A few suggest that the cultural dualities are not be inherently injurious, and in conditions of economic and societal development can become sources of creativity and renewal. The chapter concludes by focusing on these differing views.

My own study of identity development suggests that young adults in MENA societies may not have more difficulty forming identities that synthesize or balance these dualities than do Americans in reconciling the dualities in which they live. In MENA societies, however, economic and political underdevelopment renders many unable to anchor their identities in life structures that affirm and sustain them. The chronic struggle for identity that ensues—and may continue through the twenties and thirties—differs from the acute "crisis" often associated with first formulating one, in ways that Western theories do not understand well. Several studies suggest that young adults often combine the emerging family-based achievement orientation with religious piety to form a synthesis that resembles Weber's description of the "Protestant ethic." This orientation to "modernize within tradition" may partly underlie youths' return to religion in many MENA societies.

Introduction ❀

There is a large literature on identity in MENA societies (see the discussion of sources at the end of this chapter). Once again, little of it is by psychologists, but political scientists and anthropologists have provided rich observations about the psychological aspects of identity development. These writings suggest that the internalization of cultural constructions of *social personae* in accordance with the imperatives of honor-modesty and Islam does not assign identities, but challenges individuals to fashion them in terms set by these two value systems. The development of the third level of personality organization—for which I use Erikson's term *identity*—begins with the individual taking up the challenge to prove that he or she can live up to the culturally assigned ideals, or to revise or reject those ideals.

Writings on identity in MENA tend to emphasize its multiplicity—both of the identities available in the culture[1] and of the self-representations fashioned by single individuals. In addition, most observers emphasize the extent to which identity has become a contentious, politicized matter, animating cultural strife on the one hand and personal ambivalence on the other. Throughout this century, colonization, independence movements, and Western cultural domination have transformed both the social and the psychological character of identity. In a series of provocative works written during Algeria's war of liberation, the psychiatrist Franz Fanon explored the sense of inferiority inflicted on indigenous peoples by European colonization.[2] Fanon believed that the colonized strive to repair their dignity either by abandoning their "backward" traditions and showing they can become as "civilized" as the colonizers, or by revitalizing and defending their own "authentic" traditions against the colonizers' alien culture.[3] These two responses have defined the cultural dialogue about identity in MENA societies, and in the postindependence decades they have been set into play against each other. In the mid-1990s Akbar Ahmed wrote:

> A few decades ago, Nasser talked of three concentric circles that provide the Egyptian identity: Arabian, African, and Islamic. Today the West has penetrated and scrambled the circles. Egyptians may say they hate the West because of its imperialism, in particular Britain and France, but they are also fascinated by it. Education at the American University in Cairo is seen as a right step in the marriage market. Young men wear jeans and American consumerism is the rage among the middle class. Nasser's circles today would be replaced by two opposed positions: Islam and the West.[4]

My own "study of lives" research on identity in Morocco further demonstrates the multiplicity of self-representations and the importance of "traditional"/Muslim versus "modern"/Western dualities.[5] This research also suggests that many individuals experience important disjunctions between more truly traditional features of their personalities and the modernist identities they seek to fashion.

Studies of identity thus make it clear that young adults in MENA societies do not simply assimilate culturally constituted selves but actively select elements from their hybrid cultural heritage and combine them in innovative ways. Many individuals adopt *both* modernist and traditionalist identities and shift between them in smoother or more conflictual ways, sometimes ignoring their contradictions or thriving on their ambiguity. But it is important not to minimize the contradictions: Western and Islamic models diverge radically on how the body, psyche, soul, and social relations should be experienced and managed. Many writers emphasize the difficulty of reconciling these models, describing the duality as "schizophrenic"[6] or as tying life into a "knot." The chapter will focus on the character of these "knots."

After briefly reviewing Western theories of identity, part 1 of this chapter examines accounts of male and female identity in traditional milieus. Part 2 considers contemporary contexts in which traditional and traditionalist identities (those seeking to embrace "authentic" traditions) vie with "modern" and "Western" ones, and discusses some of the developmental discontinuities experienced by those who grow up in more traditional conditions but come of age in modernizing or underdeveloping ones. It concludes by taking up the crucial question posed by Abdelkrim Ghareeb,[7] about whether identity formation in a "composite" society provides rich opportunities for creativity or causes fragmentation and incoherence.

Western Theories of Identity

G. H. Mead's "Social Self"

Two of the pioneers of American psychology—William James and George Herbert Mead—theorized that self-conceptions arise from belonging to groups and emphasized that because individuals play many roles or belong to several groups, they develop multiple self-conceptions. Mead went on to argue that because roles and groups are ultimately integrated in an encompassing social structure, individuals gradually develop overarching self-conceptions that integrate the specific group-based roles they play. As described in chapter 3, he likened this to the learning of a sports game with positions and roles, suggesting that self-conceptions arise from viewing oneself from the perspective of the whole—by taking the point of view of the "Generalized Other." In this manner the self comes to be organized as a social structure. But Mead did not believe that all of an individual is encompassed by the self seen in the mirror of the Generalized Other, and so he distinguished between a socially constructed "Me" pole of the self and a subjective "I" pole that can react to the various "Me" construals.

I have suggested that the "Me" self (which I have termed "social persona" or "social self") more or less consolidates by early adolescence, as the maturing child comes to automatically see himself or herself in the light of cultural values and etiquettes, and experiences a set of sentiments and motives that have been shaped by these. As described in chapter 3, MENA cultures encompass two overlapping but also conflicting systems of values: the honor-modesty system and Islam. Yet the "Me" selves formed by these systems do not provide ready-made identities; rather they *challenge* individuals to fashion identities in their terms. That is, the Generalized Other becomes a kind of internalized grand inquisitor, demanding "You must become this . . . " or "Prove that you are this . . ." To view identity development in Mead's terms: during adolescence the games of childhood turn real, and in later adolescence and early adulthood the "I" must respond to the challenge(s) by fashioning what Erik Erikson terms a "psycho-social identity." In more traditional milieus, this often meant (for men) demonstrating honor-building prowess tempered by piety, and (for women) demonstrating fertility safeguarded by honorable modesty. In contemporary milieus, it has come to mean weaving together stands of modernity and tradition, individual achievement and family loyalty, Western and Muslim ways of life.

Erikson's Theory of Identity

What Erikson's theory adds to Mead's account is the observation that the "task" of forming an identity is typically triggered by the biological and cognitive changes associated with puberty, which often are timed with changes in social roles. These combine to disequilibrate the personality organization developed in late childhood. The task of identity formation requires building both self-conceptions and a worldview that integrates the near-adult's new body, new feelings, new ways of thinking, and new social roles—*in a meaningful way*. The new organization comes to be anchored in a system of beliefs, values, and practices: a worldview fashioned both as a map *of* reality and a model *for* constructing reality.[8] The "newness" of this organization derives from its anchoring in an ideological/ethical system, which individuals typically develop in late adolescence and early adulthood. For some individuals this leads to a sharp break with their past. For others it entails a deepening or broadening of their values and commitments: *proving* that one can become the "Me" demanded by the Generalized Other(s).

Built of cultural symbols and metaphors fused with personal feelings and images, identity as a belief system defines a cosmology that shows the temporal, spatial, and causal organization of one's world.[9] The sociologist S. N. Eisenstadt has studied generational relations and youth cultures cross-culturally and believes that an individual's transformation in adolescence provokes a need to find meaning in larger patterns of change, in "cosmic and societal time": "The attempt to find some meaning in personal temporal transition may often lead to identification with the rhythms of nature or history, with the cycles of the seasons, with the unfolding of some cosmic plan (whether cyclical, seasonal, or apocalyptic), or with the destiny and development of society."[10] Thus the child in late adolescence turns into a philosopher and myth-maker—or at least into someone in need of a philosophical-mythical system to live by, something to "stand for," a way to make one's life matter in the larger scheme of things. By linking one's place in the world with what one aspires to make of one's self, *identity* ideally brings the elements of life into coherence.[11]

Above all, an identity coalesces as a moral system and a political ideology—and Erikson insists that these are intimately related. Identity embraces some of one's feelings, motives, and self-images as worthy and empowering, and typically associates these with one's culture or in-group. At the same time it condemns other feelings, motives, and self-images as unworthy and dangerous, and associates these with groups held to be inferior.[12] Identity thus integrates by creating a broadened sense of "We," but almost invariably in contrast to an immoral or abject "They," who stereotypically come to represent the undesirable qualities or potentials of one's own personality. Erikson repeatedly underscores the group-based character of identity, and the crucial role played by culture and history in providing young adults with the structure of in-group versus out-group comparisons most rely on to organize their personalities. He sees the promise of youth as residing in its potential to struggle for more encompassing "wholistic" identities and cultures, and the danger of youth as lying in its liability to formulate "totalistic" identities that rigidly reaffirm prevailing prejudices or support totalitarian movements in the persecution of deviants and out-groups.

Narrative Theories of Identity

Recent narrative theories hold that people organize identities as life-stories or as "discourses" that position them in history and in relationships with real and fictional Others. In general accordance with Erikson's view, evidence is accumulating that people begin to synthesize readily tellable life-stories—and a set of early memories that loosely anchor them in a childhood origin—in adolescence.[13] Theorists diverge, however, about the nature of narrative self-representation. Jerome Bruner believes that it is a *life-story* with good plot structure that brings coherence to personality, and that people construct these mainly by adopting plot-lines and metaphors provided by their culture.[14] Dan McAdams also emphasizes the integrative importance of *story-structure*, but he sees these as encompassing a variety of scripts, imagos, and motivational themes that may configure several identities as elements of an overarching life-story.[15] In contrast to plot-structure theories, Hubert Hermans and Harry Kempen draw on the work of the literary theorist Mikhail Bakhtin to argue that identity is organized as the inner (and sometimes public) *dialogue* people stage among contrasting self-representations, or between the self and others who represent contrasting sides of their character—usually without recognizing that the Other they debate represents aspects of "Me."[16] My own theory of identity holds that identity tends to be anchored in an often small set of culturally prominent symbols, metaphors, and motifs, from which people may "generate" a variety of stories and dialogues.[17]

All three of these views capture important features of identity as imagined and rehearsed inwardly and as performed in daily life: key symbols, self-metaphors, and motifs, life-story structure, and dialogue among "sides" of one's character. All emphasize the crucial role of culture in providing and sometimes imposing the elements with which individuals compose identities, and they recognize that people typically fashion several contrasting identities, which may be brought into greater or lesser coherence within a life-story.

Daniel Levinson's Theory of "Life Structures"

Daniel Levinson and his colleagues have built on Erikson's theory and added several notions important for cross-cultural research.[18] Based on life-history studies of 40 American men, they identify four key "tasks" of later adolescence and early adulthood: forming (1) a "dream" for one's life, (2) mentor relationships, (3) an occupation, and (4) love relationships, marriage, and family. The "dream" forms the core of *identity*.

It has the quality of a vision, an imagined possibility that generates excitement and vitality. At the start it is poorly articulated and only tenuously connected to reality, although it may contain concrete images such as winning the Nobel Prize or making the all-star team. It may take a dramatic form as in the myth of the hero: the great artist, business tycoon, athletic or intellectual superstar performing magnificent feats and receiving special honors. It may take mundane forms that are yet inspiring and sustaining: the excellent craftsman, the husband-father in a certain kind of family, the highly respected member of one's community.[19]

The other three elements anchor a *life structure*, consisting of the vocation, relationships, and the life-style a person works out to pursue his or her "dream." Levinson emphasizes the difference between the psychological work that goes into forming a "dream" and the more practical efforts it takes to assemble a life structure: that is, deciding that one wants to become a doctor forms a 'dream'; getting into and through medical school anchors it in a life structure. Developing an identity can become a crisis not only because of the psychological confusions Erikson studied but because a young person may not be able to assemble a *life structure* that can sustain his or her "dream." This occurred to most of the blue-collar workers in Levinson's study: they succeed in developing "fantasies about exciting kinds of work and accomplishment," he writes, "but the incipient Dream cannot be articulated or explored. It is gradually covered over by the more immediate problems of survival."[20] In MENA societies—as in "majority" cultures around the globe—modernization has unleashed new "dreams," but conditions of underdevelopment dash many of them. Western psychology may well understand the normal and usually healthy "identity crisis" of youth but not the crisis of identity brought about by the inability to pursue "dreams" in conditions of underdevelopment.

Part 1: Identity in Traditional Milieus

Selves and Antiselves

As I discussed in chapter 7, many features of traditional MENA cultures provide continuous and often smooth transitions through a brief or nonexistent adolescence. At the same time, an array of forces can subject youths to significant strife and stress. Divisions of households, deaths, and disasters can fracture relationships they desperately want to sustain, and the decisions of patriarchs can force upon them relationships they dread, dash dreams that arise from a florescence of talent, or thwart romances nurtured from afar. Injuries and illnesses often frustrate the simple yearning to fulfill one's destiny as a fertile woman or an honorable man. Many scholars note that the culture's "sociocentric" emphasis on familial loyalty coexists with powerful individualistic imperatives, and these readily come into conflict in late adolescence and early adulthood. The majority of young men and women resolve these in favor of family loyalties, making the key psychological "task" one of renouncing individualistic strivings—rather than that of separating from familial interdependencies and achieving autonomy, as Western theories assume.

In traditional milieus, then, adolescents become full participants in the honor-modesty system and Islam. They began developing *expertise* at these discourses, which appear to anchor their identities in the richly elaborated symbolic and ritual forms linking male and female bodily processes with ethical ideals, social roles, and grand patterns of nature and history. These symbolic and ritual forms provide an array of contrasts by which selves can be defined in contrast to antiselves that embody despised and feared qualities. For men, the honor system traditionally set out not only prototypes of gentlemanly men but also an idealized *complement*, the modest and fecund woman, and a number of abject *opposites*, especially the weak, cowardly, or unbalanced man and the dishonorable and/or barren woman. The image of woman as polluting, lacking reason (*'aqel*), subject to desire (*nafs*) and therefore a source of chaos and discord (*fitna*) provides men with a ready vehicle for projectively denying their own negative qualities as they define their identities in terms of purity, reason, and self-control.

Women can define themselves as honorably modest in worthy contrast to abject images of dishonorable women, and as honorable complements to honorable men. It is not clear how women in traditional milieus "use" images of men to define themselves as women, but the many ethnographies that capture and translate women's voices make it clear that they have no difficulty disdaining men as flawed, inferior creatures and celebrating the virtues of women. But they also appear to internalize the stereotypes of themselves as weak, impure, and troublesome. Boddy reports that Hofriyati women frequently said of themselves "Nihna bahaim," or "We are cattle" (which we often heard from Imeghrani women), which grows from a deep self-defining association of woman with nature—as near-sacred source of fecundity and nurturance but also as bestial. Boddy emphasizes the meaningful ambiguity of this metaphor: that women use it both in resentment that "they live like their goats, pent up in tiny crowded rooms and hoshes in the dust of the desert, tethered to men by the nuptial rope, forced to subsist on the poorest of foods" but also to describe their value: "They are the inner core of village life: fertile, enclosed, domesticated. . . . Hofriyati women bestow the effects of generative and socially reproductive power onto men."[21] And, as mentioned in the last chapter, the symbols of gender differentiation— white versus red, meat versus milk, exposure versus concealment, right versus left, interior versus exterior spaces within the house, village, or neighborhood—appear to provide the materials from which women (and men) traditionally fashioned identities.[22] These assign more positive qualities to men, but women can reconfigure them to articulate contradictory identities: as superior, precious, and sacred on the one hand and as inferior, worthless, and profane on the other.

It is motherhood, of course, that affirms this rich reproductive symbolism. If marriage traditionally served as a rite of passage for women around the time of puberty, it did not yet confer an identity but challenged them to prove their fertility by bearing children—especially boys who survived. Motherhood then secured a woman's marriage, established her status in her new family, and affirmed her identity. "The birth of the first boy is much more important than marriage," writes Lacoste-Dujardin, as it marks the great turning point in a woman's life: "conferring the only status possible for a woman, the only permitted identity."[23] As El Khayat-Bennai points out, a mother usually takes a "teknonym," so that if she has given birth to "Mohammed" she comes to be known as "um-Mohammed" or "Mother of Mohammed"[24]— this, along with clothing, color, and spatial symbolism, anchors her identity. As Marcia Inhorn and others report, women who fail to conceive or whose infants die find their marriages, statuses, and identities in desperate jeopardy, and some percentage live broken lives with no respected social role and with "spoiled" identities. But she also found that a surprising number of infertile poor couples in Egypt resisted family pressures to divorce and chose to "nurture conjugal relationships characterized by love, involvement, and commitment."[25]

As described in chapter 3, Islam provides another set of ideal and antiself images. The Prophet perfectly combines honor and piety and provides the model all should seek to emulate. Earlier prophets, later religious leaders, and a great variety of saints provide additional models, each embodying a few admired powers or virtues. A set of prominent antiself images take shape in the *jahiliyya*, or "time of ignorance," before the revelation of the Quran to the Prophet. This is widely viewed as a time when all the impulses antithetical to civilization were given free rein: violence, idolatry, infanticide, tyranny, intoxication, illicit fornication, and so on. The same impulses also are associated with non-Muslims who live outside the house of Islam, such as supposedly primitive Africans, cow-worshiping Hindus, and pork-eating, whiskey-drinking, body-exposing Europeans. The beliefs and practices of Islam thus construct a sense of self-mastery and control (*'aqel*) over desires (*nefs*) that are perceived to be indulged by non-Muslims. These contrasts also get drawn *within* the Muslim world as well: other families, villages, tribes, and nations can be accused of being "not real Muslims" or "children of sin." Religious reformers have long made use of this rhetoric, as Islamist activists effectively do today, casting the present era as having devolved into a new *jahiliya* of ignorance and unbelief, its rulers acting as "pharaohs," the archetype of pagan tyranny.[26]

The *jinn* spirits also provide an important repertoire of traditional antiself images, as their habits and tastes are exactly the opposite of civilized humans.

Their characters range from mischievous to malevolent, they serve as agents of sorcery, and they indulge desires for the forbidden, drinking the blood of butchered animals and seducing humans in their sleep. The purity, self-control, and licit behavior of a believer, then, appears in contrast to the world of *jinns*, where representations of impure, chaotic, illicit impulses can be projectively set into play. And, as Crapanzano and Boddy point out, in spirit possession, the structure terrifyingly reverses as an antiself enters and takes control.

Gender Ideology in Afghanistan

In the mid-1970s, Audrey Shalinsky explored gender ideology in Afghanistan, and she makes two important observations about how men and women flexibly use it to organize identities.[27] First, she found that the ideology has two aspects, between which Afghans switch: one based in stereotypes about the essential "nature" of men and women, and one based on evaluations of specific men's and women's actions. Second, she found that the stereotypes are often linked with ethnic and human-*jinn* contrasts: the most negative, abject, and fearful representations tend to be located in *other* ethnic groups, and in the image of the *almasti*, a "witch-like" *jinn* figure. According to the view of the psyche taught by local religious authorities, desire (*nafs*) must be controlled by reason (*'aqel*), or chaos and disorder (*fitna*) will result. This provides the basis for everyday judgments of morality and character. But the ideology also associates men with reason and women with desire and disorder: "Men may consistently increase their *'aqel* through their lifetime by the study of the Qur'an, while women who have more *'aqel* in childhood lose it after marriage as their sexual desires awaken."[28] (Daisy Dwyer reports this belief from southern Morocco.)[29] Yet among themselves, women often reverse these images, emphasizing their self-control and indicting men for being ruled by their desires.

When they speak of men and women "in the abstract," Shalinsky observes, Afghans make rich use of the stereotypes; but when they speak of "specific cases," they tend to use the ideology in a gender-neutral way. In addition, men "do not necessarily think that their own women are as uncontrolled as the abstract statements indicate. It is the women from other ethnic groups who are the temptresses."[30] Women similarly fear the "wild and evil" men from neighboring ethnic groups. In classic stereotypic form, "negative sexuality, *nafs*, is attributed to the opposite sex or to those outside the ethnic group."[31] Negative sexuality is most vividly represented in the figure of the *almasti*, a wild, evil, non-Muslim, female, *jinn*-like being that she says resembles the North African Aisha Qandisha *jinniya* (believed there to have come across the desert from Sudan). Men thus associate unconstrained desire with women, women associate it with men, and both attribute it to outgroups and non-Muslim spirit beings.

Shalinsky's account of the way people shift between using their theory of the psyche in a flexible, nonstereotypic way when they deal with individual cases and in stereotypic ways when they deal with others as groups fits well with the "social identity theory" developed by Henri Tajfel.[32] In a now classic series of laboratory and cross-cultural studies, Tajfel and his colleagues have shown that when relationships are construed as person to person, individuals represent them in terms of individual characteristics. But as soon as relationships are construed as group to group, people shift to stereotypic representations: first depersonalizing others by ignoring their individuating qualities and then repersonalizing them in a prejudicial way by attributing purported group qualities to them. Shalinsky shows that men and women use the shared view of the human psyche to monitor their inner lives and evaluate the character of others. But *identity* tends to be anchored in the matrix of group stereotypes, built of gender, ethnicity, and religious oppositions, that define a moral, orderly, pure self ruled by reason (*'aqel*), in contrast to stereotypic images of immoral, impure Others who, ruled by desire (*nafs*), spread chaos.

Poetic Constructions of Identity

Ethnographies repeatedly suggest that traditional identities do not consist *only* of these social oppositions but also of more individual qualities. Individuals develop reputations for personal traits, talents, and peculiarities and often get nicknames based on these that stick throughout their lives. They also may perform what Meeker terms "glorious acts" that win them honor,[33] or they may fail to meet a challenge and dishonor themselves. Young adults also traditionally began participating in the poetic life of their community, and various forms of oral poetry and song provided them opportunities to assert their individual qualities. Bedouin societies are renowned for their improvisational poetry, song, and epic, and the oral arts permeate all aspects of life—as they do nearly as much for villagers and city-dwellers. Not only do one's actions count toward a reputation but so does one's poetic skill at dramatizing them.

Steven Caton studied how the poetry contests at weddings in Yemen (termed *balah*) enable men to construct individualized selves. After a drum signal, a group of men form a circle with their arms linked around each other's waists. One begins a tune, and the others may join in:

> The circle of men acts as a chorus in the performance. One half of the chorus chants a standard refrain line, the other half picks up part of the poetic turn delivered by a poet in the center of the circle, and together they alternate in the chanting of refrain and verse until a new poet or the same one enters the circle to take another performance turn. . . . Ideally, everyone should try to compose at least one verse as a "gift" to the groom.[34]

The verses are highly formulaic but also allow latitude for individual expression, and poets soon begin a "challenge and retort" period in which they tease and provoke each other:

> Herein, it is said by tribesmen, comes the real test of the oral poet: that is, has he not only mastered the traditional rhetorical devices but does he also possess the wit, imagination and stamina to compose verse lines in an improvisational manner? . . . Only the best and bravest poets dare to enter the circle when it is clear to everyone that a contest of challenge and retort has begun. . . . Built into the composition of the poem is an exchange of challenges between equals which is exactly parallel to the exchange of glorious deeds between honorable men. What is created in this performance is not only a poem, it is also social honor . . . an honorable self.[35]

Caton draws on G. H. Mead's distinction between the socially constructed "Me" and individual "I" to describe how this form of Arab poetry provides conventions (organizing the "Me" pole) within which improvisational freedom encourages individualistic assertions (of the "I" pole):

> This "I" emerges in the course of a *balah* performance when an opponent challenges the honorable self of an individual in a nonformulaic, particularly witty or otherwise spontaneous fashion, and the "I" of that individual's self must devise an apt reply. . . . The construction of the honor-bound self depends largely on the poetic "I" rather than the poetic "me" responsible for the formulaic, predictable parts.[36]

John Anderson explored constructions of self—he prefers the term *persona*—in *jinn* beliefs, love poems, proverbs, and Quranic verses that enliven everyday speech among the Pakhtun in Afghanistan.[37] These operate with the same theory of *'aqel* (reason, social maturity) and *nafsh* (desire), described by Shalinsky. In what Anderson terms the "discourse of affliction," *jinns* are blamed for breakdowns in social life: illnesses, accidents, strife, outbursts of temper, sexual deviance, and so on. The *jinns* represent "disorderliness in the form of random vitality," he writes, so "the actions of *jinn* on humans are opposed to states of grace articulated by *'aqel*," and the disruptions they cause stand out as "counterpoints to the ideology of honor, which stresses orderly presence and composed personae."[38] In the "discourse of love," a genre of rhymed couplets known as *landay* give voice to "an erotic sentimentality of bursting passions . . . they are the preferred voice for speaking of vitality, passion, exuberance and other qualities made problematic by *'aqel*."[39] Proverbs bring a kind of streetwise cynicism into everyday conversation: sometimes they express the urgings of love, as do *landay* couplets, but more often "they are used to emphasize regardfulness and sanction respect for values."[40] Quotations from the Quran and *hadith* (teachings of the Prophet) state the core moral imperative for reason to rule desire. Each of these discourses entails a "dialectic of *'aqel* and *nafsh*" that recruits the vital but disorderly forces of desire to different purposes—constructing different personae in the process. Anderson does not view any of these as expressing an "inner self" as against an "outer experience," or a personal "I" against a social "Me," as does Caton. Rather, he sees each as fashioning a persona: "Multiple discourses mark the multiplicity of personae" that one can enact in different social settings.[41]

Abu-Lughod emphasizes a different function of the *ghinnawa* genre of poetry she studied among Bedouin women in Egypt: that it gives voice to sentiments of weakness and vulnerability that are silenced by the core values of honor and modesty (see chapter 3). Sung at weddings and spontaneously in the company of some family and friends, these have both formulaic structures and freedom for improvisation, allowing women, juniors, and sometimes adult men to voice personal and subversive feelings. They form a "discourse of defiance" that is not condemned or even grudgingly tolerated but "culturally elaborated and sanctioned."[42]

> People are thrilled by poetry. They are drawn to *ghinnawa*s, and at the same time they consider them risque, against religion, and slightly improper—as befits something antistructural. . . . People admire poetry in the same way they secretly admire youths' or women's refusals to submit to tyranny or to accept domination by the system or its representatives.[43]

Especially for women and juniors who cannot fully participate in men's game of honor, Abu-Lughod sees the *ghinnawa* as providing a vehicle for individual creativity.

Islam similarly provides a wealth of concepts, symbols, and paths of piety with which individuals can tailor belief and practice to their idiosyncratic qualities. As described in chapter 3, the contrast between more orthodox and mystical forms of Islam stretches back to the Prophet and across the breadth of the Muslim world. Individuals differ in the importance they give prayer, fasting, the *jinns*, and purification, and in which suras from the Quran and which incidents in the life of the Prophet they find moving and meaningful. Many young men traditionally have joined Sufi orders or religious brotherhoods, and in the personal relationships they form with a teacher and the order's patron saint, they find their own path toward *hasana*, self-improvement and virtue. Many women (and some men) have dreams in which a saint appears, and they subsequently become "tied" to the saint—following his (or occasionally her) teachings, praying to him as an intercessor, and making pilgrimages to his tomb. All of these provide material for individualizing traditional identities. Thus the cultural systems that seem to stamp individuals with preformed identities—especially gender and religion—either incorporate or exist alongside other discourses that facilitate the expression and recognition of idiosyncratic, personal qualities.

Traditional MENA societies appear to have shared the anchoring of identity in elaborately symbolized gender, religion, and age contrasts with most other preindustrial cultures, though MENA's specific constructions were distinctive. Nearly all ethnographers concur that African family systems and gender constructions differ from those typical of MENA (and of Eurasian "classic patriarchy" in general). Given that sub-Saharan Africa was home to a great many "little tradition" cultures with their own languages and cosmologies, it appears probable that the "ethnic" group was a more salient ingredient of identity there than in most of MENA. And many sub-Saharan African societies had age-grade systems, which probably highlighted age in defining identities. In Hindu India, the caste system and its related marriage and pollution-purification practices undoubtedly played a central role in identity. The gender and age contrasts of preindustrial Mediterranean Europe appear to have been quite similar to those found in MENA: MENA differed from bordering culture areas most distinctively in its Muslim cosmology and practices. Until their Islamization, African cultures tended to be "animist," with invisible realms populated by ghosts and witches rather than jinns and the Evil Eye. The Hindu cosmology provided a dramatically different scheme of time and space, and thousands of divinities to which an individual might be "devoted."

Part 2: Identity in "Modernizing" Milieus ❈

Multiple Self-Representations

As Halim Barakat points out, MENA cultures have never been repositories of traditions resisting innovation but always were animated by struggles between the old and the new.[44] In this century, colonialism, nationalism, and globalization have redrawn the lines of this struggle, pitting Islam against the West. Aziz Krichen is correct to see that there are now two ways to do everything, from dressing, eating, and speaking to managing one's sexuality and interpreting one's dreams.[45] This has become the matrix of conflicting values, styles, and symbols within which young people fashion identities. The traditional repertoire (male versus female, right versus left, white versus red, Muslim versus nonbeliever, human versus jinn, and so on) has not been displaced but incorporated within the new, while some elements have faded in salience and others assumed new prominence, and all have been redefined in relation to the "modern" and the Western.

Not only do individuals take up different positions within this matrix—some more "modern," others more "traditional," some staking out middle grounds—but many develop contrasting or contradictory identities among which they shift. There is nothing specifically modern or Middle Eastern about shifting among multiple self-representations, as identity everywhere coalesces as a kind of dialogue among contrasting and often opposed voices.[46] Typically an individual presents some of the voices as alternative representations of his or her "true self," and other voices as radically Other "antiselves." What is distinctive about MENA cultures is (1) the *content* of self and antiself representations, and (2) the kinds of *dialogue, cacophony,* or *synthesis* among voices that individuals work out. Interestingly, the fundamental polarity described by Ibn Khaldun in the fourteenth century—between strong, virile, ascetic Bedouins and senescent, corrupt, indulgent urbanites, or (to view it from the city-dwellers' point of view) between civilized, sophisticated, cultured urbanites and ignorant, brutish, bestial Bedouins—continues to appear in many forms. Not only may rural peoples and urbanites still hold these stereotypes of each other but the commoners and Westernized elites may contrast themselves in similar terms.

Social Identity in Cairo

Sawsan El Messiri's study of social identities in Egypt examined the idealized character of Cairo's popular or working classes—*ibn al-balad,* or "son of the homeland"—and how this character is defined in contrast to the upper-class *effendi,* who adopted the "foreign" ways of their Turkish rulers, and to the *fellahin,* the rural peasants whom the *effendi* see as backward, naive, and crude. The image of the *ibn al-balad* took shape in response to the centuries-long domination by foreign rulers (Turks, French, and British), as "it was in the face of these alien Cairo-based elements that the indigenous inhabitant sought to preserve and assert his particular identity."[47] This image coalesced from a cast of folk characters, "rebel heroes resisting the exploiting foreign elite, protecting the weak and poor, and dispensing justice amongst their people."[48] The *ibn al-balad* is the "real," authentic Egyptian, who speaks the Egyptian dialect of Arabic (rather than classical Arabic or Arabic mixed with foreign phrases), wears a *djellaba* robe and *teqiya* headcap (rather than a Western suit) in a clean, stylish, and elegant fashion (in contrast to the peasants' dirty garb). He works as a small merchant or craftsman (rather than as a bureaucrat or farmer), has a shrewd and clever intellect (rather than the elites' educations or the peasants' simple-mindedness). He shows manly strength and courage (unlike the "cowardly," "weak," "effeminate" elite and the passive peasants), and he practices religion (as opposed to the elite, who have abandoned it, and the peasants, who do not understand what they practice).

The *ibn al-balad* are the *futuwa* (tough youths—chapter 7) grown into adults, and El Messiri writes that the most prominent traits forming their character are gallantry, cleverness, and masculinity: "Many interviews described the *ibn al-balad* as 'the person who is manly.'"[49]

He is particular about his behavior and his appearance. He never shaves his moustache, nor plucks his eyebrows. He will not walk in the street arm in arm with a friend nor talk in a soft manner or tone. . . . This strong awareness of his manliness is expressed in his relation to others, especially his wife. Most of the interviewees thought of the *ibn al-balad* as the person who has complete authority in his home and who keeps his home and his wife completely under control.[50]

As one *bint al-balad* ("daughter of the homeland") commented on an elite man whose wife carried on an affair, "as long as the husband is soft, the woman will do what she wants. Unless he is like a 'lion,' the woman will neither fear nor respect him."[51] Yet women also embrace lion-like qualities, and the *bint al-balad* also sees herself as "courageous and outspoken in words and actions"—like the woman El Messiri interviewed who recounted attacking and beating a man who harassed her on the street, forcing him to move out of the neighborhood in shame. By contrast, the *bint al-balad* regards the peasant woman "as awkward, inept, stupid and narrow-minded" and views "her aristocratic counterpart as one who wears an elegant exterior to cloak an immoral self 'of which only God is aware.'"[52] The *ibn al-balad*, El Messiri explains, regard themselves as repositories of authentic Egyptian values and the foreignized elite as "the source of corruption and immorality in Egyptian society."[53]

El Messiri ends by noting that this identity has been undergoing change, especially in the post–World War II decades. As important segments of the popular classes have obtained educations and office jobs, they have sought to "negate" their *ibn al-balad* identities and "relate themselves to a completely Western frame of reference." They increasingly have seen themselves as a vanguard of modernization, and "Western education, fashions and life styles became means and symbols of status and progress." The *ibn al-balad* have increased in number but declined in status. Independence and nationalism led paradoxically to "a reinforcement of the Western elitist tendencies rather than those emanating from the masses," he writes, ending the book in the mid-1970s with the prescient observation that "when and how the traditional past will meet with the modern present to produce an authentic identity is the dilemma of the *awlad al-balad* [children of the homeland], and perhaps this is also the main crisis of Egyptians in the twentieth century."[54]

Acculturation in Algeria

A little-known study of psychological "acculturation" in 1950s Algeria ends with some provocative observations about the duality of identity created by French colonization and popular resistance. Horace Miner and George

DeVos's *Oasis and Casbah* embodies much that was wrong with the "basic personality" approach, but the researchers creatively rethought their data when it failed to confirm their main hypotheses. They initially asked a Rorschach expert unfamiliar with North Africa to formulate a series of predictions about personality differences between men living in a southern oasis community and their neighbors who had moved to urban Algiers. They hired French-speaking Algerian assistants to administer Rorschach tests and conduct brief life-history interviews with 20 men in the oasis and 26 in Algiers. They then had the Rorschach protocols blind-scored and coded for the relevant traits, and statistically tested the hypotheses.

Though Miner did fieldwork in the sites, neither spoke Arabic, and by current standards they had little familiarity with MENA cultures. Perhaps as a consequence, the book is rife with what today appear to be "Orientalist" statements (the Algerians exhibit "a tendency . . . toward illogical, rather than systematic thought"[55]). But when statistical tests confirmed only a chance percentage of the predictions, Miner and DeVos concluded that a range of religious and social attitudes can change (for the city-dwellers did espouse generally more "modern" views in a number of areas) without concomitant changes in deeper layers of personality. They then conducted post hoc analyses of their data to identify Algerian versus American and rural versus urban differences, and wrote a series of case histories to illustrate the diversity of personal adaptations.

First of all, they report finding more signs of psychological distress and constriction among Algerians than among "normal" Americans. This may well reflect only the Eurocentric norms of Rorschach interpretation and the greater anxiety experienced by the Algerians in the testing situation. But populations that experience malnutrition, a 20 percent childhood mortality rate, a high prevalence of chronic and debilitating diseases, and a century of colonial despoliation and military oppression may indeed be expected to experience higher levels of psychological distress and constriction. Miner and DeVos also found greater use of externalizing and projective defenses among Algerians, which may again reflect Eurocentric norms but also might be predicted where parents teach children to fear invisible beings and where there is greater physical suffering, emotional loss, and political oppression.

Second, contrary to the Rorschach expert's prediction, Miner and DeVos found an association between *dis*belief in supernatural forces (*jinn* spirits, ogres, and the like) and higher levels of psychological distress—mostly among residents of Algiers: "The attenuation of traditional beliefs among the urbanized Arabs is related to increasing intrapsychic tensions. . . . The minority position of the more acculturated urban Arab is reflected in his perception of the social environment as hostile and threatening."[56] While this correlation could be an artifact of other associations, Miner and DeVos also might be correct to argue that *dis*belief increases distress: "The decline of supernatural beliefs decreases the protection from stress that they provide in the oasis."[57]

As Franz Fanon argued, belief in supernatural beings integrates individuals into traditional communities, and because these beliefs come with protective rituals, they may provide an important source of psychological security. Many of the adolescents studied by Davis and Davis[58] and most of the young Moroccans I interviewed were troubled by uncanny experiences—nightmares, "hysterical" paralyses, illicit sexual thoughts, accidents and injuries, impotence, and so on—that in traditional milieus would have been explained as caused by Satan, the Evil Eye, sorcery, or *jinns.* Their educations had led them to reject supernatural explanations, but they searched in vain for modern, scientific interpretations. They appeared to be caught in an important developmental disjunction: their early training in attributing anxiety to external forces led them to have uncanny experiences for which they had no "modern" explanation or means of self-protection. Since religious practice provides protection (see chapter 3), the need to interpret and manage uncanny experiences may be an important motive drawing young people back to Islam—a motive unrecognized by most observers of the "Islamic revival."

Third, as brief and clinical as are the case histories, Miner and DeVos suggest that the researchers were intrigued by the Algerian men's attempts to work out niches in the colonial world, several of them struggling to define themselves in terms of symbols of Frenchness and Algerianness. They describe "Ali" as traditional in most features of his personality and beliefs, but after he had worked for four months in France, they said,

> we see him as a teen-aged, oasis youth who intensely desires to identify with the French way of life. He uses a mixture of European and Arab dress and is vain about his wristwatch, a certain mark of French contact. He wears a fez like an Arab urbanite and swears that he will never wear the more rural turban. . . . Beneath the clothes and speech, however, we find a core of cultural belief that is characteristically like that of the unacculturated oasis Arabs.[59]

"Ahmed" spent only a few years in the local French school but more skillfully blends French and Arab elements. He is an innovator in the oasis community: they note that he shifts between emphasizing one style or the other according to circumstances. "Benazouz" was a young nationalist; they suspect that he perished in the subsequent war of independence. They describe him as having an "ambivalent" social identity, as "looking both ways in his acculturation." By this they mean that while he was highly Westernized in many respects, he vehemently defended Arab culture and orthodox Islam, "looking down on groups he consider[ed] primitive or simple"—which included "backward" Arabs, the "Negro" heads he perceived in one of the Rorschach ink blots, and American Indians.

The case studies show that Miner and DeVos were most struck by the struggle for identity they saw being waged in terms of French versus Arab cultural concepts, styles, and symbols. The portraits outline the binary (self versus antiself) and shifting nature of self-representation: Ali strives to be solidly "French, not-Arab"; Ahmed mixes cultural genres and shifts flexibly between "French, not-Arab," and "Arab, not-French"; and Benazouz vehemently asserts himself to be "Arab/Muslim" and "not French" in some contexts and "not-primitive" in others. The portraits provide precious few details but enough to see that prominent self symbols (clothes, manners of speech, stereotypic group representations, and so on) sometimes mean French versus Arab, sometimes Muslim versus heathen, sometimes urban modernity versus rural backwardness.

The Politics of Clothing in Turkey

Historical events in Turkey and Iran show how contentious the wearing of clothes symbolizing "tradition" and "modernity" can become. In the 1920s Mustafa Kamal ("Ataturk"), set out to modernize the country along European lines. Writing in the 1950s, Daniel Lerner praised Ataturk's attack on "the 'oriental mentality' that interdicted republican development":

> Ataturk aimed at nothing less than reshaping a traditionalized society by transforming the daily deeds and desires of the people—first the new elite, then the ancient mass. From the very start, Ataturk preoccupied himself with details of deportment that seemed picayune to his more rigidly ideological contemporaries. . . . His model was the "modern Western style" and his method was the production of "new Turks."[60]

In addition to adopting a new legal code modeled on the Swiss, creating a compulsory public education system, building a network of roads, providing villages with radios, and closing down religious shrines and brotherhoods, Ataturk set out to modernize the fine details of dress. In 1925 the "Hat Law" prohibited men from wearing the traditional Fez and designated European-style hats as the official headwear. Ataturk explained in a 1927 speech:

> Gentlemen, it was necessary to abolish the fez, which sat on the heads of our nation as an emblem of ignorance, negligence, fanaticism, and hatred of progress and civilization, to accept in its place the hat, the headgear used by the whole civilized world, and in this way to demonstrate that the Turkish nation, in its mentality as in other respects, in no way diverges from civilized life.[61]

The law also allowed women not to veil, and Western-style dress soon became the norm for urban men and women.

Turks transformed the minutest details of their comportment, the sociologist Nilufer Gole writes, "as if European eyes are watching over their daily lives."[62] She cites the writings of Ahmet Tanpinar as capturing the psychological duality introduced by Westernism—at times intensifying into a "psychosis" affecting the "inner self." "We have moved toward the West with a will reinforced by the requirements of history," Tanpinar wrote, "yet at the same time, we own a past such that it is impossible to close our ears once it starts to talk to us with all its quality." The duality of inner voices ties life into a "knot," so that the Turk lives "in the middle of two different but overlapping worlds, unaware of each other."[63] In popular speech the duality came to be known by borrowed French terms: *alafranka* (European) ways versus *alaturka* (Turkish) ways.[64]

The Kemalists maintained one-party rule until the 1950s, when, as the historian Hugh Poulton describes, "the continuing Islamic sensibilities of the large majority of the population began to make themselves evident."[65] In the 1970s, cultural and political strife grew intense, with leftists, rightists, and religious activists attacking the Western-oriented government and conflict intensifying between the Kurdish minority and Turkish majority and between the Alevi (Shi'i) minority and Sunni majority. Nearly all features of dress became political symbols, and "by the end of the decade," Emelie Olson writes, "even the curve or droop of a man's mustache was carefully calibrated for its political significance."[66] As street violence, terror attacks, and assassinations escalated toward civil war, the military seized power in 1980 and used force to impose order. To defuse the explosive identity politics, it issued a "Dress and Appearance Regulation" for all public employees that prohibited men from wearing mustaches, beards, or long hair and women from wearing short skirts, low-cut dresses, or headscarves.

But as part of the regime's effort to counter the leftists, it also reintroduced religious instruction in the public schools—and this, combined with the success of the revolution in Iran, strengthened the Islamists. In 1984, newspapers carried stories about the valedictorian of the University of Ankara medical school, who was not allowed to give a graduation address because she insisted on wearing a headscarf, and then about an engineering professor who was threatened with dismissal because she wore a headscarf while teaching. These set off what came to be known as the "headscarf" dispute, in which large numbers of women students protested and demonstrated to win the right to veil. Westernized students and professional women opposed them, and the entire nation debated the matter. As Gole points out, paradoxes abound: that women's bodies have reemerged as the foci of morality and politics shows the strength of tradition beneath decades of state-imposed modernism; but that the Islamist women are taking fully modern roles in the public political process shows that modernism has triumphed. The self-conscious veiling of students and professional women differs in both style and meaning from that practiced as custom by village and poor urban women. Though defending the "authenticity" of tradition, the professionals condemn truly traditional veiling styles as not reflecting true Islam, and their veiling appears as a fully modern statement of fashion-based identity and political commitment.

The headscarf dispute signaled another round in the politicization of dress—which affects men's clothing and hairstyles as well—and the latest "reemergence" of Islam as a cultural and political movement. In 1994 the Islamic Welfare party won many local elections, including the mayorships of Istanbul and Ankara, and in 1995 got over 20 percent of the vote in parliamentary elections. The struggle between Western-style modernity and Turkish backwardness has refused to go away and has grown into a conflict between Western and Muslim visions of modernity.

In the 1950s Lerner believed that his survey data showed that between the "moderns" and the "traditionals" were a large group of "transitionals," who

> exhibit ambivalent feelings about the choices between old and new. It is this conflict of values—continued loyalty to the old, growing desire for the new—that differentiates the decisions and shapes the behavior of the Transitionals. The conflict exhibits various forms. Sometimes ambivalence takes the form of uncertainty and indecision. . . . Ambivalence also takes the form of self-contradictory preferences. . . . Among younger Transitionals, ambivalence often shows itself in incompleteness and inconsistency of attitudinal structures.[67]

Poulton believes that much of the populace supports the "Turkish-Islamic synthesis" promoted as a middle course by governments in the 1980s, and that most are willing to ignore the contradictions between the Kemalists' Turkish nationalism and Islamism in order to embrace features of both.[68] But a great many remain ambivalent. "There is a readily observable struggle in process for 'the soul' of Turkey," he writes toward the end of the 1990s, "between the previous Kemalist elites, who for decades have been used to paternally defining the essence of 'Turkishness,' even down to what constitutes 'real Turkish music,' and the new Islamic challengers."[69] This struggle forms the primary axis of identity, along which Turks can move in either direction: overcoming backward *alaturk* traditions and becoming modern in accordance with the Kemalist program of *alafrank* Westernization, or resisting the corrupt influences of the West and becoming authentic by revitalizing Islam.

"Euromania" in Iran

In 1925, the year of the "Hat Law" in Turkey, the commander of Persia's Cossack Brigade, Reza Pahlavi, became shah of shahs—king of kings—and began a similar program of modernization in the nation he insisted be called Iran. He first built a modern army, and used it to settle the nomads, crush resistance, and mobilize the population for government projects. Taking many of Ataturk's reforms as examples, he put in place new Western-style legal, financial, and education systems and began building an infrastructure of roads, communications lines, and factories. In 1929 his government ordered men to dress in Western clothes and in 1936 became the first to outlaw veiling. His soldiers and police enforced these rules, sometimes tearing veils off women in the streets. There was one religious protest, in which a large crowd came to one of Iran's holiest shrines to hear preachers criticize the shah's policies: "When they did not disperse, Reza Shah's troops mounted machine guns on the roofs overlooking the courtyard and opened fire. Over one hundred people were killed. Three soldiers who had refused to fire were shot. No further hostile religious demonstrations of any significance took place in Reza Shah's reign."[70]

The shah and his followers also developed what Roy Mottahedeh calls a "cult" of Iran's pre-Islamic past to legitimate the ruler's kingship and to provide a nationalist, nonreligious identity onto which Western ways might be grafted. Mostafa Vaziri has traced how they were inspired by German theories of nation-building and followed the racist theories of nineteenth-century Western "Orientalist" scholars who argued that an Iranian nation had been founded in the sixth century B.C. by light-skinned Aryans who were superior to the darker Semitic Arabs to the West and Dravidian Indians to the East. The shah's regime celebrated the heroes of the national epic, *The Book of Kings*: the new public school texts gave pride of place to the kingdom founded by Cyrus in the sixth century B.C.; and Arabic words were purged from the language in favor of "pure" Farsi. Vaziri writes:

> The constitution of a national memory of the glorious past was a central element of Pahlavi policies designed to give a distinct sense of identity to the people of Iran. Pre-Islamic Zoroastrian emblems appeared on government agencies and buildings and special attention was paid to Zoroastrian festivals—all in order to revive the past and to connect with it.[71]

Mottahedeh describes how the naming of children inscribed the hopes of modernization in new identities:

> From the 1930s on, middle- and upper-class Iranians, duly impressed by the role of Iran in ancient history, gave their sons such names as Cyrus and Cambyses, names that would have been outlandish and virtually meaningless to Muslim Iranians before the translation of modern European books in the nineteenth century. In fact, by the next generation, when the Cyruses of the 1930s had grown up and had named many of their children after ancient Iranians, the newly engrafted historicist cult seemed to have taken.[72]

After the World War II, Mohammed Reza Shah continued his father's programs of modernization, Westernization, and propagation of a pre-Islamic ideology. In 1971 he celebrated the twenty-five-hundredth anniversary of Iranian kingship, and "at the ceremony that was meant to be the symbolic heart of the celebration, the shah stood before the tomb of Cyrus and said, 'Sleep easily, Cyrus, for we are awake.'"[73] Then:

In the boldest gesture of all, the government changed the calendar from the Islamic era to an era based on the supposed date of the foundation of Iranian kingship by Cyrus. In 1976 Iranians found themselves no longer in 1355 of the Islamic era but in 2535 of "the era of the King of Kings." It was an act of defiance to religion that only a time like the French Revolution could produce in the West.[74]

In spite of the state's massive propaganda, Mottahedeh writes that "the third generation of Cyruses does not seem to have been significantly larger than the second. . . . Something had gone sour."[75] The most influential diagnosis came from Al e Ahmad, an educator from a rural village who eventually studied in Moscow and at Harvard, who came to feel alienated in Teheran and spent most of the 1950s studying and writing about village life. He saw an authenticity in the villages that had been lost in the modern cities, and in 1962 wrote a book entitled *Gharbzadegi*—literally "West-stricken-ness"—to describe the "illness" that afflicted Iran: "I say that *gharbzadegi* is like cholera [or] frostbite. But no. It's at least as bad as sawflies in the wheat fields. Have you ever seen how they infest wheat? From within."[76] Mottahedeh explains:

> To be "stricken" in Persian means not only to be afflicted with a disease or to be stung by an insect but it also means to be infatuated and bedazzled; "West-stricken-ness," therefore, has sometimes been translated as "Westoxication." But a less outlandish word, "Euromania," captures enough of the sense of the Persian to be a passable stand-in for the nearly untranslatable Persian original.[77]

Al e Ahmad wrote that Satan's modern incarnation is the machine, manufactured in the West, which enslaves those who consume its products. Even more powerful forms of enslavement come from the superficial cravings Westernization implants in Iranian minds, and from the way Iranians come to see and know themselves through the gaze of Europeans. The Euromaniac "has no personality—he is an object with no authentic origin."[78] And in spite of Al e Ahmad's dislike for the rigidity of the religious elite, he believed that traditional Islam remained the reservoir of Iranian authenticity.

Especially with modernization so brutally enforced by Reza Shah's army and Mohammed Shah's secret police (SAVAK), Al e Ahmad's *Westoxication* struck responsive chords. In the following two decades—leading to the 1979 revolution—it provided much of the language adopted by nearly all opposition groups, from leftists to Islamists. His heritage quickly "split into a hundred parts espoused by a hundred groups," Mottahedeh writes, "all of which were against Euromania but otherwise agreed on very little."[79] Many modernized urbanites continued to support the shah's Westernization programs, even if they opposed his dictatorship, and this then formed the highly charged matrix of identity for the prerevolutionary generation. An Iranian could opt for Western-style modernization in opposition to "backward" and "super-stitious" traditions or "fanatical" religious movements. Or he or she could choose "authentic" tradition over the soulless materialism of Euromania. Vaziri describes this as a form of "cultural schizophrenia" in which many Iranians "endorsed both Aryanism and Shi'ism as their source of identity."[80] Shayegan similarly describes the "cultural schizophrenia" of

> the individual clamped in the jaws of this split and wrestling with a contradictory double fascination: the enchanted vision of a world still infused with the aura of collective memory, and the equally compelling allure of the new and unknown . . . racked between new ideas that evaporate for lack of a context and ancient ideas arthritic with the failure to adapt.[81]

Mottahedeh writes as a historian, not a psychologist, but he points out that while some Iranians played out the role of pious believer and others the role of modernizer, a great many found ways to combine and move between the two poles. He repeatedly comments on the Iranian "love of ambiguity" that enabled the majority of Iranians to "shift roles from devotee to cynic," from Cyrus (the pre-Islamic king) to Hosein (the Shi'i martyr), from the modern to the traditional—a "freedom" he believes the revolution brought to an end. The polarization prior to it forced choices and hardened identi-ties, and the revolutionary government quickly set about reversing the half-century of state-directed Westernization. A great many Westernized Iranians left the country, and the revolutionary government enforced the purity of Islamic tradition on those who remained. "The inner spaces created by am-biguity no longer exist," Mottahedeh writes, "and the attraction of ambigu-ity is forever dead."[82]

Religious Revival in Egypt

In the decades since El Messiri wrote about the gathering crisis of the *awlad al-balad*, Egyptian society became more Westernized but also emerged as a center of Islam's resurgence. Egypt has developed MENA's largest media industry, and its movies and TV shows—the vast majority depicting West-ernized styles of life—are avidly watched throughout the region. At the same time, Egypt saw the emergence of the first and still-prototypic Islamist po-litical movement, whose activists assassinated Anwar Sadat in 1981 and staged spectacular attacks on tourists and government officials in the 1990s. "Egypt has since the end of the eighteenth century born the brunt of the intercultural confrontation between the technological-scientific West and the preindustrial Middle East," Bassam Tibi writes, and "Cairo still remains by and large the center of religio-ideological reaction against European in-cursion into the region."[83] This reaction is most readily seen in the history of the Muslim Brotherhood and other activist groups, but it also has been occurring among the great number of Egyptians who have turned to piety as part of a less visible but more steady grassroots movement. Still following Islamist doctrines but rejecting armed attacks, Geneive Abdo describes this "popular Islam" as aiming "to transform the social structure of Egyptian society from the bottom up, creating an Islamic order."[84]

From the 1880s through the 1930s, a line of theologians at Egypt's al Azhar University—especially Jamal al-Afghani, Muhammad 'Abduh, and Mohammad Rida—argued for resisting Western domination by revitalizing Islam. Even many secular nationalists came to appreciate the power of invoking Islam to mobilize popular support. But religious renewal went much further than recruitment to anticolonialism, and nationalist movements in most MENA societies also entailed efforts to purify Islam of the unorthodox practices that were seen to have made it vulnerable to Western powers. "Purified," "real" Islam—a modern creation—became the tradition that modernizing peoples rallied to defend.[85]

Hasan Banna was a devout young teacher from a rural village who came to Cairo to study and participated in the 1919 uprising against British rule. Ten years later, in his post in a village near the Suez Canal, he founded the Muslim Brotherhood (*ikhwan muslimun*) when a handful of laborers working at a British camp came to him and took an oath to be "troops for the message of Islam." They began recruiting and soon expanded to Cairo, where by the late 1940s they had a half million members and branches in other countries.[86] The *ikhwan* were suppressed in 1949, and Banna was assassinated. It reemerged and was suppressed again by Nasser in the 1960s, and its leader, Siyyid Qutb, was hanged. It was again allowed to organize a few years later by Sadat, in the hope that it might offset a growing leftist movement.

Gilles Kepel describes how Islamism found roots in the 1970s among the youth of a new generation suffering from "profound malaise." The 1967 and 1973 wars with Israel had rendered the ideologies of Westernization, Arab nationalism, and Soviet communism all hollow and served as a catalyst for the religious revival. According to Fadwa El Guindi, "in the aftermath of the 1967 Arab-Israeli War a climate of intense and visible religiousness developed in Egypt that continues up to the present among the urban population in general. . . . Women resumed veiling after the 1973 Ramadan War."[87] Economic growth failed to keep pace with population growth. Kepel writes:

> It was in this period that the first generation coming out of the demographic explosion and the rural exodus became adults—the first generation never to have known direct colonial domination and to be massively literate (at least the males). Arriving on the labor market, they faced the bitter experience of general underemployment . . . which was all the more painful owing to its contrast with the hopes placed in education as a means to upward mobility, hopes fostered by the rhetoric of the post-independence regimes.[88]

The *ikhwan* offered this postindependence generation a new rhetoric and grew in the 1970s by propagating Siyyid Qutb's view that Egypt (and other Muslim societies) had fallen into a new state of *jahiliya*—the term used for the pre-Islamic era of "ignorance"—ruled by a corrupt "pharaoh" against whom a new *jihad* (holy war) must be waged.

The Brotherhood thus appears to have captured the historical *ibn al-balad* resentment of the foreignized elite and refashioned it in sharply religious terms. The Islamist critique begins, writes Richard Mitchell, in "the cultural, religious, societal, or personal question of inferiority and humiliation—an angry response to the conspicuous contempt of the foreign 'economic overlord' for the Egyptian."[89] This critique indicts the West for its cultural "materialism" and its international "greed and tyranny," counterposing to it the moral and spiritual superiority of indigenous religion and culture—at least in the era of the Prophet and his successors. It indicts as apostates the Egyptian elites who adopt Western ways.

Many observers have seen Islamism as a "nativist movement" resembling revivals of tradition in the face of Western domination[90] that have been studied in many non-Western societies, including Japan,[91] India,[92] New Guinea,[93] and among Native Americans.[94] While many of the leaders have been professionals, technicians, and students, the movement has found great popular support among the recently urbanized, whether they be students, day laborers, or unemployed residents of the sprawling shantytowns. The multitudes who find themselves trapped in underdevelopment while others enjoy the fruits of modernization especially perceive Islam to be "the heart of a heartless world," Gilsenan writes, providing a dignified identity and the promise of a better eternal life.[95] Studies of students who join and support Islamist groups find that many come from rural villages or families that recently moved into cities, and have high aspirations for school and career achievement, often in scientific and technical fields. For both men and women, less educated mothers appeared to have been sources of traditional and religious values. Leila Ahmad writes:

> Joining Islamic groups or, as is the case for most women, informally affiliating with the trend, then, evidently carries the comfort of bringing the values of home and childhood to the city and its foreign and morally overwhelming ways. This psychological and social dimension appears to be among the most important elements underlying the trend. Inner ease and resolution, often described as a feeling of peace, of centeredness, brought about by the formal or public aligning of oneself with Islam, are prominent features of women's and men's accounts.[96]

Young women who veil also say it protects them from the nearly constant harassment unveiled women receive in public and enables them to engage men as equals in classroom and campus conversation. Like many observers,

Ahmed points out that women are "returning" to the veil to claim their right to traditionally male public spaces, schools, and jobs:

> Islamic dress can be seen as the uniform, not of reaction, but of transition; it can be seen, not as a return to traditional dress, but as the adoption of Western dress—with modifications to make it acceptable to the wearer's notions of propriety. Far from indicating that the wearers remain fixed in the world of tradition and the past, then, Islamic dress is the uniform of arrival, signaling entrance into, and determination to move forward in, modernity.[97]

Ali Lila shows how an earlier generation of Egyptian youth led the adoption of Western ways in rejection of seemingly backward traditions, while the current one is leading the religious revival. But he too sees continuity in their striving for modernization: against the apparent failure of Nasser's socialism and Sadat's and Mubarek's capitalism—both Western imports—the religious revival is being animated by the decisions of many youth to "progress from within our tradition."[98]

Professionals and Saints in Pakistan

Katherine Ewing has been one of the few anthropologists to investigate the cultural shaping of self by studying individual life-histories, and to show the importance of multiple, often contradictory self-representations. In "The Illusion of Wholeness," she analyzes interviews she conducted with Shamim, a Pakistani woman studying for her doctorate and struggling both to chart her own life and remain a dutiful daughter. These show her "rapidly shifting self-representations," mainly between "two self-images that are based on inconsistent premises. At some moments she presents an image of herself as a good, obedient daughter who will, hopefully, become a good wife. At other times her self-representation is that of a 'politician' who can employ various strategies to meet her personal needs and wishes."[99] The first is rooted in the sociocentric concept of personhood familiar throughout South Asia, Ewing writes, "in which persons are regarded, not as individuals with personal needs, but rather as units of the social order." This self is articulated in terms of Muslim principles of filial piety and control of *nafs* (desire) by *'aqel* (reason/social maturity).[100] The second draws on a cultural model of everyday political maneuvering, according to which "each person operates to maximize his or her advantage (or that of his or her family) vis-à-vis others in order to realize personal or familial wishes and goals."[101] These juxtaposed "good Muslim" and "clever politician" models (which roughly parallel the contrast I have described as between "piety" and "honor") cause conflict and guilt for many Pakistanis, Ewing observes, and lead Shamim and others to see the same qualities and acts from contrasting perspectives: "the good Muslim may explain manifestations of 'political' action as the excessive indulgence of a person's *nafs*. Alternatively, from the political standpoint a person's actions, though proper behavior for a good Muslim, might be branded as 'boorish' or stupid or, more benignly, labeled 'simple.'"[102] Ewing notes that when Shamim changes self-images, she also changes her images of her parents and the personal memories that go with them, so that each of the two self-representations constitutes a complete "frame of reference." Because she (and others) generally are unaware of their shifts, each frame of reference creates a feeling—or illusion—that the self is whole:

> People construct a series of self-representations that are based on selected cultural concepts of person and selected "chains" of personal memories. Each self-concept is experienced as whole and continuous, with its own history and memories that emerge in a specific context, to be replaced by another self-representation when the context changes.[103]

In a subsequent article, "The Dream of Spiritual Initiation," Ewing shows how educated Pakistanis may develop contrasting "modern" and "traditional" self-representations, and how dreams about Sufi *pirs* (masters) may bring about a reorganization of the prominence given to each. In postcolonial Pakistan, she writes,

> many people are forced into situations in which they must organize strands of their lives that are highly inconsistent with one another. Many Pakistanis have found that self representations developed in a traditional Muslim family are difficult to reconcile with those formed in British-dominated educational, governmental, and business settings.[104]

She presents the life-histories of two Western-educated Pakistani professional men for whom the duality had become conflict, though she points out that many individuals shift so smoothly between even "radically inconsistent" self-representations that they do not notice themselves doing so. These men, however, struggled consciously with the conflict, and ultimately resolved it in favor of traditional religion by means of a centuries-old cultural schema in which they dreamed of a Sufi master and then became his disciple. Where they previously gave priority to their Westernized professional self-representations, the dreams served as catalysts for reversing the emphasis and bringing their religious selves into the foreground. Together these papers show not only how contrasting cultural models may be internalized as contrasting identities but also how traditional contrasts ("good Muslim" versus "clever politician") may be transformed by colonial and postcolonial influences into modern ones ("Westernized modernity" versus "traditional religiosity").

Mounia Bennani-Chraibi had begun a study of youth and media in Morocco when youth-led riots broke out at the end of 1990, attacking "the material symbols of 'modernity'." The next year a series of antigovernment, anti-Western demonstrations were staged in response to the Gulf War that also were dominated by teen-agers and young adults. She quickly broadened the scope of her inquiry, interviewing participants in the demonstrations and some of those arrested, and three years later published her observations on this generation's struggle with modernity and tradition, as *Soumis et Rebelles.* Traditional family and kin-groups are decreasing in size and importance, she believes, bringing about a "birth of the individual." Individuals, however, are growing into an overpopulated world of economic underdevelopment and political oppression, where only a few can achieve the careers and living standards that are the promise of modernization. These conditions embroil youth in two related struggles: one in the social realm for the educations and steady jobs that would enable them to help support their parental families, marry, and begin families of their own—in Levinson's terms, for a *life- structure*; the other in the realm of ideas, values, and meanings—in Erikson's terms, for *identity.* The realm of values has quite literally become a marketplace:

> In the marketplaces of the great cities, Oum Kaltoum, Michael Jackson, and reciters of the Quran battle for the field of sound; Islamic literature published in Cairo or Casablanca sits side by side with *Playboy* and *Femme Actuelle. . . .* During the month of Ramadan, feverish nights of pleasure and encounters follow austere days of fasting. In summer, young people on their way back from the beach stop to pray in one of the mosques they pass on their way.[105]

Bennani-Chraibi found young people "fascinated" with the West, as "at the same time a model and a counter-model," alternating between "attraction and repulsion," "idealizing" and "demonizing" the West. They often described Europeans as possessing the virtues Moroccans lack:

> The West offers the image of a universe where the blossoming/developing individual is also an accomplished citizen. . . . The myth of development prevails with all of its apparatus: science, technology, media, the moon, rocket ships, oceanographic research. . . . These descriptions are almost always accompanied with "not like among us," "not like here," "not like us."[106]

Yet nearly all of those she interviewed also rejected European ways as decadent and dissolute—affirming the superiority of Morocco's familial and spiritual values.

As they "compartmentalize" these contrary attitudes, many appear to allot "transgressive" behaviors and religious devotion their separate times and spaces. A few had become more permanently "marginalized" in their delin-quencies, and some turned to Islamism to live piously all day, every day. The vast majority approved of the mixing of males and females in schools, work settings, and public and wanted to choose their own spouses. But like Davis and Davis, Ouzi, and Schade-Poulsen, she found that male-female relation-ships were characterized by anxiety and mistrust. Boys have to establish them-selves financially before they can marry, while most girls still rely on marriage to provide them a place in society. For most boys, "feminine sexuality and nonvirginity constitute a blot and a taboo, whereas sexual experience acquired by a man is a natural and indispensable thing."[107] The majority of girls con-cur and oppose premarital sexuality, and "virginity is the weapon of a young woman in the war of the sexes."[108] Yet many young women in their later teens and early twenties also have relationships with boys that involve some sexual play, though usually not intercourse. She quotes a 25-year-old Casablanca secretary who argued that sex is "natural," an important part of a girl's matu-ration, and that girls have the same right to pleasure as boys. When the in-terviewer asked, "And virginity?" she vehemently responded, "Ah, virginity before everything," and launched into a speech on the importance of main-taining virginity until marriage, couched in terms of religious values and fam-ily obligations absent from her earlier defense of pleasure. She even justified the killing of a daughter who loses her virginity before marriage. Bennani-Chraibi writes: "The young girl is subject to two types of value systems: one dominated by individualism and hedonism, the other fundamentally social in that the person is legitimately subjected to the law of the collective. These two systems are not opposed in their eyes."[109] She thus found idealization and demonization of the West side by side, and many of those who condemned religious regimes (Iran, Saudi Arabia) and movements (Algeria) as "not true Islam" also idealized the state of justice that "true Islam" would bring. The demonstrations and riots united socialist, democrat, Islamist, and apolitical youth in an inchoate spirit of rebellion fueled by their forced submission and seclusion. In the end, she sees Moroccan youth as caught up in tumultuous struggle with dual identities, carried on in usually "cold" times beneath sur-faces of calm.

This is precisely what I found in the life-history interviews I conducted with 18- to 28-year-old "young adults" in rural southern Morocco.[110] Their life-narratives resemble those of Americans I have interviewed[111] in the ways they shift between contrasting identities, and in their use of cultural symbols and metaphors to define who they are and what they stand for. But where the American narratives draw heavily on images of self and Other related to social class, race, and subcultural "life-style," the Moroccan narratives de-fine contrasting identities primarily in terms of "modern" Westernized and "traditional" Moroccan/Muslim images. All appeared to be familiar with the yearning that Orhan Pamuk's journalist imagines Master Bedii's mannequins feel—to escape from the dusky basement of tradition and come to new life by copying the (Western) Other—but at the same time with the feeling of estrangement Al e Ahmad described as "Euromania," which evokes yearnings to embrace one's authentic traditions.

Individuals varied greatly in the personal meanings and the symbols they associated with "modernity" and "tradition," and in the dialogues they set in motion between them. A few firmly defined themselves at one pole, in contrast to antiself representations that delineated the contrasting pole—as did my interviewee Mohammed, who hoped one day to head a religious school and defined his "pure," "well-ordered" self in contrast to the "dirty," "wild" delinquent he had been in high school. Several wove both poles into remarkably smooth complementarities—especially a pious high school French teacher, who was both the most "modern" and most "traditional" of all those I interviewed. Many ambivalently embraced both poles, as did Hussein, who cycled between describing himself as fleeing the disempowering world of "backward" patriarchal tradition for empowering modern "urbanity" and fleeing the disempowering modern world of anomic, stressful bureaucracy for the health-bestowing simplicity of family ties and tradition. The greatest conflict was experienced by a secretary who described herself as split into "European" and "Muslim" personalities, unable to be either without the other forcibly intruding.

It is difficult to ascertain whether young MENA adults typically experience greater conflict between identities than do "average" Westerners whose struggles gave rise to the notion of "identity crisis." But identity conflicts are probably intensified by conditions of underdevelopment. Bennani-Chraibi does not attribute the tumult she observed to the mere coexistence of Western and traditional/Muslim models of self, but rather to the slow pace of economic and political development that leaves so many young people unable to anchor their lives in either traditional or modern social institutions. The difficulties they face in fashioning "life structures" that embody their "dreams"—to use Levinson's terms—certainly can turn the transitional task of identity formation into chronic tumult.

Developmental Discontinuities and a "Muslimist Ethic"?

The life-narratives I elicited further suggest that the "task" of identity development is often shaped by several important developmental themes that take distinctive forms in MENA societies. Three in particular appear to be related to developmental discontinuities that have arisen from rapid social change, and especially from the intermixing of "modernization" and "underdevelopment." First, many members of this generation appear to experience an important developmental discontinuity concerning belief in "supernatural" forces and the use of protective rituals to defend against them. In traditional milieus, this complex provided a system of psychological self-care in which some feelings of anxiety, vulnerability, and weakness are externalized and attributed to *jinns,* the Evil Eye, Satan, sorcery, and so on, and managed by protective and purificatory practices. Having spent their childhoods in traditional milieus, most of the young adults I interviewed appeared to have internalized the core of this complex—externalization—and to quite automatically experience some forms of distress as issuing from invisible forces. But their modern educations have led them to reject belief in invisible beings and to eschew the minirituals traditionally used to keep them under control. Many thus have disturbing dreams, physical symptoms, deviant thoughts, and uncanny experiences that are traditionally attributed to spirit beings but, in the absence of the "pop psych" theories Westerners use to explain these away, find themselves with no interpretation or recourse. As Fanon wrote, belief in the spirit beings provides an important security system, and Miner and DeVos may be correct to infer that disbelief leads to higher levels of manifest anxiety, at least in the short-run, until individuals or the culture develop new systems of self-care. Several of those I interviewed had become more religious in their late teens and early twenties in part to help manage disturbing experiences of this sort, and I suspect this may be an important but generally unrecognized motive for the "return" of many young people to devout religiosity.

Second, another important discontinuity appears with regard to the role of the honor-modesty system and religious piety in the world of achievement and "modern" life-styles. The life-narratives show young Moroccans automatically configuring their relationships and comportment in terms of the imperatives of honor and modesty but rarely employing the explicit rhetorics associated with them. While they continued to practice many traditional etiquettes of deference, their lives in "modern" apartment blocks, "modern" towns, "modern" schools and offices, and "modern" clothes no longer embodied the rich color, grooming, and spatial symbolism that traditionally organized daily life in accordance with the generational and gendered honor-modesty system. No longer engaged in agriculture, pastoralism, raiding, or traditional crafts, most town- and city-dwelling young people are now removed an important degree from the traditional anchorage points of that system, and they now watch TV, play sports, and listen to music cassettes rather than participate in the raids and poetic performances that stake personal claims to honor.

With the exception of areas caught up in military struggles, the main "glorious deed" a young person can perform to honor his or her family is to pass the college entrance exam. Honor and modesty remain central to the (level 2) sentiments, motives, and social selves of youths, but (level 3) identities are now being defined in terms of educational and economic achievement and modern/Western versus traditional/Muslim ways of life. In response, the honor-modesty system is being transformed into a family-based achievement ethic—in a manner resembling that studied in Japan and other Asian cultures. The overarching developmental "task" faced by MENA adolescents and young adults can be described as fashioning an honorable and proprietous life in terms of school and career achievement.

Third, the life-narratives indicate that Islam also is being transformed, as young people are weaving it into their drive for achievement. For my interviewee Rachida, it is piety that brings *natija*—a word that refers to the "yield" of crops and to one's "outcome" or "grade" at school—while impiety leads to "failure." Hussein formulated an identity during his second (and last) year in college, when he decided to become a defense attorney and fight to "restore the rights" of the oppressed and unjustly accused and thereby himself maintain "an innocent relationship with God." Most of those I interviewed[112] articulated their striving for achievement as a kind of divine "calling" that requires self-mastery and "this-worldly asceticism." These are Max Weber's terms for the Protestant ethic, and the life-narratives support the suggestion of several scholars that education and economic opportunity are catalyzing the development of an analogous "Muslimist ethic" that synthesizes honor, piety, achievement, and redemption.[113] This ethic differs markedly from versions of Enlightenment liberalism that we commonly identify with Western *modernity*, especially by virtue of the central place accorded to faith and of the primacy given to religious and familial authority over individual freedom. Religious piety appears not just as a spiritual complement to a secular modernity but as a primary vehicle for "becoming modern."

The interviews I conducted contain very little of the explicit "rhetoric of *self*-cultivation" so characteristic of American life-narratives, and they are not modern in that particular twentieth-century, Western, middle-class sense of self-consciously seeking "self-actualization." Nor do they evince the individualist modernism of Bentham and J. S. Mill, as the Moroccans I interviewed rarely took their eyes off familial obligations, and only a few of the narratives make much of rational self-interests or free pursuits of happiness. Rather, they more closely echo the early Protestant notion that one's earthly ambitions should be pursued as a synthetic Good Work, witnessed by God and rewarded in the afterlife.

Robert Bellah has shown how the dissemination of the samurai class's *bushido* code and the emergence of new religious movements throughout the Tokugawa period facilitated Japan's modernization, as did the Protestant ethic in Europe.[114] He traces how the broad diffusion of the *bushido* ethic and consequent synthesis of "Shinto nationalism" promoted a melding of modernist social ambitions and religious values, symbolized by the mission and power of a state headed by a divine emperor who would foster development at home and expel the "barbarians" from abroad. John Waterbury has shown how the Berbers of the Moroccan Sous region developed a Protestant ethic–like variant of Islam as they became famously successful self-sacrificing entrepreneurs and merchants.[115] Ernest Gellner has described this sort of "Weberian ethic" in his discussion of "Algerian Puritanism,"[116] and Ellis Goldberg has drawn attention to the ways Islamic activists resemble Protestant reformers.[117]

These parallels can be overstated, but they have an important implica-
tion: the cultural synthesis of modernism and religion has a personal side,
which appears in the form of a modernist family-based achievement orientation, and a political side, which appears as a kind of "natural" support for
a number of key Islamist themes. Political Islam may be the media-visible
tip of an iceberg, the submerged six-sevenths consisting of the large numbers of MENA youths who fashion "Muslim ethicist" identities as they struggle
against unfavorable odds to succeed in the educational system and open doors
into the economy's modern sector. It is in this discourse that many seek to
resolve the conflict of "individualistic" achievement motives and "collectivist" responsibilities to kin, and to synthesize potentially conflicting indigenous
and Western ways. For the practitioner of the "Muslim ethic," individual
achievement can "honor" one's family, maintain an "innocent relationship
with God," and help build the nation and the House of Islam. And it takes
but a short step to turn this personal synthesis into religiously inspired ac-
tivism, especially for those whose "dreams" appear to be dashed or to turn
hollow in the hallways of modern bureaucracies. The tension that MENA
youth so acutely experience is not that between "traditional" religion and
"modern" secular individualism, as it is so often misportrayed by Western
media. Rather, it is between the dream of modernity and the reality of
underdevelopment.

Debate: Creative Synthesis or Fragmentation? ⊛

Journalists reporting on MENA societies have fostered a debate about whether
young adults there are eager to embrace Western-style modernity or remain
so weighed down by the momentum of tradition that they cling to the obsolete values of the honor code and conservative Islam. By contrast, ethnographers have generally recognized (1) that the "traditions" many young people
embrace as their authentic culture are not truly traditional but fully modern
reformulations of traditional values and motifs, and (2) that perhaps the great
majority of young people develop an ambivalent duality of modern/Western
and traditional/Muslim identities. In this case, the scholars simply have it
right, and the journalists misunderstand. Life-narratives especially show
that identities often take shape as dialogues between these two self-
construals. Some individuals appear to work out creative syntheses or easy
complementarities; others appear to struggle in destructive turmoil.

Here a crucial divergence of views appears. On one side are researchers
(including Ewing, the Davises, Kagitcibasi, and myself) who tend to view
cultural duality as presenting challenges that most MENA youth can creatively
manage. With them are those (including Hamid Ammar and Mustafa Hijazi)
who view the originally destructive imposition of Western culture as ultimately enabling MENA youth to free themselves from "frozen," "calcified"

traditions and to revitalize their heritages. The Lebanese novelist Amin Maalouf recently blamed the desire for a single fixed identity, in response to the loss of self threatened by Western-style modernization, for intolerance and violence and urged Arabs to seek identities that encompass multiple affiliations, cultures, and languages.[118] This camp tends to blame the "crisis" of youth on economic and political underdevelopment rather than cultural duality. On the other side are researchers (including Lila, Shayagen, Ouzi, and Haddiya) who see the cultural dualities as dooming youth to fragmented identities and never-ending struggles for identity.

Abdelkrim Ghareeb recently captured this divergence by considering the identity dilemma of youth from the perspective of four theorists.[119] The Moroccan nationalist leader Allal Al-Fassi described youth as torn between their indigenous culture and the European implant, such that "the individual in Moroccan society finds himself lost and alternating in his choices and decisions."[120] He hoped education would enable youth to adapt and adopt Arab-Muslim high culture, but he suspected that the apparent weakness of their own heritage would motivate them to imitatively opt for the European model. The sociologist Paul Pascon similarly pointed out that 50 years of colonialism had turned Morocco into a "composite" society: a mixture of Moroccan and French cultures and of indigenous and Western orders of knowledge, manifest in the shifting, "composite" behavior of individuals. Pascon acknowledged that this causes strife, but where al-Fassi saw *only* discord, Pascon saw composite culture as animating creativity and development. For his third perspective, Ghareeb takes a Freudian point of view to describe youth as alternating between two egos—a "Moroccan-culture ego" anchored in identification with the father and a "Western-culture ego" based on rejection of the father and identification with Western figures—setting up disturbingly contradictory relations with the id. Finally he outlines a Piagetian analysis that shows youth not passing through a brief disequilibrium at the onset of formal operational thinking but trapped in an interminable disequilibrium caused by being embedded in the contradictory orders of indigenous and Western knowledge. He draws these analyses together to raise the question of whether postcolonial composite culture dooms individuals to inner strife and disequilibrium or whether this may be a "transitional" period (though now decades long) in which youths suffer and sacrifice as they work creatively to invent new forms of cultural coherence.

It may help to view this debate about "composite" selves in the light of contemporary models of self in cross-cultural psychology. Harry Triandis led many researchers beyond the simple contrast of "individualistic" versus "collectivistic" cultures and selves by suggesting that people have "private," "public," and "collective" selves, with differences in social ecology determining which come to the fore.[121] A consensus now appears to be emerging that people in all cultures develop multiple self-conceptions that are called into play in different contexts.[122] Studies by Hazel Markus and her colleagues have emphasized a "repertoire of schemata" view of self, some investigating relationships among "possible selves."[123] These views converge with recent theories of acculturation, which no longer treat this process as a unidimensional one, in which individuals gradually lose their immigrant identities as they develop a majority culture identity, but propose "alternation"[124] models to account for multiple "bicultural"[125] and "hybrid"[126] identities.

These views also converge with theories of ethnic identity that follow the writings of W.E.B. DuBois and Malcolm X to recognize that minorities often develop dual identities—internalizing both their in-group's standards and the majority group's stereotypes of them. These models propose that individuals go through dramatic shifts in reference groups and identities, ideally progressing toward a bicultural maturity.[127] Several recent studies find that bicultural individuals can master and shift identities between "cultural frames" with relative ease.[128] In this framework, the identity-development task of MENA youth in the Western-dominated world may resemble that of immigrants or ethnic minorities who seek to embrace both cultural frameworks, along developmental paths made torturous by unending battle with majority stereotypes and a potentially corrosive sense of backwardness.[129]

Erikson saw the "crisis" of identity as tapping the creative potential of youth to reinvigorate their cultures with new syntheses of values. But he also emphasized that they often experience the identity-formation "task" as demanding they become a single, authentic character, which can lead to dangerous "totalistic" resolutions in which incompatible features of personality are projected onto deviants or out-groups, who then become targets of persecution. He insisted that history plays the decisive role for each generation, noting that political polarization easily intensifies the pressure on young people to "stand for" one thing in a pure and totalistic manner. The "intense struggle of becoming" Barakat describes appears to turn up or down these pressures in one country after another, depending on whether cultural-political strife is, as Bennani-Chraibi phrases it, latent and "cool" or manifest and "hot."

Sources ❀

The anthropologist Katherine Ewing has used life-history interviews to study identity in Pakistan, and her article "The Illusion of Wholeness" presents an important model of how multiple self-representations may be organized. Audrey Shalinsky's "Reason, Desire, and Sexuality" (in Afghanistan), John Anderson's "Sentimental Ambivalence and the Exegesis of 'Self' in Afghanistan," and Steven Caton's "The Poetic Construction of Self" (in Yemen) all indicate that multiplicity characterizes both more traditional and more modern milieus, as does Janice Boddy's research on spirit possession in Sudan[130] and Lila Abu-Lughod's on Bedouin ethics and poetry.[131]

The sociologist Sawsan El Messiri's *Ibn al-Balad* provides an excellent introduction to the cultural landscape of identity, as it traces how the ordinary "authentic" people of Cairo delineated an identity in contrast to unsophisticated village-dwellers on one side and foreignized elites on the other. In spite of its deep flaws, Horace Miner and George DeVos's study of urban "acculturation" in Algeria in the early 1950s—*Oasis and Casbah*—ends with some important observations about the effects of French colonization and resistance on young men's identities. Studies of unveiling and reveiling in Turkey by Emelie Olson,[132] Nilufer Gole,[133] and Hugh Poulton[134] show how details of fashion and grooming became politicized markers of identity, and have remained so throughout the century. The historians Roy Mottahedeh's *Mantle of the Prophet* and Mostafa Vaziri's *Iran as Imagined Nation* recount the modernization forced on Iranians by Reza Shah and his son Mohammed Shah, and the critique of "Westoxication" or "Euromania" that inspired resistance and eventually revolution. Ali Mirsepassi's *Intellectual Discourse and the Politics of Modernization* and Daryush Shayegan's *Cultural Schizophrenia* further explore the dualities created in Iran's encounter with Western powers and values. Bassam Tibi's *Islam and the Cultural Accommodation of Social Change*, Richard Mitchell's *The Society of the Muslim Brothers*, Henry Munson's *Islam and Revolution in the Middle East*, Gilles Kepel's *Muslim Extremism in Egypt*, and Michael Gilsenan's *Recognizing Islam* provide descriptions of the development of Islamism in Egypt, and explore the character of the Muslim identity it opposes to Westernization. Ali Lila's *Al-shabab al-'arabi* (Arab Youth) traces the social history of Egyptian youth and its key role in recent decades' "religious revival." Katherine Ewing's study of the transformative effects of "spiritual initiation" dreams in Pakistan shows how Western and traditional self-representations may coexist and come into conflict even for men with advanced educations and professional careers.[135] Mounia Bennani-Chraibi's *Soumis et Rebelles* describes a similar ambivalence and duality of self-representations among young Moroccans. My own "study of lives" research on identity in Morocco further demonstrates the multiplicity of self-representations and the importance of "traditional"/Muslim versus "modern"/Western dualities.[136] In *Ai namoudhaj li-al-tawafiq lada al-shabab al-maghrebi* (What Model for Moroccan Youth?) Abdelkrim Ghareeb poses the crucial question of whether these cultural contradictions condemn youth to fragmented and unstable identities or potentially provoke creative syntheses that could move MENA cultures beyond neocolonial dualities.

CHAPTER 9

Mature Adulthood

Western theories of adult development appear to have limited applicability to MENA societies. While little research has been conducted specifically on development, four key issues emerge from studies of adults. First, MENA psychologists have adapted Western measures of several important personality traits (specifically intraversion-extraversion, neuroticism, and the "Big Five" traits), and also found evidence that anxiety levels are higher in MENA than in Western and some other developing societies.

    Second, while little studied, the individualism versus collectivism of MENA societies emerges as an important topic of discussion, especially since they are assumed to be "collectivist." Cross-cultural psychologists have come to regard this as perhaps the central dimension on which the world's cultures vary, with Westerners being more "egocentric" and non-Westerners more "sociocentric" in their social relationships and selves. Several Asian and Indian psychologists have criticized the validity of this continuum and collected data showing that Japanese, Koreans, and Indians possess both types of self-representations and can call either into play according to circumstance. Kagitcibasi and Joseph similarly argue that MENA societies cannot be termed "collectivist" but that they foster forms of "connectivity" or "interrelatedness" in some spheres of life and individualism in others.

    Third, studies of MENA women show that they often acquire a good deal of power and prestige in mid life and later. These accounts parallel David Guttman's theory that many cultures script a kind of gender reversal in midlife, in which men reintegrate "feminine" characteristics they suppressed in order to play strongly masculine roles in their teens and twenties, while women similarly reintegrate "masculine" qualities they suppressed during the same period to emphasize feminine-nurturant characters. While "gender reversal" is not an appropriate term, MENA cultures do appear to foster a shift in gender roles that can enlarge men's and women's interaction styles and self-conceptions.

The fourth topic—crucial to development throughout the life-span—consists of Arab scholars' analyses of the psychological effects of economic underdevelopment and political subjugation prevailing in many MENA societies. These writings began with Hamid Ammar's essays on traditional and modern personality styles in Egypt, and multiplied as part of the widespread "self-critique" set off by the 1967 "Six-Day" war. Several of these scholars—including Mustafa Hijazi, Ali Zayour, and Hisham Sharabi—emphasize the role that oppressive rule has played over centuries in shaping culture, family organization, and psychological functioning. These writers believe that the humiliation, insecurity, and fear that some regimes deliberately create undermine both societal and psychological development by causing people to (1) retreat to the protection of traditional-appearing social groups, (2) adopt magical and superstitious methods of protecting themselves and influencing their conditions, (3) turn to violence in cathartic attempts to overcome humiliation, and (4) identify with the aggressor, internalizing the Leader's, the Party's or the secret police's surveillance and adopting authoritarian styles in their familial and occupational relationships. Western psychology knows little about these processes, and I end by suggesting that the theory of societal development proposed by Amartya Sen (and adopted by the authors of the 2002 UN Arab Human Development Report), combined with the philosopher Axel Honeth's theory of societal effects on personal trust, identity, and self-regard, could provide a framework for investigating what Hijazi terms the "psychology of subjugation."

Introduction ❀

A good deal of research has been conducted in MENA societies on the psychological characteristics of adults, but very little on *development* during adulthood (see the discussion of sources at the end of this chapter). Adult development was long a neglected topic in Western psychology, and it is easy to appreciate the priority MENA researchers have given to childhood and adolescence, especially in light of the youthfulness of their populations and the hopes placed on rising generations. Most of the psychological research on adults has entailed adapting Western measures of personality traits (such as introversion and extraversion, anxiety, and depression) and exploring their associations with schooling, clinical symptoms, family and peer relations, and so on. This is important work, which lays a groundwork for cross-cultural comparisons. But the studies that speak most directly to the shaping of psychological characteristics distinctive of MENA societies are the ethnographies that describe how the honor-modesty system and Islam are internalized until they have a "second nature," "grammar of everyday life"–like influence on thinking and emotion. I discussed how these two value systems appear to shape sentiments, motives, and social personae—McAdams's level 2 of personality organization—in chapter 3.

This chapter begins with a brief review of Western theories of adult development—especially those of Carl Jung, Erik Erikson, Daniel Levinson, and Dan McAdams—and considers their limited applicability to MENA societies. It then examines four issues that bear on psychological development in adulthood: (1) the status in MENA societies of personality traits studied by Western psychologists; (2) the "sociocentrism" versus "egocentrism" of MENA culture and self; (3) culturally patterned shifts in gender orientations in mid- and later life; and (4) the psychological effects of economic and political underdevelopment. This fourth section—summarizing Arab scholars' writings on the "psychology of underdevelopment"—is the heart of the chapter, and in some respects of the book, since my own research convinces me that prevailing conditions of *societal underdevelopment* profoundly influence *psychological development* throughout the life-span. I will end by focusing on the key question of causality raised by these writings: is it mainly "culture" (for example, values, beliefs, and norms) that shapes psychological development, or rather the power of nature and the authority of rulers, to which many features of "culture" should be seen as attempts at psychological adaptation?

Western Theories of Adult Development ❁

The most influential Western theories of development in adulthood have their roots in the notion that each person emerges from childhood with a set of core life themes that define the directions of future development, *if* the individual chooses to answer their beckoning, and *if* the environment allows their pursuit. This vision of an "organic unfolding" of personality first appeared in the tragedies of the German Romantic writer Goethe, and especially in his *bildungsroman* ("novel of development") *Wilhelm Meister's Years of Apprenticeship*. Goethe saw the unfolding as an inherently tragic process, in which every life project is doomed to collapse because it overreaches toward its unfulfillable ideal or because it withers with the birth of a new project. Marshall Berman I believe correctly sees this vision—that each individual should gain the freedom to recognize and pursue his or her inner direction—as the psychological essence of modernity.[1] The preeminent theorists of adult development—especially Carl Jung, Erik Erikson, and Daniel Levinson—have seen this process as the primary motor of adult development. Their models conceptualize adulthood as consisting of a series of stages, each defined by specific developmental processes or tasks. While all have tried to incorporate historical and cross-cultural perspectives, the content and timing of the stages they propose remains closely linked to the life patterns of modern,

Western, often middle-class milieus. It is not clear which features of these theories fit MENA life patterns.

Carl Jung

Jung pioneered theorizing about development during adulthood. One of his key disputes with Freud centered on his view that psychological turmoil stemmed less from fixation on childhood repressions than from conflicts over trajectories of adult development. In Jung's view, the unconscious contains a kind of developmental blueprint that maps out paths toward self-realization. It is as if events in adulthood "switch on" unconscious symbols and images,[2] which then serve as signs drawing an individual toward the directions his or her development should take. People project these *archetypes* into the world and then find themselves drawn toward them in fascination, but without recognizing that they originate from their own psyches. Jung believed archetypes also appear in symptoms, dreams, free associations, and artistic creations, which he viewed not only as expressing residues of childhood "fixations" (as did Freud) but as speaking of the future an individual should pursue. He believed that socialization leads to the development of a persona, a kind of mask of conventionality molded from the stamp of culture. In the process, it forces important features of the self—usually those incongruent with the persona—to be denied, split off, or repressed. These return in the form of archetypes, and much of adult development consists of reintegrating them and achieving more and more inclusive forms of wholeness.

Jung gave particular importance to three sorts of archetypes he thought to be universal: the *shadow,* the *anima/animus,* and the *self.* He believed that the *shadow* embodies "darker" aspects of repressed sexuality and aggression, excluded from the persona. People typically feel ambivalently repulsed by their shadow figure and attracted to it. Jung clearly had the Christian devil in mind, as well as similar figures from other cultures and from his patients' hallucinations, dreams, and fantasies. Some people try to protect themselves from the shadow with rigid defenses that block development: others may try to destroy it (one might see "the Jew" as the Nazis' collective shadow figure); and a few try to become their shadow figure, either literally or vicariously. Growth proceeds by engaging the shadow in a kind of dialogue, demystifying it, and gradually reintegrating one's own antisocial sexuality and aggression—not as the wild, terrifying forces they initially appear to be but as human impulses that can be controlled.

The anima emerges in the form of a woman for a man, representing an amalgam of maternal images and his own feminine qualities that have been repressed in the process of forming a masculine persona. The animus takes a similar male form for women. Jung believed that men and women often fall in love with people who initially appear to match these archetypal figures, and then find themselves disappointed when the real people don't live up to the character they have imagined by projection. Some people may go from partner to partner in an endless and unsatisfying search for their fantasy turned real, while others may be frightened away from those who resemble their archetype and seek partners who appear to embody opposite qualities. Again, healthy development—and "true" love—proceeds via relationships with archetype-resembling figures that allow one to discover the "real" person beneath the projections and reintegrate one's own repressed femininity or masculinity.

Self symbols emerge later in life, often in the form of sages and wise persons, and in yin-yang or mandala-like symbols representing wholeness and a unity of opposites. Engagement with these figures can develop the spiritual dimensions of the self, and lead toward a full self-realization. Jung termed this whole process *individuation,* and he believed it begins in early adulthood after the consolidation of a persona solidifies the repressions and renunciations required by cultural convention. Jung did not see individuation as requiring separation and an individualist system of values, and he believed that the religious systems of some traditional cultures support it better than do modern Western ones.

Erik Erikson

Erikson's signal contribution to psychology was to revise Freud's stage theory of child development and extend it throughout the life-span. As described in chapter 8, the formation of identity becomes the crucial psychological "task" at the entrance to adulthood, and Erikson believes this leads to the task of developing a set of intimate relationships rather than suffering isolation.[3] This underlies the capacity to sustain a career of productive work and mutually fulfilling intimacy, which leads to the support and nurturing of a new family. His theory that "generativity" emerges as the main psychological task of midlife may have greater relevance for MENA societies. Jung believed that people begin to turn inward in their forties or fifties, disengaging to some extent from their social responsibilities to follow more personal or spiritual interests. Erikson views withdrawal more negatively, believing that the developmental challenge consists of finding new forms of "generative" engagement. Generativity entails a commitment to "establishing and guiding the next generation,"[4] which encompasses not only one's own children but all those who come after one. It may express itself through face-to-face mentoring of juniors or through work that is done for the sake of the future. Erikson believes generativity enriches and enlivens the individual at a time when he or she otherwise may become "stagnant" and "isolated."

Research by McAdams and others has found evidence that concerns with generatively are present throughout adulthood but peak in the thirties and forties, and that individuals with stronger generative concerns and commitments tend to have higher psychological well-being.[5] Stewart and Vandewater propose a model in which the "desire for generativity" declines from early adulthood to later adulthood, while "generativity accomplishment" increases, such that the "felt capacity for generativity" peaks in midlife.[6] While women generally have greater generative concerns and commitments than men, several studies suggest that generativity is not closely associated with parenthood but rather with a broadening of care beyond one's own children.[7] Other studies indicate that, as Erikson and McAdams theorize, generativity develops not simply as an individual trait but in response to social roles and cultural models that both expect it and provide opportunities for enacting it. If the development of generativity is a universal midlife "task," then cultures should vary in the nature and timing of their expectations for it. At the present time, however, there is little cross-cultural research on generativity.

Erikson also theorizes that aging brings another developmental stage, in which the "task" is to achieve a sense of *ego integrity* that goes with "the acceptance of one's one and only life cycle as something that had to be and that, by necessity, permitted of no substitutions"[8] and not fall into the *despair* of fearing death or regretting one's life. Like Jung, Erikson associates ego integrity with the development of "wisdom"—with forms of knowledge and styles of relationship that differ from the practical life-skills relied on through the more productive decades of adulthood. And this may encompass the sense of "wholeness" of self that Jung believed the later-life process of "individuation" seeks. Western research on aging has increased dramatically during the last two decades, but relatively few studies have sought to assess "integrity," and only in recent years have researchers begun to investigate the nature of "wisdom."

Daniel Levinson

On the basis of interview studies of American men[9] and women,[10] Levinson has proposed a model of adulthood based on "eras" of "life structure" (as shown in table 9.1). He believes that both men and women pass through the same schedule of stages, but due to the "gender splitting" of social roles and psychological orientations, they experience different developmental tasks in each. Many researchers find his claim that the eras correlate closely with age ranges to be unconvincing, and there is no evidence that it holds in other cultures. But his notion of *life structure* is an important one, especially as it distinguishes between a person's identity and the nexus of relationships and commitments in which identity is embedded and affirmed.

The psychological character of Levinson's midlife and late adult transitions roughly correspond to Erikson's notion that generativity and integrity are at stake. Levinson's early adult transition is primarily about establishing an identity—and I have followed him in viewing identity as mainly an "early adult" task rather than an adolescent one. Levinson also diverges from Erikson in viewing the twenties as mainly about not intimacy versus isolation but consolidating a life structure in congruence with one's identity. He also be-

Table 9.1 Eras in the Male Life-Cycle

Age	Period
65–	Late adulthood
60–65	Late adult transition
45–60	Middle adulthood
40–45	Midlife transition
22–40	Early adulthood
17–22	Early adult transition
4–17	Childhood and adolescence

After D. Levinson, *The Seasons of a Man's Life* (New York: Ballantine, 1978), p. 200.

lieves that the transition for men at age 30 primarily concerns "settling down," in the sense of intensifying their commitments to their career paths and often to their families. For both homemaker and career women, however, he found this to be a period of questioning and often of changing family and career commitments they had made in their twenties.[11]

Adult Development in MENA Societies

It is not clear what aspects of these theories may applicable to adult development in MENA societies. I know of no Jungian writings on the region (except for David Gutman's cross-cultural study of gender roles, which I describe below) or studies of Levinson's "life structures." A few researchers are currently conducting cross-cultural studies of "generativity" and "wisdom," but not in MENA societies. In addition, the organization of adult lives and MENA cultural models of adulthood and aging differ significantly from those in the Western societies that gave rise to these theories, and it remains for researchers in the region to judge their usefulness. At the present time, only speculation can be offered.

Erikson's theory that achieving "intimacy" forms the main developmental "task" of early adulthood has been criticized for failing to account for women's development,[12] and it clearly reflects the Western middle-class organization of the life-cycle: go to school and find one's self, move away from home and begin a career, fall in love and get married, start a family. Anthony Giddons has described how modern societies have so separated marital and friendship relations from those of work and politics that they become "pure relationships"—stripped of any basis other than the exchange of affection and mutual enjoyment.[13] It should be no surprise, he suggests, that pure relationships tend to be unstable and fragile. And it should be no surprise that this cultural situation should make achieving intimacy into a key developmental "task." Patterns of intimacy differ so greatly in traditional MENA societies from the industrialized West (few relationships are "pure," and intimacy is expected to grow *from* marriage rather than lead *to* it) that it is difficult to see Erikson's "intimacy versus isolation" as the key developmental "task" of the people in their twenties and thirties.

Traditional MENA cultures certainly provide men in their forties and fifties with ample opportunities—as they assume more responsibility for the well-being of their families and communities—for the development and expression of "generativity." But other psychological characteristics, associated with authority, honor, and perhaps religion may be equally or more important. Women have ample opportunities for "generativity" from the age of about seven, when they typically begin taking care of their siblings, so it's not clear that this schema applies to women at all. As in many traditional societies, men and women traditionally aged in their families, being cared for and respected by them. One would expect this to facilitate the development of "ego integrity" and "wisdom" much more readily than in Western societies, where aging parents often live in isolation or in nursing homes. And the religious study and devotion that many men and women undertake after midlife certainly provides a rich arena in which to "individuate" and develop the more wholistic selves of which Jung wrote.

The timing and content of Levinson's "life-stages" is clearly anchored in Western middle-class and professional career paths (he points out that the working-class men he studied fit the pattern less well), and there is no reason to expect traditional MENA lives to follow them. However, I believe that Levinson's "life structure" concept, in the ways it differs from Erikson's notion of "identity," can help make a distinction that is crucial for investigating adult development in MENA societies. That is, the task of forming an identity differs significantly from the task of forming a life structure that can confirm and sustain it. I suggest that late teens and young adults may not experience much more "crisis" in *developing* identities—in spite of clashing value systems—than do youths in most other cultures, including those of the industrialized West. But many are thrown into "crisis" when they cannot form *life structures* that confirm and sustain their identities—when they cannot get a stable vocation that would allow them to marry, have children, and be welcomed into their families and communities as adults. This is a direct consequence of population growth and economic underdevelopment. They indeed experience "crises of identity" that cut to the core of self and personality, but I believe these have a different character from the initial process of creating an identity that Erikson studied. Many young adults in MENA find themselves shifting from one provisional and partial life structure to another, often into their late twenties or early thirties, with none of them embodying the "dreams" they developed toward the end of adolescence.[14] "Identity development" then appears not as a transitional task of the late teens or early twen-

Traditional MENA cultures provide most older adults with respected family and community roles.

ties but as a chronic and troubled labor that psychologically dominates what should be—according to both MENA and Western models of the life-span—the first decade or more of adulthood.

Personality Traits ❀

Several personality traits identified by Western psychologists also have been studied in MENA societies. Since these are covered by Abdel-Khalek's chapter entitled "Personality" and Abou el Nil's chapter entitled "Cross-Cultural Psychology" in Ahmed and Gielen's *Psychology in the Arab Countries*, I will give only a brief summary of research on basic personality traits (introver-

*Older women—especially
mothers of adult men—often
acquire a good deal of power
and prestige.*

sion-extraversion and neuroticism; the "Big Five" traits) and on anxiety. Large studies of Egyptians,[15] Saudis,[16] and Iranians[17] have found support for the existence of introversion-extraversion and neuroticism, adding to the large body of research that suggests these are probably inherited dimensions of personality. Most of these studies did not compare MENA versus Western cultures on the *strength* of these traits, though Ibrahim found Egyptians higher on neuroticism than British or Americans, and lower on extraversion.[18] A pair of recent studies found evidence for the existence of the "Big Five" traits in Turkey,[19] and Aziz and Jackson's study of Pakistani business students found evidence for both Eysenck's three traits and the Big Five.[20] But three large studies of Kuwaitis by Al Ansarey did not find clear support for the Big Five traits.[21] It is not yet clear how well either model describes basic dimensions of personality in MENA.

Khalifa and Radwan recently carried out a multistage study of Egyptian personality traits that may represent an important step toward creating an

Rural villages now have many educated young men, unhappily doing farm work because they cannot find modern jobs in the cities. Others are frequently on the move, combining short-term or seasonal city jobs with farm work in their home villages.

indigenous psychology.[22] They first used focus-group-like discussions and individual interviews to identify 37 trait-like characteristics, then developed 133 questions to assess these, and in the last stage surveyed 662 university students and 565 white-collar employees' perceptions of how well they describe Egyptians. Factor analyses identified bipolar trait dimensions they believe to be universal, including one resembling Eysenck's "neuroticism," one similar to the "agreeableness" factor from the Big Five, one an achievement motivation dimension, and one an optimism/self-confidence dimension. They also found evidence for more culturally specific characteristics, including a dimension of "belonging and conservatism versus selfishness and self-love," one of "sociable and civil versus opportunistic and un-sociable," and a group of positive and negative traits resembling Hamid Ammar's description of the "Fahloui personality" type (discussed later).[23]

In addition to these studies, several scales measuring depression and anxiety have been adapted and validated.[24] These have generally shown anxiety levels to be higher in MENA than in Western samples, and than in some other developing societies, including China, Korea, Czechoslovakia, and Brazil. Abdel-Khalek suggests that "the low economic level in Egypt in comparison to that in the U.S.A. may raise the Egyptians' anxiety level."[25] However, Rien Van Dam-Baggen and colleagues recently found higher levels of social anxiety among Americans than among Dutch or Turkish samples.[26] Together, these studies provide relatively strong evidence that general anxiety levels tend to be higher in MENA societies than in Western ones, and higher than in at least some other developing societies—though most of the studies sample only high school and university students. It is not clear why. Economic underdevelopment or conditions in the schools may turn out to provide a full explanation, but other cultural factors or conflicts also may play a role.

Individualism and Collectivism

During the last decade, Western psychologists have come to a near consensus that individualism versus collectivism ("I" versus "C") is the primary psychological dimension on which the world's cultures vary. An impressive array of data—mainly based on paper-and-pencil measures of values or attitudes—shows that modern Western societies are predominantly individualist, and premodern and non-Western cultures mainly collectivist. Japan often appears to be the archetypal sociocentric culture. Little of this research has been conducted in MENA, but data from Hofstede's global survey of IBM managers found those in Arab countries to be more "collectivistic" than Americans,[27] as did Buda and Elsayed-Elkhoula's survey of Egyptian, Gulf state, and American managers.[28] Al-Zahrani and Kaplowitz also found Saudi university students more collectivistic than American students.[29] There are many reasons, however, to resist terming MENA cultures "collectivistic."

There can be little doubt that the West's official ideology is highly individualist, and that the official ideologies of most Eastern societies (China, Japan, India)—and MENA—are highly collectivist. These differences clearly matter in family and personal relationships, and in the decisions that chart life-courses. But the notion that they create fundamentally different psyches or selves has been frequently criticized,[30] and the widespread notion that "individuality" first developed in the West during the Renaissance or Enlightenment appears to be simply incorrect.[31] Dwight Reynolds's recent study of 140 premodern Arabic autobiographies shows that this genre was established by the eleventh century, with many writers using its conventions to voice distinctive personalities and life-stories.[32] Recent studies of premodern Chinese, Japanese, and Tibetan autobiographies reach similar conclusions.[33]

Several non-Western psychologists have argued that individualism and collectivism do not form a continuum on which cultures can be ranked, and proposed either that (1) I and C are specific to *domains* of life, or (2) I and C form independent *dimensions,* so a person can be "high" or "low" on both. Sinha and Tripathi, for example, maintain that both "individualist" and "collectivist" are "inappropriate for designating Indian cultural and social reality," since both have permeated Indian psyches.[34] A survey they conducted showed 12 percent of Indian undergraduates to be solidly "individualists," 1 percent solidly "collectivist," and 87 percent "mixed." Ho and Chiu similarly reject "individualist" or "collectivist" as appropriate characterizations of Chinese culture, arguing that "there is no necessary contradiction in holding individualist and collectivist views at the same time."[35] They studied Hong Kong students' outlooks in five domains—values, autonomy/conformity, responsibility, achievement, and self-reliance/interdependence—and found the students could be termed "collectivist" only in the area of achievement.[36] Harry Triandis, one of the first psychologists to study I versus C, recently wrote: "The current view of I/C theory is that it consists of a set of contrasting elements that operate like ambiguous pictures. Just as in perceptual psychology one might see a 'lady' or a 'pot' in a particular picture, so a person can sample a collectivist or individualist element to construct a social situation."[37] Oyserman and colleagues' recent metaanalysis of cross-cultural studies supports Triandis's conclusion, finding that not even America and Japan can be contrasted as "individualist" versus "collectivist."

The psychologist Cigdem Kagitcibasi has discussed this issue with regard to Turkey, MENA, and what she terms "majority" (non-Western) cultures.[38] She concurs with the notion that individualism versus collectivism is perhaps the most salient dimension on which cultures differ, but not that this forms a single dimension that characterizes all social domains. Studies in Turkey show that the material interdependence of extended family members is decreasing, but not emotional interdependence, which she believes is deeply rooted in the culture and family system.[39] In contrast to Western cultures that have both material and emotional independence, and to many "majority" cultures that have both material and emotional interdependence, she proposes a third type of society: material independence with emotional interdependence. This predominates in urbanized Turkey, she believes, and "in the more developed urban areas of the majority World with cultures of relatedness."[40]

She further believes that the psychological orientations of "separatedness and relatedness" coexist in most individuals, who can experience them either in conflict or confluence. Imamoglu has found evidence that many Turkish students achieve "optimal development" by synthesizing "interrelatedness" with "individuation."[41] Karakitapoglu-Aygun's survey of American and Turkish students also "supported the coexistence of individuational and interrelational orientations in the same individual."[42] Most important, Kagitcibasi believes that urbanized Turkish youth tend to "combine individual and group loyalties into a 'social achievement motivation'" that contrasts with the

West's individualist achievement orientation, and more closely resembles that described for Japan, India, and China.[43]

Suad Joseph makes similar observations based on her studies of Lebanese families, and uses the term "connectivity" to describe the strongly interdependent bonds that develop in Arab families. These differ from Western ideals of nuclear family relations, in that they emphasize group ties over individuality and in that they blend bonds of love and nurturing with the "patriarchal" authority of men over women and seniors over juniors. It is this blending of affection and authority, she believes, which makes the patriarchal system so resilient: "in patriarchal societies connectivity can become a psychodynamic instrument of domination."[44] But she argues against conceptualizing MENA cultures or selves in terms of the I-versus-C continuum: "Connectivity exists side by side with individualism in the same culture, and perhaps even in the same person," she writes: "these are not oppositional polarities."[45] In the Arab world especially, "forms of individualism also thrive and receive support."[46] Al-Zahrani and Kaplowitz's data appears to support this. They failed to find evidence of several group-oriented attributional styles they expected to be associated the Saudi students' collectivist values, and they suggest this is probably due to the fact that "strength and honor are more important than harmony" and often set individuals in open competition.[47]

In an intriguing series of studies of bilingual students in America, Japan, and MENA (Jordan and Egypt), Kuroda and Suzuki found value patterns that differed from the common I-versus-C contrast. While the Americans voiced "individualist" and "optimistic" values, the Japanese were "contextualist" (rather than "collectivist") and "holistic," and the Arabs "rationalist" and "traditional."[48] More important, they found that the Japanese and Arab students who responded to English versions of the survey expressed more "American" values than those who answered in their native languages, as the Americans who responded in Japanese expressed more "Japanese" values—indicating that "language is definitely more crucial than nationality in determining students' response patterns."[49]

In particular, Arab students responding in Arabic more strongly endorsed "filial piety" and less strongly endorsed "individual rights" and "individual freedom." And in rating the "ideal personality," the Arab students who responded in English valued "rational decision according to principle" and less highly valued "interpersonal harmony." "In general," Kuroda and Suzuki conclude, students responding in Arabic are "more likely to think of traditional Arab values such as loyalty and honor more often than when they are thinking in a foreign language, English."[50] Kuroda and Suzuki believe that learning a language teaches the culture's "implicit designs for living," and this can change overall values (the Arab students most fluent in English have more "American"-like values, even when responding in Arabic). But the changes "are not necessarily all prevailing," and may "show up only when they are speaking in one or the other language."[51] The bilingual education (and media) provided in MENA societies (Arabic and French or English) thus probably enhances the value dualities described in chapter 8, the shifting between "cultural frames," and the coexistence of individualist and collectivist outlooks.

In addition to the coexistence of "I" and "C" values, perhaps the most important point in Kagitcibasi's and Joseph's discussions concerns the formation of achievement orientations that are motivated by familial relatedness and attachment to the larger household. Phalet and Claeys's large survey study found Turkish youth showing stronger achievement orientations than Belgian youth and combining "individualistic Self-Realization with collectivist Group Loyalty" in ways that "support the concept of a collectivist work ethic: Achievement motive appears to be tied up with filial loyalty and with the prospect to gratify one's family for their sacrifices and to live up to their pride by being successful and responsible."[52] This was evident in many of the life-histories I elicited and appeared to resemble Asian forms of achievement motivation[53] more closely than "individualist" American forms.[54] As I suggested in chapter 8, I believe that this represents a transformation of the traditional honor-modesty system into an honor-fueled achievement motivation, and that many young people combine this with religious piety to form "Muslim ethicist" value systems. These syntheses—of egocentric and sociocentric orientations, and of honor and religion—probably provide important forms of "ego integration" throughout adulthood, though conflict may be as common as smooth synthesis.

Gender Differentiation and Reversal ❀

Susan Davis was one of the first anthropologists to show that senior women in traditional milieus often acquire significant power and influence.[55] Deniz Kandiyoti's and Camille Lacoste-Dujardin's more recent accounts of women's life-cycles also emphasize their frequent midlife increase in power and prestige.[56] They report that much of a girl's socialization explicitly prepared her for her marriage, which then served as her rite of transition into adulthood, around the time of puberty. As a new bride she entered her husband's household at the bottom of its hierarchy, servant to her mother-in-law and insecure until she gave birth to a boy (see chapter 8). But achieving this honored status enables her to begin accruing prestige and influence. Her alliance with her son(s) typically deepens as she becomes his (their) refuge from the often confrontative world of peers and the authority of senior men, sometimes serving as his protector and intermediary. Her influence increases steadily as her son(s) grow and bring daughters-in-law into the house, and as she increasingly takes charge of organizing domestic affairs. Postmenopausal women can exercise a good deal of "countervailing power" to that of the men. Davis writes:

Besides controlling all the women's activities, a woman occasionally has economic power over the entire group. . . . At this stage of her life she is able to express herself freely; there is no more expectation of shy, demure behavior. . . . Thus "sexless," women are allowed and even expected to be loud and boisterous, and to talk and tease about immodest topics even in the presence of men.[57]

Kandiyoti writes:

A woman's life-cycle in the patrilocally extended family is such that the deprivation and hardship she may experience as a young bride are eventually superseded by the control and authority she will have over her own daughters-in-law. The powerful postmenopausal matriarch thus is the other side of the coin of this form of patriarchy.[58]

Lacoste-Dujardin similarly writes that the mother of sons often matures into an impressive personage, becoming, "socially the most masculine of women, the most converted to serving the patrilineal group, and the closest to the men."[59]

This indicates that a shift in gender roles often takes place in midlife, providing important developmental opportunities for women—at least for those who have succeeded at living the cultural ideal. David Gutmann argues that a kind of "gender reversal" takes place around midlife in many cultures, with men becoming more passive and "feminine" and women more assertive and "masculine."[60] He has used interviews and Thematic Apperception Tests (TATs) to study men's midlife shifts in psychological themes among suburban Americans, Navaho communities, Maya in Chiapus and Yucatan, and Druze (an Arabic-speaking Shi'ite minority living in Syria, Lebanon, and Israel). He marshals his data to propose a Jungian account of adult gender development: that in adaptation to highly separate parental roles, men and women specialize their psychological orientations in their late teens and early twenties, with men suppressing their more "feminine" qualities and women their more "masculine" qualities. In middle age, with the "phasing out of the parental emergency," Gutmann writes, "post-parental men and women can reclaim the sexual bimodality that was hitherto repressed and parceled out between husband and wife."[61] Thus "a significant sex-role turnover takes place. . . . Just as men in latter middle life reclaim title to their denied 'femininity,' middle-aged women repossess the aggressive 'masculinity' that they once lived out vicariously through their husbands."[62] This entails developmental shifts in ego styles, for men from "active mastery" to "passive mastery," and vice versa for women. "Across cultures and with age," he writes, women "seem to become more authoritative, more effective, and less willing to trade submission for security.[63]

Gutmann's research has been criticized by some who doubt the validity of TAT measures, and his interpretations have been criticized by feminist scholars for suggesting that the gendered division of psychological labor is wired into the species as an evolutionary adaptation to parenting. They also have criticized him for using ideologically "loaded" terminology: if the essence of "femininity" in young adulthood is to specialize in nurturing others, it may not be appropriate to view older men's desire to be nurtured as a recovery of their "femininity." And it is probably not appropriate to describe women's early adult adaptation as "passive mastery," for it is difficult to see either child-caretaking or heavy burdens of agricultural and household work as "passive." These are serious problems. But Gutmann's data, combined with other ethnographic accounts, warrant an interpretation that follows the general lines he lays out: as in many cultures that emphasize more "machismo" ideals of manhood, in MENA, gender differentiation appears to peak in early adulthood. Then in midlife, men and women may begin to develop in ways that can be construed as significant modifications, if not reversals, of the "masculinity" and "femininity" they fashioned as young adults.

Ethnographies clearly show that MENA societies do not have a *single* cultural construction of masculinity and femininity but one that scripts change in roles and psychological orientations over the life-span. For both men and women, the role changes in midlife present both developmental challenges and opportunities for empowerment and individuation. Paradoxically, however, senior women's power ultimately tends to support the patriarchal system, as they exercise their power largely to safeguard and perpetuate it. Lacoste-Dujardin writes: "Delegees of masculine authority, they become complicit in the patriarchal order from which their authority proceeds."[64] Kandiyoti concurs: "The cyclical nature of women's power and their anticipation of inheriting the authority of senior women encourages a thorough internalization of this form of patriarchy."[65]

Toward a Psychology of Underdevelopment ❁

As I have described throughout this book, MENA societies are both "becoming modern" and "underdeveloping." Increasing numbers of educated city-dwellers enjoy comfortable life-styles and cosmopolitan cultures, but the majority of families live in conditions of economic and political underdevelopment. With per capita GDP at 14 percent of those of the OECD countries (and lower in the nonoil states), most people are poor, and about one-third live in "absolute poverty." In many nations oppressive regimes rule with intimidation and violence. The UN's 2002 *Arab Human Development Report* begins by pointing out: "The wave of democracy that transformed governance in most of Latin America and East Asia in the 1980s and Eastern Europe and much of Central Asia in the late 1980s and early 1990s has barely reached the Arab States."[66] The report also indicates that MENA scores much lower on indices of "freedom" and "voice and accountability" than any other region on the globe. This has important psychological consequences, about which Western psychology knows alarmingly little.

The Enlightenment architects of the West's liberal democracies believed that civil rights and political participation were essential to individual "pursuits of happiness." Western social critics have shared this view, indicting the class system, the "fetishism of commodities," the "iron cage" of bureaucracy, the "anomie" of disintegrated communities, and the "one-dimensional" world of media-driven consumerism that deny individuals the social and political opportunities they need to fully develop their personalities. Nazism forced these issues onto psychologists' agendas, and in the 20 years after World War II, researchers carried out classic studies of the authoritarian personality, ethnic prejudice, dogmatism, and social conformity. Scholars from various disciplines sought to define the "open-minded" or "democratic" personality and to study the conditions promoting its development. Interest in these topics then waned, and during the last 30 years mention of political and economic influences on psychological development has all but disappeared from professional journals and textbooks.

During the same decades, anthropologists and political scientists studying Latin America have come to see the violence inflicted by colonial rulers and military regimes as so pervasively shaping some societies that they can be termed "cultures of terror." A handful of European and American psychologists have assisted their Latin American colleagues in providing therapy to torture victims and relatives of the "disappeared," and some of their observations may apply to MENA societies as well. In MENA, social scientists have been analyzing the workings of authority, and debating the extent to which "authoritarianism" may have cultural and psychological roots (see chapter 6). Here I will focus on those who have written on the effects of underdevelopment and tyrannical rule on MENA cultures and psyches.

National Character as an Adaptation to Tyranny

Hamid Ammar followed his study of child-rearing with a pair of essays on psychological modernization. In *Al-shakhsiyya fahlaoui* ("The 'Fahlaoui' Personality"), he described and criticized a personality "type" that he believed had become common in Egypt in response to millennia of harsh village life and tyrannical rule by pharaohs, sultans, and foreign conquerors.[67] "Fahlaoui" is an Egyptian term describing a commonly recognized style of social behavior, whose central traits, according to Ammar, were (1) a "rapid adaptability" that had developed to adjust to the unpredictable conditions of peasant life, and (2) a type of intelligence oriented to practical cleverness (rather than theoretical abstraction) that was crucial to negotiating social relations. Both had negative sides: adaptation could be superficial and designed to present expected appearances, and cleverness could turn manipulative. The "Fahlaoui" also tended to "exaggeration" in self-presentation—to theatrical displays of ability and importance, which resemble the performance of honor-claiming masculinity described by many ethnographers (see chapter 3). Ammar thought that this "type" worked well in conditions of peasant and "popular" urban life but that in the postindependence period it had become an obstacle to modernization. Superficial displays of conformity, clever manipulation, and false displays of prowess would no longer get the job done, when the job was applying technology and building rational institutions.

His second essay, *Al-shakhsiyya al-intaji* ("The Productive Personality"),[68] described the "type" that he saw emerging in response to modernizing conditions, and that he hoped would lead the transformation of Egyptian society. This type embodies the kind of traits that Alex Inkeles and other classic "modernization theorists" hold to characterize "modernity": rationality, achievement orientation, a linear sense of time rooted in long-term planning, cooperative social relations, and so on. These essays amounted to an exhortation: the future belongs to the "effective/productive" type.

Soon after Ammar's essays, the 1967 Arab-Israeli war triggered a wave of "self-criticism" by Arab scholars, some of it psychological. A 1969 issue of the journal *Fikr ma'asr al-qahiria* (Contemporary Thought in Cairo) was dedicated to the Egyptian personality, with an outpouring of criticism.[69] Saddiq Adim's *An-naqd al-dhati ba'd al-hazima* (Self-Critique After the Defeat) blamed Ammar's "Fahlaoui" mentality for Egypt's defeat in the war. The Israeli scholar Rafael Patai picked up Ammar's and Adim's portraits of the "Fahlaoui" and presented it his book *The Arab Mind* as *the* Arab character, which he also blamed for Arabs' economic stagnation and military defeats.[70] And as I showed in chapter 1, some Western journalists subsequently adopted and further popularized Patai's analysis.

In the early 1970s, Egypt's Institute of Policy and Strategic Studies commissioned social scientists to study both Arab and Israeli societies. As part of that work, Sayyid Yassin studied Western, Israeli, and Arab writings on the Arab "national character"[71] and found them to describe overlapping clusters of mostly negative traits. He identified four recurrent themes: weak social bonds, dissimulation and exaggeration, free-floating hostility, and self-inflation.[72] He viewed these as stereotypes arising from misunderstandings of social interaction styles[73] and criticized Adim's use of the "Fahlaoui" concept to explain the military defeat.[74] Ahmad Zaid subsequently conducted a public opinion survey with 900 Egyptians to assess the extent to which their attitudes matched a set of alleged national character traits.[75] His respondents confirmed some traits: they indeed valued piety and expressed mistrust of people outside their family networks. But the survey did not confirm that patience/endurance (*saber*) and fatalism—alleged by several writers to impede individual initiative and retard social development—are prominent personality traits. Egyptians saw patience/endurance as a religious notion applicable to some situations but not a general value, and a majority endorsed the view that a person's life is determined mainly by his effort rather than "fate," saying they turn to God not in dependency but to strengthen their resolve in the face of obstacles.[76] Finally, the respondents voiced "negativity," but not as a general outlook: it was focused on their alienation from authorities and political institutions. Most were engaged in "personalistic politics" rather than civil life.[77]

In a parallel investigation, the rural sociologist Mahmoud 'Awda undertook an "archaeology of the Egyptian personality," reviewing all of the writings on this topic from ancient and medieval travelers to twentieth-century Western, Russian, and Egyptian social scientists.[78] He too identified a set of recurring stereotypes, including cheerfulness, laziness, lying, suspicious and hostile social relations, superstitiousness, and fatalism. These appeared in the recent writings as well as older ones, but 'Awda notes that the precolonial writings tended to be even more negative than those of colonial "Orientalists." 'Awda regards some of these as stereotypes but suggests that others contain grains of truth—especially suspicious and hostile social relations, superstitiousness, and a combination of passivity, laziness, and dissimulation, which he sees as forms of resistance to despotic authority. He proposes that four historical epochs have ruptured and transformed Egyptian culture,[79] but that the exploitative and brutal relation of state to citizen has remained across the centuries as the foundation of psychological adaptation. Each transformation added a layer of culture atop the others, and the *actual* Egyptian personality is built of roles from all of these layers, such that most individuals shift among them depending on context. Jamal Hamdan also took a geographic approach, arguing that the oppressive conditions of peasant agriculture along the Nile fostered dependency, resignation, quietude, and negativity.[80]

Khalifa and Radwan's recent book reviews these and other studies of Arab and Egyptian "national character,"[81] documenting how the "distorted" portraits published by outsiders and the negative self-critiques written in the aftermath of the 1967 defeat gradually turned more balanced after victories in the 1973 war. And while many interpretive works continued to emphasize the negative, most empirical studies have found mixtures of positive and negative traits—as did their own study of educated Cairenes' perceptions of Egyptian traits.[82] Khalifa and Radwan concur with 'Awda's historical and Jabar's and Hamdan's geographic approaches, and suggest that some of the trait dimensions they identified probably took shape as adaptations to Egyptian social environments.

Yassin, 'Awda, Khalifa and Radwan, and others suggest that many of the *stereotypes*—especially laziness, cheerfulness, lying, suspicion, and fatalism— arise from misinterpretation of behavioral styles developed in response to harsh living conditions and exploitative tyranny. Indeed, these styles may be common to peasantries in feudal-like systems. Fromm and Maccoby,[83] George Foster,[84] and Oscar Lewis[85] reported similar clusters of styles in Mexican peasant communities, with Lewis controversially suggesting that these form a "culture of poverty." Eric Wolf described similar styles among feudal European peasants,[86] and James Scott identified a similar set of styles as strategies of peasant resistance to landlords in Southeast Asia.[87] Even Henri Ayrout (whose *Egyptian Peasant* has been a much-cited source of stereotypes) often explains negative traits as adaptations to oppression. These ethnographers of peasant life thus reverse the commonly pointed arrows of causality: predominant behavioral styles often interpreted as "national character" do not arise as consequences of infant and child-care practices but develop as strategies to deal with exploitative tyranny. These strategies then shape family life, social relations, and child-rearing.

Tyranny as the Preserver of Tradition

In the 1960s Franz Fanon presciently described new forms of tyranny as the fate of most postcolonial peoples:

> In a certain number of underdeveloped countries the parliamentary game is faked from the beginning. . . . The state, which by its strength and discretion ought to inspire confidence and disarm and lull everybody to sleep, on the contrary seeks to impose itself in spectacular fashion. It makes a display, it jostles people and bullies them, thus intimating to the citizen that he is in continual danger.[88]

In his *Torture and Modernity*, Darious Rejali documents how the Shah's and then Ayatollah's regimes in Iran have not continued the traditional forms of grotesque public punishments practiced by their predecessors but have created institutions of surveillance and torture that are distinctively modern in their bureaucratic organization.[89] Three decades ago, Fuad Ajami wrote that the citizenry of many MENA nations "wish only to be left alone, and they shelter themselves from the capricious will of the state."[90] In his 1998 *Dream Palace of the Arabs* he writes about the loss of his generation's confidence in modernization, and he quotes the Iraqi poet Buland Hadari's expression of despair that the region had been engulfed in an "ocean of terror."[91]

Mohammed Shah in Iran, Saddam Hussein in Iraq, and perhaps Hafiz Assad in Syria and Israeli forces in the occupied Palestinian territories have created conditions that deserve to be termed "cultures of terror."[92] Other nations have experienced briefer reigns and lower daily levels of terror, and the wars in Lebanon, Afghanistan, and Algeria have inflicted terror of a prolonged but more diffuse sort. Even many "moderate" regimes curtail freedom of the press, assembly, and speech and other civil rights, maintain widespread secret police surveillance, and make periodic use of violence and threats. The effects of political terror are amplified in some areas by the nearly unchecked latitude of local officials and police to use violence and intimidation for corrupt as well as "legitimate" purposes. Police in some countries routinely beat petty criminals upon arrest and sometimes torture them to extract confessions.[93] Western psychologists still lack concepts to describe the corrosive atmosphere of fear this creates.

Ahmad Zaid's large national survey found Egyptians low in trust and participation in political institutions.[94] Barakat writes of this "alienation" and "powerlessness":

> Arab citizens have been rendered powerless by their exclusion from the processes of conducting their own affairs and by deprivation of their right to active and free participation in political movements. . . . The tyranny of the state and the ruler over civil society is a central cause of the condition of alienation felt by so many Arabs.[95]

Sharabi gives special emphasis to the pernicious role of the *mukhabarat*, the secret police: "Ordinary citizens not only are arbitrarily deprived of some of their basic rights but are the virtual prisoners of the state, the objects of its capricious and ever-present violence."[96] He believes this forces people to rely on forms of association that undermine the development of civil society: "Isolated, estranged, and suppressed, the individual subject was driven back to the primary social structures—the family, the ethnic community, the tribe, the religious sect—for security and for survival."[97] Hijazi and Hammoudi describe similar processes by which individuals may seek protection from hostile authorities in traditional social groupings, and by which undemocratic regimes may rehabilitate traditional forms of authority and patronage. This is the essence of political underdevelopment: not that traditional social structures stubbornly endure by the force of their momentum but that deliberately created fear drives people to re-form them—hence Sharabi's use of the term *neo*patriarchy in contrast to traditional *patriarchy*.

The Psychology of Subjugation

One of the first and still most frequently cited analyses of the psychology of underdevelopment comes from the Lebanese psychotherapist Mustafa Hijazi's *Al-takhaluf al-ijtima'i: Sikologia al-insan mqahor* (Societal Underdevelopment: The Psychology of Subjugation). His term *takhaluf* can be rendered as either "backwardness" or "underdevelopment," and he uses it in both senses to refer to more traditional forms of MENA society, to conditions of colonization, and to the postindependence conditions Sharabi terms *neo*patriarchy. His central thesis is that the psychology of underdevelopment *is* the psychology of subjugation, which consists of human weakness before the uncontrollable forces of nature on one side and before despotic rule on the other. This combination can reign over life in traditional milieus, in the form of floods, droughts, illnesses, and deaths on the one hand, and of rapacious sultans, beys, pashas, and landlords on the other. And it can reign over life in modernizing milieus in the form of poverty and insecurity driven by market forces, and of intimidation by dictators, corrupt officials, and secret police.

Hijazi believes weakness before nature and tyrants creates psychological injuries at deep levels, undermining the subjugated person's basic sense of security, efficacy, and self-regard and evoking pervasive fear and anxiety. As in many cultures, nature tends to be richly symbolized as a "Mother," and so weakness before "her" reevokes the feelings of separation anxiety, maternal neglect, and rejection that accompany even the best mothering. Authorities are symbolized as fathers (especially as they deliberately adopt paternal symbols), and so subjection to despots reevokes feelings of emasculation experienced in the face of angry, punishing fathers. The subjugated person's life thus comes to be colored by infantilizing regression to these childhood fears. Above all, because authority is exercised directly, blatantly, and with the intent of humiliating, it combines with weakness before nature to produce intolerable feelings of shame, embarrassment, sin, and resentment. In response to these wounds to narcissism and potency, people resort to a variety of defensive strategies that give at least temporary illusions of psychological equilibrium.

Hijazi proposes three "stages" of response to subjugation, but he often speaks of these less as stages than as stances or attempts at adaptation a person might adopt. The first is simple *subordination* wrought by naked force, which produces the most intense and conscious feelings of insufficiency, humiliation, and resentment. This "shame complex" affects everyone, he writes, even the patriarchs and Big Men who subjugate others, as they are in turn subjugated by more powerful ones. The intolerable nature of conscious shame, sin, and anxiety leads to a second psychological strategy, which sets up an internal order of self-subjugation. This is based on *repression* of the feelings of inferiority and typically is accomplished by identifying with the authority, projecting the shame and sin onto others (most prominently women) and displacing the resentment as punitive hostility toward sinners. This stage/stance provides a semblance of psychological equilibrium that may last through a lifetime or extend over generations. But it is always an unstable equilibrium that may lead, when individual and social circumstances allow, to *rebellion*. Here Hijazi cites Fanon at length on the psychologically reparative effects of taking up arms against the oppressor. The subjugated person who conquers his or her fear of death and confronts the tyrant restores a sense of dignity and efficacy.

But Hijazi does not stop the dialectic with the healing effects of violence. At the beginning of revolt, he writes, only a few take up arms, and these become heroes and then leaders to the masses who follow. The heady effects of empowerment and leadership easily lead to narcissistic aggrandizement, and violence comes to have magical self-inflating properties that deflect it from the goal of liberation and give it a life of its own. Heroic leader-follower relations are re-created, daily life comes to be lived in a "clan-like" style, subverting in practice the vision of liberation that first drove the rebels to fight. Hijazi later carried out field studies of militia fighters in the Lebanese civil war, and he describes in detail how their violence became "magical" acts of self-reparation via mutilation of victims. He points out that their popular warrior nicknames, composed with the prefix "abu"- ("father of"-), expressed an unconscious identification with old-style paternal prowess, for which these young men apparently yearned. He also found that they took on roles of traditional patriarchs, including arranging marriages.[98] Subjugation forms a total psychological system, he concludes, even generating rebellion that re-creates the very forms it initially seeks to destroy. Only different kinds of change, about which he declines to speculate, can transform the self-replicating totality.

Hijazi then describes four main types of defense mechanisms that subjugated persons adopt to bear their shame, fear, and rage: (1) withdrawal into self (including dreaming of the glorious past and "dissolving" into family and kin-groups); (2) identification with authority; (3) mythic/superstitious control of fate (achieving an illusion of efficacy and security by protecting one's self from the *jinns*, Satan, and Evil Eye and by practicing sorcery and fortune-telling); and (4) violence (sometimes directed self-destructively inward but more often displaced outward, readily taking "paranoid" and "fascist" forms). He argues that the whole symbolic complex by which men dominate women serves as the key equilibrium-restoring mechanism for men, as it creates an illusory dignity of exercising authority, no matter how strongly they themselves may be subjected to the authority of other men. Yet none of these defenses provide a satisfactory equilibrium, and so people typically shift among them according to temperaments and circumstance.

The analyses of the psychotherapist Ali Zayour and the historian Hichem Djait parallel Hijazi's in many respects. Zayour terms the no longer traditional but not modern condition a "deformed" or "degraded" society, and Djait refers to the postcolonial cultural mixture as an incoherent "mongrel" structure. Both criticize traditional forms of family and political authority for instilling feelings of weakness, for blocking individual initiative, and for embedding the individual in a realm of mythical beings, forces, and thinking. "The sultan and the father and the husband and the fqih," Zayour writes, "add up to a picture of the unified structure, characterized by repression and severity."[99] Djait especially criticizes the networks of patron-clientage created within new state institutions, reinforcing the "prestige complex" and complementary styles of "ingratiation" he believes have become features of the "basic personality."[100] Both scholars also emphasize the sense of insufficiency inflicted by colonialism, which has continued after independence as the wealthy and powerful West has become the standard of comparison by which Arabs evaluate their lives and selves, and judge them inferior. This does not affect children in the first years of life, Zayour points out, but comes into play in later childhood, gradually deepening the "wounds" to the self inflicted by traditional authorities and setting off a struggle to recover one's "standing." Here Zayour's analysis also resembles writings by W.E.B. DuBois, Malcolm X, Ralph Ellison, and others on the wounds inflicted by racism as minority children come to see themselves reflected negatively in the eyes of whites. Like Hijazi (and the writers on racism), he believes this typically leads to a variety of defensive maneuvers, often to blanket rejection of tradition in favor of Western-style modernity, or to reactionary adherence to tradition—both of which subvert efforts to modernize the Arab cultural heritage.

The Republic of Fear

Perhaps the most provocative study of state terror is Kanan Makiya's *Republic of Fear*, about Saddam Hussein's regime in the 1980s.[101] Makiya traces how, from its seizure of power in 1968, Hussein's Ba'th Party created a new Iraqi society, based on three principles. First, it gained control of Iraq's oil revenues, and launched massive development projects that came to employ 60 percent of the urbanized workforce. The state thus created the modern sector as a kind of vast patronage system, and instead of fostering the institutions of "civil society" that provide the infrastructure of democracy, it destroyed all but the party's own training and propaganda groups. Militia, military, police, and intelligence agencies were expanded until by 1980 they employed a fifth of all working Iraqis.[102] By providing modern jobs but preventing the development of modern forms social relationships, they created a mass of isolated individuals.

Second, the party deployed an extensive system of surveillance and terror among the masses, and ferreted out so-called enemies and betrayers at will—executing some of them publicly, torturing and murdering others secretly:

> The pattern is for agents to pick someone up from work, or at night from his house. No explanations are proffered as there would be in an official killing. Unlike Central American "disappearances" in which the state denies complicity, the Ba'th give the event a macabre twist. What one assumes to be the corpse is brought back weeks or maybe months later and delivered to the head of the family in a sealed box. A death certificate is produced for signature to the effect that the person has died of fire, swimming, or other such accident. Someone is allowed to accompany police and box for a ceremony, but at no time is he or she permitted to see the corpse. The cost of the proceedings is demanded in advance, and the whole thing is over within hours of the first knock on the door.[103]

This produced an "all-embracing atmosphere of fear,"[104] a "Kafkaesque" world in which people feel they are being watched and judged in secret: "The system functions like a concentration camp: inmates are played off against one another (enemies are invented) and children are tortured (for a 'higher' purpose) as the whole thing spins wildly out of control in a closed world all of its own making."[105] Mistrust and suspicion seeps into every relationship, so that "nothing is as it seems and nothing can be taken for granted."[106]

Saddam Hussein himself supplied the third element: the Leader who inspires fear but, even more important, appears to the frightened public as their sole hope for security. Makiya sees this as the psychological genius of the system, which he describes by analogy to Thomas Hobbes's theory of the founding of government in a tacit social contract. The "state of nature" before government, Hobbes reasoned, was one of war "of each against all," in which life was "nasty, brutish, and short." In order to create peace and security, people turn their natural rights to defend their property and take vengeance over to a sovereign, who enforces order in their stead. The Ba'th turned this around and *manufactured* a Hobbesian world in which each feared all, and *only* the state then appeared to provide protection. The Leader who metes out terror thus comes to embody each individual's hope for security. Iraqis learned quickly to fear Hussein, Makiya writes, but soon "these same people were 'choosing' to surround themselves with pictures of Saddam in their homes and offices, hoping in this way to 'ward off evil.'"[107]

Makiya is not a psychologist, and he does not make the relevant point that this attachment resembles that of abused children to the parents who abuse them. This kind of attachment has been repeatedly noted in protracted hostage situations and described in conjunction with state terror elsewhere. Writing of Latin America, the psychotherapist Nancy Hollander explains:

> Identification with the aggressor was an important defense against the fear and anxiety stimulated by the continuous flow of disappearances and rumors of torture. For the witness/victim citizens who survived in the violence of everyday life, identification, at both the unconscious and conscious levels, with an arbitrary state power enacting its wrath on the *desaparecidos* permitted them to symbolically choose victims outside themselves to sacrifice—*algo habra hecho* [he or she must have been up to something].[108]

Makiya sees the Iraqi public as having become complicitous in precisely this manner.

Importantly, Makiya does not see Iraq's "Republic of Fear" as a remnant of tradition undermining modernity or as a manifestation of an underlying authoritarian personality. Rather, he shows how the Ba'th Party forged a *new* form of society and authority: "Their project was to destruct the social reality they inherited into a new set of equally weighted constituent elements—frightened, rootless individuals, alienated from their traditional groups (kin, tribe, sect, class)—and then to reassemble these fragments within a new state-centralized network of relationships."[109] The "Leader syndrome" diffused through these relationships "was a *new* conception of authority for modern Iraq uniquely associated with Ba'thi experience."[110] Shadowy state terror thus created a new social psychological field within which frightened citizens identify with the ubiquitous Leader, and gain a measure of protection from feelings of catastrophic vulnerability by believing that it is the victims—people *un*like themselves—who represent the threat. In addition to identification with the aggressor, Makiya repeatedly cites fear, isolation, vulnerability, and suspicion as psychological consequences of terror, forming "the psychological constitution of citizenship."[111] This also echoes reports from Latin America, which Hollander summarizes as follows.

> Citizens were compelled to feel that their homes, their jobs, their loved ones, their own lives were in jeopardy. They came to trust no one, to confide in no one, to seek preservation in isolation. Contact with others endangered everyone. Citizens' fearful hypervigilance resembled a kind of paranoid character disorder that was so widespread it looked like a national trait.[112]

Debate: Tyranny and Psychological Development ❀

A divergence of views appears throughout all of the writings on psychological patterns in MENA societies, as to the direction of causality. Many scholars treat the family as society's core or "kernel" unit from which other features of the culture (myth, poetry, religion, politics, etc.) derive. Others—including myself in this book—view the family and its values as adapted to its social ecology, so that it serves as the main *agent* of socialization but is not necessarily the *source* of the culture it inculcates. I have followed Schneider and others in viewing family structure and the values of honor and modesty as adaptations to the arid/semiarid MENA-Mediterranean zone that supported a mixture of pastoral, agricultural, and urban ways of life. I have followed LeVine in treating the MENA's pediatric model of infant care as an adaptation to conditions of poor nutrition, high infant mortality, and hot climates. I have followed Boserup, Goody, and Kandoyati in treating the "patriarchal" control of women as originally rooted in the agricultural and inheritance systems of "Eurasia," and I have followed Herdt and Gilmore in viewing men's often "harsh" treatment of boys as rooted in the imperative to toughen them for raiding, feuding, and defending their families' honor.

The writings on "neopatriarchy" and the "psychology of subjugation" describe another important characteristic of the social ecology of development, which acts both directly on adolescents and adults and indirectly on children through its effects on families and schools. Many features of MENA's traditional social ecology are receding in importance, but tyranny has taken distinctly modern forms and in many areas extended and intensified its intimidation. In this historical context it is essential to distinguish between "bottom-up," family-based influences on psychological development and "top-down" economic and political influences. This is a challenging task, especially since the networks of patron-client relations at the heart of MENA social structure tend to entail protection and nurturance couched in familial terms on the one side and humiliating "domination and subordination" on the other (see chapters 2 and 3). Yet, however difficult, it is vitally important to disentangle "bottom-up" from "top-down" influences in MENA societies.

In some passages Hijazi, Zayour, Bouhdiba, and Sharabi appear to take a "family socialization" view, regarding the traditional patriarchal family as the source of an authoritarianism that spreads throughout social institutions. In other passages, however, they take a "top-down" perspective, describing family patriarchy as developing in response to subjugation. Similarly, in some passages Hammoudi seems to see the "master-disciple" schema as originating in the father-son relationship, but in others as stemming from the political style of rural "notables." Msefer and Dachmi see beliefs in *jinns*, the Evil Eye, Satan, and sorcery as arising from the "splitting" of maternal imagoes in response to symbiotic mothering terminated by abrupt weaning, while Hijazi and Zayour see them as projections of fears and hostilities that arise from subjugation, and as magical attempts to restore the security that tyranny undermines. Certainly these scholars emphasize that the culture forms a *system* in which causal influence runs both up from families toward politics and down from politics toward families. But, as they themselves sometimes point out, such a view of cultural coherence runs the risk of portraying it as more integrated and static than it is. And it runs the even greater risk of failing to recognize the extent to which people turn to some institutions and values—especially family and religion—to seek refuge from powerlessness and to resist tyranny.

It may be impossible to assess the effects of "top-down" subjugation and terror on psychological development, but perhaps because I have seen the fear, powerlessness, and hypervigilance evoked by a regime (Morocco under Hassan II) that was truly "moderate" by comparison to the Shah's Iran or Hussein's Iraq, I am convinced that their effects can be profound. There is not much "scientific" research on these matters, however, since undemocratic regimes rarely allow psychologists to study how they effect their populaces. And after a few controversial experiments on authority and total institutions in the 1950s and 1960s, research ethics were tightened to stop realistic laboratory simulations. But we can perhaps extrapolate some other lines of research to sketch a framework for the question.

Studies of posttraumatic stress disorder clearly demonstrate that prolonged exposure to threat produces anxious, hypervigilent alertness, chronic tension, dissociative withdrawal, various strategies of emotional "numbing," and occasionally outbursts of violence.[113] Studies by Mirowsky[114] and Mirowsky and Ross[115] show that social powerlessness is associated with styles of seemingly "paranoid" thinking, but no psychological theory adequately captures what Makiya terms the "Kafkaesque" quality that daily life can suddenly take on under the threat of terror. Hollander cites a Chilean therapist who explained that during the terror, "the boundaries between the real, the possible, and the imaginary were all erased, and reality thus became confused and threatening, no longer able to guide subjective perception."[116] This is a crucially important part of the picture, perhaps captured best in "magical realist" literary works, such as those by Milan Kundera, Gabriel Garcia Marquez, and Salman Rushdie.

The sociologist Anthony Giddons calls attention to the sense of trust and regularity that, however illusory, societies must foster as the precondition for ordinary social relationships and personal identities.[117] He links this to D. W. Winnicott's and Erik Erikson's accounts of the "basic trust" that must be established in infancy to ground healthy development. It consists of a core sense that needs will be met, discomforts soothed, and attachments sustained, a sense that enables a child to bear frustration and move into the wider world with a feeling of confidence. Winnicott believed most mothers provide "good-enough" mothering to build basic trust, and Giddons seems to suggest that most cultures provide good-enough culturing to sustain it among adults. In ordinary times people take this foundation of their lives largely for granted, and do not notice how fragile it in fact is. But as torture shatters forever the basic trust of its victims,[118] so terror can disrupt it for entire populaces. Tyranny and terror evoke the most basic anxieties and needs, psychologically "infantilizing" people (Hollander also makes this point)[119] and setting off efforts to "repair" a sense of self-security. Reparation may entail dissociative withdrawal, rigid self-restraint, "magical" protective techniques (it is not only a joke to note that people hang pictures of the Leader to "ward off evil"), and identification with the aggressor. These are precisely the processes Hijazi describes. And in their recent review of research, "The Psychological Underpinnings of Democracy," Sullivan and Transue cite high "interpersonal trust" and low "perceived threat" as the primary determinants of tolerance and democratic orientations, as identified by 50 years of research. The research also shows that trust and threat are influenced both by child-rearing practices (harshness lowers trust and raises perceived threat) and by participation in civil associations (which raises trust and lowers perceived threat); undemocratic regimes typically suppress such participation.

We also can point to studies of the Evil Eye, which Hijazi and Zayour see (along with beliefs in other invisible forces) as defensive responses to tyrannical authority and to helplessness before Nature. Recall that Roberts found the Evil Eye complex to be associated with a set of societal characteristics typical of the circum-Mediterranean and MENA, including patrilineal descent, inequality, and concentrated authority (see the introduction to part II). It was not associated with infant-care practices that would support a "paranoia" interpretation, but rather with later-childhood practices linked to authority: paternal distance, corporal punishment, sexual restraint, circumcision or genital mutilation, and emphasis on obedience, responsibility, industry, and aggression.[120] Focusing on the way the "Evil Eye complex" centers on defensive measures, Garrison and Arensberg attribute the complex mainly to the "risk of seizure" that permeates networks of "patronal dependency" and exploitative states.[121] While we cannot necessarily extrapolate the research on the Evil Eye to *jinns* and other invisible forces, Hijazi, Zayour, El Khayat-Bennai, Lacoste-Dujardin, Bouhdiba, Boddy, and others all point out that it is women who are most engaged with them, and these researchers argue that such engagement represents "magical" attempts to control nature (especially fertility and infants' health) and exert indirect resistance to the direct power of men. Further, Schneider, Ortner, and Kandiyoti all argue that the "classic" forms of family patriarchy found in the Mediterranean and MENA—entailing close surveillance, control, and often harsh discipline of women and junior men—evolved from the labor demands of peasant agriculture combined with states making family heads responsible for the behavior of family members and for paying tribute.[122] All of these point toward the kind of "top-down" effects of subjugation on family organization and psychological processes that Hijazi, Zayour, and Sharabi describe.

I believe the writings on "neopatriarchy," the "psychology of subjugation," and the "republic of fear" make strong cases that tyranny and terror affect psychological development in important ways. In the absence of research, we know little about their specific effects, though they probably follow the contours of posttraumatic syndromes and include hypervigilant arousal, dissociative withdrawal, and intrusive reexperiencing of real or imagined scenes of violence. They also probably "wound" the self (undermining "self-efficacy" and "self-esteem," if one prefers those terms) and arouse feelings of powerlessness and shame. Surveillance and intimidation undermine the "basic security" on which ordinary social life depends, amplifying generalized anxiety and tendencies to suspicious and "paranoid" thought. Common psychological responses to these "infantilizing" conditions appear to include (1) retreat to the protection of traditional-appearing social groups, (2) adoption of magical and superstitious means of protection and of influencing threatening conditions, (3) turns to violence in cathartic attempts to overcome humiliation, and (4) identification with the aggressor, which may initially be adopted as a provisional response to fear but may coalesce over time into a more permanent personality organization.

In addition, as observers of many armed conflicts in MENA have noted, violence reinforces "Strong Man"-centered patronage networks[123] and intensifies the more "machismo" constructions of masculinity, invariably to the detriment of women.[124] Both Hijazi and Makiya believe that subjugation and terror insidiously work their way into the home, and Makiya hypothesizes that "growing cruelty toward Arab women has accompanied the modernization of the Arab world."[125] Further, as Zayour describes it, the sense of inferiority vis-à-vis the neighboring West—created by colonial rule and sustained today by Western prosperity, military might, and consumerist marketing— parallels the internalization of negative identities among ethnic minorities as they see themselves through the eyes of prejudiced majorities, a process documented by a host of studies of ethnic identity and acculturation.[126]

Toward a Psychology of Modernization and Underdevelopment

The theory of societal development proposed by the economist Amartya Sen—adopted by the Arab scholars who prepared the 2002 United Nations *Arab Human Development Report*—might provide a broad framework for investigating the psychological consequences of tyranny.[127] His theory gauges development by a set of freedoms[128] that promote the growth of individual capabilities and agency.[129] Market economies and rising GNPs can promote this development, but in a series of studies Sen has shown that they do not automatically bring it about, and that increased freedoms, capabilities, and agency often serve as the *precursors* of economic growth. These are fundamentally psychological characteristics, and even when Sen speaks of money, material goods, and information, his ultimate concern is with how these translate into capabilities and agency. He therefore redefines poverty as "capability deprivation,"[130] pointing out that in societies with basic freedoms, low incomes can translate into high capabilities (that then catalyze economic growth), while in unfree societies even high incomes may not enable people to develop capabilities and agency. He thus emphasizes the psychological importance of *relative deprivation*: that physical and mental health, sense of efficacy, and self-respect appear more strongly related to a person's perceived *relative* status in society than to his or her objective wealth.[131] Sen's theory of development thus focuses precisely on forms of social capability and agency that Hijazi and others see as compromised by economic underdevelopment, political subjugation, and neopatriarchal social relations.

Sen's theory of freedoms, capabilities, and agency can be made more psychologically specific by incorporating concepts from the political philosopher Axel Honneth, who draws on Hegel, Erik Erikson, and G. H. Mead to formulate a theory of social influences on the development of self-regard.[132] Honneth argues that in preindustrial societies, individual development ideally culminated in a sense of "honor" rooted in the face-to-face relations of family, kin-group, and village or band. The institutions of industrial societies eclipse these groupings, and he sees self-regard in modern states as rooted in three forms of "recognition" that affirm a person's worth: (1) love and nurturance within families provides the foundation for "basic self confidence," equivalent to Giddons's "basic trust"; (2) the guarantee of civil rights by representative governments provides the foundation for "self-respect"; and (3) the solidarity that comes with acquiring a valued status in the larger community provides the foundation for a more individuated "self-esteem." Each of these forms of recognition can be threatened: basic self-confidence by threats to one's physical integrity; self-respect by denial of rights or exclusion; self-esteem by denigration or insult.[133] These concepts can provide an initial framework for distinguishing the effects of family socialization from those of government actions and from those of the larger social and cultural order. They can help distinguish, for example, between the effects of economic underdevelopment (for example, unemployment denies the "self-esteem" that comes with acquiring a valued social status), of the absence of civil rights and representative institutions (for example, denying "self-respect"), and of surveillance and torture (for example, undermining "basic self-confidence").

Throughout this book I have taken a developmental approach to cultural influences on psychological processes, covering the life-span from infancy through mature adulthood. Even though I have tried to view development in the context of its "social ecology," this organization by life-stage promotes a "bottom-up" perspective, which focuses on patterns of face-to-face family, kin-group, and community relationships. It is important to end this book by focusing on the "top-down" influences that, by acting directly on adults, tune all of the milieus in which infants, children, adolescents, and adults develop. If we are to understand the "struggle of becoming" that Barakat describes as preoccupying MENA peoples (see chapter 1), it is crucial to give priority to economic and political underdevelopment.

In agreement with Sen, I believe that development—both societal and individual—need not be a "fierce" process that pits modernity and tradition against each other in desperate and sometimes armed combat.[134] With economic opportunities and political freedoms, "modernization within tradition"[135] can become a largely creative rather than a "wounding," "fragmenting," or "schizophrenic" undertaking. It becomes all of these in the conditions of underdevelopment or "neopatriarchy" prevailing in many MENA societies. Sen's and Honeth's conceptions may provide a framework within which to investigate the psychological responses to underdevelopment described by the many Arab writers reviewed in this chapter. And following the lead of the *Arab Human Development Report*, these conceptions may provide a framework for examining the effects of economic and political modernization on psychological development throughout the life-span.

Sources

The ethnographies I have reviewed throughout this book describe the patterns that organize adult lives, and while none specifically examine adult development, many contain life-histories that illustrate developmental paths. Autobiographies by "ordinary" people provide informative portraits of the life-course—such as Fadhma Amrouche's *My Life Story*, Brick Oussaid's *Mountains Forgotten by God*, Nayra Atiya's collection of five Egyptian women's life stories, *Khul-Khaal*, and Afsaneh Najmabadi's book *Women's Autobiographies in Contemporary Iran*. So do several life-history-based studies, including Mottahedeh's *Mantle of the Prophet*, Kevin Dwyer's *Moroccan Dialogues*, Henry Munson's *House of Si Abd Allah*, Antoun's *Muslim Preacher in the*

Modern World, Gilsenan's *Lords of the Lebanese Marches*, Lois Beck's *Nomad*, Katherine Ewing's *Arguing Sainthood*, and Uni Wikan's *Tomorrow, God Willing*. And especially for an outsider, Mahfouz's Cairo Trilogy may provide the best introduction to the cultural forces shaping development during adulthood, and to the range of individual variation that emerges in response to them.

MENA psychologists have carried out many studies of personality traits first identified by Western psychologists, either by translating and adapting Western scales or devising new ones. Ahmad Abdel-Khalek, Ihsan Al-Issa, G. Ghareeb, J. Beshai, M. Farrag, and Abdul Ibrahim have made substantial contributions to this project, which generally provide evidence for the universality of many traits, and for the importance of assessing them with culturally adapted (and not just translated) scales. Abdel-Khalek's chapter on "Personality" and Abou el Nil's chapter "Cross-Cultural Psychology" in Ahmed and Gielen's *Psychology in the Arab Countries* cover most of this work, and Abdelatif Khalifa and Sha'ban Radwan's recent *Al-shakhsiyya al-misriyya* (The Egyptian Personality) reviews these and many other studies, and presents findings from their own multistage study of Egyptian characteristics.

For the past 20 years, cross-cultural psychologists have studied the "individualism" versus "collectivism" of cultures and selves, generally finding that the West's "egocentrism" contrasts with the "sociocentrism" of East and South Asia (mainly Japan, China, Korea, and India). Several researchers have criticized these conceptions,[136] and Daphna Oyserman's recent metaanalysis of the quantitative studies casts their findings into doubt.[137] I have located only two studies that measure these in MENA societies, but the Turkish psychologist Cigdem Kagitcibasi discusses them in her *Family and Human Development Across Cultures*, as does the Egyptian sociologist Suad Joseph in her *Intimate Selving*. There is a large literature on "patriarchal" gender relations, and, in addition to the more psychological analyses I have reviewed in previous chapters, several recent works explore the cultural construction of masculinity, including Fedwa Malti-Douglass's *Women's Body Women's Word*, Deniz Kandoyati's *Paradoxes of Masculinity*, and Asfaneh Najmabadi's "Reading 'Wiles of Women' Stories as Fictions of Masculinity." David Gutmann's studies of shifts in gender roles with aging included a sample of Druze, and may help to see MENA patterns in a broad cross-cultural framework.[138]

Finally, there are a number of important psychologically oriented works by MENA scholars, most written as part of a broad cultural "self-criticism" undertaken in the 1970s and 1980s. These include Bouhdiba's *Sexuality in Islam* and Sharabi's *Neopatriarchy*, as well as Hamid Ammar's *Fi bina' al-bashar* (On the Building of Persons), Mahmoud 'Awda's *al-takayyuff wa al-muqawamah* (Adaptation and Resistance), Hichem Djait's *Al-Shakhsiyya al-'arabiyya al-islamiyya wal-masir al-'arabi* (Arab-Islamic Personality and Arab Destiny), Ali Zayour's *Al-tahlil al-nafsi li-al-dhat al-'arabiyya* (Psychoanalysis of the Arab Ego), Sayyid Yassin's *al-shakhsiyya al-'arabiyya* (The Arab Personality), and Mustafa Hijazi's *Al-takhaluf al-ijtima'i* (Societal Underdevelopment). Even when these works "import" Western theories, they explore psychological consequences of economic and political underdevelopment that Western psychologists have almost entirely ignored.

CHAPTER 10

Patterns and Lives
Development Through the Life-Span

Patterns ❀

One could distill from the previous chapters a "typical" MENA path of development through the life-span. But this would amount to another "national
character" stereotype, to which no life would correspond. Not only does socialization vary from milieu to milieu but twists of fate often make it impossible for families to follow cultural models of child-rearing and for young
adults to take up the roles and identities their culture prescribes. Differences
in temperament, birth order, intelligence, and family organization exert such
profound effects that the cultural patterns that create shared experiences simultaneously provoke diverging reactions to them. Individuals also person-
alize their culture as they internalize it, in such idiosyncratic ways that "the"
culture is not so much shared by all its members as it is distributed among
them. Daily life is animated by dialogues and disputes among those living by
different interpretations of their culture's values.

Still, MENA societies constitute a "culture area" with distinctive influences on psychological development. This culture area is not defined by a clear
boundary separating it from its neighbors but by the intersection of patterns
it historically has shared with them: peasant agriculture with all Eurasia;
nomadic pastoralism with the arid and semiarid zones surrounding the Sahara and stretching into Central Asia; a pediatric (and "sling-carrying") model
of infant care with much of sub-Saharan Africa and South Asia; the honor-
modesty system with the preindustrial Mediterranean; Islam with societies
now stretching from Nigeria to the Philippines. It is the *conjunction* of these
patterns in the MENA region that gives it its distinctive cultural psychology.

To synthesize psychological studies of the region, I have used a model
that distinguishes three levels of personality organization, which correspond
to major transitions in biological, cognitive, and social development. These
are: (1) a *core self* shaped mainly in infancy and early childhood by the

interaction of inherited temperament and child care (roughly correspond-ing to LeVine's "personality genotype" and McAdams's level 1 characteris-tics); (2) *social personae* that consolidate mainly in late childhood as the child comes to perceive his or her social roles from the point of view of society as a whole (corresponding to G. H. Mead's "social self" and McAdams's level 2); and (3) an *identity* that typically forms in late adolescence and early adult-hood (corresponding to LeVine's "personality phenotype" and McAdams's level 3). The most prominent cultural influences on these levels can be sketched as follows.

Level 1: Core Self

In MENA societies, core selves appear to be shaped within the context of a "pediatric" model of infant care that fosters the development of a secure and intense maternal bond, often transformed abruptly by weaning and a dimi-nution of maternal caretaking. This discontinuity creates for both the infant and its family the developmental "task" of facilitating a transition to wider familial attachments. When made successfully, the establishment of wider attachments—primarily with household women—solidifies the foundation of a matrifocal interdependence that will be sustained throughout life, and perhaps of a household-based "group self" anchored in the culture's rich maternal symbolism that thrives at the core of its patriarchal ideology.[1] Pe-diatric styles of caretaking also may lay the foundation for "feminine" gen-der identity, which circumcision near the end of early childhood ritually reverses for boys, though masculinity remains to be achieved and proven in subsequent periods. Where it is practiced, female circumcision, or "female genital cutting," provides girls with ritual confirmation of their femininity,[2] though this too remains to be achieved with motherhood. In traditional and perhaps poor urban milieus, other experiences common during the first years of life probably shape emotions, motives, and defenses in ways that are little studied and poorly understood by Western psychology. In those environments, hunger, suffering associated with illnesses and injuries, and the instilling of fear of "supernatural" beings and forces may foster an "ex-ternalizing" style of emotional self-management.

Level 2: Sentiments, Motives, and Social Personae

The development of social personae—forming a second level of personality organization—begins in early childhood with the learning of family interac-tion styles. It greatly intensifies in late childhood with the mastery of social etiquettes associated with the honor-modesty system and the self-care prac-tices associated with Islam. As in many traditional societies, the pediatric model evolves into an "apprenticeship and obedience" model that resembles child-rearing styles observed in many preindustrial societies. Boys (and girls less so) often experience a second significant discontinuity[3] as they move from the world of women to that of men. At the same time, their fathers—reported by nearly all observers to have warm and nurturing interactions with infants and toddlers—assume more distant, formal, demanding, and often punitive roles. Authority typically becomes "patriarchal" and, by most accounts, harsh. Many researchers describe paternal authority as becoming "authoritarian" during this period and as creating a widespread tendency toward authoritarianism that has undermined democratization of the region. Others, however, argue that traditional patriarchal authority was not "authoritarian" in the sense described by Western theorists but that recent decades of underdevelopment and family instability may be fostering Western-style authoritarianism.

By puberty most children have mastered and internalized the values, etiquettes, and self-care practices of honor-modesty and Islam. It appears likely that this process shapes universal emotions, traits, and self-representations into culturally distinctive *sentiments, motives,* and *social personae.* Following G. H. Mead, I suggest that social selves consolidate as children learn to take the perspective of the "Generalized Other" on their own social roles and relationships. Psychologists have studied this process little, but anthropologists have provided rich descriptions that suggest that honor-modesty and Islam are sufficiently autonomous value-etiquette systems that each can provide a Generalized Other, facilitating the consolidation of a pair of social selves that sometimes converge and sometimes conflict. Conflicting honor-based and religion-based imperatives appear to animate many of the social dramas that form the texture of daily life, and to inspire popular poetry, epic, and tragic literary works. The internalization of two sets of societal expectations also appears to set the challenge that will become the main developmental "task" of adolescence and early adulthood: creating an identity that affirms, modifies, or resists the socially expected roles and that balances or synthesizes the values of honor-modesty and Islam.

Level 3: Identity

In traditional milieus, identity appears to be anchored in a richly elaborated symbolism associated with gender and age that organizes household and public spaces, styles of dress and grooming, and interaction etiquettes. Within this framework, marriage and parenthood serve as credentials to valued identities. Marriage in the early teens creates a sharp disjunction and developmental task for many girls, with motherhood crucial to establishing a young woman's status and identity. Men's development of masculinity, which began with circumcision, may not be fully completed until they become fathers. Men generally find a wider field for fashioning identities than do women, via their honorable deeds and "performance of manhood" in the larger kin-group and community. Religious practice, often associated with saints and/or "Sufi" brotherhoods, and genres of popular poetry appear to provide both men and women with opportunities for personalizing their identities, and perhaps for psychological individuation.

In modernizing milieus, schooling often creates disjunctions with the family-based honor-modesty system, which some observers suggest is being transformed into an achievement orientation driven by familial attachments and honor—and supported by an achievement-oriented, "Muslim ethic" piety. Nearly all researchers report that the saturation of MENA societies with Western values and life-styles fosters the development of contradictory motives and self-representations, which most see as causing inner strife and subverting the formation of coherent identities. I suggest, however, that chronic strife over identity may be due less to the existence of cultural dualities than to the inability of many young adults in conditions of underdevelopment to create *life structures* (based on educational success, occupations, and marriages) that can sustain the balances or syntheses they often successfully work out as their desired identities.[4]

Levels and Life-Spans

The development of each of these three levels corresponds to major transitions in bodily maturation, cognitive ability, and social roles. Within any society, some of these transitions typically come to take the form of culturally patterned discontinuities, which present growing individuals with culturally specific developmental tasks. In traditional MENA milieus, these appear to occur at weaning, circumcision (mainly for boys), the shift from maternal to paternal authority, and early teen marriage (mainly for girls). These discontinuities may be decreasing in modernizing milieus, while others are emerging, especially between (1) the honor-modesty system learned in families and local communities and the achievement orientation learned in schools, and (2) the "externalizing" styles of emotional self-management learned in childhood and the scientific worldview learned in schools that rejects "superstitious" belief in *jinn* spirits and other invisible forces. Some scholars also see a discontinuity between the interdependent loyalties typically developed in childhood and individualist orientations fostered by schools and careers. Most scholars, however, reject the simple notion that traditional MENA culture was "collectivist" and is under assault by modern "individualism." Ethnographies and my own life-history study of identity suggest that the widespread return to religion among youth, especially in "Muslimist ethic" forms that resemble the "Protestant ethic" Max Weber described in early modern Europe and Robert Bellah in Tokugawa-era Japan, may provide resolutions for these discontinuities.

Also according to the model, each level builds upon and transforms the earlier, but, especially where development entails discontinuities, earlier patterns also may remain "beneath" later ones, as latent but active influences in psychological functioning. As anthropologists have argued for many cultures, an early "feminine" sense of self may persist throughout the course of men's development of masculinity, motivating defensive antipathy to femininity and fostering misogynist gender ideologies. Similarly, psychological strivings regarded as "masculine" may persevere in latent form after their suppression in girls (at least in traditional milieus) and appear in disguised forms in spirit possession and perhaps in the bodily symptoms that ethnographers report many women seek to cure by visiting religious healers or saints. The cultural model of mid- and later-life development then may facilitate older men's reincorporation of supposedly "feminine" orientations and postmenopausal women's reincorporation of supposedly "masculine" orientations as part of a process of individuation. As suggested earlier, in modernizing milieus, the most important characteristics that may remain latent but active concern (1) externalizing styles of emotion management developed in infancy and early childhood that are not easily incorporated into the "scientific" identities many adolescents and young adults seek to fashion, and (2) sentiments and motives associated with honor-based social personae that may not be easily incorporated into achievement-oriented identities and enacted in modern bureaucratic organizations.

Finally, it is important to point out that, as in all cultures, development continues throughout adulthood, and at all three levels of personality organization. Identities may be more elaborately articulated or dramatically remade. Social personae may change as a person adapts his or her enactment of honor-modesty etiquettes to new family statuses or reputation-changing events, and as his or her style of religious devotion shifts. As discussed in chapter 3, the imperatives of honor-modesty and Islam often can conflict, and the task of balancing or synthesizing these may continue throughout the life-span. Even "deep" characteristics of the core self can be affected by changes in a person's basic bodily, emotional, and interpersonal conditions. And in addition to the blows or blessings of fate that may change personality at all levels, Islam appears to provide both men and women with important opportunities for mid- and late-life "individuation," which can take place even as they enact prescribed social roles in accordance with prevailing "collectivistic" values, and maintain familial interdependencies and "group selves" cultivated since infancy. At the same time, however, the economic underdevelopment, political tyranny, and violence that has profoundly affected many MENA societies during recent decades impose serious constraints on development and inflict stresses and traumas that can disorganize all three levels of personality. Analyses by a number of Arab social scientists suggest that in some MENA regions these have been so acute and chronic as to have traumatizing effects, forcing individuals to make regressive and sometimes authoritarian adaptations to insecure, threatening, humiliating conditions.

These culturally patterned continuities and discontinuities influence development through the life-span in ways distinctive of the MENA "culture area." They certainly influence the *likelihood* that a person will have some experiences (for example, one to two years of "on-demand" breast-feeding), and they define the meanings these experiences typically take on (for example, maternal compassion that anchors a bond of reciprocal protection and indebtedness). But the patterns by no means give every person similar developmental experiences, or even guide them along parallel developmental pathways. As my own life-history research abundantly shows, the life-course of every individual is marked by deviations from culturally expected paths and by unexpected events. A few lives followed cultural models fairly closely, but many did not. One man had been sent to stay with relatives after weaning to "forget his mother's milk," and then for reasons he never understood, was left to be raised by them. As a young adult he did not feel strongly attached to either his biological or foster mother. Another's father had been too old and ill to impose his authority, so his mother stepped into that role, for which he still bore her some resentment. One woman's seriously disturbed mother had repeatedly abused her, and her father played a comforting and nurturing role, even supporting her ambition to have a career and live a Westernized life-style against her mother's insistence she prepare herself for marriage and a life of motherhood and housework.

In addition, all of an individual's formative experiences are shaped by his or her idiosyncratic temperament. Where one young man I interviewed clearly had fashioned an honor-modesty-based social persona to sustain familial attachments against deeper (for example, core self) anxieties about abandonment, another had tailored a social persona around nearly identical principles of honor and modesty in order to acquire a sense of prowess and defend against deeper anxieties about weakness and injury. One man, fueled by a misanthropic rage he attributed to his mother's death and his father's neglect, pursued the "daring deeds" and "tough guy" components of the honor-modesty system into a period of delinquency that destroyed his once bright prospects. It took a religious reconversion to bring him back to his family responsibilities. This kind of individual variation in temperaments and deviations from expected pathways guarantees that even the most robust cultural patterns do not yield shared personality types.

The anthropologist Kevin Dwyer's interviews with a southern Moroccan farmer named *fkir* Mohammed illustrate some of the ways individuals may struggle both to achieve and to resist their culture's ideals. In his sixties when Dwyer recorded their conversations, the *fkir* was a successful farmer, head of an extended household, a leader of his community, a devout member of the Tijanniya "Sufi" brotherhood (hence his title *fkir*, "the poor one"), and in every respect a cultural exemplar. Yet it hadn't always been that way.

His father died when he was a child, and he repeatedly rejected his mother's attempts to control him: "My mother would just tell me, 'Go there,' or 'Do this,' or 'Do that.' And I couldn't tolerate that at all, that she would direct me. . . . So I did what I wanted, myself."[5] When he reached "the age of fasting" (puberty) he began to have "wayward thoughts" and waste time "running around": "I began to think only . . . that I be really good-looking, better than everyone else; and tougher than everyone else; and a bigger operator than everyone else."[6]

Though he casts his "wild" adolescence as lying far in his past, he recalls it as if it were yesterday. He fell in love with a disreputable young woman who probably worked as a prostitute in the nearest town, and in desperation to have him be not so "distracted," his family agreed to their marriage. Three years later, however, he divorced her. He first offered Dwyer a stereotypic explanation: "Well, a marriage without good roots is no good. You know, our acquaintance wasn't made in the right way, it was made in the street. We got to know each other in the wrong way."[7] But then it became clear that the real reason was that she bore no children, and his family became increasingly angry with her. "She understood that because there were no children, people would be disrespectful toward her," he explained, so "if the commotion was going to continue, then I had to take her back. If it had quieted down, I wouldn't have taken her away." Then the *fkir* spoke of her with fondness:

> We had been together for three years, she and I. And I found her good, she had taken root in me. She didn't hold herself back from me. . . . For a time I was looking for a reason to let her go, for some defect in her, but I couldn't find one. She was fine. . . . [Perhaps she had put a spell on you?] . . . The most powerful spell is the one that works on your will. . . . We were entangled, tied together.[8]

After they divorced the *fkir* went into a three-year period of angry withdrawal. "After that divorce, it was exile!" he says, "I was in anger. For two years, I couldn't stand talking to anyone. . . . I was like an animal. I didn't want people, no one at all. No one at all." Finally he decided to take up his responsibilities, and within a year accepted an arranged marriage that soon yielded children:

> All that noise, all that waste, that wild life. I need, for myself, to become humble, to make do with what is here. And to marry someone humble. That is how I saw things then. . . . [I wanted a woman] of a small mind, without the build or the style of a city woman. You know the type. She should be a country woman and humble like us. . . . And I said to myself, "This way, I'll be in peace."[9]

He joined the Tijanniya brotherhood at the same time.

Throughout the series of interviews, the *fkir* appears as a man who has run his household with dedication, generosity, and firmness but relatively little emotional involvement. He appears to have developed his richest emotional bonds with his religious brothers, his Tijanniya sheikh (teacher), and the Prophet. "Always my mind is focused on my sheikh," he tells Dwyer: "We say, you know, that there are three benedictions: There is that of God, there is that of your parents, there is that of your sheikh."[10] He had listened to the Tijanniya litany as a child when his father and uncle chanted it with the village brothers, but he paid it little attention until he was nearly forty: "Even though I heard it when I was young, I had no interest in it, because I saw no purpose to it. Then, when I reached a certain age, I had to [learn it]. . . . We say that it was written, inscribed, in early times. Inscribed, written. What the Lord inscribes for you comes to appear."[11]

Forced out of the cultural pattern by his father's death, the *fkir* struck out to live a life different from the culturally prescribed one he now so exemplifies. His family abandoned the ideals of honor to accept his marriage-for-love to a woman he met "in the street," but then her infertility doomed them. Several years of sullen withdrawal (perhaps clinical depression) followed, until he decided to become "humble," accept an arranged marriage, step into his patriarch role, and shift his emotional life to the Tijanniya. "What the Lord inscribes for you comes to appear"—Jung saw reconversion to the religion of one's youth as a common developmental pattern, and termed it *apococastasis*: a sudden transformation that restores an earlier structure. Yet the *fkir*'s descriptions of his relationships within the Tijanniya suggest it also provides a rich venue for *individuation*, even as he subordinates his life to his family and acts as an embodiment and upholder of cultural tradition.

Cultural psychologists often err in the power they accord culture to recruit the allegiance of individuals to its prevailing values, ideals, and norms. Individuals repeatedly fail to become what the "Generalized Other" demands of them, and equally often they resist becoming it. None of the young Moroccans I interviewed had easily assimilated and lived out prevailing cultural models, from Mohammed, the well-bred and devout son of the village imam who as a teen turned into a "wild/rapid" fighting, drinking delinquent, to Rachida, the arch-defender of cultural tradition who violently fought off her parents' attempts to marry her in order to stay in school and have her own career. Unlike the rules of grammar, cultural patterns are not simply learned and automatically followed; they are powerful because they are enforced by people who can make life miserable for those who resist or deviate.

The texture of life and drama of development in MENA societies—as in all societies—derives from individuals' struggle to acquire and resist the patterns of their culture. An array of forces impels individual lives away from the prevailing patterns and then back toward them, provoking them to overshoot the mark and then to correct course, to resist conformity and then to crave what has been "inscribed." By improving overall living conditions and health, modernization has greatly reduced the disruptions traditionally wrought by illnesses, deaths, and the forces of nature. But underdevelopment and "Westernization" have created new disruptions, so that psychological development now often becomes embroiled in religious and political strife. Economic growth and democratization would enable individuals' struggles for development to be carried on in cooler conditions, where youths' goal of "modernizing within tradition" might be more readily and less violently achieved.

Afterword
A Research Agenda

It is not an outsider's place to prescribe a research agenda for MENA or for any other culture area. But at the completion of a review like this, it may be appropriate to participate in the discussion, especially by reporting what MENA psychologists are writing about their priorities. In that spirit, I offer three sorts of observations, as follows, on:

1. Some of the crucial research questions that appear in the literature I have reviewed
2. Recent lines of research in cultural psychology that might be carried out in MENA societies
3. The range of approaches being taken by MENA psychologists to create indigenous psychological theories

I will focus on culture-specific influences on development, as I have throughout the book, and not on the entire field of psychology. I again urge the reader to see Ahmed and Geilen's *Psychology in the Arab World* and Ihsan Al-Issa's *Al-Junun: Mental Illness in the Islamic World* for reviews of fields I have not covered.

I have shown that there is a rich literature on psychological development in MENA societies, most of it by MENA scholars writing in Arabic or English, and some in French. Many of the studies are qualitative in nature, written by anthropologists, sociologists, and psychotherapists, and in some cases by historians, political scientists, and literary critics. Data from the available quantitative studies generally support the patterns described in the qualitative writings, though the numbers sometimes require the picture to be revised (as was shown, for example, with regard to the duration of breast-feeding and mothers' use of physical punishment). "Verifying" these patterns with more sophisticated field observation and quantitative methods will continue to be an important priority.

Developmental Periods ❀

The studies reviewed in the previous chapters suggest several research priorities in each developmental period.

Infancy

First, in light of the debate over whether "symbiotic" infant care culminating in abrupt weaning undermines individuation or supports interdependent loyalties and builds resilience to childhood stresses, the nature of attachment and separation in traditional milieus deserves a good deal of research attention. Second, while available data make it clear that a transition is underway from *pediatric* toward *pedagogic* models of infant care, it is not clear whether a Western-style pedagogic model is emerging or a distinctive MENA style that might, as Kagitcibasi suggests, provide the foundation for a balance of autonomy and interdependence that Western societies seem to lack. Third, little appears to be known at the present time about infant-care practices among the growing numbers of urban poor, who may lack the social resources to either continue traditional pedagogic styles or adopt modern pedagogic ones.

Early Childhood

Many ethnographers report that the years from age two to five appear to be especially difficult, at least in traditional milieus, where many recently weaned toddlers experience a significant diminution in maternal caretaking—often described as a *dethronement*—along with increased exposure to less sanitary conditions and foods. In addition to the discontinuity that comes with weaning, a number of observers note that children appear to develop styles of *assertive dependency* as they strive to evoke caretaking from their mothers and from extended family members. These styles of assertive dependence appear to develop into components of the interdependent attachments said to characterize MENA families. This period therefore deserves research attention from perspectives of both physical health and psychological development.

This also tends to be a period in which children—at least in traditional and poor urban milieus—endure often unrelieved *physical discomforts* caused by illnesses, injuries, and environmental conditions, the effects of which are poorly understood by Western psychologists. Research on parents' responses to these discomforts, and on the short- and long-term consequences for children, could significantly contribute to psychological understanding of the conditions still faced by a majority of the world's children. Finally, given its cultural importance, it is perhaps surprising that the circumcision of boys and "female genital cutting" (where it is practiced) have rarely been studied. This would appear to be a critical topic for understanding personality development in general, and gender development in particular.

Late Childhood

There are still traditional rural and urban sectors in many MENA societies in which children receive little or no formal schooling and spend late childhood learning agricultural or craft skills by working alongside adults and older children. These provide rapidly vanishing opportunities to study *apprenticeship learning*, which some developmental psychologists believe has positive features lacking in school-based formal instruction. Little also is known about the extent to which schoolchildren participate in apprenticeship learning during the hours when they are not at school, and to what extent this enhances or detracts from school achievement.

A second issue concerns the extent to which attaining mastery of the etiquettes associated with the honor-modesty system and with Islam facilitate the coalescing of relatively independent *social selves*—the "Me" poles of the self that G. H. Mead describes as arising from seeing one's self from the perspective of the social Generalized Other. Ethnographers suggest that the internalization of these value systems (and associated self-care practices and self-presentational styles) deeply shapes psychological functioning, giving psychologists a number of strong hypotheses to investigate about the formation of culturally distinctive sentiments and motives.

And in light of the ongoing political struggles in many MENA societies, the most urgent priority concerns the nature and consequences of *patriarchal* or *authoritarian* parenting styles. Western norms are probably not directly applicable to MENA families, and the studies reviewed here provide a foundation for reconceptualizing forms of familial authority and authoritarianism that are distinctive to MENA cultures.

Adolescence

Many scholars suggest that it is adolescents who are most intensely caught in the crucible of social change. At a time when bodily, emotional, and social role changes destabilize childhood personality organizations, MENA youth also find themselves moving between "traditional" and "modern" institutions that offer contradictory worldviews and values—often in conditions of uncertainty about gaining any adult status. Perhaps the most critical issue raised by these writings concerns the fate of traditional family bonds. While many researchers see widespread family strife and psychological dis-organization, others see family loyalties as sustaining forms of interdependence or "connectivity" that Western societies have lost. If infant and child care lay a foundation for this interdependence, adolescence appears as the period in which familial bonds become especially important (and perhaps most strained) in the face of the fragmenting forces of "modernization" and "underdevelopment." Adolescents' reactions to these circumstances are now a high research priority, and should continue to be so. A closely related issue—the formation of family-based forms of achievement motivation, perhaps forged from a reinterpretation of the honor-modesty system—deserves the kind of research attention it has received in Asian cultures.

Nearly all researchers describe romantic relationships during adolescence as charged with anxiety and suspicion; especially in light of heated public debates about "re-segregating" the sexes, this calls for more intensive study. Dramatic differences among MENA nations in gender segregation would appear to provide a kind of natural laboratory for comparative studies.

Identity

Nearly all researchers emphasize that the process of identity formation takes place in cultural environments of intense dispute between indigenous and Western-oriented ways of life. Most also report that a great many individuals internalize and shift between contrasting indigenous and Western identities. Scholars differ, however, on the question of whether this multiplicity of identities reflects a loss of authenticity that causes *psychological fragmentation* or provides opportunities for synthesizing *bicultural* or *hybrid* identities and creating an authentic new cosmopolitan culture. There also can be little doubt that conditions prevailing in many MENA societies turn what Western psychologists tend to see as an acute "crisis" of identity into a chronic labor with but provisional resolutions. It may therefore be crucial for psychologists to distinguish between an initial formation of identity as described by Erikson and a different sort of "identity crisis" that arises when people cannot sustain their chosen identities by anchoring them in occupations, marriages, and communities—in what Levinson termed a *life structure*. Both life-narrative and quantitative methods are available to study identity formation and its outcomes, and could be adapted to investigate these crucial questions.

Mature Adulthood

At the present time, there appears to be growing cross-cultural interest in studying factors that facilitate the development of *generativity* in midlife and *wisdom* in later life. These concepts potentially provide a framework for research on adult development that could facilitate comparing MENA with other non-Western "developing" societies.[1] Especially as education and technology often shift power and status from seniors to youth, concepts of generativity and wisdom could prove useful in assessing the consequences of "modernization" for men and women in mid- and later life.

Finally, as the UN's 2002 *Arab Human Development Report* emphasizes, the overriding issue for the MENA region concerns the effects of economic and political underdevelopment on people's capabilities and sense of self-efficacy. Investigating these effects is not easy, especially where governments maintain surveillance and control over researchers, and neither Western psychology nor recent cross-cultural psychology has much to offer by way of concepts or methods. Here the writings of MENA scholars, perhaps combined with Amartya Sen's theory of capabilities and freedoms, could provide a starting point.

Cultural Psychology ❀

Unfortunately, few MENA psychologists have been able to participate in the last two decades' growth of cultural psychology as an international undertaking, based increasingly on the work of cross-cultural teams of researchers. As Abou el Nil points out (see his "Cross-Cultural Research" for a review and critique of studies by Arab psychologists), the obstacles are mainly economic: the costs of books, journals, international conferences, and travel for collaboration are too high for most universities, institutes, and scholars. The Sudanese psychologist Omar Khaleefa notes that the membership dues for the main international psychology associations are each equivalent to a month's salary, and that attending an international conference would cost him four years' salary.[2] As a result, several of the main topics currently under cross-cultural investigation have received little attention in MENA societies. The studies I have reviewed in this book suggest that three lines of research could facilitate the investigation of characteristics distinctive to MENA societies: research on individualism versus collectivism, on the cultural shaping of emotion, and on acculturation and biculturalism.

Individualism and Collectivism

Perhaps the single most studied topic by cultural psychologists over the last 20 years has been societal differences in "individualism" (or "egocentrism") versus "collectivism" (or "socio-centrism"). These have been studied as evident in values, styles of interpersonal relationship, and forms of self-conceptions (see chapter 9). Researchers now appear to have moved beyond the simple notion that cultures or selves can be ranked on a single "I"-versus-"C" dimension to study the cultural contexts that evoke "individualist" versus "collectivist" orientations. This work appears to be related to an important and controversial issue in MENA societies: while some scholars believe that traditional culture suppresses individuality and undermines individuation (Hijazi, Sharabi, Msefer, Dachmi), others argue that modernization undermines the solidarities on that healthy development and authentic identities depend (especially Al-e Ahmad). Kagitcibasi makes the intriguing suggestion that MENA and other "majority" cultures might be evolving toward a balance of individualism in the public sphere and "relationality" in the family sphere that has escaped the West. Japanese, Chinese, Korean, and Indian psychologists have developed a variety of concepts and methods for studying this issue, and these could help compare MENA with developing East and South Asian societies as well as with the West. In addition, research on this issue could enable psychologists to contribute to the public debates underway about the consequences of modernization and underdevelopment for family relationships and social values.

Reviewing anthropological studies of MENA culture, I suggested that internalization of the region's honor-modesty system and Islam form "social selves," coexisting in different form and balance in each person. Recent approaches to cultural values and self-cognition tend to view the self as composed of a *repertoire of schemata*, and these could be adapted to investigate the organization and activation of self-construals defined by honor-modesty schemata and of self-construals defined by religious belief and practice.

Culture and Emotion

One of the most active and fruitful areas of research during the last two decades has used new methods of assessing perceptions of facial expressions and other stimuli to investigate the universality versus cultural specificity of emotions. In general, these studies have found evidence both for the universality of a set of core emotions and for the role of culture in shaping the "display rules" that modify their expression and confer culturally distinctive meanings on them. In accordance with this model, I suggested that the region's two primary values systems (honor-modesty and Islam) probably shape universal emotions into culturally distinctive *sentiments*. David Matsumoto's *Unmasking Japan* shows how quantitative research can yield a rich profile of emotional expression in a single culture, revising and supplementing the qualitative accounts of ethnographers. These methods readily could be used in MENA cultures, similarly testing, modifying, and extending qualitative interpretations of sentiments, and perhaps providing new sources of data on regional, gender, and urban-rural differences. I also suggested that the honor-modesty system and Islam shape universal traits into culturally distinctive *motives* (see chapter 3), and I believe the logic of the cross-cultural research on emotion could be extended to study the basic motives constituting personality as well.

Acculturation

One weakness of my treatment of MENA societies as forming a "culture area" is that it underappreciates the flow of people, goods, and values across increasingly porous boundaries—especially those between MENA and Europe and MENA and South Asia. Because of the saturation of MENA cultures with Western values and life-styles, combined with the emigration of millions of "guest workers" to Europe, perhaps all members of MENA societies now live in conditions of *acculturation*: of acquiring a second or new culture. And because they are continually confronted by a Euro-American cultural hegemony, perhaps all MENA people now live to some extent as ethnic minorities in the globalized world.

In the last two decades, research on acculturation has shifted from linear models holding that immigrants/emigrants more or less successfully replace their original culture with a new one to models of "hybridity," in which the most successful individuals master and shift between "cultural frames." These models of acculturation converge with several developed from studies of minority ethnic identity that emphasize the development of dual identities. The recent theories take account of the considerable psychological stress associated with cultural dualism and minority ethnic status, especially for those who are targets of ethnic stereotyping and prejudice. But theorists also have moved toward viewing some forms of multicultural or dual identity as the healthiest and most empowering developmental outcome.

These newer models, developed from research on acculturating and ethnic minority groups around the globe, could provide innovative ways to study what so many researchers describe as the "contradiction" of values and lifestyles in MENA cultures. And they could help link the experiences of MENA peoples with those of other non-Western cultures. Both the acculturation and ethnic identity literatures take account of the alternating tendencies to reject one's original or minority culture and fully assimilate to the new or majority culture, and to reject the new or majority culture and fully embrace one's culture of origin or ethnic culture. Some models propose that these phases occur as developmental stages, leading toward synthetic forms of maturity. As pointed out in chapter 9, many MENA psychologists see the region's cultural dualities as destructive to identity development, but at least a few have raised the possibility that they could present opportunities for creative development as well. The newer "hybridity" and "shifting frames" models could facilitate studying the conditions that make cultural duality destructive and those that can make it creative.

These three lines of research could enhance the ability of psychologists to conduct more empirical investigations—both qualitative and quantitative—of the important interpretations proposed by ethnographers about MENA's cultural psychology. The quantitative methods used in these programs of research could provide an important complement to qualitative ethnographic and clinical studies, and perhaps help resolve some of the differences in interpretation. Further, the newer models have been devised by or with the active collaboration of non-Western psychologists, and they would enable researchers to view their findings in MENA in contrast not just with Western norms but also with other "majority" cultures, especially India, China, Japan, and Korea, where much of the last two decades' of cross-cultural research has been carried out.

Indigenous Psychology ⊛

At the present time, the highest priority for MENA psychologists has to be the creation of an *indigenous psychology*—or, perhaps more accurately, of *indigenous psychological theories*.[3] As in many developing societies, psychology was first established by importing Western theories and methods. But the Eurocentric biases of imported theories then set off a phase of "indigenization" in which psychologists began drawing psychological concepts from their own philosophical, literary, and "folk" traditions. This process appears to be most advanced in Japan, China, and India, and to have begun somewhat later in MENA. At the present time, however, many MENA psychologists linked in loose collaboration are contributing to the creation of indigenous theories, terminologies, and therapies.

Their efforts perhaps can be seen as falling on a continuum from more secular to more religious theories (though none entirely reject secular or religious concepts). At the secular end of this continuum, Mustafa Hijazi outlines an approach[4] that extends the approach he took in his *Al-takhaluf al-ijtima'i* (Societal Underdevelopment—see chapter 9). He criticizes Arab psychologists for uncritically adopting Western theories and for imitatively repeating the kinds of studies done in the West. His strategy would embrace much of Western psychology, including psychoanalytic theory, but with the recognition that many MENA social conditions and psychological processes differ from those studied in the West. He believes original research on these distinctive MENA characteristics will entail revising the Western theories and devising new indigenous concepts.

At the center of this continuum, psychologists including Mohammed Nablusi,[5] Fuad Abu Hateb,[6] and Ali Zayour[7] urge more cautious and selective borrowing of Western theories, combined with studies of the Arab-Muslim intellectual heritage to provide psychological concepts that can be used to create indigenous theories.[8] Nablusi spells out the dangers of adopting Western theories—and especially Western approaches to child-rearing and psychotherapy—that are not appropriate to MENA societies. At the same time, he argues that traditional forms of child-rearing and therapy need to be either established on a scientific foundation or transformed. He also calls attention to the problems associated with translating Western terms, pointing out that translators often differ in their choices of Arabic equivalents, and that some have kept the Western terms in Arabic transcription. He calls for the establishment of an Arab psychological institute where researchers could consider the appropriateness of popular versus scholarly Arabic terms versus transliterations of the Western-language terms, and reach consensus on appropriate translations.

At the more religious end of the continuum, two of the most influential writers are the psychologist Mohammed Najati and the physician Mustafa Mahmoud. Najati's *'Ilm al-nafs al-islami* (Islamic Psychology) criticizes the philosophical foundations of Western psychology and all of its major theories (behavioral, psychoanalytic, and humanist) for neglecting the spiritual character of the psyche. He draws on both Quranic passages and Muslim philosophers (such as al-Farabi, Ibn Sina, and al-Ghazali) to sketch a spiritual conception of the psyche and to specify the orthodox religious practices that foster emotional health.

Mustafa Mahmoud is a retired physician who gained a public reputation in the 1950s and 1960s by writing newspaper columns advocating a Western-style scientific worldview. Since becoming deeply religious, he has founded a popular mosque and hospital in Cairo, and written a series of books, including 'Ilm nafs qur'ani jadid (A New Quranic Psychology). While continuing to advocate scientific progress, he argues that psychology is inherently not scientific but a product of culture. Drawing almost exclusively on Quranic passages, Mahmoud sharply criticizes Freudian psychology and argues that humans achieve emotional health by resisting their desires and feeling guilt over their wayward thoughts and acts. He argues that people have an instinct of faith (rather than sex and aggression) and that religious practice strengthens the spiritual self in its struggle against desire. Religion recognizes that the spiritual self communicates with an invisible world, and recognizes that the intruding inner voices Freudian psychology treats as superego and id are actually of those of angels and the devil. Rather than seeking to cure distress by recovering the memories of traumas and repressed desires, religion encourages a person to continually "remember" God and live consciously in the "circle of light" rather than unconsciously in the "circle of darkness."

Mahmoud's descriptions of the faithful and mentally healthy person emphasize the qualities of calmness, compassion, modesty, patience, hard work, and perseverance. Most important, unlike the "materialist," the person of faith demonstrates self-control in restraint of immediate gratification, confident of reward in the afterlife. This appears to parallel the kind of achievement-oriented asceticism Weber saw as characterizing "Protestant ethic" piety, and this may give Mahmoud's Quranic psychology widespread appeal among those seeking to fashion modern achievement-oriented life-styles while resisting temptations to Western-style hedonism and conserving what they perceive to be their authentic traditions.

Strategies for indigenizing psychology thus range widely from more secular approaches that adopt much of Western psychology, but put it to different uses, to approaches that seek to synthesize some Western psychological concepts with theories derived from humanist Muslim philosophers, to approaches that largely reject Western theories and offer modernized styles of religious self-care based on Quranic passages. This resembles the array of strategies pursued in Japan, India, China, and other developing regions,[9] and holds out the dual promises of (1) contributing to scholarly psychology in MENA societies, as well as in the West, and (2) providing increasingly literate publics with a variety of modernized "popular" psychological theories.

NOTES

INTRODUCTION

1. See Hermans and Kempen, "Moving Cultures."
2. Jabar, "Dirasat muqarana fi al-shakhsiyya al-qatariyya wa al-'iraqiyya wa al-misriyya wa al-amrikiyya" (Comparative Study of Personality in Qatar, Iraq, Egypt, and America). See chapter 2 for a discussion of this study. His study of parental attitudes among Egyptians, Qataris, and Palestinians similarly found "more similarities than differences." Jabar, "Dirasat muqarana fi itijahat al-walidayn wa asalib al-tenshi'a al-ijtima'iyya li-thalath 'ayinat 'arabiyya" (Comparative Study of Parental Orientations and Style of Socialization in Three Arab Samples).
3. Ortner, "The Virgin and the State"; Kandiyoti, "Bargaining with Patirarchy" and "Islam and Patriarchy." See also Papanek and Minault, *Separate Worlds.*
4. Kandiyoti, "Islam and Patriarchy," p. 28.
5. See especially Abrahim, Yassin, and Qaziha, *Itijahat al-rai al-'am al-'arabi nahoua mas'alat al-wihda* (Orientation of Arab Attitudes Toward Unity). This survey of over 5,000 citizens in 10 countries from Morocco to Yemen found widespread popular belief that the region forms a single culture.
6. Ibid., pp. 63–64.
7. On a distributed model of culture, see Wallace, *Culture and Personality,* and Schwartz, "Where *Is* Culture?"
8. Patai, *Arab Mind* (2002), p. x.
9. Bouhdiba, *Sexuality in Islam.*
10. See Abou el Nil, "Cross-Cultural Research."
11. Psychology books published in Egypt and Morocco, for example, cost roughly $4 to $8, and are affordable on a professor's salary. Western books at $25 to $60 and journals costing hundreds of dollars are not. Most universities cannot afford the PSYCHINFO database routinely used by Western psychologists to locate studies in their area.
12. Khaleefa, "Predicament of Euro-American Psychology in a Non-Western Culture."
13. I have declined to cover a good number of publications, both qualitative and quantitative, because of doubts about their methodological soundness. This does

not mean, however that I can vouch for the methodological soundness of all the studies I do cover.

14. As will be discussed in detail in chapter 5, boys are circumcised in all MENA societies, but girls in only a few.

15. MENA psychologists have made great progress in developing the discipline in many countries, where students receive excellent training and researchers conduct high-quality work on topics central to societal development. They have done especially strong work to support the development of educational systems, studying the causes of school success and failure, the needs of handicapped and gifted children, and the causes of delinquency and drug abuse among teen-agers. They also have studied the effects of occupation and violence on Palestinian children, often in difficult circumstances.

16. Erikson, *Childhood and Society*; *Identity: Youth and Crisis*; and *Toys and Reasons*.

17. Whiting, *Culture and Human Development*; Whiting and Whiting, *Children of Six Cultures*; Whiting and Edwards, *Children of Different Worlds*.

18. LeVine and LeVine, "Nyansongo"; LeVine, *Culture, Behavior and Personality* and "Infant Environments in Psychoanalysis"; LeVine et al., *Child Care and Culture*.

19. McAdams, *Power, Intimacy, and the Life Story* and "What Do We Know When We Know a Person?"

20. Doi, *Anatomy of Dependence* and *Anatomy of Conformity*.

21. Obeysekere, *Medusa's Hair*; "Depression, Buddhism, and the Work of Culture in Sri Lanka"; and *Work of Culture*.

22. Kakar, *Inner World*; Nandy, *At the Edge of Psychology* and *Intimate Enemy*.

23. Herdt, *Guardians of the Flutes* and "Sambia Nosebleeding Rites and Male Proximity to Women."

24. I treat his second and third stages as "early childhood," and his seventh and eighth stages as "mature adulthood."

25. This follows the lead of LeVine, *Culture, Behavior and Personality,* and McAdams, "What Do We Know When We Know a Person?"

26. See Ahmed and Gielen, *Psychology in the Arab Countries*; Ahmed, "Psychology in the Arab Countries"; Abu Hateb, "*'Ilm al-nafs wa qadhaya al-mujtama'at al-mu'asira* (Psychology and Contemporary Social Issues).

27. Kagitcibasi, "Individual and Group Loyalties" and *Family and Human Development Across Cultures*; Joseph, "Theories and Dynamics of Gender, Self, and Identity in Arab Families" and "Brother-Sister Relationships."

28. See Matsumoto, *Handbook of Culture and Emotion.*

CHAPTER 1

1. See Jones, Kanoure, Kelley, Nisbett, Valins, and Weiner, *Attribution*; Tajfel, *Human Groups and Social Categories* and *Social identity and Intergroup Relations*; Pettigrew, "Ultimate Attribution Error."

2. See Adorno Frenkel-Brunswik, Levinson, and Sanford, *Authoritarian Personality*; Sniderman and Piazza, *The Scar of Race*; Altemeyer, *Authoritarian Specter*; Young-Breuhl, *The Anatomy of Prejudice.*

3. Moughrabi, "Arab Basic Personality."

4. Barakat, "Beyond the Always and the Never."

5. Yassin, *Al-shaksiyya al-'arbiyya* (Arab Personality).

6. Hijazi, "Al-shakhsiyya al-misriyya bayn al-silbiyya wa al-ijabiyya" (Egyptian Personality Between the Negative and the Positive).

7. 'Awdah, *Al-takayyuff wa al-maqawamah* (Adaptation and Resistance).

8. He especially focuses on how Saddiq 'Adim, in his influential *Al-naqed dhati b'ad al-hazima* (Self-Critique After the Defeat), made use of Hamid Ammar's analysis of the "Fahlaoui personality," *Fi bina' al-bashar* (On Building Human Character), to account for some glaring lapses in military preparedness and response. Hijazi (*Al-shaksiyya al-misriya bin es-silbia ou al-ijabiyyia*, Egyptian Personality Between the Negative and the Positive) and others subsequently criticized both Ammar's conception and 'Adim's misuse of it, but their points were not picked up by Western writers (Yassin, *Al-shaksiyya al-'arbiyya* [Arab Personality], pp. 225–240).

9. Quoted in Said, *Orientalism*, pp. 38–39.

10. Servier, *Islam and the Psychology of the Musulman*, pp. 2–3.

11. Ibid., p. 11.

12. Ibid., p. 13.

13. Ibid., p. 194.

14. Ibid., p. 271.

15. Lerner, *Passing of Traditional Society*, p. 45. Lerner here approvingly cites von Grunebaum on the nature of modernity's "challenge."

16. Lerner, "Nasser's Officialdom," p. 25.

17. Geertz, "From the Natives' Point of View."

18. Geertz, *Islam Observed*, p. 69.

19. Patai, *Arab Mind*, p. 163.

20. Quoted in Said, *Orientalism*, pp. 46–47.

21. Pryce-Jones, *Closed Circle*, p. 13.

22. Ibid., p. 51.

23. Said, *Orientalism*, p. 82.

24. Wharton, *In Morocco*, p. 79.

25. Ibid., p. 213.

26. Ibid., pp. 221–222.

27. These writers often voiced contempt for village- and city-dwelling Arabs, but Western colonists and travelers commonly imagined finding noble savages somewhere amid the savages.

28. A region in northern Afghanistan and northwest Pakistan.

29. Quoted in Tidrick, *Heart Beguiling Araby*, p. 72.

30. Ibid., p. 72.

31. Quoted in ibid., pp. 100–101.

32. Quoted in ibid., p.118.

33. Quoted in ibid., p. 124.

34. Quoted in ibid., p. 172.

35. Many more belonged to the Grange, Knights of Labor, insurance cooperatives, and other groups that also held initiations (Carnes, *Secret Ritual and Manhood in Victorian America*, p. 1).

36. Hodson, *Lawrence of Arabia and American Culture*, p. 33–35.

37. Ibid., p. 66.

38. Ibid., pp. 67–68.

39. Ibid., pp. 124–125.
40. Quoted in Kabbani, *Europe's Myths of Orient*, p. 21.
41. Ibid., p. 22.
42. Ibid., p. 48–49.
43. Quoted in Said, *Orientalism*, p. 182.
44. De Nerval, *Journey to the Orient*, p. 48.
45. Ibid., pp. 58–59.
46. Ibid., p. 77.
47. Said, *Orientalism*, p. 190.
48. Books like *The Lustful Turk* and *The Sultan's Reverie* are offered as "classics" by some publishers.
49. Alloula, *Colonial Harem*, p. 118.
50. Ibid., p. 122.
51. Coco, *Secrets of the Harem*, p. 10.
52. Ibid., p. 48.
53. Ibid., p. 126.
54. Ibid., p. 45.
55. Ibid., pp. 22, 95.
56. Ibid., p. 123.
57. Ibid., p. 112.
58. Ibid., p. 66.
59. Ibid., p. 162.
60. Ibid., p. 177.
61. Ibid., p. 185.
62. Simon, *Middle East in Crime Fiction*, p. vii.
63. Ibid., p. 7.
64. Also see Shaheen, *TV Arab* and *Arab and Muslim Stereotyping in American Popular Culture*.
65. Shaheen, *Arab and Muslim Stereotyping in American Popular Culture*, p. 14. In the 1980s, he writes, "ten features, including *The Ambassador* (1984), *The Delta Force* (1986), *Wanted Dead or Alive* (1987), and *Ministry of Vengeance* (1989), made the Palestinian Muslim Enemy Number One. The 1990s saw more of the same, including *Navy SEALs* (1990), *True Lies* (1994), and *Executive Decision* (1996)."
66. Shaheen, *Reel Bad Arabs*, p. 11.
67. Or to know the Indians or the Chinese or the Kenyans, for that matter.
68. Mackey, *Passion and Politics*, p. 13.
69. Ibid., p. 14.
70. Pryce-Jones, *Closed Circle*, p. 19.
71. Ibid., p. 33.
72. See Peters, "Proliferation of Segments in the Lineage of the Bedouin of Cyrenaica"; Sahlins, "Segmentary Lineage"; Galaty, "Models and Metaphors."
73. See, for example, Hart, *Dada 'Atta and His Forty Grandsons*.
74. Mackey, *Passion and Politics*, p. 23.
75. Ibid., pp. 26–27.
76. Ibid., p. 24.
77. Ibid., p. 29.
78. Pryce-Jones, *Closed Circle*, p. 35.

79. Ibid., p. 38.

80. Ibid., pp. 402–403.

81. Goldenweiser, "Loose Ends of a Theory on the Individual, Pattern, and Involution in Primitive Society," p. 99.

82. See Hofstede, *Culture's Consequences;* Markus and Kitiyama, "Culture and the Self"; Triandis, *Individualism and Collectivism;* Kagitcibasi, *Family and Human Development Across Cultures.*

83. Abu-Lughod, *Veiled Sentiments,* p. 88.

84. Philipchalk, *Invitation to Social Psychology.*

85. Herzfeld, "Honor and Shame" and *Poetics of Manhood.*

86. Patai, *Arab Mind,* p. 310.

87. Berger, *Arab World Today,* p. 175.

88. Hamady, *Temperament and Character of the Arabs,* p. 185.

89. Ibid., p. 188.

90. Ibid., p. 189.

91. Ibid., p. 185.

92. And, to their credit, the journalists Pryce-Jones and Mackey.

93. Fakhouri, *Kafr El-Elow,* p. 41.

94. Salt deposits in the area had been mined for the trans-Saharan gold trade for centuries, and it was nearly impossible to predict where the groundwater would be "sweet."

95. Faced with limited resources and corrupt officials, many Imeghrani entrepreneurs chose to invest elsewhere. One group of five families even formed a partnership and bought land in the Sous valley and trucked vegetables to Imeghrane's tribal markets each week.

96. Waterbury, *North for the Trade,* p. 96.

97. Patai, *Arab Mind,* pp. 279–280.

98. Hobbs, *Bedouin Life in the Egyptian Wilderness,* p. 54.

99. Pamuk, *Black Book,* p. 56.

100. Critchfield, *Shahhat,* p. xiii.

101. Ibid., p. xvi.

102. I will give citations to Critchfield's and Ayrout's books, but most of the quotations appear in Mitchell, "Invention and Reinvention of the Egyptian Peasant."

103. Ayrout, *Egyptian Peasant,* p. 150.

104. Mitchell, "Invention and Reinvention of the Egyptian Peasant," pp. 145–146.

105. Hobbes, *Bedouin Life in the Egyptian Wilderness.*

106. And modern Western societies don't much resemble the ideal of secular humanism. They remain profoundly religious and encompass all manner of back-to-tradition and authoritarian movements. Nazism and the Holocaust were as much modern creations as are science and doctrines of human rights.

107. See Hobsbawm and Ranger, *Invention of Tradition;* Anderson, *Imagined Communities.*

108. Laroui, *Crisis of the Arab Intellectual,* p. 42.

109. This is admittedly a complex issue, and a degree of collective responsibility for the acts of a few should not be cursorily dismissed—any more than America's widespread racism should be ignored as creating a cultural atmosphere in which a few deliver actual blows. The complexity also can be seen in the recently re-ignited debate over whether the Holocaust should be blamed on a totalitarian

party that usurped power or on deep-seated authoritarianism and anti-Semitism in the German populace.

110. Laquer, *Age of Terrorism.*
111. Pape, "Strategic Logic of Suicide Terrorism."
112. Clark, "Patterns in the Lives of ETA Members."
113. Post, "Terrorist Psycho-Logic," pp. 25–40.
114. Smith, *From Words to Action.*
115. Drummond, "From the Northwest Imperative to Global Jihad."
116. For an excellent summary of research on these processes, see Kelman and Hamilton, *Crimes of Obedience.*
117. McCauley points out that "every army aims to do what the terrorist group does. . . . Every army cuts trainees off from their previous lives so that the combat unit can become their family" ("Psychology of Terrorism," p. 3).
118. Nordland and Wilkinson, "Inside Terror, Inc."
119. Rubin, *Revolution Until Victory?* p. 19.
120. Lamb, *Arabs,* p. 89.
121. El-Sarraj has conducted several studies of Palestinian children. See Punamaeki, Qouta, and El-Sarraj, "Resiliency Factors Predicting Psychological Adjustment After Political Violence Among Palestinian Children," and Qouta, El-Sarraj, and Punamaeki, "Mental Flexibility as Resiliency Factor Among Children Exposed to Political Violence." See also see El-Sarraj, "Wounds and Madness," and Bond, "Psychology of Conflict."
122. Fields, Elbedour, and Abu Hein, "Palestinian Suicide Bomber."
123. Pryszczynski, Solomon, and Greenberg, *In the Wake of 9/11,* p. 155, suggest that the *absence* of "an effectively functioning cultural system" has been an important root of "Islamic terrorism." Post, "Terrorist Psycho-Logic," pp. 28–31, reports that terrorists disproportionately come from social margins and fragmented families. Drummond, "From the Northwest Imperative to Global Jihad," p. 72, sees a kind of "double marginalization" in the histories of American and Middle Eastern terrorists.
124. Feldman, *Formations of Violence.*
125. Hage, "Comes a Time We Are All Enthusiasm."
126. Peteet, "Male Gender and Rituals of Resistance in the Palestinian Intifada," pp. 108–109.
127. Hage, "Comes a Time We Are All Enthusiasm," p. 77.
128. Ibid., p. 79.
129. Barak, "Palestinians Oppose Suicide Missions by Children."
130. Ibid., p. 78.
131. Ibid., pp. 80–83. Hage's analysis parallels that of the psychiatrist James Gilligan, who argues that all acts of personal violence—which excludes "official" and "instrumental" violence—represent attempts to annul humiliation. See Gilligan, *Violence.*
132. See Taussig, *Shamanism, Colonialism, and the Wild Man.*
133. After studying Shii suicide attacks, Ariel Merari concludes that "culture in general and religion in particular seem to be relatively unimportant in the phenomenon of terrorist suicide" ("Readiness to Kill and Die," p. 206).
134. Richards and Waterbury, *Political Economy of the Middle East,* pp. 64–65.
135. Al-Khalil, *Republic of Fear,* p. 40.

136. Zaid, "Al-islam wa tanaqudhat al-hadatha" (Islam and the Contradictions of Modernity), pp. 41–74.
137. Sharabi, *Neopatriarchy*, p. 22.
138. Ibid., p. 4.
139. Ibid., p. 7.
140. Quoted in ibid., p. 8.
141. Barakat, *Arab World*, p. 276.
142. United Nations Development Program, *Arab Human Development Report*, p. 2.
143. Ibid., executive summary, p. 1.
144. Ibid., pp. 274–275.
145. Ibid., p. 204.

CHAPTER 2

1. Hsu, *Under the Ancestors' Shadow*, p. 8.
2. Giddons, *Modernity and Self-Identity*, pp. 87–98.
3. Bourdieu, *Outline of a Theory of Practice*.
4. Ibid., p. 184.
5. Ibid.
6. Wolf, "Kinship, Friendship, and Patron-Client Relations in Complex Societies."
7. Ibid., p. 176.
8. Eickelman, *Middle East*, emphasizes this point.
9. Agriculture has been greatly expanded and mechanized in the most productive areas, but marginal regions—like in the Moroccan Imeghrane confederation we studied—continue to depend on subsistence agriculture and pastoralism practiced with essentially Neolithic techniques.
10. See Nelson, *Desert and the Sown*.
11. See Khazanov, *Nomads and the Outside World*.
12. Ibid.
13. Asad, "Beduin as a Military Force."
14. Lewis, *Nomads and Settlers in Syria and Jordan*.
15. Hart, *Aith Waryaghar of the Moroccan Rif*.
16. Sweet, "Camel Raiding of North Arabian Bedouin."
17. Meeker, *Literature and Violence in North Arabia*.
18. Ibid., pp. 8–9.
19. Ibid., p. 10 (emphasis added).
20. Rodinson, *Islam and Capitalism*.
21. Wolf, "Social Organization of Mecca and the Origins of Islam."
22. Ibn Khaldun, *Moqqademah*, p. 93.
23. Ibid., p. 94.
24. Ibid., pp. 105–106.
25. Goody, *Oriental, the Ancient, and the Primitive*.
26. Ibid., p. 484.
27. Boserup, *Women's Role in Economic Development*.
28. Bridewealth payments typically provide a fund that can be used to obtain an additional wife or a wife for a man's son, and so tend to circulate in a direction counter to the movement of women.
29. Goody, *The Oriental, the Ancient, and the Primitive*.

30. Ortner, "The Virgin and the State," p. 25.
31. Kandiyoti, "Islam and Patriarchy," pp. 31 and 27.
32. A society need not be *either* patrilineal or matrilineal. Many pass some properties, rights, and duties along the male line and other properties, rights, and duties along the female line—and so mix patrilineal and matrilineal principles.
33. The most prominent exception are the Saharan Tuareg, who, while strongly patriarchal, have a predominantly matrilineal kinship system and combine matrilocal and patrilocal residence in complex ways. See Nicolaisen, *Ecology and Culture of the Pastoral Tuareg.*
34. It is important to recognize that a lineal kinship system (as opposed to a kindred) need not be entirely patri- or matrilineal. Some relationships in a predominantly patrilineal society may be traced along the matriline, and some rights or goods inherited from mothers.
35. See especially Bouhdiba, *Sexuality in Islam,* and Mernissi, *Beyond the Veil,* discussed in chapter 4.
36. Bourdieu, *Outline of a Theory of Practice.*
37. Levi-Strauss, *Elementary Structures of Kinship.*
38. Barth, *Nomads of South Persia,* p. 41.
39. Cohen, *Arab Border Villages in Israel,* pp. 109–110.
40. Sharabi, *Neopatriarchy,* p. 245.
41. Levi-Strauss, *Elementary Structures of Kinship.*
42. Murphy and Kasdan, "Structure of Parallel Cousin Marriage."
43. Barth, *Nomads of South Persia.*
44. Holy, *Kinship, Honour, and Solidarity,* p. 113.
45. Ibid., p. 121.
46. Ibid., p. 126.
47. Tillion, *Republic of Cousins.*
48. She recognizes, of course, that not every society cleanly fits these types.
49. Tillion, *Republic of Cousins,* p. 61.
50. Schneider, "Of Vigilance and Virgins," pp. 1, 2.
51. Ibid., p. 11.
52. Ibid., p. 11.
53. Ibid., pp. 21–22.
54. Bourdieu, "Sentiment of Honour in Kabyle Society."
55. Herzfeld, *Poetics of Manhood.*
56. See chapter 6 of Eickelman, *Middle East,* for an excellent account of the history of this notion in anthropology.
57. Evans-Pritchard, *Nuer.* See also Smith, "Segmentary Lineage Systems."
58. See Eickelman, *Middle East,* or Lindholm, *Islamic Middle East,* for diagrams and explanations of segmentary theory.
59. Peters, "Proliferation of Segments in the Lineage of the Bedouin of Cyrenaica."
60. Marx, "Tribe as a Unit of Subsistence."
61. Ibn Khaldun, *Moqqademah,* p. 99.
62. Sahlins, "Segmentary Lineage," p. 323.
63. Hijazi, "'Ilm al-nafs fi al-'alam al-'arabi" (Psychology in the Arab World).
64. Martinez, *Algerian Civil War 1990–1998*; Kouaouci, "Transitions, chomage des jeunes, recul du marriage et terrorisme en Algeria."

65. In some regions, alliances ramify across tribal boundaries, so that, for example, half of the clans in each village will be allied with "alliance A" and half with "alliance B." See Montagne, *Les Berberes et le Makhzen dans le Sud au Maroc.*

66. See Hart, *Aith Waryaghar of the Moroccan Rif* and *Dada 'Atta and His Forty Grandsons.*

67. Geertz, "Meanings of Family Ties."

68. Ibid., p. 339.

69. Ibid., p. 327.

70. Ibid., pp. 340–341.

71. Ibid., p. 350.

72. Cohen, *Arab Border Villages in Israel* and "Politics of Marriage in Changing Middle Eastern Stratification Systems."

73. Ibid., pp. 315–316.

74. Eickelman, *Middle East,* pp. 178–179 (emphasis added).

75. There are regions, such as parts of Lebanon, where a feudal-like system developed, and in many areas, groups that have an under-caste status.

76. See especially Benedict, *Chrysanthemum and Sword,* Lebra, *Japanese Patterns of Behavior,* and Nakane, *Japanese Society.*

77. Doi, *Anatomy of Dependence.*

78. Sharabi, *Neopatriarchy.*

79. Hammoudi, *Master and Disciple.*

80. Suad Joseph also provides an excellent account of how kinship terms and etiquettes are extended to encompass patron/client relations that provide security but keep people in bondage. Joseph, "Family as Security and Bondage."

81. Khuri, *Tents and Pyramids,* p. 11.

82. Ibid., pp. 11–12.

83. Ibid., p. 24.

84. Ibid., p. 27.

85. Ibid., p. 28.

86. Ibid., pp. 126–127.

87. Ibid., pp. 15, 132, 133.

88. Richards and Waterbury, *Political Economy of the Middle East,* p. 310.

89. Ibid.

90. Ibid., p. 311.

91. Ibid., p. 312.

92. Lindholm, *Islamic Middle East,* p. 259.

93. The samples were not large: 67 Qataris, 96 Iraqis, and 144 Egyptians.

94. Ibid., p. 493.

95. Richards and Waterbury, *Political Economy of the Middle East,* p. 48.

96. Ibid., p. 49.

97. Ibid., p. 64; United Nations Development Program, *Arab Human Development Report 2002,* p. 88.

98. United Nations Development Program, *Arab Human Development Report 2002,* p. 89.

99. Hauchler and Kennedy, *Global Trends,* p. 62.

100. United Nations Development Program, *Arab Human Development Report 2002,* p. 90.

101. Ibid., p. 158; Hauchler and Kennedy, *Global Trends*, pp. 126–134.

102. Hauchler and Kennedy, *Global Trends*, pp. 126–134.

103. Richards and Waterbury, *Political Economy of the Middle East*, p. 68.

104. Ibid., pp. 252–253.

105. Ibrahim, "Urbanization in the Arab World," p. 137.

106. Ibid., p. 105; United Nations Development Program, *Arab Human Development Report 2002*, p. 38.

107. Ibid., p. 39.

108. Ibid., p. 40.

109. Richards and Waterbury, *Political Economy of the Middle East*, p. 114. All percentages are rounded.

110. United Nations Development Program, *Arab Human Development Report 2002*, p. 52.

111. Richards and Waterbury, *Political Economy of the Middle East*, pp. 141–142.

112. Ibid., p. 139.

113. United Nations Development Program, *Arab Human Development Report 2002*, reports a general decline in the ability of governments to rely on oil revenues or foreign aid to provide public sector employment. This may lead on the one hand to greater government reliance on taxes and a greater voice in government by taxpayers and on the other hand to the enlarging of "informal" economic sectors, which tend to operate by more traditional and conservative principles.

114. Ibid., p. 374.

115. Mostyn and Hourani, *Cambridge Encyclopedia of the Middle East and North Africa*, p. 116.

116. Ibid., p. 363, 372. United Nations Development Program, *Arab Human Development Report 2002*, pp. 65–72.

117. Hauchler and Kennedy, *Global Trends*, pp. 153, 157.

118. Guessous, "Al-tatawurat al-'a'iliyya wa al-tenshaia al-ijtima'iyya li-al-tifl al-maghribi" (Family Changes and Socialization of the Moroccan Child).

119. Haddiya, *Al-tanshi'a al-ijtima'iyya wa al-hawiyya* (Socialization and Identity).

120. Haddiya, *Processus de la Socialisation en Milieu Urbain au Maroc*.

121. Quoted in Burgat and Dowell, *Islamic Movement in North Africa*, p. 45.

122. Fanon, *Wretched of the Earth*, pp. 149–152.

123. Ibid., p. 169.

124. Hauchler and Kennedy, *Global Trends*, pp. 94–103.

125. United Nations Development Program, *Arab Human Development Report 2002*, especially pp. 2–5.

126. Lila, *Al-shebab al-'arbi* (Arab Youth).

127. Goethe, *Wilhelm Meister's Years of Apprenticeship*, pp. 347, 474.

128. Ibid., p. 427.

CHAPTER 3

1. Patai, *Arab Mind*, is one of the most objectionably reductionistic and ethnocentric works on Arab "national character." It nonetheless advances some useful formulations, including, I believe, this one.

2. Dumont, *Homo Hierarchicus*.

3. Many, like Michael Meeker, believe that nomadic pastoralism was the key catalyst for this system of values, at least in MENA. Meeker, *Literature and Violence in North Arabia*, pp. 10–11.
4. Peristiany, *Honor and Shame*, pp. 10, 13.
5. Ibid., p. 14. See also Peristiany, "Honour and Shame in a Cypriot Highland Village."
6. Plato, *Republic*, 581b.
7. Ibid., 440d.
8. See the story of Leontius, *Republic*, 439e.
9. Ibid., 375a.
10. Ibid., 375b.
11. Ibid., 586d.
12. Richard Nisbett's research on the honor code of the American South is an important exception. See his 1996 *Culture of Honor*.
13. Peristiany, *Honor and Shame*, pp. 11, 15.
14. Campbell, *Honour, Family, and Patronage*, pp. 268–271.
15. Abou Zeid, "Honour and Shame Among the Bedouins of Egypt."
16. Ibid., p. 246.
17. Ibid., p. 253.
18. Ibid., p. 247.
19. Ibid.
20. Bourdieu, "The Sentiment of Honour in Kabyle Society," p. 197.
21. *Nif* literally means "nose."
22. Bourdieu, "The Sentiment of Honour in Kabyle Society," pp. 204, 208.
23. Ibid., pp. 216–217.
24. See his "The Kabyle House or The World Reversed."
25. Bourdieu, "The Sentiment of Honour in Kabyle Society," p. 220.
26. Ibid., p. 223.
27. Ibid., p. 224.
28. Ibid., pp. 231–232.
29. Bourdieu, *Outline of a Theory of Practice*.
30. Peristiany, *Honor and Shame*, p. 10.
31. Abou Zeid, "Honour and Shame Among the Bedouins of Egypt," p. 259. He goes on to insist that "the line does exist and society knows how to evaluate the same action in different contexts," but this is precisely what critics have questioned.
32. Pitt-Rivers, "Honour and Social Status," p. 45.
33. Ibid., p. 68.
34. Ibid., p. 43.
35. Ibid., p. 58.
36. Ibid., p. 72.
37. Peristiany, "Honour and Shame in a Cypriot Highland Village," p. 188.
38. Wolf, "The Social Organization of Mecca and the Origins of Islam."
39. Rodinson, *Mahomet*.
40. Campbell, "Honour and the Devil," p. 167.
41. Ibid., p. 167.
42. Ibid., p. 169.

43. Ibid., pp. 168–169.
44. Herzfeld, "Honor and Shame."
45. Bourdieu, "The Sentiment of Honour in Kabyle Society,"p. 193.
46. Herzfeld does not describe *egoismos* as "masculine assertiveness" but says it is associated "not only with the defence of household and village, but also with the assertiveness that goes with being a member of one of the larger agnatic lineages" (p. 346).
47. I have slightly abridged this table. See ibid., p. 348, for his exact formulation.
48. Herzfeld, *Poetics of Manhood*, p. 16.
49. Ibid., pp. 53–54
50. See Tajfel, *Human Groups and Social Categories.*
51. Abu-Lughod, *Veiled Sentiments*, pp. 87–88.
52. Ibid., p. 81–82.
53. Eickelman, *The Middle East*, p. 178.
54. Abu-Lughod, *Veiled Sentiments*, pp. 112–113.
55. Ibid., p. 79.
56. Ibid., p. 187.
57. Ibid., p. 234.
58. Ibid., p. 248.
59. Ibid., p. 250.
60. Ibid., p. 250.
61. Ibid., pp. 251–252.
62. Ibid. p. 256.
63. Ibid. p. 259.
64. Ibid.
65. See especially the social psychologist Zajonc, "Emotional Expression and Temperature Modulation."
66. See, for example, Izard, *Human Emotions*; Tomkins, "Affect as the Primary Motivational System"; Ekman, "Biological and Cultural Contributions to Body and Facial Movements in the Expression of Emotions." Also see chapters 7 through 15 of Lewis and Haviland, *Handbook of Emotion*, and Matsumoto, *Handbook of Culture and Emotion.*
67. Lutz, "Domain of Emotion Words on Ifaluk," p. 113. See also Harre, *Social Construction of Emotion*, especially Claire Armon-Jones, "Thesis of Constructionism."
68. Shweder, "Cultural Psychology of Emotion."
69. Ekman, "Biological and Cultural Contributions to Body and Facial Movements in the Expression of Emotions."
70. See Matsumoto, *Handbook of Culture and Emotion.*
71. See Obeyesekere, "Depression, Buddhism, and the Work of Culture in Sri Lanka."
72. LeVine, *Culture, Behavior, and Personality.* LeVine terms these levels "genotypic" and "phenotypic" by an *analogy* to the biological distinction between an organism's inherited characteristics and those that, under the influence of its environment, it actually displays. But he does not use "genotypic" literally to mean "inherited." To avoid confusion, I use the terms "core" and "identity." See the introduction to part II.
73. McAdams, "What Do We Know When We Know a Person?" p. 365. Level 3 consists of identity, as embedded in one's life-narrative.

74. McDougall, *An Outline of Psychology*, p. 418. A few other psychologists have used the term to refer to larger or more "molar" constellations of emotion and value—such as Pradines, "Feelings as Regulators," and Peters, "Education of the Emotions"—but students of emotion have preferred to focus on more "molecular" states. Henry Murray occasionally used the term "sentiment" in a similar manner to McDougall (Murray and Morgan, "Clinical Study of Sentiments," pp. 3–311) but mainly used the terms "need" and "motive" to refer to even broader constituents of personality.

75. Ibid.

76. Again, it is crucial to keep in mind that Middle Easterners experience an array of sentiments in addition to these, and that many situations may not evoke honor-related sentiments.

77. For summaries see Wiggins, *Five-Factor Model of Personality*, and Wiggins and Trapnell, "Personality Structure."

78. Each of these higher-order traits is held to be composed of several more specific traits.

79. See Murray, *Explorations in Personality*; Kluckhohn and Murray, *Personality in Nature, Society, and Culture*.

80. See Emmons, "Exploring the Relations Between Traits and Motives" and "Motives and Life Goals."

81. Winter, Stewart, and Duncan, "Traits and Motives," p. 238.

82. Aboulafia, *Mediating Self*.

83. This differs profoundly for men and women, not only because men must do it with *machismo* and women with modesty but because women must also do it by proving their fertility, by giving birth to children.

84. Quoted in von Grunebaum, *Muhammadan Festivals*, p. 12.

85. Brohi, "Spiritual Dimension of Prayer," p. 134.

86. Ibid., p. 58.

87. The Saudi government now collects, refrigerates, and distributes this food.

88. Von Grunebaum, *Muhammadan Festivals*, p. 45.

89. Quoted in ibid., p. 49.

90. Peters, *A Reader on Classical Islam*, p. 51.

91. Ibid., pp. 53–54.

92. Brohi, "Spiritual Dimension of Prayer," p. 132.

93. Nelson, *Art of Reciting the Quran*, p. 13.

94. See Nelson, *Art of Reciting the Quran*, pp. 89–100.

95. Ibid., p. 99.

96. Ibid., pp. 99–100.

97. Nasr, *Islamic Spirituality*, p. 64.

98. Schimmel, *And Muhammad Is His Messenger*, p. 4, 55.

99. Antoun, *Muslim Preacher in the Modern World*, pp. 118–119.

100. Ibid., p. 109.

101. Unlike Catholicism, Islam has no official mechanism for designating "sainthood."

102. Gilsenan, *Recognizing Islam*, p. 99.

103. Ibid., p. 105.

104. Ibid., pp. 99–100.

105. Ibid., p. 102.

106. Ibid., pp. 102–103.
107. Ali, trans., *Holy Quran*, p. 1220, 1222.
108. Crapanzano, *Hamadsha*, p. 23.
109. As a psychologist I must profess my skepticism about the reality of invisible beings. But I also want to emphasize that when supposedly modern Westerners turn inward to explain their anxieties in terms of intrapsychic or interpersonal conflicts, we are likely to come up with no less mythic interpretations. Indeed, "the unconscious" may be our term for a concept of an invisible mythic reality behind the world of appearances.
110. See especially Bouhdiba, *Sexuality in Islam*.
111. Gilsenan, *Recognizing Islam*, pp. 120, 123.
112. Mernissi, *Beyond the Veil*.

PART II INTRODUCTION
1. LeVine, *Culture, Behavior and Personality*, p. 116.
2. Stern, *Interpersonal World of the Infant*.
3. McAdams, "What Do We Know When We Know a Person?"
4. LeVine, *Culture, Behavior and Personality*, pp. 121–122.
5. Erikson, *Identity: Youth and Crisis*.
6. LeVine, *Culture, Behavior and Personality*, pp. 122–123.
7. Obeyesekere, *Work of Culture*.
8. As McAdams emphasizes it would be wrong to think of these levels as forming, "a tight hierarchy in which traits give rise to mores specific personal concerns, which ultimately coalesce to form a life story" ("What Do We Know When We Know a Person?" p. 386). Rather, each level forms as a new organization, which incorporates and transforms the previous.
9. This model also facilitates viewing the widening social contexts as shaping "zones of proximal development" in which interpersonal styles and forms of emotional expression are learned. See Vygotsky, *Mind in Society,* and Wertsch, *Vygotsky and the Social Formation of Mind*.
10. Whiting, "Environmental Constraints on Infant Care Practices."
11. Whiting, *Culture and Human Development;* Whiting and Whiting, *Children of Six Cultures;* and Whiting and Edwards, *Children of Different Worlds*.
12. Whiting, *Culture and Human Development*, p. 132.
13. Ibid., p. 133.
14. See Chodorow, *Reproduction of Mothering*.
15. See Herdt, "Sambia Nosebleeding Rites and Male Proximity to Women" and *Guardians of the Flutes*.
16. Gilmore, *Manhood in the Making*, p. 223.
17. See the map of cradle and sling practices in Whiting, "Environmental Constraints on Infant Care Practices," pp. 120–122.
18. Edgerton, *Individual in Cultural Adaptation*, p. 279.
19. Ibid., p. 275.
20. Ibid., p. 279.
21. Ibid, p. 280.
22. Ibid., p. 195.
23. Berry, Child, and Bacon, "Relation of Child Training to Subsistence Economy"; Munroe and Munroe, "Obedience Among Children in an East African Society."

24. Ibid., p. 176.
25. The term "transhumant" refers to pastoralists who move their herds through a relatively short-range series of pastures—often into mountain valleys during the summer and onto plains in the winter. They usually also have homes in villages, where other family members practice settled agriculture.
26. See Spooner, "Evil Eye in the Middle East"; Donaldson, "Evil Eye in Iran."
27. For ethnographic descriptions and a range of theories, see the articles collected in Maloney, *Evil Eye*, and Dundes, *Evil Eye*.
28. See for example, Roheim, "Evil Eye," and Kearney, "World-View Explanation of the Evil Eye."
29. Foster, "Cultural Responses to Expressions of Envy in Tzintzuntzan" and "Anatomy of Envy."
30. This contrasts with the swidden or "slash-and-burn" agriculture, pastoralism, and hunting-and-gathering foundation of most sub-Saharan African societies. These subsistence systems may not produce the surpluses that settled agriculture can, but they more readily expand or contract their resource base to changing labor supplies. Jack Goody has argued that settled agriculture historically gave rise to common marriage systems throughout "Eurasia" that contrast with those of Africa and other nonagricultural societies. Goody, *The Oriental, the Ancient, and the Primitive.*
31. Foster, "Anatomy of Envy," p. 168.
32. Ibid., pp. 168–169.
33. Roberts, "Belief in the Evil Eye in World Perspective."
34. Ibid., p. 250.
35. Ibid., p. 262.
36. Garrison and Arensberg, "Evil Eye: Envy or Risk of Seizure?"
37. Ibid., p. 290.
38. See Harfouche, "Evil Eye and Infant Health in Lebanon."
39. Hsu, "Kinship and Ways of Life," and "Passage to Understanding."
40. See Mernissi, *Beyond the Veil*; Msefer, *Sevrages et Interdependence*; Bouhdiba, *Sexuality in Islam*; Sharabi, *Neopatriarchy*; Joseph, "My Son/Myself, My Mother/Myself"; Dachmi, *De La Seduction Maternelle Negative*; Chamcham, "L'enfant marocain"; Chaouite, "L'enfant marocain."
41. See, for example, El Khayat-Bennai, *Le Monde Arabe au Feminin*, pp. 88–90.
42. See especially Bouhdiba, *Sexuality in Islam,* and Sharabi, *Neopatriarchy.*
43. See Joseph, "Brother-Sister Relationships."
44. LeVine, Dixon, LeVine, Richman, Leiderman, Keefer, and Brazelton, *Child Care and Culture,* p. 47.

CHAPTER 4
1. LeVine, Dixon, LeVine, Richman, Leiderman, Keefer, and Brazelton, *Child Care and Culture,* p. 248.
2. Ibid., pp. 249–250.
3. LeVine, Miller, and West, *Parental Behavior in Diverse Societies,* p. 7.
4. Ibid.
5. LeVine, Dixon, LeVine, Richman, Leiderman, Keefer, and Brazelton, *Child Care and Culture,* p. 249.
6. Ibid., p. 251.

7. Ibid., p. 212.
8. Ibid.
9. Ibid., p. 215.
10. Ibid., p. 216.
11. Richman, Miller, and Soloman, "Maternal Behavior to Infants in Five Cultures," p. 82.
12. LeVine, Dixon, LeVine, Richman, Leiderman, Keefer, and Brazelton, *Child Care and Culture*, discuss cultural models that rely on apprenticeship learning and emphasize obedience, but they do not use this terminology.
13. Ammar, *An Egyptian Village Growing Up*.
14. Dawood, trans., *Koran*.
15. Granqvist, *Birth and Childhood Among the Arabs*.
16. Delaney, *Seed and the Soil*.
17. Boddy, *Wombs and Alien Spirits*.
18. Friedl, *Children of Deh Koh*, pp. 30, 32–33.
19. Granqvist, *Birth and Childhood Among the Arabs*, pp. 36–37.
20. Ibid.
21. Ammar, *Growing Up in an Egyptian Village*, p. 88.
22. See Al Nawayseh, *Al-tifl fi al-hiyat al-sha'biyya al-urdunyya* (Child in Popular Life in Jordan), pp. 25–28.
23. Friedl, *Children of Deh Koh*, p. 36.
24. See Delaney, *Seed and the Soil*, pp. 59–64.
25. Friedl, *Children of Deh Koh*, p. 57. Omidsalar reports that an Iranian woman who dies in childbirth "is considered a martyr whose sins are all forgiven"; "Childbirth in Modern Persian Folklore," p. 406.
26. Ibid., p. 59.
27. Al Nawayseh, *Al-tifl fi al-hiyat al-sha'biyya al-urdunyya* (Child in Popular Life in Jordan), p. 30; Sa'idallah, "Dirasat anthrobologia muqarana li-anmat al-tanshi'a al-ijtima'iyya fi mujtama' mahali badawi wa mujtama' mahali rifi fi misr"(Comparative Anthropological Study of Socialization Patterns in Bedouin and Rural Societies in Egypt), pp. 192–193.
28. Ammar, *Growing Up in an Egyptian Village*, p. 91.
29. Ammar, *Egyptian Village Growing Up*, pp. 188–189.
30. Al Nawayseh, *Al-tofal fi al-hiyat al-sh'abia al-ardania* (Child in Popular Life in Jordan), and Shakri, "Al-tanshi'a al-ijtima'iyya" (Socialization), pp. 89–90.
31. Sa'idallah, "Dirasat anthrobologia muqarana li-anmat al-tanshi'a al-ijtama'iyya fi mujtama' mahali badawi wa mujtama' mahali rifi fi misr" (Comparative Anthropological Study of Socialization Patterns in Bedouin and Rural Societies in Egypt), p. 193.
32. Al-Sa'ti, "Asma' al-misriyyin wa al-taghir al-ijtima'i" (Egyptian Names and Social Change), p. 182.
33. Ammar, *Egyptian Village Growing Up*, p. 189.
34. This is reported throughout the Middle East, and by Cederblad for Arabs in Sudan. Cederblad, *Child Psychiatric Study on Sudanese Arab Children*, p. 52.
35. See Boddy, *Wombs and Alien Spirits*, pp. 249–250, Shakri, "Al-tanshi'a al-ijtima'iyya" (Socialization), pp. 87–88, Friedl, *Children of Deh Koh*, p. 34, and Delaney, *Seed and the Soil*.
36. The dangers this "nafasa" period is reported by Shakri for Egypt, by Boddy for

the Sudan, and Delaney for Turkey—the latter noting that women specifically associate the danger with the "open womb."

37. Granqvist, *Birth and Childhood Among the Arabs*, p. 104; Delaney, *Seed and the Soil*, p. 68.
38. Ammar, *Egyptian Village Growing Up*, p. 197.
39. Whiting, *Culture and Human Development*.
40. LeVine et al., *Child Care and Culture*.
41. Swaddling for periods during the first months is now recommended by many American pediatricians.
42. Prothro, *Child Rearing in Lebanon*, p. 57.
43. Granqvist, *Birth and Childhood Among the Arabs*, p. 100.
44. Shakri, "Al-tanshi'a al-ijtima'iyya" (Socialization).
45. Davis, *Patience and Power*, pp. 149–151.
46. Williams, *Youth of Haouch el Harimi*, p. 26.
47. Ibid., p. 27.
48. Gorer and Rickman, *People of Great Russia*, pp. 128–129.
49. Ammar, *Growing Up in an Egyptian Village*, p. 102.
50. Granqvist, *Birth and Childhood Among the Arabs*, p. 107.
51. Cederblad, *Child Psychiatric Study on Sudanese Arab Children*, p. 55.
52. Williams, *Youth of Haouch el Harimi*, pp. 29, 37.
53. Davis, *Patience and Power*, p. 149.
54. Friedl, *Children of Deh Koh*, p. 108.
55. Al Nawayseh, *Al-tofal fi al-hiyat al-sh'abia al-ardania* (Child in Popular Life in Jordan), p. 39.
56. Dachmi, *De La Seduction Maternelle Negative*, pp. 45–49; Qabaj, *Al-tifl al-maghribi*, (The Moroccan Child), p. 85.
57. Williams, *Youth of Haouch el Harimi*, p. 30.
58. Sa'idallah, "Dirasat anthrobologia muqarana li-anmat al-tanshi'a al-ijtama'iyya fi mujtama' mahali badawi wa mujtama' mahali rifi fi misr" (Comparative Anthropological Study of Socialization Patterns in Bedouin and Rural Societies in Egypt), p. 195.
59. Shakri, "Al-tanshi'a al-ijtima'iyya" (Socialization), p. 98.
60. Ammar, *Egyptian Village Growing Up*, p. 251.
61. Badri, *Child-Rearing Practices in the Sudan*, pp. 72–74 and 205.
62. Akin, Bilsborrow, Guilkey, and Popkin, "Breastfeeding Patterns and Determinants in the Near East."
63. Shakri, "Al-tanshi'a al-ijtima'iyya" (Socialization), pp. 94–106.
64. Ibid., p. 100.
65. Ammar, *An Egyptian Village Growing Up*, p. 252.
66. Shakri, "Al-tanshi'a al-ijtima'iyya" (Socialization), p. 73.
67. Granqvist, *Birth and Childhood Among the Arabs*.
68. Ammar, *Growing Up in an Egyptian Village*, p. 99.
69. Boddy, *Wombs and Alien Spirits*.
70. Ammar,*Growing Up in an Egyptian Village*.
71. Shakri, "Al-tanshi'a al-ijtima'iyya" (Socialization), pp. 91–92; Dachmi, *De La Seduction Maternelle Negative*, pp. 35–48.
72. Cederblad, *A Child Psychiatric Study on Sudanese Arab Children*, p. 55.
73. Egyptian researchers confirm all of these as components of the cultural model,

at least in traditional milieus (see Shakri, "Al-tanshi'a al-ijtima'iyya" [Socialization]), as do North African researchers (see Dachmi, *De La Seduction Maternelle Negative*, Qabaj, "Al-tifl al-maghribi" [The Moroccan Child], Bouhdiba, *Sexuality in Islam*, Lacoste-Dujardin, *Des Meres Contre les Femmes*, Msefer, *Sevrages et Interdependence*). However, a surprisingly high percentage of Sudanese mothers told Badri they often leave their infants to cry during the day (one-third of urban mothers; two-thirds of rural ones), though all said they comfort and/or nurse them at night. It is not clear whether mothers answered about infants or toddlers, but their responses prompt caution about the universality of comforting (Badri, *Child-Rearing Practices in the Sudan*, p. 57).

74. Friedl, "Child Rearing in Modern Persia," p. 413.
75. See Shakri, "Al-tanshi'a al-ijtima'iyya" (Socialization), pp. 116–128.
76. Dachmi, however, argues from his clinical observations that it does produce development-retarding passivity. See Dachmi, *De La Seduction Maternelle Negative*.
77. Brink, "Changing Child-Rearing Patterns in an Egyptian Village," p. 85.
78. There are about 7 percent fewer females than males in India, about 4 percent fewer in North Africa. Sen, *Development as Freedom*, p. 104.
79. Seymour, "Caste/Class and Child-Rearing in a Changing Indian Town," p. 788.
80. De La Ronciere, "Notables on the Eve of the Renaissance," p. 220.
81. Shahar, *Childhood in the Middle Ages*.
82. In MENA, wet-nurses traditionally were sought for infants whose mothers died or lacked sufficient milk—the most famous example being the Prophet—but were not routinely used by elite families.
83. Lacoste-Dujardin, *Des Meres Contre les Femmes*, pp. 57–68.
84. Sen, *Development as Freedom*, pp. 104–105.
85. Dachmi, "Troubles du Sommeil au Feminin."
86. Carstairs, *Twice-Born* ; Kakar, *Inner World* ; Roland, *In Search of Self in India and Japan* ; Kurtz, *All the Mothers Are One*.
87. Doi, *Anatomy of Dependence*; Beardsley, Hall, and Ward, *Village Japan*; DeVos, *Socialization for Achievement*; Lebra, *Japanese Patterns of Behavior*.
88. Antoun, *Muslim Preacher in the Modern World*.
89. This belief and practice appears throughout MENA and is reported for the Arabs Cederblad studied in the Sudan as well (p. 51). See El Khayat-Bennai, *Le Monde Arabe au Feminin*, p. 89.
90. Ammar, *Growing Up in an Egyptian Village*, p. 103.
91. Cederblad, "Child Psychiatric Study on Sudanese Arab Children," p. 55.
92. Davis, *Patience and Power*, pp. 152, 151.
93. Shakri, "Al-tanshi'a al-ijtima'iyya" (Socialization), pp. 102–105.
94. Sa'idallah, "Dirasat anthrobologia muqarana li-anmat al-tanshi'a al-ijtima'iyya fi mujtama' mahali badawi wa mujtama' mahali rifi fi misr" (Comparative Anthropological Study of Socialization Patterns in Bedouin and Rural Societies in Egypt), p. 195.
95. Al Nawayseh, *Al-tifl fi al-hayat al-sha'biyya al-urduniyya* (The Child in Popular Life in Jordan), pp. 39–40.
96. Prothro, *Child Rearing in Lebanon*, p. 78.
97. Ibid., p. 77.
98. Ibid., pp. 77–78.
99. Friedl, *Children of Deh Koh*, pp. 109–110.

100. Albine and Thompson, "Effects of Sudden Weaning on Zule Children"; Ainsworth, *Infancy in Uganda.*
101. See LeVine et al., *Child Care and Culture,* for a summary, p. 45.
102. Ibid., p. 260.
103. Friedl, *Children of Deh Koh,* p. 110.
104. Several Egyptian investigators clearly believe gradual weaning results in less distress, but they have not suggested that abrupt weaning may cause serious disruption in attachment or basic trust. See Shakri, "Al-tanshi'a al-ijtima'iyya" (Socialization).
105. Dachmi, Lacoste-Dujardin, Bouhdiba, and El Khayat-Bennai also hold this view.
106. Msefer, *Sevrages et Interdependence,* pp. 68, 67.
107. Ibid., p. 13.
108. Ibid., p. 67.
109. Ibid., p. 86.
110. Chamcham, "L'enfant marocain," p. 74 (my translation).
111. Dachmi, *De La Seduction Maternelle Negative.* See especially pp. 41–52.
112. Ibid., p. 98.
113. Lacoste-Dujardin, *Des Meres Contre les Femmes,* pp. 88–91, 113–116.
114. El Khayat-Bennai, *Le Monde Arabe au Feminin,* pp. 89–90.
115. Lacoste-Dujardin, *Des Meres Contre les Femmes,* p. 90.
116. Chaouite, "L'enfant marocain," pp. 52, 53 (my translation).
117. Ibid., p. 53 (my translation).
118. Ibid., p. 55 (my translation).
119. Ainsworth, Blehar, Waters, and Wall, *Patterns of Attachment*; Ainsworth, "Development of Infant-Mother Interaction Among the Ganda."
120. Cassidy and Berlin, "Insecure/Ambivalent Pattern of Attachment."
121. Colin, *Human Attachment*; Posada, Goa, and Posada, "Secure-Base Phenomenon Across Cultures."
122. In this procedure, mothers and their children are observed as the mother twice leaves her child alone or with a stranger, and then returns. Behaviors at separation, during separation, and at reunion are all coded to determine attachment style.
123. Cederblad, "Behavioural Disorders in Children from Different Cultures," p. 91.
124. Granqvist, *Birth and Childhood Among the Arabs.*
125. Ammar, *Growing Up in an Egyptian Village.*
126. Prothro, *Child Rearing in Lebanon.*
127. Abdelqader and Ali, "Asalib al-rida'a wa al-fitam al-shai' fi al-thaqafa al-misriyya wa atharuha 'ala shakhsiyyiat al-tifl" (Styles of Nursing and Weaning Widespread in Egyptian Culture and Their Influence on the Personality of Children); Abdelqader and 'Afifi, " Al-dirasa al-midaniyya 'an al-asalib al-sha'ia al-ijtima'iyya fi al-rif al-misri" (Field Study of Socialization in Rural Egypt).
128. Askandar, 'Amad, and Rachdi, *Kayfa nurabi atfalana* (How We Raise Our Children).
129. Al-markaz al-Qaumi li-al-Buhouth (National Center for Research), *Beheth ahtiajiat al-tufula fi jumhuriyyat misr al-'arabiyya iyia* (Study of the Needs of Children in the Arab Republic of Egypt).
130. Shakri, "Al-tanshi'a al-ijtima'iyya" (Socialization).
131. Sa'idallah, "Dirasat anthrobologia muqarana li-anmat al-tanshi'a al-ijtima'iyya

fi mujtama' mahali badawi wa mujtama' mahali rifi fi misr" (Comparative Anthropological Study of Socialization Patterns in Bedouin and Rural Societies in Egypt).

132. Al-Sa'ti, *Asma' al-misriyyin wa al-taghir al-ijtima'i* (Egyptian Names and Social Change).

133. Cederblad, "Behavioural Disorders in Children from Different Cultures."

134. Badri, *Child-Rearing Practices in the Sudan.*

CHAPTER 5

1. Qabaj, "Al-tifl al-maghribi" (The Moroccan Child).

2. LeVine repeatedly uses these two terms to contrast African and Western child-rearing but does not specifically use the phrase "apprenticeship-and-obedience."

3. See Rogoff, *Apprenticeship in Thinking.*

4. Whiting and Whiting, *Children of Six Cultures.*

5. Davis, *Patience and Power*, pp. 23–25 and 156–157.

6. See Sa'idallah, "Dirasat anthrobologia muqarana li-anmat al-tanshi'a al-ijtima'iyya fi mujtama' mahali badawi wa mujtama' mahali rifi fi misr" (Comparative Anthropological Study of Socialization Patterns in Bedouin and Rural Societies in Egypt); Abdelqader and Ali, "Asalib al-rida'a wa al-fitam al-shai' fi al-thaqafa al-misriyya wa atharuha 'ala shakhsiyyiat al-tifl" (Styles of Nursing and Weaning Widespread in Egyptian Culture and their Influence on the Personality of Children); Askandar, *Kayfa nurabi atfalana* (How We Raise Our Children); Shakri, "Al-tanshi'a al-ijtima'iyya" (Socialization); Brink, "Changing Child-Rearing Patterns in an Egyptian Village."

7. When women do work outside, as they do seasonally in many agricultural communities, they try to leave their infants and toddlers inside with other women.

8. Davis, *Patience and Power*, p. 148.

9. Badri, *Child-Rearing Practices in the Sudan*, p. 145.

10. Ibid.

11. Prothro, *Child Rearing in Lebanon*, p. 135.

12. Williams, *The Youth of Haouch el Harimi*, pp. 35–36.

13. Friedl, "Child Rearing in Modern Persia," p. 413.

14. Badri, *Child-Rearing Practices in the Sudan*, pp. 60–61.

15. Prothro, *Child Rearing in Lebanon*, pp. 65–66.

16. Sigman and Wachs, "Structure, Continuity, Nutritional Correlates of Caregiver Behavior Patterns in Kenya and Egypt."

17. Ibid., p. 133.

18. Beals, *Gopalpur.*

19. Brink, "Changing Child-Rearing Patterns in an Egyptian Village," pp. 85–86.

20. Ibid.

21. Shakri, "Al-tanshi'a al-ijtima'iyya" (Socialization), pp. 135–137.

22. Al Aharas, "Terkib al-'ai'la al-'arabiyya wa wada'ifha" (Organization and Functions of the Arab Family).

23. Friedl, "Child Rearing in Modern Persia," p. 413.

24. Birth order, gender, household composition, and the mother's and child's health, of course, introduce tremendous variation. Mothers can have greater or lessor burdens of work; those in nuclear families may have no help with their children; wealthy families may have servants who do most of the household

work and child care; boys usually get more maternal care than girls; and last-borns may get prolonged maternal attention.

25. Ammar, *Egyptian Village Growing Up*, p. 224.
26. Hamid Ammar *Growing Up in an Egyptian Village*, p. 112.
27. LeVine, Dixon, LeVine, Richman, Leiderman, Keefer, and Brazelton, *Child Care and Culture.*
28. Cederblad, *Child Psychiatric Study on Sudanese Arab Children,* pp. 91–92.
29. Friedl, *Children of Deh Koh,* p. 131.
30. Ibid., p. 132.
31. Ammar, *Growing Up in an Egyptian Village,* pp. 134–135.
32. Ibid.
33. Williams, *The Youth of Haouch al Harimi*, p. 38.
34. Ammar, *Growing Up in an Egyptian Village*, p. 115.
35. Prothro, *Child Rearing in Lebanon*, p. 81.
36. Ammar, *Growing Up in an Egyptian Village*, p. 34.
37. Prothro, *Child Rearing in Lebanon*, p. 83.
38. Ibid., p. 154.
39. Darain, "Growing Up in India," pp. 139–140.
40. Ibid., p. 94.
41. Ammar, *Growing Up in an Egyptian Village*, pp. 108–109.
42. Ibid., p. 110.
43. Prothro, *Child Rearing in Lebanon*, p. 94.
44. Ammar, *Growing Up in an Egyptian Village*, pp. 110–111.
45. Ammar, *Egyptian Village Growing Up*, p. 272.
46. Prothro, *Child Rearing in Lebanon.*
47. Whiting and Whiting, *Children of Six Cultures*, p. 71.
48. Ammar, *Growing Up in an Egyptian Village*, p. 30.
49. Williams, *The Youth of Haouch al Harimi*, pp. 36–37.
50. Davis, *Patience and Power*, pp. 21 and 155.
51. Whiting and Whiting, *Children of Six Cultures*, p. 114.
52. Ibid., p. 123.
53. Ibid., p. 120, 125.
54. See especially Papanek and Minault, *Separate Worlds,* and Mandelbaum, *Women's Seclusion and Men's Honor.*
55. Whiting and Whiting, *Children of Six Cultures*, p. 122.
56. Askandar, Ismail, and Rachid, *Kayfa nurabi atfalana* (How We Raise Our Children).
57. Sa'idallah, "Dirasat anthrobologia muqarana li-anmat al-tanshi'a al-ijtima'iyya fi mujtama' mahali badawi wa mujtama' mahali rifi fi misr" (Comparative Anthropological Study of Socialization Patterns in Bedouin and Rural Societies in Egypt), p. 209–210.
58. See Haddiya, "Howl al-tanshi'a al-ijtima'iyya li-al-tifl al-qarawi" (Socialization of Rural Children), pp. 50–52.
59. See especially Shakri, "Al-tanshi'a al-ijtima'iyya" (Socialization), pp. 123–128 and 135–137.
60. Kagitcibasi, *Family and Human Development Across Cultures.*
61. Ben Jalloun, *Al-tifl wa tandhim al-majal fi al-ma'mar al-maghribi* (Children and the Organization of Space in Moroccan Buildings).

62. See, for example, Wikan, *Tomorrow, God Willing*.

63. Sa'idallah, "Dirasat anthrobologia muqarana li-anmat al-tanshi'a al-ijtima'iyya fi mujtama' mahali badawi wa mujtama' mahali rifi fi misr" (Comparative Anthropological Study of Socialization Patterns in Bedouin and Rural Societies in Egypt), p. 208.

64. Badri, *Child-Rearing Practices in the Sudan*, p. 141.

65. Grotberg and Badri, "Sudanese Children in the Family and Culture," p. 229.

66. Lacoste-Dujardin reports five to eight as typical of rural North Africa in the 1970s; *Des Meres Contre les Femmes*, p. 115.

67. Hicks, *Infibulation*, pp. 19–20; 184–209.

68. Granqvist, *Birth and Childhood Among the Arabs*, pp. 184–209.

69. Hicks, *Infibulation*.

70. Boddy *Wombs and Alien Spirits*, p. 51.

71. Ibid., p. 50.

72. Ibid., p. 52.

73. Ibid., p. 55.

74. Ibid., p. 74.

75. Ammar, *Growing Up in an Egyptian Village*, p. 118.

76. El Saadawi, pp. 8–9.

77. Cansever, "Psychological Effects of Circumcision"; Ozturk, "Ritual Circumcision and Castration Anxiety."

78. Davis and Davis, *Adolescence in a Moroccan Town*; Crapanzano, "Rite of Return."

79. Crapanzano, "Mohammed and Dawia," p. 169.

80. See Granqvist's description of ceremonies in a Palestinian village, *Birth and Childhood Among the Arabs*, and Davis and Davis's in a Moroccan small town, *Adolescence in a Moroccan Town*.

81. Crapanzano, "Rite of Return," p. 31.

82. Cansever, "Psychological Effects of Circumcision," p. 327.

83. Ibid.

84. Ibid., p. 328.

85. Ibid., p. 329.

86. Ozturk, "Ritual Circumcision and Castration Anxiety," p. 54.

87. Ibid., p. 55.

88. He also instructed residents at the psychiatric hospital where he worked to carefully interview newly admitted patients, and he reports that records of 11 years showed nearly no "clinical evidence of circumcision-related psychopathology." Ibid., p. 56.

89. Ibid., p. 57.

90. Ibid., p. 57.

91. Ibid., p. 58.

92. Crapanzano, "Rite of Return," p. 32.

93. Ozturk, "Ritual Circumcision and Castration Anxiety," pp. 56–57

94. See Kluft, *Childhood Antecedents of Multiple Personality Disorder*, and Putnam, *Diagnosis and Treatment of Multiple Personality Disorder*.

95. I will not discuss the development of sexual orientation here.

96. See Chodorow, *Reproduction of Mothering*.

97. Ibid., p. 169.

98. Gilligan, *In a Different Voice.*

99. Herdt, "Sambia Nosebleeding Rites and Male Proximity to Women."

100. Gilmore, *Manhood in the Making*, pp. 28–29.

101. Ibid., p. 224.

102. Whiting, *Culture and Human Development.* This association did not appear in Amazonian societies, where Whiting finds evidence for the intriguing hypothesis that ritualized identification with women (in the form of men suffering birth pains during their wives' childbirth)—ritually enacting rather than rejecting the feminine—can provide an alternative solution to the "cross-sex" conflict.

103. It is common for mothers to carry boys home on their backs, but highly unlikely that these men were carried naked against their mothers' naked backs.

104. Hijazi, *Al-takhaluf al-ijtima'i* (Underdeveloped Society); Bouhdiba, *Sexuality in Islam*; Hammoudi, *Master and Disciple.*

105. Coaches often "motivate" players by insulting them as "girls" and "pussies," and teams congratulate dramatic plays with "You're the man!" The pro football coach Bill Parsels caused a row when he pointedly referred to an underperforming player in a TV interview as "she." A recent Marine Corps ad showed rugged training scenes while the narrator offered "And kiss your mama good-bye!" See also Gibson, *Warrior Dreams.*

106. Najmabadi, "Reading 'Wiles of Women' Stories as Fictions of Masculinity," pp. 150–151.

107. Boddy, *Wombs and Alien Spirits*, pp. 125–131, 289–292. Some are possessed by female spirits, most notably Ethiopian prostitutes.

108. This does not just occur in Hofriyat. The teenage daughter of an Imeghrane neighbor of ours was said to be possessed by an Israeli commando *jinn.*

109. Badri, *Child-Rearing Practices in the Sudan*; Grotberg and Badri, "Sudanese Children in the Family and Culture."

110. Al-Aharas, " Terkib al-'ai'la al-'arabiyya wa wada'ifha" (Organization and Functions of the Arab Family) .

111. Whiting and Child's data from the Human Relations Area Files showed that Western society is an outlier among the world's cultures in how early and harshly parents toilet-train their toddlers. This suggests that the West distinctly patterned toilet-training as a strife-provoking procedure, and that Freud perhaps treated its deleterious effects. See Whiting and Child, *Child Training and Personality.*

112. Davis, *Patience and Power*, p. 153.

113. Badri, *Child-Rearing Practices in the Sudan*, pp. 90–92. He found, however, that a majority of Sudanese mothers said they scolded or hit children who soiled themselves after they had been toilet-trained.

114. Abdelqader and 'Affifi, "Al-dirasa al-midaniyya 'an al-asalib al-sha'ia al-ijtima'iyya fi al-rif al-misri" (Field Study of Socialization in Rural Egypt).

115. Sa'idallah, "Dirasat anthrobologia muqarana li-anmat al-tanshi'a al-ijtima'iyya fi mujtama' mahali badawi wa mujtama' mahali rifi fi misr" (Comparative Anthropological Study of Socialization Patterns in Bedouin and Rural Societies in Egypt), p. 197.

116. Askandar et al., *Kayfa nurabi atfalana* (How We Raise Our Children).

117. Dachmi, *De La Seduction Maternelle Negative.*

118. It is not clear, however, whether this is a technique of toilet-training or punishment for soiling after toilet-training has been completed. Shakri concludes that urban middle-class families begin and complete toilet-training earlier but rely mainly on communication and encouragement (Shakri, "Al-tanshi'a al-ijtima'iyya" [Socialization] pp. 114–117).

CHAPTER 6

1. LeVine, Dixon, LeVine, Richman, Leiderman, Keefer, and Brazelton, *Child Care and Culture.*
2. Again, this is my term, but based on LeVine, Dixon, LeVine, Richman, Leiderman, Keefer, and Brazelton, *Child Care and Culture.*
3. Johari, "Al-tifl fi al-turath al-sha'bi" (Child in Popular Tradition), p. 62.
4. Grotberg and Badri, "Sudanese Children in the Family and Culture," p. 216.
5. Shakri, "Al-tanshi'a al-ijtima'iyya" (Socialization).
6. Sharabi and Ani, "Impact of Class and Culture on Social Behavior"; Askandar, Isma'il, and Rachdi, *Kayfa nurabi atfalana* (How We Raise Our Children); Bouhdiba, *Sexuality in Islam*; Nurdin, *Awladuna akbaduna* (Our Children Our Hearts). Shakri writes: "It appears clearly that all of the studies agree—across the different environments they have been conducted in—that Egyptian parents depend primarily on hitting" (Shakri, "Al-tanshi'a al-ijtima'iyya" [Socialization], p. 137). Al-Mofti writes that "physical punishment is used by the majority of Egyptian familes of lower social levels, both rural and urban, and by both mothers and fathers" (*Derasat moqarana al-tanshi'a al-ijtim'iyya fi al-rif wa al-hadar al-misri* [Comparative Study of Socialization in Rural and Urban Egypt], p. 496). She also points out that the "atmosphere of sternness" in many families may interfere with the development of important capabilities (*Anmat al-tanshi'a al-ijtima'iyya fi bilad al-nuba* [Pattern of Socialization among the Nuba], p. 10).
7. Ammar, *Growing Up in an Egyptian Village*, p. 126.
8. Ammar, *Egyptian Village Growing Up*, p. 257.
9. Sharabi, *Neopatriarchy*, p. 41.
10. Guessous, "Al-tatawurat al-'a'iliyya wa al-tenshaia al-ijtima'iyya li-al-tifl al-maghribi" (Family Changes and Socialization of the Moroccan Child); Haddiya, *Al-tanshi'a al-ijtima'iyya wa al-hawiyya* (Socialization and Identity) and "Tatallu'at al-shabab" (Aspirations of Youth).
11. In addition, while no statistics on MENA societies are available, it is not clear that "child abuse" occurs more frequently in them than in the United States.
12. Edgerton, *Individual in Cultural Adaptation.*
13. Williams, *The Youth of Haouch el Harimi*, p. 39.
14. Sharabi and Ani, "Impact of Class and Culture on Social Behavior."
15. Williams, *The Youth of Haouch el Harimi*, p. 39.
16. Ammar, *Growing Up in an Egyptian Village*, p. 131.
17. Williams, *The Youth of Haouch el Harimi*, pp. 39–40.
18. Ammar, *Growing Up in an Egyptian Village*, p. 133.
19. Ibid.
20. Joseph, "Brother-Sister Relationships."
21. Williams, *The Youth of Haouch el Harimi*, p. 39.
22. For Mead, this constitutes the "Me" pole of the self, opposed to the "I."

23. See the theoretical framework presented in the introduction to part II of this book.
24. Brink, "Changing Child-Rearing Patterns in an Egyptian Village," p. 86.
25. Ouzi, *Saykulujiyyat al-murahiq* (Psychology of Adolescence), pp. 217–218.
26. Ibid., p. 50.
27. Eickelman, *Knowledge and Power in Morocco*, pp. 50–51.
28. Williams, *The Youth of Haouch el Harimi*, p. 38.
29. Friedl, *Children of Deh Koh*, pp. 192–193, 195.
30. Ammar, *Growing Up in an Egyptian Village*, p. 141.
31. Ibid., p. 139.
32. Ibid., p. 135, 139.
33. Ibid., pp. 137–138.
34. Oussaid, *Mountains Forgotten by God*, pp. 48, 50.
35. Ibid., p. 47.
36. Ghallab, *Le Passe Enterre*, p. 73. My translation.
37. Mahfouz, *Palace Walk*, p. 19.
38. Chairbi, *Simple Past*, pp. 2, 3. It should be noted that this novel probably comments not only on Moroccan family relationships but on political relationships as well.
39. Friedl, *Children of Deh Koh*, p. 193.
40. Al-Mofti, *anmat al-tanshi'a al-ijtima'iyya fi bilad al-nuba* (Pattern of Socialization among the Nuba), pp. 9–10.
41. See for example, Wilson, *Good Company*.
42. See Carstairs, *Twice-Born*; Kakar, *Inner World*.
43. It should be noted that arranged marriages and traditional gender roles are often thought to inhibit emotional ties between spouses, but our observation of many deeply bonded couples in Imeghrane villages leads us to wonder whether the Western romantic model fosters lasting intimacy with any greater frequency.
44. Aisha Bela'rbi also describes this pattern as typical of the Moroccan families she and her students have studied. She also suggests that the intimacy mothers cultivate with their children may partly serve as a compensation for what they lack with their husbands" (Ishkaliyyat al-tawasul dakhil al-usra al-maghrebiyya" [Forms of Communication in the Moroccan Family]).
45. See Ouzi, *Saykulujiyyat al-murahiq* (Psychology of Adolescence), pp. 215–216.
46. Lacoste-Dujardin, *Des Meres Contre les Femmes*, p. 116.
47. Mahfouz, *Palace Walk*, p. 4.
48. Ibid., p. 3.
49. Ibid., pp. 14–15.
50. Ibid., p. 52.
51. Bouhdiba, *Sexuality in Islam*, pp. 220–221.
52. Prothro, *Child Rearing in Lebanon*, pp. 70, 106–109, 143. Caution should be used in interpreting these findings, as the samples and rating procedures were analogous but not strictly comparable, and the observed differences may be due more to differences in family size, health, wealth, and other "confounding" factors.
53. Bouhdiba, *Sexuality in Islam*, p. 221.
54. See Boddy, *Wombs and Alien Spirits*, and Bourdieu, "The Kabyle House or The World Reversed."
55. Whiting, *Culture and Human Development*.

56. Ammar, *Growing Up in an Egyptian Village*, p. 128.
57. Ibid., pp. 128–129.
58. Harris, *Nurture Assumption*.
59. Ammar, *Growing Up in an Egyptian Village*, p. 156; Friedl, *Children of Deh Koh*, pp. 219, 236.
60. Friedl, *Children of Deh Koh*, p. 235.
61. Ammar, Growing Up in an Egyptian Village, p. 156.
62. Ibid., p. 157.
63. "It cannot be mere accident that most of the games, especially boys' games, although co-operative within the term, are directed mainly in their execution towards a highly competitive goal. While it cannot be firmly established, there is a strong suggestion that the village's social structure, with the solidarity of family, clan, and division combined with the rivalry between the various families, clans and the two divisions, favours the adoption of such games" (Ibid., p. 160).
64. Ibid.
65. Ibid., pp. 151–153.
66. Ibid., p. 156.
67. Ammar, *Growing Up in an Egyptian Village*, p. 159.
68. Dundes, "Strategy of Turkish Boys' Verbal Dueling Rhymes."
69. Ibid., p. 326.
70. Ibid., p. 347.
71. Ammar, *Growing Up in an Egyptian Village*, p. 135.
72. Friedl, *Children of Deh Koh*, p. 237.
73. Ammar, *Growing Up in an Egyptian Village*, p. 150.
74. Ibid., pp. 236–237.
75. Hart, *Aith Waryaghar of the Moroccan Rif*, p. 123.
76. Ibid., p. 124.
77. Chaqueri, *Beginning Politics in the Reproductive Cycle of Children's Tales and Games in Iran*, p. 108.
78. Ibid., pp. 101–102.
79. Ibid., p. 110.
80. Davis, *Patience and Power*.
81. And street gangs.
82. Zaid, "Ba'dh khasa'is al-shakhsiyya al-qawmiyya al-mesriyya bayn al-aftradat al-nadharijyya wa al-waqa' al-ambiriqi" (Some Characteristics of the Egyptian National Character), p. 194.
83. Mottahedeh, *Mantle of the Prophet*, p. 99.
84. Radi, "Processus de socialisation de l'enfant marocain," p. 48.
85. Said to have been spoken by the ruler Harun al Rashid to his son's tutor. Ammar, *Growing Up in an Egyptian Village*, p. 206.
86. El Khayat-Bennai, *Le Monde Arabe au Feminin*, p. 92.
87. Ammar, *Growing Up in an Egyptian Village*, p. 211.
88. Mottahedeh, *Mantle of the Prophet*, p. 30.
89. Ibid., pp. 203–204.
90. Fernea, "Childhood in the Muslim Middle East," p. 9.
91. Al-Aharas, "Terkib al-'ai'la al-'arabiyya wa wada'ifha" (Organization and Functions of the Arab Family).

92. Al-Aharas, "Terkib al-'ai'la al-'arabiyya wa wada'ifha" (Organization and Functions of the Arab Family). Badri, "Child-Rearing Practices in the Sudan,"
pp. 116, 122–123, 160; Grotberg and Badri, "Sudanese Children in the Family and
Culture"; Jabar, "Dirasat muqarana fi itijahat al-walidayn wa asalib al-tenshi'a
al-ijtima'iyya li-thalath 'ayinat 'arabiyya" (Comparative Study of Parental Orientations and Style of Socialization in Three Arab Samples); Al-Mofti, "Derasat
moqarana al-tanshi'a al-ijtim'iyya fi al-rif wa al-hadar al-misri" (Comparative
Study of Socialization in Rural and Urban Egypt), pp. 496–499.

93. Al-Mofti, "Derasat moqarana al-tanshi'a al-ijtim'iyya fi al-rif wa al-hadar al-
misri" (Comparative Study of Socialization in Rural and Urban Egypt), p. 498;
Jabar, "Al-itijahat al-walidia fi tenshia al-atfal" (Parental Orientations to the
Socialization of Children); Grotberg and Badri, "Sudanese Children in the Family and Culture."

94. Cederblad and Rahim, "Effects of Rapid Urbanization"; Rahim and Cederblad,
"Effects of Rapid Urbanization" (1986).

95. Haddiya, "Howl al-tanshi'a al-ijtima'iyya li-al-tifl al-qarawi" (Socialization of
Rural Children), "Al-tanshi'a al-ijtima'iyya bayna al-usra wa al-dirasa fi al-wasat
al-qarawi" (Socialization Between the Family and School in a Rural Area), and
Al-tanshi'a al-ijtima'iyya wa al-hawiyya (Socialization and Identity).

96. Haddiya, *Al-tanshi'a al-ijtima'iyya wa al-hawiyya* (Socialization and Identity),
pp. 167, 169.

97. Ibid., pp. 159, 161.

98. Ibid., pp. 190–206.

99. Miller, "Classroom 19," pp. 152–153.

100. Inkeles and Smith, *Becoming Modern*; Inkeles, *Exploring Individual Modernity*.

101. DeVos, *Socialization for Achievement*.

102. Goldberg, "Smashing Idols and the State"; Gellner, "Unknown Apollo of
Biskra"; Bellah, *Tokugawa Religion*.

103. Fromm, *Escape from Freedom*.

104. Adorno, Frenkel-Brunswik, Levinson, and Sanford, *Authoritarian Personality*.

105. Altermeyer, *Authoritarian Specter*.

106. Doty, Peterson, and Winter, "Threat and Authoritarianism in the United States,
1978–1987."

107. Baumrind, "Child Care Practices Anteceding Three Patterns of Preschool
Behavior."

108. Baumrind, "Effective Parenting During the Early Adolescent Transition."

109. Barakat, *Arab World*, pp. 175, 116–117.

110. Sharabi, *Neopatriarchy*, pp. 64, 7.

111. Bouhdiba, *Sexuality in Islam*, pp. 319–320.

112. Wilson, "Jobless Ghettos and the Social Outcomes of Youngsters."

113. Chao, "Beyond Parental Control and Authoritarian Parenting Style."

114. Prothro and Melikian, "California Public Opinion Scale in an Authoritarian
Culture." Melikian, "Authoritarianism and Its Correlates."

115. This may have been due to less cultural familiarity with the conceptions employed in some of the less direct questions.

116. Milikian, "Authoritarianism and Its Correlates," p. 67. Milikian also found positive correlations of authoritarianism with measures of psychological health in

the Egyptian sample, in contrast to negative correlations observed in some U.S. samples, suggesting that authoritarian attitudes provide better adjustment to Egyptian culture than they do in the United States.

117. Kagitcibasi, "Social Norms and Authoritarianism."

118. El-Keky, "Patterns of Parental Control in Kuwaiti Society."

119. Karakitapoglu-Aygun, *Self-Construals, Perceived Parenting and Well-Being in Different Cultural and Socio-Economic Contexts.*

120. Ibid., p. 193.

121. A study by Siyd Ma'taz takes a potentially fruitful indigenous approach, studying *'asabiyya,* or "solidarity," rather than the Western notion of authoritarianism. ("Al-itjahat al-tea'sbia" [Orientations of Solidarity]).

122. Sharabi, *Neopatriarchy.*

123. See Gregg, "Patterns of Authority in the Life Histories of Young Moroccans."

124. Dabashi, *Authority in Islam,* pp. 152, xvii.

125. Ibid., pp. xii–xiii.

126. Ibid., p. 156.

127. Khuri, *Tents and Pyramids,* pp. 123–124.

128. Al-Khalil, *Republic of Fear,* p. 124 (emphasis added).

129. Ibid., p. 128.

130. Ibid.

131. Hammoudi, *Master and Disciple,* p. ix.

132. Ibid., p. 41.

133. Kohn, *Class and Conformity;* Strauss and Mathur, "Social Change and Trends in Approval of Corporal Punishment from 1968 to 1994," pp. 91–105.

134. Cederblad and Rahim, "Effects of Rapid Urbanization"; Rahim and Cederblad, "Effects of Rapid Urbanization" (1986).

135. Al Aharas, "Terkib al-'ai'la al-'arabiyya wa wada'ifha" (Organization and Functions of the Arab Family).

136. Askandar, Isma'il, and Rachdi, *Kayfa nurabi atfalana* (How We Raise Our Children).

137. Sa'idallah, "Dirasat anthrobologia muqarana li-anmat al-tanshi'a al-ijtima'iyya fi mujtama' mahali badawi wa mujtama' mahali rifi fi misr" (Comparative Anthropological Study of Socialization Patterns in Bedouin and Rural Societies in Egypt).

138. Abdelqader and 'Afifi, "Al-dirasa al-midaniyya 'an al-asalib al-sha'ia al-ijtima'iyya fi al-rif al-misri" (Field Study of Socialization in Rural Egypt); Abdelqader and Ali, "Asalib al-rida'a wa al-fitam al-shai' fi al-thaqafa al-misriyya wa atharuha 'ala shakhsiyyiat al-tifl or atfal" (Styles of Nursing and Weaning Widespread in Egyptian Culture and their Influence on the Personality of Children).

139. Al-markaz al-Qaumi li-al-Buhouth (National Center for Research), *Beheth ahtiajiat al-tufula fi jumhuriyyat misr al-'arabiyya iyia* (Study of the Needs of Children in the Arab Republic of Egypt).

140. Al-Mofti, "Derasat moqarana al-tanshi'a al-ijtim'iyya fi al-rif wa al-hadar al-misri" (Comparative study of socialization in rural and urban Egypt).

141. Al-Mofti, *Anmat al-tanshi'a al-ijtima'iyya fi bilad al-nuba* (Pattern of Socialization among the Nuba).

142. Haddiya, "Howl al-tanshi'a al-ijtima'iyya li-al-tifl al-qarawi" (Socialization of Rural Children), "Al-tanshi'a al-ijtima'iyya bayna al-usra wa al-dirasa fi al-wasat

al-qarawi" (Socialization Between the Family and School in a Rural Area), *Al-tanshi'a al-ijtima'iyya wa al-hawiyya* (Socialization and Identity), and "Tatallu'at al-shabab" (Aspirations of Youth).

CHAPTER 7

1. Davis and Davis, *Adolescence in a Moroccan Town*, p. 182.
2. Nancy Chodorow, Carol Gilligan, and others have criticized the "achieving autonomy" theories of adolescence as incorrect even for girls in Western societies.
3. Ouzi, *Temthal al-tifl fi al-mujtama' al-maghribi* (Representation of the Child in North African Society) and *'Ilm al-nafs wa qadhaya al-mujtma'at mu'asira* (Psychology and Contemporary Social Issues), pp. 117–123.
4. Schlegel and Barry, *Adolescence*.
5. Wikan, *Behind the Veil in Arabia*.
6. Naamane-Guessous, *Au-dela de Toute Pudeur*, p. 21.
7. Schlegel and Barry, *Adolescence*, p. 40.
8. Ibid.
9. Though many observers note a "double standard" for boys.
10. Schlegel and Barry, *Adolescence*, p. 56.
11. Wikan, *Behind the Veil in Arabia*, pp. 86–87.
12. Ibid.
13. Naamane-Guesseus, *Au-dela de Toute Pudeur*, pp. 19–20.
14. Saadawi, "Growing Up Female in Egypt," p. 113.
15. Delaney, *Seed and the Soil*, p. 95.
16. Abu-Lughod, *Veiled Sentiments*, p. 130.
17. Ibid., p. 131. This is not universal: Imeghrani women wear white shawls.
18. Wikan, *Behind the Veil in Arabia*, p. 216.
19. Abu-Lughod, *Writing Women's Worlds*, p. 55.
20. Fernea, *Guests of the Shiekh*, pp. 155–156.
21. Hazelton, "Jawazi al-Malakim," pp. 265–266.
22. Davis, "Zahrah Muhammad," p. 205.
23. Euloge, *Les Chants de la Tassaou* , p. 133.
24. El Khayat-Bennai, *Le Monde Arabe au Feminin*, pp. 70–74.
25. Abu-Lughod, *Writing Women's Worlds*, p. 171.
26. Ibid., p. 190.
27. Ibid., pp. 201–202.
28. Atiya, *Khul-Khaal*, pp. 14–15.
29. Ibid., pp. 134–138.
30. Delaney, *Seed and the Soil*, pp. 273–274.
31. Boddy, *Wombs and Alien Spirits*, pp. 187–188.
32. See Bourdieu, "The Kabyle House or The World Reversed."
33. Meeker, *Literature and Violence in North Arabia*.
34. Ammar, *Growing Up in an Egyptian Village*, p. 190.
35. Bourdieu, "The Sentiment of Honour in Kabyle Society," Hart, *Aith Waryaghar of the Moroccan Rif*.
36. El Messiri, *Ibn al-Balad*, p. 4.
37. Ibid., pp. 64–65.
38. Ibid., p. 67.
39. Ibid., p. 68.

40. Hammoudi, *Victim and Its Masks.*
41. Gilsenan, *Lords of the Lebanese Marches,* p. 120.
42. Hammoudi, *Master and Disciple,* p. 5.
43. Ibid., p. 139.
44. Ibid., p. 140.
45. Ibid., p. 140.
46. Ibid., p. 137.
47. Ibid., p. 137.
48. Ibid., p. 137.
49. Ibid, p. 152, 153.
50. Meeker, *Literature and Violence in North Arabia.*
51. Lindholm, *Islamic Middle East.*
52. Antoun, *Muslim Preacher in the Modern World,* pp. 78–79.
53. 'Amad, Jabar, Rachdi, Labib, and Lily, "Al-sera'a al-qaimi bin al-ab wa al-abna wa 'alaqatuha bi-tawafiq al-abna al-nafsi" (Conflict of Values Between Parents and Children and Its Relationship with Agreement Among Children).
54. Mensch, Ibrahim, Lee, and El-Gibaly, "Gender-Role Attitudes Among Egyptian Adolescents," p. 16.
55. Ibid., pp. 14–16. Schooling was (weakly) associated with some more "modern" attitudes for girls, though not for boys.
56. Haddiya, "Al-tanshi'a al-ijtima'iyya bayna al-usra wa al-dirasa fi al-wasat al-qarawi" (Socialization Between the Family and School in a Rural Area).
57. Haddiya, "Tatallu'at al-shabab" (Aspirations of Youth), p. 31.
58. Davis and Davis, *Adolescence in a Moroccan Town,* pp. 59, 61.
59. See especially De Vos, *Socialization for Achievement,* and Lebra, *Japanese Patterns of Behavior.*
60. Williams, *The Youth of Haouch el Harimi,* p. 58.
61. Haddiya, *Processus de la Socialisation en Milieu Urbain au Maroc.*
62. Davis and Davis, *Adolescence in a Moroccan Town,* p. 64.
63. Ibid., p. 142.
64. Davis and Davis, *Adolescence in a Moroccan Town,* mention these complaints (p. 142), as do Pascon and Bentahar in their 1960s survey of rural Moroccan youths, "Ce Que Disent 296 Jeunes Ruraux."
65. Ouzi, *Saykulujiyyat al- murahiq* (Psychology of Adolescence), p. 206.
66. Haddiya, *Processus de la Socialisation en Milieu Urbain au Maroc.*
67. Ouzi, *Saykulujiyyat al- murahiq* (Psychology of Adolescence), p. 197.
68. Davis and Davis, *Adolescence in a Moroccan Town,* p. 82.
69. Abdel-Khaleq and Abou el Nil, "Al-daf'iya al-injaz wa 'ilaqatuha bi-ab'ad mutaghayirat al-shakhsiyya lada 'ayina min talamidh al-madaris al-ibtida'iyya wa al-tilmithat bi-dawlat qatar" (Achievement Motivation and Its Relationship with Personality Variables in a Sample of Qatari Students). Ghareeb points out that the gender differences in anxiety he found in a sample of 450 United Arab Emirates youth are similar to those found in Indian and European societies, and might be due either to biological differences or to greater social stresses on girls ("Al-qalaq lada al-shabab fi dawlat al-imarat la-'arqbiyya al-muttahida fi merhalqtqi al-tq'lim qabl al-jqmi'q wa al-ta'lim al-jami'i" [Anxiety Among Pre-University and University Students in U.A.E.]).
70. El Saadawi, *The Hidden Face of Eve,* pp. 116–117.

71. Bouhdiba, *Sexuality in Islam,* p. 90.
72. Ibid., p. 98.
73. Ibid., p. 30.
74. Ibid., p. 31.
75. Ibid., p. 127.
76. Ibid., p. 131.
77. Ibid., p. 130.
78. Ibid., pp. 169–170.
79. Davis and Davis, *Adolescence in a Moroccan Town.*
80. Ben Jalloun, "Al-tifl wa tandhim al-majal fi al-ma'mar al-maghribi" (Children and the Organization of Space in Moroccan Buildings).
81. Davis and Davis, *Adolescence in a Moroccan Town,* pp. 113–114.
82. Pascon and Bentahar, "Ce que disent 296 jeunes ruraux."
83. Ibid., p. 112.
84. Ibid., p. 218.
85. Davis and Davis, *Adolescence in a Moroccan Town,* p. 112.
86. Observers report this configuration of attitudes in Syria, Morocco, Iran, and the Middle East generally. See Schmitt and Sofer, *Sexuality and Eroticism Among Males in Moselm Societies.*
87. Wikan, *Behind the Veil in Arabia,* pp. 176–177.
88. Bouhdiba, *Sexuality in Islam,* p. 192.
89. Ibid., p. 194.
90. Ibid., p. 193–194.
91. Pascon and Bentahir, "Ce que disent 296 jeunes ruraux," pp. 218–219.
92. Davis and Davis, *Adolescence in a Moroccan Town,* p. 111.
93. Wikan, *Behind the Veil in Arabia,* pp. 143–147.
94. Noting that sociological studies have found prostitutes to be mostly in their forties, Bouhdiba believes that many teenage boys gain their sexual experience from women who are mother figures, which entails a "systematic infantilization and regression" and contributes to men's misogyny (Bouhdiba, *Sexuality in Islam,* p. 195).
95. Williams, *The Youth of Haouch el Harimi,* p. 94.
96. Davis and Davis, *Adolescence in a Moroccan Town,* p. 117.
97. Ouzi, *Saykulujiyyat al- murahiq* (Psychology of Adolescence), pp. 118–121; 210–212.
98. Ibid., p. 210.
99. Davis and Davis, *Adolescence in a Moroccan Town,* pp. 119–120.
100. Ibid., p. 119.
101. Friedl, *Children of Deh Koh,* p. 270.
102. Davis and Davis, *Adolescence in a Moroccan Town;* Bouhdiba, *Sexuality in Islam;* Bennani-Chraibi, *Soumis et Rebelles Les Jeunes au Maroc;* Mernissi, *Beyond the Veil.*
103. *Rai* means "my opinion" or "my view" and is sung in many songs in the way "yeah, yeah, yeah ... " is often used in Western rock music.
104. Schade-Poulsen, *Men and Popular Music in Algeria ,* p. 62.
105. Ibid., p. 63, 136.
106. Ibid., p. 134.
107. Ibid., p. 138.

108. Ibid., p. 155.

109. Ibid., pp. 161–165.

110. Ibid., p. 30.

111. Ibid., p. 94, 138.

112. Ibid., p. 93.

113. Ibid., p. 167.

114. Ibid., p. 187.

115. Ibid., p. 187.

116. Ibid., p. 195.

117. Ibid., p. 152.

118. Lila, *Al-shabab al-'arabi* (Arab Youth).

119. Mitchell, *The Society of the Muslim Brothers*, p. 234.

120. Ouzi, "Saykulujiyyat al-murahiq," p. 217–218.

121. Ahirshaw, "Al-montor sikologiyya li-azmat al-shabab fi al-watan al-'arabi" (Psychological Theories of the Crisis of Arab Youth), pp. 104–106.

122. Lila, *Al-shabab al-'arabi* (Arab Youth).

123. Shebshun, "Hawiyyat al-shabab al-tunisi" (Identity of Tunisian Youth).

124. Ahirshaw, "Waqa' thaqafat al-tifl al-maghrebi wa afaq tanmiyatiha" (Cultural Situation of the Moroccan Child and the Horizon of Its Development).

125. Ouzi, "Temthal al-tifl fi al-mujtama' al-maghribi" (Representation of the Child in North African Society).

126. Rabia', "Al-shabab " (Youth).

127. Lila, *Al-shabab al-'arabi* (Arab Youth).

128. Bennani-Chraibi, *Soumis et Rebelles Les Jeunes au Maroc.*

129. Kouaouci, "Transitions, chomage des jeunes, recul du marriage et terrorisme en Algeria."

130. For a review of writings on Arab youth, see Booth, "Arab Adolescents Facing the Future."

131. Sharabi, *Neopatriarchy.*

132. Barakat, *Arab World.*

133. Bouhdiba, *Sexuality in Islam.*

134. Mernissi, *Beyond the Veil.* She does use letters written to a religious counseling TV show, mostly from teen-agers and young adults, as a source of data on the younger generation's "sexual anomie."

135. Ahmad, *Women and Gender in Islam.*

136. Fernea, *Children in the Muslim Middle East.* Jenny White's *An Unmarried Girl and a Grinding Stone* describes a typical day in the life of a 16–year-old girl in a traditional Turkish family (pp. 257–268), Kari Karame's *Girls' Participation in Combat* describes Lebanese girls' participation in combat (pp. 378–391), and Farhad Khosrokhavar's *Attitudes of Teenage Girls to the Iranian Revolution* presents interviews with two Iranian girls about the revolution and war with Iraq (pp. 392–409).

137. Ammar, *Growing Up in an Egyptian Village*, p. 190.

138. Mensch, Ibrahim, Lee, and El-Gibaly, "Gender-Role Attitudes Among Egyptian Adolescents."

139. Pascon and Bentahar, "Ce que disent 296 jeunes ruraux."

140. Haddiya, *Processus de la Socialisation en Milieu Urbain au Maroc,* and *Al-tanshi'a al-ijtima'iyya wa al-hawiyya* (Socialization and Identity).

141. Schade-Poulsen, *Men and Popular Music in Algeria*.
142. Lila, *Al-shabab al-'arabi* (Arab Youth).
143. Bennani-Chraibi, *Soumis et Rebelles Les Jeunes au Maroc*.

CHAPTER 8
1. The political scientist Bernard Lewis even titled his 1999 book *The Multiple Identities of the Middle East*.
2. Fanon, *Wretched of the Earth* and *Black Skin White Masks*.
3. Ashis Nandy develops a similar interpretation of Indian responses to British colonization. See *Intimate Enemy*.
4. Ahmed, *Living Islam*, p. 129.
5. Gregg, "Culture, Personality, and the Multiplicity of Identity."
6. Shayegan, *Cultural Schizophrenia*.
7. Ghareeb, "Ai namoudhaj li-al-tawafiq lada al-shabab al-maghrebi" (What Model for Moroccan Youth?).
8. Geertz, "Religion as a Cultural System."
9. See Gregg, *Self-Representation* and *Culture and Identity in Morocco*.
10. Eisenstadt, "Archetypcal Patterns of Youth," p. 31.
11. Critics have objected that Erikson's emphasis on identity reflects Western society's preoccupation with autonomy and individualism, and he sometimes does write in romantic ways about the individualistic character of the quest for identity. But even more often he emphasizes the cultural and group-based nature of identity in the face of America's rhetoric about the "self-made man."
12. Ibid., p. 83.
13. Habermas and Bluck, "Getting a Life."
14. Bruner, *Acts of Meaning*.
15. McAdams, *Power, Intimacy, and the Life Story* and "Psychology of Life Stories."
16. Hermans and Kempen, *Dialogical Self*, and Hermans, "Voicing the Self."
17. Gregg, Self-Representation," Multiple Identities and the Integration of Personality," and "Culture, Personality, and the Multiplicity of Identity."
18. Levinson, Darrow, Klein, Levinson, and McKee, *Seasons of a Man's Life*; Levinson and Levinson, *Seasons of a Woman's Life*.
19. Levinson, Darrow, Klein, Levinson, and McKee, *Seasons of a Man's Life*, p. 91.
20. Ibid., p. 97.
21. Boddy, *Wombs and Alien Spirits*, pp. 113–114.
22. See Lacoste-Dujardin, *Des Meres Contre les Femmes*, pp. 98–111, for a description of the circum-Mediterranean fecundity-related symbolism associated with women's identity in rural Algeria.
23. Ibid., p. 87.
24. El Khayat-Bennai, *Le Monde Arabe au Feminin*, p. 91.
25. Inhorn, *Infertility and Patriarchy*, p. 9.
26. It is important to note that Middle Easterners also are quick to reverse these characterizations in acts of self-criticism, holding up the virtues of non-Muslims to show their own shortcomings.
27. Shalinsky, "Reason, Desire, and Sexuality."
28. Ibid., p. 326.
29. Dwyer, *Images and Self-Images*.
30. Ibid., p. 330.

31. Ibid., p. 332.
32. Tajfel, *Human Groups and Social Categories* and *Social Identity and Intergroup Relations.*
33. Meeker, *Literature and Violence in North Arabia.*
34. Caton, "Poetic Construction of Self," p. 143.
35. Ibid., pp. 145, 146.
36. Ibid., p. 148.
37. Anderson, "Sentimental Ambivalence and the Exegesis of 'Self' in Afghanistan."
38. Ibid., pp. 205–206.
39. Ibid., pp. 206–207.
40. Ibid., p. 207.
41. Ibid., p. 208.
42. Abu-Lughod, *Veiled Sentiments,* p. 251.
43. Ibid., p. 252.
44. Barakat, *Arab World.*
45. Krichen, "Les problemes de la langue et l'intelligensia."
46. Hermans and Kempen, *Dialogical Self.*
47. El Messiri, *Ibn al-Balad,* p. 4.
48. Ibid., pp. 4–5.
49. Ibid., p. 45.
50. Ibid., p. 51.
51. Ibid., p. 98.
52. Ibid., pp. 89–90.
53. Ibid., p. 85.
54. Ibid., pp. 104–105.
55. Miner and DeVos, *Oasis and Casbah,* p. 126.
56. Ibid., pp. 185–186.
57. Ibid., p. 189.
58. Davis and Davis, *Adolescence in a Moroccan Town.*
59. Miner and DeVos, *Oasis and Casbah,* p. 148.
60. Lerner, *Passing of Traditional Society,* p. 112.
61. Olson, "Muslim Identity and Secularism in Contemporary Turkey," p. 164; quoted from Lewis, *Emergence of Modern Turkey,* p. 268.
62. Gole, *Forbidden Modern,* p. 15.
63. Quoted in ibid., pp. 57–58.
64. Ibid., p. 15.
65. Poulton, *Top Hat, Grey Wolf and Crescent,* p. 318.
66. Ibid., p. 163.
67. Lerner, *Passing of Traditional Society,* pp. 160–161.
68. Poulton, *Top Hat, Grey Wolf and Crescent,* p. 200.
69. Ibid., p. 206.
70. Mottahedeh, *Mantle of the Prophet,* p. 60.
71. Vaziri, *Iran as Imagined Nation,* p. 197.
72. Mottahedeh, *Mantle of the Prophet,* p. 311.
73. Ibid., p. 327.
74. Ibid., p. 329.
75. Ibid., p. 312.
76. Ibid., p. 296.

77. Ibid.
78. Ibid., p. 299.
79. Ibid., p. 323.
80. Vaziri, *Iran as Imagined Nation*, p. 208, 211.
81. Shayegan, *Cultural Schizophrenia*, pp. 5, 10.
82. Mottahedeh, *Mantle of the Prophet*, pp. 379–380.
83. Tibi, *Islam and the Cultural Accommodation of Social Change*, p. 135.
84. Abdo, *No God But God*, p. 5.
85. Laroui, *Crisis of the Arab Intellectual*.
86. Munson, *Islam and Revolution in the Middle East*, p. 77.
87. El Guindi, "Veiling Infitah with Muslim Ethic," pp. 469, 465.
88. Kepel, *Muslim Extremism in Egypt*, p. 11.
89. Mitchell, *Society of the Muslim Brothers*, p. 222.
90. Tibi, *Islam and the Cultural Accommodation of Social Change*, and Munson, *Islam and Revolution in the Middle East*.
91. Bellah, *Tokugawa Religion*.
92. Nandy, *At the Edge of Psychology*.
93. Lawrence, *Road Belong Cargo*; Worsley, *Trumpet Shall Sound*.
94. Jorgensen, *Sun Dance Religion*.
95. Gilsenan, *Recognizing Islam*, p. 44.
96. Ahmad, *Women and Gender in Islam*, p. 223.
97. Ibid., p. 225.
98. Lila, *Al-shabab al-'arabi* (Arab Youth), p. 111.
99. Ewing, "Illusion of Wholeness," p. 259.
100. Ibid.
101. Ibid., p. 260.
102. Ibid., p. 261.
103. Ibid., p. 253.
104. Ewing, "Can Psychoanalytic Theories Explain the Pakistani Woman?" p. 59.
105. Ibid., pp. 11–12.
106. Ibid., p. 76.
107. Ibid., pp. 116–117.
108. Ibid., p. 125.
109. Ibid., p. 123.
110. All of those I interviewed lived in villages and small towns in the pre-Saharan province of Ouarzazate and had at least high school educations. The interviews ranged from 6 to 20 hours, and, in addition to eliciting the respondent's life-history, they included a series of projective tests, questions about childhood memories, and discussion of religious experiences and beliefs. See Gregg, "Culture, Personality, and the Multiplicity of Identity" and "Themes of Authority in Life-Histories of Young Moroccans."
111. Gregg, *Self-Representation* and "Multiple Identities and the Integration of Personality."
112. Khadija, the woman most torn between "French" and "Muslim" identities, was a notable exception.
113. Gregg, *Culture and Identity*. For a detailed discussion of Weber's interpretations and misinterpretations of Islam, see Turner, *Weber and Islam*.
114. Bellah, *Tokugawa Religion*.

115. Waterbury, *North for the Trade.*
116. Gellner, "The Unknown Apollo of Biskra."
117. Goldberg, "Smashing Idols and the State."
118. Maalouf, *In the Name of Identity.*
119. Ghareeb, "Ai namoudhaj li-al-tawafiq lada al-shabab al-maghrebi" (What Model for Moroccan Youth?).
120. Ibid., p. 127.
121. Triandis, "Self and Social Behavior in Differing Cultural Contexts." See also Trafimow, Triandis, and Goto, "Some Tests of the Distinction Between the Private Self and the Collective Self"; Ybarra and Trafimow, "How Priming the Private Self or Collective Self Affects the Relative Weights of Attitudes and Subjective Norms."
122. See especially Sinha and Tripathi, "Individualism in a Collectivist Culture," Ho and Chiu, "Component Ideas of Individualism, Collectivism, and Social Organization," and Triandis, "Theoretical and Methodological Approaches to the Study of Collectivism and Individualism," all in Kim, Triandis, Kagitcibasi, Choi, and Yoon, *Individualism and Collectivism.*
123. Oyserman and Markus, "Possible Selves and Delinquency"; Cross and Markus, "Possible Selves Across the Life Span."
124. La Fromboise, Coleman, and Gerton, "Psychological Impact of Biculturalism."
125. See Tasi, Ying, and Lee, "Meaning of 'Being Chinese' and 'Being American'"; Oyserman, "Lens of Personhood."
126. Oyserman, Sakamoto, and Lauffer, "Cultural Accommodation"; Hermans and Kempen, "Moving Cultures."
127. Phinney, "Ethnic Identity in Adolescents and Adults."
128. Hong, Morris, Chiu, Bennet-Martinez, " Multicultural Minds"; Verkuyten and Pouliasi, "Biculturalism Among Older Children."
129. See Phinney, "Ethnic Identity in Adolescents and Adults"; Oyserman, Gant, and Ager, "A Socially Contextualized Model of African American Identity"; La Fromboise, Coleman, and Gerton, "Psychological Impact of Biculturalism"; and Verkuyten and Pouliasi, "Biculturalism Among Older Children."
130. Boddy, *Wombs and Alien Spirits.*
131. Abu-Lughod, *Writing Women's Worlds.*
132. Olson, "Muslim Identity and Secularism in Contemporary Turkey."
133. Gole, *Forbidden Modern.*
134. Poulton, *Top Hat, Grey Wolf and Crescent.*
135. Ewing, "Illusion of Wholeness."
136. Gregg, "Themes of Authority in Life Histories of Young Moroccans," and *Culture and Identity.*

CHAPTER 9
1. Berman, *All That Is Solid Melts into Air.*
2. This is my analogy, not Jung's.
3. See Erikson, *Childhood and Society,* especially p. 263.
4. Ibid., p. 267.
5. See de St. Aubin, McAdams, and Kim, *Generative Society.*
6. Steward and Vandewater, "Course of Generativity."
7. See especially Keyes and Ryff, "Generativity in Adult Lives."

8. Erikson, *Childhood and Society*, p. 268.
9. Levinson, Darrow, Klein, Levinson, and McKee, *Seasons of a Man's Life*.
10. Levinson and Levinson, *Seasons of a Woman's Life*.
11. Ibid.
12. See Gilligan, *In a Different Voice*.
13. Giddons, *Modernity and Self-Identity*.
14. This is not uncommon among working-class and poor people in the modernized West.
15. Abdel-Khalek, "Extraversion and Neuroticism as Basic Personality Dimensions in Egyptian Samples."
16. Farrag, "Dimensions of Personality in Saudi Arabia."
17. Eysenck, Makaremi, and Barret, "A Cross-Cultural Study of Personality."
18. Ibrahim, "Extraversion and Neuroticism Across Cultures." He also found support for the third dimension hypothesized by Eysenck, psychoticism (p. 209), and both he and Eysenck report higher "social desirability" among Egyptians and Iranians than British. See also Ibrahim, "Factorial Structure of the Eysenck Personality Questionnaire Among Egyptian Students."
19. The "Big Five" traits are extraversion, neuroticism, openness, agreeableness, and conscientiousness (Somer and Goldberg, "Structure of Turkish Trait-Descriptive Adjectives").
20. Aziz and Jackson, "A Comparison Between Three and Five Factor Models of Pakistani Personality Data."
21. Al Ansarey, "Meda kefaa qa'imat al-'awamal al-khamsa al-kabri li-al-shakhsiyya fi al-mujtama' al-kuwaiti" (Psychometric Properties of the Five-Factor Inventory in the Kuwaiti Society).
22. Khalifa and Radwan, *Al-shakhsiyyia al-misriyya* (Egyptian Personality).
23. Ibid., pp. 410–416.
24. See Ghareeb and Beshai, "Arabic Version of the Children's Depression Inventory"; Abdel-Khalek, "Development and Validation of an Arabic Form of the STAI"; Al Issa, Bakal, and Fung, "Beck Anxiety Inventory Symptom Comparisons Between Students in Lebanon and Canada"; Al Issa, Al Zubaidi, Bakal, and Fung, "Beck Anxiety Inventory Symptoms in Arab College Students"; El-Zahhar and Hocevar, "Cultural and Sexual Differences in Test Anxiety, Trait Anxiety and Arousability"; Ahlawat, "Psychometric Properties of the Yarmouk Test Anxiety Inventory"; Beshai and Templer, "American and Egyptian Attitudes Toward Death"; Abdel-Khalek, "Death Anxiety in Egyptian Samples" and "Normative Results on the Arabic Fear Survey Schedule III."
25. Abdel-Khalek, "Development and Validation of an Arabic Form of the STAI," p. 284.
26. Van Dam-Baggan, Kraaimaat, and Elal, "Social Anxiety in Three Western Societies."
27. Hofstede, *Culture's Consequences*.
28. Buda and Elsayed-Elkhouly, "Cultural Differences Between Arabs and Americans."
29. Al-Zahrani and Kaplowitz, "Attributional Biases in Individualistic and Collectivistic Cultures."
30. Spiro, "Is the Western Conception of the Self 'Peculiar' Within the Context of the World Cultures?"; LeVine, "Infant Environments in Psychoanalysis." See

also Murray, "What Is the Western Concept of the Self?"; Holland and Kipnis, "Metaphors for Embarassment and Stories of Exposure"; Ewing, "Can Psychoanalytic Theories Explain the Pakistani Woman?"

31. Many scholars regard St. Augustine's *Confessions* as the originating work of Western autobiographical consciousness, apparently ignoring the fact that he was a North African Berber.

32. Reynolds, *Interpreting the Self*.

33. Wu, *Confucian's Progress*; Maraldo, "Rousseau, Hakuseki, and Hakuin"; J. Gyatso, "Autobiography in Tibetan Religious Literature," cited in Reynolds, *Interpreting the Self*, p. 32.

34. Sinha and Tripathi, "Individualism in a Collectivist Culture."

35. Ho and Chiu, "Component Ideas of Individualism, Collectivism, and Social Organization," p. 138.

36. Ibid., p. 154.

37. Triandis, "Theoretical and Methodological Approaches to the Study of Collectivism and Individualism," p. 42.

38. Kagitcibasi, *Family and Human Development Across Cultures*.

39. Ibid., p. 86.

40. Ibid., p. 87.

41. Imamoglu, "Individualism and Collectivism in a Model and Scale of Balanced Differentiation and Integration."

42. Karakitapoglu-Aygun, "Self-Construals, Perceived Parenting and Well-Being in Different Cultural and Socio-Economic Contexts," p. 182.

43. Ibid., pp. xvii–xviii and 68.

44. Joseph, "Theories and Dynamics of Gender, Self and Identity in Arab Families," p. 13. She emphasizes that connectivity need not be paired with patriarchy but is so paired throughout MENA societies.

45. Joseph, "My Son/Myself, My Mother/Myself," p. 189.

46. Joseph, "Theories and Dynamics of Gender, Self and Identity in Arab Families," p. 9.

47. Al-Zahrani and Kaplowitz, "Attributional Biases in Individualistic and Collectivistic Cultures."

48. Kuroda and Suzuki, "Arab Students and English" and "A Comparative Analysis of the Arab Culture." The authors caution that the samples are neither representative nor equivalent, and not all of the Cairo sample's responses match those of the Amman sample.

49. Kuroda and Suzuki, "A Comparative Analysis of the Arab Culture," p. 39.

50. Kuroda and Suzuki, "Arab Students and English: The Role of Implicit Culture," pp. 34 and 35.

51. Ibid., p. 38.

52. Phalet and Claeys, "A Comparative Study of Turkish and Belgian Youth."

53. DeVos, *Socialization for Achievement*.

54. Atkinson and Raynor, *Motivation and Achievement*.

55. Davis, *Patience and Power*.

56. Lacoste-Dujardin, *Des Meres Contre les Femmes*; Kandiyoti, "Bargaining with Patirarchy" and "Islam and Patriarchy."

57. Davis, *Patience and Power*, p. 44.

58. Kandiyoti, *Islam and Patriarchy*, p. 32.

59. Lacoste-Dujardin, *Des Meres Contre les Femmes,* p. 136. My translation.
60. Gutmann, "Alternatives to Disengagement,"*Reclaimed Powers,* and *Human Elder in Nature, Culture, and Society.*
61. Ibid., p. 203.
62. Ibid., p. 203.
63. Lacoste-Dujardin, *Des Meres Contre les Femmes,* p. 133.
64. Ibid., p. 131. My translation.
65. Kandiyoti, *Islam and Patriarchy,* pp. 32–33.
66. United Nations Development Program, *Arab Human Development Report 2002,* p. 2.
67. In Ammar, *Growing Up in an Egyptian Village,* pp. 80–91.
68. Ibid., pp. 92–108.
69. See 'Awda, *Al-takayyuff wa al- muqawamah* (Adaptation and Resistance), Yassin, *Al-shakhsiyya al-'arabiyya* (Arab Personality, and Khalifa and Radwan, *Al-shakhsiyyia al-misriyya* (Egyptian Personality), for discussions of these self-critical writings.
70. Patai, *Arab Mind.* See chap. 4, "Under the Spell of Language," especially pp. 49–65.
71. Yassin, *Al-shakhsiyya al-'arabiyya* (Arab Personality).
72. Ibid., pp. 19–150.
73. They are easily seen as misreadings of self-presentational styles associated with competition for male honor and indirect resistance to landlords and rulers found throughout the Mediterranean (see chapter 3).
74. Yassin suggests that the "Fahlaoui" portrait fits some members of Egypt's middle class, but not Egyptians generally. Ammar did not present it as an account of "national character," but he also did not add caveats about its limited applicability.
75. Zaid, *Ba'dh khasa'is al-shakhsiyya al-qawmiyya al-mesriyya* (Some Characteristics of the Egyptian National Character).
76. Ibid., p. 197–198.
77. Ibid., pp. 193–194.
78. 'Awda, *Al-takayyuff wa al-muqawamah* (Adaptation and Resistance).
79. The establishment of agriculture under Pharaonic rule, Islamization and Arabization, the development of commerce, and colonization.
80. Hamdan, *Shakhsiyyat misr* (Egyptian Personality).
81. Khalifa and Radwan, *Al-shakhsiyyia al-misriyya* (Egyptian Personality). See especially chapter 3.
82. Khalifa and Radwan, *Al-shakhsiyyia al-misriyya* (Egyptian Personality), found the educated Cairenes perceived the "Egyptian personality" to be constituted mainly of positive traits, especially civility, piety, moral virtue, family centeredness, cultural conservatism, and social adaptability (though women saw more positive characteristics than men, and students more positive ones than employees)—a finding that they suggest fits with Halim Barakat's description of Arab culture as emphasizing group membership, affiliation, and conformity over individuality (pp. 388–389). Some of the more prominent stereotypes, such as laziness, hostility, lying, and superstitious thinking were not perceived to be widely shared by Egyptians (p. 402).
83. Fromm and Maccoby, *Social Character in a Mexican Village.*

84. Foster, "Peasant Society and the Image of Limited Good."

85. Lewis, *Children of Sanchez*. Lewis's descriptions are not entirely free of stereotyping.

86. Wolf, *Europe and the People Without History*.

87. Scott, *Weapons of the Weak*.

88. Fanon, *Wretched of the Earth*, pp. 164–165.

89. Rejali, *Torture and Modernity*. The Islamic regime performs some public punishments, but these differ in important respects from those of the Qajar era.

90. Ajami, *Arab Predicament*, p. 32.

91. Ajami, *Dream Palace of the Arabs*, pp. 7–8.

92. There is a large and growing research literature on the effects of occupation on Palestinian children and adolescents. See Punamaki, Qouta, and El-Sarraj, "Resiliency Factors Predicting Psychological Adjustment After Political Violence Among Palestinian Children," and Thabet, Abed, and Vostanis, "Emotional Problems in Palestinian Children Living in a War Zone," for two recent studies and references. El-Sarraj has suggested that many of the teens and young adults carrying out "terrorist" attacks on Israelis are committing acts of vengeance and reparation for trauma they suffered as children. (Palestinian attacks also may create conditions akin to a "culture of terror" in Israeli areas.)

93. Open windows in a police station in the Moroccan city of Taza one evening allowed me (and many others) to hear a petty criminal being tortured, and the man's animal-like screams remain as vivid in my memory as 20 years ago.

94. Zaid, *Misr al-mu'asira* (Modern Egypt).

95. Barakat, *Arab World*, p. 175, 177.

96. Sharabi *Neopatriarchy*, p. 7.

97. Ibid., p. 66.

98. Hijazi, "'Ilm al-nafs fi al-'alam al-'arabi" (Psychology in the Arab World).

99. Zayour, *Al-tahlil al-nafsi li-al-dhat al-'arabiyya* (Psychoanalysis of the Arab Self), p. 44.

100. Djait, *Al-shakhsiyya al-'arabiyya al-islamiyya wal-masir al-'arabi* (Arab-Islamic Personality and Arab Destiny), pp. 220–21.

101. Al-Khalil, *Republic of Fear*. Al-Khalil was the pseudonym Makiya used to publish this book.

102. Ibid., p. 38.

103. Ibid., p. 64.

104. Ibid., p. 47.

105. Ibid., p. xviii.

106. Ibid., p. 63.

107. Ibid., p. 111.

108. Hollander, *Love in a Time of Hate*, p. 114.

109. Makiya, *Cruelty and Silence*, p. 128.

110. Ibid., p. 124.

111. Ibid., p. 275.

112. Hollander, *Love in a Time of Hate*, p. 111.

113. See Herman, *Trauma and Recovery*.

114. Mirowsky, "Disorder and Its Context," pp. 185–204.

115. Mirowsky and Ross, "Paranoia and the Structure of Powerlessness," pp. 228–238.
116. Hollander, *Love in a Time of Hate*, p. 113.
117. Giddons, *Modernity and Self-Identity*. See especially chap. 2.
118. See Scarry, *Body in Pain*.
119. Hollander, *Love in a Time of Hate*, p. 114.
120. Roberts, "Belief in the Evil Eye in World Perspective."
121. Garrison and Arensberg, "Evil Eye."
122. Schneider, "Of Vigilance and Virgins"; Ortner, "The Virgin and the State"; Kandiyoti, "Islam and Patriarchy."
123. See especially Hijazi, "'Ilm al-nafs fi al-'alam al-'arabi" (Psychology in the Arab World), and Martinez, *Algerian Civil War*.
124. See especially Accad, *Sexuality and War*, on the civil war in Lebanon; also Sayigh, "Researching Gender in a Palestinian Camp"; Peteet, "Male Gender and Rituals of Resistance in the Palestinian Intifada."
125. Makiya, *Cruelty and Silence*, p. 299.
126. For recent studies and reviews, see Phinney, "Ethnic Identity and Acculturation"; Berry, "Conceptual Approaches to Acculturation"; Hermans and Kempen, "Moving Cultures"; and Oyserman, Gant, and Ager, "A Socially Contextualized Model of African American Identity."
127. Sen, *Development as Freedom*.
128. Sen identifies five key types of freedom: political (democratic institutions and civil rights), economic (aggregate wealth and just distribution), social (access to education and health care), transparency (openness of governing and economic institutions), and protective security (a social safety net for the vulnerable and aged).
129. The capabilities entail key forms of social participation that integrate one into a community and develop individuals' agency, which consists mainly of a sense of self-efficacy, an achievement orientation, and self-respect.
130. Sen, *Development as Freedom*, pp. 87–110.
131. See Wilkinson, "Epidemiological Transition"; Marmot, Bobak, and Davey Smith, "Explanations for Social Inequalities in Health"; Kawachi, "Income Inequality and Health."
132. Honneth, *Struggle for Recognition*.
133. Ibid. See especially fig. 2 on p. 129.
134. Sen, *Development as Freedom*, chap. 2.
135. Lila, *Al-shabab al-'arabi* (Arab Youth).
136. See Moghrabi, "Arab Basic Personality," Barakat, "Beyond the Always and the Never," Yassin, *Al-shakhsiyya al-'arabiyya* (Arab Personality), 'Awda, *Al-takayyuff wa al-muqawamah* (Adaptation and Resistance), Hijazi, "Al-shakhsiyya al-misriyya bayn al-silbiyya wa al-ijabiyya" (Egyptian Personality Between the Negative and the Positive).
137. Oyserman, Coon, and Kemmelmeier, "Rethinking Individualism and Collectivism." See also Fiske, "Using Individualism and Collectivism to Compare Cultures"; Miller, "Bringing Culture to Basic Psychological Theory"; and Matsumoto, "Culture and Self ."
138. Gutmann, "Alternatives to Disengagement" and *Human Elder in Nature, Culture, and Society*.

CHAPTER 10

1. The patriarchal ideology appears to be learned in late childhood, and internalized as a key feature of social selves based both on honor-modesty and Islam.
2. Female circumcision/genital cutting rites are often performed later in childhood, or even early adolescence.
3. The first occurs at weaning.
4. That is, I believe the widespread distress over identity stems not so much from the task Erikson described as *identity formation* but from embedding identities in what Levinson termed a *life structure*.
5. Dwyer, *Moroccan Dialogues*, p. 25.
6. Ibid, p. 23.
7. Ibid., p. 26.
8. Ibid., p. 27.
9. Ibid., pp. 30–31.
10. Ibid., p. 44.
11. Ibid., p. 42.

AFTERWORD

1. See especially de St. Aubin, McAdams, and Kim, *Generative Society*.
2. Khaleefa, "The Predicament of Euro-American Psychology in Non-Western Culture."
3. This section was written with Hala Mahmoud, a student at the American University in Cairo who is studying efforts to create an indigenous Arab or Muslim psychology.
4. Hijazi, "'Ilm al-nafs fi al-'alam al-'arabi" (Psychology in the Arab World).
5. Nablusi, *Nahwa saykulujiyya 'arabiah* (Toward an Arab Psychology).
6. Abu Hateb, *Mushkilat 'ilm al-nafs fi al-'alam al-thaleth hala al-watan al-'arabi* (Problems of Psychology in the Third World and Arab Countries).
7. Zayour, *Al-tarbiya wa 'ilm nafs al-waled fi al-dhat al-'arabiyya* (Child-Rearing and Child Psychology with Regard to the Arab Self).
8. As examples, the April 1989 issue of the Moroccan journal *Derasat al-nafsiya wa al-terbouia* (Psychological and Educational Studies) was devoted to articles on Muslim theories of child development and child-rearing, and Zayour's 1985 book examines conceptions of childhood and child-rearing in the writings of classical-era Muslim thinkers.
9. See Kim and Berry, *Indigenous Psychologies*.

REFERENCES

Abdelqader, Mahmoud, and 'Afifi, Al-Ham. (1975, January). "Al-dirasa al-midaniyya
'an al-asalib al-sha'ia al-ijtima'iyya fi al-rif al-misri" (Field Study of Socialization in Rural Egypt). *Al-majala al-ijtima'iyya al-qaumiyya* (Journal of the National Society).
Abdelqader, Mahmoud, and Ali, Mohammed. (1967, May). "Asalib al-rida'a wa al-
fitam al-shai' fi al-thaqafa al-misriyya wa atharuha 'ala shakhsiyyiat al-tifl or
atfal" (Styles of Nursing and Weaning Widespread in Egyptian Culture and
Their Influence on the Personality of Children). *Al-majalla al-ijtima'iyya al-
qaumiyya* (Journal of the National Society).
Abdel-Khalek, Ahmed. (1981). "Extraversion and Neuroticism as Basic Personality Dimensions in Egyptian Samples." *Personality and Individual Differences*
2: 91–97.
Abdel-Khalek, Ahmed. (1986). "Death Anxiety in Egyptian Samples." *Personality and
Individual Differences* 7, no. 4: 479–483.
Abdel-Khalek, Ahmed. (1989). "The Development and Validation of an Arabic Form
of the STAI: Egyptian Results." *Personality and Individual Differences* 10, no. 3:
277–285.
Abdel-Khalek, Ahmed. (1994). "Normative Results on the Arabic Fear Survey Schedule III." *Journal of Behavior Therapy and Experimental Psychology* 25, no. 1: 61–67.
Abdel-Khaleq, Ahmad, and Nil, Maissa. (2002a). "Al-Daf'iya al-injaz wa 'ilaqatuha
bi-ab'ad mutaghayirat al-shakhsiyya lada 'ayina min talamidh al-madaris al-
ibtida'iyya wa al-tilmithat bi-dawlat Qatar" (Achievement Motivation and Its
Relationship with Personality Variables in a Sample of Qatari Students). In
A. Abdel Khalek and M. Nil, *Dirasat fi shakhsiyyat al-tifl al-'arabi* (Studies of
the Personality of Arab Children). Cairo: maktabat al-injelou al-misriyya,
pp. 199–233.
Abdel-Khaleq, Ahmad, and Nil, Maissa. (2002b). *Derasat fi shakhsiyyat al-tifl al-'arbi*
(Studies of the Personality of Arab Children). Cairo: maktabat al-injelou al-
misriyya.
Abdo, Geneive (2000). *No God But God.* Oxford: Oxford University Press.
Abou el Nil, Mahmoud. (1998). "Cross-Cultural Research." In Ramadan Ahmed and

Uwe Gielen, eds., *Psychology in the Arab Countries.* Egypt: Menoufia University Press, pp. 519–548.

Abou Zeid, Ahmed. (1966). "Honour and Shame Among the Beduoins of Egypt." In J. G. Peristiany, ed., *Honour and Shame.* Chicago: University of Chicago Press, pp. 243–260.

Aboulafia, Mitchell. (1986). *The Mediating Self: Mead, Sartre, and Self-Determination.* New Haven, CT: Yale University Press.

Abrahim, S'ad al-Din, Yassin, Sayyid, and Qaziha, Walid. (1981). *Itijahat al-rai al-'am al-'arabi nahoua mas'alat al-wihda: Derasat maydaniyya* (Orientation of Arab Attitudes Toward Unity: A Field Study). Beirut: markaz al-dirasat al-'arabiyya.

Abu Hateb, Fuad. (1993). *Mushkilat 'ilm al-nafs fi al-'alam al-thaleth hala al-watan al-'arabi* (Problems of Psychology in the Third World and Arab Countries). In *'Ilm al-nafs wa qadhaya al-mujtam'at al-mu'asira* (Psychology and Contemporary Social Issues). Rabat: kulliyat al-adab, pp. 9–32.

Abu-Lughod, Lila. (1986). *Veiled Sentiments.* Berkeley: University of California Press.

Abu-Lughod, Lila. (1993). *Writing Women's Worlds.* Berkeley: University of California Press.

Accad, Evelyne. (1990). *Sexuality and War.* New York: New York University Press.

'Adim, Saddiq. (1968). *An-naqd al-dhati ba'd al-hazima* (Self-Critique After the Defeat). Beirut: dar at-tali'a.

Adorno, T. W., Frenkel-Brunswik, E., Levinson, D., and Sanford, R. (1950). *The Authoritarian Personality.* New York: Norton.

Ahirshaw, al-Ghali. (1994a). "Al-Montor sikologiyya li-azmat al-shabab fi al-watan al-'arabi" (Psychological Theories of the Crisis of Arab Youth). In *Waq'a al-tajriba al-sikologiyya fi al-watan al-'arabi* (Realities of Psychological Experience among Arab Peoples). Beirut: al-markaz al-thaqafi al-'arabi, pp. 89–110.

Ahirshaw, al-Ghali. (1994b). *"waqa' al-tajribah al-saykulujiyyah fi al-watan al-'Arabi"* (Realities of Psychological Experience among Arab Peoples). Beirut: al-Markaz al-thaqafi al-'arabi.

Ahirshaw, al-Ghali. (1997). "Waqa' thaqafat al-tifl al-maghrebi wa afaq tanmiyatiha" (Cultural Situation of the Moroccan Child and the Horizon of Its Development). In A. Dachmi, *Al-tifl wa al-tanmiya* (The Child and Development). Rabat: kulliyat al-adab, pp. 17–22.

Ahlawat, K. S. (1989). "Psychometric Properties of the Yarmouk Test Anxiety Inventory." *Advances in Test Anxiety Research.* Lisse, Netherlands: Swets and Zeitlinger, vol. 6, pp. 263–278.

Ahmad, Leila. (1992). *Women and Gender in Islam.* New Haven, CT: Yale University Press.

Ahmed, Akbar. (1994). *Living Islam.* London: BBC Books.

Ahmed, Ramadan. (1992). "Psychology in the Arab Countries." In U. P. Gielen, eds., *Psychology in International Perspective.* Amsterdam: Swets and Zeitlinger, pp. 127–150.

Ahmed, Ramadan. (1997). An Interview with Mustapha Soueif. *World Psychology* 4, nos. 1–2: 13–28.

Ahmed, Ramadan, and Gielen, Uwe, eds. (1998). *Psychology in the Arab Countries.* Egypt: Menoufia University Press.

Ainsworth, M. (1973). "The Development of Infant-Mother Interaction Among the

Ganda." In D. Foss, ed., *Determinants of Infant Behavior.* New York: Wiley, vol. 2, pp. 67–104.

Ainsworth, Mary. (1967). *Infancy in Uganda.* Baltimore: Johns Hopkins University Press.

Ainsworth, M. D., Blehar, M., Waters, E., and Wall, S. (1978). *Patterns of Attachment.* Hillsdale, NJ: Erlbaum.

Ajami, Fuad. (1967). *The Arab Predicament.* Cambridge, UK: Cambridge University Press.

Ajami, Fuad. (1998). *The Dream Palace of the Arabs.* New York: Vintage Books.

Akin, John, Bilsborrow, R., Guilkey, D., and Popkin, B. (1986). "Breastfeeding Patterns and Determinants in the Near East." *Population Studies* 40: 247–262.

Al-Aharas, Mohammed. (1979). "Terkib al-'ai'la al-'arabiyya wa wada'ifha" (Organization and Functions of the Arab Family). In L. Melikian, ed., *Qira'at 'ilm al-nafs al-ijtama'i fi al-watan al-'arabi* (Readings in Social Psychology in the Arab Countries). Cairo: al-hiyya al-mesriyya al-'ama li-al-kitab, vol. 3, pp. 125–135.

Al Ansarey, Badr. (1997). "Meda kefaa Qa'imat al-'awamal al-khamsa al-kabri li-al-shakhsiyya fi al-mujtama' al-kuwaiti" (The Psychometric Properties of the Five-Factor Inventory in the Kuwaiti Society). *Derasat nafsiyyah* (Psychological Studies) 7, no. 2: 277–310.

Albine, R. C., and Thompson, V. J. (1956). "The Effects of Sudden Weaning on Zule Children." *British Journal of Medical Psychology* 29: 177–210.

Ali, Maulana Muhammad, trans. (1994). *The Holy Quran.* Columbus, OH: Ahmadiyyah Anjuman Isha'at Islam.

Al-Issa, Ihsan, Bakal, Donald, and Fung, Tak. (1999). Beck Anxiety Inventory Symptom Comparisons Between Students in Lebanon and Canada. *Arab Journal of Psychiatry* 10, no. 1: 24–30.

Al-Issa, Ihsan, Al Zubaidi, A., Bakal, D., and Fung, T. (2000). Beck Anxiety Inventory Symptoms in Arab College Students. *Arab Journal of Psychiatry* 11, no. 1: 41–47.

Al-Issa, Ihsan (2000). *Al-Junun: Mental Illness in the Islamic World.* Madison, WI: International Universities Press.

al-Khalil, Samir. (1989). *Republic of Fear.* New York: Pantheon Books.

Alloula, Malek. (1986). *The Colonial Harem.* Minneapolis: University of Minnesota Press.

Allport, Gordon. (1979). *The Nature of Prejudice.* Reading, MA: Addison-Wesley.

Al-markaz al-Qaumi li-al-Buhouth (National Center for Research). (1974). *Beheth ahtiajiat al-tufula fi jumhuriyyat misr al-'arabiyya iyia* (Study of the Needs of Children in the Arab Republic of Egypt). Cairo: manuscript.

Al-Mofti, Maissa. (1988). *Derasat moqarana al-tanshi'a al-ijtim'iyya fi al-rif wa al-hadar al-misri* (Comparative Study of Socialization in Rural and Urban Egypt). Fourth Research Conference of Psychology in Egypt. Cairo: 'Ayn Shems University, pp. 489–522.

Al-Mofti, Maissa. (n.d.). *Anmat al-tanshi'a al-ijtima'iyya fi bilad al-nuba* (Pattern of Socialization among the Nuba). Manuscript.

Al Nawayseh, Naif. (1997). *Al-tifl fi al-hayat al-sha'biyya al-urduniyya* (The Child in Popular Life in Jordan). Amman: Ministry of Culture.

Al-Sa'ti, Samia Hassan. (1979). "Asma' al-misriyyin wa al-taghir al-ijtima'i" (Egyptian Names and Social Change). In L. Metikian, ed., *Qira'at 'ilm al-nafs al-ijtima'i fi al-watan al-'arbi* (Readings in Social Psychology in the Arab Countries). Cairo: al-hiyya al-misriyya al-'ama li-al-kitab, vol. 3, pp. 165–185.

Altemeyer, Bob. (1996). *The Authoritarian Specter.* Cambridge: Harvard University Press.

Altermeyer, Bob. (1981). *Right Wing Authoritarianism.* Winnipeg: University of Manitoba Press.

Al-Zahrani, S., and Kaplowitz, S. (1993). Attributional Biases in Individualistic and Collectivistic Cultures: A Comparison of Americans with Saudis. *Social Psychology Quarterly* 56, no. 3: 223–233.

'Amad, Al-din Sultan, Jabar, Abdelhamid, Rachdi, Labib, and Abdeljouad, Lily. (1979). "Al-sera'a al-qaimi bin al-ab wa al-abna wa 'alaqatuha bi-tawafiq al-abna al-nafsi" (Conflict of Values Between Parents and Children and Its Relationship with Agreement Among Children). In Louis Melikian, ed., *Qira'at 'ilm al-nafs al-ijtima'i fi al-watan al-'arabi* (Readings in Social Psychology in the Arab Countries). Cairo: al-haya al-mesriya al-'amma li al-kitab, vol. 3, pp. 145–163.

Ammar, Hamid. (1954). *Growing Up in an Egyptian Village.* London: Routledge and Kegan Paul.

Ammar, Hamid. (1964). *Fi bina' al-bashar* (On Building Human Character). Cairo: sirs allayan.

Ammar, Nawal. (1988). *An Egyptian Village Growing Up.* Ph.D. dissertation, University of Florida.

Amrouche, F. (1989). *My Life Story.* New Brunswick, NJ: Rutgers University Press.

Anderson, Benedict. (1983). *Imagined Communities.* London: Verso.

Anderson, Jon. (1985). "Sentimental Ambivalence and the Exegesis of 'Self' in Afghanistan." *Anthropological Quarterly* 58, no. 4: 203–211.

Antoun, R. (1989). *Muslim Preacher in the Modern World.* Princeton, NJ: Princeton University Press.

Armon-Jones, Claire. (1986). "The Thesis of Constructionism." In R. Harre, ed., *The Social Construction of Emotion.* Oxford: Blackwell, pp. 32–56.

Asad, Talal. (1973). "The Beduin as a Military Force." In C. Nelson, ed., *The Desert and the Sown: Nomads in the Wider Society.* Berkeley: University of California Press, pp. 62–64.

Asano-Tamanoi, Mariko. (1987). "Shame, Family, and State in Catalonia and Japan." In D. Gilmore, ed., *Honor and Shame and the Unity of the Mediterranean.* Washington, DC: American Anthropological Association.

Askandar, Naguib, 'Amad, Isma'il, and Rachdi, Falam. (1966). *Kayfa nurabi atfalana: Al-tensh'a al-ijtima'iyya li al-tifl fi al-usra al-arbiyya* (How We Raise Our Children: Child Socialization in Arab Families). Cairo: dar al-nahda al-'arabiyya.

Atiya, Nayra. (1982). *Khul-Khaal: Five Egyptian Women Tell Their Stories.* Syracuse, NY: Syracuse University Press.

Atkinson, John, and Raynor, Joel, eds. (1974). *Motivation and Achievement.* New York: Wiley.

'Awdah, Mahmud. (1995). *Al-takayyuff wa al- muqawamah: Al-judhur al-ijtima'iyya wa al-siyasiyya al-shakhsiyya al-mesriyya.* (Adaptation and Resistance: The Social and Political Basis of the Egyptian Personality). Cairo: al-majlis al-a'la lil-thaqafah.

Ayrout, Henry. (1963). *The Egyptian Peasant.* Boston: Beacon Press.

Aziz, Shagufta and Jackson, Chris. (2001). "A Comparison Between Three and Five

Factor Models of Pakistani Personality Data." *Personality and Individual Differences* 31, no. 8: 1311–1319.

Badri, Gasim. (1979). *Child-Rearing Practices in the Sudan: Implications for Parent Education.* Ph.D. dissertation, Stanford University.

Banuazizi, Ali. (1977). "Iranian 'National Character': A Critique of Some Western Perspectives." In L. Brown and N. Itzkowitz, eds., *Psychological Dimensions of Near Eastern Studies.* Princeton, NJ: Darwin Press, pp. 210–239.

Barak, Omar. (2002, May 11). "Palestinians Oppose Suicide Missions by Children." *Ha'aretz Daily.*

Barakat, Halim. (1976). "Socio-Economic, Cultural and Personality Forces Determining Development in Arab Society." *Social Praxis* 2, nos. 3–4: 179–204.

Barakat, Halim. (1990). "Beyond the Always and the Never: Critique of Social Psychological Interpretations of Arab Society and Culture." In H. Sharabi, ed., *Theory, Politics and the Arab World.* New York: Routledge, pp. 132–159.

Barakat, Halim. (1993). *The Arab World.* Berkeley: University of California Press.

Barth, Frederik. (1961). *Nomads of South Persia.* Prospect Heights, IL: Waveland Press.

Bates, Daniel, and Rassam, Amal. (1983). *Peoples and Cultures of the Middle East.* Englewood Cliffs, NJ: Prentice-Hall.

Baumrind, D. (1967). "Child Care Practices Anteceding Three Patterns of Preschool Behavior." *Genetic Psychology Monographs* 75: 43–88.

Baumrind, D. (1971). "Current Patterns of Parental Authority." *Developmental Psychology Monographs* 1: 1–103.

Baumrind, D. (1991). "Effective Parenting During the Early Adolescent Transition." In P. Cowan and E. Hetherington, eds., *Family Transitions.* Hillsdale, NJ: Erlbaum, pp. 111–164.

Beals, A. (1962). *Gopalpur: A South Indian Village.* New York: Rinehart and Winston.

Beardsley, R., Hall, J., and Ward, R. (1959). *Village Japan.* Chicago: University of Chicago Press.

Beck, Lois. (1991). *Nomad: A Year in the Life of a Qashqa'i Tribesman in Iran.* Berkeley: University of California Press.

Beck, Lois, and Keddie, Nikki, eds. (1978). *Women in the Muslim World.* Cambridge: Harvard University Press.

Bela'rbi, Aisha. (1992). "Ishkaliyyat al-tawasul dakhil al-usra al-maghrebiyya." (Forms of Communication in the Moroccan Family). In *Al-usra wa al-tifl fi al-mujtama'at al-maghrebiyya al-mu'asira.* (Family and Child in Contemporary A Moroccan Society). Rabat: kulliyat al-adab wa al-'ilm al-insani, pp. 79–89.

Bellah, R. (1957). *Tokugawa Religion: The Values of Preindustrial Japan.* Boston: Beacon Press.

Ben Jalloun, Juad. (2001). "Al-tifl wa tandhim al-majal fi al-ma'mar al-maghribi" (Children and the Organization of Space in Moroccan Buildings). In Abdelkarim Ghareeb and Abdelkarim Flio, eds., *Al-Tufoula wa al-murahaqa* (Childhood and Adolescence). Dar al-beida: n.p., pp. 215–222.

Ben Jelloun, Tahar. (1987). *The Sacred Night.* San Diego: Harcourt, Brace.

Benedict, R. (1934). *Patterns of Culture.* Boston: Houghton Mifflin.

Benedict, R. (1946). *The Chrysanthemum and the Sword: Patterns of Japanese Culture.* Cleveland, OH: World.

Bennani-Chraibi, Mounia. (1994). *Soumis et Rebelles Les Jeunes au Maroc.* Paris: Editions le Fennec.

Bennett, John. (1946). "The Interpretation of Pueblo Culture: A Question of Values." *Southwestern Journal of Anthropology* 2: 361–374.

Berger, M. (1964). *The Arab World Today.* New York: Doubleday.

Berque, Jacques. (1965). *The Arabs.* New York: Praeger.

Berry, H., Child, I., and Bacon, M. (1959). "Relation of Child Training to Subsistence economy." *American Anthropologist* 61: 51–63.

Berry, John. (2003). "Conceptual Approaches to Acculturation." In K. Chun, P. Organista, and F. Marin, eds., *Acculturation.* Washington, DC: American Psychological Association, pp. 17–37.

Beshai, J. A., and Templer, D. I. (1978). "American and Egyptian Attitudes Toward Death." *Essence* 2: 155–158.

Boddy, Janice . (1989). *Wombs and Alien Spirits.* Madison: University of Wisconsin Press.

Bond, M. (2002). "Psychology of Conflict." *Resurgence Magazine On Line*; available online at: http://resurgence.gn.apc.org/issues/bond215.htm (accessed Nov. 16, 2004).

Booth, Marilyn (2002). "Arab Adolescents Facing the Future." In B. Brown, R. Larson, and T. Saraswathi, *The World's Youth: Adolescence in Eight Regions of the Globe.* Cambridge, UK: Cambridge University Press, pp. 207–242.

Boserup, Esther. (1970). *Women's Role in Economic Development.* London: Allen and Unwin.

Bouhdiba, A. (1985). *Sexuality in Islam.* London: Routledge and Kegan Paul.

Bourdieu, P. (1966). "The Sentiment of Honour in Kabyle Society." In J. Peristiany, ed., *Honor and Shame: The Values of Mediterranean Society.* Chicago: University of Chicago Press, pp. 191–241.

Bourdieu, P. (1970). "The Kabyle House or The World Reversed." In *Algeria 1960.* Cambridge, UK: Cambridge University Press, pp. 133–153.

Bourdieu, P. (1984). *Distinction: A Social Critique of the Judgment of Taste* (R. Nice, trans.). Cambridge: Harvard University Press.

Bourdieu, Pierre. (1977). *Outline of a Theory of Practice.* Cambridge, UK: Cambridge University Press.

Brandes, Stanley. (1987). "Reflections on Honor and Shame in the Mediterranean." In D. Gilmore, ed., *Honor and Shame and the Unity of the Mediterranean.* Washington, DC: American Anthropological Association.

Brink, Judy. (1995). "Changing Child-Rearing Patterns in an Egyptian Village." In Elizabeth Fernea, ed., *Children in the Muslim Middle East.* Austin: University of Texas Press, pp. 84–92.

Brohi, Allahbakhsh. (1987). "The Spiritual Dimension of Prayer." In Seyyed Hossein Nasr, ed., *Islamic Spirituality.* New York: Crossroad.

Brown, L., and Itzkowitz, N., eds. (1977). *Psychological Dimensions of Near Eastern Studies.* Princeton, NJ: Darwin Press.

Bruner, Jerome. (1990). *Acts of Meaning.* Cambridge: Harvard University Press.

Buda, R. and Elsayed-Elkhouly, S. (1998). "Cultural differences between Arabs and Americans: Individualism-Collectivism revisited." *Journal of Cross-Cultural Psychology* 29(3): 487–492.

Burgat, Francois and Dowell, William. (1993). *The Islamic Movement in North Africa*. Austin: University of Texas Center for Middle Eastern Studies.

Campbell, J. K. (1964). *Honour, Family, and Patronage*. Oxford: Clarendon Press.

Campbell, J. K. (1966). "Honour and the Devil." In J. G. Peristiany, ed., *Honour and Shame*. Chicago: University of Chicago Press, pp. 139–170.

Campbell, Joseph. (1949). *The Hero with a Thousand Faces*. Princeton, NJ: Princeton University Press.

Cansever, Gocke. (1965). "Psychological Effects of Circumcision." *British Journal of Psychology* 38: 321–331

Carnes, Mark. (1989). *Secret Ritual and Manhood in Victorian America*. New Haven, CT: Yale University Press.

Carstairs, G. (1967). *The Twice-Born*. Bloomington: Indiana University Press.

Cassidy, J. and Berlin, L. (1994). "The Insecure/Ambivalent Pattern of Attachment: Theory and Research." *Child Development*. 65: 971–991.

Caton, Steven. (1985). "The Poetic Construction of Self." *Anthropological Quarterly* 58, no. 4: 141–150.

Cederblaad, Marianne. (1968). "Child Psychiatric Study on Sudanese Arab Children." Copenhagen: *Acta Psychiatrica Scandinavica* supplementum 200.

Cederblad, Marianne. (1988). "Behavioural Disorders in Children from Different Cultures." *Acta Psychiatrica Scandinavia* 78: 85–92.

Cederblad, Marianne, and Rahim, Idris. (1986). "Effects of Rapid Urbanization on Child Behaviour and Health in a Part of Khartoum, Sudan, part 1, Socio-Economic Changes 1965–1980." *Social Science and Medicine* 22, no. 7: 713–721.

Chamcham, Rouchdi. (1987). "L'enfant marocain: Entre la dependance d'hier, la detresse d'aujourd'hui et l'autonomie de demain." In M. Dernouny and A. Chaouite, eds., *Enfance Maghrebines*. Casablanca: Afrique Orient, pp. 67–79.

Chao, Ruth. (1994). "Beyond Parental Control and Authoritarian Parenting Style." *Child Development* 65: 1111–1119.

Chaouite, Abdellatif. (1987). "L'enfant marocain: Horizon d'une pensee psychologique." In M. Dernouny, and A. Chaouite, eds., *Enfance Maghrebines*. Casablanca: Afrique Orient, pp. 41–66.

Chaqueri, C. (1992). *Beginning Politics in the Reproductive Cycle of Children's Tales and Games in Iran*. Lewiston, NY: Mellen Press.

Chairbi, Driss. (1990). *The Simple Past*. Washington, DC: Three Continents Press.

Chodorow, N. . (1978). *The Reproduction of Mothering*. Berkeley: University of California Press.

Clark, R. (1983). "Patterns in the Lives of ETA Members." *Terrorism*. 6:423–454.

Coco, Carla. (1997). *Secrets of the Harem*. New York: Vendome Press.

Cohen, Abner. (1965). *Arab Border Villages in Israel*. Manchester, UK: Manchester University Press.

Cohen, Abner. (1970). "The Politics of Marriage in Changing Middle Eastern Stratification Systems." In L. Plotnicov and A. Tuden, eds., *Essays in Comparative Social Stratification*. Pittsburgh: University of Pittsburgh Press, pp. 195–210.

Cole, Donald. (1975). *Nomads of the Nomads*. Arlington Heights, IL: Harlan Davidson.

Colin, V. (1996). *Human Attachment*. New York: McGraw-Hill

Combs-Schilling, M. E. (1989). *Sacred Performances: Islam, Sexuality, and Sacrifice*. New York: Columbia University.

Connelly, B. (1986). *Arab Folk Epic and Identity*. Berkeley: University of California Press.

Crapanzano, Vincent. (1973). *The Hamadsha: A Study in Moroccan Ethnopsychiatry*. Berkeley: University of California Press.

Crapanzano, Vincent. (1980). *Tuhami*. Chicago: University of Chicago Press.

Crapanzano, Vincent. (1981). "Rite of Return: Circumcision in Morocco." In W. Muensterberger and L. Boyer, eds., *The Psychoanalytic Study of Society*, vol. 9, pp. 15–36.

Crapanzano, Vincent. (1992). "Mohammed and Dawia." In *Hermes' Dilemma and Hamlet's Desire*. Cambridge: Harvard University Press, pp. 155–187.

Critchfield, Richard. (1978). *Shahhat: An Egyptian*. Syracuse, NY: Syracuse University Press.

Cross, S., and Markus, H. (1991). Possible Selves Across the Life Span. *Human Development* 34: 230–255.

Dabashi, H. (1989). *Authority in Islam*. New Brunswick, NJ: Transaction.

Dachmi, Abdeslam. (1995). *De La Seduction Maternelle Negative*. Rabat: Faculte des Lettres et des Sciences Humaines.

Dachmi, Abdeslam. (1997). "Troubles du Sommeil au Feminin." In A. Dachmi, ed., *Enfance et Development*. Rabat: Faculte des Lettres et Sciences Humaines.

Darain, D. (1964). "Growing Up in India." *Family Process* 3, no. 1: 127–154.

Davis, Susan. (1977). "Zahrah Muhammad: A Rural Woman of Morocco." In E. Fernea and B. Bezirgan, eds., *Middle Eastern Muslim Women Speak*. Austin: University of Texas Press, pp. 201–218.

Davis, Susan. (1983). *Patience and Power: Women's Lives in a Moroccan Village*. Rochester, VT: Schenkman.

Davis, Susan, and Davis, Douglas. (1989). *Adolescence in a Moroccan Town*. New Brunswick, NJ: Rutgers University Press.

Dawood, N., trans. (1983). *The Koran*. New York: Penguin Books.

Delaney, Carol. (1991). *The Seed and the Soil: Gender and Cosmology in Turkish Village Society*. Berkeley: University of California Press.

de La Ronciere, Charles. (1988)."Tuscan Notables on the Eve of the Renaissance." In P. Aries and G. Duby, eds., *A History of Private Life*. Vol. 2, *Revelations of the Medieval World*. Cambridge: Harvard University Press.

de St. Aubin, E., McAdams, D., and Kim, T., eds. (2004). *The Generative Society*. Washington, DC: American Psychological Society.

Devereux, George. (1951). *Realty and Dream*. New York: International Universities Press.

DeVos, George. (1973). *Socialization for Achievement*. Berkeley: University of California Press.

Diqs, Isaak. (1967). *A Bedouin Boyhood*. London: George Allen and Unwin.

Djait, Hichem. (1984). *Al-Shakhsiyya al-'arabiyya al-islamiyya wal-masir al-'arabi* (Arab-Islamic Personality and Arab Destiny). Beirut: Dar at-tali'a. Translation of *La Personnalite et le Devenir Arabo-Islamiques*. Paris: Editions du Seuil.

Doi, Takeo. (1973). *The Anatomy of Dependence* (J. Bester, trans.). New York: Harper and Row. (Original work published 1971.)

Doi, Takeo. (1986). *The Anatomy of Conformity: The Individual Versus Society*. Tokyo: Kadansha.

Donaldson, Bess. (1992). "The Evil Eye in Iran." In Alan Dundes, ed, *The Evil Eye: A Casebook*. Madison: University of Wisconsin Press, pp. 66–77.

Doty, R., Peterson, B., and Winter, D. (1991). "Threat and Authoritarianism in the United States, 1978–1987." *Journal of Personality and Social Psychology* 61, no. 4: 629–640.

Drummond, J. (2002). "From the Northwest Imperative to Global Jihad." In Chris Stout, ed., *The Psychology of Terrorism* . Westport, CT: Praeger, vol. 1, pp. 49–96.

Drummond, J. (2004, March 13). "Which Ones Will Be Violent?" Paper presented to Colloquium on the Strategic Importance, Causes, and Concsequences of Terrorism, University of Michigan, Ann Arbor.

Dumont, L. (1970). *Homo Hierarchicus: The Caste System and Its Implications* (M. Sainsbury, L. Dumont, and B. Gulati, trans.). Chicago: University of Chicago Press. (Original work published 1966.)

Dundes, Alan. (1971). "The Strategy of Turkish Boys' Verbal Dueling Rhymes." *Journal of American Folklore* 83, no. 329: 325–349.

Dundes, Alan, ed. (1992). *The Evil Eye: A Casebook*. Madison: University of Wisconsin Press.

Dwyer, Daisy. (1978). *Images and Self-Images*. New York: Columbia University Press.

Dwyer, Kevin . (1982). *Moroccan Dialogues*. Baltimore: Johns Hopkins Press.

Edgerton, R. (1971). *The Individual in Cultural Adaptation*. Berkeley: University of California Press.

Eickelman, Dale. (1976). *Moroccan Islam*. Austin: University of Texas Press.

Eickelman, Dale. (1981). *The Middle East: An Anthropological Approach*. 1st ed. Englewood Cliffs, NJ: Prentice-Hall.

Eickelman, Dale. (1985). *Knowledge and Power in Morocco*. Princeton, NJ: Princeton University Press.

Eisenstadt, S. N. (1965). "Archetypcal Patterns of Youth." In Erik Erikson, ed., *The Challenge of Youth*. Garden City, NY: Anchor.

Ekman, P. (1980). "Biological and Cultural Contributions to Body and Facial Movement in the Expression of Emotions." In A. Rorty, ed., *Explaining Emotions*. Berkeley: University of California Press.

El Guindi, Fadwa. (1981). "Veling Infitah with Muslim Ethic: Egypt's Contemporary Islamic Movement." *Social Problems* 28, no. 4: 465–485.

El-Keky, Hamed. (1991). "Patterns of Parental Control in Kuwaiti Society." *International Journal of Psychology* 26, no. 4: 485–495.

El Khayat-Bennai, Ghita. (n.d.). *Le Monde Arabe au Feminin*. Casablanca: EDDIF.

El Messiri, Sawsan. (1978). *Ibn al-Balad: A Concept of Egyptian Identity*. Netherlands: Brill.

El Saadawi, Nawal. (1985). "Growing Up Female in Egypt." In E. Fernea, ed., *Women and Family in the Middle East*. Austin: University of Texas, pp. 111–120.

El Saadawi, Nawal. (1981). *The Hidden Face of Eve*. Boston: Beacon Press.

El Sarraj, Eyad. (2002). "Wounds and Madness: Why We've Become Suicide Bombers." Available online at: http://jerusalem.indymedia.org/news/2002/04/4731/php (accessed Nov. 16, 2004).

El-Zahhar, Nabil, and Hocevar, Dennis. (1991). "Cultural and Sexual Differences in Test Anxiety, Trait Anxiety and Arousability." *Journal of Cross-Cultural Psychology* 22, no. 2: 238–249.

Emmons, R. (1989). "Exploring the Relations Between Traits and Motives: The Case of Narcissism." In D. M. Buss and N. Cantor, eds., *Personality Psychology: Recent Trends and Emerging Issues*. New York: Springer-Verlag.

Emmons, R. (1997). "Motives and Life Goals." In R. Hogan, J. Johnson, and S. Briggs, eds., *Handbook of Personality Psychology*. San Diego: Academic Press.

Erikson, Erik. (1950). *Childhood and Society*. New York: Norton.

Erikson, Erik. (1958). *Young Man Luther*. New York: Norton.

Erikson, Erik. (1968). *Identity: Youth and Crisis*. New York: Norton.

Erikson, Erik. (1977). *Toys and Reasons*. New York: Norton.

Euloge, Rene. (1972). *Les Chants de la Tassaout*. Casablanca: Maroc Editions. (Translated by Elizabeth Fernea and reprinted in E. Fernea and B. Bezirgan, eds., *Middle Eastern Muslim Women Speak*. Austin: University of Texas Press.)

Evans-Pritchard, E. E. (1940). *The Nuer*. New York: Oxford University Press.

Ewing, Katherine. (1991). "Can Psychoanalytic Theories Explain the Pakistani Woman?" *Ethos* 19, no. 2: 131–160.

Ewing, Katherine. (1990). "The Illusion of Wholeness: Culture, Self, and the Experience of Inconsistency." *Ethos* 18, no. 3: 251–278.

Ewing, Katherine. (1997). *Arguing Sainthood: Modernity, Psychoanalysis, and Islam*. Durham, NC: Duke University Press.

Eysenck, Sybil, Makaremi, Azar, and Barret, Paul. (1994). "A Cross-Cultural Study of Personality: Iranian and English Children." *Personality and Individual Differences* 16, no. 2: 203–210.

Fakhouri, Hani. (1987). *Kafr El-Elow*. Prospect Heights, IL: Waveland Press.

Fanon, Frantz. (1963). *The Wretched of the Earth*. New York: Grove Press.

Fanon, Franz. (1967). *Black Skin White Masks*. New York: Grove Press.

Farrag, M. F. (1987). "Dimensions of Personality in Saudi Arabia." *Personality and Individual Differences* 8, no. 6: 951–953.

Feldman, Allen. (1991). *Formations of Violence*. Chicago: University of Chicago Press.

Fernea, E., and Bezirgan, B., eds. (1977). *Middle Eastern Muslim Women Speak*. Austin: University of Texas Press.

Fernea, Elizabeth. (1965). *Guests of the Shiekh*. Garden City, NY: Doubleday.

Fernea, Elizabeth. (1976). *A Street in Marrakech*. Garden City, NY: Doubleday.

Fernea, Elizabeth. (1995a). "Childhood in the Muslim Middle East." In *Children in the Muslim Middle East*. Austin: University of Texas Press, pp. 3–16.

Fernea, Elizabeth. (1995b). *Children in the Muslim Middle East*. Austin: University of Texas Press.

Fernea, Elizabeth, ed. (1985). *Women and the Family in the Middle East*. Austin: University of Texas Press.

Fields, R., Elbedour, S., and Abu Hein, F. (2003). "The Palestinian Suicide Bomber." In Chris Stout, ed., *The Psychology of Terrorism*. Westport, CT: Praeger, vol. 2, pp. 193–224.

Fiske, Alan (2002). "Using Individualism and Collectivism to Compare Cultures." *Psychological Bulletin* 128, no. 1: 78–88.

Foster, George. (1965a)."Cultural Responses to Expressions of Envy in Tzintzuntzan." *Southwestern Journal of Anthropology* 21: 24–35.

Foster, George. (1965b). "Peasant Society and the Image of Limited Good." *American Anthropologist* 67: 293–315.

Foster, George. (1972). "The Anatomy of Envy." *Current Anthropology* 13, no. 2: 165–202.

Foucault, Michel. (1978). *The History of Sexuality.* Vol. 1. New York: Pantheon.

Foucault, Michel. (1986). *The Care of the Self.* New York: Pantheon.

Friedl, Erika. (1991). *Women of Deh Koh.* New York: Penguin Books.

Friedl, Erika. (1997). *Children of Deh Koh.* Syracuse, NY: Syracuse University Press.

Friedl, Erika. (1992). "Child Rearing in Modern Persia." In E. Yarshater, ed., *Encyclopedia Iranica.* Costa Mesa, CA: Mazda, vol. 5, pp. 412–416.

Fromm, Erich. (1965). *Escape from Freedom.* New York: Avon.

Fromm, Erich, and Maccoby, Michael. (1970). *Social Character in a Mexican Village.* Englewood Cliffs, NJ: Prentice-Hall.

Fuller, Anne. (1970). *Buarij: Protrait of a Lebanese Muslim Village.* Cambridge, MA: Harvard University Press.

Galaty, John. (1981). "Models and Metaphors: On the Semiotic Explanation of Segmentary Systems." In L. Holy and M. Stuchlik, eds., *The Structure of Folk Models.* New York: Academic Press.

Garrison, Vivian, and Arensberg, Conrad. (1976). "The Evil Eye: Envy or Risk of Seizure? Paranoia or Patronal Dependency?" In Clarence Maloney, ed., *The Evil Eye.* New York: Columbia University Press.

Geertz, C. (1968). *Islam Observed.* Chicago: University of Chicago Press.

Geertz, C. (1973). *The Interpretation of Cultures.* New York: Basic Books.

Geertz, C. (1979). "Suq: The Bazaar Economy in Sefrou." In C. Geertz, H. Geertz, and L. Rosen, *Meaning and Order in Moroccan Society.* New York: Cambridge University Press, pp. 123–244.

Geertz, C. (1984). "From the Natives' Point of View." In R. Shweder and R. LeVine, eds., *Culture Theory.* Cambridge: Harvard University Press, pp. 123–136.

Geertz, Clifford. (1973). "Religion as a Cultural System." In *The Interpretation of Cultures.* New York: Basic Books, pp. 87–125.

Geertz, Hildred. (1979). "The Meanings of Family Ties." In C. Geertz, H. Geertz, and L. Rosen, *Meaning and Order in Moroccan Society.* New York: Cambridge University Press, pp. 315–392.

Gellner, Ernest. (1969). *Saints of the Atlas.* Chicago: University of Chicago Press.

Gellner, Ernest. (1981a). *Muslim Society.* Cambridge, UK: Cambridge University Press.

Gellner, Ernest. (1981b). "The Unknown Apollo of Biskra: The Social Base of Algerian Puritanism." In E. Gellner, *Muslim Society.* Cambridge, UK: Cambridge University Press, pp. 149–173.

Ghallab, Abdelkrim. (1987). *Le Passe Enterre.* Mohammedia, Morocco: Fedala.

Ghareeb, Abdelkrim. (1996). "Ai namoudhaj li-al-tawafiq lada al-shabab al-maghrebi" (What Model for Moroccan Youth?). In M. Rabia', *Al-shabab al-maghribi* (Moroccan Youth), Rabat: kulliyyat al-adab, pp. 117–134.

Ghareeb, Abdelkrim, and Fliou, Abdelkrim, eds. *Al tufoula wa al murahaqa* (Childhood and Adolescence). Casablanca: no publisher information.

Ghareeb, G. A., and Beshai, J. A. (1989). "Arabic Version of the Children's Depression Inventory: Reliability and Validity." *Journal of Clinical Child Psychology* 18, no. 4: 323–326.

Ghareeb, Ghareeb. (1994). "Al-qalaq lada al-shabab fi dawlat al-imarat la-'arabiyya al-muttahida fi merhalqtqi al-ta'lim qabl al-jami'a wa al-ta'lim al-jami'i"

(Anxiety Among Pre-University and University Students in U.A.E.). In Louis Melikian, *Qira'at 'ilm al-nafs al-ijtima'i fi al-watan al-'arabi* (Readings in Social Psychology in the Arab Countries). Cairo: al-hiyah al-mesriyya al-'ama li-al-kitab, vol. 7, pp. 301–318.

Gibson, James. (1994). *Warrior Dreams: Paramilitary Culture in Post-Vietnam America.* New York: Hill and Wang.

Giddons, A. (1991). *Modernity and Self-Identity.* Stanford: Stanford University Press.

Gielen, U., Adler, L. and Milgram, L., eds. (1992). *Psychology in International Perspective.* Amsterdam: Swets and Zeitlinger.

Gilligan, Carol. (1982). *In a Different Voice.* Cambridge: Harvard University Press.

Gilligan, James. (1996). *Violence.* New York: Putnam.

Gilmore, David. (1990). *Manhood in the Making.* New Haven, CT: Yale University Press.

Gilmore, D., ed. (1987). *Honor and Shame and the Unity of the Mediterranean.* Washington, DC: American Anthropological Association.

Gilsenan, Michael. (1990). *Recognizing Islam.* London: Tauris.

Gilsenan, Michael. (1996). *Lords of the Lebanese Marches.* Berkeley: University of California Press.

Giovannini, Maureen. (1987). "Female Chastity Codes in the Circum-Mediterranean: Comparative Perspectives." In D. Gilmore, ed., *Honor and Shame and the Unity of the Mediterranean.* Washington, DC: American Anthropological Association.

Goethe, Johann. (1977). *Wilhelm Meister's Years of Apprenticeship.* 3 vols. London: Caldor.

Goldberg, Ellis . (1992). "Smashing Idols and the State: Protestant Ethic and Egyptian Sunni Radicalism ." In J. Cole, ed., *Comparing Muslim Societies.* Ann Arbor: University of Michigan Press, pp. 195–236.

Goldenweiser, A. (1936). "Loose Ends of a Theory on the Individual, Pattern, and Involution in Primitive Society." In R. Lowie, ed., *Essays in Anthropology.* Freeport, NY: Books for Libraries Press.

Gole, Nilufer. (1996). *The Forbidden Modern: Civilization and Veiling.* Ann Arbor: University of Michigan Press.

Goody, Jack. (1990). *The Oriental, the Ancient, and the Primitive.* Cambridge, UK: Cambridge University Press.

Gorer, Geoffrey, and Rickman, John. (1949). *The People of Great Russia.* New York: Norton.

Granqvist, Hilma. (1947). *Birth and Childhood Among the Arabs.* Helsinki: Soderstrom.

Greenwood, Bernard. (1981). "Cold or Spirits? Choice and Ambiguity in Morocco's Pluralistic Medical System." *Social Science and Medicine* 158: 219–235.

Gregg, G. (1990). "Underdevelopment in a North African Tribe: Toward a Psychology of Peripheral Social Orders." *Journal of Social Issues* 46, no. 3: 71–91.

Gregg, G . (1991). *Self-Representation: Life Narrative Studies in Identity and Ideology.* New York: Greenwood Press.

Gregg, G. (1995). "Multiple Identities and the Integration of Personality." *Journal of Personality* 63, no. 3: 617–641.

Gregg, G. (1998). "Culture, Personality, and the Multiplicity of Identity." *Ethos* 26, no. 2: 120–152.

Gregg, G. (1999). "Themes of Authority in the Life Histories of Young Moroccans." In R. Bourgiba and S. Milller, eds., *In the Shadow of the Sultan*. Cambridge: Harvard University Press, pp. 215–242.

Gregg, G. (2005). *Culture and Identity*. Manuscript.

Gregg, G., and Geist, A. (1988). "Socio-Economic Organization of the Ait Imeghrane." Final Report to Moroccan Ministry of Agriculture. Ouarzazate, Morocco: O.R.M.V.A.O.

Grotberg, Edith, and Badri, Gasim. (1992). "Sudanese Children in the Family and Culture." In U. Gielen, L. Adler, and N. Milgram, eds., *Psychology in International Perspective*. Amsterdam: Swets and Zeitlinger, pp. 213–232.

Guessous, Mohammed. (1982, January). "Al-tatawurat al-'a'iliyya wa al-tenshaia al-ijtima'iyya li-al-tifl al-maghribi" (Family Changes and Socialization of the Moroccan Child). *Al-dirassat al-nafsiyya wa al-tarbawiyya* (Psychological and Educational Studies) 1: 55–65.

Gutmann, D. (1974). "Alternatives to Disengagement: The Old Men of the Highland Druze." In R. LeVine, ed., *Culture and Personality: Contemporary Readings*. Chicago: Aldine, pp. 232–246.

Gutmann, David. (1987). *Reclaimed Powers*. New York: Basic Books.

Gutmann, David. (1997). *The Human Elder in Nature, Culture, and Society*. Boulder, CO: Westview Press.

Habermas, T., and Bluck, A. (2000). "Getting a Life: The Emergence of the Life Story in Adolescence." *Psychological Bulletin* 125, no. 5: 748–769.

Haddiya, el Mostafa. (1982). "Howl al-tanshi'a al-ijtima'iyya li-al-tifl al-qarawi" (Socialization of Rural Children). *Al-dirassat al-nafsiyya wa al-tarbawiyya* (Psychological and Child-Rearing Research) 2: 47–50.

Haddiya, el Mostafa. (1992). "Al-tanshi'a al-ijtima'iyya bayna al-usra wa al-dirasa fi al-wasat al-qarawi." (Socialization Between the Family and School in a Rural Area). In *Al-usra wa al-tifl fi al-mujtama' al-maghribi al-mu'asir* (Family and Child in Contemporary Moroccan Society). Rabat: kulliyyat al-adab wa al-'ilm al-insani, pp. 101–107.

Haddiya, el Mostafa. (1995). *Processus de la Socialisation en Milieu Urbain au Maroc*. Rabat: College of Humanities.

Haddiya, el Mostafa. (1996a). *Al-tanshi'a al-ijtima'iyya wa al-hawiyya* (Socialization and Identity). Rabat: kulliyyat al-adab.

Haddiya, el Mostafa. (1996b). "Tatallu'at al-shabab" (Aspirations of Youth). In M. Rebi'a, ed., *Al-shebab al-maghrebi fi afaq al-qarn al-hadi wa al-a'shir* (North African Youth on the Horizon the twenty-first Century.) Rabat: kulliyyat al-adab, pp. 27–33.

Hage, Ghassan (2003). "Comes a Time We Are All Enthusiasm." *Public Culture* 15, no. 1: 65–89.

Hamady, S. (1960). *Temperament and Character of the Arabs*. New York: Twayne.

Hamdan, Jamal. (1980). *Shakhsiyyat misr* (Egyptian Personality). Al-Qahira: 'Alam al-kitab.

Hammoudi, Abdullah . (1974). "Segmentarite, Stratification Sociale, Pouvoir Politique et Saintete." *Herperis-Talmuda* 15: 147–179.

Hammoudi, Abdullah. (1993). *The Victim and Its Masks*. Chicago: University of Chicago.

Hammoudi, Abdullah. (1997). *Master and Disciple: The Cultural Foundations of Moroccan Authoritarianism*. Chicago: University of Chicago Press.

Harfouche, Jamal. (1981). "The Evil Eye and Infant Health in Lebanon." In Alan Dundes, ed., *The Evil Eye: A Casebook*. Madison: University of Wisconsin Press, pp. 86–106.

Harre, R., ed. (1986). *The Social Construction of Emotion*. Oxford: Blackwell.

Harris, Judith. (1998). *The Nurture Assumption*. New York: The Free Press.

Hart, David. (1976). *The Aith Waryaghar of the Moroccan Rif*. Tucson: University of Arizona Press.

Hart, David. (1981). *Dada ʿAtta and His Forty Grandsons*. Cambridge, UK: Middle East and North African Studies Press.

Hart, David. (1984). *The Ait ʿAtta of Southern Morocco*. Cambridge, UK: Middle East and North African Studies Press.

Hauchler, Ingomar, and Kennedy, Paul. (1994). *Global Trends*. New York: Continuum.

Hazelton, Elaine. (1977). "Jawazi al-Malakim: Settled Bedouin Woman." In E. Fernea and B. Bezirgan, eds., *Middle Eastern Muslim Women Speak*. Austin: University of Texas Press, pp. 265–266.

Herdt, G. (1981). *Guardians of the Flutes*. Chicago: University of Chicago Press.

Herdt, Gilbert. (1990). "Sambia Nosebleeding Rites and Male Proximity to Women." In J. Stigler, R. Shweder, and G. Herdt, eds., *Cultural Psychology*. Cambridge, UK: Cambridge University Press, pp. 366–400.

Herman, Judith. (1992). *Trauma and Recovery*. New York: Basic Books.

Hermans, H., and Kempen, H. (1993). *The Dialogical Self*. San Diego: Academic Press.

Hermans, Hubert. (1996). "Voicing the Self." *Psychological Bulletin* 119, no. 1: 31–50.

Hermans, Hubert, and Kempen, Harry. (1998). "Moving Cultures: The Perilous Problems of Cultural Dichotomies in a Globalizing Society." *American Psychologist* 53, no. 10: 1111–1120.

Herzfeld, M. (1980). "Honor and Shame: Problems in the Comparative Analysis of Moral Systems." *Man* 15: 339–351.

Herzfeld, M. (1985). *The Poetics of Manhood*. Princeton, NJ: Princeton University Press.

Hicks, Esther. (1993). *Infibulation: Female Mutilation in Islamic Northeastern Africa*. New Brunswick, NJ: Transaction.

Hijazi, ʿAzet. (1969). "Al-shakhsiyya al-misriyya bayn al-silbiyya wa al-ijabiyya" (The Egyptian Personality Between the Negative and the Positive). *Majallat al-fikr al-muʾasir* (Journal of Modern Thought) 50: 42–49.

Hijazi, Mustafa. (1970). *Al-takhaluf al-ijtimaʾi* (Underdeveloped Society). Beirut: maʾhad al-inmaʾ al-arabi.

Hijazi, Mustafa. (1993). "ʿIlm al-nafs fi al-ʿalam al-ʿarabi" (Psychology in the Arab World). In *ʿIlm al-nafs wa qadaya al-mujtamʾat al-muʾasira* (Psychology and Contemporary Social Issues). Rabat: College of Letters and Sciences, pp. 33–57.

Ho, D., and Chiu, C. (1994). "Component Ideas of Individualism, Collectivism, and Social Organization." In U. Kim, H. Triandis, C. Kagitcibasi, S. Choi, and G. Yoon, eds., *Individualism and Collectivism: Theory, Method, and Applications*. Thousand Oaks, CA: Sage, pp. 137–156.

Hobbs, Joseph. (1989). *Bedouin Life in the Egyptian Wilderness*. Austin: University of Texas Press.

Hobsbawm, Eric, and Ranger, Eric, eds. (1983). *The Invention of Tradition*. Cambridge, UK: Cambridge University Press.

Hodson, Joel C. (1995). *Lawrence of Arabia and American Culture*. Westport, CT: Greenwood Press.

Hofstede, Geert. (1980). *Culture's Consequences*. Beverly Hills, CA: Sage.

Holland, D., and Kipnis, A. (1994). "Metaphors for Embarassment and Stories of Exposure: The Not-So-Egocentric Self in American Culture." *Ethos* 22, no. 3: 316–342.

Hollander, Nancy. (1997). *Love in a Time of Hate: Liberation Psychology in Latin America*. New Brunswick, NJ: Rutgers University Press.

Holy, Ladislav. (1989). *Kinship, Honour, and Solidarity*. Manchester, UK: Manchester University Press.

Hong, Ying-yi, Morris, M., Chiu, C., and Bennet-Martinez, V. (2000). "Multicultural Minds: A Dynamic Constructivist Approach to Culture and Cognition." *American Psychologist* 55, no. 7: 709–720.

Honneth, Axel. (1995). *The Struggle for Recognition*. Cambridge: MIT Press.

Hoodfar, Homa. (1995). "Child Care and Child Health in Low-Income Neighborhoods of Cairo." In Elizabeth Fernea, ed., *Children in the Muslim Middle East*. Austin: University of Texas Press.

Hourani, Albert. (1991). *A History of the Arab Peoples*. Cambridge: Harvard University Press.

Hsu, Francis. (1971). *Under the Ancestors' Shadow*. Stanford: Stanford University Press, 1971.

Hsu, Francis. (1972). "Kinship and Ways of Life: An Exploration." In Francis Hsu, ed., *Psychological Anthropology*. Cambridge: Schenkman, pp. 509–572.

Hsu, Francis . (1978). "Passage to Understanding." In G. Spindler, ed., *The Making of Psychological Anthropology*. Berkeley: University of California Press, pp. 142–173.

Huntington, Samuel. (1993). "Clash of Civilizations?" *Foreign Affairs* 72, no. 3: 22–50.

Ibn Khaldun. (1967). *The Moqqademah*. Princeton, NJ: Princeton University Press.

Ibrahim, Abdel. (1979). "Extraversion and Neuroticism Across Cultures." *Psychological Reports* 44, no. 3: 799–803.

Ibrahim, Abdul. (1982). "The Factorial Structure of the Eysenck Personality Questionnaire Among Egyptian Students." *Journal of Psychology* 112, no. 2: 221–226.

Ibrahim, Saad. (1985). "Urbanization in the Arab World." In N. Hopkins and S. Ibrahim, eds., *Arab Society*. Cairo: American University in Cairo Press, pp. 123–147.

Imamoglu, E. O. (1988). "Individualism and Collectivism in a Model and Scale of Balanced Differentiation and Integration." *Journal of Psychology* 132, no. 1: 95–105.

Inhorn, Marcia. (1996). *Infertility and Patriarchy*. Philadelphia: University of Pennsylvania.

Inkeles, Alex. (1983). *Exploring Individual Modernity*. New York: Columbia University Press.

Inkeles, Alex, and Smith, David. (1974). *Becoming Modern*. Cambridge: Harvard University Press.

Izard, C. (1977). *Human Emotions*. New York: Plenum.

Izard. C. (1992). "Basic Emotions, Relations Among Emotions, and Emotion-Cognition Relations." *Psychological Review* 99: 561–565.

Jabar, Abdelhamid. (1978a). "Dirasat muqarana fi itijahat al-walidayn wa asalib al-tenshi'a al-ijtima'iyya li-thalath 'ayinat 'arabiyya" (Comparative Study of Parental Orientations and Style of Socialization in Three Arab Samples). In A. Jabar and S. Al-Shiekh, eds., *Dirasat nafsiyya fi al-shakhsiyya al-'arabiyya* (Psychological Studies of Arab Personality). Cairo: Scientific Books, pp. 42–74.

Jabar, Abdelhamid. (1978b). "Dirasat muqarana fi al-shakhsiyya al-qatariyya wa al-'iraqiyya wa al-misriyya wa al-amrikiyya" (Comparative Study of Personality in Qatar, Iraq, Egypt, and America). In A. Jabar and S. al-Shiekh, eds., *Dirasat nafsiyya fi al-shakhsiyya al-'arabiyya* (Psychological Studies of Arab Personality). Cairo: Scientific Books, pp. 479–499.

Jabar, Abdelhamid. (1978c). "Al-itijahat al-walidia fi tenshia al-atfal" (Parental Orientations to the Socialization of Children). In J. Jabar and S. al-Shiekh, *Dirasat nafsiyya fi al-shakhsiyya al-'arabiyya* (Psychological Studies of Arab Personality). Cairo: Scientific Books, pp. 85–96.

Jacques-Muenie, D. (1958). "Hierarchie Sociale au Maroc Presaharien." *Hesperis* 45: 239–269.

James, William. (1981). *Principles of Psychology.* Cambridge: Harvard University Press.

Jamous, Raymond. (1981). *Honneur et Baraka.* Cambridge, UK: Cambridge University Press.

Johari, Mohammed. (1992). "Al-tifl fi al-turath al-sha'bi" (The Child in Popular Tradition). In Mohammed Johari, 'Alia Shakri, Najoui Abdelhamid, and Mina Fernouani, eds., *Dirasat fi al-anthrubuuzhiya al-ijtima'iyya: al-tifl wa al-tanshi'a al-ijtima'iyya* (Anthropological Studies of Society: Children and Socialization). Alexandria, Egypt: dar al-ma'rifah al-jami'iyah, pp. 9–78.

Jones, Edward, Kanouse, David, Kelley, Harold, Nisbett, Richard, Valins, Stuart, and Weiner, Bernard, eds. (1971). *Attribution.* Morristown, NJ: General Learning Press.

Jorgensen, Joseph. (1972). *The Sun Dance Religion.* Chicago: University of Chicago Press.

Joseph, Suad. (1977). "Family as Security and Bondage." In N. Hopkins and S. Ibrahim, eds., *Arab Society.* Cairo: American University in Cairo Press, pp. 241–256.

Joseph, Suad. (1999a). "Brother-Sister Relationships." In Suad Joseph, ed., *Intimate Selving in Arab Families.* Syracuse, NY: Syracuse University Press, pp. 113–140.

Joseph, Suad. (1999b). "My Son/Myself, My Mother/Myself." In Suad Joseph, ed., *Intimate Selving in Arab Families.* Syracuse, NY: Syracuse University Press, pp. 174–190.

Joseph, Suad. (1999c). "Theories and Dynamics of Gender, Self and Identity in Arab Families." In *Intimate Selving in Arab Families.* Syracuse, NY: Syracuse University Press, pp. 1–20.

Joseph, Suad, ed. (1999). *Intimate Selving in Arab Families.* Syracuse, NY: Syracuse University Press.

Jung, Carl. (1959). *Aion.* Princeton, NJ: Princeton Unversity Press.

Jung, Carl. (1968). *Man and His Symbols.* New York: Dell.

Kabbani, Rana. (1986). *Europe's Myths of Orient.* Bloomington: Indiana University Press.

Kagitcibasi, Cigdem. (1970). "Social Norms and Authoritarianism: A Turkish-American Comparison." *Journal of Personality and Social Psychology* 16, no. 3: 444–451.

Kagitcibasi, Cigdem. (1987). "Individual and Group Loyalties: Are They Compatible?" In C. Kagitcibasi, ed., *Growth and Progress in Cross-Cultural Psychology.* Berwyn, PA: Swets North America, pp. 94–103.

Kagitcibasi, Cigdam. (1996). *Family and Human Development Across Cultures.* Mahwah, NJ: Erlbaum.

Kakar, Sudhir. (1978). *The Inner World.* Delhi: Oxford University Press.

Kandiyoti, Deniz. (1988). "Bargaining with Patriarchy." *Gender and Society* 2, no. 3: 274–290.

Kandiyoti, Deniz. (1991). "Islam and Patriarchy." In N. Keddie and B. Baron, eds., *Women in Middle Eastern History.* New Haven, CT: Yale University Press, pp. 23–42.

Kandiyoti, Deniz. (1994). "The Paradoxes of Masculinity." In A. Cornwall and N. Lindisfarne, eds., *Dislocating Masculinity: Comparative Ethnologies.* London: Routledge, pp. 197–213.

Karakitapoglu-Aygun, Zahide. (2002). "Self-Construals, Perceived Parenting and Well-Being in Different Cultural and Socio-Economic Contexts." Ph.D. dissertation, Middle East Technical University, Ankara.

Karami, Kari. (1995). "Girls' Participation in Combat." In E. Fernea, ed., *Children in the Muslim Middle East.* Austin: University of Texas Press.

Katakura, Motoko. (1977). *Bedouin Village.* Tokyo: University of Tokyo.

Kawachi, Ichiro (2000). "Income Inequality and Health." In L. Berkman and I. Kawachi, *Social Epidemiology.* Oxford: Oxford University Press, pp. 76–94.

Kearney, Michael. (1976). "A World-View Explanation of the Evil Eye." In Clarence Maloney, ed.,*The Evil Eye.* New York: Columbia University Press, pp. 175–192.

Keenan, Jeremy. (1977). *The Tuareg.* New York: St. Martin's Press.

Kelman, Herbert, and Hamilton, Lee. (1989). *Crimes of Obedience.* New Haven, CT: Yale University Press.

Kepel, Gilles. (1984). *Muslim Extremism in Egypt: The Prophet and Pharaoh.* Berkeley: University of California.

Keyes, C., and Ryff, C. (1998). "Generativity in Adult Lives: Social Structural Contours and Quality of Life Consequences." In D. McAdams and E. de St. Aubin, eds., *Generativity and Adult Development.* Washington, DC: American Psychological Association Press, pp. 227–263.

Khaleefa, O. (1997). "The Predicament of Euro-American Psychology in Non-Western Culture: A Response from the Sudan." *World Psychology* 3, nos. 1–2: 29–64.

Khalifa, Abdelatif, and Radwan, Sh'aban. (1998). *Al-shakhsiyyia al-misriyya* (The Egyptian Personality). Cairo: dar gharib.

Khatibi, Abdelkebir. (1990). *Love in Two Languages.* Minneapolis: University of Minnesota Press.

Khazanov, A. (1983). *Nomads and the Outside World.* Cambridge, UK: Cambridge University Press.

Khosrokharar, Farhad. (1995). "Attitudes of Teenage Girls to the Iranian Revolution." In E. Fernea, ed., *Children in the Muslim Middle East.* Austin: University of Texas Press.

Khuri, Fuad. (1990). *Tents and Pyramids: Games and Ideology in Arab Culture from Backgammon to Autocratic Rule.* London: Saqi.

Kim, U., and Berry, J. (1993). *Indigenous Psychologies.* Newbury Park, CA: Sage.

Kim, U., Triandis, H., Kagitcibasi, C., Choi, S., and Yoon, G., eds. (1994). *Individualism and Collectivism: Theory, Method, and Applications.* Thousand Oaks, CA: Sage.

Kluckhohn, Clyde, and Murray, Henry. (1956). *Personality in Nature, Society, and Culture.* New York: Knopf.

Kluft, Richard, ed. (1987). *Childhood Antecedents of Multiple Personality Disorder.* Washington, DC: American Psychological Association.

Kohn, Melvin. (1969). *Class and Conformity.* Homewood, IL: Dorsey Press.

Kouaouci, Ali. (2002). "Transitions, chomage des jeunes, recul du marriage et terrorisme en Algeria." Paper delivered at Conference on Algeria, Center for Middle Eastern and North African Studies, Ann Arbor, MI, Sept. 27–28.

Krichen, Aziz. (1987). "Les problemes de la langue et l'intelligensia." In C. Michel, ed., *La Tunisie au Present.* Paris: CNRS Presses.

Kritzeck, James. (1964). *Anthology of Islamic Literature.* (Ameen Rihani, trans.) New York: Holt, Rinehart and Winston,

Krohn, Alan. (1978). "Hysteria: The Elusive Neurosis." New York: International Universities Press.

Kuroda, Y., and Suzuki, T. (1991a). "Arab Students and English: The Role of Implicit Culture." *Behaviormetrika* 29: pp. 23–44.

Kuroda, Y., and Suzuki, T. (1991b). "A Comparative Analysis of the Arab Culture." *Behaviormetrika* 30: 35–53.

Kurtz, Stanley. (1992). *All the Mothers Are One.* New York: Columbia University Press.

Lacoste-Dujardin, Camille. (1986). *Des Meres Contre les Femmes.* Paris: Editions la Decouverte.

La Fromboise, T., Coleman, H., and Gerton, J. (1993). "Psychological Impact of Biculturalism: Evidence and Theory." *Psychological Bulletin* 114, no. 3: 395–412.

Lamb, David. (1987). *The Arabs: Journeys Beyond the Mirage.* New York: Random House.

Lancaster, William. (1981). *The Rwala Bedouin Today.* Cambridge, UK: Cambridge University Press.

Laquer, Walter. (1987). *The Age of Terrorism.* Boston: Little, Brown.

Laroui, Abdallah. (1976). *The Crisis of the Arab Intellectual.* Berkeley: University of California Press.

Laroui, Abdallah. (1977). *The History of the Maghrib.* Princeton, NJ: Princeton University Press.

Lasch, Christopher. (1978). *Culture of Narcissism.* New York: Norton.

Lawrence, Peter. (1964). *Road Belong Cargo.* Atlantic Highlands, NJ: Humanities Press.

Lebra, T. (1976). *Japanese Patterns of Behavior.* Honolulu: University of Hawaii Press.

Lerner, Daniel. (1958). *The Passing of Traditional Society.* Glencoe, IL: Free Press.

Lerner, Daniel. (1957, June 17). "Nasser's Officialdom." *New Leader* 40: 25–26.

Leveau, Remy. (1976). *La Fellah Marocain.* Paris: Presses de la Fondation Nationale des Sciences Politiques.

LeVine, R. (1973). *Culture, Behavior and Personality.* Chicago: Aldine.

LeVine, R. (1974). "Parental Goals: A Cross-Cultural View." *Teachers College Record* 76, no. 2: 226–239

LeVine, R. (1990). "Infant Environments in Psychoanalysis: A Cross-Cultural View." In J. Stigler, R. Shweder, and G. Herdt, eds., *Cultural Psychology*. Cambridge, UK: Cambridge University Press.

LeVine, R., Dixon, S., LeVine, S., Richman, A., Leiderman, P., Keefer, C., and Brazelton, T. (1994). *Child Care and Culture: Lessons from Africa*. New York: Cambridge University Press.

LeVine, R., and LeVine, B. (1963). "Nyansongo: A Gusii Community in Kenya." In B. Whiting, ed., *Six Cultures: Studies of Child Rearing*. New York: Wiley, pp. 19–202.

LeVine R., Miller, P., and West, M., eds. (1982). *Parental Behaviors in Diverse Societies*. San Francisco: Jossey-Bass.

LeVine, S. (1979). *Mothers and Wives: Gusii Women of East Africa*. Chicago: Chicago University Press.

Levinson, D. (1978). *The Seasons of a Man's Life*. New York: Ballantine.

Levinson, Daniel, and Levinson, Judy. (1996). *The Seasons of a Woman's Life*. New York: Knopf.

Levi-Strauss, Claude. (1969). *The Elementary Structures of Kinship*. Boston: Beacon Press.

Lewis, Bernard. (1968). *The Emergence of Modern Turkey*. New York: Oxford University Press.

Lewis, Bernard. (1998). *The Multiple Identities of the Middle East*. New York: Schocken.

Lewis, M., and Haviland, J., eds. (1993). *Handbook of Emotion*. New York: Guilford.

Lewis, Norman. (1987). *Nomads and Settlers in Syria and Jordan, 1800–1980*. Cambridge, UK: Cambridge University Press.

Lewis, Oscar. (1961). *Children of Sanchez*. New York: Random House.

Lifton, Robert . (1986). *The Nazi Doctors*. New York: Basic Books.

Lila, Ali. (1993). *Al-shabab al-'arabi: Ta'amulat fi dawahir al-'ihya' al-dini wa al-'unf* (Arab Youth: Reflections on the Phenomenon of Religious Renewal and Violence). Cairo: dar al-ma'arif.

Lindholm, Charles. (1996). *The Islamic Middle East*. Oxford: Blackwell.

Lutz, C. (1982). "The Domain of Emotion Words on Ifaluk." *American Ethnologist* 9, no. 1: 113–128.

Maalouf, Amin. (1996). *In the Name of Identity*. New York: Arcade.

Mackey, Sandra. (1992). *Passion and Politics*. New York: Penguin Books.

Maher, Vanessa. (1974). *Women and Property in Morocco*. Cambridge, UK: Cambridge University Press.

Mahfouz, Naguib. (1981). *Midaq Alley*. New York: Quality Paperback.

Mahfouz, Naguib. (1990). *Palace Walk*. New York: Doubleday.

Mahfouz, Naguib. (1991). *Palace of Desire*. New York: Doubleday.

Mahfouz, Naguib. (1992). *Sugar Street*. New York: Doubleday.

Mahler, Margaret. (1975). *The Psychological Birth of the Human Infant*. New York: Basic Books.

Mahmoud, Mustafa. (1998). *'Ilm nafs qur'ani jadid* (A New Quranic Psychology). Cairo: akhbar al-yawm.

Makiya, Kanan. (1993). *Cruelty and Silence*. New York: Norton.

Maloney, Clarence, ed. (1976). *The Evil Eye*. New York: Columbia University Press

Malti-Douglas, Fedwa. (1991). *Woman's Body, Women's Word*. Princeton, NJ: Princeton University Press.

Mandelbaum, David. (1988). *Women's Seclusion and Men's Honor.* Tucson: University of Arizona Press.

Mannoni, O. (1964). *Prospero and Caliban: The Psychology of Colonization.* New York: Praeger.

Maraldo, J. (1994) "Rousseau, Hakuseki, and Hakuin: Paradigms of Self in Three Autobiographies. In R. Ames, ed., *Self as Person in Asian Theory and Practice.* Albany: State University of New York Press, pp. 57–79.

Markus, H., and Kitiyama, S. (1991). "Culture and the Self: Implications for Cognition, Emotion, and Motivation." *Psychological Review* 98, no. 2: 224–253.

Marmot, M., Bobak, M., and Davey Smith, G. (1995). "Explanations for Social Inequalities in Health." In B. Amick, S. Levine, A. Tarlov, and D. Walsh, eds., *Society and Health.* New York: Oxford University Press, pp. 172–210.

Martinez, Luis. (2000). *The Algerian Civil War.* New York: Columbia University Press.

Marx, Emmanual. (1977). "The Tribe as a Unit of Subsistence." *American Anthropologist* 79, no. 2: 343–363.

Ma'taz, Siyd Abdellah. (1990). "Al-itjahat al-tea'sbia: aham askalha wa mda a'mumiatha" (Orientations of Solidarity: Important Forms and Extent of their Generality). In Louis Melikian, ed., *Qira'at 'ilm al-nafs al-ijtima'i fi al-watan al-'arabi* (Readings in Social Psychology in the Arab Countries). Vol. 5. Cairo: al-hiia al-misriyya al-'ama li-al-kitab, pp. 13–37.

Matsumoto, David. (1996). *Unmasking Japan.* Stanford, CA: Stanford University Press.

Matsumoto, David. (1999). "Culture and Self: An Empirical Assessment of Markus and Kitayama's Theory of Independent and Interdependent Self-Construals." *Asian Journal of Social Psychology* 2: 289–310.

Matsumoto, David, ed. (2001). *Handbook of Culture and Emotion.* New York: Oxford University Press.

Maxwell, Gavin. (1966). *Lords of the Atlas.* London: Longmans

McAdams, D. (1988). *Power, Intimacy, and the Life Story.* New York: Guilford.

McAdams, D. (1995). "What Do We Know When We Know a Person?" *Journal of Personality and Social Psychology* 63, no. 3: 365–396.

McAdams, D. (2001). "The Psychology of Life Stories." *Review of General Psychology* 5, no. 22: 100–122.

McCauley, Clark. (2004). "The Psychology of Terrorism." Social Science Research Council. Available online at: www.ssrc.org/sept11/essays (accessed Nov. 16, 2004).

McDougall, William. (1923). *An Outline of Psychology.* London: Methuen.

Mead, G. H. (1934). *Mind, Self, and Society.* Chicago: University of Chicago Press.

Meeker, Michael. (1979). *Literature and Violence in North Arabia.* Cambridge, UK: Cambridge University Press.

Melikian, L. (1959). "Authoritarianism and Its Correlates in the Egyptian Culture and in the United States." *Journal of Social Issues* 15: 58–75.

Melikian, Louis, ed. (1979). *Qira'at 'ilm al-nafs al-ijtima'i fi al-watan al-'arabi* (Readings in Social Psychology in the Arab Countries). Vol. 3. Cairo: al-hiia al-misriyya al-'ama li-al-kitab.

Melikian, Louis, ed. (1985). *Qira'at 'ilm al-nafs al-ijtima'i fi al-watan al-'arabi* (Readings in Social Psychology in the Arab Countries). Vol. 4. Cairo: al-hiia al-misriyya al-'ama li-al-kitab.

Melikian, Louis, ed. (1990). *Qira'at 'ilm al-nafs al-ijtima'i fi al-watan al-'arabi* (Readings in Social Psychology in the Arab Countries). Vol. 5. Cairo: al-hiia al-misriyya al-'ama li-al-kitab.

Melikian, Louis. (1994). *Qira'at 'ilm al-nafs al-ijtima'i fi al-watan al-'arabi* (Readings in Social Psychology in the Arab Countries). Vol. 7. Cairo: al-hiia al-misriyya al-'ama li-al-kitab.

Mensch, B., Ibrahim, B., Lee, S., and El-Gibaly, O. (2003). "Gender-Role Attitudes Among Egyptian Adolescents." *Studies in Family Planning* 34, no. 1: 8–18.

Mernissi, Fatima. (1975). *Beyond the Veil*. Cambridge: Schenkman.

Mernissi, Fatima. (1984). *Woman in the Muslim Unconscious*. New York: Pergamon Press. (Under the pseudonym Fatna Sabbah.)

Mernissi, Fatima. (1994). *Dreams of Trespass*. Reading, MA: Addison-Wesley.

Mernissi, Fatima. (1992). *Islam and Democracy*. Reading, MA: Addison-Wesley.

Merari, Ariel. (1990). "The Readiness to Kill and Die: Suicidal Terrorism in the Middle East." In W. Reich, ed., *Origins of Terrorism*. Washington, DC: Woodrow Wilson Center Press, pp. 192–207.

Metwalli, Ahmed. (1971). *The Lure of the Levant*. Ph.D. dissertation, State University of New York, Albany.

Milgram, Stanley. (1969). *Obedience to Authority*. New York: Harper and Row.

Miller, Gerald. (1977). "Classroom 19: A Study of Behavior in a Classroom of a Moroccan Primary School." In L. Bown and N. Itzkowitz, eds., *Psychological Dimensions of Near Eastern Studies*. Princeton, NJ: Darwin Press, pp. 152–153.

Miller, Joan. (2002). "Bringing Culture to Basic Psychological Theory: Beyond Individualism and Collectivism." *Psychological Bulletin* 128, no. 1: 97–109.

Miner, H., and DeVos, G. (1960). *Oasis and Casbah: Algerian Culture and Personality in Change*. Museum of Anthropology Papers no. 15. Ann Arbor, MI: Museum of Anthropology.

Minoura, Yasuko. (1992). "A Sensitive Period for the Incorporation of a Cultural Meaning System." *Ethos* 20, no. 3: 304–339.

Mirowsky, John. (1985). "Disorder and Its Context: Paranoid Beliefs as Thematic Elements of Thought Problems, Hallucinations, and Delusions Under Threatening Social Conditions." *Community and Mental Health* 5: 185–204.

Mirowsky, John, and Ross, Catherine. (1983). "Paranoia and the Structure of Powerlessness." *American Sociological Review* 48: 228–238.

Mirsepassi, Ali (2000). *Intellectual Discourse and the Politics of Modernization*. Cambridge, UK: Cambridge University Press.

Mitchell, Richard. (1969). *The Society of the Muslim Brothers*. New York: Oxford University Press.

Mitchell, Timothy. (1990). "The Invention and Reinvention of the Egyptian Peasant." *International Journal of Middle Eastern Studies* 22: 129–150.

Moghaddam, F., Taylor, D., and Wright, S. (1993). *Social Psychology in Cross-Cultural Perspective*. New York: Freeman.

Montagne, Robert. (1930). *Les Berberes et le Makhzen dans le Sud au Maroc*. Paris: Felix Alcan.

Mostyn, T., and Hourani, A., eds. (1988). *Cambridge Encyclopedia of the Middle East and North Africa*. New York: Cambridge University Press.

Mottahedeh, R. (1985). *The Mantle of the Prophet*. New York: Pantheon Books.

Moughrabi, Fouad. (1978). "The Arab Basic Personality: A Critical Survey of the Literature." *International Journal of Middle East Studies* 9: 99–112.

Msefer, Assia. (1985). *Sevrages et Interdependence.* Casablanca: Editions Maghrebines.

Munroe, R., and Munroe, R. (1972). "Obedience Among Children in an East African Society." *Journal of Cross-Cultural Psychology* 3: 395–399.

Munson, Henry. (1984). *The House of Si Abdullah.* New haven: Yale University Press.

Munson, Henry. (1988). *Islam and Revolution in the Middle East.* New Haven, CT: Yale University Press.

Murphy, Robert, and Kasdan, Leonard. (1959). "The Structure of Parallel Cousin Marriage." *American Anthropologist* 61: 17–29.

Murray, D. W. (1993). "What Is the Western Concept of the Self? On Forgetting David Hume." *Ethos* 21, no. 1: 3–23.

Murray, H., and Morgan, C. (1945). "A Clinical Study of Sentiments." *Genetic Psychology Monographs* 32: 3–311.

Murray, Henry. (1938). *Explorations in Personality.* New York: Oxford Unversity Press.

Muslim Child Rearing. (1989, April). Al-dirasat al-nafsiyya wa al-tarbaiyya (Psychological and Educational Studies) 9. Special issue.

Naamane-Guessous, Soumaya. (1988). *Au-dela de Toute Pudeur.* Mohammadia, Morocco: SODEN.

Nablusi, Muhammad. (1990). *Nahwa saykulujiyya 'arabiah* (Toward an Arab Psychology). Beirut: dar al-tali'ah li-al-tiba'ah waal-nashr.

Najati, Mohammed. (1974). *Al-madaniyya al-hadithah wa-tasamuh al-walidayn* (Modernization and Parental Permissiveness). Cairo: al nahda el 'arabia.

Najati, Mohammed (2001). *'Ilm al-nafs al-islami* (Islamic Psychology). Cairo: dar al-shuruq.

Najmabadi, Afsaneh. (2000). "Reading 'Wiles of Women' Stories as Fictions of Masculinity." In Mai Ghoussoub and Emma Sinclair-Webb, eds., *Imagined Masculinities.* London: Saqi, pp. 147–168.

Najmabadi, Afsaneh, ed. (1990). *Women's Autobiographies in Contemporary Iran.* Cambridge: Harvard University Center for Middle Eastern Studies.

Nakane, Chie. (1970). *Japanese Society.* Berkeley: University of California Press.

Nandy, Ashis. (1980). *At the Edge of Psychology: Essays in Politics and Culture.* Delhi: Oxford University Press.

Nandy, Ashis. (1983). *The Intimate Enemy.* Delhi: Oxford University Press.

Nasr, S. (1987). *Islamic Spirituality.* New York: Crossroad.

Nelson, C. (1973). *The Desert and the Sown: Nomads in the Wider Society.* Berkeley: University of California Press.

Nelson, Kristina. (1985). *The Art of Reciting the Quran.* Austin: University of Texas Press.

Nerval, Gerard de (2001). *Journey to the Orient.* London: Owen.

Nicolaisen, Johannes. (1963). *Ecology and Culture of the Pastoral Tuareg.* Copenhagen: Copenhagen National Museum.

Nisbett, Richard. (1996). *Culture of Honor.* Boulder, CO: Westview Press.

Nordland, R., and Wilkinson, R. (1986, April 7). "Inside Terror, Inc." *Newsweek* 107: 25–28.

Nurdin, Mohammed. (2001). "Awladuna akbaduna" (Our Children Our Hearts). In A. Ghareeb and A. Flio, eds., *Al-tufula wa al-murahaqa* (Childhood and Adolescence). Casablanca: n.p., pp. 91–115.

Obeysekere, G. (1981). *Medusa's Hair*. Chicago: Chicago University Press.

Obeysekere, G. (1985). "Depression, Buddhism, and the Work of Culture in Sri Lanka." In A. Kleinman and B. Good, eds., *Culture and Depression*. Berkeley: University of California Press.

Obeysekere, G. (1990). *The Work of Culture*. Chicago: University of Chicago Press.

Olson, Emelie. (1985). "Muslim Identity and Secularism in Contemporary Turkey: 'The Headscarf Dispute.'" *Anthropological Quarterly* 58, no. 4: 161–170.

Omidsalar, M. (1992). "Childbirth in Modern Persian Folklore." In E. Yarshater, ed., *Encyclopedia Iranica* (vol. 5). London: Routledge & Keegan Paul, pp. 404–406.

Ortner, Sherry . (1973). "On Key Symbols." *American Anthropologist* 75: 1338–1346.

Ortner, Sherry. (1978). "The Virgin and the State." *Feminist Studies* 4, no. 3: 19–35

Oussaid, Brick. (1989). *Mountains Forgotten by God*. Washington, DC: Three Continents Press.

Ouzi, Ahmad. (1986). *Saykulujiyyat al- murahiq* (Psychology of Adolescence). Rabat: majallat dirasat nafsiyya wa tarbawiyya.

Ouzi, Ahmad. (1993). "Temthal al-tifl fi al-mujtama' al-maghribi" (Representation of the Child in North African Society). In *'Ilm al-nafs wa qadhaya al-mujtama'at al-mu'asira* (Psychology and Contemporary Social Issues). Rabat: kulia al-adab, pp. 117–123.

Oyserman, D., and Markus, H. (1990). "Possible Selves and Delinquency." *Journal of Personality and Social Psychology* 59, no. 1: 112–125.

Oyserman, D., Sakamoto, I., and Lauffer, A. (1998). "Cultural Accommodation: Hybridity and the Framing of Social Obligation." *Journal of Personality and Social Psychology* 74, no. 6: 1606–1618.

Oyserman, Daphna. (1993). "The Lens of Personhood: Viewing the Self and Others in a Multicultural Society." *Journal of Personality and Social Psychology* 65, no. 5: 993–1009.

Oyserman, Daphna, Coon, H., and Kemmelmeier, M. (2002). "Rethinking Individualism and Collectivism." *Psychological Bulletin* 128, no. 1: 3–72.

Oyserman, Daphna, Gant, Larry, and Ager, Joel. (1995). "A Socially Contextualized Model of African American Identity." *Journal of Personality and Social Personality* 69, no. 6: 1216–1232.

Ozturk, Orhan. (1973). "Ritual Circumcision and Castration Anxiety." *Psychiatry* 36: 49–60.

Pamuk, Orhan. (1994). *The Black Book*. San Diego: Harcourt, Brace.

Papanek, Hanna, and Minault, Gail. (1982). *Separate Worlds: Studies of Purdah in South Asia*. Columbia, MO: South Asia Books.

Pape, Robert. (2003). "The Strategic Logic of Suicide Terrorism." *American Political Science Review* 97, no. 3: 343–361.

Pascon, Paul, and Bentahar, Mekki. (1978). "Ce que disent 296 jeunes ruraux." In A. Khatabi, ed., *Etudes Sociologiques sur le Maroc*. Rabat: Bulletin Economique et Social du Maroc, pp. 145–287.

Patai, Raphael. (1973). *The Arab Mind*. New York: Scribner's. Reprint, Long Island City, NY: Hatherleigh Press, 2002.

Peristiany, J. G. (1966). "Honour and Shame in a Cypriot Highland Village." In J. G. Peristiany, ed., *Honour and Shame*. Chicago: University of Chicago Press.

Peristiany, J. G., ed. (1966). *Honour and Shame*. Chicago: University of Chicago Press.

Peteet, Julie. (2000). "Male Gender and Rituals of Resistance in the Palestinian Intifada." In M. Ghoussoub and E. Sinclair-Webb, eds., *Imagined Masculinities*. London: Saqi, pp. 103–126.

Peters, Emrys. (1960). "The Proliferation of Segments in the Lineage of the Bedouin of Cyrenaica." *Journal of the Royal Anthropological Institute* 90, no. 1: 29–53.

Peters, F. E. (1994). *A Reader on Classical Islam*. Princeton, NJ: Princeton University Press.

Peters, R. (1970). "The Education of the Emotions." In M. Arnold, ed., *Feelings and Emotions*. New York: Academic Press.

Pettigrew, Thomas. (1979). "The Ultimate Attribution Error." *Personality and Social Psychology Bulletin* 5, no. 4: 461–476.

Phalet, K., and Claeys, W. (1993). "A Comparative Study of Turkish and Belgian Youth." *Journal of Cross-Cultural Psychology* 24, no. 3: 319–343.

Philipchalk, R. (1995). *Invitation to Social Psychology*. Fort Worth, IN: Harcourt Brace College.

Phinney, Jean. (1990). "Ethnic Identity in Adolescents and Adults: Review of Research." *Psychological Bulletin* 108, no. 3: 499–514.

Phinney, Jean. (2003). "Ethnic Identity and Acculturation." In K. Chun, P. Organista, and G. Marin, eds., *Acculturation*. Washington, DC: American Psychological Association, pp. 63–81.

Piers, Gerhart, and Singer, Milton. (1953). *Shame and Guilt*. New York: Norton.

Pitt-Rivers, Julian. (1966). "Honour and Social Status." In J. G. Peristiany, ed., *Honour and Shame*. Chicago: University of Chicago Press, pp. 19–78.

Posada, G., Gao, Y., Wu, F., and Posada, R. (1995). "The Secure-Base Phenomenon Across Cultures." *Monographs for the Society for Research on Child Development*, vol. 60 (nos. 2–3): 27–48.

Post, J. (1990). "Terrorist Psycho-Logic: Terrorist Behavior as a Product of Psychological Forces." In W. Reich, ed., *Origins of Terrorism*. Washington, DC: Woodrow Wilson Center Press, pp. 25–40.

Poulton, Hugh. (1997). *Top Hat, Grey Wolf and Crescent: Turkish Nationalism and the Turkish Republic*. New York: New York University Press.

Pradines, M. (1968). "Feelings as Regulators." In M. Arnold, ed., *The Nature of Emotion*. Baltimore: Penguin Books.

Prothro, Edward. (1961). *Child Rearing in Lebanon*. Cambridge: Harvard University Press.

Prothro, T., and Melikian, L. (1953). "The California Public Opinion Scale in an Authoritarian Culture." *Public Opinion Quarterly* 17: 353–362.

Pryce-Jones, David. (1991). *The Closed Circle: An Interpretation of the Arabs*. New York: Harper.

Punamaki, R., Qouta, S., and El-Sarraj, E. (2001). "Resiliency Factors Predicting Psychological Adjustment After Political Violence Among Palestinian Children." *International Journal of Behavioral Development* 25, no. 3: 256–267.

Putnam, Frank. (1989). *Diagnosis and Treatment of Multiple Personality Disorder*. New York: Guilford Press.

Pyszczynski, T., Solomon, S., and Greenberg, J. (2003). *In the Wake of 9/11: The Psychology of Terror*. Washington, DC: American Psychological Association.

Qabaj, Mohammed. (2001). "Al-tifl al-maghribi" (The Moroccan Child). In

A. Ghareeb and A. Flio, eds., *Al-Tofoula wa al-mrahaqa* (Childhood and Adolescence). Casablanca: n .p., pp. 83–89.

Qouta, S., El-Sarraj, E., and Punamaeki, R. (2001). "Mental Flexibility as Resiliency Factor Among Children Exposed to Political Violence." *International Journal of Psychology* 36, no. 1: 1–7.

Rabia', Mbarek. (1996). "Al-shabab: Al-tahawwul wa siraa' al-qiyam" (Youth: Transformation and the Struggle of Values). In M. Rabia', *Al-shabab al-maghribi* (Moroccan Youth). Rabat: kulliyyat al-adab, pp. 17–26.

Radi, Abdelwahad. (1968). "Processus de socialisation de l'enfant marocain." *Annales Marocaines de Sociologie* 1: 48.

Rahim, Idris, and Cederblad, Marianne. (1984). "Effects of Rapid Urbanization on Child Behaviour and Health in a Part of Khartoum." *Journal of Child Psychology and Psychiatry* 25: 629–641.

Rahim, Idris, and Cederblad, Marianne. (1986). "Effects of Rapid Urbanization on Child Behaviour and Health in a Part of Khartoum, Sudan, part 2, Psycho-Social Influences on Behaviour, 1965–1980." *Social Science and Medicine* 22, no. 7: 723–730.

Rejali, Darius. (1994). *Torture and Modernity: Self, Society, and State in Modern Iran.* Boulder, CO: Westview Press.

Reynolds, Dwight. (2001). *Interpreting the Self.* Berkeley: University of California.

Richards, Alan, and Waterbury, John. (1996). *A Political Economy of the Middle East.* Boulder, CO: Westview Press.

Richman, A., Miller, P., and Soloman, M. (1988). "Maternal Behavior to Infants in Five Cultures." In R. LeVine, P. Miller, and M. West, eds., *Parental Behaviors in Diverse Societies.* San Francisco: Jossey-Bass, pp. 65–74.

Roberts, John. (1976). "Belief in the Evil Eye in World Perspective." In C. Maloney, ed., *The Evil Eye.* New York: Columbia University Press, pp. 223–278.

Rodinson, Maxime. (1961). *Mahomet.* Paris: Éditions du Seuil.

Rodinson, Maxime. (1974). *Islam and Capitalism.* New York: Pantheon.

Rogoff, Barbara. (1990). *Apprenticeship in Thinking.* London: Oxford University Press.

Roheim, Geza. (1981). "The Evil Eye." In A. Dundes, ed., *The Evil Eye: A Casebook.* Madison, WI: University of Madison Press, pp. 211–222.

Roland, Alan. (1988). *In Search of Self in India and Japan.* Princeton, NJ: Princeton University Press.

Rosen, Lawrence. (1979). "Social Identity and Points of Attachment." In C. Geertz, H. Geertz, and L. Rosen, *Meaning and Order in Moroccan Society.* New York: Cambridge University Press, pp. 19–122.

Rosen, Lawrence. (1984). *Bargaining for Reality.* Chicago: University of Chicago Press.

Rubin, Barry. (1994). *Revolution Until Victory? The Politics and History of the PLO.* Cambridge: Harvard University Press.

Sa'idallah, Najoui. (1992). "Dirasat anthrobologia muqarana li-anmat al-tanshi'a al-ijtima'iyya fi mujtama' mahali badawi wa mujtama' mahali rifi fi misr" (Comparative Anthropological Study of Socialization Patterns in Bedouin and Rural Societies in Egypt). In Mohammed Johari, 'Alia Shakri, Najoui Abdelhamid, and Mina Fernouani, eds., *Dirasat fi al-anthrobologia al-ijtima'iyya.* (Studies in Social Anthropology). Alexandria: dar ma'rifa jam'aia, pp. 173–263.

Sahlins, Marshall. (1961). "The Segmentary Lineage: An Organization of Predatory Expansion." *American Anthropologist* 63: 322–345.

Said, Edward. (1978). *Orientalism.* London: Routledge.

Sapir, E. (1918). "Culture, Genuine and Spurious." *American Journal of Sociology* 29: 401–429.

Sayigh, Rosemary. (1996). "Researching Gender in a Palestinian Camp." In D. Kandiyoti, ed., *Gendering the Middle East.* Syracuse, NY: Syracuse University Press, pp. 145–167.

Scarry, Elaine. (1985). *The Body in Pain.* New York: Oxford University Press.

Schade-Poulsen, Marc. (1999). *Men and Popular Music in Algeria.* Austin: University of Texas Press.

Schimmel, Annemarie. (1985). *And Muhammed Is His Messenger.* Chapel Hill: University of North Carolina Press.

Schimmel, Annemarie. (1989). *Islamic Names.* Edinburgh: Edinburgh University Press.

Schlegel, Alice, and Barry, Herbert. (1991). *Adolescence: An Anthropological Inquiry.* New York: Free Press.

Schmitt, A., and Sofer, J., eds. (1992), *Sexuality and Eroticism Among Males in Moselm Societies.* New York: Harrington Park.

Schneider, J. (1971). "Of Vigilance and Virgins: Honor, Shame and Access to Resources in Mediterranean Societies." *Ethnology* 10: 1–24.

Schwartz, T. (1972). "Distributive Models of Culture in Relation to Societal Scale." Manuscript. (Published in 1978 as "The Size and Shape of a Culture," in F. Barth, ed., *Scale and Social Organization.* Helsinki: Norwegian Research Council, pp. 215–252.)

Schwartz, T. (1978). "Where Is Culture? Personality as the Distributive Locus of Culture." In G. Spindler, ed., *The Making of Psychological Anthropology.* Berkeley: University of California Press, pp. 419–441.

Scott, James. (1985). *Weapons of the Weak.* New Haven, CT: Yale University Press.

Sears, R., Maccoby, E., and Levin, H. (1957). *Patterns of Child Rearing.* Oxford: Row, Peterson.

Sen, Amartya. (1999). *Development as Freedom.* New York: Knopf.

Servier, Andre. (1924). *Islam and the Psychology of the Musulman.* London: Chapman and Hall.

Seymour, Susan. (1976). "Caste/Class and Child-Rearing in a Changing Indian Town." *American Ethnologist* 3, no. 4: 783–796.

Shahar, Shulamith. (1990). *Childhood in the Middle Ages.* New York: Routledge.

Shaheen, J. (1984). *The TV Arab.* Bowling Green: Popular Press.

Shaheen, J. (1997). *Arab and Muslim Stereotyping in American Popular Culture.* Washington, DC: Georgetown University.

Shaheen, J. (2001). *Reel Bad Arabs: How Hollywood Vilifies a People.* New York: Olive Branch Press.

Shakri, 'Alia. (1992). "Al-tanshi'a al-ijtima'iyya." ("Socialization"). In Mohammed Johari, 'Alia Shakri, Najoui Abdelhamid, and Mina Fernouani, eds., *Dirasat fi al-anthropologia al-ijtima'iyya: al-tifl wa al-tanshi'a al-ijtima'iyya* (Anthropological Studies of Society: Children and Socialization). Alexandria, Egypt: dar safra al-ijtima'iyya, pp. 89–182.

Shalinsky, Audrey. (1986). "Reason, Desire, and Sexuality: The Meaning of Gender in Northern Afghanistan." *Ethos* 14, no. 4: 323–343.

Sharabi, Hisham. (1988). *Neopatriarchy.* New York: Oxford University Press.

Sharabi, Hisham, and Ani, Mukhtar. (1977). "The Impact of Class and Culture on Social Behavior: The Feudal-Bourgeois Family in Arab Society." In L. Brown and N. Itzkowitz, eds., *Psychological Dimensions of Near Eastern Studies.* Princeton, NJ: Darwin Press.

Shayegan, Daryush. (1992). *Cultural Schizophrenia: Islamic Societies Confronting the West.* Syracuse, NY: Syracuse University Press.

Shebshun, Ahmad. (1996). "Hawiyyat al-shabab al-tunisi" (Identity of Tunesian Youth). In A. Dachmi and M. Haddiya, *Indimaj al-shabab wa waqi'iyyat al-hawiyya* (Integration of Youth and the Problem of Identity). Rabat: kulliyyat al-adab, pp. 57–61.

Shouby, E. (1951). "The Influence of the Arabic Language on the Psychology of the Arabs." *Middle East Journal* 5, no. 3: 284–302.

Shweder, R. (1991). "Rethinking Culture and Personality Theory." In *Thinking Through Cultures.* Cambridge: Harvard University Press, pp. 269–312.

Shweder, R. (1993). "The Cultural Psychology of Emotion." In M. Lewis and J. Haviland, eds., *Handbook of Emotion.* New York: Guilford, pp. 417–434.

Shweder, R., and Bourne, E. (1984). "Does the Concept of the Person Vary Cross-Culturally?" In R. Shweder and R. LeVine, eds., *Culture Theory.* Cambridge, UK: Cambridge University Press, pp. 158–199.

Sigman, Marian, and Wachs, Theodore. (1991). "Structure, Continuity, Nutritional Correlates of Caregiver Behavior Patterns in Kenya and Egypt." In M. Bornstein, ed., *Cultural Approaches to Parenting.* Hillsdale, NJ: Erlbaum, pp. 123–137.

Sijilmassi, Mohamed. (1984). *Enfants du Maghreb.* Mohammadia, Morocco: SODEN.

Simon, Reeva. (1989). *The Middle East in Crime Fiction.* New York: Barber Press.

Sinha, D., and Kao, H. (1988). *Social Values and Development.* New Delhi: Sage.

Sinha, D., and Tripathi, R. (1994). "Individualism in a Collectivist Culture: A Case of Coexistence of Opposites." In U. Kim, H. Triandis, C. Kagitcibasi, S. Choi, and G. Yoon eds., *Individualism and Collectivism: Theory, Method, and Applications.* Thousand Oaks, CA: Sage, pp. 123–136.

Smith, Alison (2003). *From Words to Action.* Ph.D. dissertation, University of Michigan, Ann Arbor.

Smith, M. G. (1956). "Segmentary Lineage Systems." *Journal of the Royal Anthropological Institute* 86: 39–80.

Sniderman, P., and Piazza, T. (1993). *The Scar of Race.* Cambridge: Harvard University Press.

Somer, O., and Goldberg, L. (1999). "The Structure of Turkish Trait-Descriptive Adjectives." *Journal of Personality and Social Psychology* 76, no. 3: 431–450.

Spiro, M. (1993). "Is the Western Conception of the Self 'Peculiar' Within the Context of the World Cultures?" *Ethos* 21, no. 2: 107–153.

Spooner, Brian. (1976). "The Evil Eye in the Middle East." In C. Maloney, ed., *The Evil Eye.* New York: Columbia University Press, pp. 76–84.

Stadler, C. (1996). *The Nation as Idea.* Ph.D. dissertation, New York University.

Stern, Daniel. (1985). *The Interpersonal World of the Human Infant.* New York: Basic Books.

Steward, Abigail, and Vandewater, Elizabeth. (1998). "The Course of Generativity." In D. McAdams and E. de St. Aubin, eds., *Generativity and Adult Development*. Washington DC: American Psychological Association Press, pp. 75–100.

Straus, Murray, and Mathur, A. (1996). "Social Change and Trends in Approval of Corporal Punishment From 1968 to 1994." In D. Frehsee, W. Horn, and K. Bussmann, eds., *Violence Against Children*. New York: de Gruyter, pp. 91–105.

Sullivan, J., and Transue, J. (1999). "The Psychological Underpinnings of Democracy." *Annual Review of Psychology* 50: 625–650.

Sweet, Louise. (1970). "Camel Raiding of North Arabian Bedouin: A Mechanism of Ecological Adaptation." In L. Sweet, ed., *Peoples and Cultures of the Middle East*. Garden City, NY: Natural History Press, pp. 265–289.

Sweet, Louise, ed. (1970). *Peoples and Cultures of the Middle East*. 2 vols. Garden City, NY: Natural History Press.

Tajfel, Henri. (1981). *Human Groups and Social Categories*. Cambridge, UK: Cambridge University Press.

Tajfel, Henri. (1982). *Social Identity and Intergroup Relations*. Cambridge: Cambridge University Press.

Tasi, J., Ying, Y., and Lee, P. (2000). "The Meaning of 'Being Chinese' and 'Being American.'" *Journal of Cross-Cultural Psychology* 31, no. 3: 302–332.

Taussig, Michael. (1987). *Shamanism, Colonialism, and the Wild Man: A Study in Terror and Healing*. Chicago: University of Chicago Press.

Taussig, Michael. (1993). *Mimesis and Alterity*. New York: Routledge.

Thabet, A., Abed, Y., and Vostanis, P. (2002). "Emotional Problems in Palestinian Children Living in a War Zone." *Lancet* 359: 1801–1804.

Tibi, Bassam. (1991). *Islam and the Cultural Accommodation of Social Change*. Boulder, CO: Westview Press.

Tidrick, Kathryn. (1981). *Heart Beguiling Araby*. London: Tauris.

Tillion, Germaine. (1966). *The Republic of Cousins*. London: Saqi.

Tomkins, S. (1970). "Affect as the Primary Motivational System." In M. B. Arnold, ed., *Feelings and Emotions*. New York: Academic Press, pp. 101–110.

Trafimow, D., Triandis, H., and Goto, S. (1991). "Some Tests of the Distinction Between the Private Self and the Collective Self." *Journal of Personality and Social Psychology* 60, no. 5: 649–655.

Trapnell, P. (1997). "Personality Structure: The Return of the Big Five." In R. Hogan, J. Johnson, and S. Briggs, eds., *Handbook of Personality Psychology*. San Diego: Academic Press, pp. 737–766.

Triandis, H. (2001). "Individualism and Collectivism." In Matsumoto, D., ed., *Handbook of Culture and Psychology*. New York: Oxford University Press.

Triandis, H. (1988). "Collectivism and Development." In D. Sinha and H. Kao, eds., *Social Values and Development*. New Delhi: Sage, pp. 283–303.

Triandis, H. (1994). "Theoretical and Methodological Approaches to the Study of Collectivism and Individualism." In U. Kim, H. Triandis, C. Kagitcibasi, S. Choi, and G. Yoon, eds., *Individualism and Collectivism*. Thousand Oaks, CA: Sage, pp. 41–51.

Triandis, H. (1995). *Individualism and Collectivism*. Boulder, CO: Westview Press.

Triandis, Harry. (1989). "The Self and Social Behavior in Differing Cultural Contexts." *Psychological Review* 96, no. 3: 506–520.

Turner, Bryan. (1974). *Weber and Islam*. London: Routledge and Kegan Paul.

United Nations Development Program. (2002). *Arab Human Development Report 2002*. New York: Author.

Van Dam-Baggan, Rien, Kraaimaat, Floris, and Elal, Gueliz (2003). "Social Anxiety in Three Western Societies." *Journal of Clinical Psychology* 59, no. 6: 673–686

Vaziri, Mostafa. (1993). *Iran as Imagined Nation*. New York: Paragon House.

Verkuyten, Maykel, and Pouliasi, Katerina (2002). "Biculturalism Among Older Children." *Journal of Cross-Cultural Psychology* 33, no. 6: 596–609.

von Grunebaum, G. E. (1951). *Muhammadan Festivals*. London: Curzon.

Vygotsky, L. S. (1978). *Mind in Society*. Cambridge: Harvard University Press.

Wallace, A. (1961). *Culture and Personality*. New York: Random House.

Waterbury, John. (1972). *North for the Trade: The Life and Times of a Berber Merchant*. Berkeley: University of California Press.

Weber, Max. (1958). *The Protestant Ethic and the Spirit of Capitalism*. New York: Scribner's.

Wertsch, James. (1985). *Vygotsky and the Social Formation of Mind*. Cambridge: Harvard University Press.

Wharton, Edith. (1996). *In Morocco*. Hopewell, NJ: Ecco Press.

White, Jenny. (1995). "An Unmarried Girl and a Grinding Stone." In E. Fernea, ed., *Children in the Muslim Middle East*. Austin: University of Texas Press.

Whiting, Beatrice, and Edwards, Carolyn. (1988). *Children of Different Worlds*. Cambridge: Harvard University Press.

Whiting, Beatrice, and Whiting, John. (1975). *Children of Six Cultures: A Psycho-Cultural Analysis*. Cambridge: Harvard University Press.

Whiting, J. (1994). *Culture and Human Development* (E. Chasdi, ed.). Cambridge, UK: Cambridge University Press.

Whiting, J. (1994). "Environmental Constraints on Infant Care Practices." In *Culture and Human Development*. Cambridge, UK: Cambridge University Press, pp. 107–134.

Whiting, J., and Child, I. (1953). *Child Training and Personality*. New Haven, CT: Yale University Press.

Wiggins, J., and Trapnell, P. (1997). "Personality Structure: The Return of the Big Five." In R. Hogan, J. Johnson, and S. Briggs, eds., *Handbook of Personality Psychology*. San Diego: Academic Press, pp. 737–766.

Wiggins, J., ed. (1996). *The Five-Factor Model of Personality*. New York: Guilford.

Wikan, Unni. (1982). *Behind the Veil in Arabia*. Chicago: University of Chicago Press.

Wikan, Unni. (1995). "The Self in a World of Urgency and Necessity." *Ethos* 23, no. 3: 259–285.

Wikan, Unni. (1996). *Tomorrow, God Willing*. Chicago: University of Chicago Press.

Wilkinson, Ray, and Nordland, Rod. (1986, April 7). "Inside Terror, Inc." *Newsweek* 107: 25–28.

Wilkinson, Richard. (1994). "The Epidemiological Transition." *Daedalus* 123, no. 4: 61–78.

Williams, Judith. (1968). *The Youth of Haouch el Harimi, A Lebanese Village*. Cambridge: Harvard University Press.

Williams, Raymond. (1973). *The Country and the City*. New York: Oxford University Press.

Wilson, Monica. (1951). *Good Company*. Boston: Beacon Press.

Wilson, W. (1995). "Jobless Ghettos and the Social Outcomes of Youngsters." In P. Moen, G. Elder, and K. Luscher, eds., *Examining Lives in Context.* Washington, DC: American Psychological Association, pp. 4257–4544.

Winnicott, D. W. (1989). *Psychoanalytic Explorations.* Cambridge: Harvard University Press.

Winter, D., John, O., Stewart, A., Klohne, E., and Duncan, L. (1998). "Traits and Motives: Toward an Integration of Two Traditions in Personality Research." *Psychological Review* 105, no. 2: 230–250.

Wolf, E. (1951). "The Social Organization of Mecca and the Origins of Islam." *Southwestern Journal of Anthropology* 7, no. 4: 329–356.

Wolf, E. (1977). "Kinship, Friendship, and Patron-Client Relations in Complex Societies." In S. Schmidt, L. Guasti, and J. Scott, eds., *Friends, Followers, and Factions* . Berkeley: University of California Press, pp. 167–177.

Wolf, Eric. (1982). *Europe and the People Without History.* Berkeley: University of California.

Worsley, Peter. (1968). *The Trumpet Shall Sound.* New York: Schocken Books.

Wu, Pei-Yi. (1990). *The Confucian's Progress: Autobiographical Writings in Traditional China.* Princeton, NJ: Princeton University Press.

Yassin, Sayyid. (1974). *Al-shakhsiyya al-'arabiyya: Bayn al-mafhoum al-isra'ili wa al-mafhoum al-'arabi* (The Arab Personality: Between the Israeli Conception and the Arab Conception). Cairo: Pyramid Commercial Press.

Ybarra, Oscar, and Trafimow, David. (1998). "How Priming the Private Self or Collective Self Affects the Relative Weights of Attitudes and Subjective Norms." *Personality and Social Psychology Bulletin* 24, no. 4: 362–370.

Young-Bruehl, Elisabeth. (1996). *The Anatomy of Prejudices.* Cambridge: Harvard University Press.

Zaid, Ahmad. (1990). *Misr al-mu'asira* (Modern Egypt). Al-Qahira: Al-markaz al-qawmi li-al-buhouth al-ijtima'iyya wa al-jema'iyya.

Zaid, Ahmad. (1994a). "Ba'dh khasa'is al-shakhsiyya al-qawmiyya al-mesriyya bayn al-aftradat al-nadharijyya wa al-waqa' al-ambiriqi" (Some Characteristics of the Egyptian National Character: Between Theoretical Hypotheses and Empirical Realities). In L. Melikian, *'Alim al-nafs al-ijtima'ai fi al-watan al-'arabi* (Readings in Social Psychology in the Arab Countries). Vol. 7. Cairo: al-hiia al-misriyya al-'ama li-al-kitab, pp. 185–207.

Zaid, Ahmad. (1994b, July). "Al-islam wa tanaqudhat al-hadatha" (Islam and the Contradictions of Modernity). *Al-majalla al-ijtima'iyya al-qawmiyya* (Journal of the National Society) 31, no. 1: 41–74.

Zajonc, R. (1994). "Emotional Expression and Temperature Modulation." In S. van Goozen, N. Van De Poll, and J. Sergeant, eds., *Emotions: Essays on Emotion Theory.* Hillsdale, NJ: Erlbaum, pp. 3–27.

Zayour, Ali. (1977). *Al-tahlil al-nafsi li-al-dhat al-'arabiyya* (Psychoanalysis of the Arab Self). Beirut: dar al-tali'ah.

Zayour, Ali. (1985). *Al-tarbiya wa 'ilm nafs al-waled fi al-dhat al-'arabiyya* (Child-Rearing and Child Psychology with Regard to the Arab Self). Beirut: dar andelus.

INDEX

Abdel-Khalek, Ahmed, 272, 333, 336, 357
Abdelqader, Mahmoud, 210–211, 251
Abdo, Geneive, 312
Abou el Nil, Mahmoud, 373
Abou Zeid, Ahmed, 94–96, 103
Aboulafia, Mitchell, 111
Abu-Hateb, Fuad, 8, 376
Abu-Hin, Fadal, 40
Abu-Lughod, Lila, 29, 97, 100–103, 106, 109, 259, 262, 286, 300, 323
acculturation, 9, 303, 305, 323, 354, 374–375
achievement, 30, 32–33, 77, 108–109, 158, 163, 190, 194, 209, 241–242, 271, 284, 291, 313, 319–321, 335, 337, 339, 343, 362–363, 371–372, 377
Adim, Saddiq, 343
Adorno, Theodore, 242, 246
'Afifi, al-Ham, 21–211
agriculture, 4, 46, 50–56, 62, 75, 84, 144–147, 151, 216, 264, 283, 344, 351, 354, 359
agro-pastoralism, 32, 51–53, 66, 83
Ahirshaw, al Ghali, 284, 287
Ahmed, Akbar, 290
Ahmed, Leila, 285, 313–314
Ahmed, Ramadan, 7, 8, 333, 357, 369
Ainsworth, Mary, 166, 175
Ajami, Fuad, 345
Akin, John, 177
Al Ansarey, Badr, 334

Al Nawayseh, Naif, 164, 171, 177
Al-Aharas, Mohammed, 210, 239, 251
Al-Issa, Ihsan, 8, 369
Al-Khalil, Samir, 41–42, 81, 248
Alloula, Malek, 23
Allport, Gordon, 138
Al-Sa'ti, Samia, 161, 177
Altermeyer, Robert, 243
Al-Zahrani, S., 336, 338
Ammar, Hamid, 7, 159–161, 165–167, 171, 180, 185–190, 198–199, 208, 210–211, 215, 217, 222, 224, 230–233, 236–238, 250–251, 264, 266, 284–286, 321, 335, 342–343, 357
Ammar, Nawal, 159–167, 177, 185, 190, 210–211, 215, 250–251
Amrouche, Fadhma, 356
Anderson, John, 299
Ani, Mukhtar, 216
Antoun, Richard, 121, 228, 268, 356
anxiety, 127–128, 131, 187, 200–202, 272, 277–279, 304–305, 318–319, 335, 347–348
apprentice learning, 47, 49, 158, 181, 214, 215, 229, 239–341, 371
apprenticeship and obedience model, 150, 158, 181, 194, 214, 239, 360
Arab Human Development Report, 43, 82–83, 87, 341, 355–356, 372
Arensberg, Conrad, 147–148, 353
Askander, Naguib, 193, 210–211, 251

assertive dependence, 185, 190–192, 194, 204, 218, 236, 257, 370
Atiya, Nayra, 262, 356
attachment, 106, 110, 137, 146, 151, 154, 166–177, 181–185, 205–208, 225–228, 339, 353, 360, 364, 370
authoritarianism, 7, 31, 43, 87, 192–193, 215, 221–225, 228, 233, 234, 235, 242–250, 342, 350, 352, 361, 363, 371
Aryrout, Habib, 31–35, 345
'Awda, Mahmoud, 344, 357
Aziz, Shagufta, 334

Badri, Gasim, 164, 178, 182–183, 195, 210–211, 214, 220, 251
Bakhtin, Mikhail, 293
Bandura, Albert, 203
baraka (blessedness), 113, 115, 116, 119, 122–128, 131–133, 166, 188–189, 225, 239, 263, 266
Barakat, Halim, 14, 43, 49, 243, 249, 251, 285, 301, 323, 346, 356
Barber, Samuel, 3
Barry, Herbert, 256, 286
Barth, Fredrick, 59–60
Bates, Daniel, 49
Baumrind, Diana, 243–246
Beardsley, Richard, 170
Beck, Lois, 257
Bellah, Robert, 320, 362
Ben Jalloun, Juad, 194, 274
Benedict, Ruth, 142
Bennani-Chraibi, Mounia, 285, 287, 316–318, 323
Bentahar, Mekki, 274–275, 286
Berger, Morroe, 31
Beshai, J., 357
"Big Five" personality traits, 108, 334–335
birth, 159–162
Boddy, Janice, 159, 166, 196–198, 203, 210–211, 258, 264, 286, 295, 297, 323, 354
Boserup, Esther, 56, 351
Bouhdiba, Abdelwaheb, 7, 208–209, 225–229, 244, 251, 273–276, 285, 352, 354, 357
Bourdieu, Pierre, 48, 59, 63, 95–98, 101, 106, 110, 264

Brink, Judy, 167, 177, 184, 189, 192, 210, 221, 251
Brohi, Allahbakhsh, 113
Brown, L. Carl, 136
Bruner, Jerome, 293
Buda, R., 336
Burton, Richard, 17–18, 22, 210

Campbell, J.K., 94, 98–99
Cansever, Gocke, 199, 201, 203, 211
Carnes, Mark, 19
Carstairs, G., 170
Caton, Steve, 298–300, 323
Cederblad, Marianne, 163, 166, 171, 176, 178, 186, 240, 251
Chamcham, Rouchdi, 174, 178
Chao, Ruth, 244, 246
Chaouite, Abedlatif, 174–176, 178
Chaqueri, Cosroe, 232–236, 251
China, 4, 55, 57, 146, 170, 215, 246, 256–257, 336, 338, 357, 373, 375–377
Chiu, C., 337
Chodorow, Nancy, 143, 205–209, 232
Chraibi, Driss, 223–224, 251, 324
circumcision, 7, 112, 181, 195–203, 207–211, 229, 240, 262–263, 360–362, 370
Claeys, W., 339
clientage, 27, 42, 50–51, 66, 69–75, 81–82, 85, 87, 97, 103, 115, 192, 218, 219, 241, 249, 255, 269, 348, 351
Coco, Carla, 23
Cohen, Abner, 60, 70
collectivism, 9, 29, 47, 70, 76–77, 145, 254–255, 295, 314, 317, 321–322, 327, 336–339, 357, 362–363, 373
colonization, 14, 19, 23, 29, 35–36, 40–41, 77, 86–87, 91, 219, 282, 284, 289, 304–305, 312, 315, 322, 342–345, 348, 354
core personality, 138–142, 177, 181, 213, 359–360
Crapanzano, Vincent, 127, 199–203, 208–211, 297
Critchfield, Richard, 34–35
culture area, 4–6, 46, 53–54, 76–77, 136, 364, 374–375
culture and emotion. *See* emotion and culture
culture and personality, 5, 49, 104–111

cultural dualities, 84–85, 91–92, 269–283, 291–293, 303–318, 374–375

Dabashi, Hamid, 247–248
Dachmi, Abdeslam, 164, 170, 174, 176, 178, 208, 211, 225, 352, 373
Davis, Douglas, 254, 270–278, 282, 284, 286, 305, 317, 321
Davis, Susan, 162, 164, 167, 171, 177, 182, 192, 199, 210–211, 236, 254, 261, 270–278, 282, 284, 286, 305, 317, 321, 339
deference, 19, 49, 71–73, 91, 97, 100–103, 155, 212, 218–219, 229, 235, 257, 266–268, 319
Delaney, Carol, 159, 162, 258, 263, 286
De La Ronciere, Charles, 169
De Nerval, Gerard, 22
dethronement, 183, 370
developmental discontinuity, 175–176, 183, 204, 209–210, 229, 290, 304–305, 318–321, 360–362, 370
DeVos, George, 170, 303–305, 319, 324
Djait, Hichem, 348, 357
Doi, Takeo, 8, 72, 170
dreams, 25, 85, 113, 128, 188, 225, 300–301, 315, 318–319, 328
Drummond, Jonathan, 38
Dumont, Louis, 91
Dundes, Alan, 233, 251
Durkheim, Emile, 64
Dwyer, Daisy, 297
Dwyer, Kevin, 356, 364–366

Edgerton, Robert, 144–145, 148
Eickelman, Dale, 49, 69, 72, 221, 223, 236, 249, 251
Eisenstadt, S. N., 292
Ekman, Paul, 105
El-Feky, Hamed, 245–246
El Guindi, Fadwa, 312
El Khayat-Bennai, Ghita, 174, 178, 225, 262, 286, 296, 354
El Messiri, Sawsan, 265, 281, 285, 302–303, 311, 324
El Mofti, Maissa, 224, 251
El Saadawi, Nawal, 198–199, 211, 249, 258, 272
El-Sarraj, Eyad, 39

El Sayed-Elkhoula, S. 336
emotion and culture, 9, 49, 91, 107–110, 130–133, 144, 213, 360–361, 374
endogamy, 50, 59–63, 66, 69, 74–75, 197, 248
Erikson, Erik, 8, 37, 88, 106, 111, 136–140, 170, 176, 254, 255, 285, 291–293, 316, 323, 327–332, 353, 355, 372
etiquettes, 49–50, 71, 92, 97, 101, 105, 110, 126, 130, 215–220, 224, 239, 255, 257, 266, 291, 319, 360–361, 363, 371
Eurasia, 55–56, 257, 301, 351, 359
Euromania, 308–311, 318
Evans-Pritchard, E. E., 64, 65
evil eye, 98, 113, 125–128, 131, 145, 147, 154, 160–162, 174, 181, 186, 225, 301, 305, 319, 348, 352–354
Ewing, Katherine, 314–315, 321–324, 357
Eysenck, Hans, 334–335

Fahlaoui personality, 335, 342–343
Fakhouri, Hani, 32
family, 28, 46–50, 55–71, 76, 83–84, 98–103, 148–150, 155–156, 166–167, 173–177, 191–195, 216–228, 242–250, 254, 268–269, 278, 283–285, 316, 320–321, 337–341, 351–354, 360, 370–374
Fanon, Franz, 86–87, 289, 305, 319, 345, 347
Farrag, M., 357
fasting, 114–115, 131, 239, 256, 365
fatalism, 30–34, 343–344
fear, 185–187, 222–224, 227, 233, 239, 271, 346–353
Feldman, Allen, 40
Fernea, Elizabeth, 136–137, 238, 260, 285
FGC (female genital cutting ritual), 195, 203, 209, 360, 370
fitna (disorder, chaos), 131–132, 239, 264, 295, 297
Flaubert, Gustav, 22
Foster, George, 146–147, 344
Freud, Sigmund, 14, 29, 88, 141, 203–205, 213, 254, 328–329, 377
Freidl, Erika, 159–162, 164, 167, 171, 173, 177, 183–186, 189, 210, 222, 224, 232–236, 251, 278, 285
Fromm, Erich, 242, 246, 344

Garrison, Vivian, 147–148, 353
Geertz, Clifford, 16, 69, 72
Geertz, Hildred, 69–72
Gellner, Ernest, 320
gender development, feminine, 195–199,
    203–210, 258–264, 339–342, 363
gender development, masculine, 19, 92,
    100, 103, 143, 149, 195–210, 233, 235,
    264–267, 285, 302, 339–342, 354, 357,
    360–361, 363
gender differences, 181, 192–193, 195, 215,
    228, 232, 236, 241, 257, 272, 297–298,
    339–341, 360–361
generalized other, 110–112, 133, 220, 236,
    239, 291–292, 361, 366, 371
Ghallab, Abdelkrim, 223, 251
Ghareeb, Abdelkrim, 290, 322, 324, 357
Gibson, James, 93
Giddons, Anthony, 47–48, 331, 353, 355
Gielen, Uwe, 8, 333, 357, 369
Gilligan, Carol, 206
Gilmore, David, 143, 206, 207, 229, 232, 351
Gilsenan, Michael, 124, 130, 266, 285, 313,
    324, 357
Goethe, Johann, 87–88, 327
Goldberg, Ellis, 320
Goldenweiser, Alexander, 29
Gole, Nilufer, 306–307, 324
Goody, Jack, 55–56, 351
Gorer, Geoffrey, 163
Granqvist, Hilma, 159, 162–163, 166, 177,
    196
Grotberg, Edith, 195, 210, 214, 251
group self, 175–176, 218, 360
Guessous, Mohammed, 83
Gutmann, David, 331, 340–341, 357

habitus, 96, 105, 130
Haddiya, Mustafa, 83, 193, 241, 251, 270–
    272, 286, 322
Hage, Ghassan, 40
Hamady, Sania, 31, 33
Hamdan, Jamal, 344
Hammoudi, Abdallah, 73–74, 208, 244,
    249–250, 266–268, 285, 346, 352
Harris, Judith, 231
Hart, David, 234, 251, 265
Hazelton, Elaine, 260

Herdt, Gilbert, 8, 143, 206, 232, 351
Hermans, Hubert, 293
Herzfeld, Michael, 30, 64, 98–99, 109
Hicks, Ester, 211
Hijazi, Azet, 14
Hijazi, Mustafa, 7, 14, 66, 87, 208, 244, 249,
    321, 346–348, 352–355, 358, 373, 376
Ho, D., 337
Hobbs, Joseph, 33, 35
Hodson, Joel, 20
Hofstede, G., 336
Hollander, Nancy, 350–352
Holy, Landislav, 37, 61, 67
Honneth, Axel, 355–356
honor, 42, 60, 93, 97–98, 101, 217, 235,
    263, 269, 274, 298, 319, 321, 338, 343
honor code, 27–33, 54, 63, 91–103, 129, 321
honor-modesty system, 17, 29–30, 53–54,
    62–64, 91–92, 95, 101–112, 118, 129–133,
    140, 181, 203, 209, 213, 218, 224, 228,
    232, 236, 242, 255, 257, 271, 281, 284,
    289, 291, 295, 300, 319, 326, 339, 351,
    359–364, 371–374
Hoodfar, Homa, 177
Hsu, Francis, 45–46, 148, 217
Huntington, Samuel, 3

Ibn, Khaldun, 27, 54–55, 65, 77–78, 264–
    265, 302
Ibrahim, Abdel, 334, 357
identity, 4, 37–38, 63, 91, 100, 105, 106, 111,
    129, 139–142, 197, 205, 254–255, 264–
    265, 270, 289–323, 329–332, 360–362,
    372, 375
Imamoglu, E., 337
Imeghrane, 4, 32, 35, 50, 60, 66–70, 82,
    163, 166, 172, 175, 186, 188, 192, 200, 263,
    266
India, 4, 5, 8, 21, 46, 49, 52, 55, 57, 59, 68,
    77, 91–92, 146, 158, 161, 168–170, 181,
    185, 189, 192–193, 210, 215, 224, 256–257,
    274, 284, 301, 313, 336–338, 357, 359, 373,
    375–377
indigenous psychology, 335, 376–377
individualism, 9, 29, 47, 63, 70, 76–77,
    88, 91, 145, 254–256, 261, 268–269, 295,
    299, 314, 317, 321–322, 327, 336–339, 357,
    362, 373

individuation, 154, 174, 329–330, 337, 341, 362–363, 366, 370–373
Inhorn, Marcia, 296
Inkeles, Alex, 35, 242, 343
interdependence, 166–177, 182–185, 194, 225–228, 255, 295, 337, 362, 370
Islam, 36, 42, 53–54, 56, 76, 78, 92, 97, 103, 106, 112–133, 181, 213, 215, 236–239, 242, 255, 273–274, 289, 291, 295–296, 300–301, 305, 313, 317–321, 359–363, 371, 374
Islamism, 79, 125, 130, 253, 279, 282–283, 308, 311–317, 321

Jabar, Abdelhamid, 4, 77, 251, 269, 344
Jackson, Chris, 334
James, William, 19, 291
Japan, 8, 30, 72, 154, 170, 242, 246, 313, 319–320, 336–338, 357, 362, 373–377
jinn, 85, 113, 124–133, 147, 150, 154, 160, 162, 174, 181, 186–187, 194, 197, 200, 210, 222, 225, 229, 296–301, 304–305, 319, 348, 352, 354, 362
Johari, Mohammed, 177, 214
Joseph, Suad, 9, 149, 284, 338–339, 357
Jung, Carl, 88, 327–332, 366

Kabbani, Rana, 21–22
Kagitcibasi, Cigdem, 9, 145, 194, 215, 245–246, 284, 321, 337, 339, 357, 370, 373
Kakar, Sudhir, 8, 170
Kandiyoti, Deniz, 4, 56, 339–341, 351, 354, 357
Kaplowitz, S., 336, 338
Karakitapoglu-Aygun, Zahide, 245–246, 337
Kardiner, Abram, 205
Kasdan, Leonard, 60
Kempen, Harry, 293
Kepel, Gilles, 312, 324
Khaleefa, Omar, 7, 373
Khalifa, Abdelatif, 5, 334, 344, 357
Khazanov, A., 51
Khuri, Fuad, 7, 71–75, 97, 100, 103, 190, 247–248
kinship, 55–67, 148–150, 216–221
Kouaouci, Ali, 66, 285
Krichen, Aziz, 84–85, 301

Kuroda, Y., 338
Kurtz, Stanley, 170

Lacoste-Dujardin, Camille, 174, 225–226, 286, 296, 339–341, 354
Lamb, David, 39
Lane, Edward, 22
Laquer, Walter, 37
Laroui, Abdullah, 36
Lawrence, T. E., 17–18, 20
Lebra, T., 170
Lerner, Daniel, 15, 306, 308
level I personality, 106, 138–142, 181, 360
level II personality, 106, 108–109, 138–142, 182, 319, 327, 360–361
level III personality, 138–142, 319, 361–362
LeVine, Robert, 8, 106, 136–140, 149–150, 154–157, 162, 166, 172, 174, 181, 185, 214, 351, 360
Levinson, Daniel, 293–294, 316, 318, 327, 330, 332, 372
Levi-Strauss, Claude, 59–60
Lewin, Kurt, 138
Lewis, Oscar, 344
life structure, 294, 316, 330, 332, 362, 372
Lila, Ali, 29, 87, 282, 284, 286–287, 314, 322–324
Lindholm, Charles, 76, 268
lineage, 54, 58–70, 94–95, 101, 193, 232

Maalouf, Amin, 322
Maccoby, Michael, 344
Mackey, Sandra, 26–29
Mahfouz, Naguib, 43, 111, 130, 132, 221, 223–224, 226–229, 246, 249, 251, 254, 273, 357
Mahmoud, Musafa, 14, 177, 344, 376–377
Makiya, Kanan, 248–250, 349–354
Malti-Douglass, Fedwa, 357
Markus, Hazel, 322
marriage, 50, 55–61, 260–263
Martinez, Luis, 66
Marx, Emmanual, 65–66
Matsumoto, David, 374
McAdams, Dan, 8, 106, 109, 136, 139–140, 293, 327–330, 360
McDougall, William, 107

Mead, G. H., 110, 111, 133, 136, 140, 218, 220, 236, 239, 291, 299, 355, 360–361, 371
Mead, Margaret, 142, 180
Mediterranean, 6, 30, 46, 50, 61–63, 91–93, 97–99, 104–105, 122, 136, 143, 145, 147, 161, 169, 170, 176, 206, 208, 214, 224, 258, 275, 278, 283, 301, 351, 353, 359
Meeker, Michael, 53, 264, 268, 285, 298
Melikian, Louis, 244–245
Mensch, B., 269, 286
Mernissi, Fatima, 131, 225, 285
Miller, Gerald, 241
Miner, Horace, 303–305, 319, 324
Mirowsky, John, 352
Mirsepassi, Ali, 324
Mitchell, Timothy, 34–35, 283, 313, 324
modernity (modernizing social milieus), 3, 9, 16, 25–37, 43, 46, 70–72, 77–89, 154, 194, 215, 239–242, 250, 269, 270, 279, 283–285, 294, 301–323, 341–356, 362–363, 366, 371–374
modesty, 21, 53, 92, 97, 101, 103, 105, 130, 182, 193, 235
Moghrabi, Fouad, 14
Morgan, Lewis Henry, 19
motives, 106–110, 113, 131–132, 136, 140, 181, 213, 239, 242, 271, 291–292, 319, 321, 327, 339, 360–363, 371, 374
Mottahedeh, Roy, 237, 251, 309–311, 324, 356
Msefer, Assia, 173, 176, 178, 225, 352, 373
Munson, Henry, 324, 356
Murphy, Robert, 60
Murray, Henry, 77, 108–109
Muslim ethic, 32–33, 242, 284, 318, 321–323, 339, 362

Naamane-Guesseus, Soumaya, 258, 286
Nablusi, Mohammed, 8, 376
Najati, Mohammed, 376
Najmabadi, Afsaneh, 209, 356–357
naming, 120, 161, 190, 217, 296, 298, 309, 348
Nandy, Ashis, 8
Nasr, Seyyed Hosein, 119
Nelson, Kristina, 117–118
neopatriarchy, 42, 246, 351, 354, 356
Nil, Maissa, 272, 333, 357

Nuwaisa, Naif, 177
nursing, 163–166
nurturance, 221, 224–228, 239, 257
nutrition, 157, 186

Obeysekere, Gannanath, 8, 140
Olson, Emelie, 307, 324
Ortner, Sherry, 4, 56, 314
Oussaid, Brick, 223, 356
Ouzi, Ahmed, 221, 225, 256, 270–272, 278, 284, 286, 317, 322
Oyserman, Daphna, 357
Ozturk, Orhan, 199–203, 208, 211

Pamuk, Ohran, 34, 317
Pascon, Paul, 274–276, 286, 322
pastoralism, 4, 34, 46, 50–54, 59, 62, 75, 94, 144–145, 151, 195, 216, 218, 264, 268, 285, 351, 359
Patai, Raphael, 7, 16, 28, 31, 33, 91, 343
patronage, 27, 32, 42, 50, 55, 67–82, 97, 101, 103, 115, 123, 147, 218–219, 241, 248–249, 255, 269, 346–349, 351, 354
patronymic association, 50, 69–72, 75, 82, 112, 115, 176, 218, 220, 241, 255, 257
pedagogic model (of child care), 154–159, 167, 181–182, 193–195, 214, 370
pediatric model (of child care), 154–159, 166–173, 177, 181, 193–195, 208, 214, 351, 359–360, 370
Peristiany, J. G., 92–93, 96–97, 109, 111
personality, levels, 8–9, 104–111, 130–133, 138–142, 150–151, 213, 359–363
personality genotype, 138–139, 360
personality phenotype, 139, 360
personality theories, 8–9, 46–47, 136–142, 153–159, 203–208, 254–256, 291–294, 327–331
Peteet, Julie, 40–41
Peters, Emerys, 64, 66
Phalet, K., 339
Piaget, Jean, 255, 322
Pitt-Rivers, Julian, 96–97
play (children's), 230–236
pollution, 112–113, 128–132, 162, 197, 225, 238–239, 258, 263–264, 274, 295, 297, 301
Poulton, Hugh, 307–308, 324

prayer, 127, 131, 238
Protestant ethic, 32, 242, 320, 362, 377
Prothro, Edward, 162–164, 171, 177, 183, 188–190, 210, 220, 228, 244–245, 251
Pryce-Jones, David, 7, 16, 26–28, 30
purification, 94, 97, 112, 133, 116, 127–132, 160, 181, 197, 203, 225, 238–239, 259, 262–264, 274, 295, 297, 301, 319

Qabaj, Mohammed, 164, 180
Quran, 112–121, 125–129, 133, 160, 237–239, 266, 273, 296, 299–300, 316

Rabia', Mbarik, 284
Rabinow, Paul, 72
Radi, Abdelwahad, 237
Radwan, Sh'aban, 5, 334, 344, 357
Rahim, Idris, 251
Rassam, Amal, 49
recitation (of Quran), 116–119, 131–133, 238–239
Rejali, Darius, 345
Reynolds, Dwight, 336
Richards, Alan, 42, 74, 79
Roberts, John, 147, 353
Rodinson, Maxime, 53, 97
Rogoff, Barbara, 181
Roland, Alan, 170
Rosen, Lawrence, 69, 72
Ross, Catharine, 352
rural social milieus, 5, 18, 31, 50–55, 61–63, 75–84, 98, 112, 156–159, 161–171, 185–186, 190, 193, 197, 220, 232, 238–242, 261, 264, 270–272, 276, 284, 297–307, 313, 317–318, 343–345

S'aidallah, Najoui, 164, 171, 177, 193, 211, 251
Sahlins, Marshall, 65–66
Said, Edward, 15–17, 22
Sapir, Edward, 142
Satan, 85, 113, 125–133, 147, 181, 274, 305, 319, 348, 352
Sati, Samia, 177
Schade-Poulsen, Marc, 279–283, 287, 317
Schimmel, Annemarie, 120
Schlegel, Alice, 256, 286
Schneider, Jane, 62–63, 92, 99, 145, 351, 354
schools, 239–242, 270–273

Scott, James, 345
seclusion, 62, 91, 97, 193, 256, 258, 286
segmentary organization, 50, 64–68, 75–76, 95
self, 16, 29, 91–92, 103, 105–106, 109–113, 130–131, 210, 213, 217, 236–264, 268, 290–291, 295, 298–299, 302, 315, 319, 322, 336, 338, 357, 361, 363, 371–374
Sen, Amartya, 169, 355–356, 373
sentiments, 24, 30, 64, 93–96, 101–110, 113, 118, 131–132, 136, 181, 213, 239, 271, 291, 300, 319, 327, 361, 363, 371, 374
Servier, Andre, 16
Shahar, Shulamith, 25
Shaheen, Jack, 25
Shakri, Alia, 162, 177, 210, 214, 251
Shalinsky, Audry, 297–299, 323
shame, 28–29, 42, 53, 93–94, 97–98, 101, 105, 108, 190, 217, 258, 263, 274, 347–348
Sharabi, Hisham, 42, 43, 60, 73, 215–216, 225, 244, 246–251, 285, 346, 352, 354, 357, 373
Shayagen, Daryush, 311, 322, 324
Shebshun, Ahmad, 284
Shweder, Richard, 104
sibling rivalry, 189–191
Sigman, Marian, 183
Sijelmassi, Mohamed, 177
Simon, Reeva, 24
Smith, David, 35, 242
social class, 71, 81, 84, 158, 164–167, 193, 201, 211, 239, 244, 250, 302
social interaction (children's), 189–195
social persona, 92–93, 106, 109–111, 132, 136, 140, 142, 181, 213, 220, 255, 271, 289, 291, 327, 360–364
social self, 99, 106, 109–111, 140, 213, 218, 220, 236, 239, 291, 360
Stewart, A., 329
sub-Saharan Africa, 5, 46, 52, 56, 59, 77, 79–80, 91–92, 136, 138, 146, 149, 199, 154–158, 162, 166, 168, 172, 174, 181, 183, 185, 193, 195, 199, 208, 224, 256, 284, 301, 359
Sullivan, J., 353
Suzuki, T., 338
swaddling, 162–163

Tajfel, Henri, 100, 298
terrorism, 37–41
Tibi, Bassam, 311, 324
Tidrick, Kathryn, 17–19, 25
Tillion, Germaine, 61–62
tradition (traditional social milieus), 41–
46, 80, 87, 165, 194, 215–242, 249, 256–
269, 284–285, 294–301, 350, 352, 356,
370–371
traditionalism, 35–36, 290
traits (personality), 14, 104–108, 132, 136,
138, 140, 245, 326–327, 333–334, 336–
339, 343, 345, 357, 361, 374
transhumance, 51–52
Transue, J., 353
Triandis, Harry, 322, 337
tribe, 26–27, 41, 51–53, 64, 68, 75, 78, 83,
147

underdevelopment, 3–4, 7, 9, 26, 30–33,
41–42, 46, 70, 74, 77, 85–89, 154, 241,
250, 253–254, 270, 284–285, 294, 313,
316, 318, 321–322, 327, 332, 336, 341–342,
346, 355–356, 361–363, 367, 371–374
urban social milieus, 4–5, 27, 35, 37, 42,
44, 46, 50–55, 62, 75, 78–85, 112, 145,
148, 150, 157, 159, 161–167, 171, 177, 186,
193–194, 197, 228, 230, 239–241, 265,
269–273, 284, 302–307, 319, 343, 351,
360, 370–371, 374

Van Dam-Baggan, Rien, 336
Vandewater, E., 329
Vaziri, Mostafa, 309, 311, 324
veil, 23, 36, 62, 78, 258, 263, 281, 306–307,
313

Wachs, Theodore, 183
Wallace, Anthony, 514
Waterbury, John, 32–33, 42, 74, 79, 320
weaning, 163–177, 194
Weber, Max, 32, 242, 320, 362, 377
Westernization, 36, 42, 308–312, 367
Wharton, Edith, 17
Whiting, Beatrice, 8, 143, 182, 184, 191–
193, 210
Whiting, John, 8, 143, 162, 182, 191–193,
207, 209, 229, 232
Wikan, Uni, 258, 260, 274–276, 286, 357
Wilkinson, Ray, 39
Williams, Judith, 162–164, 183, 187, 192,
210, 216–217, 220, 222, 251, 271, 277,
284, 286
Winnicott, D., 173–175, 353
Wolf, Eric, 49, 53, 97, 345

Yassin, Siyyid, 14, 343, 344, 358

Zaid, Ahmad, 42, 343, 346
zar, 125, 162, 203, 210
Zayour, Ali, 7, 244, 348, 352–354, 358, 376

CPSIA information can be obtained
at www.ICGtesting.com
Printed in the USA
BVHW062252281122
653010BV00002B/4

9 780195 171990